GW00602709

TEACHERS
AND THE LAW

TEACHERS AND THE LAW

Sixth edition

G. R. Barrell
formerly Headmaster, Sir John Cass's Foundation and
Red Coat Church of England Secondary School, London;
Adviser in Educational Law to the College of Preceptors

and

J. A. Partington
Senior Lecturer in Education, University of Nottingham

Methuen

First published in 1958 by
Methuen & Co. Ltd
11 New Fetter Lane
London EC4P 4EE

Sixth edition published 1985
© 1985 John Partington

Printed in Great Britain
at the University Press, Cambridge

All rights reserved. No part of this book may be reprinted or
reproduced or utilized in any form or by any electronic, mechanical
or other means, now known or hereafter invented, including
photocopying and recording, or in any information storage or
retrieval system, without permission in writing from the publishers.

British Library Cataloguing in Publication Data
Barrell, G. R.
    Teachers and the law.—6th ed.
    1. Law—England
    I. Title   II. Partington, J.A.
    344.204'78   KD532

ISBN 0–416–42170–9
ISBN 0–416–39530–9 (Pbk)

For Jane

For Jane

Contents

Note to the sixth edition

The education service noted Geoffrey Barrell's death in 1983 with sincere regret. A former well known headmaster, he was one of the very first some thirty years ago to recognize that the law would come to play an increasing role in teachers' professional lives. Today this is taken for granted and his book, on which he was working at the time of his death, has almost trebled in size since its first edition in 1958. It is no mean achievement that so many thousands of teachers recognize immediately the advice 'Look it up in Barrell'.

Since the last edition of the book appeared in 1978 the education service has continued to take the strain of two major pressures, falling rolls and financial cutbacks. These have been unprecedented in their severity and even the most senior teachers and administrators have little previous experience upon which to rely. DES Circular 2/81 reported that the school population of about 9 million in 1979 will fall to about 7 million by 1990. Among other things this has consequences for teachers' conditions of service, redundancy, redeployment and early retirement. Following hard on the heels of comprehensive reorganization, local education authorities have been faced with the pressing need to reorganize their schools to cope with rapidly falling numbers of classes, starting with primary schools and working through to the current issue of sixth form reorganization. Financially hardpressed schools have had to look to other sources of funding. The urgent need to shed academic staff brought about by scarcity of funds has caused the government to look hard at the whole question of tenure for academic staff in universities. These are the sorts of issues on which the law has been called to pronounce and are included in this edition.

The picture is however not entirely negative. Spare places in many schools have created a situation where parental choice of school can become a reality, and the Education Act of 1980 has responded to this. The size of the teaching force has not declined as quickly as numbers of pupils, so that classes are generally smaller. The bridge between the maintained and non-maintained sectors which threatened to vanish with the phasing out of the direct grant system of funding has been partly restored by the assisted places scheme. Perhaps most significantly of all, the Education Act of 1981 has given renewed impetus to the education of children with special educational needs.

This edition went to print in May 1985. 'The law', says Lord Denning in his recent *Landmarks in the Law*, 'never stands still. It goes on apace. You have to run fast to keep up with it.' Parliament is currently debating a government Bill which will permit parents to exempt their children from corporal punishment in schools; yet decisions pending at the European Court of Human Rights at Strasbourg may render this Bill pointless even before it reaches the statute book. The means by which teachers' salaries and conditions of service are negotiated are currently under close scrutiny. The law on copyright, substantially unrevised since the principal Act of 1956, will probably have to be amended to take account of changed circumstances. Some of these matters may be resolved even before this edition appears in print.

Finally, so many people, sometimes voices at the other end of the telephone only, have had a hand in producing and commenting on the material upon which this book is based that sheer lack of space makes it impossible to thank them all by name. I would, however, particularly like to thank Graham

Clayton, Solicitor at the National Union of Teachers, Paul Vaughan, Head of Division of Law at Thames Polytechnic, and Pat Partington, Nottinghamshire County Secretary of the National Association of Head Teachers, all of whom read through the final typescript and put me right in many places. I also owe a particular debt of thanks to Hilda Ratcliffe whose skill in deciphering my handwriting while typing leaves me speechless with admiration.

John Partington
Nottingham 1985

Preface

This book is intended to help the teacher through some of the many legal pitfalls which beset his path today. It is hoped, also, that it may be of some use to students in training so that they may be both forewarned and forearmed. Whilst some of the subject matter is primarily the concern of heads, a great deal more is part and parcel of the everyday life of the assistant teacher. Furthermore, school governors often have to deal with matters of a legal nature and, in any case, need some knowledge of the structure of the educational system in which they are playing an increasingly important part. The book has been so arranged that it provides a quarry of material to which quick and easy reference may be made by those whose concern with education is limited to their spare time, and whose training is in other disciplines.

The first part of the book is devoted to a simple outline of the educational system in England and Wales as established by law. Teachers often have hazy ideas about those parts of the national system of education with which they are not in close contact, and of their own place, rights and responsibilities within it. A teacher's employment is subject to the terms of his contract and this, in turn, depends upon the common law, statutes and a host of regulations made under the authority of those laws. Whilst it is hardly possible to commend Statutory Instruments as soothing bedside reading, it is highly desirable that teachers should understand the conditions upon which they are employed.

At common law a teacher is *in loco parentis* and whilst a child is in his care some of the privileges of the natural parent are delegated or transferred to him in order that he may carry out his duties. In return, the teacher must assume certain responsibilities and must recognize that these obligations, partly legal and partly moral, rest upon him in every aspect of his work. The second part of the book deals with the way in which some of these matters affect the teacher in his professional capacity.

The common law requires that since the teacher is *in loco parentis* he should take such care of his pupils as a prudent father would take. It does not demand more; it will not be satisfied with less. Most of us would agree that caring for other people's children is morally a greater burden than looking after our own. The law does not explicitly take this view, but it does expect that we should take at least the same care.

Many of the problems covered in this book are illustrated by actual cases which have been before the courts. It should be remembered that the law, as promulgated in Acts of Parliament, is stated in very general terms for it would be quite impossible to frame a statute which would meet every conceivable set of circumstances – and some circumstances are almost inconceivable. It is the duty of the courts to apply the test of law to the facts of a particular case and the decisions thus made, provided they have not been appealed against successfully, become case law and may be quoted as precedents in similar proceedings.[1]

It would be foolish to pretend that the aim of this book is to make every teacher his own lawyer. No two cases are exactly alike in their circumstances, and the differences are often so subtle that only a trained legal mind can recognize them. It is intended as a general guide to help teachers to unravel some of the simpler problems, and to warn them of the existence of some of the graver dangers. Most teachers manage to pass from training to retirement without being personally concerned in any major legal problems; others are not so fortunate, and may become involved in wrangling over the tenure of their appointment or a complaint by a contentious parent which has arisen through no fault of their own. If serious trouble threatens, a wise teacher will take two precautions.

First, he should immediately inform his superior and discuss the matter fully and frankly with him. For teachers this means the head; depending on the problem, a head will go either to the chairman of his governors or, if he deems it wise, to the local education authority, or both. If legal action is probable, a superior has a right to be forewarned. Moreover, such action is in the teacher's own interest since he is much less likely to receive sympathetic treatment when concealed trouble bursts like a bolt from the blue or when the passage of time has seriously restricted the help which can be given to him. It is useless and unwise for an assistant teacher to try to persuade a complaining parent to drop a matter he is threatening to report. If the teacher has acted reasonably, he has little to fear from an investigation; if, on the other hand, the parent suspects that he fears any probing into his work, it is highly probable that the same complaint, or another, will be raised at a later date. Almost inevitably the teacher's earlier attempt to hush things up will then be revealed, with disastrous effects on his professional reputation.

The second precaution is to report the whole affair to his professional association. Some teachers will say that they are not 'union minded' and that they prefer not to join such an organization. Moreover, there is no 'closed shop' in the profession. However, quite apart from the fact that many of the privileges of the profession are due to the activities of the associations, there are many practical advantages to be gained from membership, and not the least of these is the provision of legal advice to members faced with litigation. When an important issue is at stake the associations will spare no time, trouble or money to safeguard their members' interests.[2] This book is not intended as a substitute for service of this kind; the teacher faced with a lawsuit should consult his association at once and, having received advice, he should follow it. This applies even when the advice is unpalatable, and the member is advised not to pursue a line of action which he was proposing to take. Only the association's solicitor, in possession of all the facts of the case and the records of many more relevant cases than could be included in a book of this scope, can weigh the various factors and advise the member how best he can act in his own interests.

A teacher charged with an offence before the courts should seek the advice of his professional association before entering any plea. Even though the nature of the charge may not be such that the association can accept responsibility for fighting the teacher's case, it will put him in touch with a solicitor if necessary, and will be ready to deal with any professional implications which may arise should he plead or be found guilty. The teacher may, for example, be asked to show cause why the Secretary of State should not withdraw his recognition as a qualified teacher. In some instances this result would be inevitable, but there is an undefined area where a person is not necessarily unfit to be a teacher merely because he has been convicted of an offence, and his professional association may be able to plead extenuating circumstances. A teacher can employ a solicitor privately to plead his case and pay the cost. An association provides the service free of charge.

This is not intended to be a standard work on the law of education so much as a handbook of professional advice on points at which the law touches teachers. Therefore, where it has seemed worthwhile to do so, the opportunity has been taken of including some material which is purely professional in character, but which has a bearing on the main theme.

Finally, section 1(2) of the Interpretation Act 1889 applies to this book with the effect that, 'unless the contrary intention appears, words importing the masculine gender shall include females'.

References

1. For an outline of the doctrine of the binding force of precedent, see G. R. Barrell, *Legal Cases for Teachers* (Methuen, 1970), pp. 11–12.
2. It should be remembered that professional associations will undertake to defend their members only in connection with matters arising after they join. It would be unfair to other members if it were possible to take up membership because it is already certain that free assistance is needed.

Introduction:
Statute and common law

The law affects teachers at practically every turn in their professional lives, whether they realize it or not. There are two main strands in English law: the older, the common law, and the newer statute law, rooted in Acts of Parliament, and it is important to understand the way in which those two strands follow teachers into school each day.

So far as statute law is concerned, the basis is the Education Act 1944, to which has been added a number of amending Acts. No statute can take account of every single set of circumstances which can possibly arise, and Parliament has never striven to achieve this detailed perfection. It would be quite foolish, even presumptuous, because conditions vary from one part of the country to another and from time to time during the currency of the Act. Therefore a statute is cast in very general terms. But most statutes, including the Education Act 1944, give the power to competent government departments such as the DES to make regulations; and these regulations, if they are made within the powers given by the Act, and if they are neither contrary to law nor repugnant to public policy, have the force of law and form part of the statutory law of the realm. They are known as Statutory Instruments (S.I.).

This is what is called delegated legislation, and the Act naturally gives power in the first instance to the Secretary of State to make such regulations. For example, there are the Education (Schools & Further Education) Regulations 1981 which lay down in a little more detail how schools which are within the maintained system shall be governed. It is these regulations, for example, which include amongst many other things the rules relating to the number of teaching sessions per year. Then there are the recent regulations dealing with such matters as the composition of governing bodies, school premises, and the information about local schools which must be made available to parents. These are made by the Secretary of State; Parliament has the opportunity of questioning them before they are put into force, and they then have the effect of law. There should be copies in every school; all too often there are not.

The second level to which legislation in education is delegated is the local education authority and, within the framework of the Act and the Secretary of State's regulations, a local education authority may make regulations in more detail dealing with the conduct of its schools. Once again, if they are not beyond the authority's legal powers (*ultra vires*) they are binding, and these regulations vary quite considerably from one authority to another. This is part of the wisdom of Parliament in that, having given the provision of the public sector of education into the hands of local education authorities, it then leaves to those authorities quite a wide discretion as to how the duties bound upon them by the Act are to be carried out to take account of local needs.

There is, however, another level at which there is a delegation of the authority to make regulations and this is an important one from the teacher's point of view. Under section 17 of the Act of 1944 and section 1 of the Education Act of 1980 it is provided that every school shall be conducted in accordance with Articles of Government. The Articles of Government define the relationship and the duties of the local education authority, the governors, and the head of the school. There are references in them to the appointment and dismissal of the teaching staff, and there is a standard provision that the assistant staff shall have the opportunity to make their views known, but the functions and the duties of the staff, other than the head, are not dealt with in the Articles. In law they are appointed under contract to carry out the reasonable directions of the head.

One of the standard provisions is that the head teacher 'shall control the internal organization, management and discipline of the school, shall exercise supervision over the teaching and non-teaching staff, other than the clerk to the governors, and shall have the power of suspending pupils'. This places the whole burden of running the school professionally in the hands of the head and of no one else; and it is part of the recognized system of justice in this country that if you place a duty on someone you must give him the necessary discretion to carry it out. There is no point in placing an obligation on any person, and preventing him from discharging it by bonds which cannot be broken.

To carry out his duty the head of a school must have a code of rules. These may be formulated in different ways: they may not be called rules in every school; they may be written, or they may be the accumulation of a large number of oral precepts which become, so to speak, the tradition of the school. No matter what form the rules take, they are part of the system by which the head discharges his legal obligation to control the internal organization, management and discipline of the school and they have for the members of that school the force of law. Reasonable school rules as such have been upheld in courts of justice.

For example, in 1929 there was a rule at Newport Grammar School in Shropshire that pupils of the school should not smoke within the school precincts or in public during term time. One afternoon, two boys left school and smoked as they strolled through the streets. They were seen by prefects who reported them to the headmaster, and the headmaster decided that they should be caned for breach of a school rule. One boy took his punishment 'like a man', but the other objected. He said that his father had given him permission to smoke, it was no concern of the head whether he did or not, and that the head could not make a rule which flouted the father's authority. Moreover it had happened away from the school premises, and after school hours. The head got two masters to hold the boy down and administered the beating. The father thereupon summoned the headmaster before the magistrates, and the case was dismissed. The father then asked the justices to state a case for the consideration of the Divisional Court of the King's Bench Division. The justices at first refused, holding the application to be frivolous, but in due course they had to comply. The Lord Chief Justice, Lord Hewart, said at the hearing in the King's Bench Division:[1]

> There was at the school a school rule forbidding smoking by pupils at the school during the school term and on the school premises and in public. That was a reasonable rule. The boy deliberately broke the rule, being aware of it, and the head master caned him. Such punishment was a reasonable punishment for the breach of the school rule, and the father's application to the court must be dismissed.

The court was quite clearly upholding a school rule, whether the members of that court or indeed the boy's father approved of smoking or not.

Some years later, in the early 1950s, came the case of *Spiers v. Warrington Corporation*.[2] A 13-year-old girl named Eva Spiers was a pupil at a secondary school in Warrington, and turned up at school in clothing which the headmistress considered as unsuitable. She came, in fact, in jeans. There was a school rule relating to the suitability of clothing in the school. The mother's excuse was that the girl had had two bouts of rheumatic fever. She had been advised by a doctor that the girl's kidneys should be kept warm, and believed that jeans keep kidneys warmer than skirts. The headmistress thereupon asked the mother to produce a medical certificate to this effect.

No such certificate was forthcoming, and the headmistress entered her repeatedly for medical examinations in school, but Eva failed to turn up. The headmistress then decided to take a well charted but fairly exceptional course. Every time Eva came to school in slacks the headmistress said to her, in effect: 'Now run along home dear and come back properly dressed. As soon as you do, you can come into school.' But Eva stayed at home for the morning and arrived at school again in the afternoon. The same conversation would take place and Eva would return the next morning. This went on for some months until the County Borough of Warrington decided to prosecute the father for failing to send his child to school as was his duty. The magistrates found him guilty and fined him.

Mr Spiers appealed, maintaining that the magistrates were wrong in law, that he had sent his child to school; and that it was the perversity of the headmistress which was preventing Eva from receiving her education, the education to which she was entitled.

The West Derby Quarter Sessions Appeals Committee quashed the conviction, believing that the parents were acting reasonably in the interests of their child. The local education authority thereupon appealed to the Queen's Bench Division, which did not agree.

Lord Chief Justice Goddard considered the clause in the Articles of Government which said: 'The Head Mistress shall control the internal organization, management and discipline of the school.' He commented: 'The Head Mistress obviously has the right and the power to prescribe the discipline for the school.... There must be somebody to keep discipline, and of course that person is the Head Mistress.... The question is: was the Head Mistress in communicating her refusal to allow the girl to come to school in this way acting within her rights? We hold that she was not only within her rights, but that it was her duty; and the parent, knowing that the child would not be admitted, and insisting on her being dressed in this way ... committed an offence.'

Once again, the court upheld the school rule, and said that for Eva Spiers the rule relating to dress was part of the law of the land and justiciable before the courts.

This does not mean, however, that any school rule, however capricious, is lawful. Rules must be reasonable: it is possible that in the 1980s a judge with a trendy teenage daughter of his own might decide, while still accepting the overall authority of the head, that to exclude a pupil *on grounds of dress* was unreasonable. A rule must also not be contrary to the law as a whole: it was finally held on appeal in 1982 that a Birmingham head could not ban a Sikh boy from wearing a turban to school, because such a ban was contrary to the Race Relations Act of 1976.[3]

Returning to the common law, it must be noted that much of the education of children is entrusted to the schoolmaster and, if he is to carry out his obligations, some of the rights and some of the duties of the natural parent must be transferred or delegated to him so far and for so long as may be necessary for him to carry out his duty. In other words the schoolmaster is said, to that extent, to be *in loco parentis*. He may chastise the child; if he does so unreasonably he is accountable to the law. He must take care of the child, and if he fails to do so reasonably he is accountable to the law. Indeed, this question of the care of children really lies at the root of many of our problems, because a large number of the restraints which we place on children are placed upon them for their own good, or for the good of other pupils. In the late nineteenth century there was a case in what we should now call an independent boarding school where some boys exploring the school conservatory found some phosphorus and started to play about with it. They had an accident, and one boy was very badly burnt. The parent brought a successful action for damages in what is known as negligence against the school[4] and in the course of the hearing Mr Justice Cave asked: 'What is the duty of a schoolmaster?' 'The duty of a schoolmaster', he continued, 'is to take such care of his boys as a careful father would take of his boys.'

That is the basic duty *in loco parentis*, and the courts have generally borne in mind that wise, prudent and careful parents do not have thirty children! But there has been a tendency in the courts since the war to raise the standard of care in all cases of negligence. So far as education cases are concerned, this trend started with a case in Middlesex in 1962 arising out of an incident when two boys had been playing a game of ring-a-ring-o'-roses round the changing rooms of the gym, until one put his fist through a pane of glass and cut his arm badly. In *Williams v. Eady* Mr Justice Edmund Davies considered that the schoolmaster's duty of care involved caring for his boys as a careful father would: not a careful father thinking in relation to events at home, but a careful father applying his mind to school life where there is 'more skylarking and a bit of rough play'. He therefore awarded very heavy damages to the boy.[5]

There have been other cases in which the standard of care has been raised, one of the most important being one in which the learned judge restated the rule in *Williams v. Eady* in more specific terms, and then inquired into the school's disciplinary system in detail.[6]

As has been said earlier, a head must make rules in order to perform his duty to control the discipline of the school under the Articles of Government. These rules form part of the school's system, one of the functions of which is to take all reasonable steps to prevent any untoward event which a reasonable person might foresee, or which is preventable, and which might cause injury to any person. There must be, of course, the provision of an adequate degree of supervision to make the system work. This, in turn, will usually necessitate a requirement that the assistant staff will assist the head by undertaking such duties as he may require.

When it is alleged that a school has been negligent in caring for its pupils, the court examines the system in detail. Having first satisfied themselves that the school has an adequate system, the court will then inquire whether, on the occasion in question before them, the system at that particular point was being maintained at full efficiency.

In *Beaumont v. Surrey County Council* it was established that during break there were two masters on duty, four prefects, four sub-prefects and four monitors – fourteen people. It should have been adequate. On the day in question, when an accident happened, the two masters (whose duty it was also to clear the school at the beginning of break) did not, in fact, emerge into the playground until about eight minutes after the break began. The accident had already happened. This was a breakdown of the system, with the result that the decision went against the Authority.[7]

In his judgment Mr Justice Geoffrey Lane said that the duty of a headmaster is to protect his pupils from inanimate objects, from the actions of their fellow pupils or from a combination of the two.

So the two strands of the law meet. On the one hand there is the duty deriving from statute under the Articles of Government; on the other, duty at common law. In all that is often written about the excessive powers of the head, one must never forget, as the law stands at present, the inescapable burden of duty and responsibility placed upon him and, to a lesser degree, upon every teacher. No one can continue to carry out that duty or exercise that responsibility unless he has the necessary discretion: so one must talk in terms of the discretion necessary to carry out a duty, rather than in terms of power. Without it a teacher cannot fulfil his obligations in law.

It should be noted that a deputy head teacher takes on all the obligations of the head when acting on the head's behalf.

References

1. R *v.* Newport (Shropshire) Justices *ex parte* Wright [1929] 2 KB 416; LCT 237.
2. [1954] 1 QB 61; LCT 165.
3. Mandla *v.* Dowell Lee (1983) 1 All ER 1062 HL.
4. Williams *v.* Eady (1893) 10 TLR 41 CA; LCT 240.
5. Lyes *v.* Middlesex County Council (1963) 61 LGR 443; LCT 198.
6. Beaumont *v.* Surrey County Council (1968) 66 LGR 580; LCT 246.
7. The failure of supervision, however, was not the only element of negligence in this case. By putting the elastic which later caused the injury into the wastepaper basket, the master had created an 'allurement' to children; and moreover, this had been allowed to remain for a considerable period. This case is discussed later in chapter XIV.

PART I
TEACHERS
AND THEIR
EMPLOYERS

I
The organization
of education

1 Statutory provisions

The organization of the public system of education in England and Wales is laid down in detail in the Education Act 1944, commonly called the Butler Act after Lord Butler who, as President of the Board of Education, piloted it through Parliament and subsequently became the first Minister of Education.

The Act of 1944 is cited as the principal Act. It has, however, been amended and supplemented by the Education Act 1946, the Education (Miscellaneous Provisions) Acts of 1948 and 1953, the Education Acts of 1959, 1962, 1964, 1967, 1968, 1973, 1975, 1976, 1979, 1980, 1981, the Remuneration of Teachers Act 1965, the Education (No. 2) Act 1968, the Education (Work Experience) Act 1973 and the Education (School Leaving Dates) Act 1976. These later statutes were largely designed to make amendments in the light of experience of the working of the principal Act. The statutes are cited as the Education Acts 1944 to 1981. The Education (Grants and Awards) Act of 1984 permits the Secretary of State to make grants to local education authorities for purposes defined in regulations.

4 Teachers and the Law

In addition, there are other Acts which affect the administration of the educational system, either by specific reference or because their provisions apply across the whole spectrum of society. Examples of the first category are the London Government Act 1963 which included educational reorganization in the general reconstruction of the capital's local government, and the Local Government Act 1972 which did the same in the rest of England and Wales. In the second group are such measures as the Health and Safety at Work, etc. Act 1974, the Sex Discrimination Act 1975, the Race Relations Act 1976 and the Employment Protection (Consolidation) Act 1978.

2 The Secretary of State

The 1944 Act provided that there should be a Minister of Education 'to promote the education of the people of England and Wales and the progressive development of institutions devoted to that purpose, and to secure the effective execution by local authorities, under his control and direction, of the national policy for providing a varied and comprehensive educational service in every area'.[1]

The Minister replaced the former President of the Board of Education and took over all the functions formerly exercised by him. The Secretary of State for Education and Science Order, 1964,[2] transferred the functions of the Minister of Education and Science to a Secretary of State, and the Ministry of Education became the Department of Education and Science (commonly called the DES).

The Secretary of State is a member of the government of the day and is answerable to Parliament for the actions of his department.[3] He is assisted by Under-Secretaries of State.

3 The powers of the Secretary of State

The Secretary of State influences the work of local education authorities in several different ways: for example, through specific powers granted under Acts of Parliament (approval of capital expenditure on schools, power to approve the reorganization of schools and so on), through statutory instruments (regulations binding on local education authorities), through circulars (policy statements) and through administrative memoranda (change of detail, alterations to procedure).

The Secretary of State also has the power to ensure that local education authorities act 'reasonably',[4] and that they carry out the requirements of the Acts of Parliament.[5] If appealed to, the Secretary of State can 'give directions' to the defaulting local education authority, governors or any person to ensure compliance with the law.

The significance of the term 'reasonable' as used in the 1944 Act was the subject of legal interpretation in 1976.[6] Political control of the Tameside local education authority changed after the authority had gained approval from the Secretary of State for a plan of comprehensive reorganization, but before the plan was implemented. Although the incoming political party claimed an electoral mandate *not* to introduce comprehensive schools, the Secretary of State ruled that failure to implement the approved plans would be 'unreasonable' under section 68.

The local authority appealed to the courts. In the Court of Appeal, Lord Denning quoted Lord Hailsham in another case on the interpretation of 'reasonable': 'Two reasonable persons could perfectly reasonably come to opposite conclusions on the same set of facts without forfeiting their right to be regarded as reasonable. It was one thing to say to a person: "I think that you are wrong: I do not agree with you"; it was quite another to say to him "You are being quite unreasonable about it".'

On the facts of the case, therefore, it was not unreasonable of Tameside not to proceed with comprehensive reorganization, however much the Secretary of State might *disagree* with the authority. It seems that the courts are willing to intervene between the Secretary of State and local education authority if the Secretary of State confuses disagreement with local authorities with unreasonable behaviour on their part.

4   The Department of Education and Science

The DES has a large permanent staff under the control of the Secretary of State and carries on the day-to-day routine of the latter's functions as laid down in the Act, in accordance with the wishes of Parliament. It correlates the work of the various education authorities and examines their schemes involving capital expenditure. Regulations made by the Secretary of State in accordance with the powers given by the Act are prepared, in the first instance, by the permanent staff.

All the teachers in schools within the statutory system of education must be recognized by the DES, which is the keeper of their professional records. Modern statistical methods have enabled the DES to replace teachers' service books by service cards, which contain all the information previously contained in book form relating to qualifications, details of service from year to year, and matters concerning salary and superannuation. Arrangements are made for teachers to obtain copies of their service cards. In the meantime, the employing authority will provide a certified statement of service at a nominal charge.

The Act provides that the Secretary of State shall 'cause inspections to be made of every educational establishment at such intervals as appear to him to be appropriate, and to cause a special inspection of any such establishment to be made whenever he considers such an inspection to be desirable'.[7] For this purpose he recommends to the Crown the appointment of inspectors whose duties are to visit the schools in order to consider whether they are complying with the regulations, and to report upon their general efficiency.

Her Majesty's Inspectors (commonly known as HMIs) deal with a wide range of subjects including not only the actual teaching work of the school but also the state of the buildings and the provision of facilities generally. They may not inspect religious education of a denominational character in voluntary schools. They make periodic routine visits to the schools under their care and, although regular, full inspections have been discontinued, they may still take place from time to time. They can also inspect local education authorities and are increasingly involved with initial teacher training. Over the years the HMI's function has changed in emphasis and greater stress is now laid on the advisory side of this work. Although the inspectoral element has diminished, however, it still remains a basic part of HMI's duties when appropriate. A review of the functions of the inspectorate may be found in *The Work of H.M. Inspectorate in England and Wales.*[8]

Since January 1983 the DES has made public the content of HMI reports on educational institutions and local authorities.[9]

It is an offence to obstruct any person authorized to make an inspection, the penalty being a fine for the first offence or, for subsequent offences, a fine with or without a maximum of three months' imprisonment.[10]

The Act also set up two advisory councils, one for England, the other for Wales.[11] The function of these bodies is 'to advise on educational theory and practice as they think fit and on any questions referred to them' by the Secretary of State. Members of the councils are appointed by the Secretary of State and must include persons with educational experience outside the statutory system. They replaced the former Consultative Committee which issued such far-reaching documents as the Hadow Report on The Education of the Adolescent and the Spens Report on Secondary Education. From the Advisory Councils came the Crowther and Newsom Reports on secondary education (*15 to 18* and *Half Our Future*) and the Plowden Report, *Children and their Primary Schools*. The panels have not been reconstituted since 1967, but their structure remains on the statute books. More recently, Secretaries of State have called for reports on the education of ethnic minorities (Rampton, later Swann) and the teaching of mathematics (Cockcroft).[12]

5   Local education authorities

It is a characteristic British anomaly that, although there is a statutory system of education, there are no state schools. The actual provision and administration of education, other than the universities and voluntary establishments, is in the hands of local education authorities.[13] The whole structure of local government in England and Wales has, however, been altered since the passage of the 1944 Act, and little remains of the local education authorities established at that time. In 1944 the local administration of education was entrusted to the councils of counties and county boroughs; and the county authorities, other than London, were required to prepare schemes for dividing their areas into smaller units each with a divisional executive committee. In addition, some non-county boroughs and urban districts were given the status of an excepted district which enabled them to act as the divisional executive committee for their areas.

Reorganization of local government in Greater London took effect in 1964; and a decade later county boroughs, divisional executives and excepted districts were swept away by the Local Government Act 1972 which came into force in 1974. As a result, thirty-nine authorities with populations below 100,000 disappeared, together with all statutory intermediate bodies between the authority's education committee and the then managing and governing bodies of schools.

Local education authorities appoint education committees to discharge their functions under Part II of the first schedule to the 1944 Act. A majority of the members of the education committee must be members of the authority itself, but it is laid down that the composition must include persons of experience in education and persons acquainted with the educational provisions prevailing in the area for which the committee acts.

Local education authorities are required to provide an adequate number of school places, a sufficient supply of teachers in the various categories, and the equipment needed for their work. These duties are bound upon them by the Act.[14] Beyond this they have an overriding obligation to see that the school system runs smoothly. When in 1979 schools in Haringey were closed during industrial action by school caretakers, a group of parents protested to the Secretary of State that the local authority was failing in its duty to educate children. The Secretary of State replied that, in her view, the local authority

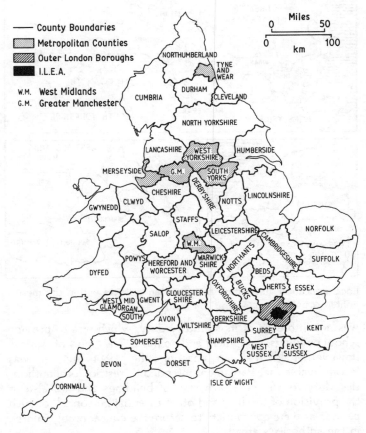

Local education authorities: counties. In the metropolitan counties (shaded on the map) education is the responsibility of the metropolitan districts.

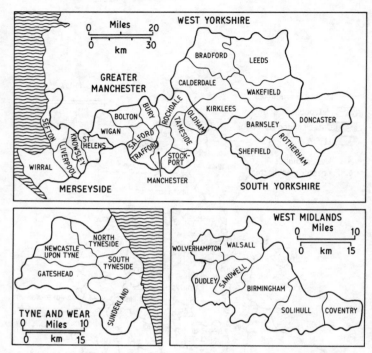

Local education authorities: metropolitan districts within the metropolitan counties.

was not in breach of its statutory duty, which was to provide
school buildings, equipment and no more. The Court of Appeal,
however, held that, in enacting the 1944 Act, it was
inconceivable that Parliament intended to restrict local authorities' duty to the mere provision of buildings and not also to
the provision of teachers and other essential personnel for such
periods as were appropriate to secure the education of children
in the authority's area.[15]

NON-METROPOLITAN COUNTIES

There are forty-seven non-metropolitan counties, of which
thirty-nine are in England and eight in Wales. The counties

Local education authorities: Greater London. The Inner London Education Authority is responsible for education in the central, shaded area. Each of the outer boroughs is a separate local education authority.

are divided into districts, but the latter have no powers in relation to education.

METROPOLITAN COUNTIES

Six areas of dense population – Tyne and Wear, Merseyside, Greater Manchester, West Yorkshire, South Yorkshire and West Midlands – have been designated as metropolitan counties. They are divided into metropolitan districts which are the local education authorities in these areas. The metropolitan county councils have no educational functions.

GREATER LONDON

The London Government Act 1963, which abolished at a blow
the London and Middlesex County Councils, introduced a
unique system for the administration of education in the Greater
London area. Since its provisions took effect the whole of the
area until then administered by the London County Council
has been controlled by the new Greater London Council, acting
by means of a special committee. Each of the new outer London
boroughs became a local education authority in its own right.
The special committee for the central area consists of the
members of the Greater London Council for that area, one
representative of each inner London borough council appointed
by that council from among its members, and one representative
of the Court of Common Council of the City of London
appointed from among its members. When acting in this
capacity the body is known as the Inner London Education
Authority, usually referred to as ILEA. The Act provided that
the Secretary of State should review the situation by 1970 to
determine whether all or part of this service should be
transferred to the City and the inner London Boroughs,[16] but
Mr Anthony Crosland announced on 18 November 1965 that
legislation would be introduced to repeal this section. This was
done, and London's educational administration has survived
the Local Government Act 1972. The situation is not static,
however. During 1983 the Government announced its intention
ultimately to abolish the metropolitan county authorities, and
to hold direct elections to the ILEA, making it into an *ad hoc*
education authority.[17]

In addition to schools, local education authorities provide a
wide range of ancillary services ranging from school meals to
libraries, grants for further education, and the service of youth.
They must make provision for the education of children who
are handicapped physically or mentally, and for those who are
deprived of a normal home environment or who are maladjusted.
They may appoint their own inspectorate to advise and report
on the work of their schools.[18] The penalties for obstructing
these officers are the same as in the case of HMIs.

Some local education authorities maintain colleges in which specialist training for teachers is provided. Entry to such colleges is not restricted to those living in the authority's area, neither are those trained in them necessarily employed later in the service of that authority.

One of the duties of a local education authority is the appointment of a Chief Education Officer.[19] This official is responsible for the administration of the authority's education service under the direction of the education committee. The requirement that the authority should consult the Secretary of State before making an appointment has been repealed.[20]

Local education authorities may make such rules as they consider necessary for the good conduct of their schools and the guidance of those who work in them. These regulations must not conflict with the provisions of the Acts, nor with any rules made by the Secretary of State under the Acts.

6   Local authority finance

Expenditure by local authorities has three sources: approximately 30 per cent comes from local rates, 20 per cent from fees and charges (council house rents, admission charges, school lettings, fees for further education courses, and so on) and 50 per cent from government grants.

As part of a general policy of reducing public expenditure, the present government is reducing in percentage terms its grants to local authorities – the rate support grant. The government can inhibit local authorities from increasing rates, perhaps to compensate for the reduction in rate support grant, by enabling the Secretary of State for the Environment to limit specific local rate levels by law, and to require local authorities to consult local industry before determining their level of rates. The latter is deemed to be necessary because local industry cannot as such vote in local elections, and yet must pay rates.

In carrying out this overall policy, the government has taken steps to remove from local authorities the statutory obligation to provide certain services.[21] In the education field, the Education Act of 1980 removed the obligation to provide milk, school meals or other refreshment and made it instead discretionary.[22] Pupils whose parents are in receipt of supplementary benefit or family income supplement must, however, continue to be offered these benefits.[23] Furthermore, local education authorities can make such charges as they think fit for school meals,[24] or none at all.[25] The government also intended in the 1980 Act to permit local education authorities to charge for transport to and from school, but these provisions were removed by the House of Lords during the passage of the Bill. It was felt that such charges would fall inequitably on those parents who chose denominational schools, since their children tend on average to travel further to school.

Against this background of financial restrictions, in 1980 Hereford and Worcester local education authority introduced charges for tuition in musical instruments in their schools. A parent of two daughters with musical aptitude challenged the lawfulness of this in court. Mr Justice Forbes held that under the 1944 Act[26] 'no fees shall be charged by a local authority ... in respect of the education provided in any such school.' He rejected the argument that the Act was concerned with education and not with training, which was what the local education authority believed instrumental tuition to be. 'The Act of 1944 dealt with education as if it were synonymous with instruction and training and there was a clear distinction between that and the provision of facilities for recreation and social and physical training referred to in section 53 of the Act.' Such charges on parents, he ruled, are therefore not lawful: if any local education authority could not provide such tuition for financial reasons, it should cease to, and the court would not interfere.[27] Charges for swimming lessons would no doubt be similarly regarded.

There is, however, nothing unlawful in parents making voluntary contributions over and above what is provided by the authority. It was reported in 1980 that one local education authority school was inviting parents to pay a contribution of £9 per year towards the cost of school books; the DES is reported to have taken the view that section 8 of the 1944 Act '... did not lay down that every child should have individual copies of textbooks',[28] so that failure to provide books free of charge from the school would not invite censure from the DES.

In 1981 a group of Northamptonshire parents appealed to the Secretary of State to use his powers under s. 68 or s. 99 of the 1944 Act[29] to declare the local authority to be in default of its duty under section 8 to provide sufficient schools 'in number, character and equipment to afford for all pupils opportunities for education offering such variety of instruction and training as may be desirable in view of their different ages, abilities and aptitudes'. The point at issue was whether financial cuts had reduced the quality of the education service to below a reasonable standard, and below the standards required by the 1944 Act.

The appeal did not succeed. The DES view, as reported, was that the Secretary of State would act 'only if there was evidence of a "systematic dismantling of the curriculum"."A secondary school which provided no modern languages and no science for any of its pupils — that would constitute a breach under section 8."' The section 'was drafted in such terms that the Secretary of State was required to examine an authority's total provision ... a school would be unlikely to be regarded by the Department as in breach of the Act if it abolished, say, modern languages if schools nearby continued to offer them, but there might be a case to answer if a school serving a wide rural area systematically and as a matter of policy refused to offer modern languages.'[30]

7 Ultra vires

Powers are granted by Parliament to public bodies such as government departments (the DES) and to local authorities (local education authorities). Such bodies can exercise only the powers they have been given, and only within any limits set by Parliament to those powers. If a public body attempts to do something for which it has no such statutory authority, any aggrieved and injured party can seek a declaration from the courts that the act complained of is *ultra vires* (beyond its powers). The High Court may order the act to be quashed or prohibited.

Perhaps the most famous *ultra vires* action in the history of the education service was the so-called 'Cockerton case' which reached the Court of Appeal in 1901.[31] The then London School Board was held to have no statutory authority for the vast sums of public money which it had spent on non-elementary education in its schools: this was despite the fact that the Education Department (the forerunner of the DES) had known about and even encouraged the expenditure.

More recently, in the Tameside case the authority of the Secretary of State to give instructions to local education authorities was challenged and redefined. Similarly in *Coney v. Choyce*[32] the *ultra vires* doctrine was shown to be fairly and reasonably flexible. The school authorities for Roman Catholic schools in the north of Nottinghamshire failed to publish details of their proposed comprehensive reorganization precisely in the manner laid down by regulations. A particular bone of contention was the failure to post notices of reorganization near the entrances of the affected schools. The court held, however, that the intention of the Education Act 1944 of ensuring that all interested parties knew the details of the proposed reorganization had nevertheless been met, despite the irregularities, and refused to declare the reorganization null and void.

8   Diocesan education committees

Voluntary schools are provided, so far as the buildings are concerned, by various bodies. In the case of Church of England schools, however, the close relationship between Church and State has involved the creation of diocesan education committees by a Measure of the former Church Assembly which gives them a statutory existence.[33] This Measure provides for the creation of such committees in every diocese except that of Sodor and Man.

The majority of Church schools were once parochial in character and were provided out of funds raised in the parish.

Before the war, many of these buildings had long ceased to conform to modern standards and the cost of putting them in order was far beyond the means of the ordinary parish.

Moreover, in large cities the shift of population and the development of local authorities' housing schemes meant that some Church schools were no longer required, whereas neighbouring parishes badly needed new schools. So long as the trusts were on a parochial basis, it was almost impossible to close down a school in one place and apply its funds elsewhere.

The diocesan education committees can redeploy the educational resources of a whole diocese in accordance with an overall plan. This enables the most urgent modernizations to be carried out, and many new schools have been built which would not have been possible before the creation of the committees. The value of the diocesan education committees has been particularly evident in the establishment of new Church secondary schools which, by their nature, usually serve a much wider area than one parish.

The functions of the diocesan education committees are laid down as follows:[34]

(a) to take such steps as may appear to the Committee to be conducive to the promotion of religious education according to the faith and practice of the Church of England, and to watch the interest of Church schools;

(b) to take such action as may appear desirable to provide new schools;

(c) to promote, and to co-operate with other religious bodies and with local education authorities in promoting, religious education within the diocese;

(d) to give advice, as and when the Committee thinks fit, to trustees or owners, and governors, of Church schools and others concerned as to any matters affecting Church schools within the diocese, and also to the governing bodies of Church educational endowments as to any matters affecting Church educational endowments within the diocese;

(e) to make plans calculated, in the opinion of the Committee, to further the development and organization of religious education in the diocese, and in particular of instruction in religious education according to the faith and practice of the Church of England, after consultation with such trustees or owners and governors of Church schools within the diocese and with such other persons as, in the opinion of the Committee, are interested or as may be in any way affected thereby.

Trustees or owners and governors of Church schools are required to consult the diocesan committee before concluding any agreement dealing with the restoration, rearrangement, continuance, discontinuance, closing, sale or lease of any Church school.

The constitution of the committees is laid down in a schedule to the Measure.

A Church school is now defined as a voluntary school, including its site and buildings, which is held on trust for the purposes of primary or secondary education together with instruction (whether as part of, or in addition to, such primary or secondary education) in accordance with the principles and practice of the Church of England. A school may fall within this definition by statute or charter, by a scheme, order, or other instrument deriving from a statute or other authority, by usage or repute, or by any combination of these authorities.[35]

Providing bodies other than the Church of England, such as the Roman Catholic Church, have their own arrangements which are determined by the varying structures of the bodies concerned.

9   Age, ability and aptitude

The 1944 Act states that 'the schools available for an area shall not be deemed to be sufficient unless they are sufficient in number, character and equipment to afford for all pupils such variety of instruction and training as may be desirable in view of their differing ages, abilities and aptitudes'. The 1981 Act added to this the requirement that local education authorities should secure 'that special educational provision is made for pupils who have special educational needs'.[36]

The organization of schools to meet these needs is laid down as follows: 'The statutory system of public education shall be organized in three successive stages to be known as primary education, secondary education and further education.'[37]

The primary stage of education covers nursery schools or classes, infants' schools and junior schools. It is defined as 'full-time education suitable to the requirements of junior pupils who have not attained the age of 10 years and 6 months, and full-time education suitable to the requirements of junior pupils who have attained that age and whom it is expedient to educate together with junior pupils who have not attained that age'.[38] A junior pupil is a child who has not attained the age of 12 years.[39]

There is no statutory obligation on local authorities to provide nursery education, although a number do. Nor is there any obligation to admit under-5s to reception classes in primary schools.[40]

At the secondary stage there are several different kinds of schools. Secondary education is 'full-time education suitable to the requirements of senior pupils, other than such full-time education as may be provided for senior pupils in pursuance of a scheme made under the provisions of this Act relating to further education, and full-time education suitable to the requirements of junior pupils who have attained the age of 10 years and 6 months and whom it is expedient to educate together with senior pupils'.[41] A senior pupil is a person who has attained the age of 12 years, but has not attained the age of 19 years.[42]

During the first twenty years following the passage of the 1944 Act many local education authorities found the somewhat precise definition of the frontier between primary and secondary education unduly restrictive. In some areas it was difficult to move towards comprehensive secondary education and, at the same time, to make an economical use of the existing buildings. Some educationalists questioned whether the statutory age of transfer was psychologically the best time for transition to a new school environment. Both these considerations pointed towards the development of middle schools which would cater for pupils at the upper end of the primary and the lower end of the secondary categories as defined in the 1944 Act.

The 1944 Act met these difficulties by permitting proposals to be put forward, either for county or voluntary schools, which specify that a school will provide full-time education for pupils below the age of 10 years and 6 months and over the age of 12. The upper and lower age limits must be precisely stated. The Secretary of State, when giving his approval to any particular application, will specify whether the school is to be a primary or a secondary school.[43] Under the Education (Middle School) Regulations of 1980 a middle school in which the age range of pupils above the age of 11 is greater than the age range below it is regarded as a secondary school. If the age range below it is greater, the school is deemed to be primary. Where the balance is equal, the Secretary of State decides.

Further education comprises all vocational and non-vocational education provided for young people after they have left school, and for adults. Until 1944 this field was not among those where authorities were bound to act, although all had some system of further education; but provision of this type is now general. Vocational education is covered by technical, commercial and art courses, many non-vocational courses are arranged, county colleges may eventually be established and the service of youth provides a wide range of recreational facilities. Children in their last year of compulsory education at school may attend a college of further education in the evenings with their head's permission.

One aspect of the problem of falling rolls is that the traditional sixth form in 11–18 comprehensive and grammar schools has become less and less viable, both on educational and economic grounds. Local authorities have powers to establish separate sixth-form colleges, as do diocesan authorities. These colleges are for the full-time education of pupils who have attained the age of 16 but are below 19 years of age. In

1983 there were about 100 such colleges in England and Wales providing education, both academic and non-academic, for about 60,000 students.

Another recent development has been the tertiary college which provides a full range of further education courses, as well as sixth-form type courses, for students over 16. In 1983 there were some fifteen tertiary colleges with some 15,000 students.

Sixth-form colleges are deemed to be secondary schools:[44] a tertiary college is conducted under further education regulations and thus students are deemed not to be at school.

Local authorities are not compelled to provide full-time education in any particular establishment.

10   Parental choice

Parliament provided in 1944 that pupils are to be educated in accordance with the wishes of their parents.[45] This general principle was subject to the proviso that such education should be compatible with efficient instruction and training, and that it should not cause unreasonable public expenditure.

It has been held that this section does not inhibit a local education authority from modifying any development plan for its schools nor from changing the fundamental character of its schools by introducing a system of comprehensive education, for example. When the officer of the Joint Parents Committee of the Ealing Grammar Schools asked the courts to restrain comprehensive reorganization of secondary education in the borough, Mr Justice Goff said:

> There is, in my judgment, no prima facie case of a breach of section 76, since in administrative matters the obligation means no more than that the authority must take into account the general principle, weighing it in the balance against other considerations.... Moreover, I cannot find anywhere in the Act any obligation on the local education authority to consult parents on the revision of the development plan.... The general principle is confined to the wishes

of particular parents in respect of their own particular children.... In my judgment, education in section 76 must refer to the curriculum, and if it includes any, and if so what, religious instruction, and whether co-educational or single-sex, and matters of that sort, and not to the size of the school or the conditions of entry.[46]

The Education Act of 1980 introduced major changes[47] to the law affecting parental choice, building on the principles outlined above. Every local education authority must now make arrangements for all parents in their area to express a preference as to the schools they wish their children to attend, and to give the reasons for their choice. Prior to this change, the onus often lay with parents to initiate their exercise of choice. Moreover, local education authorities must now publish the arrangements made for parents to express their choice.[48] Furthermore, whereas previously local education authorities were required only 'to have regard to the general principle' of parental choice,[49] and might therefore quite reasonably have regard to other matters as well,[50] they now have a *duty* to follow parents' choice.[51] The duty is limited, however, if compliance with the parents' choice:

(a) would prejudice the provision of efficient education or the efficient use of resources.

(b) runs counter to any agreement made between the local education authority and the governors of an aided or special agreement school for which a preference has been expressed.

(c) would conflict with arrangements for selection by reference to ability or aptitude; i.e. in schools providing specialist facilities in music or dancing, or in areas where comprehensive reorganization is not complete.[52]

This duty, and the limitations on it, cover also parents who express a preference for a school outside the area covered by the local education authority in which they reside.[53]

11   Schools appeals panels

Prior to the passing of the 1980 Act a parent whose choice of school had been refused could appeal only directly to the Secretary of State. Under the 1980 Act a local education authority is required to establish procedures for parents to ask for a review of any decision by the authority itself, or by the governors of a county or controlled school, which has resulted in a child not being accepted at the school of his parents' choice. The governors of aided and special agreement schools are required to make similar arrangements. Objections by parents must be in writing. If parents are still dissatisfied after such a review, they may appeal to the Secretary of State on the grounds that the decision was not consonant with the authority's published admission arrangements, or that the authority or governors have failed to comply with the statutory requirements as to published information, or that no arrangements have been made for parents to express a choice.[54] An appeals committee's decision can also be reviewed by the courts in the same way as any other type of quasi-judicial review. The court will look at procedural defects and whether the appeals committee has behaved reasonably. A parent can also complain to the 'Ombudsman' (the Commissioner for Local Administration). The decision of an appeals committee is, however, binding on the local authority and on governors.[55]

During 1982 doubt was expressed by several local authorities that the Secretary of State retained the power to consider appeals, since Parliament had set up a separate appeals machinery under the 1980 Act.[56] It seems, however, that the power of the Secretary of State to act against local authorities or governors who behave 'unreasonably' is paramount.[57]

There is a code of practice for appeals committees. As guarantee of their independence, appeals committees are subject to the supervision of the Council on Tribunals,[58] and not of local education authorities. The Council participated with local authority associations and representatives of the voluntary bodies in drawing up a code of practice covering appeals committees. The full text of the original code can be found in

County and Voluntary Schools by Brocksbank, Revell, Ackstine and Bailey (Society of Education Officers, 6th edition 1982), Appendix F.

Some dissatisfaction has been expressed, however, by the Ombudsman and the courts arising from teething troubles with the new legislation. In *R. v. South Glamorgan Appeals Committee,* ex parte *Evans* heard in May 1984, the judge held that an appeals committee must first decide as a matter of fact whether there would be 'prejudice to efficient education or efficient use of resources' (the wording of the 1980 Act) if the child were to be admitted. This prejudice must be *proved* by the local education authority, *not merely accepted.* After that it must be shown that to add a pupil would be to aggravate the situation to an unacceptable degree. The judge observed that an appeals committee would probably find it hard to reach a conclusion without hearing evidence from the teachers actually affected by its decision. A revised version of the code of practice for appeals committees will be published during 1985.

The admission arrangements in the 1980 Act do not apply to those pupils who are under 5 at the time of their proposed admission unless the local authority agrees or has a general policy of admitting under-5s.[59]

12 Information for parents about schools

In order that parents can make informed choices about schools, the 1980 Act[60] gave the Secretary of State power to make regulations determining the information about schools which is to be published.[61]

Local education authorities must send out the prescribed information free to parents whose children are moving to middle or secondary schools and to other parents on request. It must be available for reference both at local education authority offices and public libraries, and, of course, in schools.

The 'general information' may be summarized as follows:

1. addresses and telephone numbers of the offices of the authority;

2. name, address and telephone number of each maintained school;
3. size of each school and its age range;
4. classification (comprehensive, co-educational, single sex, etc.) and denominational affiliation of each school;
5. arrangements for transport, school meals and milk, school clothing and other welfare grants;
6. entering pupils for public examinations.

In the case of aided or special agreement schools either the governors are responsible for disseminating this information or the relevant LEA does it on their behalf.

The information which must be published in respect of individual schools is considerable. It must be available in schools for distribution, without charge, to parents on request 'and for reference by parents and other persons'. The material must state the school year to which it applies and must contain a warning that 'though the particulars were correct in relation to that year ... it should not be assumed that there will be no change affecting the relevant arrangements ... before the start of or during the school year or in relation to subsequent school years'.

The details for each school must include:

DESCRIPTION

The name, address and phone number of the school; the names of the head teacher and of the chairman of the governors; the classification of the school, for example county, primary, comprehensive, co-educational, boarding; where there are arrangements for parents considering sending their child to the school to visit it, particulars of those arrangements.

CURRICULUM

Curriculum for different age groups; subject choices; arrangements for 'education as respects sexual matters'; for secondary schools, the levels to which particular subjects are taught and the careers education provided; arrangements for RE and whether the school has a religious affiliation; whether there are arrangements for pupils in particular groups including those with special educational needs.

ORGANIZATION

Details of arrangements for streaming and setting and homework; arrangements for pastoral care; the organization of school discipline including corporal punishment; the main societies and activities and facilities available to pupils at school 'otherwise than as part of the education provided therein'; policy on school uniform including the cost of the uniform; for secondary schools, arrangements for careers guidance.

EXAMINATIONS

In the case of schools with children of 15 and over details have to be given of the policy on entering pupils for public examinations; the names of the examinations; the year pupils will generally take such an exam; and, in the case of O and A level and CSE, the numbers of appropriate year groups who, subject by subject, attained each grade in each such examination, and the total number of pupils in each of those year groups on the third Thursday (or in the case of a school in Wales, the third Friday) in January of the specified year.

SPECIAL SCHOOLS

In addition, authorities also have to publish details of their arrangements and policies on special education, such as identification and assessment of children with special needs and parental involvement. Copies will be distributed free to parents on request and be available for reference at education offices, maintained schools and public libraries. Information about individual special schools will be available to parents from the schools or the education offices.

WALES

In all the Welsh LEAs the information put out by the authority will have to detail the use of Welsh as a language in which instruction is given, any normal requirement that pupils should learn Welsh, and the circumstances in which they may be excepted. The Secretary of State has power to make regulations under which he may make grants towards the teaching of Welsh or of other subjects through the medium of Welsh.[62] Much the same information must be distributed by each individual school. If Welsh is used as the language of instruction, then the school must state the extent, if any, to which alternative instruction in English is available in that subject. It must be stated also the extent, if any, to which Welsh is the normal language of communication at the school.

The Regulations also say that if a Welsh local education authority or the governors of an aided or special agreement school in Wales think that documents should be published in Welsh, then they should do so.

The regulations stipulate the minimum information which must be made available to parents. Schools may, of course provide more, particularly where local circumstances make this desirable.

13 Parental choice in practice

The DES Manual of Guidance *Choice of School* (1953), giving guidelines for local education authorities, has been withdrawn,[63] but there is no reason to believe that the general commonsense principles which it contained have been totally abandoned. They included such matters as the choice of a school on denominational grounds, educational considerations to be taken into account, the accessibility of a particular school, the existence of special facilities, and parental preferences for a single-sex or mixed school. The manual also suggested that a journey, from door to door, of more than forty-five minutes for primary pupils or seventy-five minutes for secondary pupils is a reasonable limit. In terms of mileage the DES considered that such journeys would, in general, limit the catchment area of a primary school to five or six miles; and of a secondary school to its defined catchment area, or ten miles, whichever is the less.

A further consideration is the avoidance of unreasonable public expenditure such as would be implicit in journeys of greater length; although it is recognized that in such cases parents may opt to pay the fares themselves where there is no other objection to the choice. It would also be unreasonable to take up places at independent schools either where the requisite educational facilities can be provided in grant-aided schools, or where an independent school would not provide an education suitable to the needs of the child.

The right of a parent under section 76 of the 1944 Act to choose a particular school for his children was the subject of a lawsuit in 1955.[64] The Watt twins passed the 11-plus examination and, as there was no grammar school in their part of the county, the local education authority offered to pay their fees at Stamford School, an independent Church of England foundation. The boys were Roman Catholics and the father sent them to Roman Catholic schools in Monmouthshire and Northamptonshire, demanding from the Council payment of the full fees. He based his claim on the authority's duty to educate children in accordance with the wishes of their parents as laid down in section 76. The Court of Appeal upheld the decision of Mr Justice Ormerod that the Council had not failed to comply with the section by refusing to pay. Section 76 did not give a parent the right to choose his children's school at the public expense, subject to two conditions; it only laid down a general principle. In this particular case the public expenditure would have been unreasonable. Leave was given to appeal to the House of Lords, but the parent dropped the case at this point.

Another case connected with section 76 of the Act came before Lord Chief Justice Parker, Mr Justice Ashworth and Mr Justice Hinchcliffe in the Queen's Bench Division in 1962.[65] The Hertfordshire local education authority had decided that Bonnygrove Primary School, Cheshunt, was overcrowded, and

that the 6-year-old children concerned must attend Burleigh
Primary School. The parents wished their children to attend
the former school, which was only a hundred yards from their
homes, whereas the school named by the authority was a mile
away and involved crossing the Great Cambridge Road.

Mrs Darling and Mrs Jones persuaded their husbands to
make them the temporary heads of their families, and kept the
children away from school after the Minister had made a
School Attendance Order under section 37 of the Act.[66] In
November 1961 both mothers were fined ten shillings for
failing to send their children to school. They had arranged for
three hours' tuition a week, which was all they could afford.

In the Queen's Bench Division they applied for an extension
of time for leave to apply for an order of certiorari to quash
the decision of the Secretary of State. For the parents, Mr
R. K. Brown QC agreed that section 37(3) of the Act gave
the Secretary of State the power to name a school if he
considered the school chosen by the parent to be unsuitable
or to involve unreasonable public expense, but pointed out
that overcrowding was not mentioned as a ground for this
action.

Lord Parker asked what the Secretary of State could do if
the nearest school was overcrowded, and Mr Brown replied
that the authority could adjust its pupils' list so that children
could be moved to another school. The Court granted the
extension of time, but refused leave to apply for the order of
certiorari. The effect of this decision was to limit the parents'
right to choose if the Secretary of State deemed the school so
selected to be overcrowded. Moreover, the Secretary of State's
decision could not be challenged in the courts.

Section 37 of the 1944 Act was in effect a kind of loophole
for determined parents. By keeping their child away from
school, they were able to force a dispute over choice of school
to a point where the dispute received rather different treatment
from that given to similar disputes which had not gone as far
as involving school attendance proceedings. The section
permitted the Secretary of State to refuse the school desired

by the parent *only* if the admission of one child to that school would cause unreasonable public expenditure.[67]

The 1980 Act has changed this. A local education authority must now notify the parent which school (or schools) they are willing to name in a school attendance order. Parents must accept one of the schools offered or seek admission to another within 14 days. If the application is turned down, they can appeal in the normal way.[68] If the application is successful, that school is named in the attendance order. If not, the local education authority names the school, or one of the schools originally proposed.

14   Choice and denominational schools

The denominational problem was thrown into sharp relief in Birkenhead through the authority's fear that, unless all the first-year places in Roman Catholic secondary schools were taken up, there would be a serious shortage of places in other secondary schools. Accordingly, circulars were issued to the parents of children preparing to leave Roman Catholic junior schools restricting their choice to Roman Catholic schools, but adding that reallocation would be considered in special cases. In the High Court action which followed, it was claimed that the authority had acted *ultra vires* in issuing the circulars, that the plaintiffs had a right to express a preference unfettered by any question of religious affiliation, and that the authority was in breach of its duty under sections 8 and 76 of the 1944 Act.[69]

Mr Justice Ungoed Thomas did not agree. Rejecting the plaintiffs' claim, he held that the authority's duty was to provide 'sufficient schools', not to pay regard to religious differences, and the only remedy lay in appeal to the Secretary of State under section 99 for default of statutory duty by the authority. The limiting factor was a lack of places in county schools, except for pupils leaving Church of England or county primary schools.

In a judgment in the Court of Appeal the Master of the Rolls, Lord Denning, upheld this decision. The authority had the power and duty to allocate children, and must exercise a proper administrative discretion in doing so:

> If this education authority were to allocate boys to particular schools according to the colour of their hair, or, for that matter, the colour of their skin, it would be so unreasonable, so capricious, so irrelevant to any proper system of education that it would be altogether *ultra vires*, and this court would strike it down at once. But if there were valid educational reasons for a policy as, for instance, in an area where immigrant children were backward in the English tongue and needed special teaching, then it would be perfectly right to allocate those in need to special schools where they would be given extra facilities for learning English.... [The authority's action] is a sound administrative policy decision to which no objection can be taken, especially when it is realized that in exceptional cases the authority are ready to reconsider the position of any particular pupil. In my opinion, there is no ground for saying that the education authority have acted beyond their powers. If they have done anything wrong at all — and I do not suggest that they have — it is not a matter which comes within the jurisdiction of these courts. If complaint is to be made, it should be made to the Secretary of State, and not to us.

An unusual objection by a parent was revealed when a Muslim father pleaded guilty to a charge of failing to cause his daughter to receive efficient full-time education suitable to her age, ability and aptitude.[70] The family lived in Blackburn, where all the secondary schools are co-educational, and the father believed that, having regard to the tone of present-day society, she would lose her virtue and become unmarriageable under Muslim law. The court imposed a fine of £5.

Under the Education Act 1980, aided and special agreement schools must publish information for parents and details of admission procedures as in county schools. There is also similar appeals machinery.

15 Choice and the curriculum

A parent may be expected to take the curriculum into account in choosing a school for his child. The responsibility for the organization of the curriculum lies with the head teacher and the governing body where it is charged under the Articles of Government with the 'oversight of the curriculum', or some other similar phrase.

A parent cannot therefore demand a particular curriculum for his child as of right in a particular school. Where the curriculum of a school is demonstrably unsuited to a child's 'ability and aptitude' the parent might in law be in breach of his statutory duty to educate 'efficiently' and should move the child elsewhere.[71]

A parent may approach those responsible for the organization of the curriculum (e.g. in connection with the options system in secondary schools) with a view to negotiation. There is, however, no statutory obligation on schools to consult parents when the curriculum is being planned, although schools may consider it courteous and helpful to do so. 'The 1944 Act leaves to local education authorities a broad discretion to choose what, in their judgement, are the means best suited to their areas for providing the variety of instruction called for by ... (the Act).'[72]

The curriculum must, however, not unlawfully discriminate (see chapter XIII). An appeal to the Secretary of State might also be possible.[73]

16 The primary stage

NURSERY SCHOOLS

Nursery schools are designed for children under 5. Where it is not expedient to provide a separate school, nursery classes may be formed within the framework of a larger primary school. There is no statutory duty requiring local education authorities to provide nursery education.[74] They, or the governors of a voluntary school with a nursery class, may make a teacher available to a day nursery established under the National Health Service Act 1977. Such teachers must already be employed in a nursery school or a primary school with a nursery class and must themselves agree to the arrangement. The authority may also provide equipment for teaching and may define the prospective functions of the teacher and the person in charge of the day nursery. Such a teacher will remain on the staff of the school to which he is appointed.[75] A local social services committee may make charges for nursery education.

PRIMARY SCHOOLS

These may take the form of separate infants' and junior schools although falling rolls in recent years have brought about a spate of amalgamations into 'all-through' primary schools. Children become of statutory school age at the beginning of the term after they attain the age of 5. They may be admitted earlier at the discretion of the local education authority.

17 The secondary stage

Secondary school provision has been historically of three kinds — grammar, technical and modern. These distinctions, however, were not legislative; the 1944 Act made no stipulation as to the structure of secondary education. For a time after 1944 most children were drafted at the age of 11 plus to a grammar school or a modern school, but within a short time some local education authorities began to experiment with various forms of comprehensive schools designed to accept all secondary pupils from a given area. The move towards comprehensive secondary education gathered momentum in the 1950s and 1960s and, in principle, gained official support from both sides of the House of Commons.

In the summer of 1965 the Secretary of State issued Circular 10/65, *The Organization of Secondary Education*, asking all local education authorities to re-examine their development plans, and to submit proposals for ending selection. The circular suggested half a dozen ways in which this might be done in varying circumstances. Some authorities tended to drag their feet, and two attempts were made to introduce legislation designed to outlaw all forms of selection for different kinds of secondary education. A general election resulting in a change of government frustrated these intentions, and Circular 10/70 stated that the Secretary of State would adopt a more flexible attitude towards the reorganization of secondary education. Reorganization continued during the first half of the 1970s, but the tempo slowed appreciably.

Successive governments had sought to influence local authorities towards or away from comprehensive reorganization by DES Circulars, which in law have no real 'teeth'. In 1976, however, the then government enacted the Education Act 1976 which stated that 'local education authorities shall, in the exercise and performance of the powers and duties relating to secondary education, have regard to the general principle that such education is to be provided only in schools where the arrangements for the admission of pupils are not based (wholly or partly) on selection by ability or aptitude'.[76] The sections of the 1976 Act which related to comprehensive education were then repealed by the Education Act of 1979. The present position is similar to that of the post-1944 period, in that local education authorities have discretion as to the form of schools which best suits their area. The view of the government is currently that no pattern of secondary education has in itself overriding advantages or disadvantages of principle.[77] There are still those, however, who are convinced that comprehensive education is not necessarily the best form of secondary organization in their areas, and it would be idle to pretend that the last shots in this battle have yet been fired.

In the meantime there remain some grammar schools designed for the top academic flight of children. Traditionally they were the principal means of entry to the universities and professions. In those areas where reorganization is not complete there are also secondary modern schools catering for about four-fifths of the secondary school population, and providing a much more practical approach to school work. Over the years, however, there has been a growing tendency for all schools to offer opportunities for their more able pupils to sit for public examinations, notably the Certificate of Secondary Education which was introduced in 1965, and, to a lesser extent, for the General Certificate of Education. Falling rolls in recent years have produced a situation in which many schools have found it difficult to staff both CSE and GCE courses in the same subjects and this has contributed to pressure to merge the two examinations into a common system of examining at 16 plus.

Falling rolls and the need to close or amalgamate schools have led to renewed consideration by most local education authorities of how best to organize secondary schools in their area. Several have discussed the possibility of reintroducing selective schools but none has, as yet, taken the idea very far. In 1982 there were fewer than 200 maintained grammar schools remaining.

Side by side with the debate on the organization of secondary schools there has been, since the mid-1960s, a further discussion about the internal organization of these schools. If it is wrong, some have asked, to segregate children by ability in different schools, can it be right to segregate them in different classes in the same school? However, streaming, setting and mixed-ability groups are not matters of legislation and this is not the place to pursue the arguments.

18 Special educational needs

Local education authorities have a duty to provide facilities for children who need specialized treatment in some form or another. In many cases these arrangements have traditionally been made by the provision of special schools, e.g. ESN schools for the mentally retarded, open air schools for the delicate, and special provision for the physically handicapped. A number of authorities maintain boarding schools for pupils whose well-being will be promoted by residential school life. Special schools are also provided for maladjusted children. Special education, however, need not take place in a special school, or even in school at all. There is a growing belief among many educationalists that handicapped children need to grow up among normal classmates, and there is evidence that some local education authorities are considering reducing the number of their special school places in order to provide for handicapped children in ordinary schools. Special units, e.g. for partially-hearing children, may be attached to ordinary schools, and individual tuition provided for severely handicapped children.

Such integration is the keynote of the Education Act 1981, based on the recommendations of the Warnock Committee.[78] The Act contains three definitions:

1. *A learning difficulty*: where a child has 'significantly greater difficulty in learning than the majority of children of his age' or '*has a disability* which either prevents or hinders him from making use of educational facilities of a kind generally provided in schools, within the area of the local authority concerned, for children of his age' or is '*aged under 5 and falls into one of these categories* or is likely to later if special educational provision is not made'.

    However, a child is not to be taken as having a learning difficulty because the language or form of language used at home is different to that used in school.

2. *Special educational provision*: for children aged under 2 means any educational provision; for children aged 2 and over it means 'educational provision which is additional to or otherwise different from the educational provision made generally for children of his age in schools maintained by the local education authority concerned'.

3. *Special educational needs*: a child has special educational needs if he has a learning difficulty which calls for special educational provision to be made.[79]

Local authorities now have a statutory duty in providing primary and secondary schools to have regard to 'the need for securing that special educational provision is made for children who have special educational needs'.[80] Subject to three conditions local authorities must secure that such provision is made 'in an ordinary school'. The conditions are that such integration is compatible with (i) the child receiving the special educational provision which s/he requires; (ii) the provision of 'efficient education' for children with whom s/he will be educated; (iii) the efficient use of resources.

Those responsible for providing education for children with special needs in ordinary schools must secure that 'the child engages in the activities of the school together with children who do not have special educational needs', provided the conditions are met and it is 'reasonably practicable'.[81] Furthermore, governors of county and voluntary schools (and the local education authority in the case of its nursery schools) must use their 'best endeavours' to ensure that special education provision is made in their schools for those who need it.[82] Head teachers (or the governing body in the case of voluntary schools) must be informed by the local education authorities of registered pupils who are deemed to have special educational needs, as must 'all who are likely to teach him'.[83] A local education authority may, if they feel it to be appropriate, provide for special educational provision to be made wholly or partly 'otherwise than in a school'.[84]

Parents' rights and duties are also affected by the 1981 Act. Parents' basic educational duty has been amended to read: 'It shall be the duty of the parent of every child of compulsory school age to cause him to receive efficient full-time education suitable to his age, ability and aptitude and to any special educational needs he may have either by regular attendance at school or otherwise.'[85] There are new rights for parents to make their views known, to be involved in assessments, to be given copies of reports provided in the course of formal assessments, and to know who to go to for help and information.

The overriding principle, which continues to apply to all the powers and duties of authorities, is that 'so far as is compatible with the provision of efficient instruction and training and the avoidance of unreasonable public expenditure, pupils are to be educated in accordance with the wishes of their parents'.[86]

The duties in the 1981 Act to take parents' views into account are in addition to this basic duty.[87]

The explanatory DES Circular stresses: 'In looking at the child as a whole person, the involvement of the child's parent is essential. Assessment should be seen as a partnership between teachers, other professionals and parents, in a joint endeavour to discover and understand the nature of the difficulties and needs of individual children. Close relations should be established and maintained with parents and can only be helped by frankness and openness on all sides.'[88]

There is no provision in English law to ensure that the subjects of education decisions, the young people themselves, are involved in the making of these decisions. None of the new rights for parents in the new Act is exercisable by pupils, unlike the new law for children with special educational needs in Scotland, which transfers some parental rights to young people who are able to express views at the age of 16.[89] However, 'the feelings and perceptions of the child concerned should be taken into account, and the concept of partnership should wherever possible be extended to older children and young persons'.[90] Parents have a duty to co-operate with local education authorities' assessment procedures. If an authority decides to examine a child it must send the parent a formal notice of purpose, time and place. The parent has a right to attend. Failure to co-operate in the examination without reasonable excuse, can render the parent liable to an appearance in court and a fine of up to fifty pounds.[91]

Basically, the requirements of the 1981 Act are that where a local education authority is 'of the opinion' that a child has special education needs, it is their duty to make an 'assessment'.[92] If the needs are established, the local education authority must 'make a statement of his special educational needs'.[93]

Lack of space prevents a detailed exposition here of the thorough and complex procedures now to be adopted by local education authorities in assessing and making formal statements about children with special educational needs. Most local education authorities will by now have issued guidelines to their schools about the procedures under the Act. Readers' attention is drawn to the *Special Education Handbook* published by the Advisory Centre for Education, and to the major DES policy documents:

1. The Education (Special Educational Needs) Regulations 1983 bring into force provisions of the Education Act 1981 on 1 April 1983. They deal with the procedure for the assessment of children with special needs. They reproduce the Form of Statement of Special Educational Needs.

2. Circular 1/83: *Assessment and Statements of Special Educational Needs*. This considers the implications of the Education Act 1981 and of the Education (Special Educational Needs) Regulations 1983 for the assessment of a broad range of special educational needs. It offers advice to assist local education authorities in reviewing and revising their procedures in consultation with district health authorities (DHAs) and social services departments (SSDs). This Circular should be read in conjunction with Circular 8/81 which explains the provisions of the 1981 Act. It is available from DES, Honeypot Lane, Canons Park, Stanmore, Middlesex.

In the final resort, a parent has an appeal against the making of a statement, although 'the Secretary of State hopes that appeals will seldom prove necessary'. A parent may appeal to a panel constituted as under the Education Act 1980[94] but in considering appeals under the 1981 Act the panels have fewer powers. A panel can do no more than either uphold the local authority or refer the matter back to them for reconsideration.[95] However, a parent dissatisfied with an appeal under the Education Act 1981 has the specific right[96] to appeal further to the Secretary of State, who may either confirm the statement, amend it as he or she thinks appropriate, or direct the local authority to cease to maintain the statement.[97]

The DES has issued guidance on the conditions for the approval of special schools to local education authorities and governing bodies of non-maintained special schools. Regulations covering the new requirements aim to achieve greater uniformity in the treatment of ordinary and special schools.

The conditions of approval for special schools – including those located in hospitals – and the statutory procedures for withdrawal of approval are set out. The regulations say what provision is to be made about: admissions and pupils; health, meals and milk; religious worship; maintenance of reports and records; teaching and non-teaching staff; and accounts of non-maintained schools.

Non-maintained special schools must ensure that their governing bodies include parent, teacher and local education authority representatives. They must also publish annually information about schools, including details of the curriculum and arrangements for discipline.

There are about 180 independent schools that are not approved as special schools, but which provide mainly for children with special educational needs. Regulations dealing with the standards which these schools must meet if they take children with statements of special educational needs are in existence.[98]

19   Direct grant and independent schools

The category of school which received financial assistance directly from the Secretary of State, instead of from a local education authority, was known as 'direct grant'. In 1975 the government decided to phase out the direct grant grammar schools, but not the special schools, of which there are 130. Over 100 of the grammar schools decided to become independent. Fifty-one schools joined the maintained sector.[99]

The direct grant list has since been abolished and all such schools which survived until the autumn of 1980 are now regarded as independent. The independent schools stand outside the statutory system of education. They range from those well known public schools which are administered under a trust deed, to small schools conducted for private profit. Parliament has taken cognizance of the existence of all such schools.[100] Section 70 of the Act, which provides for the registration and inspection of all independent schools, was implemented in the autumn of 1957. In 1979 the Secretary of State announced that Her Majesty's Inspectors would no longer inspect independent schools with a view to ascertaining their efficiency, but the provision of the 1944 Act exempting certain independent schools from registration has now been abolished[101] and the regulations relating to the information to be given in applications for registration or in annual returns have been strengthened.[102] The independent schools are currently engaged in establishing their own system of inspection.

The Independent Schools Tribunal has discretion to disqualify a person from being a proprietor of an independent school, without disqualifying that person from being a teacher in any school. This was held by the Queen's Bench Division in 1968. A husband and wife were equal shareholders and directors of an independent school near Salisbury. When the husband was jailed for assault and cruelty to his pupils, the Secretary of State served a notice of complaint on the wife, alleging that as a director she was responsible for her husband's employment and for his conduct as headmaster. The Independent Schools Tribunal disqualified her from being the proprietress of any independent school, but did not disqualify her from being a teacher. The Divisional Court held that she was an equal party in running the school, and responsible for what had happened. There was some evidence she had contributed to the good academic record which, in some respects, the school had, and it was unnecessary to bring her teaching career to an end provided that the management of any school in which she was a teacher was in other hands.[103]

In April 1970 Mr Chaim Grunhut and Mr Mervyn Warner were charged with conducting an unregistered school on premises disqualified under the Education Act 1944. In 1968 a notice of complaint had been served because of the inadequate secular education at the school. Religious lessons were given in the mornings by three rabbis and Mr Warner, the headmaster, gave secular instruction to thirty-five boys in the afternoons. A notice of closure in August 1969 was ignored. Mr Grunhut, a member of the managing committee, maintained that he had resigned before the offences were committed and was acquitted. Mr Warner said he believed that an appeal was still possible after the notice had been served, so he had continued to work part-time although he no longer considered himself responsible for the running of the school. He was fined on each summons.[104]

In 1984 the head teacher of a small private school continued to operate her school after school inspectors had recommended withdrawal of recognition for failing to carry out improvements. She admitted breaching section 70(3)(a) of the 1944 Act and the magistrates imposed a fine of £250 and £250 in costs.[105]

The Education Act of 1976 enabled the Secretary of State to revoke any approval previously given by him to arrangements made by local education authorities for assisting non-maintained schools or for the payment of fees and expenses of pupils attending such schools.[106] In an interesting attempt to circumvent the application of legislation, the Greater Manchester Metropolitan County Council in April 1978 set up a scheme to provide free or assisted places at independent schools for children resident in their area, by making a grant to trustees to provide bursaries payable over seven years. The Manchester City Council appealed ultimately to the House of Lords on the grounds that such a grant lay outside the authority of the Greater Manchester Council and was therefore unlawful; moreover, the Greater Manchester Council was not, by law, an education authority. The House of Lords noted that the purpose of the fund was to ensure that there was no interruption during the seven-year period of the education of pupils entering independent schools in the one year, 1978. The Lords held that the scheme fell within the Local Government Act of 1972,[107] even though the council was not an education authority, and that the council had not unlawfully delegated its powers over the money to the trustees, even though the council had no longer any right in law to exercise direct control over the trustees.[108]

The Education Act of 1976 empowered the Secretary of State to pay remuneration and allowances to members of Independent Schools Tribunals under Part 3 of the Education Act 1944.[109]

A legal action was commenced in 1984 which, although as yet not fully heard, may have considerable implications for the relationship of independent schools with the DES. An independent school run by an ultra orthodox Jewish trust, the Talmud Torah Machzikei Hadass School, applied for registration under section 70 of the 1944 Act and was inspected by HMI. Subsequently the Secretary of State issued a complaint under section 71 of the Act 'that efficient and suitable instruction is not being provided at the school, having regard to the ages and sex of the pupils attending thereat'. The major objections were that insufficient secular education was provided and no music (the latter being against the religious beliefs of the community).

The trust argued before Mr Justice Taylor that the Secretary of State was guided by an erroneous view of the law, namely that he was entitled to direct an amount of secular instruction *irrespective of the purpose for which the school is established*. DES regulations affecting secular instruction in maintained schools were not binding on independent schools, and could not therefore be used as a norm in determining their curriculum. It was further argued that since 1944 very many special communities had grown up in the United Kingdom who seek to preserve their way of life and cultural heritage, and the notion that there should always be some basic agreed notion of what should be taught in schools of all types and established for whatever purpose was now open to question. Mr Justice Taylor gave leave to take the matter before the High Court for a decision on the law. There Mr Justice Woolf held that there had been no error of law on the part of the Secretary of State and referred the matter to the Independent Schools Tribunal. He expressed the view that schools catering for minority sects could be held to be within the meaning of Section 71 (1)(c) of the 1944 Act.

20   The assisted places scheme

The assisted places scheme was one of the most controversial parts of the Education Act of 1980.[110] The scheme is designed to allow the Secretary of State to make participation agreements with independent schools, under which schools would remit fees (in whole or part) for pupils accepted under the scheme. The remitted fees would then be reimbursed to the schools by the Secretary of State. Grants made by the schools for expenses and any incidental charges remitted are also recoverable.[111] Participation agreements may be terminated by the Secretary of State or the school, but the ending of the agreement may not act to the detriment of any pupil holding an assisted place at the time.

The regulations[112] made by the Secretary of State under the 1980 Act stipulate that, in order to participate in the scheme, a child must be ordinarily resident in the United Kingdom, the Channel Islands or the Isle of Man throughout the three years preceding the 1st January in the year the place would be taken up; and the child must be 11 years of age or older before 31st July of the first assisted year. Only children eligible for fee remission in their first year are eligible. The selection of pupils from those eligible under the scheme is the responsibility of the school. Furthermore the requirements of the 1980 Act as to the publication of information to parents, including examination results, must be observed by participating schools, and at least 60 per cent of assisted place holders at a school are to be children from maintained schools. The Secretary of State has powers also to prevent, postpone or restrict a proposed increase in fees for assisted pupils.

A further regulation stipulates that a pupil registered at a maintained school is eligible for selection for an assisted place at sixth form level only if the local education authority in question is in agreement. This clause shows due deference to local authorities who during consultation over the scheme expressed alarm that their already dwindling sixth forms could be adversely affected by an exodus of pupils to independent schools.

In 1982 a pupil at a maintained 11–16 comprehensive school was unable to find a place in a maintained sixth form to study for A-levels in chemistry, economics, physics and music, and therefore sought an assisted place at a local independent school which was able to offer an appropriate programme. The local education authority, which did not approve of the assisted places scheme on principle, refused permission to the pupil on the grounds that the chosen combination of subjects was 'sufficiently unusual that they could not approve the application'.[113] The Secretary of State issued a Section 68 notice,[114] declaring that the local education authority was acting 'unreasonably' and requiring the authority to allow the pupil to take up the place.

Since the scheme came into operation, more than one local education authority has sought to instruct head teachers not to give any information to parents about it, and in particular not to supply reports on pupils seeking assisted places in independent schools. Although such an instruction has not been tested as such in court, it is of doubtful legality. The spirit of the 1980 Act is to increase parental choice and the new scheme is part of that Act also. It is most unlikely that Parliament intended that its plans might be obstructed in such a way. An aggrieved parent might also be able to bring such obstruction to the attention of the Ombudsman as possible maladministration.

However, there is no obligation on head teachers to provide special tuition or adjust curricula to cope with selection procedures adopted by independent schools participating in the scheme.

21   The careers service

Until March 1974, local education authorities were required to provide a careers service for persons under 18 and for those over that age who were for the time being attending school.[115] The service had no functions in relation to young people over 18 who were receiving further education or who were at universities. A good many youngsters in this category made unofficial use of the service but, because this was unauthorized, careers officers were not equipped or staffed adequately to deal with these clients.

From 1 April 1974 the responsibilities of the service were expanded and it is now responsible for assisting full-time and part-time students attending educational institutions 'to determine what employments will, having regard to their capabilities, be suitable for them and available to them when they leave the institutions'.[116]

The Youth Employment Service has, therefore, ceased to exist not only in law but in fact. The new job centres of the Employment Service Agency, of which it is expected there will be 800 by 1985, will be equipped to help people of any age in full-time or part-time education.

Within the secondary schools there has been an increasing tendency in recent years to appoint members of staff with the special additional responsibility of advising pupils about careers, the opportunities available to them and the qualifications they need. In many schools, however, provision of this kind is given inadequate preparation and thought. In colleges of further education even less formal help is given and, although some have counsellors, much of the internal advice is given on an *ad hoc* basis by students' personal tutors.

To some extent the work of the local education authority careers officer in the school is helped or hindered by the quality of the careers teacher. Ideally, much of the careers education should be undertaken by the teacher, the careers officer's educational function being largely consultative with an emphasis on interviews and individual counselling. It remains to be seen how effectively the new organization will work, but the indications are that success will depend on a trained, dedicated and sympathetic careers teacher whose teaching load is light enough to enable him to give sufficient time and energy to his vocational guidance.

Whereas the former Youth Employment Service was administered by local education authorities on behalf of the Department of Employment, the new careers service is entirely the responsibility of the local education authorities. Advice given by the Secretary of State for Employment will be of a general character.

22   The school milk and meals service

The Education Act 1980[117] abolished the mandatory requirement that local education authorities should provide pupils
with a midday meal and such other refreshment as might be
necessary.

The provision of milk, meals and other refreshment for
registered pupils at maintained schools is now a discretionary
power. Local education authorities must, however, continue to
make adequate provision for pupils whose parents are in receipt
of supplementary benefit or family income supplement; and
must provide such facilities as the authority consider appropriate
for the consumption of any meals or other refreshment brought
to the school by pupils.[118] School governors must co-operate
fully with local education authorities in this but the governors
of aided schools are not required to incur expenditure in doing
so.[119]

The charge made by an authority for school milk or meals
is now decided by the authority and not centrally. It must be
waived in whole or in part in appropriate cases.

Teachers can no longer be required to supervise the midday
meal.[120]

23   Provision of clothing

A local education authority may provide clothing, including
boots or shoes, for any pupil who is maintained as a boarder
at an educational institution by the authority, or who is a pupil
in a maintained nursery school or class, or for a pupil for
whom they are providing board and lodging otherwise than
at an educational institution if that pupil is receiving special
educational treatment.

If it appears to the local education authority that any pupil
not falling within the categories listed above, and who is a
pupil of a maintained school or of a special school (whether
maintained or not), is unable to take full advantage of his
educational opportunities because of inadequate or unsuitable

clothing, the authority may provide necessary clothing to remedy the deficiency.

Physical education clothing may be provided for pupils in schools, at county colleges, or taking advantage of other physical education facilities provided by the authority.

The authority may determine whether it confers a right of property, or of user only, when providing such clothing. The authority may require a parent to pay such a sum as he is able to find without hardship.[121]

24   Non-maintained schools and ancillary services

A local education authority may, with the consent of the proprietor of any school not maintained by the authority,[122] make arrangements for the provision of milk (within the limitations outlined above), meals and other refreshment for pupils at that school, and for the supply of clothing for the benefit of registered pupils at that school. The financial arrangement must be such that the cost to the authority is no greater than it would have been if the service were being provided for a pupil in one of its own schools.[123]

The Secretary of State for Health and Social Services may charge for the provision in such schools of medical and dental inspection and treatment.[124]

25   The Ombudsman

During the post-war period there was a growing body of opinion that citizens who believed they had been victims of administrative malpractice should have facilities to make a formal complaint which could be investigated and determined impartially.

The Parliamentary Commissioner Act 1967 provided arrangements for complaints against government departments. The Commissioner is appointed by Letters Patent and may, subject to certain specific exceptions, investigate any action taken by (or on behalf of) a government department or any other authority to which the Act applies, provided that action has been taken in the course of its administrative functions. The complaint must be made in writing to a Member of Parliament by the person who is aggrieved and the Commissioner may not examine it unless a Member of Parliament refers it to him with the complainant's assent and the Member's request that it be investigated. A complaint may not normally be used to oust the jurisdiction of statutory or prerogative tribunals or of the courts. The Commissioner reports to the Member of Parliament who has transmitted the complaint and to the principal officer of the department against which the allegation has been levelled. If he thinks that an injustice will not be remedied, he may lay a report before both Houses of Parliament. All proceedings before the Commissioner are protected by absolute privilege.

The Local Government Act 1974 established bodies of Commissioners for Local Administration in England and Wales. The Local Commissioner may, subject to specified exceptions, investigate allegations of administrative malpractice. Complaints must be made in writing by a member of the public through a member of the local authority concerned. If he is satisfied that a local authority member who has received a complaint has smothered it, the Commissioner may himself initiate an investigation. The local authority must have had a reasonable time to consider the complaint itself before it is investigated by the Commissioner. Complaints about matters affecting all or most of the inhabitants of an area are not open to investigation. The Commissioner's report is made to the member who referred the complaint, the complainant, and the local authority. All proceedings are protected by absolute privilege.

Any action concerning the giving of secular or religious instruction, or the conduct, curriculum, internal organization, management or discipline of any maintained school or college is expressly excluded from the Local Commissioner's purview. Teachers, therefore, will not find themselves hauled before him. The Local Commissioner has investigated a considerable number of complaints against local education authorities, many of them concerned recently with the refusal of admission to schools under the 1980 Education Act and alleged maladministration of appeals panels.[125]

26   The Council of Europe

In Britain great stress is laid on the sovereignty of Parliament and the rule of law. For many Britons the age of legal idealism dawned at Runnymede in 1215, and they sometimes forget that the privileges of freedom and of equality before the law have not been shared so widely, or for so long, in some other countries.

Moreover two world wars have drawn the nations of Europe more closely together. Britain's entry into the three European Communities in 1973 is still a matter of debate, and one of the favourite arguments of opponents of the Common Market is the loss of Parliamentary sovereignty. The Council of Europe, however, which was born in London on 5 May 1949, 'to achieve a greater unity among its members for the purpose of safeguarding and realizing the ideals and principles which are their common heritage' is conveniently forgotten. At present there are twenty-one member nations,[126] and throughout its history the Council has striven to ensure that fundamental human rights are secured for every citizen in each of the member states.

The principles which lie behind these rights are enshrined in the European Convention on Human Rights, which, together with its watchdogs, the European Commission of Human Rights and the European Court of Human Rights came into force on 3 September 1953. The Convention has been ratified by all the member states except France and Switzerland, and fourteen members (including the United Kingdom) have recognized the competence of the Commission to receive individual as well as inter-state applications.

There have been five Protocols (supplementary conventions). Education is dealt with in the first of these, which was signed in Paris on 20 March 1952, ratified by the United Kingdom on 3 November in the same year, and entered into force on 18 May 1954. Article 2 provides:

No person shall be denied the right to education. In the exercise of any functions which it assumes in relation to education and to teaching, the State shall respect the right of parents to ensure such education and teaching in conformity with their own religious and philosophical convictions.

Quite clearly, the United Kingdom, as a signatory, can neither make a new law nor attempt to enforce existing law in a way which is contrary to the spirit of this article. Indeed, for the individual, this safeguarding may be of greater importance now, in an increasingly multicultural society (where, for example, strict Muslims refuse on religious grounds to send their daughters to co-educational schools) than it was when it was drafted.

Several educational issues have been referred to the Commission. Between 1962 and 1964 six groups of francophone residents in Flemish Belgium and the Brussels area claimed that the linguistic system for education in Belgium was incompatible with the Convention. The court found that there had been discriminatory treatment, and new legislation was introduced in Belgium. Of four other linguistic cases, two were declared inadmissible.

In *Karnell and Hardt v. Sweden*, filed in 1971, members of the Evangelical-Lutheran Church of Sweden complained that parents of children belonging to that Church were prevented from giving their children appropriate religious instruction as the children were obliged to attend religious instruction in school. The Church had been refused permission to provide alternative religious instruction. The application was eventually withdrawn, following a decree by the King-in-Council that, at their parents' request, children belonging to the Evangelical-Lutheran Church could be exempted from compulsory religious instruction, which should not take place in classes where they were present, and that such pupils should not suffer any disadvantage.

In *Kjeldsen v. Denmark*, the parents of a 10-year-old girl complained that a law making sex education compulsory was a violation of their right not to have their daughter educated contrary to their religious and philosophical convictions. Optional sex education had been common in Denmark for many years; the new law made it obligatory, not as a separate subject but integrated with the teaching of other subjects. The Danish government maintained that the parents had not exhausted all the domestic remedies (which must be done before a case is referred to the Commission), that they could legally educate her at home (which they had been doing for some time), and that there were plenty of private schools near the parents' home. The matter was eventually referred to the Court, which decided that the legislation 'in no way amounts to indoctrination advocating a specific kind of sexual behaviour', and that it 'does not affect the right of parents to enlighten and advise their children' or to 'exercise with regard to their children natural parental functions as educators'. There had been no breach of the Convention.

The *Little Red Schoolbook* made its first appearance in Denmark in 1968, and translations were subsequently published in a number of European countries. An English edition was prepared for publication in 1971 but, following seizure by the police of more than a thousand copies, the publisher was convicted of possessing an obscene book likely to deprave or corrupt a substantial number of readers for whom it was intended. In the London Sessions Appeals Committee Judge Hines QC said:

> The *Book* is a great embarrassment to the impartial judgement of children, and the Committee finds it subversive to authority. It throws over the old concepts of affection and love, and tends to suggest only restraint to the individual in sexual intercourse and not to the community. Children were advised to have sexual intercourse or to smoke pot without any reference to the fact that it is illegal. The appellant has not established a statutory defence under the Obscene Publications Act that it was in the public interest to publish the book.

The publisher thereupon complained to the European Commission that a large number of his rights, including freedom of expression, freedom of thought, freedom from discrimination and the right to enjoyment of his property, had been violated. The Court ruled that the destruction of the copies as ordered by the courts amounted to deprivation of property, but that it was not contrary to the Convention as the contracting states may waive rights for the protection of health or morals. (*Handyside v. UK.*)

Perhaps the greatest impact on the British education scene has been made by the judgments of the European Court affecting the use of corporal punishment in United Kingdom schools: these are considered later in Chapter XV. It seems, too, that the European Court is becoming increasingly involved in matters of parental choice of school. In 1981 the parents of three children who were attending the Rudolf Steiner school in Edinburgh sought a declaration that Article 2, Protocol 1 to the Convention (*supra*) imposed an obligation on the state either to subsidize the school, or to provide financial assistance with the fees. The application to the Court was declared inadmissible. The Commission considered that whilst the state must not by action prevent parents from exercising the right expressed, it is sufficient that the state 'evidence respect for the religious and philosophical beliefs of parents within the existing and developing system of education'. However, there is no obligation on the state to set up or to support any educational establishment serving particular religious or philosophical beliefs or convictions. The Commission observed that the United Kingdom had shown 'respect' for the Rudolf Steiner school by granting it charitable status and making it eligible under the assisted places scheme.

It was reported in 1982 that Wiltshire parents were to claim a breach of the Convention in that their daughter had been denied both selective and single-sex education by their local education authority. But the Commission ruled again (in 1984) that the state was not obliged to establish at their expense any particular type of education in order to respect parents' wishes.[127]

In the mid-1970s, the world is shrinking, there is greater mobility between countries, economic ties are becoming closer and there is a wider appreciation of human dignity and human rights. The privileges which for centuries the Britisher has enjoyed before the law are now much more universally accepted. Before long, the EEC will have to consider the validation of academic qualifications among its members. English educational organization is still basically the concern of Westminster, but Parliament in its turn must ensure that its legislation and practice are acceptable not only in these islands, but also in a wider context.[128] Many lawyers see it as an anomaly that Britons can sue their public authorities in Strasbourg for infringements of human rights even where they have no remedy in the British courts: it may be that a future Parliament will enact the European Convention as part of the law of the United Kingdom.

27 The organization and working of the European Court of Human Rights

The Court consists of a number of judges equal to that of member states of the Council of Europe (currently twenty-one). No two judges may be nationals of the same state.

The judges are elected by the Consultative Assembly, for a period of nine years, from a list of persons nominated by member states of the Council of Europe; they may be re-elected. The judges sit on the Court in their individual capacity and they enjoy full independence in the discharge of their duties.

The Court elects its president and vice-president. The Court's members receive an allowance for each day of duty and its expenses are borne by the Council of Europe. The Court is assisted by a registry coming under its direct control. The Court itself elects its registrar and deputy registrar after having consulted the Secretary General of the Council of Europe. The other officials in the registry are appointed by the Secretary General with the agreement of the president or the registrar.

The jurisdiction of the Court in contentious matters extends to all cases concerning the interpretation and application of the Convention. It can, however, be exercised only with regard to states which have either declared that they recognize it as compulsory *ipso facto* or given their consent to a particular case being referred to the Court. To date, eighteen states have accepted the Court's compulsory jurisdiction, namely, Austria, Belgium, Cyprus, Denmark, France, the Federal Republic of Germany, Greece, Iceland, Ireland, Italy, Luxembourg, the Netherlands, Norway, Portugal, Spain, Sweden, Switzerland and the United Kingdom.

According to the Convention, any case submitted to the Court necessarily originates in an application lodged with another body, the European Commission of Human Rights, by a state or by a person, non-governmental organization or group of individuals. The Commission deals first with the admissibility of the application. If it accepts the application, it ascertains the facts and tries to reach a friendly settlement. Should this attempt fail, the Commission draws up a report containing both a statement of the facts and an opinion as to whether the facts found disclose a breach by the respondent state of its obligations under the Convention. The report is transmitted to the Committee of Ministers of the Council of Europe, whereupon the case may be brought before the Court, within three months, by the Commission and/or by any contracting state concerned. If this does not occur, the Committee of Ministers decides whether there has been a violation of the Convention.

For the consideration of each case brought before it, the Court sits in a chamber of seven judges including, as *ex officio* members, the president or the vice-president and the judge who is a national of any state party concerned. If the 'national' judge is unable to sit or withdraws, or if there is none, the state in question is entitled to appoint in his stead a member of the Court (an elected judge of a different nationality) or a person from outside the Court (an *ad hoc* judge). The names of the other judges are chosen by lot by the President before the opening of the case.

28   Children's rights

Whether children should have autonomous substantive rights in law, or whether such rights should be given to parents to exercise on their children's behalf is a perennial dilemma for those in the education service. A. S. Neill (at Summerhill) and others sought to free the child to make its own decisions and to minimize interference by adults. At the other end of the spectrum, the United Kingdom education system may be seen as paternalistic, seeking to protect children not only from themselves but also from allegedly bad influences. The system is criticized also for creating vested interests in head teachers, teachers and administrators. The issue flared up prominently in 1983 during the public discussion surrounding the High Court judgment that it was not unlawful for medical practitioners to prescribe the contraceptive pill to girls under 16 without the prior knowledge of the child's parent or guardian.[129] On appeal the High Court reversed the earlier judgment: at the time of writing the Department of Health and Social Security has taken the matter before the House of Lords but no decision has been reached. If it is finally held that parents must be consulted, it is likely that part at least of schools' sex education curriculum will have to be subject to parental approval. Some concern has been caused by Lord Justice Eveleigh's statement in the Court of Appeal that parents had a 'parcel of rights' over their children which could in general be neither abandoned nor transferred, and with which only the courts might interfere.

In recent years there has been a slight shift in the general direction of children's autonomous rights. Where care proceedings in the juvenile courts are being heard, for example, a child is entitled to request that his or her parent does not speak for them.[130] The child, not the parent, is entitled to legal aid for professional representation. Similarly, the local authority is required to 'so far as is practicable, ascertain the wishes and the feelings of the child regarding the decision and give due consideration to them, having regard to his age and understanding'.[131]

The European Convention on Human Rights may also come

to be interpreted in such a way as to further the cause of children's rights. The matter of corporal punishment in schools and the European Court is dealt with in another chapter.[132] However, English law allows anyone over 16 who is caring for a child to use reasonable physical punishment. This may be a breach of Article 3 of the Convention: 'No one shall be subjected to torture, or to inhuman or degrading treatment or punishment'. Article 4: 'No one shall be held in slavery or servitude; no one shall be required to perform forced or compulsory labour' may affect parents, for example, who make their children earn pocket money by doing 'paper rounds' and weekend jobs. Similarly, government proposals to reduce social security payments to young people who refuse to join training schemes may be affected. Article 6: 'In the determination of his civil rights and obligations, or of any criminal charge against him, everyone is entitled to a fair and public hearing within a reasonable time by an independent and impartial tribunal established by law ...' When pupils are suspended or expelled from school it is usually only the parents who are given the right of appeal under the Articles of Government. Article 6 however extends the right to 'everyone'. Whether the bodies to whom parents may currently appeal are 'independent and impartial' is also open to question. It is also probably against the spirit of Article 6 that children have no right to have their views represented when decisions about custody, access and maintenance are being made following separation or divorce. Article 10: 'Everyone has the right to freedom of expression ... to receive and impart information and ideas without interference ...' In schools, many young people would regard this article as breached daily with regard to bans on styles of dress and badges, on some books and organizations. Article 14: 'The enjoyment of the rights and freedoms set forth in this Convention shall be secured without discrimination on any ground such as sex, race, colour, language, religion ...' Although the United Kingdom has statutes dealing with racial and sex discrimination, young people with mental or physical disabilities may also currently be denied access to 'ordinary' institutions and given relatively limited access to training and education.

In a case heard by the European Commission on Human Rights in 1975, one of the Commissioners expressed an opinion, concurring with his colleagues, which seems to indicate the emphasis which the European Court may be expected to place on children's rights:

> ... the majority opinion ... does not to my mind put sufficient stress on the right of the child itself. Article 2 gives the impression that parents shall have not only a prior right but an unconditional right to decide in educational matters on the basis of their own religious and philosophical convictions, and that states have to exempt children, e.g. from compulsory public education, if their parents allege a conviction that such education is contrary to their religious and philosophical beliefs.
>
> It is obvious that such an interpretation cannot be accepted. Apart from the restrictions imposed by Article 17 of the Convention, there must necessarily be certain other factors which have to be considered. First and foremost it is the respect for the right of the child. It is hardly conceivable that the drafters would have intended to give parents something like dictatorial powers over the education of their children. But it is equally inconceivable that society shall not have anything at all to say in educational matters.... It can furthermore hardly have been intended that a child up to the formal age of majority shall be under the unfettered powers of its parents in these matters. In my opinion one therefore has to pay attention to the interest of the child.... A child who has reached a certain maturity has often a legal right to be heard and also in some cases to have his views respected. In some countries it would for instance not be possible to take away, against his wish, a 12- to 13-year-old child from foster parents with whom he has been living over a number of formative years.... In the field of convictions – religious or others – it may also be held that a child of a certain age can command respect for his views.

In other words, such a child has become an individual who has his own rights under the Convention. And it would, of course, be wrong to say that a child who holds another philosophical conviction than his parents must abide by their decision in educational matters in this field.[133]

Furthermore in the International Year of the Child, 1979, the Committee of Ministers took the first steps towards a European Charter on the Rights of the Child: the text adopted by the Parliamentary Assembly on 4 October 1979 included as its first general principle: 'Children must no longer be considered as parents' property, but must be recognized as individuals with their own rights and needs ...'

The Children's Legal Centre opened in 1981, initiated as the major UK project of the International Year of the Child. It is a registered charity, funded by grants from central government, and from trusts and foundations, and by sales of publications and training activities. The Centre's management committee is composed of individuals who have experience of work with or for children and young people.

The Centre's free and confidential advice and information service covers all aspects of law and policy affecting children and young people in England and Wales. It is open to young people, and to parents, professionals, other adults working with young people, agencies and organizations. When enquiries do not come directly from young people the Centre may require confirmation that they consent to the approach being made on their behalf. When very young children are involved the Centre would ascertain that parents are aware of the enquiry.

In some instances, cases are pursued beyond initial advice, by making representations to central or local government or institutions, or acting as advocate at case conferences, reviews etc. The Centre is also able, if necessary, to take cases to court.[134]

The Centre also publishes a charter, constitution or bill of rights setting out a framework of positive rights and responsibilities for all members of the school community, together with systematic methods for consultation and participation by all members of the school community, and a model grievance procedure. This document takes into account the provision of the European Convention and considers also the experience of the USA in this field.

References

1. Education Act 1944, s. 1(1).
2. S.I. 1964, no. 490.
3. Education Act 1944, s. 5.
4. Education Act 1944, s. 68.
5. Education Act 1944, s. 99.
6. Secretary of State for Education and Science v. Tameside Metropolitan Borough Council [1977] AC 1014; The Times, 26 July 1976.
7. Education Act 1944, s. 77.
8. HMSO, 1983.
9. Available from DES Publications Despatch Centre, Honeypot Lane, Stanmore, Middx HA7 1AZ.
10. Education Act 1944, s. 77.
11. Education Act 1944, s. 4. The constitution of the advisory councils is laid down in the Central Advisory Councils for Education Regulations, 1945 and 1951.
12. All such reports are available from HMSO.
13. Education Act 1944, s. 6(1) and (2).
14. Education Act 1944, ss. 8 and 41.
15. Meade v. Haringey London Borough Council [1979] 1 WLR 637; 77 LGR 577 CA.
16. London Government Act 1963, ss. 30–4.
17. White Paper: Streamlining the Cities, Cmnd 9063, HMSO, 1983.
18. Education Act 1944, s. 77(3) and (4).
19. Education Act 1944, s. 88.
20. Local Government Act 1972, Schedule 30.
21. White Paper: Central Government Controls over Local Authorities, Cmnd 7634, HMSO, 1980.
22. Education Act 1980, s. 22(1)(a).
23. Education Act 1980, s. 22(2).
24. Education Act 1980, s. 22(3)(a).
25. Education Act 1980, s. 22(3)(b).
26. Education Act 1944, s. 61(1).

27. R. *v.* Hereford & Worcester Local Education Authority *ex parte* Jones [1981] 79 LGR 490.
28. *The Teacher*, 27 June 1980.
29. See p. 5.
30. *Education*, 22 May 1981.
31. R. *v.* Cockerton [1901] 1 KB 726; 84 LT 488 CA.
32. Coney *v.* Choyce [1975] 1 WLR 422; All ER 979.
33. Diocesan Education Committees Measure 1955.
34. Diocesan Education Committees Measure 1955, s. 2(1).
35. Diocesan Education Committees Measure 1955, s. 3(1).
36. Education Act 1944, s. 8(1) and Education Act 1981, s. 2(1).
37. Education Act 1944, s. 7.
38. Education (Miscellaneous Provisions) Act 1948, s. 3(2).
39. Education Act 1944, s. 114(1). The Education Act 1964 provided that schools might be established at which the age of transfer does not correspond to the ages laid down in the 1944 Act.
40. Education Act 1980, s. 24.
41. Education Act 1944, s. 8(1)(b) and Education (Miscellaneous Provisions) Act 1948, s. 3(3).
42. Education Act 1944, s. 114(1).
43. Education Act 1964, s. 1.
44. Education Act 1944, ss. 8(1)(b) and 114(1).
45. Education Act 1944, s. 76.
46. Wood and others *v.* Ealing London Borough Council [1967] Ch 364; LCT 143.
47. Education Act 1980, s. 6. See also DES Circular 1/81 on the Education Act 1980.
48. Education Act 1980, s. 8(1)(c).
49. Education Act 1944, s. 76.
50. Watt *v.* Kesteven County Council [1955] 1 All ER 473; LCT 136.
51. Education Act 1980, s. 6(2).
52. Education Act 1980, s. 6(3).
53. Education Act 1980, s. 6(5) and Education (Areas to which pupils belong) Regulations 1980.
54. Education Act 1980, s. 7.
55. Education Act 1980, s. 7(5).
56. *Times Educational Supplement*, 11.6.82; 18.6.82; 27.8.82.
57. Education Act 1944, ss. 68 and 99.
58. Tribunal and Enquiries Act 1971.
59. Education Act 1980, s. 9.

60. Education Act 1980, s. 8.
61. Education (School Information) Regulations 1981: see also DES Circular 15/77: *Information to Parents*.
62. Education Act 1980, s. 21.
63. Circular 1/81.
64. Watt *v*. Kesteven County Council [1955] 1 All ER 473; LCT 136; see also Winward *v*. Cheshire County Council, *The Times*, 21 July 1978.
65. Darling *v*. Minister of Education; Jones *v*. Minister of Education (1962) *The Times*, 7 April 1962; LCT 139.
66. See p. 318.
67. See chapter XI, 'School attendance'.
68. See p. 23.
69. Cumings and others *v*. Birkenhead Corporation (1971) 69 LGR 444 CA.
70. *Daily Mail*, 3 November 1972. See also p. 327.
71. Education Act 1944, s. 36 as amended by the Education Act 1981.
72. Lord Diplock in Secretary of State *v*. Tameside [1976] 3 All ER 665. The point was made also in Winter *v*. Swallow and Essex County Council (1980) (unreported).
73. See p. 4.
74. Education Act 1980, s. 24.
75. Education Act 1980, s. 26.
76. Education Act 1976, s. 1.
77. DES Circular 4/82.
78. *Special Educational Needs, Report of the Committee of Enquiry into the Education of Handicapped Children and Young People*, Cmnd 7212, HMSO, 1978.
79. Education Act 1981, s. 1.
80. The Education Act 1944, s. 8 has been amended to include this duty.
81. Education Act 1981, s. 2(3).
82. Education Act 1981, s. 2(5)(a).
83. Education Act 1981, s. 2(5)(b).
84. Education Act 1981, s. 3.
85. Education Act 1944, s. 36 as amended.
86. Education Act 1944, s. 76.
87. Education Act 1981, s. 2(3).
88. DES Circular 1/83: *Assessments and Statements of Special Educational Needs* (jointly with DHSS).

89. Education (Scotland) Act 1981.
90. DES Circular 1/83.
91. Education Act 1981: Schedule 1, Part 1.
92. Education Act 1981, s. 5.
93. Education Act 1981, s. 7.
94. See p. 23.
95. Education Act 1981, s. 8.
96. Education Act 1981, s. 8(6).
97. Education Act 1981, s. 8(7) and Education Act 1980, s. 34(1).
98. DES Circular 6/83: *The Approval of Special Schools*. The Education (Approval of Special Schools) Regulations 1983.
99. Direct Grant Grammar Schools (Cessation of Grant) Regulations 1975.
100. Education Act 1944, ss. 70–5.
101. Education Act 1980, s. 34(2–4).
102. Education (Particulars of Independent Schools) Regulations 1982, S.I. no. 1730.
103. Byrd *v.* Secretary of State for Education and Science; Secretary of State for Education and Science *v.* Byrd, *The Times*, 22 May 1968.
104. *Times Educational Supplement*, 3 April 1970 .
105. *Guardian*, 22 March 1984.
106. Education Act 1976, s. 5 (now repealed).
107. Local Government Act 1972, s. 137(1).
108. Manchester City Council *v.* Greater Manchester Metropolitan County Council and others, *The Times*, 10 July 1980; 78 LGR 560 HL.
109. Education Act 1976, s. 6.
110. Education Act 1980, ss. 17–18.
111. Education (Assisted Places) (Incidental Expenses) Regulations 1981, as amended.
112. Education (Assisted Places) Regulations 1980.
113. *Education*, 3 December 1982.
114. See p. 4.
115. Employment and Training Act 1948, s. 7.
116. Employment and Training Act 1973, s. 8.
117. Education Act 1980, s. 22(1)(a).
118. Education Act 1980, s. 22(1)(b).
119. Education Act 1980, s. 22(4).
120. See p. 411.
121. Education (Miscellaneous Provisions) Act 1948, s. 5, as amended

64   Teachers and the Law

by the Education (Provision of Clothing) Regulations 1980 and the Education Act 1980, s. 29.

. e.g. an independent school.
123. Education Act 1944, s. 78(2) and Education (Miscellaneous Provisions) Act 1948, s. 5(4).
124. National Health Service Reorganization Act 1973, s. 3(3).
125. Education Act 1980, s. 7.
126. Austria, Belgium, Cyprus, Denmark, the Federal Republic of Germany, France, Greece, Iceland, Ireland, Italy, Liechtenstein, Luxembourg, Malta, the Netherlands, Norway, Portugal, Spain, Sweden, Switzerland, Turkey and the United Kingdom.
127. *Times Educational Supplement*, 17 December 1982: *Daily Telegraph*, 17 August 1984.
128. Readers who are interested in this subject are recommended to read G. R. Barrell: 'Teachers and the European Law' (College of Preceptors: *Education Today*, Vol. 26, No. 2, Summer 1976, pp. 2–20).
129. Gillick *v.* West Norfolk and Wisbech Area Health Authority, *The Times*, 27 July 1983.
130. Magistrates Court (Children and Young Persons) Rules 1970.
131. Child Care Act (1980), s. 18.
132. See p. 456.
133. Kjeldsen, Busk Madsen and Pedersen *v.* Denmark (1975). Report of the Commission, pp. 41–2.
134. The Children's Legal Centre Ltd, 20 Compton Terrace, London N1 2UN.

II
The conduct of schools

1 Primary schools

Primary schools are conducted by a body of governors who are appointed under an Instrument of Government which is made by the local education authority in the case of county schools and by the Secretary of State for voluntary schools.[1] Their powers are defined by Articles of Government drawn up by the local education authority. The principal executive officer of the governors is known as the correspondent or the clerk.[2]

The distinction between 'managers' for primary schools and 'governors' for secondary schools was abolished by the Education Act 1980.[3] Before that date public elementary schools, whether primary, senior (for pupils over 11) or all-age, had managers; and secondary (or grammar) schools had governors. The distinction between managers and governors appears to have arisen from a wish not to discard either term, although their functions have been largely similar since 1944. The Taylor Report[4] recommended the universal use of the word 'governor'.

2   Secondary schools

Secondary schools are conducted by a body of governors who are appointed under an Instrument of Government which is made by the local education authority in the case of county schools and by the Secretary of State for voluntary schools.[5] Their powers are defined by Articles of Government which are made by the local education authority (with the Secretary's approval) for county schools, and by an order of the Secretary of State for voluntary schools. Such Articles determine the respective functions of the local education authority, the board of governors and the head of the school. The principal officer is known as the clerk to the governors.

3   All-age schools

All-age schools, where they still exist, containing pupils of both primary and secondary school ages, are conducted administratively in all respects as though they were primary schools.[6]

4   Middle schools

The Education Act 1964 enabled the establishment of schools which would include pupils both of primary and secondary school age.[7] The Act provides that, when giving his approval of an application to set up such a school, the Secretary of State will designate it as a primary or secondary school, currently under the terms of the Education (Middle Schools) Regulations 1980.

Although the term 'middle school' is in common use as a matter of convenience, it has no statutory existence with reference to a distinct stage of education. The three stages — primary, secondary and further — remain the legal divisions, and middle schools developed under the 1964 Act in order to facilitate reorganization in areas where this would otherwise have been impracticable. In practice schools for pupils from 8 to 12 years of age are designated as primary; those for pupils from 9 to 13 are secondary.

5   Maintained and other schools

Maintained schools are those which are maintained by local education authorities, and both county and voluntary schools are in this sector. The whole cost of running a maintained school,[8] including the salaries of the staff, is met by the authority. County schools are provided by a local education authority and voluntary schools by a voluntary body which may be a religious denomination, a city company or an educational trust. An incorrect distinction is often made between 'maintained' and 'voluntary', instead of between county and voluntary, schools.

Independent schools are outside the maintained sector. Sometimes called 'private' schools, and including some of the 'public' schools, they receive no grants from public funds. Independent schools must rely entirely upon their fees and any endowments which they may have for their income. Those which are registered charities, however, enjoy a favourable tax position, and pupils' fees may be subsidized under the assisted places scheme.[9]

6   County schools

The governors of county schools are appointed in accordance with the Instrument of Government made by the local education authority.[10]

Religious education and worship must be undenominational in character, and in accordance with the Agreed Syllabus.[11]

7   Aided schools

An aided school is a voluntary school, that is, one not established by a local education authority, in which the governors are able and willing to find 15 per cent of the cost of improving or enlarging the school to bring it up to the standards laid down. If it be a new school the governors are required to find 15 per cent of the cost of building.

The governing bodies of aided schools contain a number[12] of so-called foundation governors, whose particular duty is to ensure that the school is conducted in accordance with the terms of any trust deed. A trust deed may be well over a hundred years old but is nevertheless binding in law. If the Secretary of State considers that anything included in an Instrument or Articles of Government (or about to be included) is inconsistent with the trust deed, he can modify the trust deed if he thinks it just and expedient to do so.[13] He must however first consult all interested parties and bear in mind the way in which the school has been conducted traditionally.[14]

Governors of aided schools must comply with parental preference as regards choice of school, subject to the statutory limitations[15] under the 1980 Act. They must treat applications from outside the local education authority area in similar fashion.[16]

The cost of improving or enlarging the school building,[17] including the cost of a new site, is the responsibility of the governors,[18] subject to a maintenance contribution of 85 per cent from the Secretary of State.[19] Other buildings or capital expenditure, e.g. playing fields, canteens, kitchens, etc., must be provided by the local education authority: in such cases, all additions to the site (other than playing fields) must be conveyed to the trustees.[20] New voluntary-aided secondary schools, designed to accommodate children who have attended primary schools belonging to the same religious denomination, were envisaged by the Education Act 1959. Popularly known as 'matching schools ', they also rank for a maintenance grant of 85 per cent.[21]

Religious education is under the control of the governors and must be in accordance with the trust deed or, where there is no deed, in accordance with the practice in the school before it became aided. Agreed Syllabus instruction must be provided for children who cannot be conveniently educated elsewhere, if their parents request it.[22] The secular instruction in an aided primary school is under the control of the local education authority, in secondary schools of the governors.[23]

Teachers are appointed by the governors[24] subject to the establishment and educational qualifications prescribed by the local education authority, which may prohibit the appointment of any particular person to be employed for giving secular instruction, or require his dismissal if, in the authority's opinion, he is unsuitable for that purpose. Teachers are the servants of the governors and not of the authority[25] although, since their salaries form part of the authority's liability in maintaining an aided school, they are usually paid direct by the authority. However, for the purposes of protecting their rights against unfair dismissal, teachers in aided schools are regarded as being employed by the local education authority.[26]

The schoolkeeping staff is appointed by governors, subject to the general requirements of the authority.[27] The school meals staff is appointed by the local education authority in accordance with the Secretary of State's regulations. The appointment of secretarial staff is in accordance with the Articles of Government.

In general, the governors are responsible for the exterior maintenance and repair of the building (with an 85 per cent maintenance contribution from the Secretary of State), the local education authority for the interior. The local education authority maintains the playground and playing fields.[28]

The local education authority may require the free use of the buildings for any educational purpose or for the welfare of the young on not more than three days in any week, when they are not in use as a school, provided that no other suitable accommodation is available.[29]

8 Controlled schools

The term 'controlled school' is not defined in the 1944 Act, but it may be said to be a voluntary school which is neither an aided nor a special agreement school. It is a voluntary school – that is, a school not provided by a local education authority – where the governors are unable or unwilling to find the required proportion of the cost of improving or enlarging the school,[30] or of building a new voluntary school to provide for the closure or reorganization of existing voluntary schools.[31] The Instrument of Government is made by an order of the Secretary of State.[32]

The local education authority bears the whole cost of improvements and additions to the school[33] and, if these are on the original site, their ownership must be vested in the trustees. This need not be done, however, in the case of a new controlled school.

Religious education must be in accordance with an Agreed Syllabus,[34] but denominational instruction must be provided, for not more than two periods a week, for those pupils whose parents request it.[35] The nature of the daily act of worship is not specified but, unless the Secretary of State makes a direction to the contrary, it may be in accordance with the trust deed or, if there is no deed, in accordance with the practice in the school before it became controlled.

Teachers are appointed by the local education authority which must, however, consider representations from the foundation governors in appointing the head. Reserved teachers must be appointed.[36]

The whole cost of the maintenance of the school and the buildings is borne by the local education authority,[37] which also appoints the non-teaching staff.[38]

The use of the school is reserved to the foundation managers on Sundays, and on Saturdays if it is not required by the local education authority for the purposes of school activities or the welfare of the young.[39]

9 Special agreement schools

The constitution of governing bodies is the same as in the case of an aided school.[40]

In the case of a new school, capital expenditure on the building is met by the voluntary body with a grant of not more than 85 per cent from the local education authority.[41] Where the special agreement school is to provide accommodation for displaced pupils, the cost is met by the voluntary body with a grant of not more than 85 per cent from the Secretary of State towards such part as he may determine to be attributable to the provision of places for displaced pupils.[42]

The provisions for religious instruction are as in the case of an aided school.[43] The position with regard to worship, however, is the same as in a controlled school.[44] Except as may be otherwise provided in the Articles of Government, secular instruction is under the control of the local education authority.[45]

The teaching staff is appointed under the same conditions as in a controlled school,[46] with similar provisions regarding the appointment of the head and of reserved teachers. The proportion of reserved teachers, however, is not fixed by the Act, and is determined jointly by the proposers of the school and the local education authority. 75 per cent is a usual figure.

The non-teaching staff is appointed by the local education authority.[47] The arrangements for the maintenance of the premises are the same as in the case of an aided school.[48]

The local education authority may require the use of the premises for educational purposes or for the welfare of children when they are not in use as a school. Such use is limited to not more than three days in any one week, and conditional upon there being no suitable alternative accommodation available.[49]

10 Minor authorities

A minor authority, in relation to a school maintained by a local education authority,[50] is one of the following:

(a) the parish council (in England) or the community council (in Wales) which appears to the local education authority to be the council of the area served by the school;
(b) the parish meeting where a school is situated in a parish which has no council;
(c) the district council where a school is situated in a community

(in Wales) which has no council, or (in England) neither in a parish nor a metropolitan county;

(d) the parish or community council or councils, the parish meeting or meetings, or the district council or councils acting jointly where a school appears to serve more than one minor authority area.[51]

It is not necessary that a representative governor should be a member of the body which appoints him.

11   Grouping of schools

A number of schools may be grouped together under the same body of governors but this requires the approval of the Secretary of State who may impose conditions.[52] Where this is done, the schools are generally, though not necessarily, of a similar kind. Primary and secondary schools are not usually grouped together although the 1944 Act expressly states that this may be done. As a rule, it is not practicable to group county and voluntary schools under the same body, and such a scheme requires the consent of the local education authority, the Secretary of State and the governors of the schools concerned.[53] Community homes and remand homes are maintained by an authority by virtue of its powers under the Children and Young Persons Acts, and are therefore not the responsibility of the education committee.

The report of the Taylor committee[54] recommended that each school should have its own governing body. The Education Act 1980 has gone a long way to securing this.

12   Instruments of government and the composition of governing bodies

The instrument defines the constitution of the governing body and lays down the procedure by which its members are appointed. Instruments vary somewhat to suit particular circumstances.

	Instrument	*Articles*
PRIMARY		
County	LEA	LEA
Voluntary:		
Controlled	S of S	LEA
Special Agreement	S of S	LEA
Aided	S of S	LEA
SECONDARY		
County	LEA	LEA*
Voluntary:		
Controlled	S of S	S of S
Special Agreement	S of S	S of S
Aided	S of S	S of S

* With the Secretary of State's approval.

Responsibility for making instruments and articles of government.

The Education Act 1980 laid down new minimum requirements for the appointment and composition of governing bodies.[55] The requirements came into force in July 1981 and apply if the local education authority makes a new instrument (e.g. in the case of a new or reorganized school) or if the Secretary of State decides to apply the requirements to any particular school or schools.[56] The new-style governmental regulations apply to maintained special schools from September 1984.[57]

The Secretary of State has announced that from September 1985:[58]

(a) the governing bodies of all maintained schools must conform with the requirements of the Education Act 1980; and

(b) each school must have its own governing body except in the case of two primary schools or as otherwise approved by the Secretary of State.

The new minimum requirements for governing bodies are:[59]

(a) Governors appointed by the local education authority.

(b) If there is a minor authority for the area served by the school, at least one governor appointed by the minor authority.

(c) Parent governors, elected by parents of registered pupils and themselves at the time parents of pupils at the school:
County and controlled schools: at least 2 parent governors.
Aided and special agreement schools: at least 1 parent governor.

(d) Teacher governors, elected by teachers at the school and themselves teachers at the school. At least two teacher governors unless the school has fewer than 300 registered pupils, in which case at least one teacher governor.

(e) The head teacher shall be a governor, unless he elects not to be. In any case, he has a right to attend meetings.

(f) Foundation governors (in the case of voluntary schools):
   (i) *Controlled schools*: at least one fifth of the members of the governing body shall be foundation governors.
   (ii) *Aided or special agreement schools*: the foundation governors shall outnumber the other members of the governing body by two, if that body has eighteen or fewer members and by three if it has more. At least one of the foundation governors must on appointment be a parent of a registered pupil at the school.

Arrangements for the election of parent and teacher governors are the responsibility of local education authorities and the governors of aided or special agreement schools.[60]

The Act stresses that its requirements with regard to representation are minima, and additional representation is permitted.[61] It was reported, for example, that the local education authority for Birmingham has made parents the biggest group on governing bodies for its area.[62]

There is no positive provision in the Act for pupil governors, but no pupil may hold this office until he has attained the age of 16.

Although the matter has not been formally tested in the courts, doubt has been expressed as to whether pupils under

18 can lawfully be appointed as school governors. Whereas there would undoubtedly be legal difficulties if they were to vote on the expenditure of money, it seems that the governing bodies of county schools do not spend funds in their own right — they merely advise their local education authority as to how the authority might spend its funds. This remains true even if as a matter of policy a local education authority places a sum annually at the disposal of governing bodies, perhaps for minor maintenance work.

The governors of voluntary aided and special agreement schools do, however, have certain financial obligations in regard to the upkeep of their buildings and this would seem to disqualify pupils from being governors.

13   Regulations affecting governing bodies

The Education Act of 1980 conferred on the Secretary of State the power to make regulations as to the meetings and proceedings of governing bodies.[63]

The regulations,[64] which came into force in August 1981, contain the following provisions:

(i)   DISQUALIFICATION OF GOVERNORS

No person may serve on more than five governing bodies: for this purpose, the governing body of an approved group of schools is regarded as one body. A bankrupt is ineligible, as is anyone with a criminal conviction who has served a sentence of three months or longer (even if suspended) without the option of a fine. The sentence must be served either during the period of governorship or within five years of appointment. If a governor, other than an ex-officio governor, is absent from governors' meetings for a continuous period of twelve months without the governors' consent, then he shall cease to hold office, but may be re-elected or reappointed.

(ii)   CONDUCT OF MEETINGS

A governing body must elect a chairman and vice-chairman from their number, either at the first meeting of the school year or at a time specified in the Instrument of Government. Any member of the governing body is eligible, with the exception of teacher and pupil governors.

The governing body must meet at least once a term. Any three members of the governing body are able to requisition a meeting. The quorum for a meeting is three or, where greater, one third of the membership of the governing body.

(iii)   PROCEEDINGS AND MINUTES

The proceedings of a governors' meeting are not invalidated by any defect in the appointment, election or qualification of any member, nor by any unfilled vacancy. The chairman, if necessary, can use a second or casting vote.

Where the governing body are considering disciplinary action against a teacher or other school employee, or against a pupil arising out of an incident involving a pupil, then the regulations impose no restriction on the governing body allowing the teacher or pupil concerned to be heard, the person who has made relevant allegations to present these allegations or a material witness to give relevant evidence.

Copies of the agenda and signed minutes of every meeting must be readily available at school for inspection by any teacher, employee or any parent of a pupil. Any minute relating to (a) a named teacher, employee or proposed employee at the school; (b) a named pupil or candidate for admission to the school; (c) any matter which the governing body consider to be confidential, can be excluded from the minutes.

(iv)   TENURE OF OFFICE

Parent governors cease to hold office on the first day of the school year in which they no longer have a child as a registered pupil of the school.

Teacher governors, and governors elected from the non-teaching staff of a school, cease to hold office on ceasing to be employed at the school.

A head teacher who elects to be a governor, or elects not to be a governor, must do so in writing to the clerk to the governing body. A head is entitled at any time to change his decision. Whether or not he elects to be a governor, a head is entitled to attend all meetings unless the circumstances decree his withdrawal.[65]

(v) PROVISIONS APPLYING TO VOLUNTARY SCHOOLS

A resignation or removal from office of a governor shall take effect when the clerk to the governing body receives written notice.

Where a casual vacancy occurs on a governing body, the clerk shall notify the appointing group or body.

When convening a meeting, a clerk must comply with any direction given by: (a) the governing body at a previous meeting; (b) the chairman or vice-chairman of the governing body, unless this is inconsistent with (a).

Every member of the governing body, the head teacher and the Chief Education Officer must receive seven clear days' notice of the meeting together with the agenda, unless there are matters demanding urgent attention and justifying shorter notice. The convening of a meeting and its proceedings will not be invalid even if proper notice is not given to all those concerned.

A resolution to rescind or vary a resolution carried at a previous meeting must be specifically included in the agenda.

If a quorum of governors is not present at the beginning of a meeting or during it, or if it is so resolved, the meeting shall be terminated. If all business on the agenda for that meeting has not been transacted, then a special meeting must be called for that purpose at a time and date specified by the resolution.

The local education authority shall have access to the minutes and, on request by the Chief Education Officer, the local authority must be supplied with any or all minutes of meetings.

The minutes must record the names of all governors present and include the head teacher even if he has elected not to be a governor.

(vi)   PROVISIONS FOR WITHDRAWAL FROM MEETINGS

A person shall withdraw from participation in a governors' meeting if:

(a) he or she has any direct pecuniary interest in any matter under consideration.

(b) the matter under consideration is that person's or a relative's appointment to a post as a teacher or otherwise at the school or transfer to another post in the school, promotion or retirement.

(c) the person could be a candidate for the vacancy created by the transfer, promotion or retirement of another teacher which is under consideration at the meeting.

(d) he or she is involved either as a teacher, pupil, parent or relative in disciplinary proceedings against a pupil or teacher or other employee at the school.

(e) he or she is employed as a teacher, or otherwise employed at the school, and his or her conduct, continued employment or the appointment of a successor is being discussed.

(f) he or she is a parent of a child whose admission to school is being considered.

In 1984 the Court of Appeal held that a teacher governor who should have withdrawn from an appointments meeting but voted at it, had thereby invalidated the proceedings.[66]

The DES has produced, as a guide to local education authorities, a model Instrument of Government which takes account of the Education Act of 1980.[67] This replaces the model Instrument which accompanied the Education Act of 1944.[68]

(vi) SPECIAL SCHOOLS

The Secretary of State has power to refuse to recognize a non-maintained special school if he is not satisfied with the composition and function of the governing body.[69]

14 Articles of Government

These are binding on governors in the conduct of schools. They define the functions of governors, the relationship between the governing body, the local education authority and the head, and between the governing body and the school. Articles vary somewhat from place to place and according to the type of school, but the following are among the matters usually included:

1. The conduct of the school must be in accordance with the Education Acts, the appropriate regulations of the Secretary of State and, except in the case of voluntary-aided schools, the regulations of the local education authority.
2. The governors are responsible for certain matters connected with maintenance and for obtaining the necessary estimates.
3. The respective functions of the governors and the local education authority in connection with the appointment and dismissal of teaching and non-teaching staff are defined.
4. In county and controlled schools the correspondent or clerk to the governors is appointed by the authority; in aided and special agreement schools, the governing body may appoint.
5. The governors have general control of the school and must take appropriate action within their powers; in matters where they have no power to act they must notify the local education authority of anything requiring attention.
6. The educational character of the school is determined by the local education authority.
7. Responsibility for the internal organization, management and discipline of the school is vested in the head, together with the supervision of both teaching and non-teaching staff, and the power to suspend pupils from attendance.

8. Provision is made for full consultation between the head, the governors and the local education authority; and opportunity is given for the assistant staff to make representations either through, or with the knowledge of, the head.
9. The head is entitled to attend throughout the meetings of governors unless excluded for good cause during the discussion of specific business.
10. Holidays are, in general, determined by the local education authority; the granting of some occasional closures usually being within the discretion of the governors.
11. The governors must furnish the local education authority with such returns as may be required.
12. A copy of the Articles of Government must be given to every teacher on appointment, or he must be given facilities for acquainting himself with them.

Where proposals for a significant change in the character of a school are approved under the Education Act 1980, section 12, the Secretary of State may make such variations in the Articles of Government (if the school is a secondary school) or modifications of the trust deed which appear to him to be required.

15   The powers of governing bodies

Statutory bodies may delegate the exercise of their powers to subordinate bodies. When they have done so absolutely, it is not possible for them to claw back these powers as a matter of convenience or in an attempt to remedy a defect. There have been cases in which disciplinary proceedings have been stopped in these circumstances.

CURTIS v. MANCHESTER CITY COUNCIL

A group of teachers made a complaint under the model grievance procedure about the educational philosophy and administrative methods of their headmistress. The issues were examined by a panel which reported 'that the conditions existing at the school are such that urgent action is necessary'. The headmistress, Mrs Curtis, was suspended on full pay from June 1975, and the education committee decided to establish a sub-committee to examine the matter. Mrs Curtis objected to the procedures which were being employed on the grounds that the grievance (as distinct from the disputes) procedure was not intended to be used for collective complaints, and also that the sub-committee which had been set up had no jurisdiction to conduct a disciplinary hearing. Her objections were overruled, and she applied to the Chancery Division for an injunction to restrain the authority from holding, or proceeding with, the disciplinary inquiry.

The school's Articles of Government provided that the headmistress 'except when otherwise determined by the local education authority, shall not be dismissed except upon the recommendation of the governors'. Although the Articles of Government specified the functions of the governing body, no governors had, in fact, been appointed. Mrs Curtis claimed that she was entitled by the Articles to have the question of her dismissal considered by the governors and that, in the absence of a governing body, the authority could not establish a substitute. In support of this, her counsel cited Lord Denning: 'The jurisdiction of a domestic tribunal, such as the committee of the Showmen's Guild, must be founded in contract. Outside the regular courts of this country, no set of men may sit in judgment on their fellows except so far as Parliament authorizes it, or the parties agree to it.' The Articles of Government formed part of the headmistress's contract.

The authority rested its case on the four words 'except when otherwise determined', maintaining that it had so determined through its properly constituted education committee which had power, under the Local Government Act 1972, section 101, to delegate its functions. In those circumstances the recommendations of a governors were no longer relevant.

Mr Justice Slade felt there was a triable issue, and that one arguable interpretation of the Article was that there had always to be a recommendation from the governors before the education authority could dismiss: the four words merely left it open to the authority to disregard the recommendation. He accepted that the authority had done their best to secure a fair hearing, but they had not gone the right way about it. Mrs Curtis was entitled to an interlocutory injunction.[70]

WINDER v. CAMBRIDGESHIRE COUNTY COUNCIL

In April 1976 six members of the teaching staff at the Isle of Ely College of Further Education in Wisbech complained about the principal. During an investigation by six of the governors complaints were made about Mr Winder, the head of department of building and engineering, who had been on the staff for twenty years. The committee recommended that the principal and Mr Winder should be required to answer certain charges, and both were suspended. The governors set up a disciplinary committee of three of their number who had not taken part in the inquiry, but this committee's recommendation that the principal should be dismissed was not accepted by the governing body.

It was at this point that the procedures ran into trouble. The governors decided that it would not be right for the disciplinary committee to deal with the complaints against Mr Winder as they had already heard certain evidence about him; on the other hand they did not have enough eligible members who had not already been involved in the proceedings to form a new committee. They asked the local education authority to take over the case and the chairman of the authority's further education sub-committee was authorized to appoint a disciplinary committee of the authority.

The Articles of Government for the college set out the respective functions of the authority, the governors and the academic board,[71] and empowered the governors to dismiss members of the teaching staff, other than the vice-principal, subject to the consent of the authority. Mr Winder sought an injunction against the authority to restrain them from prosecuting disciplinary charges against him and a further injunction against one of the governors to prevent him from delegating his duties under the Articles. He contended that, on the plain language of the scheme, only the governors could dismiss him, and the authority's function was limited to confirming (or not confirming) that decision. It was argued for the authority that, as the contractual employer, they were entitled to dismiss.

Granting both injunctions, the deputy judge said that the Act, in bringing about a division of functions, said that the Articles 'shall determine the functions to be exercised respectively'. Those words were sufficiently broad and mandatory to empower an authority to give exclusive power to another body to carry out any function, including appointment and dismissal. That had been done in the present case. The expression of a specific power excludes others: if the power to appoint was vested in the governors, so was the power to dismiss. Nor would it be right to put a gloss on the word 'empowered' by implying that that power was concurrent with an implied power in the council. Nothing would have been easier than to have made express provision for a residual or concurrent power to be given to the council.

Any other construction would lead to situations which, if not absurd, would be highly undesirable. Thus the governors could appoint a teacher one week and the county council dismiss him the next, or vice versa.[72]

However, the local education authority succeeded in its appeal. The Court of Appeal held that the governing body could still either accept or reject its findings. There was therefore no question that powers had been delegated to the local education authority. Moreover, even if the local education authority had in fact been invited to dismiss Mr Winder because the governing body had been unable to set up its own sub-committee, the local education authority would have had to step in at some point in the interests of keeping the college running smoothly.[73]

16   Governing bodies in the future

The White Paper[74] which followed consultation about the Taylor report indicated that there was no general agreement about what power governing bodies should have: 'Most people ... see the nature of the relationship between the governing body and the school as something organic which is individual to each school. Where the relationship works, it does not need any over-elaborate delegation of statutory powers, and where it does not work, no amount of formal statutory power will increase its usefulness or its influence.'

Against this background of thinking, the 1980 Act contained no provisions about the powers to be given to governors. However a White Paper in 1985 stated that the government was considering enacting explicit powers to governing bodies to prepare annual estimates for their schools' budgets, to define curriculum guidelines and policy and to make regular reports on meeting them to annual meetings of parents.[75]

There are already signs that the DES is seeking to involve governing bodies more with the curriculum of their schools. Recent Circulars on the school curriculum which invited local education authorities to review their curriculum policy specifically asked for governing bodies to be consulted.[76]

It seems likely, too, that the influence of parents on governing bodies will be strengthened. The composition of governing bodies proposed in the White Paper is given in the table on the facing page.

In advance of any legislation it seems that the DES is already thinking of stimulating an increased role for governing bodies. In July 1984 it was reported that the Secretary of State had refused to amend the Articles of Government of schools in Newcastle upon Tyne to give the final say on policy matters to the education authority rather than to individual governing bodies.[77]

The White Paper proposes an increase in training for school governors. It also suggests that local education authorities should be empowered to pay subsistence and travelling allowances to all governors attending meetings. At present

The proposed composition of governing bodies for county, voluntary controlled and maintained special schools

Size of school:	Elected by and from parents[b]	Appointed by LEA	Head-teacher[c]	Elected by and from teachers	Co-opted[d] or, for controlled schools: Foundation		Co-opted[d]	Total
fewer than 100 pupils	2	2	1	1	2	3	1	9
100–299 pupils	3	3	1	1	3	4	1	12
300 pupils or more[a]	4	4	1	2	4	5	1	16
600 pupils or more[a]	5	5	1	2	4	6	2	19

Notes (a) the LEA would be free to choose either composition for schools with 600 or more pupils.

(b) where insufficient parents stood for election (or, in any case, for schools with at least 50 per cent boarders) the LEA would appoint parent proxies to fill vacancies. LEA members and employees and co-opted members of the Education Committee would be ineligible for such proxy appointments.

(c) the head teacher would be able to choose not go be a governor.

(d) the number of co-optees would be reduced by one to allow for the addition shown in the following mutually exclusive circumstances:

(i) one representative of the minor authority (or minor authorities, acting jointly) in the case of a county or controlled primary school serving an area in which there is one or more minor authorities;

(ii) one representative of the District Health Authority in the case of a hospital special school;

(iii) one representative of a relevant voluntary organisation in the case of any other maintained special school.

Source: 'Better Schools' (1985) HMSO Cmnd 9469.

local authorities have discretion to pay such allowances only to councillors and co-opted members of councils who are also school governors, under the Local Government Act 1972.

17   Confidentiality at governors' meetings

In order to ensure full and frank discussion, discussion at governors' meetings should be regarded as confidential. What is said, unless spoken in malice, attracts qualified privilege.[78]

It is important to note that all governors are representatives and not delegates of those who appoint them. Unauthorized 'reporting back' may remove the protection of privilege and pave the way for action for defamation. The channel of communication between governing bodies and the community is the publication of the minutes, as laid down by regulations.[79]

It should be noted that the regulations refer to the publication of the signed minutes. Although this can cause some delay in publication, it affords the governing body the opportunity to scrutinize what is to be published in their name.

18   The reorganization of schools

The procedures established by the 1944 Act[80] for the establishment, discontinuance and alteration of schools were the subject of much interpretation by the courts and amendment by Parliament during the years 1944–80, largely provoked by disputes between parents, governors and local education authorities about the reorganization of secondary schools along comprehensive lines.

The government's declared intention of taking controls off local authorities, the need, brought about by falling rolls, to streamline the procedures and the urgent need to take school places out of commission, led to the simplified procedures of the Education Act 1980.[81] In essence the 1980 Act states that:

(a) if a local education authority wishes to start or cease to maintain a county school, or to make a significant change in its character or a significant enlargement of it, they must publish their proposals.[82] The public notices are usually referred to as 'Section 12 notices'.[83] Governors of voluntary schools must publish notices similarly, after consultation with the local education authority. Copies of all such proposals must be submitted to the Secretary of State, together with the dates of intended implementation. Nursery schools are not covered by this procedure.

(b) The Secretary of State has power to determine what constitutes a significant enlargement in each set of circumstances. A change of character is defined in the 1980 Act as a change in the age range of pupils for whom the school is intended, a change from or to co-education, and the making or alteration of arrangements for the admission of pupils by reference to ability or aptitude.[84]

(c) Within two months of the submission of proposals to him, the Secretary of State may rule that the proposals require his approval. If he has received objections, the proposals automatically require his approval. However, the local education authority may negotiate with objectors with a view to withdrawing their objections.

(d) The local education authority must implement approved proposals. If circumstances have changed during the period of approval, the local education authority may ask the Secretary of State to approve minor modifications, but not substantial changes.

Against the background of rapidly falling school rolls, it is necessary for local education authorities very carefully to balance the consequences of free exercise of parental choice of school against the need to keep as many schools educationally viable as possible with an eye to future needs. Local education authorities have authority to impose admission limits on their schools, as do governors in aided schools. Under the Education Act 1980[85] the standard number of pupils admitted (i.e. the number of pupils *in any age group* who were admitted in the school year 1979) may be reduced at local education authority or voluntary school governors' discretion in future years by no more than 20 per cent without going through the Section

12 procedure. The consultative procedures must apply to greater reductions.

School appeals panels[86] have power to admit pupils to any school or schools in excess of any admission limit, although the existence of such limits must be considered by the panel.

The procedures for closing special schools are rather different.[87] The local education authority need not publish Section 12 notices. It must however notify, in writing, the Secretary of State, all parents affected, all other LEAs who make use of the school, teachers' associations and any local voluntary bodies concerned with the handicap for which the school caters. It must also explain why it is necessary to discontinue the school, and what arrangements are to be made to cater for the special educational needs of pupils who would otherwise have attended the school.

19 Requirements for school premises

There are detailed regulations covering curriculum needs, land needs, teaching areas, staff and ancillary accommodation and boarding provision.[88] They are too extensive to reproduce here; however, the latest amendments (1982) are:

(i) 'Sufficient' land must be provided for the building, roads, delivery bays, parking, recreation, play and outdoor education.

(ii) Playing fields should be able to withstand at least 7 hours use per week. Unsuitable terrain (e.g. woodland) does not count towards the minimum provision.

(iii) Teaching space for upper junior and middle school pupils has been increased.

(iv) Suitable changing accommodation must be provided for children of 8 and upwards.

(v) The requirement to provide school kitchens is removed. LEAs have discretion as to how best to provide for their reduced obligation under the 1980 Act as regards school meals.

However, a ten-year transitional period is envisaged, since

premises cannot be brought into line immediately. New schools must meet the requirements immediately, existing premises will not have to conform to the new higher standards until 1991.

References

1. Education Act 1944, s. 17 as amended.
2. In county schools this is normally the Chief Education Officer, who may perform the duties by deputy.
3. Education Act 1980, s. 1.
4. *A New Partnership for Our Schools* (HMSO, 1977). Appendix B of the report (pp. 141–94) includes an excellent historical account of the history of school government from 597 to 1945.
5. Education Act 1944, s. 17.
6. Education Act 1944, s. 31(2). Now spent.
7. Education Act 1964, s. 1.
8. No fees may be charged.
9. See p. 43.
10. Education Act 1944, s. 17.
11. Education Act 1944, s. 26.
12. See p. 72.
13. Education Act 1944, s. 17(4).
14. Education Act 1944, s. 17(5).
15. See p. 21.
16. Education Act 1980, s. 6(5).
17. School buildings are defined as any building, or part of a building, forming the school premises except those required only as a caretaker's dwelling, in connection with school playing fields, for medical purposes or for the provision of milk, meals or other refreshment (Education Act 1946, s. 4(2)).
18. Education Act 1944, s. 15.
19. Education Act 1944, ss. 102, 103 and 105, as amended by the Education (Miscellaneous Provisions) Act 1953, s. 8, the Education Act 1967, s. 1, the Education Act 1968, Schedule 2, and the Education Act 1975, s. 3.
20. Education Act 1946, s. 3 and Schedule I.
21. The provisions of the 1959 Act have been superseded by the enlarged powers of the Secretary of State to make grants under the Education Act 1967, s. 1, as amended by the Education Act 1968, Schedule 2, and the Education Act 1975, s. 3.

22. Education Act 1944, s. 28.
23. Education Act 1944, s. 23(1) and (2).
24. Education Act 1944, s. 24(2).
25. Crocker *v.* Plymouth Corporation [1906] 1 KB 494, LCT 69.
26. Employment Protection (Consolidation) Act 1978, s. 80.
27. Education Act 1944, s. 22(4).
28. Education Act 1944, s. 15(3).
29. Education Act 1944, s. 22(2), and Education Act 1967, ss. 2 and 3.
30. Education Act 1944, s. 15(3).
31. Education (Miscellaneous Provisions) Act 1953, s. 2, as amended by the Education Act 1968, Schedule 2.
32. Education Act 1944, s. 17.
33. Education Act 1944, s. 15(3).
34. Education Act 1944, s. 27(6).
35. Education Act 1944, s. 27(1).
36. Education Act 1944, s. 27(2) to (5). For a discussion of the position of reserved teachers, see p. 121.
37. Education Act 1944, s. 15(3).
38. Education Act 1944, s. 22(4).
39. Education Act 1944, s. 22(1).
40. See pp. 72.
41. Education Act 1944, Schedule III, as amended by the Education (Miscellaneous Provisions) Act 1948, s. 11(1) and Schedule I.
42. Education Act 1967, s. 1, as amended by the Education Act 1968, Schedule 2.
43. See p. 330.
44. See p. 328.
45. Education Act 1944, s. 23(1).
46. See p. 69.
47. Education Act 1944, s. 22(4).
48. See p. 67
49. Education Act 1944, s. 22(2).
50. See p. 71.
51. Local Government Act 1972, s. 192(4).
52. Education Act 1980, s. 3(6). Two primary schools may be grouped without approval, provided neither is a special school, s. 3(2).
53. Education Act 1980, s. 3(3).
54. *A New Partnership for Our Schools* (HMSO, 1977).
55. Education Act 1980, s. 2.

56. Education Act 1980, s. 2(11)(b).
57. DES Circular 7/83.
58. Letter to local education authorities and governors of voluntary schools, January 1984 and DES Circular 7/84.
59. Education Act 1980, s. 2.
60. Education Act 1980, s. 2(9)(b).
61. Education Act 1980, s. 2(10).
62. *Times Educational Supplement*, 28 December 1979.
63. Education Act 1980, s. 4(1) and (2).
64. Education (School Governing Bodies) Regulations 1981.
65. Education Act 1980 s. 2(8) and Education (School Governing Bodies) Regulations 1981.
66. Noble *v.* ILEA (1984) 82 LGR 291 CA.
67. DES Circular 4/81.
68. Education Act 1944, Schedule IV.
69. Education (Approval of Special Schools) Regulations 1983: Schedule 2.
70. Curtis *v.* Manchester City Council, *The Times*, 27 May 1976.
71. Pursuant to the Education (No 2) Act 1968, s. 1(3).
72. Winder *v.* Cambridgeshire County Council, *The Times*, 24 May 1977.
73. Winder *v.* Cambridgeshire County Council (1978) 76 LGR 549 CA.
74. White Paper: *The Composition of School Governing Bodies*, Cmnd 7430, HMSO, 1979.
75. *Parental Influence at School: A New Framework for School Government*, Cmnd 9242, HMSO, 1984. (Green Paper): Better Schools, Cmnd 9469 HMSO 1985 (White Paper).
76. DES Circulars 65/81 and 8/83.
77. *Guardian*, 28 July 1984. The issue was corporal punishment.
78. See p. 598.
79. See pp. 75–9.
80. Education Act 1944, s. 13 as amended.
81. Education Act 1980, ss. 12–16.
82. Education Act 1980, s. 12.
83. The distribution of these notices is regulated by the Education (Publication of School Proposals) Regulations 1980.
84. Education Act 1980, s. 16(2).
85. Education Act 1980, s. 15.
86. See p. 23.

87. DES Circular 3/82: *The Discontinuance of Maintained Special Schools.*
88. Education (School Premises) Regulations 1981.

III
The status of teachers

1 Duties of local education authorities

The Secretary of State's requirements concerning the staffing of schools are binding upon all maintained schools as follows:[1]

(a) every school must have a head;
(b) every school must have a qualified teaching staff which is suitable and sufficient in numbers for the purpose of securing the provision of education appropriate to the ages, abilities, aptitudes and needs of its pupils.

The teachers employed must be qualified, but the regulation provides for certain relaxations:

(a) unqualified teachers in service before 1 April 1945 in schools maintained or aided by a former authority, or in receipt of a grant from the Secretary of State, may continue to be employed, if the teacher is a supplementary teacher (but such a teacher may not be appointed after 8 April 1982, and after a break in service, without the approval of Her Majesty's Inspectorate);
(b) student teachers and 'instructors' may be employed in accordance with the regulations;

(c) a person who is not a qualified teacher may, with the permission of the Secretary of State, be appointed to the assistant staff of a nursery school or class if she has satisfactorily completed a course of instruction in the care of young children.

2   Qualified teachers

In 1977 the DES announced that courses leading to the Certificate of Education would be phased out from 1979 as a stage in the establishment of a fully graduate entry to the teaching profession.

The definition of the term 'qualified teacher' is to be found in the Education (Teachers) Regulations 1982. Any person employed as a teacher must:

(a) have been notified in writing, by or on behalf of the Secretary of State, that he is a qualified teacher.
(b) have successfully completed a course for the Bachelor of Education, the Certificate in Education, the Postgraduate Certificate in Education or a comparable academic award. The award must be of a university or the Council for National Academic Awards, and the course for initial teacher training must be approved by the Secretary of State.
(c) from 1st September 1984, have attained 'O' level passes in English and mathematics (Grade C) or Grade 1 in those subjects in the examinations for the CSE.

Qualified teacher status is also extended to:

(a) persons with special qualifications.
(b) certificated and supplementary teachers employed before 1 April 1945 who have completed twenty years service as teachers.
(c) a teacher who possesses a qualification approved in his case on the recommendation of a local education authority, and has at least ten years (or such shorter period as may

for special reasons be approved) service as a teacher or of other experience, may be approved.

(d) a teacher who obtained either (i) the Diploma in the Teaching of Mentally Handicapped Children; or (ii) the Declaration of Recognition of Experience of the Training Council for Teachers of the Mentally Handicapped; or (iii) an equivalent diploma of the said Council awarded in recognition of some other diploma awarded before the establishment of that Council and has at least five years satisfactory service as a teacher in a special school since obtaining the Diploma or Declaration.

In 1978 a former polytechnic lecturer who falsely claimed to hold an honours degree in an application for another post was fined £400 with £100 costs for the deception.[2]

3   Approved courses of training

Until 1975 the professional initial training of teachers was conducted in polytechnic or university postgraduate departments of education, or in colleges of education which were concerned only with teacher education. The general oversight of these institutions was the responsibility of the area training organizations.

In 1972 the report of a committee under the chairmanship of Lord James[3] criticized the existing system on a number of grounds, and in the following December the Government issued a White Paper[4] proposing the abolition of colleges providing only initial training for teachers. Some were to become more closely involved with universities, most were to be assimilated into the maintained sector of higher education, and those which were to remain exclusively concerned with teachers were to have a commitment to in-service training.

The intention that 'outside the universities teacher education and higher education should be assimilated into a common system'[5] was given legal form in the Further Education Regulations 1975. The Area Training Organizations began to be phased out, and there has been a continuing programme of amalgamation, reorganization and closure. The Secretary of State let it be known that she did not intend to replace the Area Training Organizations at that time, and there have been protracted negotiations. Some of the ATOs' functions were taken over by the Regional Advisory Councils which had been in existence for many years in higher and further education.

Similarly, no detailed requirements were laid down at that time for the recognition of courses in such details as duration, or the minimum age and qualifications for admission. Institutions were asked to 'continue to ensure that persons who are unsuitable on grounds of character or health are not admitted to courses which include practical experience in schools'.

In England and Wales, courses recognized by the General Teaching Council for Scotland are accepted as approved initial training; and the following courses approved by the Ministry of Education for Northern Ireland and leading to recognition as a teacher in primary, intermediate or grammar schools in that country are also recognized by the Secretary of State:

Queen's University, Belfast
New University of Ulster, Coleraine
Stranmillis College, Belfast
Saint Joseph's College of Education, Belfast
Saint Mary's College of Education, Belfast
Ulster College of Physical Education, Jordanstown, Co. Antrim
Belfast Training College for Teachers of Domestic Economy

In 1983 the Government announced the establishment of the Council for the Accreditation of Teacher Education, whose function is to advise the Secretary of State for Education in England and Wales on the approval of initial teacher training courses, and to assess courses both in the university and public sectors. To date the Council has produced criteria by which Postgraduate Certificate in Education courses will be assessed: one such criterion is that PGCE courses must be of at least 36 weeks duration.

The authority of the Secretary of State to influence initial teacher training courses lies in the power to recognize courses for the purpose of granting qualified teacher status.[6]

4 Special approved qualifications

Graduates of universities within the British Isles, holders of degrees granted by the Council for National Academic Awards and those who (subject to any conditions therein mentioned) possess any of the qualifications listed in Circular 11/73 are regarded as holders of special approved qualifications.

They can, however, no longer take up a first appointment in a primary school unless they gained their special qualification before 1 January 1970 nor in a secondary school unless it was awarded before 1 January 1974.

Teachers already in service on the relevant date are not affected by the restriction.

The grant of qualified status by virtue of qualification through one of the certificates listed in the Circular does not limit the particular form of instruction which the teacher may give. It is for the employing authority to decide whether a teacher is qualified to give instruction in a particular subject or to be appointed to a particular post.

5 Special cases

If an authority wishes to appoint as a qualified teacher a person who does not possess an approved qualification, the DES must be consulted and the approach must be made by the local education authority, not by the teacher. To be granted qualified status, such a person must possess a combination of qualifications and experience. The latter must include at least ten years' teaching experience unless there are special reasons for making an exception. The probation for such teachers cannot be extended.

6 Overseas qualifications

The Secretary of State is prepared to recognize courses and qualifications taken in the British Commonwealth and in other countries if they appear to be of a standard equivalent to British qualifications. The length of the list precludes the publication of details of all the courses which have been so recognized and employing authorities should consult the DES about all qualifications, including degrees, obtained overseas.

The founding treaties of the European Community proclaim the free movement of services and people. Considerable agreement has already been reached within the medical and paramedical professions in Europe to allow members to practise freely in the Community. The teaching profession has so far been less affected, but in future may well be the subject of negotiations.

7   Verification of qualifications

An employing authority is required to verify without delay the qualifications of teachers appointed to its service.

The DES issues a notification to teachers who complete satisfactorily a course of initial training. Until 1977 the status of qualified teacher was not acquired until such a person was employed in a maintained school. Since that date, however, teachers trained in England and Wales (and those trained in Scotland or Northern Ireland who apply to the Department for qualified teacher status) are recognized on the successful completion of training. Teachers trained outside the United Kingdom are still not recognized as qualified until they are appointed to a school where this status is a requirement.

8   Probation

The initial period of service as a qualified teacher in a maintained school is probationary in character and during it the teacher must satisfy the Secretary of State of his practical proficiency as a teacher.[7]

The probationary period is designed not only to test the teacher, but also to give him a chance to 'run-in'. Local education authorities are asked to ensure that the schools in which teachers serve their probation offer favourable working conditions and the opportunities for advice and help from the head or an experienced assistant. In particular, authorities are asked not to appoint probationers to their supply staff where this would involve working in a number of schools. On the other hand a transfer should be possible if the teacher is not making the progress expected of him.

Full-time teachers trained in the United Kingdom serve one year's probation; for other full-time teachers the period is two years. Part-time teachers may be required to serve up to four years' probation. The main responsibility for its supervision rests with the local education authority which before the end of that period may recommend either that probation has been satisfactorily completed, or that a further period should be served, or that the person should no longer be employed as a qualified teacher. It is the authority's responsibility to advise the teacher if the probationary period is successful; if extension or termination is recommended, the teacher should be informed of the contents of a special report to the Secretary of State, who will make the decision. If a second, or further, extension or termination is then recommended, the Secretary of State will give the teacher an opportunity to make representations before the decision is reached.

For a teacher whose first appointment is in an independent school, in further education, or in any establishment other than a maintained school, probationary service does not begin unless and until the teacher transfers to the maintained sector. The Secretary of State has, however, advised local education authorities that if such a teacher has good experience and substantial service reliably vouched for, it would be unreasonable to require the full, or in some cases any, period of probation. An authority can, in such cases, make an early application even at the time of appointment for a reduction or waiver of probation. In suitable instances this might apply to teachers with experience overseas.

In 1983 the DES issued detailed guidelines to local education authorities on the treatment and assessment of probationary teachers. Particular points to note are:[8]

(a) New teachers and their head teachers should be informed in writing of the period of probation to be served.

(b) The duties assigned to a probationer, supervision and conditions of work should be such as to facilitate a fair and reasonable assessment of conduct and efficiency as a teacher.

(c) Probationers should have an opportunity to demonstrate their proficiency in teaching classes of a size normal for the school in which they teach and the subject they are teaching.

(d) Probationers should not be appointed as supply teachers if at all possible, nor to peripatetic posts.

(e) Probationers should be appointed to posts which closely match their training.

(f) Probationers should be made aware at the beginning of the probationary period of who particularly is to assess their work (e.g. the head teacher or local education authority advisers or inspectors), and of the criteria by which they will be assessed. These should include class management, relevant subject expertise, appropriate teaching skills, adequacy of lesson preparation, use of resources, understanding the needs of pupils, and the ability to establish appropriate relationships with pupils and colleagues.

It is particularly important that probationary teachers are informed of any formal assessments, particularly adverse ones, as soon as they are made, so that there is ample opportunity to heed advice and put matters right. In 1982 a probationary teacher was notified by the Secretary of State that the teacher had failed to satisfy him as to his practical efficiency. The teacher asked to see the local education authority's report on his work, on which the Secretary of State had based his decision. The DES replied that the report was confidential.

Mr Justice Woolf in the Queen's Bench Division[9] ruled that this was a situation which fell 'below the standard of fairness required by the rules of natural justice. ... The applicant should have been given the gist of them and the specific allegations which they contained and he should have been given an opportunity to comment on them ... there was accordingly a risk of injustice.' The decision of the Secretary of State was quashed and the matter sent back to him for further consideration, during which the probationary teacher was to be given time to study the reports and make further representations.

Finally, it should be noted that, as employees, probationary teachers have a right of appeal to an industrial tribunal under current employment protection legislation. Such tribunals will not question the professional judgement of a probationer's competence, provided that it is properly and reasonably exercised. The tribunals will, however, take great pains to see that the probationer has been fairly treated, that the guidelines above have been followed reasonably, and that adequate advice and warning on performance has been given.

A case in 1981 showed the willingness of industrial tribunals to review the treatment and evaluation of probationers.[10]

At the school where the employee worked it was thought that he was a fully qualified teacher; in fact he was a probationary teacher, and as such should have been receiving substantial advice and assistance. After about 18 months' work the true position was discovered. Reports on his performance at this stage were critical, and after visits from school inspectors the employee's probationary period was extended by 6 months. After the end of that period and a period of consultation he was dismissed for unsatisfactory performance. An industrial tribunal held that the employee had been unfairly dismissed, although they assessed his contribution to his own dismissal at one third. The employers contended that the employee had been clearly shown to be incompetent after conscientious investigation, and also was so reluctant to accept advice that it was hopeless to make any further attempt to equip him as a teacher. His incompetence was such that it would not be right to allow him to continue to teach, and that dismissal in such circumstances was fair. The Court of Appeal upheld the tribunal's decision. They pointed out that the tribunal had found that the employee had not received the advice and assistance appropriate to a probationer, either in duration or in quality, and the Court noted that this was an important factor in deciding whether it was reasonable for the employer to treat his incompetence as sufficient reason for dismissing him. The tribunal's decision was not perverse and no error of law had been shown; the decision should stand.

In 1982 an industrial tribunal rejected another appeal by a probationary teacher that he had received inadequate advice and assistance.[11]

It is currently not possible for local education authorities to make support during probation available in independent schools. Probation cannot thus be served in independent schools.

9 Special schools

Special requirements are laid down in respect of teachers in special schools.[12]

Each special school must have a head who takes an appropriate part in the teaching of the school and a staff of assistants suitable and sufficient in number to provide full-time education suitable to the ages, abilities, aptitudes and needs of the pupils.

All members of the staff must be qualified teachers within the meaning of the Education (Teachers) Regulations 1982 and, if they are teaching blind, deaf or partially-hearing children, they must have such further qualifications as may be required by the Secretary of State. Unless they are to give instruction in a craft, trade or domestic subject, they must possess (appropriate to the school in which they work) either:

(a) the Teacher's Diploma of the British Association of Teachers of the Deaf, or

(b) the Certificate for Teachers of the Deaf awarded by the University of Manchester, or

(c) the School Teachers' Diploma of the Association for the Education and Welfare of the Visually Handicapped, or

(d) the Diploma in Special Education (Visually Handicapped) awarded by the University of Birmingham, or

(e) any comparable qualification approved by the Secretary of State.

Teachers with one of these qualifications may also be employed in schools for pupils who are both blind and deaf.

Temporary unqualified appointment to special schools is also permitted, provided that the employing body is satisfied that there is an intention to acquire one of the approved qualifications.

Teachers in special schools who were qualified under the old regulations[13] are regarded as qualified under the new.

10   Student teachers

A person who is 18 years of age, and who holds one of the qualifications required for admission to an approved course of training, or possesses some other qualification acceptable to the Secretary of State, may be appointed as a student teacher.[14] A student teacher is not counted against the teaching establishment of a school. He should intend to proceed to qualified teacher status and should not be given the responsibilities of a class nor teach a subject which is not also taught by a qualified teacher at the school.

A student teacher may not be employed for longer than two years in all in maintained schools unless the Secretary of State gives specific approval. Extension of time is possible only for those who, having undertaken a course of approved training, have not completed their training satisfactorily, and is limited to the time needed for an opportunity to retrieve the failure.

11   Instructors

It sometimes occurs that no qualified teacher is available to teach some of the specialist skills which are now included in the school curriculum, e.g. playing musical instruments, office skills, sports, games and pastimes, and technical skills, some of which may be vocational in character. It is now possible to appoint an instructor who is not a qualified teacher to undertake this work until a specialist teacher is available.[15]

12   Health

Subject to the provisions of the Disabled Persons (Employment) Acts, a teacher must satisfy the Secretary of State of his health and physical capacity for teaching unless he has already done so for the purpose of the Teachers (Superannuation) Acts. This must be done at the outset of his first employment as a qualified or temporary assistant teacher.

A teacher may not continue in employment if his employing body is satisfied after proper enquiry that he has not the health or physical capacity for the work.[16]

13   Professional register

The Education (Administrative Provisions) Act, 1907, established a council representative of the teaching profession with the power to form and keep a register of qualified teachers. Registration was voluntary and subject to the payment of a life membership fee. At no time did the register contain the names of more than a small minority of teachers.

Before the passage of the 1944 Act the Board of Education had recognized only teachers in public elementary schools. From 1 April 1945, however, all teachers in maintained and assisted schools became subject to recognition by the Ministry, and in 1948 the Royal Society of Teachers ceased to accept new members. It was incorporated in the Ministry of Education, the interests of existing members being safeguarded.

In 1969 the Secretary of State, at that time the Rt Hon. Edward Short, himself a former schoolmaster, set up a working party consisting of representatives of the local education authorities and the teachers' professional associations under the chairmanship of Sir Toby Weaver of the DES. The function of the committee was to formulate proposals for the formation of a council through which teachers in England and Wales could exercise a measure of professional self-government, and for national arrangements to advise the Secretary of State on the training and supply of teachers. The working party reported within seven months.

In brief, the report recommended the establishment of a council of forty members, of whom twenty-five would be appointed by the Secretary of State on the nomination of the teachers' professional associations, and fifteen appointed by the Secretary of State to present the views of such bodies as the local authority associations, the universities and the public at large. The inclusion of the College of Preceptors, in view of its long association with efforts to enhance the status of the profession, was specifically mentioned.

The report suggested that the functions of the council would be the maintenance of a register of qualified teachers, the recommendation to the Secretary of State of standards of entry to the profession, the control of probation and the discipline of registered teachers.

The report was referred to the professional associations for comment. There was some adverse criticism, and some praise, but little has been heard of the scheme since.

14   Professional conduct

As there is at the moment no professional council to determine the standards of conduct expected of teachers in professional matters, some of the professional associations have drawn up codes specifying actions which have already been declared by them to be unprofessional, and have set up the necessary machinery for dealing with allegations that their code has been broken. The code applies, of course, only to members of the association concerned.

The code of the National Union of Teachers declares it to be unprofessional:

1. for any teacher to take an appointment from which, in the judgement of the NUT Executive, a member of the Union has been unjustly dismissed;
2. for any teacher[17] to make a report on the work or conduct of another teacher without at the time acquainting the teacher concerned with the nature of it, if it be a verbal

report, or without showing it, if it be written, and allowing
the teacher concerned to take a copy of it:[18]

3. in any case of dispute between members of the NUT settled
   by arbitrator under Rule 52 for any member not to abide
   by the decision;

4. for any teacher to censure other teachers or to criticize their
   work in the hearing of the pupils and other persons not
   directly involved in the running of the school;

5. for any teacher to seek to compel another teacher to perform
   outside the ordinary school hours any task which is
   not essentially connected with the ordinary work and
   organization of the school;

6. for any teacher to impose upon another teacher, out of the
   ordinary school hours, an excessive and unreasonable
   amount of work of any kind;

7. for any teacher to behave in a racially discriminatory manner
   or to make racist remarks directed towards or about ethnic
   minority groups or members thereof;

8. for any teacher to harass sexually another teacher or pupil.

Members of the Union who are found guilty of a breach of
professional honour may be warned, censured, fined, suspended
or expelled.

The NUT has also prepared a code of professional ethics
designed as a guide to the proper conduct of its members. A
breach of the code cannot, in itself, lead to a particular offence
or charge. Much of the code is concerned with the relationships
which should exist between colleagues, including responsibilities
towards those in a subordinate position. Stress is laid on the
need for consultation, when possible, before changes are made
in a school's organization, but it is explicitly stated that in
some situations it is not necessarily possible to consult when
an urgent decision must be made.

The code reminds teachers that they must handle carefully
any confidential information they may receive, bearing in mind
the requirements of the law and the best interests of the
children. The head, or a senior officer of the local education

authority, should be consulted before confidential information is disclosed.

Members are reminded that it is an abuse of their professional relationships:

(a) to enter into an improper relationship with a pupil;
(b) to show undue favour or disfavour towards a pupil;
(c) to commit an illegal act against a child;
(d) to endeavour to exert undue influence in personal attitudes, opinions or behaviour which are in no way connected with the work of the school.

Members are warned that they should not deliberately behave in such a way as to bring the school into disrepute.

Another code is contained in a resolution of the Incorporated Association of Assistant Masters in Secondary Schools, whose council has declared the following acts to be injurious to the interests or objects of the Association:

1. for any member to take an appointment from which, in the judgement of the executive committee, a teacher has been unjustly dismissed;
2. for any member to take an appointment in any school where, in the opinion of the executive committee, the conditions or terms of service are unsatisfactory;
3. in the case of a dispute with an employer, for any member to refuse to act on a direction from the executive committee concerning his conduct towards that employer;
4. for any teacher to make a report on the work or conduct of another teacher without at the time acquainting the teacher concerned with the nature of it, if it be an oral report, or without showing it, if it be written, and allowing the teacher concerned to take a copy of it;[19]
5. for any teacher to censure or criticize another in the presence of pupils.

The executive committee of the Association has power to suspend any member guilty of conduct injurious to the interests or objects of the Association, subject to the member's right to appeal to the council.

The Professional Association of Teachers' code of professional conduct emphasizes the professional aspects of the teacher's work:

1. Self development of the professional teacher
The professional teacher is one who keeps up to date with current educational thought and practice. It is important therefore that he takes all proper steps to maintain and improve his ability in his own subject and specialist area including, where appropriate, attendance at in-service training courses, both to maintain his professional standards and as a preparation for promotion. The professional teacher also appraises his own competence, acknowledges potential weaknesses and seeks relevant qualified advice.
2. The professional teacher and the student
Because the professional teacher is acting *in loco parentis*, meetings with parents are absolutely essential. When the student leaves the parent's care and arrives at school or college, the parent expects the teacher to take the same sort of care of the student as that undertaken by a reasonable parent. The teacher must be concerned, therefore, with every aspect of the student's welfare.

The professional teacher accepts character development as part of the task of education, promotes the highest moral standards and undertakes as his professional responsibility the guidance of each student in his care in the pursuit of knowledge and skills and in the development of his full potential so that he may become a responsible and self-supporting citizen of a democratic state.

The professional teacher recognizes the individuality of every student, respects his personality, fosters a healthy environment for education and learning, exercises authority with compassion and ensures that disciplinary or other corrective action is constructive and refrains from words or actions which are destructive or negative and respects the dignity of all concerned. The professional teacher respects the right of every student to have confidential information withheld at all times except when required by authorized agencies or by law.

3. The professional teacher and the parents

The professional teacher endeavours to maintain constructive co-operation with the parents of students in his care and welcomes their interest and support. The professional teacher keeps parents adequately informed about the progress of their child and all aspects of the educational system.

The professional teacher recognizes that the teaching profession occupies a position of public trust, and therefore his actions and conduct shall be of such a nature that he commands the respect of the community and enhances the image of the profession.

4. The professional teacher and the employer

The professional teacher is loyal to the education service by serving it to the best of his ability, by promoting its interests and objectives, obeying lawful instructions and regulations and by conducting professional business through the proper channels only.

5. The professional teacher and his colleagues

If the class contact time is to be fully productive the professional teacher cannot act in total isolation. There must be occasions when it is necessary for the teacher to consult with colleagues both informally and formally in staff and departmental meetings. The professional teacher must strive to minimize misunderstanding and promote good relations between all who work in the school or college, must consult and communicate clearly, take full account of the needs and problems, ideas and suggestions of others, be objective and constructive when giving advice or guidance in his professional capacity.

The professional teacher must be concerned in the working environment for the health, safety and wellbeing of all, especially those for whom he is responsible. Towards his subordinates the professional teacher shall be supportive and ensure that all are aware of their duties and responsibilities especially in relation to those of others and shall encourage the improved performance of subordinates and the develop-

ment of their potential, by means of training and in other
suitable ways.

He will never maliciously injure the professional reputation,
or career prospects of others.

In all of the foregoing the masculine gender also refers
to the feminine. The Association's Code of Professional
Action renounces the right to take strike action, preferring
instead to use other forms of action in support of the
Association's aims.

15   Aides

In 1967 the Plowden Committee on primary education
recommended the employment of aides to undertake some of
the routine work which is necessary to support the teaching
itself.

The aides in primary schools correspond, in some degree,
to the technicians used for many years in secondary school
laboratories and workshops.

The professional associations are naturally concerned that
ancillary staff shall not be used either to dilute the quality of
the teaching profession, or to affect pupil teacher ratios
adversely. In general it is felt that one aide could be shared
by two infants', or four junior classes.

As distinct from welfare helpers, the aides work in the
classroom situation under the control of a qualified teacher;
but they do not assume control of the class as a teaching unit.

In delegating responsibilities to aides and helpers it is
important that they should not be assigned duties which might
be considered exclusively those of a professional teacher. Many
teachers are concerned about their personal responsibility for
accidents arising from the negligence of ancillary staff to whom
they have delegated duties which involve the care of pupils.
This responsibility is neither greater nor less than is involved
in any delegation, and is considered in a later chapter.

References

1. Education (Teachers) Regulations 1982.
2. *Times Higher Education Supplement*, 6 October 1978.
3. *Teacher Education and Training* (HMSO, 1972).
4. *Education: A Framework for Expansion* (HMSO, 1973).
5. Circular 5/75: *The Reorganization of Higher Education in the non-University Sector*.
6. Education (Teachers) Regulations 1982: Schedule 5(2).
7. Education (Teachers) Regulations 1982: Schedule 6.
8. Administrative Memorandum 1/83: *The Treatment and Assessment of Probationary Teachers*. See also Circular 7/82.
9. R. *v.* DES, *ex parte* Kumar, *The Times*, 23 November 1982. See also Sandhu *v.* London Borough of Hillingdon, pp. 158–9.
10. Inner London Education Authority *v.* Lloyd [1981] IRLR 394, CA.
11. Wijesinghe *v.* London Borough of Merton, *Times Educational Supplement*, 28 May 1982.
12. Education (Teachers) Regulations 1982.
13. Handicapped Pupils and Special Schools Regulations 1959, nos 15, 16 and 16A, as amended by the Qualified Teachers and Teachers in Special Schools Regulations 1971, no 3.
14. Education (Teachers) Regulations 1982: Schedule 4(5).
15. Education (Teachers) Regulations 1982: Schedule 4(6).
16. Education (Teachers) Regulations 1982: Regulation 9.
17. Although the use of the word 'teacher' in the second Article of the code is primarily applicable to serving teachers and those actively and professionally engaged in education, the Professional Conduct Committee reserves the right to examine matters referred to it concerning members of the Union who are not so engaged.
18. Where a teacher gives the name of another teacher or member as a referee, he takes, in accordance with normal practice, a risk as to the nature and contents of the reference which the referee may give. Accordingly, any reference so given is not regarded by the Executive as a report within the meaning of the above Article, provided the candidate has nominated the referee of his own free choice. Enquiries made about a candidate of his present head are not excepted when they are made as a matter of routine by an appointing authority or other body.
19. Unlike the NUT, the Assistant Masters Association extends this

provision to references given in the course of seeking employment, whether the referee has been named by the candidate or not.

IV
Conditions of service

1 Types of appointment

Teachers may be appointed to full-time service in a number of ways:

(a) *To the staff of a school*: It is expected that teachers appointed in this way will remain at the named school: however, such appointments may nevertheless be covered by redeployment agreements.[1]

(b) *To the service of an authority*: In such cases the teacher must be prepared to serve in any school and in any teaching capacity which the employing authority may determine. A long-standing example of this kind of appointment is the London divisional staff whose members may be used anywhere in the division to which they are appointed. In practice, however, they are normally left for considerable periods in one school.

(c) *To the authority's unattached staff*: These appointments are similar to those in the last category but the teachers concerned are really 'permanent supply' teachers and are used to fill vacancies caused through the absence of regular members of the staff of a school. Some authorities also maintain a small staff of unattached heads who can be used in a similar way during the absence of the permanent head of a school.

In addition to permanent full-time service, authorities may make appointments on a permanent part-time, annual, termly, or daily or hourly paid basis.

2   Appointment

Most vacancies are advertised in the educational press. The majority are for open competition and any suitably qualified teacher may apply. In some areas, however, certain promotion appointments are limited to a particular range of candidates.

Applications must usually be made on a form provided by the authority. The information given must be accurate since it will form the basis of the contract between the authority and the successful candidate. The suppression of material facts or the inclusion of information which is false within the candidate's knowledge may lead to the withdrawal of an offer, to dismissal if the appointment has been taken up, or even to prosecution.[2] Under section 16 of the Theft Act 1968, obtaining a post by deception may carry a sentence of up to five years' imprisonment.

The DES requires a medical examination before a first appointment is taken up. Some local authorities also require a medical check-up including, in some cases, a satisfactory chest X-ray examination when a serving teacher enters their service from the area of another authority or returns after a long absence.

Sometimes an appointing committee merely has the power to recommend an appointment to the local education authority, subject to a satisfactory medical report, and a candidate may be told that it will not be possible to confirm the offer for some weeks. It may be that this delay will mean that the candidate will have to resign an existing appointment before the new one is confirmed, if he is to be free to join his new school when required. It is then reasonable to ask whether it is safe to resign. Usually it is, but there must always remain the risk that the appointment may not be confirmed.

In one case the managers of a school passed a resolution appointing a candidate. This fact was not officially communicated to the teacher but was casually mentioned to him by a manager. At a later meeting the resolution was rescinded and another candidate was appointed. The rejected candidate claimed damages for breach of contract[3] but the court held that, as the appointment had not been properly communicated, there was no concluded contract to break.

The first appointment of a qualified teacher in a maintained school is subject to probation.[4]

3 Conditions of service

Standard conditions of service have existed since 1946 for sick leave and a number of other matters. These were negotiated by the teachers' professional associations and the associations representing employing authorities. During the past few years, following the establishment of the new authorities in 1974, discussions have continued between the teachers' associations and the Council of Local Education Authorities (CLEA) with a view to codifying and updating all matters concerning conditions of service. The conditions, sometimes referred to as the Burgundy Book because of its colour, incorporate all the previous agreements, modified where necessary, and a number of more recent items dealing with such subjects as the grievance and disputes procedures, time off for professional association work and so forth. The 1968 report of the working party on school meals is also included. Negotiations are continuing on a number of other aspects of teachers' conditions of service.

The Burgundy Book is not an exhaustive list of provisions and should be read in conjunction with an authority's own conditions of service and the provisions of Articles of Government which may provide further safeguards for and obligations on the individual teacher. CLEA 'expects' local authorities, however, to adopt the agreements and to incorporate them through a model clause in the contracts of service of their teachers. Most have done so.

It is intended that the Burgundy Book should apply to all full-time qualified teachers, and to part-time teachers who are not employed on a daily or hourly rate. It does not apply to temporary teachers employed as substitutes for a term or less. Certain sections do apply to the excepted groups, however, and these are considered in the appropriate sections of this chapter.

In recent years Parliament has devoted a great deal of time to legislation designed to protect employees. The volume of law in this field is now so great that a general consideration has been deferred to the following chapter. Discrimination in employment is dealt with in chapter XIII. This chapter, therefore, is concerned only with the arrangements which are peculiar to the teaching profession. Suffice it here to note that mandatory provisions of the law relating to employment must override any conditions of service or contracts which are less favourable to employees. The various provisions of the conditions of service are included at appropriate points throughout the relevant chapters.

4   The agreement

When the appointment has been confirmed, the teacher will generally receive two copies of an agreement, one of which must be signed and returned to the authority. Alternatively, he may receive a notification of appointment under minute. A teacher must, within thirteen weeks of the beginning of his appointment, be furnished with a copy of the agreement or minute under which he is appointed, together with any regulations referred to therein, unless he is given an opportunity of acquainting himself with the rules in some other way.[5]

The candidate should read the agreement (sometimes in the form of a letter of appointment) carefully before signing it, and be certain that he understands its terms since they form the contract between him and his employer. The principal points covered in an agreement are:

(a) Date of commencement of appointment;
(b) School (if applicable) and capacity in which the teacher is to be employed, whether as head or assistant, whether full- or part-time, and whether partly as a teacher and partly in some other capacity;
(c) Reference to the regulations under which the teacher is employed;
(d) Provision for termination of the agreement by either side on giving:
   (i) two months' notice[6] terminating on 31 December or 30 April;[7]
   (ii) three months' notice[8] terminating on 31 August;
(e) There is sometimes a statement that unless the teacher is employed partly as a teacher and partly in some other capacity (or in a boarding school), he may not be required to perform any duties except such as are connected with the work of a school; nor may he be required to abstain, outside school hours, from any occupations which do not interfere with the due performances of his duties;
(f) Reference to the salary scales and the frequency of payment of salary, deductions of salary for unpaid leave without (e.g. in the case of strike action), or with, the authority's permission to be based on a daily, or part-daily, proportion of a year's salary;
(g) Provision for the suspension and dismissal of the teacher;
(h) In the case of a reserved teacher in a controlled or special agreement school, a reference to this fact and the requirements contingent upon it.

Teachers in voluntary-aided schools are appointed by the governors and the agreement is therefore made with them and not with the local education authority which maintains the school. The Articles of Government normally provide that such appointments are subject to the consent of the authority. Where, however, a teacher in a voluntary-aided school is dismissed on the requirement of a local education authority, the local education authority is regarded in law as being the employer, and the teacher's statutory employment protection rights are guaranteed against the authority.[9]

Occasionally an authority issues revised agreements in respect of all its teachers. This is done to bring existing teachers into line with new terms of service which have been agreed nationally between the local education authorities and the professional associations. Teachers' contracts of employment usually specify that any amendments will automatically be incorporated. If a contract of employment does not permit variation of a teacher's conditions of service, and an employer insists on changing them, the law regards this as dismissal, which may well be unfair. Recent case law, however, suggests that the courts may accept an employer's defence of 'some substantial reason'.

5   Indemnity against assault

The national conditions of service bind local education authorities who have accepted the Burgundy Book to indemnify members of their teaching staff or, in the event of death, their dependants, against financial loss caused by violence or criminal assault in the course of, or as a consequence of, their employment.

At the time of writing, much-enhanced compensation for victims of assault has been agreed by CLEA. The revised figures are:

(a) In the event of death within twelve months from the date of the assault and, in the opinion of the local education authority, as a direct result of the assault, where the employee has left one or more dependants, the equivalent of five years' gross salary at the rate applying at the date of the assault or £15,000 whichever is the greater. Where the employee has left no dependants, the sum of £400 shall be payable.

(b) In the event of permanent total or partial disablement as a result of the assault a percentage on a sliding scale up to five times the gross salary applying at the date of the

assault or of £15,000, whichever is the greater, provided
that such payments shall, at the discretion of the employing
authority, be reduced by the amount of any damages, or
compensation recoverable in respect of the particular
injuries.

'Dependants' is defined as (a) a spouse residing with the
employee at the date of death or, if not residing, wholly
or substantially supported by the employee and (b) a child
who has not attained the age of 19 years and is following
a course of full-time education or who is regarded as an
apprentice under the statutory provisions relating to family
allowances.

The scheme provides that payments which are expressed as a
proportion of current salary are automatically adjusted to take
account of increases, so that the need to renegotiate fixed,
specified sums at regular intervals is avoided.

6   Crimes of violence

If a teacher is absent because of injuries for which he may
make a claim to the Criminal Injuries Compensation Board and
is qualified to receive sick pay, it is recommended in the
national conditions of tenure that such sick pay should be
granted without any requirement of a refund of any part of
this in the event of an award by the Board.

If an award has been made, it is recommended that the
authority should be at liberty to discount all or part of the
sick leave, as may seem fit, in calculating the teacher's
entitlement to such leave.[10]

7   Personal property

Local education authorities are asked, in the national conditions
of tenure, to consider sympathetically loss of, or damage to,
a teacher's personal property when such losses are suffered
during duty at school or whilst taking part in out-of-school

activities, and there has been no negligence on the teacher's part.

It is recognized that the authority may have no legal liability in this matter, but some take out insurance against such contingencies whilst others make an *ex gratia* payment. It may be a condition of such cases that the head teacher must give prior approval to the use of personal property and assistants should check this carefully beforehand. However, this is currently under negotiation which may result in a contractual obligation to compensate in some circumstances.

The code does not suggest full compensation, and teachers would be well advised to cover any valuable property they may have in school by private insurance. In some cases membership of a professional association carries a limited degree of indemnity. Insurance companies, however, are reasonably careful in dealing with such claims and frequently reject those where there is an element of negligence on the owner's part. It is therefore important to take all reasonable care of personal belongings in school.

8 Loss through out-of-school activities

The national conditions lay down that teachers, or their dependants, should be entitled to compensation for death, personal loss, or injury occurring in the course of, or as a result of, voluntary approved out-of-school activities which are outside the teacher's contract of service. To qualify there must be a link between the activity and the teacher's authority or school, though this may be indirect, such as affiliation to a national organization. It is not necessary for a pupil from the teacher's own school actually to be taking part. If, however, the teacher is participating at the request of an organization which has no connection with schools maintained by his local education authority, it is the organization which is responsible for insurance, if any.

Some local education authorities may limit their liability by excluding intrinsically dangerous activities. The Burgundy Book requires that in such circumstances teachers should consult their professional associations to ensure awareness of the need for special insurance arrangements. In some cases, also, local education authorities will not cover overseas visits.

The compensation payable is as for assault (see pp. 118–19).

9 Examination duties

Paid leave is normally granted to teachers who undertake duties as examiners, moderators and so forth in connection with public examinations. They may also receive fees and expense allowances.

It is also recommended that teachers undertaking similar duties in connection with public examinations in their own schools should be paid if the work is comparable to that of an external examiner, and involves time additional to their normal teaching commitment.

10 Travelling expenses

If teachers, at the request of the local education authority or the head of the school, use their cars to facilitate the discharge of their duties, they should be paid an adequate mileage allowance to cover running costs, including insurance and depreciation.

It is recommended that the allowance be calculated locally in consultation between the teachers' professional associations and the authorities, and have some reference to the authority's casual user rate.

The position as regards income tax on allowances is discussed in chapter VII.

11 Reserved teachers

In controlled and, normally, in special agreement schools a certain proportion of the staff must be appointed as reserved teachers. These are persons specially selected for their fitness to give religious instructions according to the tenets of the providing body.[11] The local education authority must appoint in the following ratio. There is no obligation to appoint reserved teachers if a school has fewer than three teachers.

Total teaching staff	Numbers of reserved teachers
3–5	1
6–10	2
11–15	3
16–20	4

The head is not a reserved teacher, but is included in the staff for the purpose of calculating the number of reserved teachers.

In special agreement schools, the agreement will state whether reserved teachers are to be appointed, and will specify the proportion of the staff to be reserved.

Although the local education authority appoints the whole teaching staff of such schools, the foundation governors must be consulted before a reserved teacher is appointed. The foundation governors may also require the local education authority to dismiss a teacher from being a reserved teacher in their school on the grounds that he is not competent to give the religious instruction for which he was appointed. This does not, however, preclude the authority from appointing the same person as a non-reserved teacher in the same school.

12 Corruption in office

If an officer of a local authority, under colour of his employment, exacts or receives any fee or reward whatsoever other than his proper remuneration, he is liable on summary conviction to a fine.[12]

13 Pecuniary interest

It is public policy, enshrined in law, that members and officers of public authorities should not seek to take direct or indirect pecuniary advantage of their position. Pecuniary advantage is not always easy to define, although in some cases it is clear. A teacher who has written a book which he requisitions for his own school clearly has such an interest. Teachers who are in doubt about their position should consult their professional association before assuming that they have no interest. Generally speaking no difficulty should arise if the interest is declared, and the book is entirely suitable and appropriate.

If an officer of a local authority knows of a contract in which he has any pecuniary interest, whether direct or indirect, which has been (or is proposed to be) entered into by the authority, or any of its committees in office, he must, as soon as practicable, give notice of his interest to the authority in writing. The penalty for failing to do so is a fine.

Teachers who are members of the education committee of a local education authority are subject to the disabilities imposed on elected members who have a direct or indirect pecuniary interest.[13] This means that they may not speak or vote on any matter concerning a contract in which they have an interest,[14] and they are liable to a fine if they do so, unless they can prove that they did not know the matter was to be discussed at that meeting. A member with an interest must declare it at as early a stage as possible: provided he takes no further part in the proceedings, he need not withdraw unless excluded under standing orders. A general, written notice of pecuniary interest is a sufficient disclosure of matters affecting that interest if discussion thereon is likely to be frequent.[15] It is also possible to make an application to the district council (in the case of parish or community councils), or to the Secretary of State (in the case of other local authorities) to remove the section 94 disability: such a dispensation usually permits the member to speak, but not to vote, on matters affecting him, and he must declare his interest each time he speaks.[16]

In June 1975 six teacher representatives took part in the debate and voted at a meeting of the Lincolnshire education committee, which was considering a proposal to reduce the authority's points score ranges. Having argued the educational advantages of attracting skilled staff by adopting the maximum.

the representatives cast their votes, which were sufficient to swing the decision in favour of their viewpoint. At the beginning of the discussion the representatives had been warned that it was the view of the authority's legal advisers that they had a direct or indirect pecuniary interest. The police later interviewed two representatives whose wives were part-time teachers, but the Director of Public Prosecutions was of the opinion that the investigations disclosed no breach of section 94.[17] A similar issue arose elsewhere when councillors who were parents of children at school voted on the issue of whether to continue the schools meals service for their area, after such provision became discretionary under the Education Act 1980.

In the case of *Director of Public Prosecutions v. A. J. Williams* in 1981 a member of a teachers' association who was at the time taking a form of industrial action over pay and who was a member of an education committee failed to declare an interest when the dispute was discussed by the committee. He was held to have committed an offence.

14   Membership of public bodies

A paid officer of a local authority who is employed in an office to which appointment is, or may be, made or confirmed by that authority, or any of its committees or sub-committees, or by a joint board on which it is represented, or by any person who is himself employed by the authority, is disqualified from being elected or being a member of that authority.[18] Neither may a person be appointed to the service of any authority whilst he is a member of that authority, nor for twelve months afterwards.[19]

The only exceptions are a paid chairman, vice-chairman or deputy chairman of the authority.

Teachers in schools maintained, but not established, by the authority (i.e. voluntary schools) are subject to the same disqualification.[20] They may, however, be a member of any committee, as distinct from the authority itself, appointed to discharge functions with regard to education or under the Public Libraries and Museums Act 1964.[21]

A teacher employed by a county authority may be a member of a district council even though that council nominates members of the county education committee. Similarly, a teacher employed by a metropolitan district council may be a member of the county council even though the county council nominates members of the district education committee.[22]

15   Professional association representatives and members

Employers must, by law, permit their employees who are officials of independent trade unions recognized for collective bargaining purposes to have time off with pay for certain purposes.[23] The amount of time spent in this way must be reasonable and is limited by the Employment Protection (Consolidation) Act 1978 to time needed to perform duties concerned with industrial relations between the employer and his employees and to undergo training which is approved by the Trades Union Congress or the union concerned. A Code of Practice is in existence for use by employers.

In 1982 the Court of Appeal held that 'duties concerned with industrial relations' were not limited to those connected with a collective bargaining process but may include meetings concerned with the formulation of policy. 'Attendance at a meeting called solely for the purpose of exchanging information would not qualify for time off with pay under section 27(1) but would qualify for time off without pay under section 28 as a trade union activity.'[24]

A member of any appropriate trade union, that is a union which is recognized by the employer, may also have time off to take part in any activities of his union, or in any in which he represents his union. This entitlement to leave does not carry the right to pay, and must be with the consent of the employer, and in accordance with the Code of Practice.[25]

The Burgundy Book provides that, for teachers, accredited representatives are members of the national executive of a professional association, or representatives of the association on a national body, local officers negotiating at local authority level or other local officers and school representatives. Professional associations are responsible for notifying the names of representatives to their heads and the local education authority and facilities are awarded only to those so accredited.

Representatives will be concerned with such matters as the grievance and collective disputes procedures, professional association responsibilities including attendance at national conferences as delegates, the interests of their members, and the training of teachers' representatives at national, regional or local authority levels.

It is recommended that local agreements should include arrangements for discharging association responsibilities in schools, permission to leave school for association business, the provision of lists of new teachers to facilitate direct contact and of annual lists of teaching staff, the use of accommodation for association meetings, the use of the authority's internal mailing or other distribution system, and arrangements (on request, and with the individual member's consent) for the deduction of membership dues from salary. Leave of absence for association duties, up to a locally agreed maximum, should be with full pay. It is expected that local committees which require the attendance of representatives will not meet earlier than four o'clock on a school day, or later in areas where travelling times are considerable.

Within the school itself, professional association representatives deal with such matters as the recruitment and maintenance of membership, the collection of contributions, communication with their members, and matters concerned with industrial relations such as grievances. To enable them to discharge these functions, representatives should be accorded notice-board facilities (multi-association boards are recommended), the use of the telephone with reasonable privacy (outgoing calls being paid for), the use of a room for meetings on reasonable notice being given, and the use of the school's typing, duplicating and photocopying equipment, provided there is not undue interference with the work of the school and the cost of materials is reimbursed.

16 Religious opinions

No teacher may be disqualified or dismissed from appointment, receive less emolument or be deprived of promotion, purely on the grounds of holding any particular religious opinions, or because he attends (or fails to attend) any particular place of worship.[26]

This does not apply to the staffs of aided schools; nor to reserved teachers in controlled and special agreement schools who are selected for their fitness to give denominational instruction.

In spite of this clause it is still not unknown for teachers to be asked questions of this character at an interview. Whatever the candidate says, he is at a disadvantage. The safest course is to reply that the question is highly personal and, therefore, irrelevant. Strictly speaking, the governors of a county school have no right to question a candidate on his religious beliefs, even when he has applied for appointment as a scripture specialist.

The law draws a distinction between what teachers believe and what they do. A full-time teacher, a devout Muslim, absented himself for prayer at the mosque every Friday afternoon, causing considerable disruption to his school. The local education authority requested him to change from full-time employment to part-time, in fact to $4\frac{1}{2}$ days each week. He appealed to an industrial tribunal that this was constructive dismissal, and that his rights under the 1944 Act and under the European Convention of Human Rights 'to practise and observe his religion' were being infringed.

The Court of Appeal held that the teacher had not been unfairly dismissed. Section 30 of the 1944 Act was subject to the local education authority's right to his regular services under the contract of employment.[27] The European Commission on Human Rights also later rejected Mr Ahmad's appeal on the same grounds.

17   Accidents to teaching staff

At common law the relationship between employer and employee does not involve a guarantee that the former will never expose his employees to danger or risk. In accepting employment the employee willingly undertakes the risks ordinarily involved in the work and the employer is not required to indemnify him against these.

Even where negligence is proved, there is no case against the employer if the servant continues in a place where he is aware of danger. In one case a man continued to work for a railway company for a fortnight after he learned that there was danger due to the negligence of the employer. His action failed.[28]

In any case, the duties of a teacher are not very clearly defined: he is expected to do whatever he considers to be necessary for the welfare of the pupils and this will involve many things besides teaching. Indeed, the risk of accident is often greater outside the normal work of the classroom. It is possible, for a small premium, to insure against injury and the teacher may well consider it wise to make this provision, perhaps through a teachers' organization.

By the doctrine of common employment, it was once held that an employer was not liable for injury to an employee through the negligence of a fellow servant, unless he had retained the servant in his employment knowing him to be incompetent. Under the Law Reform (Personal Injuries) Act 1948, this defence has now been abolished, and all contracts or agreements are void in so far as they exclude or limit the liability of an employer by the doctrine of common employment. This applies not only to new contracts or agreements, but also to those made before the passage of the Act. As did the common law, the Health and Safety at Work etc. Act 1974 now requires all employees to take reasonable care of each other and themselves.

The employer's duty is not clearly defined,[29] but he is bound to use reasonable care to provide safe premises and appliances. The common law right to compensation requires proof of negligence, or continuation in common employment after proof of incompetence.

In county, controlled and special agreement schools, the local education authority is the employer of the teacher. In aided schools the teachers are appointed by the governors and there is no privity of employment between the teacher and the authority. Teachers in an aided school have, therefore, no claim against the authority as employer since there is no relationship as between employer and employee. The authority may, however, be liable in respect of failure to carry out repairs for which it is responsible or for dangerous apparatus which it has installed. An employer is not liable if the defective nature of the apparatus is due to the negligence of a servant, although the employer may be liable to a third party under the Defective Equipment Act.

It is probable that the success of an action would not be prejudiced by the fact that the teacher was performing a voluntary duty at the time of an accident.

18   The grievance procedure

Discussions between substantially the same bodies which drew up the recommended conditions of tenure have resulted in a standard form of grievance procedure which, with small local variations, is applied throughout the country.

The procedure is designed to deal with the grievances of individual teachers, and does not apply to collective disputes. It recognizes that grievances may arise between assistant teachers, or between assistants and the head; that they may be simple or fundamental; and that they may involve the governors and the local education authority. The scheme sets out an informal procedure which would not involve taking the matter to any subsequent more formal stage, and a formal procedure for use when the simpler form has failed. Modified procedures are outlined for heads, and a note sets out the matters which need to be taken into account in dealing with grievances in voluntary schools.

ASSISTANTS: INFORMAL PROCEDURE

If an assistant's grievance is against his governors or local education authority, he should (without involving any other member of the staff) approach the chief education officer or the governors, as may be appropriate. If his grievance involves another member of the staff, he may resolve the matter by direct approach to that person, or by discussion with the head of department concerned, some other senior colleague or the head. If a request for a discussion with one of these senior staff is received, a personal interview should be granted within five days. The senior colleague should try to resolve the matter personally, or by mutual agreement, in consultation with other members of the staff. If the head is asked to intervene he may, with mutual agreement, consult the chairman of the governors, officers of the local education authority or representatives of the appropriate professional associations.

ASSISTANTS: FORMAL PROCEDURE

If informal discussions fail, the person aggrieved should submit a formal notice of grievance to the head and the other teacher concerned. The head should make a formal written report to the governors, and send a copy to the chief education officer. The governors, in consultation with the chief education officer (if appropriate) should, with all relevant documents available, seek to settle the issue. If they wish, the parties should have an opportunity to make submissions, each being accompanied (if desired) by a friend or official representative of his professional association. This meeting should take place within ten days.

ASSISTANTS: APPELLATE PROCEDURE

The appellate procedure should be settled between the local education authority and the professional associations. All relevant documents should be submitted to the appellate body, which should then meet within ten days. Submissions and the presence of 'friends' should be permitted as at the original hearing.

HEADS: INFORMAL PROCEDURE

A head who has a grievance should try to settle it with the person concerned and, if this fails, he should discuss the matter with an advisory or administrative member of the local education authority's staff. If the problem cannot be settled in this way, the head should discuss it with the chief education officer (or his representative) who may, by mutual agreement, consult the chairman of the governors or representatives of any professional association concerned.

HEADS: FORMAL PROCEDURE

If the informal procedure is unsuccessful, the head should submit a formal written notice of the grievance to the governors and/or to the chief education officer. The governors, if the grievance lies against them, should arrange a meeting within ten days, at which the parties may make submissions and be accompanied by 'friends'. If the grievance lies against the local education authority, the chief education officer should refer it to the authority's appropriate committee, whether or not the head has sought the support of the governors. The committee should meet within ten days, the parties being given an opportunity to make submissions and to be accompanied by 'friends'.

HEADS: APPELLATE PROCEDURE

This is the same as for assistants.

APPLICATION TO VOLUNTARY SCHOOLS

Subsequent discussions with the Church of England and Roman Catholic educational bodies produced agreement on a number of points which take account of the fact that teachers in voluntary-aided schools are the employees of the governors, but that many of their conditions of employment stem from the local education authority. The modifications might also be helpful in dealing with grievances in other voluntary-aided schools, e.g. those established by City livery companies. The question of applying the modifications to controlled or special agreement schools depends on the Articles of Government.

Any procedures adopted must not conflict with the Articles of Government. The appropriate voluntary school authorities should be concerned in the establishment of any appellate body. In making an informal approach, heads should, unless it is inappropriate, consult the chairman of the governors, rather than the chief education officer. Similarly, in moving to the next informal stage, a head should discuss the matter with his chairman before going to the chief education officer. The head of a voluntary school should normally submit a written grievance to his governors; if circumstances make this inappropriate, he must send them a copy of any written notice of grievance he sends to the chief education officer. Similarly, if the grievance lies against the authority, the head should report the matter to the chief education officer, and inform his chairman. There is no procedure for submitting a complaint against the governors to the authority.

For the purpose of the grievance procedure, a teacher in a voluntary-aided school is regarded as an employee of the local education authority.

Every employee must be given a note specifying, by description or otherwise, a person to whom he can apply to seek redress of any grievance, and the manner in which he should apply. The note should indicate what steps will follow such an application or, alternatively, it should state where such information is reasonably accessible to the employee in documentary form.[30]

19 Collective disputes

The legislation does not require, but does encourage, the establishment of a procedure designed to settle collective disputes between employers and employees, as distinct from individual grievances. The Burgundy Book, however, includes a set of recommendations designed in the first instance to prevent such disputes from becoming fractious, secondly to provide for their settlement at the local level if possible, and thirdly to establish a national body as a long-stop. Matters such as salaries and superannuation for which there is statutory arbitral provision are excluded from the disputes procedure.

LOCAL CONSULTATIVE PROCEDURES

The recommendations are of the establishment of local joint consultative committees consisting of representatives of the employing authority (including members) and the teachers' professional associations. It is hoped that by following this course of action many disputes will be avoided.

LOCAL CONCILIATION

The local consultative procedures would not preclude the right of a teachers' association to negotiate directly with the authority. The scheme provides, however, that consultation should take place with other associations if discussions reach a point which would involve the integrity of an agreement to which the others are also party. If difficulties with the authority reach the stage of a dispute, the issue is referred to local conciliation, and it is stressed that both sides should try to contain the issue within the limits of their authority's area unless it appears to have national origins or overtones. The local conciliation panel may be either an ad hoc body, or drawn from a panel; it should commence its inquiry within fourteen days of a reference being made, and report within a given time or as soon as possible. If the local decision is unacceptable to either side, the matter should be referred for national conciliation.

NATIONAL CONCILIATION

The model procedure recommends the establishment of a

national conciliation panel by the associations of employers and teachers. The chairman would be required to satisfy himself either that a dispute referred to the panel is a national issue, or that all reasonable efforts have been made to settle a local issue at local level. The panel should commence its proceedings within a fortnight of reference, and its findings or recommendations should be made public. If the decision of the panel is unacceptable to either party, the authority should not implement its decision or, as the case may be, the teachers should not commence industrial action without first giving two weeks' notice. At the time of writing, such a panel has not been set up and such issues as have arisen have been referred to a conciliator.

The collective disputes procedure was invoked for example in Wiltshire at the end of 1975, when the local education authority, as a matter of economy, issued an instruction that the number of teachers allowed to have free lunches was to be limited to one for every thirty children staying for lunch, subject to a minimum of two. Prior to the instruction some 2,500 teachers in the county, out of a total of 4,400, were receiving free lunches, and the proposal would have had the effect of reducing the number of free lunches by about a fifth. The cost would still have been in the region of £170,000 a year, following a saving of £35,000. Originally the authority had intended to fix the ratio at one to forty, but had improved on this following discussions with the teachers' professional associations.

The disputes panel decided that local education authorities should not try, unilaterally, to vary the 1968 agreement on school meals.[31] By the agreement, incorporated into the Burgundy Book, teachers taking charge of pupils during the midday break, either on duty or merely overseeing their activities, are entitled to free school meals. It was suggested to the panel that the rapid increase in the number of duty meals was due to changes in the interpretation of the word 'duty'. Some schools, in an attempt to persuade teachers to stay in school during the midday break, and to avoid the difficulty of defining the word, allowed a free meal to virtually all the teachers who wanted one. The authority claimed that the 1968 agreement did not give teachers an absolute right to engage in voluntary activities. For the teachers it was said that their voluntary participation in midday supervision saved the authorities vast sums. The panel said that alterations to the 1968 agreement could be made only through national negotiations.

20 Disciplinary procedures

There is no national agreement on disciplinary procedures, but a local authority must specify to all employees the rules which are applicable to them, and the person to whom they should complain if they are dissatisfied with a decision.[32]

The Advisory Conciliation and Arbitration Service has prepared a code of practice which gives advice on the preparation and operation of disciplinary procedures.[33] The Code stresses the fact that employees should be told clearly what kind of conduct is expected of them: in particular they should be aware of the consequences of breaking rules, and of the kind of behaviour which may lead to summary dismissal.

Disciplinary procedures should:

(a) be in writing;
(b) specify to whom they apply;
(c) indicate disciplinary actions which may be appropriate;
(d) lay down the level of management at which action will be taken, immediate superiors normally not to have the power to dismiss without reference;
(e) make arrangements for individuals to be informed of complaints, and to be heard before decisions are made;
(f) provide for an employee against whom disciplinary proceedings are taking place to be accompanied by a representative of his professional organization or a fellow employee of his own choice;
(g) ensure that employees are not dismissed for a first breach, unless it be gross misconduct;
(h) prevent disciplinary action without prior careful inquiry;

(i) have arrangements for employees to be told of the reason for any penalty;
(j) include appellate rights and procedures.

It is recognized that minor warnings of an oral nature may be given from time to time. When, however, it appears that disciplinary action may be necessary a formal warning (whether oral or written) should make the nature of the offence and the probable effect of further infringements clear. At the same time the employee should be told that this is the first stage of the disciplinary procedure. A further offence may then lead to a final written warning specifying the penalty which will follow any further infraction: if this is likely to be suspension or dismissal, this should be stated. Disciplinary transfer or suspension without pay can be imposed only if they are provided for in the contract. However, such clauses are usually included nowadays. At all stages the employee should be told of any appellate rights which are open to him.

Criminal offences outside employment are not automatic grounds for dismissal unless they make a person unsuited to his work or unacceptable to his colleagues. Employees should not be dismissed merely because they are awaiting trial, whether on bail or in custody. Special considerations apply, of course, when the Secretary of State has determined that a person shall no longer be employed as a teacher.

The ACAS code recommends that confidential records should be kept of breaches of discipline, and any action which flows from them.

There are currently no nationally agreed disciplinary procedures contained in the Burgundy Book, but local education authorities work out their own in consultation with the professional associations. Space prevents a detailed examination of all the local variations. Most disciplinary procedures have the following stages in common:

1. *Informal warning* by the head teacher. This is not recorded, and the teacher is so informed. However a repeated occurrence of the conduct in question could lead to a formal warning.

2. *Formal oral warning.* A formal meeting is set up and the teacher may bring a friend. A report of the warning is placed on record, and the teacher given a copy.
3. *Formal written warning.* A formal meeting is set up and the teacher may bring a friend. A written warning is issued, and the teacher has a copy. The local education authority will also receive a copy, and could decide to set dismissal proceedings in train. Usually there is a right of appeal against the issue of a formal written warning, usually to the governing body of the school.

In general it should be noted that:

(a) the disciplinary procedure is separate and distinct from the grievance procedure which is not intended to inflict penalty on a teacher;
(b) recorded warnings are usually expunged from teachers' records after a period of one or two years has elapsed without further occurrences;
(c) in serious cases it is permissible to omit the earlier stages of the disciplinary procedures, even proceeding directly to summary dismissal. However, in appropriate cases, every opportunity should be given to the teacher to show that he has mended his ways.

The Employment Protection (Consolidation) Act 1978 accepts a 'reason related to the conduct of the employee' as grounds for fair dismissal.

21   The teacher's day and duties

The Burgundy Book states: 'There are no existing national collective agreements on these matters beyond that affecting the school midday break, which is set out in appendix VIII.'

There is general agreement that the lack of agreement about what parts of teachers' work are obligatory and which voluntary has on occasion created friction and a situation in which the efficient management of schools in the best interest of pupils has been made difficult. There is a legal tangle between duties which may be expressly contractual and those equally important duties which may be binding because of custom and practice.

In 1979 a working party[34] set up by the Council of Local Education Authorities (CLEA) considered the feasibility of a precise definition of the teacher's day and duties, a job description for teachers, and guaranteed non-teaching time. No agreement was reached, but the principles remain of general interest. Draft proposals put forward by the employers' representatives in 1980 were:

DRAFT PROPOSALS

1. *Working year* (1 September–31 August)

   Teaching year: 192 days (2 more than the school year)
   Working year: 205 days
   In-service training
   Staff meetings
   Examination administration
   The year to be defined by reference to the school in which a teacher is employed.

2. *Working week* (7 consecutive days)

   Total: 37½ hours.
   Teaching contact time (TCT) (No more than 27½ hours)
   Timetabled pedagogic contact with pupils
   Supervision of examinations
   Pastoral interviews
   Careers interviews
   Administration and organization
   Teaching support time (TST) (No more than 2½ hours between 0900 and 1600)
   Marking, etc.
   Consultation with colleagues
   Lesson preparation
      Not necessarily in contact with pupils
      Not necessarily on school premises
   Other professional duties (OPD) (7½ hours)

    Supervision (morning + afternoon breaks, lunchtime, before
      and after school)
    Staff meetings
    Consultations with parents
    In-service training
    Administration and organization
    School competitions, performances, matches, etc.

If these time allocations are exceeded, time-off in lieu may be granted.

A revised set of proposals was put forward by the employers in November 1984, and is currently under discussion. The proposed definition of teachers' duties and responsibilities *must* be seen as part of a package based on the compatibility of a common salary scale, the duties to be undertaken by teachers and the management structure within a school. At the time of writing, the Council of Local Education Authorities and the Association of County Councils have agreed to approach the Secretary of State for a review of the current negotiating arrangements for school teachers. It is possible that some provisions of the Remuneration of Teachers Act 1965 will be amended.

*Proposed limits on the performance of duties and
responsibilities (November 1984)*

(i) Although every teacher will be contractually required to prepare lessons, mark pupils' work and prepare pupil profiles and reports, these tasks cannot be constrained within any fixed weekly or annual limit. The performance of these tasks will be subject to the processes of performance appraisal and review as described at paragraphs 30 to 37 below.

(ii) In respect of all other tasks set out in the teacher's job description the total time during which the head may direct the teacher to perform them shall not exceed 1300 hours per year spread over a maximum of 195 days.

(iii) The remainder of the year shall be annual leave but leave may not be taken outside periods of school closure.

(iv) Weekly class contact timetabled for the teacher shall not exceed 25 hours. Some posts may require lower levels of class contact to enable the duties and responsibilities of the post to be carried out. [There is no intention to make a national agreement which specifies an entitlement to lower timetabled class contact in particular circumstances or for particular reasons.] Reduced class contact is a matter for the Head to determine in the light of staffing resources available to him.

(v) Each teacher in a secondary school shall be entitled to a minimum of two 35 or 40 minute periods per week during which he or she cannot be called upon to provide cover for an absent colleague. These two periods shall not be specified in the timetable but shall be the minimum number of 'free periods' to which any teacher in a secondary school is entitled each week.

(vi) Except as provided in the remainder of this paragraph the teacher shall be free from all responsibilities during the pupils' midday break. The exception is that each teacher, together with appropriate ancillary staff, shall actively supervise pupils who are on the premises, but not any who are in the dining hall or other place where pupils are required to take their meals, on not more than two days a week and then not for more than half of the pupils' midday break. On days when the teacher supervises pupils he or she shall be entitled to a free meal. No other teacher will be entitled to a free meal. The 1968 'Rosetti' agreement will cease to apply from the date of implementation of this agreement. The Annexe to the 'Rosetti' agreement will also cease to apply.

Certain aspects of teachers' duties have already been tested in court. The *Lake v. Essex* case, which decided that marking and preparation were not part of a teacher's contract and authorities could expect but not require them, is discussed in detail later.[35] A teacher who refused to supervise mid-morning breaks because he claimed it was not in his contract to do so, was held by an industrial tribunal not to have been unfairly dismissed.[36] A teacher who during a dispute over pay worked a five-hour day in accordance with the policy of his professional association, had part of his salary deducted. The local education authority claimed that the normal working day was five and a half hours. The court supported the authority:[37] the five-hour day was based on an inappropriate application of a regulation contained in the 1978 Burnham salaries document.[38] The reference merely exemplified a method for calculating the salary of a teacher employed on a short-term basis.

It must be emphasized that no agreement has yet been reached about a definition of a teacher's day and duties, nor on its possible relationship to the salaries structure. Both remain for the foreseeable future highly contentious issues.

22   Resignation

Notice of resignation should be served on the employer[39] in accordance with the terms of the agreement. Sometimes an employer will release a teacher if notice is not given by the specified date, but it should be remembered that this is an act of grace and not of right.

23   Redeployment

There is no nationally agreed redeployment scheme for teachers who are surplus to the requirements of their school. Locally agreed schemes usually contain the following principles:

(i)   Compulsory redeployment will take place only after all attempts to secure voluntary redeployment have failed.

(ii)   Teachers will be selected for redeployment on the basis of agreed criteria including the needs of the school as regards teaching expertise and subject specialisms, and the personal circumstances of the teacher. Local authorities will usually offer additional travelling expenses over a reasonable period incurred as a result of redeployment.

It would be relevant to the discussions that a teacher, for example, could not for good domestic reasons, travel far to a new school.

(iii) Salaries and status at all levels are protected on redeployment.[40]

(iv) A teacher may not be redeployed too frequently. A maximum of once in four years is considered reasonable.

(v) Redeployment may be temporary. There should be the possibility, where teachers desire it, to return to the original school after a reasonable period.

(vi) The principle of 'last in, first out' should not apply.

(vii) Probationer teachers are considered for redeployment only in exceptional circumstances.

(viii) There should be an appeals procedure for those selected for redeployment.

The extent to which teachers in aided schools are covered by such agreements is open to local negotiation between their employers and the local education authority.

Some local education authorities have amended the Articles of Government of their schools to give reasonable priority to the appointment of teachers redeployed from other schools.

24   Suspension of teachers

The terms under which teachers may be suspended are contained in the Articles of Government, and are usually set out fully in the agreement, if one is concluded.[41]

A teacher has the right to be present, accompanied by a 'friend' if he so desires, at any meeting of governors or the local education authority at which his suspension or dismissal is considered. He must be given seven days' clear notice of such meetings. The proceedings must remain confidential until a decision is reached. The teacher is entitled to a written statement of the decision and the reasons for it, but only the decision may be published. In the case of summary dismissal, for example where the teacher's conduct has effectively destroyed the employment relationship, the teacher is not entitled to the usual notice and salary may be stopped from the date of suspension.

Where, following suspension, a teacher is reinstated, arrears of salary accruing from the date of suspension to the date of reinstatement will normally be paid to the teacher. The conditions of tenure recommend, however, that payment of full salary during suspension should be regarded as the normal procedure from which departures should be made only when the employing authority decides that there is a compelling reason for so doing.

25 Dismissal

At one time the opportunities available to a dismissed employee to challenge the termination of his employment were limited to a claim that the employer's action was *ultra vires* or in bad faith. In 1971 legislation introduced the concepts of unfair dismissal and constructive dismissal, which are dealt with in chapter V.[42]

A teacher may be dismissed, provided this does not amount to unfair dismissal,[43] in accordance with the terms of his contract on the usual notice being given. The Burgundy Book requires that the hearing provided for in the disciplinary procedure should take place whatever the circumstances. Teachers who are dismissed in accordance with the terms of their contract at the end of the autumn and spring terms after serving the same employer continuously for more than one month are entitled to not less than one week's notice until two years have elapsed, and after that to one week for each year up to twelve years.[44]

A headmaster was given notice of dismissal by a local education authority following an action against him for excessive corporal punishment.[45] The magistrates had held that the punishment was excessive, although there had been great provocation, and the headmaster was bound over under the Probation of Offenders Act. His appeal to Quarter Sessions was allowed with costs. His case against the Council was that, in view of the successful appeal, the dismissal was invalid and inoperative, and he sought an injunction against the Council to prevent them from acting on the notice. He also asked for costs. The Corporation maintained that the dismissal was a valid and effective exercise of discretion and that there was no liability for restraint or damages.

Giving judgment for the Corporation, Mr Justice Clauson said that the education committee had considered whether the educational machine would not function more satisfactorily without the plaintiff. There was a difference of opinion, which went against the headmaster. There had been no suggestion of corruption and he could see no evidence of bad faith.

It will be seen from this that a breach of the local education authority's discipline, which has not involved breaking the law, may be a valid ground for dismissal.

In recent years there has been a tendency on the part of those appealing to the courts against dismissal to claim that their employers have acted 'contrary to the principles of natural justice'. These principles are not formulated in any code but are a compound of common sense and the basic principles of the common law. In ordinary speech we call them 'fair play': they include the right to know the charge and the right to answer it under a reasonably unbiased procedure.

HANNAM v. BRADFORD CORPORATION

A master in a voluntary school was dismissed by his governors, and the local education authority decided not to exercise its statutory power to prohibit the dismissal.[46] This decision was taken by the authority's staff sub-committee, three members of which at the meeting were governors of the school; but they had not attended the governors' meeting. In the county court the authority's decision was condemned, but the Court of Appeal found otherwise. Lord Justice Sachs said: 'It is not conceivable that any properly constituted sub-committee of the authority could have decided to prohibit the dismissal.' Lord Justice Cross added: 'The question is not whether the tribunal will in fact be biased, but whether a reasonable man with no inside knowledge might well think it might be biased.'

The court held that the plaintiff's right to be heard did not stem from his contract, but from the Articles of Government; consequently he could not bring an action for breach of contract against the authority.[47]

MALLOCH v. ABERDEEN CORPORATION

An important Scottish case reached the House of Lords in 1971, when one of thirty-seven teachers who had been dismissed for refusing to register with the Scottish Teachers Council won a majority decision. The plaintiff had not been present at the meeting which decided to dismiss him; and Lord Reid thought that, had he been, there was a substantial possibility that 'he might have influenced enough of the members to prevent a two-thirds majority from voting for his dismissal.... If an employer failed to take the preliminary steps which the law regarded as essential, he had no power to dismiss, and any purported dismissal was a nullity.'[48]

HADDOW v. ILEA[49]

A group of primary school teachers who had been dismissed in the wake of the William Tyndale school investigation claimed before an industrial tribunal that the dismissals were contrary to natural justice. The education officer who laid the complaints about them before the ILEA disciplinary tribunal was also available for consultation during the proceedings and wrote the report. The Employment Appeal Tribunal found that this dual function had not invalidated the proceedings of the tribunal and that the dismissal was not unfair, nor did it violate the principles of natural justice. The Employment Appeal Tribunal took into account an earlier case[50] where the presence of an assistant education officer during the deliberations of a disciplinary committee might have invalidated the process. The judge however felt that, overall, the committee had acted fairly.

WEDDELL v. NEWCASTLE-UPON-TYNE CORPORATION

The pattern is still to be set, but an industrial tribunal decided that it was not an unfair industrial practice to dismiss a teacher with fourteen years' experience who had become increasingly desperate because of his inability to control a class or to get to school on time, and whose pupils were lounging about, laughing, talking and listening to the Derby on a radio set. The chairman said: 'We are not satisfied that Mr Weddell was a bad teacher, but there were ample grounds for dismissal for unpunctuality. Also, his powers of discipline in a pretty tough class were well below average.'[51]

NEWBIGIN v. LANCASHIRE COUNTY COUNCIL

It was also not an unfair industrial practice to dismiss the head of a remedial department who believed that it was her responsibility to encourage children to find out about life by acting among themselves. The headmaster had found a thirteen-year-old girl lying flat on her back across two desks, whilst a boy lay on top of her simulating sexual intercourse. One of the bystanders, a girl, was screaming. It was also complained that the teacher allowed boys to touch her breasts and permitted them to put their hands up girls' skirts.[52]

VOGLER v. HERTFORDSHIRE COUNTY COUNCIL

When it was discovered that a schoolmaster had had sexual intercourse with a 16-year-old pupil, his headmaster made him write out his resignation. The master asked an industrial tribunal to rule that he had been unfairly dismissed, and the local education authority admitted that the headmaster had no power to terminate a teacher's employment. The authority asked for the case to be adjourned in order that they might dismiss him properly, but the tribunal rejected this and decided that the dismissal was fair.[53]

SIMPSON   v.   BRADFORD   METROPOLITAN   DISTRICT
COUNCIL

The vice-principal of Ilkley College of Education wrote to the
chief education officer asking for advice and help in connection
with difficulties at the college. Fifteen months later, the principal,
Miss Harding, made formal complaints about Miss Simpson,
alleging that she showed no reliability in her oversight of
routine matters, that she did not enjoy the confidence of her
colleagues, that her contribution to the academic work of the
college had been inadequate, and that she had played no
effective part in policy. It was another eight months before
the governors commenced an inquiry, which then occupied
nine separate days during the succeeding ten months. The
decision to dismiss her was not taken until a further eight
months had elapsed. An industrial tribunal found that she had
been unfairly dismissed: she was the first to bring the difficulties
at the college to the notice of the authorities and the tribunal
doubted 'the wisdom of letting her actions rebound on her in
the form of an accusation'. Further considerations which led to
the tribunal's decision that 'this appeal was totally unsatisfactory'
were the 'appalling delay between Miss Harding's complaints
and the governors' meetings', a statement by the deputy chief
education officer that it was his job 'to try and destroy the
applicant professionally', the presence of governors who were
not adjudicating who might have been thought to intend to
influence results, the triple role of the deputy chief education
officer as conciliator, prosecutor and witness, and the failure
of the governors to give findings of fact and reasons for
dismissal. Neither did the tribunal like the way in which the
education committee had received the appeal: documents shown
to the governors were not seen by the committee, and
the deputy chief education officer apparently succeeded in
convincing the committee that unproven charges were true.
Concluding that there was evidence to justify Miss Simpson's
removal from her post, the tribunal found that the education
committee did not, however, consider 'whether there should
be completely dismissed from their service a teacher with over

twenty years' service'. The chairman said that she should be offered an alternative post not lower than that of a Grade 2 lecturer in a college of further education, or a senior lecturer in a college of education, her vice-principal's salary being safeguarded.[54]

NOTHMAN v. LONDON BOROUGH OF BARNET

Miss Nothman, an orthodox Jewess, arrived in this country as a refugee from Hitler's Germany in 1939. She obtained a United Kingdom degree, but she was not offered a permanent post until 1974. Some of her colleagues objected to the fact that she was allowed to leave early on darker Friday afternoons to comply with the requirements relating to the Sabbath, and she had some trouble with two forms. 'I have never', she said, 'come across children who were so difficult.' In January 1976 an 'O' level form was taken away from her, and she made a complaint under the grievance procedure. This led to a disciplinary inquiry, a request for her resignation, suspension by the governors and a six-hour appearance before the education committee. She was dismissed with effect from 31 December 1976. Miss Nothman took her case to an industrial tribunal, which ruled that she was statute barred. There is a provision in the employment legislation that employees over the normal retirement age cannot complain of unfair dismissal.[55] Miss Nothman was 61, but the Act also says that the bar extends to men over 65 and women over 60. The automatic retirement age for both men and women in Barnet was 65. Miss Nothman claimed that this provision amounted to discrimination against women under the Sex Discrimination Act, but that Act does not legislate out other statutory provisions. In the Employment Appeal Tribunal, Mr Justice Kilner-Brown said this amounted to 'as glaring an example of discrimination against a woman on the grounds of her sex as there could possibly be' but the law, 'however absurd, out-of-date and unjust' it was, was clear and unambiguous, and she could not succeed. In the Court of Appeal, Lord Denning said that 'whenever the literal interpretation gives rise to an absurd or unjust situation, judges should use their good sense to remedy it. They should adopt such interpretation as would promote the general purpose underlying the statutory provisions. The present provision could be interpreted sensibly by inserting the words 'where there is no normal retiring age' before the second part of the sub-paragraph. The 'normal retiring age' is the age in any particular profession at which a person must, or should, retire. Teachers have a contractual retiring age of 65. The employee had not reached that age, and is entitled to bring her claim for unfair dismissal.'[56] The court allowed Miss Nothman's appeal. She could then be heard by the tribunal which previously refused to entertain her.

CROSBIE v. NOTTINGHAMSHIRE COUNTY COUNCIL

In 1980 a teacher of a nursery class refused to teach a class which, since financial cuts had brought about a worsening of the pupil-teacher ratio, she thought was too large for the safety and education of the children. She was dismissed and appealed to an industrial tribunal.

The teacher rested her case on the guidelines issued some years before by the DES about the size of nursery classes. The tribunal took the view that the guidelines were only advice and not mandatory. The teacher had therefore been guilty of failing to carry out her head teacher's requirement that she teach the class and her dismissal was fair.[57]

Summary dismissal may take place for wilful disobedience of a lawful order, misconduct, incompetence, permanent disability or gross moral misbehaviour which is inconsistent with the fulfilment of the conditions of service. A member of a university staff took a student into a dark lecture room where he put his arm round her and kissed her. He was dismissed by the university authorities and subsequently brought an action against them.[58] Judgment, with costs, was given for the university.

In aided schools, where the governors are the employers, there is a clause in the Articles of Government requiring them to dismiss teachers when directed to do so by the local education authority, and prohibiting the dismissal of teachers without the consent of the authority except in any cases where the governors are expressly given the power to dismiss on grounds connected with the giving of religious education. Needless to say, aided school governors should follow the normal procedures in such instances. Where a teacher in an aided school is dismissed on the requirement of a local education authority, the law regards the authority as the employer for the purposes of the employment legislation[59] and possible appeals to an industrial tribunal.

In recent years there have been instances of summary dismissal of teachers from Roman Catholic schools because they have chosen to divorce or re-marry. Offensive as this is to the tenets of the Church, the proper procedures for dismissal must be observed. A teacher was appointed head teacher of a Roman Catholic primary school and was informed that his appointment was according to enclosed conditions of tenure. These conditions stated that, as regards dismissal, the head teacher had a right to a hearing before the authority, whose consent to the dismissal was required. The head teacher divorced and re-married and was summarily dismissed: he sought an injunction from the courts to restrain the dismissal as contrary to his conditions of tenure. Finally it was held in the Court of Appeal that the school managers had wrongly purported to dismiss the head teacher by disregarding his contractual rights, and granted the injunction sought.[60]

On the other hand, an industrial tribunal upheld the summary dismissal of a teacher who wrote four words, constituting part of the answer to one question, on a candidate's 'A' level script, and at first denied doing so, causing his head to carry out a 'distressing' interview with the girl pupil.[61]

26   Convictions in court and dismissal

A disciplinary committee of a local education authority is not obliged to dismiss a teacher solely because the teacher has been convicted of some offence, placed on probation or conditionally discharged, whether on appeal or otherwise.[62]

Nevertheless, such a committee is not prevented by the maxim *nemo debet bis punire pro uno delicto* (no one should be punished twice for the same wrong) or by the powers of the Criminal Courts Act 1973, from taking into account the facts underlying that conviction.[63]

Section 13 of the Powers of Criminal Courts Act provides:

(1) a conviction of an offence for which an order is made under this Part of this Act placing the offender on probation or discharging him absolutely or conditionally shall be deemed not to be a conviction for any purpose other than the purposes of the proceedings in which the order is made and of any subsequent proceedings which may be taken against the offender under the preceding provisions of this Act ... (3) Without prejudice to the preceding provisions ... the conviction of an offender who is placed on probation or discharged absolutely or conditionally ... shall in any event be disregarded for the purposes of any enactment or instrument which imposes any disqualification or disability upon convicted persons or authorizes ... the imposition of any such disqualification or disability.

The following cases indicate the varying ways in which local education authorities and industrial tribunals have reacted to this principle.

REGINA v. POWYS COUNTY COUNCIL.[64]

In 1981 a Welsh teacher was convicted of conspiracy with others to damage telecommunications installations and was sentenced to nine months imprisonment of which, after remission, he served six months.

The council's staffing panel thought that the teacher's imprisonment amounted to a repudiation of his contract, and so informed him. He appealed to the council's appeals committee which offered him a further one-year contract. A parent of a child at the school sought to have that decision of the appeals committee quashed. The court held, refusing the application, that it was clear that the teacher's conduct amounted to a repudiation of his contract, which had been in effect accepted by the staffing panel. On a true analysis of the matter, however, the appeals committee, whilst having no jurisdiction to make any appointments of teachers, did have a jurisdiction to vary the decision of the staffing panel, and that is what happened. The appeals committee had thus been acting within its powers in varying the decision of the staffing panel, even though the effect of that variation was to create a new contract.

NORRIS v. SOUTHAMPTON CITY COUNCIL[65]

Although this case did not involve a schoolteacher, it sets out the approach to be adopted by employers when dealing with an employee convicted of a criminal offence.

In 1980 Mr Norris was convicted of driving whilst disqualified and given a six-month suspended sentence of imprisonment. His employers were aware of this conviction. Subsequently, one of the senior staff heard that Mr Norris was in trouble again and this time he expected to go to prison. Later he pleaded guilty in a magistrates' court to a charge of driving whilst disqualified and sentence was deferred until after the hearing of other charges. Subsequently he was convicted of an assault occasioning actual bodily harm and of reckless driving. He was then committed to the Crown Court for sentencing and ordered to be kept in custody. The woman with whom he was living then called at the respondents' offices and told them that Mr Norris was in prison awaiting sentence and expected to get at least six months. The following day the respondents sent him a notice of dismissal. Mr Norris was released on bail following his lodging of an appeal.

An industrial tribunal held that the employee's conduct brought about the frustration of his contract of employment, that he was not dismissed and therefore failed to establish a claim for unfair dismissal compensation. Mr Norris appealed against this decision.

Mr Justice Kilner-Brown argued: 'When considering whether or not the dismissal was unfair, the only arguable proposition in our view is that the employers here were over-hasty in

treating the contract as repudiated and impossible of performance. In considering this question the industrial tribunal will
have to remind themselves that the test is to consider the
standard of a reasonable employer in the light of his knowledge
and belief at the time of dismissal. Subsequent matters such as
the lodging of notice of appeal and the granting of bail pending
the hearing of the appeal are irrelevant considerations. If it is
argued that further inquiries should have been made, the
industrial tribunal will have to bear in mind that such inquiries
would have revealed that the appellant was in prison because
the magistrates considered that in totality he merited a sentence
in excess of their powers. In other words, on a balance of
probabilities he was likely to get a sentence of twelve months
or more. But even if this would have been the result of
inquiries, should not the employers have paused, thought more
about it and considered the advisability of making inquiries?
Even if the tribunal does come to the conclusion that the
dismissal was unfair, it would be open to them to find that the
appellant contributed wholly and to the maximum extent
to his dismissal. Ought he to get anything by way of
compensation?

These are the questions which will have to be decided by
the industrial tribunal to which this case is remitted. Our
unanimous decision is that the appeal is allowed and the case
remitted to an industrial tribunal to reconsider the case on the
lines we have indicated.'

It seems, therefore, that the doctrine of frustration of contract
(i.e. that one or more parties to a contract is unable to fulfil
it) is now inapplicable. The problem is to be resolved by
determining whether the act is intentionally repudiatory and
then examining how the employer responds to it. It remains
the case, however, that actual imprisonment for a serious
offence could bring about a frustration of contract.

GARDNER v. NEWPORT BOROUGH COUNCIL[66]

A teacher who had been convicted of gross indecency appealed
against dismissal. The tribunal argued, 'We think that a

professional man owes a duty to himself and those who employ him to observe proper standards of behaviour. There are things that can be done nowadays by professional men that could not have been done years ago, but not anything of this kind. The Education Committee in our view acted reasonably in taking the conviction seriously. They were not unreasonable in acting upon it.' The tribunal agreed that the local education authority was entitled to take into account the appellant's previous sexual misconduct, even though the evidence of it was inconclusive. The tribunal further agreed that Mr Gardner might be punished twice for the same offence, 'otherwise employers would waive consequences which the court antici- pated and allowed for in fixing its penalty'. Mr Gardner had not been excluded from teaching by the Secretary of State,[67] but this did not make it wrong to dismiss him.

NOTTINGHAMSHIRE COUNTY COUNCIL v. BOWLY[68]

A teacher was convicted of indecency in a public convenience and appealed to a tribunal which declared his subsequent dismissal to be unfair. The local education authority appealed and succeeded: 'The panel were of the opinion that there was no satisfactory evidence of any incident suggesting a risk to pupils. That seems to us to be somewhat ambiguous. True, there was nothing in the facts already summarized directly indicating from his nature and interests that Mr Bowly would be likely to commit an act of this sort against one of his pupils, in the sense that that was positively established. But, looked at negatively in the circumstances of this case at all events (and we certainly do not propose to lay down rules for other cases), it would be surely difficult to say ... that there was no risk.' Here again, the teacher was not excluded by the Secretary of State.

NORFOLK COUNTY COUNCIL v. BERNARD[69]

A teacher-adviser of drama was convicted of an offence involving cannabis, dismissed, but ultimately reinstated by the

Employment Appeal Tribunal. The Tribunal applied the test that 'If a conviction for an offence outside employment seriously and genuinely affects the employee's relationship with his fellow employees, then the dismissal might be justified. The same proposition is put forward if the nature of the offence upon which the conviction rests made the employee a danger to others, particularly children.'

The latter views no doubt motivated local education authorities to dismiss in three further reported cases: a Plymouth teacher who allegedly sniffed glue in front of a class;[70] a male teacher who allegedly wore women's clothing in class;[71] and a teacher who allegedly called for the legalization of cannabis.[72]

WISEMAN v. SALFORD CITY COUNCIL[73]

The teacher taught drama, working mainly with mature students but also to some extent with those in the 16–19 age group.

Following an incident in London involving another man in a public lavatory, the teacher was charged with committing an act of gross indecency. The charge was dismissed but he was bound over in the sum of £100 to keep the peace for twelve months.

After another incident in a public lavatory, he was again charged with gross indecency. He pleaded guilty. The case was reported in the local paper and thus came to the attention of the college authorities. During the investigations, they also learned of the earlier offence.

The teacher was dismissed following a hearing at which he was given an opportunity to present his case. One of the main reasons leading to the decision to dismiss him was the potential risk of continuing to employ him in work which involved close contact with young people. An appeal against the dismissal was turned down.

By a majority decision, an industrial tribunal found that the dismissal was reasonable in the circumstances. The main argument advanced on behalf of the teacher on appeal to the Employment Appeal Tribunal was that it is a self-evident proposition, not susceptible of dispute by a right-thinking disciplinary body or industrial tribunal, that someone who has done what the teacher admitted he had done and who takes the view that his conduct was incautious and foolish but not evil and criminal, cannot be a risk to teenage boys in his charge and, therefore, there was no basis on which the disciplinary body and the industrial tribunal could conclude that there was a risk in the continued employment of the teacher.

On appeal the Employment Appeal Tribunal held that the industrial tribunal had not erred in law in concluding that the respondents had acted reasonably in dismissing the drama teacher following two charges of indecency with men in public lavatories, on the grounds of the risk involved to young men in the 16–19 year age group whom he taught.

Contrary to the argument advanced on behalf of the teacher it is not a self-evident proposition that a man who behaved as the teacher did and who regarded his behaviour as no more than incautious and foolish could not be a risk to teenage boys in his charge. 'Although there may well be a respectable body of opinion which supports that proposition, the subject is highly controversial and the proposition is not self-evident. As the proposition was not self-evidently right, it was for the industrial tribunal to evaluate the reasonableness of the employers' action in treating the appellant's conduct as a reason for dismissal in the circumstances.' The industrial tribunal had not erred in law, therefore, in concluding that there was some risk attached to the appellant's continued employment and in finding that the dismissal was fair.

Decisions are made in each case by industrial tribunals on both the law and the facts, whereas the Employment Appeal Tribunal considers only the law. Thus in Mr Bernard's case the industrial tribunal felt that Norfolk County Council had paid too little attention to the considerable support for him expressed by parents and colleagues: in the Bowly case the Employment Appeal Tribunal would not hold that the industrial tribunal had been wrong in law. The Employment Appeal Tribunal does not re-hear the case.

CHAKKI v. UNITED YEAST CO. LTD[74]

Mr Chakki was sentenced to eleven months' imprisonment and the employers engaged a replacement on the ground that his contract of employment was frustrated by the prison sentence. Mr Chakki successfully appealed against his sentence and was placed on probation. On his complaint of unfair dismissal to an industrial tribunal it was contended that since Mr Chakki had only been in prison for twenty-four hours before being granted bail and the imprisonment had taken place during his annual holiday, the employers had dismissed him unfairly. The industrial tribunal held that the employers were justified in considering the contract frustrated and dismissed the claim. Mr Chakki appealed.

It was argued for Mr Chakki at the appeal that where an employee was imprisoned for a substantial period it was not the sentence of imprisonment but the disruption of the contractual relationship which made it impossible for him to carry out his work. The employee's short period of imprisonment was during his annual holiday. The argument that a contract was frustrated immediately a prison sentence was imposed was unconvincing. It was necessary to ascertain the moment at which the question of frustration had to be determined. The relevant questions for an industrial tribunal were: when was it necessary to decide whether a replacement had to be engaged; at the time that decision was taken what would a reasonable employer have considered to be the likely period of absence and whether it was reasonable to engage a permanent replacement rather than a temporary one. The industrial tribunal had erred in law in deciding that the contract of employment was frustrated immediately on the imposition of the prison sentence. Mr Chakki's appeal was allowed. It is important to bear in mind however that this case was heard *before* the Norris case (see p. 152) and it might now be held that his conduct in fact amounted to repudiation of contract.

27   Withdrawal of recognition

Under current legislation, an employer may dismiss an employee for reasons 'related to the conduct of the employee'.[75]

If a teacher's appointment is terminated for grave professional default, misconduct or conviction of a criminal offence, the facts must be reported to the Secretary of State. It is immaterial whether the teacher has resigned or been dismissed.[76] Convictions of teachers in service are also reported which may result in exclusion or restriction by the Secretary of State before the employer reaches a decision.

If the Secretary of State, after giving the teacher every chance of refuting the charges,[77] declares him to be unsuitable for employment as a teacher on grounds of grave professional default, or misconduct, he must not be so employed.

If the Secretary of State determines that a teacher shall be employed to a limited extent only, he may be employed only to that extent.

After giving the teacher every chance of making representations the Secretary of State may, on educational or medical grounds, require that the employment of a teacher be terminated or made subject to such conditions or qualifications as he may impose.[78]

A Punjabi teacher, with six years' experience in his own country, trained for fifteen months after coming to England. He was appointed to the staff of the London Borough of Hillingdon and placed on two years' probation, which was extended for a further six months. He was then informed that he was unsuitable for employment as a teacher, and the authority dismissed him. Before an industrial tribunal he claimed that he had not been placed in a suitable school, or provided with suitable supervision and conditions of work for a probationer. He alleged that his dismissal was because of his ethnic origins. The local education authority said that Mr Sandhu's dismissal followed from a statutory duty not to employ a person declared unsuitable to be a teacher, and in these circumstances the tribunal had no jurisdiction to hear the complaint.

Before the Employment Appeal Tribunal Mr Sandhu also alleged racial discrimination. Although the DES had been responsible for informing Mr Sandhu formally that he had failed his probation, the Appeal Tribunal paid regard to the fact that the Department's decision was based on a recommendation of the local education authority that he was unable to prepare work or to command a satisfactory degree of respect in the classroom. Mr Sandhu was also told that his pronunciation and use of English led to a 'communication problem'. Because the DES had, in accordance with current probation procedures, relied on the local education authority's report, the Appeal Tribunal was not satisfied that the Department's directive amounted to a statutory prohibition, and ordered that the issue be heard again by an industrial tribunal to determine whether Mr Sandhu had been given a fair opportunity to prove himself.[79]

Cases of misconduct come to the notice of the DES usually through reports from local education authorities or through the police who are asked to notify the DES in confidence of convictions of teachers for certain offences, particularly violence, indecency, dishonesty, drink or drugs, but excluding minor offences and all road traffic offences.

It is not possible to define precisely or give an exhaustive list of the kind of misconduct which leads to exclusion, but the following are most likely to do so:

– sexual offences and violence involving children or young people
– other serious kinds of violence
– the misappropriation of school monies
– false claims of a gravely deceptive nature as to qualifications
– repeated misconduct or multiple convictions unless of a minor kind.

If the Secretary of State finally decides on exclusion from the profession, or lays down conditions, the teacher's name, date of birth and DES reference number are entered on the so-called 'List 99' which is circulated to local education authorities to ensure that they do not appoint prohibited teachers. If the

Secretary of State has restricted employment to certain types of school, this information will also be included. Excluded teachers have no appeal as such, but may apply for re-instatement after a period, the length of which depends on the seriousness of the misconduct.

A prohibited teacher may not be employed in an independent school. Contravention of this will lead to the serving of a notice on the proprietor of the school under the Education Act 1944, section 71.

28   Supply and temporary teachers

The conditions of tenure provide that when teachers are employed at a daily or hourly rate, only the following provisions shall apply to them:

(a) suspension or termination of employment on medical grounds;

(b) the grievance procedure;

(c) the local education authority's disciplinary procedure, where one exists;

(d) leave to undertake duties in connection with external examinations, for jury and other public service, and for other purposes generally;

(e) definition of the teacher's duties and holiday entitlements;

(f) assaults on teachers, compensation for crimes of violence, loss or damage to personal property, protection in out-of-school activities;

(g) travelling allowances for official duties.

Teachers employed on a temporary basis for one term or less in substitution for absent permanent members of the staff are covered by the whole code of conditions of service, except:

(a) the section dealing with the period of notice required on termination of a teacher's employment, unless there is no other stated requirement in the contract;

(b) the provisions relating to the dismissal of teachers, unless the dismissal is on grounds of conduct or capability;

(c) the arrangements for maternity leave.

Part-time teachers who do not fall into either of these categories are protected by the whole code.

The general conditions should be as for full-time teachers, including the right to a hearing in case of termination otherwise than for redundancy. If particular hardship is claimed in a case of redundancy, the teacher should be able to make representations to the local education authority.

29   Maternity leave

Although there are provisions for maternity leave in the Burgundy Book, consideration of these is deferred to chapter VIII. All women employed continuously for two years now have the right to maternity pay, and to return to their employment after confinement. In this matter the conditions of service and the statutory provisions stand side by side and their interrelationship should be clearly understood.

30   Industrial action

In common with all other employees, teachers have the legal right to belong to a trade union, to seek and hold office in it and to take part in its activities.[80] The Employment Act of 1980 protects them against unreasonable behaviour by their union such as expulsion or arbitrary discrimination. They may, however, terminate their membership on giving reasonable notice.

Strikes and other practices such as 'working to rule' are relatively infrequent in the teaching profession, but there has been a tendency for them to increase in number recently. Working to rule is, in any case, a difficult procedure to define in a vocation which has no rule book; the general interpretation is a refusal to take part in out-of-school activities, most of which are, in any case, voluntary.

Teachers, especially heads, may find themselves in a difficult position when some form of industrial action appears to be brewing in their school. Local education authorities are, naturally, anxious that there should be as little disruption of normal work as possible; action which involves sending children home when they would normally be at school may involve risks for those pupils, and there are still many teachers who disapprove strongly of strikes and kindred activities. It is on such occasions that personal views must be subordinated to professional considerations, and there are two basic questions which must be considered. First, a head must ask himself: 'What steps must I take to ensure, so far as may be reasonably practicable, the personal safety of each pupil?' Few teachers who are planning industrial action are prepared to put children at risk, and it is usually possible to reach an agreed position which will minimize danger. The second question arises from the fact that emotional pressures tend to increase at such times. There is always the danger that precipitate and ill-considered action may polarize views, and so divide the staff that it may be many years before the damage to the school can be repaired. This question, therefore, may be formulated in these terms: 'What steps must I take to ensure that, when industrial action ceases, the school will resume a normal life in an atmosphere of good-will?'

Ultimately the head will have to take decisions. Some may be repugnant to him, but it is in such situations that the stature of headship may well be increased. The key note is consultation: consultation with representatives of any professional association meditating action, consultation with the other associations, and consultation with the chairman of the governing body and the local education authority. The questions posed in the preceding paragraph must be opened up, and the head's legal and professional duties made clear. When a course of action has been agreed, everyone must adhere to it, and unless the head's own association is involved, he should maintain a strictly neutral attitude.

Several practical points should be borne in mind. If children have to be excluded, their safety is best ensured by giving advance notice to their parents. Such warnings should be non-partisan in tone and, if different groups are to be excluded over a period, it is as well to issue a general letter as early as possible followed by specific notifications on the day prior to the actual exclusion of particular children. The lightning strike is not a weapon available to a teacher who cares for his pupils, and every effort should be made to secure that adequate advice can be given to parents in advance.

The position of the head teacher in law is currently both obscure and difficult. It was held by Lord Denning in *Meade v. Haringey London Borough Council* (1979)[81] that the duty laid upon local education authorities to provide schools *and keep them running* is absolute. An authority therefore has a right to expect its head teachers to use their best endeavours to keep the school running. It has also been argued that head teachers who are not themselves taking action but who can be shown to have assisted colleagues in furtherance of a dispute might be guilty of 'secondary action', but this has not been tested.[82]

It would be unwise of head teachers to undertake, or ask others to undertake, any teaching, duties or other action which might be construed as 'blacklegging'. This is a certain recipe for lasting damage to the school. The consultations which take place before industrial action commences should include the principles to be applied in making arrangements for any partial continuance of the school's work, and these should be applied with the utmost integrity. The only possible exception to such a course is during an emergency which poses a genuine threat of immediate physical danger.

If, for one reason or another, an excluded child appears in school, the head should take all reasonable steps to return him to his parent's care. Much will depend on the age of the child, and the home circumstances. Again, provision for this contingency should be included in the consultations and, in default of any agreement, the head should assume responsibility for the child's safety until he can be returned to the parent.

The school organization should not be used by teachers without the authority's consent for the issue of unofficial documents to parents in an attempt to canvass sympathy or support for (or disapproval of) industrial action.

Once the internal negotiations have taken place, a head

should advise his local education authority of the probable effects of industrial action and the steps he proposes to take to deal with them. If he believes that the situation will be such that he cannot perform his duty of care to his pupils either partially or at all, he should say so. If the authority is unwilling to allow him to exclude children or, if necessary, to close the school, he should consult his own professional association, and ask for support. This is particularly important if disciplinary action might follow his disregard of the authority's instructions. As one experienced headmaster said: 'It is not for a local education authority to place a head teacher in an impossible vacuum, and then seek to discipline such a person for acting carefully and professionally.'

In particular, heads should ensure that the instructions of the local education authority are given in writing. Those of a general nature should be communicated to, and discussed with, the staff. Heads should not pass on verbal warning notices to individual members of the staff.

31   Protest action and penalties

In *Crosbie v. Nottinghamshire*[83] it was said by a legal representative: 'When an employee on matters of principle withdraws his or her labour, however praiseworthy the principle, one of the possibilities which must be faced is the sack and the employee cannot then ask the industrial tribunal to decide the principle. She has only the right not to be unfairly dismissed.' Provided the local authority's agreed disciplinary procedure has been carefully followed, an industrial tribunal will not decide whether it would have come to the same decision as the internal disciplinary panels.

Employees who withdraw their labour totally receive no salary for the period concerned.

Action by teachers, however, has usually taken the form of varying the usual pattern of work: working a reduced number of hours, refusing to cover for absent colleagues, withdrawal from voluntary activities are typical examples. A case heard in

1983 casts light on how the law views employers' reactions to such actions.

On the instruction of his professional association a teacher refused to accept an increased number of children into his class. He continued to teach the original thirty-one (and undertook all his usual extra-curricular activities), but not the additional five. The local authority took the view that his action constituted a breach of his contract of employment in that the teacher was refusing to carry out the instructions of his head teacher. The authority made deductions from the teacher's salary in accordance with his conditions of service agreement (the Burgundy Book, section 5.2.2) which refers to unpaid leave of absence without the permission of the authority, and is calculated as a daily or part-daily rate based on the day's salary being 1/365th of a year for each day of the period of absence. The teacher took legal action to recover the unpaid salary.

The local authority argued in court that a teacher could not expect payment if he did only part of the work for which he was employed. 'In so doing he was seeking to impose on his employers a contract different from that into which he had entered. There was nothing in his contract to indicate that if he failed to comply with its terms he would be entitled to be paid his salary.' Furthermore, since other teachers were taking similar action, the local authority was being forced into a breach of its statutory duty to provide full-time education for all the children in its area.[84] The local authority's representative relied on a judgment by Lord Denning in another case: 'Now I quite agree that a man is not bound positively to do more for his employer than his contract requires. He can withdraw his good will if he pleases. But what he must not do is wilfully to obstruct the employer as he goes about his business.' In the same case Lord Justice Roskill had said: 'It is self-evident ... that the employee would never seek so to interpret ... the rules as to disrupt the entire ... system.'

Mr Justice Park ruled that the teacher's actions were not intended to make it impossible for the local education authority to carry out its duty to educate. 'It seems to me that on the evidence the worst that can be said is that ... (the teacher's) acts made the discharge of that duty difficult.'

He further stated: 'The education authority could have refused to allow the plaintiff to teach until he agreed to teach the class of 36. But that course was not taken.' Furthermore, 'by deciding not to suspend teachers from duty, and by allowing teachers to remain on the premises if they wished to do so, had also thereby decided (a) not to treat each threatened breach of contract by a teacher as a repudiation of it, and (b) as a teacher who was allowed to remain on the school premises was hardly likely to remain idle, to accept from him whatever duties he chose to perform.... In my judgment the defendants, by their conduct, impliedly affirmed the plaintiff's contract of employment. For this reason the plaintiff is entitled to recover at least part of his unpaid salary.'

As to the deductions made under the Burgundy Book section the judge held that the section was inapplicable to this case. 'I do not consider that ... failure to teach a class in accordance with the head teacher's instructions can be regarded as absence from the school or from his duties.' However, the judge held an agreed deduction of 5/36th of salary as appropriate.

As to the consequences of the teacher's action for the local education authority, Mr Justice Park concluded: 'The defendants have not suffered any financial loss by reason of the plaintiff's breaches of contract; for example, they have not incurred the cost of employing a teacher to teach the children whom the plaintiff had refused to teach: if they had done so, they might well have succeeded in recovering the cost of such employment; nor have they been required to meet any claim by a parent for their failure to educate a child.'[85]

It seems therefore that local authorities may lawfully make notional salary deductions in cases where teachers carry out protest action which stops short of a complete withdrawal of labour. This could include, for example, refusal to cover for absent colleagues, refusal to work to a timetable different from that drawn up at the beginning of an academic year, refusal to attend parents' evenings or staff meetings held wholly or in part outside normal timetabled hours, refusal to continue examination invigilation outside normal school timetabled hours and refusal to undertake rostered duties before and after sessions. *Royle v. Trafford* seems also to suggest that failure to make some salary deduction might be interpreted as acceptance by the local authority that the disputed action did not amount to breach of contract. CLEA wrote to LEA making these points in early 1985.

It should be remembered that local education authorities which take no action over disruptive action run the risk of court action by parents for breach of statutory duty to provide education. (See *Meade v. Haringey*, p. 8.)

32   Industrial action: the Employment Act 1982 and the Trade Union Act 1984

At the moment one can only speculate about the effects of the 1982 Act on industrial action in schools.

The Act reduces the immunity of trade unions, although the immunity of individual members of actions done 'in contemplation or furtherance of a trade dispute' remains unchanged. A trade dispute is now defined thus:

'In this Act 'trade dispute' means a dispute between workers and their employer which relates wholly or mainly to one or more of the following, that is to say,

(a) terms and conditions of employment, or the physical conditions in which any workers are required to work;

(b) engagement or non-engagement, or termination or suspension of employment or the duties of employment, of one or more workers;

(c) allocation of work or the duties of employment as between workers or groups of workers;

(d) matters of discipline;

(e) the membership or non-membership of a trade union on the part of a worker;

(f) facilities for officials of trade unions; and

(g) machinery for negotiation or consultation and other procedures, relating to any of the foregoing matters, including the recognition by employers or employers' associations of the right of a trade union to represent workers in any such negotiation or consultation or in the carrying out of such procedures.'[86]

Particular points to note are:

1. Unions which strike in sympathy with other groups of workers will no longer have total immunity from actions for damages by employers.
2. Political 'days of action', for example recently against government financial restrictions, do not appear to be covered by the new definition of a trade dispute, unless they are concerned largely with terms and conditions of service.
3. Policy disputes between teachers and their employers, for example over the reintroduction of selective secondary schools, seem similarly not to be covered, unless the meaning of the term 'conditions of service' can be stretched to cover such issues.

Action by employers to enforce their legal rights, or by interested other parties, comes under civil, not criminal, law. Those who have rights in law are not obliged to exercise them, but have discretion to do so.

Under the Trade Union Act 1984 unions must hold a secret ballot before undertaking strike action. Failure to do so puts union funds at risk if an individual or group takes legal action claiming loss of income as a result of industrial action. One possibility in the field of education would be that parents who were forced to take time away from work, or even perhaps to give up a part-time job, could sue the union. The Act permits ballots to be held on school premises.

In 1985 the Metropolitan Borough of Solihull obtained an interim injunction against the National Union of Teachers on the grounds that the Union had failed to hold a secret ballot as required by the 1984 Act. The Union had called upon its members to refuse to carry out activities connected with school which the Union regards as voluntary only.

If the matter goes to a full hearing in court the difficult issue of teachers' duties may be further clarified.

33   The European Economic Community

It is a basic principle of the Common Market that there should be complete freedom for firms, branches, agencies and individuals, belonging to any of the member states, to set up in business or practice anywhere within the EEC.[87]

This provision is intended to apply to members of the professions, as well as to those engaged in business. At present, little progress has been made, however, because of the wide variations in training, qualifications and practice in the member states. Shortage of staff is said to be one reason for the delay, but there are many problems concerned with the recognition by the member states of each other's qualification equivalents.

The European Parliament has an education committee and education ministers for the EEC meet regularly to discuss and promote policies for dealing with, for example, illiteracy and teacher unemployment. Their first directive, which originated in meetings in 1977, was enacted in this country[88] and required all member states to provide free tuition in the language of their state to immigrant children. Immigrants should also receive free teaching of their mother tongue and culture in the receiving country.

34   Independent schools

Lying outside the maintained and former direct grant sector, the independent schools are largely free to devise their own conditions of service. The terms of notice may be different, the Burgundy Book does not automatically apply, and the avenues of promotion are not the same. Some adhere to the Burnham Scale for the payment of salaries, some pay more, others less. Some do apply the Burgundy Book: in some boarding schools a lower salary is paid, but the staff enjoy the residential emoluments.

There is a growing concern on the part of the Government

to regulate certain aspects of the relationships between employers and those who work for them; where this has been done, the statutory provisions apply with equal force in independent schools. Teachers in independent schools, therefore, are advised to study chapter V, which sets out the minimum conditions of service which have been included in recent legislation on employment. In addition, some aspects of the employment cases cited in this chapter also apply to the staffs of these schools. It is particularly important that teachers in independent schools should have a statement in compliance with the requirements of the Employment Protection (Consolidation) Act 1978.

35   Secondment for service overseas

BRITISH COMMONWEALTH

The Commonwealth Education Conference which was held at Oxford in 1959 drew attention to the desperate shortage of teachers in the less developed parts of the Commonwealth. Following this, the Government agreed to stimulate recruitment for periods of teaching service overseas.

Teachers intending to participate in this scheme may apply for secondment by their local education authority or governing body for a period of one year. Provision has been made for teachers to be reinstated as far as possible in posts as nearly equivalent to their appointments at the time of secondment.

Teachers taking part in the scheme should be between the ages of 25 and 45, with at least five years' experience of which at least two years should have been with their current local education authority. Teachers are required to sign an undertaking to return to service with the same employing authority in the United Kingdom.

The scheme is administered for the DES and overseas education authorities by the League for the Exchange of Commonwealth Teachers.[89] The League also operates on behalf of the education authorities for Scotland and Northern Ireland.

EUROPE AND THE UNITED STATES OF AMERICA

The European scheme is intended mainly for teachers of modern languages. Post-to-post exchanges, usually for a term but occasionally for a year, are available. There are also arrangements which permit the unilateral exchange of teachers: in some cases teachers are paid by the authorities in the host country, and teachers should write to the pensions branch of the DES to make arrangements to safeguard their pension rights.[90] The unilateral exchanges are usually of one year's duration and involve the teaching of English as a foreign language. The participating countries are Austria, Belgium, Denmark, France, Federal Republic of Germany, Italy, Switzerland, Spain and the USSR.

Exchanges with the United States are available for a period of one year to teachers with at least three years' experience. Salary is paid by the 'home' authority and British teachers receive a tax-free grant to offset the higher cost of living in the United States.

The European and United States schemes are operated on behalf of the DES, the Scottish Education Department and the Ministry of Education by the Central Bureau for Educational Visits and Exchanges.[95]

HEALTH

The United Kingdom has reciprocal arrangements with a number of overseas countries intended to protect the interests of its citizens working abroad, but these agreements do not necessarily give complete cover. Teachers can obtain Leaflet NI38 *Social Security Abroad* from the local office of the Department of Health and Social Security. Full details of agreements with individual countries can be obtained from the Department's overseas group.[96] The benefits conferred by the various agreements are set out in the table on p. 172.

Those travelling to EEC countries are advised to obtain and complete Form E111. It should be attested before travelling. The form is not, however, necessary in Eire or Denmark where

Social Security: Reciprocal Agreements (see p. 171)

Benefits available to citizens of the United Kingdom by various reciprocal agreements.

1 Sickness Benefit
2 Industrial Injuries
3 Unemployment Benefit
4 Maternity Benefit
5 Guardian's Allowance
6 Retirement Pension
7 Death Grant
8 Widow's Benefit
9 Family Allowances

European Economic Community:

Belgium	123456789	Spain	123456789
Denmark[93]	123456789	Sweden[93]	123456 89
France	123456789	Switzerland	12 56 89
German Federal		Turkey	12 456789
Republic	123456789	*Other countries:*	
Greece	123456789	Australia[91]	1 3 56 89
Irish Republic	123456789	Austria	1234 7 9
Italy	123456789	Bermuda[92]	2 6 8
Luxembourg	123456789	Canada	
Netherlands	123456789	Finland	123456 89
Gibraltar	123456789	Israel[94]	12 456 8
Other members		Jersey &	
of the Council		Guernsey[92]	123456789
of Europe:		Jamaica	2 5678
Cyprus[92]	12345678	Mauritius	2 56 9
Malta, G.C.[92]	123 56 8	New Zealand[91 92]	1 3 56 89
Norway[93]	123456789	United States	
Portugal	12345678	of America	6 8
		Yugoslavia[93]	1234 6789

the patient's passport should be produced when seeking medical treatment. In some countries it is necessary to pay for this treatment at the time, and to seek reimbursement later. Details of the current arrangements can be obtained from the Department of Health and Social Security.[97]

References

1. See p. 141.
2. The inclusion of false testimonials may lead to a prosecution under the Servants Characters Act 1792. The whole question of testimonials and references is dealt with on pp. 607–11.
3. Powell. *v.* Lee (1908) 72 JP 353; LCT 68.
4. See p. 98.
5. Employment Protection (Consolidation) Act 1978, s. 1.
6. For heads the period of notice is one month longer than for assistants.
7. When the teacher's resignation is to take effect in April there is normally a provision that, if his new school begins the summer term before 1 May, the teacher will be released from such earlier date. After two years' continuous employment an employee is entitled by the Employment Protection (Consolidation) Act 1978: s. 49, to one week's notice for each year of that employment, to a maximum of twelve weeks. After nine years' service with the same employer, therefore, a teacher is entitled to nine weeks' notice. This overrides the two months in the standard form of contract, and rises by a week a year until the maximum is reached at the end of twelve years' service.
8. In accordance with the agreed national conditions of tenure most local education authorities include a clause providing for automatic retirement at the end of the term in which the teacher attains the age of 65. Service may be extended beyond this age by mutual agreement between the teacher and the local authority and, during such an extension, all other terms of the agreement will remain in force.
9. Employment Protection (Consolidation) Act 1978, s. 80.
10. The question of action against the parents of violent pupils is considered on p. 464.
11. Education Act 1944, s. 27(2) to (5) and s. 28(3) and (4).
12. Local Government Act 1972, s. 117.
13. Local Government Act 1972, s. 105.
14. Local Government Act 1972, s. 94.
15. Local Government Act 1972, s. 96.
16. Local Government Act 1972, s. 97.
17. *The Teacher*, 12 December 1975.
18. Local Government Act 1972, s. 80(1)(a).
19. Local Government Act 1972, s. 116.

20. Local Government Act 1972, s. 80(3).

21. Local Government Act 1972, s. 104(2).

22. Local Government Act 1972, s. 81(4).

23. Employment Protection (Consolidation) Act 1978, s. 27.

24. Beal and others *v.* Beecham Group Ltd, *The Times*, 23 April 1982, CA.

25. Employment Protection (Consolidation) Act 1978, s. 28 as amended by the Employment Act 1980, s. 19. See also Code of Practice 3: 'Time off for Trade Union Duties and Activities' (ACAS).

26. Education Act 1944, s. 30.

27. Ahmad *v.* ILEA (1978) 1 All ER 574.

28. Woodley *v.* Metropolitan District Railway Co (1877) 2 Ex. D. 384.

29. General duties are now laid upon employers by the Health and Safety at Work etc. Act 1974, and precise duties are specified in regulations. See chapter VI.

30. Employment Protection (Consolidation) Act 1978, s. 1(4)(b)(ii).

31. See p. 411.

32. Employment Protection (Consolidation) Act 1978, s. 1(4).

33. Code of Practice I: 'Disciplinary Practice and Procedures in Employment' (ACAS).

34. Conditions of Service Working Party (COSWOP).

35. See pp. 194–5.

36. *Times Educational Supplement*, 3 July 1981.

37. *Times Educational Supplement*, 2 May 1980.

38. App. IV, para. 1.

39. The governors in aided schools; the local education authority in others.

40. See p. 116.

41. In the case of teachers appointed under a minute, the letter of appointment will refer to the appropriate staff code where these conditions are set out.

42. See p. 189.

43. As defined in the Employment Protection (Consolidation) Act 1978, s. 57.

44. Employment Protection (Consolidation) Act 1978, s. 49.

45. Gill *v.* Leyton Corporation, *Education*, 14 April 1933; LCT 103.

46. Education Act 1944, s. 24(2)(a).

47. Hannam *v.* Bradford Corporation (1970) 68 LGR 498.

48. Malloch *v.* Aberdeen Corporation (1971) 2 All ER 1278.

49. Haddow v. ILEA (1979) ICR 202.
50. Ward v. Bradford Corporation (1971) 70 LGR 27.
51. Weddell v. Newcastle-upon-Tyne Corporation, *Daily Telegraph*, 8 November 1973.
52. Newbigin v. Lancashire County Council, *Daily Mail*, 14 November 1973.
53. Vogler v. Hertfordshire County Council, *The Times*, 7 and 8 November 1975.
54. Simpson v. Bradford Metropolitan District Council, *The Teacher*, 13 December 1974.
55. Employment Protection (Consolidation) Act 1978, s. 64(1)(b).
56. Nothman v. London Borough of Barnet (1977) IRLR 228.
57. Crosbie v. Nottinghamshire County Council, *Education*, 31 October 1980.
58. Jones v. University of London, *The Times*, 22 March 1922.
59. Employment Protection (Consolidation) Act 1978, s. 80.
60. Jones v. Lee (1979) 78 LGR 213.
61. *Times Educational Supplement*, 2 March 1984.
62. See Gill v. Leyton Corporation (1933): p. 143.
63. R. v. Statutory Committee of the Pharmaceutical Society of Great Britain and others, *ex parte* Pharmaceutical Society of Great Britain, *The Times*, 13 November 1980.
64. R. v. Powys County Council, *ex parte* Smith (1983) 81 LGR 342.
65. Norris v. Southampton City Council, Employment Appeal Tribunal (1982) IRLR 142.
66. Gardner v. Newport Borough Council (1974) IRLR 265.
67. See p. 158.
68. Nottinghamshire County Council v. Bowly (1978) IRLR 252.
69. Norfolk County Council v. Bernard (1979) IRLR 220.
70. *Guardian*, 2 March 1983.
71. *Daily Telegraph*, 25 July 1979.
72. *Guardian*, 10 March 1984.
73. Wiseman v. Salford City Council (1981) IRLR 202.
74. Chakki v. United Yeast Co. Ltd (1981) EAT 9 December.
75. Employment Protection (Consolidation) Act 1978, s. 57(2)(b).
76. Education (Teachers) Regulations 1982.
77. Administrative Memorandum 3/82: *Misconduct of Teachers*.
78. Education (Teachers) Regulations 1982.
79. Sandhu v. London Borough of Hillingdon, *Times Educational Supplement*, 23 September 1977; *Guardian*, 9 March 1978. See also R. v. DES *ex parte* Kumar: p. 100.

80. Employment Protection (Consolidation) Act 1978, s. 23; Employment Act 1980, s. 415.
81. See p. 8.
82. See Employment Act (1980), s. 17(3).
83. See p. 149.
84. See p. 163.
85. Royle v. Trafford Borough Council (1984) IRLR 184.
86. Trade Union and Labour Relations Act 1974, s. 29(1) as amended by Employment Act 1982, s. 18.
87. Treaty of Rome (25 March 1957), Articles 52 to 58; Treaty of Accession (January 1972).
88. Circular 5/81, *Directive of the Council of the European Community on the Education of the Children of Migrant Workers.*
89. Seymour Mews House, Seymour Mews, London W1H 9PE.
90. Department of Education and Science, Pensions Branch, Mowden Hall, Staindrop Road, Darlington, Co. Durham.
91. Some benefits are subject to a means test.
92. Members of the Commonwealth.
93. Visitors and tourists may not have to bear the full cost of treatment.
94. Sickness benefit is limited.
95. Seymour Mews House, Seymour Mews, London W1H 9PE.
96. Department of Health and Social Security, Overseas Branch, Newcastle-upon-Tyne, NE98 1YX. A separate leaflet is available for each of the countries with which there is a reciprocal social security (as distinct from medical) arrangement. It is important to specify the country to be visited when requesting literature.
97. These are obtainable from the Overseas Branch, Newcastle-upon-Tyne, NE98 1YX. Of particular interest are SA36 which deals with medical treatment for visitors to EEC countries, and SA30 which is largely concerned with territories outside the Common Market.

V
Employment legislation

1 Introduction

In recent years there has been a considerable extension of legislation in the field of employment and labour relations. General law of this kind inevitably affects all kinds of employment and teaching is no exception. It is particularly important to note that some clauses in contracts are now void, at any rate in particular circumstances, because they are less favourable to the employee than the new statutory provisions require. In such circumstances the terms of the enactment are substituted for those clauses.

Sometimes the provisions of new legislation are incorporated in new contracts; in other cases it is unnecessary to do this because the legal rights are available simply by operation of the statute. This chapter can give only a brief review of some of the statutory measures.

2 Redundancy payments

The law on this matter is to be found in the Employment Protection (Consolidation) Act 1978 as amended. Redundancy occurs when employees are dismissed because the employer has ceased (or intends to cease) business, when he moves (or intends to move) his business from the place where the employees were contracted to work, or the requirements for work of a particular kind have diminished (or are expected to do so) either in the business as a whole or at the place where the employees concerned are contracted to work.

The appropriate teachers' associations must be consulted about planned redundancies *before* redundancy notices are issued. The period in advance is usually 30 or 90 days:[1] however, compulsory redundancies amongst permanently employed teachers are to date almost unknown.

Employers are required to make lump sum payments to men under 65 and women under 60 who are dismissed because of redundancy, provided they have worked for the same employer continuously for two years. The amount of the payment is related to the employee's age, pay, and length of service with the employer. The test of redundancy is that the employer needs fewer people to do work of the same kind.

Liability to the payment is excluded if the employee is dismissed either with contractual, shorter or no notice, i.e. in cases of grave misconduct, but not if the employer fails to give a written statement of the reasons for dismissal. It is also avoided, before the notice takes effect, by a formal offer (not necessarily in writing) of re-engagement with not more than four weeks' break in service. The offer must be suitable in relation to the employee; and if it is refused reasonably by the employee, the liability to the redundancy payment may still attach. If the offer is accepted, or refused unreasonably, the entitlement to redundancy payment lapses. The Employment Protection Act 1975 introduced a 'trial period' to encourage employees to judge whether the new employment really suits them.[2] The trial period runs from the end of the original employment to the end of the fourth week of the new. If the employee does not like his new work, and the industrial tribunal holds his objection to be reasonable, he may still be eligible for a redundancy payment.[3]

Dismissal by reason of redundancy may amount to unfair

dismissal, for example if the choice of employees to be made redundant is based on unfair selection.

The detailed provisions of the scheme are complex, and readers who are interested should study the relevant legislation and official guide.[4]

TAYLOR v. KENT COUNTY COUNCIL

In 1968 the Kent County Council decided to amalgamate a boys' secondary school with a similar school for girls. The appointment of the headmaster, who had held office for ten years, was terminated. The local education authority wrote to him, stating that his salary had been safeguarded and that, as he had refused a post (which was not offered in writing) in the new school, he was offered a post in the mobile pool of teachers. This meant he might be required to serve in any capacity in such schools as the authority might require, but probably in a different part of the county from that where he was actually living.

The industrial tribunal rejected the headmaster's application for a redundancy payment, basing their decision on his age, qualifications, experience, loss of status, the safeguarding of his salary and his 'unfortunate showing at the interview': 'The fact that the offer made was less suitable does not necessarily make it unsuitable.'

The Queen's Bench Division allowed the headmaster's appeal. The Lord Chief Justice, Lord Parker, said:

> Suitability is almost entirely a matter of degree and fact for the tribunal and not a matter with which this court would wish to or could, interfere, unless it was plain that they had misdirected themselves in some way in law, or had taken into consideration matters which were not relevant for the purpose. It is to be observed that so far as age was concerned, so far as experience was concerned, they negative the suitability of this offer, because the appellant is going to be put into a position where he has to go where he is told at

any time for short periods, to any place, and be put under a headmaster and assigned duties by him.

The only matter which can be put against that as making this offer suitable is the guarantee of salary. One would think, speaking for myself, that a headmaster of this experience could think an offer which, while guaranteeing him the same salary, reduced his status, was quite unsuitable. To go to quite a different sphere of activity, a director under a service agreement is offered on dismissal a job as a navvy, and it is said: but we will guarantee you the same salary as you have been getting. I should have thought such an offer was plainly unsuitable.

Here one wonders whether one of the matters which affected the tribunal was this reference to the words 'Not forgetting the unfortunate showing at the interview'. That is a reference to when he was interviewed, not by the respondents, but by the governors of the school with a view to taking on the headmastership of the new school. One really wonders what the relevance of that was unless it be that the tribunal felt from what they had heard that he was not up to a headmastership at all. But at once one says to oneself: if that was in their minds, it was not evidence on which they could properly act, having regard to the fact that the appellant had given satisfaction for some ten years, and if he was not up to his job he could have been dismissed for that reason, and no question of redundancy could have arisen.

Mr Justice Melford Stevenson and Mr Justice Willis agreed.[5]

FISHMAN v. LONDON BOROUGH OF REDBRIDGE[6]

An industrial tribunal can determine whether an employer's changed demands on his employees are reasonable. A London teacher was appointed to be head of the resources centre in a school. Subsequently the local authority instructed the teacher to undertake eighteen hours teaching per week: she refused and was dismissed. The Employment Appeal Tribunal held her dismissal to be unfair because the change in the teacher's work took too little account of the *particular* duties for which she had been appointed.

COLE v. BIRMINGHAM DISTRICT COUNCIL[7]

A part-time needlework teacher who under her contract was paid an hourly rate in respect of 'actual attendances only', was entitled to a redundancy payment based on the full hourly rate, and the local authority were not entitled to make a deduction on the ground that part of the rate related to holiday periods when no work was done.

Mr Justice Kilner-Brown said that the local authority had tried to justify a reduction by saying that a part-time worker was paid at a higher hourly rate than a full-time worker who had other benefits such as a pension and sick pay schemes. It was said that there was a built-in increment in the hourly rate for part-time teachers which was equivalent to the proportion of a full-time teacher's pay which represented holiday pay. That had not been explained to Mrs Cole when she entered into her contract. The local authority had no right to vary her contract and the teacher's appeal would be allowed.

LEE v. NOTTINGHAMSHIRE COUNTY COUNCIL

The Court of Appeal held that the law did not require redundancy to be unexpected in order to qualify for redundancy payments. Dismissal was held to be by reason of redundancy even though termination was anticipated when the appointment was made. This case has positive implications for all teachers coming to the end of fixed-term contracts of employment.[8]

In 1985 in a case which may go to the Court of Appeal the Employment Appeal Tribunal held that if a fixed-term contract is not renewed because of a reduced demand for teachers (e.g. through falling rolls), this amounts to redundancy, and appropriate payment must be made.

3   Equal pay

The Equal Pay Act 1970 imports into every contract for the employment of a woman a clause giving her equality if any term of the contract is less favourable to her than that on which a man doing like work in the same employment is engaged. Similar provisions are included for a term determined by the rating of the work where a woman is employed on work which is rateable at the same level as a man. The Act affords the same protection to men. The equality clause, however, does not apply where there is a material difference other than sex. If it is believed that different jobs are of equal value, the law since 1983 allows for compulsory job evaluation.

In a comprehensive school in Wales the master in charge of boys' physical education was paid on Burnham Scale 3, whilst the mistress in charge of girls' physical education was on Scale 2. Neither was designated as being subordinate to the other, and the mistress brought a claim for equality of payment under the Act. The industrial tribunal found that the posts were broadly similar and rejected the authority's differentiation of the teachers on grounds both of experience and merit. There was, the tribunal said, no material difference to justify inequality of pay.[9]

4   Statement of particulars

An employer is required to give each of his employees a written statement of certain terms of his contract and this must be provided within one month of the commencement of employment.[10] The statement may, for some of the required particulars, refer to relevant documents which the employee has reasonable opportunities to read. A statement is not required in connection with service for less than sixteen hours weekly, except in the case of employees who work at least eight hours a week and have five years' continuous service with the same employer.

Some authorities and voluntary school bodies incorporate the information in their agreements or letters of appointment, others issue a separate document. When the latter is done, it must be remembered that this by itself is no more than the statement required by the Act and is not a contract. There will usually also be a reference to the Burgundy Book (by its full title): a copy should be available in every school.

Information relating to pensions need not be given in respect of a statutory scheme such as that provided by the Teachers (Superannuation) Acts, and if there is no information to be given under any head, this should be stated. References to specific schemes such as the Burnham salary scales, the authority's staff code, and so forth are sufficient.

After identifying the employer and the employee, the statement must include the following particulars:

(a) date of commencement of appointment, and whether any service with a previous employer counts for the purpose of continuous employment;
(b) the scale, or rate, of salary, or the method of calculation;
(c) the intervals at which salary is paid;
(d) working hours (for teachers there is at present no national agreement);
(e) holiday entitlement, including public holidays, holiday pay (if appropriate), sick leave and pay, and pension schemes (subject to the exception noted above in respect of statutory superannuation schemes);
(f) length of notice for determination of employment. The Act[11] requires the following minima:

Continuous employment	Weeks' notice
4 weeks–2 years	1
2–12 years	1 for each complete year
12 years or more	12

These provisions supersede those in any existing contract which are less favourable to the employee. Teachers with nine or more years' completed continuous service are therefore entitled to more than two months at the end of the autumn and spring terms.

(g) the title of the appointment;

(h) disciplinary procedures;[12]
(i) grievance procedure.[13]

Any changes during employment must be notified to the employee within one month.

5   Continuous employment

The legal definition of continuous employment is of great importance to employees: for example, a woman's entitlement to maternity leave under the agreed conditions of service is dependent on the completion of twelve months' continuous employment, though not necessarily with the same employer, immediately prior to the leave. To obtain the statutory confinement leave, however, she must have two years' continuous employment with the same employer immediately before the eleventh week before the expected confinement. Qualification for a redundancy payment also depends on continuous employment, as does the right to claim unfair dismissal. Also contingent on an appropriate period of continuous employment are the right to a written statement of employment particulars, the right to a minimum period of notice, and the right to receive a written statement of reasons for dismissal.[14]

A whole week, beginning on a Sunday, is reckonable for the purposes of continuous employment if the employee works for not less than sixteen hours. During the subsistence of a contract which normally requires work for sixteen or more hours, weeks when the employee works for less than sixteen hours, or does not work at all, because of holidays, sickness or pregnancy, also count. Weeks are also reckonable in the following circumstances:

(a) if a contract ceases to exist, e.g. after sick leave: if he is re-engaged during the next twenty-six weeks, all the intervening weeks count;
(b) if there is a temporary cessation of work which is not due to the employee being on strike;

(c) during absence, whether customary or by arrangement
     where employment is regarded as being continuous;
(d) during absence due to maternity which does not qualify
     for the right to return to work, but the employee is in fact
     re-engaged, within a period of up to twenty-six weeks.

An employee who works for the same employer for a
minimum of eight hours a week, but for less than the sixteen
hours normally required to qualify for reckonable service,
becomes qualified after five years' such service for the whole
of that period to be reckoned.

An employee who has qualified for an entitlement by
completing a period of continuous employment loses that
entitlement only if his normal working week is reduced to
fewer than eight hours, in which case it lapses immediately.
An employee whose working week is reduced to less than
sixteen hours during the qualifying period for an entitlement,
however, is regarded as having still been in continuous
employment if he returns to a sixteen-hour week within twenty-
six weeks. If his working week remains below sixteen hours
he must wait until he qualifies under the five years provision
noted above.[15]

Uncertainty about staffing levels because of falling school
rolls and financial pressures has led many authorities in recent
years to increase the numbers of supply, temporary and/or
part-time staff. Where lecturers[16] are employed on a series of
sessional contracts, it now seems from case law college holiday
periods between the end of one contract of employment and
the beginning of the next do not count as breaking continuity
of service and thus, when no further work is offered, the
provisions relating to redundancy payments and unfair dismissal
apply as under the Act.[17]

Mrs Ford was a session lecturer in ceramics at a College of
Further Education for eight successive sessions before no further
work was offered by the local authority. She claimed that her
dismissal was unfair or that she was at least entitled to a
redundancy payment under the Act. An industrial tribunal
held,[18] following earlier decisions of the Employment Appeal

Tribunal[19] and of the Scottish Court of Session,[20] that where a fixed-term contract expired and there was an interval before another fixed-term contract came into effect, the reason for the employee's absence was that there was no contract of employment, not that there was no work to do. A teacher who voluntarily takes employment for a fixed period of time with no guarantee of renewal cannot be said to be absent from work awaiting re-employment.

Mrs Ford fought her case through to the House of Lords. The five Law Lords reversed the earlier decisions against Mrs Ford by the Employment Appeal Tribunal and the Court of Appeal. 'From the fact that there is no work available for the employee to do for the employer during the whole of the interval between the end of one fixed-term contract of employment and the beginning of the next and that this was the reason for his non-employment during that interval, it does not necessarily follow that the interval constitutes a "temporary cessation of work"': however, looking back 'from the date of the expiry of the fixed-term contract ... over the whole period in which the employee has been intermittently employed by the same employer, in order to see whether the interval between one fixed-term contract and the fixed-term contract which next preceded it was short in duration relative to the combined duration of those two fixed-term contracts during which work has continued; for the whole scheme of the Act appears to me to show that it is in the sense of "transient", i.e. lasting only for a short time that the word "temporary" is used.... This was not a question to which the industrial tribunal ever addressed their minds.'

It is important to bear in mind however that the length of successive fixed-term contracts on which part-time lecturers and teachers are employed and the intervals between them vary considerably with the work involved, and that *Ford v. Warwickshire* does not automatically set a precedent. However, it is clear that employers cannot prevent employment protection rights from accruing by the use of fixed-term contracts. Short-term contracts of one or two years can be exempt from protection if the employee agrees.

Teachers in voluntary and former direct grant schools are no longer at a disadvantage. At one time, teachers whose continuous experience was in more than one type of school — for example, a number of years in a voluntary school followed by some years in a county school — were disadvantaged because the change of employer was deemed to have broken continuity of service.

From August 1983 such service has been regarded as continuous for the purposes of redundancy payments.[21]

The employers who are required to aggregate service in connection with the calculation by them of redundancy payments include the following:

(a) County Councils, the GLC, District Councils, London Borough Councils, the City of London and the Isles of Scilly.
(b) Governing bodies of voluntary schools.
(c) Proprietors of schools for the time being recognized as grammar schools for the purposes of the Direct Grant Schools Regulations.

The Order also defines the employers with whom previous service will be recognized as continuous and these employers include:

1. The bodies in paragraphs (a)–(c).
2. The Secretary of State for Defence in relation only to employees in schools administered by the Service Children's Education Authority.
3. The persons responsible for the management of an assisted community home.

6 Constructive dismissal

Dismissal is usually regarded as the act of an employer. In certain circumstances, however, it is possible for an employee to leave his work, with or without notice, by reason of the employer's conduct and to claim that he had been treated in such a way that it would have been justifiable for him to leave without notice.[22] He can then ask an industrial tribunal to declare that the employer has behaved in such a way as to construct his dismissal. To do this he must 'indicate that he regards himself as forced to leave and has to show that it was reasonable for him to do so'.[23]

Two forms of conduct can give rise to an allegation of constructive dismissal. In the first the employer shows quite clearly by his treatment of the employee that he has no intention of being bound by one or more of the terms of the contract of employment; the other occurs when the employer treats the employee in such a way that it amounts to a breach of a fundamental implied term and the employee could not be expected to continue in his work. Lord Denning clearly considers the former to be the more important: 'The new test of unreasonable conduct is too indefinite by far. It has led to findings of constructive dismissal on the most whimsical grounds.'[24] It has further been held that: 'You have to look at the conduct of the party whose behaviour is challenged and determine whether it is such that its effect judged reasonably and sensibly is to disable the other party from properly carrying out his or her obligations.'[25] Such conduct could bring about a repudiation of contract.

The availability of a complaint of constructive dismissal makes it highly desirable that employees who resign should be asked to state their reasons for doing so, and this is particularly important when the employee walks out without giving notice. If such a statement cannot be obtained in writing, a careful note should be made of any verbal explanations which are given.

In 1982 kitchen assistants at a Cambridgeshire infants' school had their working hours reduced from $17\frac{1}{2}$ to $7\frac{1}{2}$ hours per week – to below the eight hour limit prescribed in the Employment Protection (Consolidation) Act. Realizing that they would lose the right to unfair dismissal and redundancy protection, they resigned and claimed that they had been dismissed.

An industrial tribunal supported their claim. Although their contract had a clause which enabled the local authority to vary their hours, the tribunal noted that the authority could not reduce their hours below the statutory eight, 'otherwise it would enable any employer who draws up a contract with a variation clause completely to defeat the purpose of the Act.'[26] The Employment Appeal Tribunal decided that these clauses were invalid.

7 Fair and unfair dismissal

A dismissal may be fair if it is:

(a) for a reason related to the qualifications or capability of the employee for performing the work for which he is employed, assessed by reference to skill, aptitude, health or any other physical or mental quality;
(b) for a reason related to conduct;[27]
(c) because of redundancy;
(d) for contravention of a statutory duty or restriction;[28]
(e) for failure to join a union which is the subject of a union membership agreement ('closed shop') based on a valid membership agreement;[29]
(f) for some other substantial reason: an employer may advance this argument in relation to the dismissal of temporary staff, if, for example, an employee unreasonably refuses a change of employment terms.

An employee who has been dismissed may, if he has been continuously employed by the employer for sixteen hours a week for a period of twenty-six weeks, request a statement giving reasons for his dismissal. Such a statement must be given within fourteen days of the request being made, and may be produced in evidence. It is important, therefore, that it should be accurate and clear. Statements should not be given if the employee left of his own volition, i.e. when he alleges constructive dismissal. The employee should be asked to endorse the employer's copy of the statement, and a note made of any refusal to do so.

Dismissal on the following grounds is unfair:

(a) because the employee is, or proposes to become, a member of an independent trade union;

(b) because the employee has taken, or proposes to take, part at an appropriate time in the activities of an independent trade union;

(c) because the employee has refused, or proposes to refuse, to become a member of a trade union. (An independent trade union is one which is not under the domination or control of an employer, a group of employers, or one or more employers' associations, and is not subject to interference by an employer, or any such group or association.) In such cases no qualifying period of continuous employment is needed.

(d) because the employee is pregnant.

Complaints of unfair dismissal are heard by an industrial tribunal. There is an appeal, on points of law only, to the Employment Appeal Tribunal. Employer and trade union interests are represented in the membership of the tribunal at both levels, and the chairman must be legally qualified. The Employment Appeal Tribunal has the status of the High Court, and is presided over by a High Court judge.

The remedy for unfair dismissal is reinstatement or re-engagement, and the tribunal must explain this to the applicant, asking whether he wishes such an order to be made.[30] A reinstated employee must be treated in all respects as though he had never been dismissed; re-engagement requires employment in comparable, or other suitable, employment. Any detailed provisions in individual cases are specified in the order. Although an applicant may be willing for such an order to be made, the tribunal is not bound to do so if, in all the circumstances, it would not be just. There is no machinery for enforcing such an order, but a punitive award can be ordered against a recalcitrant employer. In cases involving teachers reinstatement is not very common.

If neither reinstatement nor re-engagement is appropriate, the tribunal may make a basic compensation order. In addition, there may be a compensatory award for a sum which is just and equitable in all the circumstances, to include immediate loss of wages, loss of future wages, and elements arising from the manner of the dismissal and loss of protection.[31] Such an order may not exceed the current maximum allowed.

In 1982 four 'dinner ladies' who refused to join a trade union under a 'closed shop' agreement operated by Walsall Metropolitan Borough Council were awarded a total of £10,568 in compensation and back pay, under the Employment Act 1980.[32]

In aided schools, teachers are appointed to the service of the governors although they are paid by the local education authority.

Since the Employment Act of 1980 an employee in a firm of twenty or fewer employees must complete two years' service to qualify for entitlement to bring an allegation of unfair dismissal: similarly an employer of fewer than five employees cannot be compelled to reinstate a woman at the end of her maternity leave if it is not reasonably practical for him to do so.

The effect of this would be to put at a disadvantage, *vis-à-vis* colleagues in county schools, those teachers working in small aided schools. Such teachers were brought into line with colleagues elsewhere by the Employment Act 1982.

8 Calculation of awards

An industrial tribunal calculates compensation for employment protection rights as follows:[33]

(A) UNFAIR DISMISSAL

Basic award: An award of $\frac{1}{2}$ to $1\frac{1}{2}$ weeks' pay depending on age for each year of continuous service subject to maxima of 20 years and £4,350.[34]

Compensatory award: An amount which the tribunal considers just and equitable up to £11,700.

Additional award: Where the terms of an order for re-employment are not fully complied with the tribunal may make an award up to £7,500.

Where an order for re-employment has not been complied with and the reason for dismissal was sex or race discrimination, an *additional* award of between 26 and 52 weeks' pay must be made.

Where an order for re-employment has not been complied with, and the dismissal was for some other reason, except trade union membership, activities or non-membership, an additional award of between 13 and 26 weeks must be made.

(B)   REDUNDANCY PAYMENTS

The amount of redundancy is calculated in the same way as the basic award for unfair dismissal. Many local education authorities however use the *actual* week's salary earned by the teacher, not the statutory minimum figure, which is usually lower. This is, however, at the employer's discretion, although regulations to make it mandatory have been promised.

9   Temporary staff

The first point to remember is that employment legislation does not recognize the term 'temporary staff' so commonly heard in educational circles. The Employment Appeal Tribunal, moreover, has suggested that it should not be used as it can mean different things to different people.[35] So far as the law is concerned the only relevant fact in determining whether an applicant is entitled to be heard is whether he has, or has not, acquired sufficient continuous service. It is immaterial whether his employment is described as permanent or temporary. This section is concerned with teachers whose temporary appointment is terminable by notice.

In settling the fairness or otherwise of a temporary employee's dismissal, the nature of the employment must be examined. To be fair, dismissal must be for one of the reasons laid down, and the mere fact that the engagement was of a temporary nature is not, of itself, enough. The employer must have acted reasonably in all the circumstances, and it is important that the temporary nature of engagement should be made clear at the outset. This limitation should be accepted in writing by the employee at that time and on any occasion that the contract is renewed on a temporary basis.

If a person is engaged temporarily to cover absence due to sickness, medical suspension or maternity leave, the return of the permanent member of the staff may be advanced as a substantial reason.[36] Nevertheless, the employer must have acted reasonably. It is possible that this approach might be extended by analogy to some other temporary appointments.

Temporary employees are entitled to the statutory minimum periods of notice, notwithstanding the fact that their standard conditions of service may provide for shorter periods. There is no statutory minimum for those engaged under a contract to perform a particular task which, it is expected, will last for not more than twelve weeks. If, in fact, it then lasts longer a right may be acquired.

10   Fixed-term contracts

Failure by the employer to renew a fixed-term contract is statutory dismissal and, if challenged, the employer must be prepared to justify that dismissal as fair. Many fixed-term contracts contain a provision for prior termination; it has been held that this does not in itself mean that the contract is not for a fixed term.[37]

In order to be heard in a claim for unfair dismissal in this manner an employee must, of course, have acquired the necessary period of continuous service. An employee under a fixed-term contract for one year or more can waive his unfair dismissal and redundancy rights in writing before the end of the period.

11   Part-time employees

Since 1 February 1977 employees who work for sixteen hours a week, or more, are in service which counts towards continuous employment for the assessment of entitlement to statements of particulars of employment, statutory periods of notice, maternity leave, protection against dismissal, statements of reasons for dismissal and redundancy payments. Similarly, those who work for eight hours a week but less than sixteen for the same employer for a continuous period of five years are qualified.

There are problems in connection with teachers' service as there is no definition of a teacher's hours of work. The author of the *'Education' Guide to Industrial Relations* writes:

It may probably be assumed, at least until the contrary is shown, that the appropriate hours for primary and secondary teachers are those during which the school is open and pupils are being taught, and that the lunch hour is not included. In further education the position is more complicated because of the existence of the separate concepts of contact hours and total hours. Again, it seems logical to assume initially that for those part-timers who are paid on an hourly basis, the hours of work are those for which they are paid, while for those (a minority) paid on a proportional basis, the hours will be calculated pro rata to thirty per week, which are the total hours for full-time staff under existing conditions of service.[38]

Mrs Jane Lake, a part-time teacher at Hockley in Essex from 1973 to 1976, provided the contrary evidence. Legislation at the time made it necessary to work for twenty-one hours a week in order to qualify for the right to be heard. Originally employed for about eighteen hours a week, her hours were subsequently extended to nineteen hours and twenty-five minutes. *Prima facie* she did not qualify for protection against unfair dismissal. She claimed, however, that there are other obligations which require all teachers to work outside the time during which they are on duty at school. The three hours and forty minutes 'free time' allowed during school hours were insufficient, since part of this time was spent supervising children out of class. As a result, she said, she was employed for more than twenty-one hours a week and was entitled to protection.

The Council maintained that Mrs Lake was employed to work only during the hours specified in her letter of engagement. The Employment Appeal Tribunal did not agree. Remitting the case to a different industrial tribunal to decide whether she had, in fact, worked more than twenty-one hours a week and had been unfairly dismissed, Mr Justice Bristow said:

> We take it to be clear law that what is expressed in a written contract does not necessarily include all the contractual rights and obligations of the parties.... Quite irrespective of the 'free time', if a teacher found it necessary to spend time outside her on-duty-at-school time in preparation or in marking, there must in our judgment be a contractual obligation to do so, whether it is written into her contract or not. If this headmaster had said: 'Mrs Lake, that lesson was quite insufficiently prepared', would she have retorted: 'I don't have time to prepare lessons outside school hours'? In our judgment, obviously not.
>
> Accordingly, in our judgment, Mrs Lake was under a contractual obligation to the Council to do as much work outside the school hours specified in her contract as was reasonably necessary for the proper performance of her teaching duties in school hours, and that work outside school hours was employment normally involved in the performance of her contract which must be included in the computation of the twenty-one hours for the purpose of paragraph 9(1)(f) in order to see whether her right not to be unfairly dismissed was excluded.[39]

The Court of Appeal subsequently overturned this decision. The Court felt that a term requiring a teacher to do such work as would enable him properly to perform his teaching duties is too vague to be implied in a contract between a teacher and an employer. Mr Justice Lane said: 'If Mrs Lake and Essex County Council had been asked: "if Mrs Lake did not do *all* that was necessary for efficient teaching, would she have been dismissed?" – I doubt that either party would have agreed.'[40]

12   Discrimination

The employment provisions of the Sex Discrimination Act 1975 and the Race Relations Act 1976 are considered in chapter XIII.

13   Voluntary-aided schools

UNION MEMBERSHIP AGREEMENTS

A local education authority cannot apply a union membership agreement, if it has one, to teachers in voluntary-aided schools. If, however, the Articles of Government enable the authority to determine the conditions of service of non-teaching staff, it is possible that such agreements may be imposed on such staff as part of the conditions.

DISCIPLINARY PROCEDURES

Disciplinary procedures in voluntary-aided schools come within the province of the Articles of Government. The regulations of the local education authority, as distinct from those of the Secretary of State, are not imported wholesale into the Articles, unless the Articles specifically provide for this. It is rare for the Articles of secondary schools to include such a provision. In such circumstances the local education authority's disciplinary procedures are not binding on such schools, unless they are adopted by the governors to such extent as does not conflict with the Articles.

REDUNDANCY

If a teacher in a voluntary-aided school is made redundant, and is then offered employment in a county school by the maintaining authority, that amounts to an offer of alternative employment. It therefore follows that if such an offer is refused unreasonably the teacher loses all rights to a redundancy payment.

DISMISSAL

If a teacher in a voluntary-aided school is dismissed by the governors on the instructions of the local education authority, any complaint of unfair dismissal lies against the authority. Any remedy ordered will be ordered against the authority.[41]

14   Rehabilitation of Offenders Act 1974

The provisions of this Act are important for teachers giving references for *non-teaching* posts. Rehabilitation of offenders is designed to assist those who have been in trouble with the law to make a fresh start, provided they have not been sentenced to more than two-and-a-half years' imprisonment, and also that they have not been convicted again of an indictable offence during the period of rehabilitation. At the end of this period the conviction is, for most purposes, said to be 'spent'.

The effects of this are far-reaching. Subject to certain exceptions, a spent conviction need not be disclosed in applying for work, for admission to a profession or occupation, or to join an organization. Nor need it be revealed in making a proposal for insurance or hire-purchase. A rehabilitated person may refuse to answer a question about his own, or anyone else's, spent convictions in civil proceedings in courts unless the court is satisfied that justice cannot otherwise be done. If, on the other hand, he does disclose such information on oath, he must do so truthfully. In most circumstances, therefore, a rehabilitated person who is asked whether he has ever been convicted may answer in the negative.

Similarly, no rehabilitated person may be refused employment or admission to a profession or occupation, neither may he be dismissed or prejudiced, because of spent convictions, nor because he failed to disclose any conviction which was spent at the time he was questioned. It is an offence to disclose someone else's spent conviction, whether from official records or otherwise, except in the course of duty.

Generally speaking, convictions in the armed services, and

offences committed abroad are treated similarly. In the case of foreign convictions, however, there may be no comparable arrangements in the country in which the offence was committed. In those circumstances it is not possible to treat a conviction as spent in that country. Spent convictions overseas should be disclosed in application for visas or immigration permits, as rehabilitation may not be effective in the country to which admission is sought.

The rehabilitation periods are as follows:

Sentence	Rehabilitation period	Rehabilitation period runs from
6 months–2½ years	10 years[42]	Date of conviction
6 months or less	7 years[42]	Date of conviction
Community service order, fine or order not otherwise specified	5 years[42]	Date of conviction
Absolute discharge	6 months	Date of conviction
Probation, conditional discharge, binding-over, care order	Expiry of order (minimum, 1 year)	Date of conviction
Remand home, approved school, attendance centre	1 year	Expiry of order
Hospital order	5 years (at least 2 years after expiry)	Date of conviction
Young offenders:		
Borstal	7 years	Date of conviction
Detention for 6 months–2½ years	5 years	Date of conviction
Detention for 6 months or less	3 years	Date of conviction
Detention centre	3 years	Date of conviction

If a person is convicted of an indictable offence during a period of rehabilitation, whether or not it is tried in the Crown Court, his rehabilitation period is extended if the end of rehabilitation for the second offence is later than that for the first. Neither offence is treated as spent until both rehabilitation periods have expired. A rehabilitation period is not extended on conviction of an offence which is triable only in a magistrates' court. The period following a penalty imposed for breach of probation or conditional discharge is that for the penalty imposed.

If a period of disqualification, e.g. from holding a driving licence, exceeds the rehabilitation period, the offence is not spent until the disqualification expires.

There are no provisions for rehabilitation in respect of prison sentences of more than two and a half years, life sentences, preventive detention, and their equivalents for young offenders. Suspended sentences are treated as though they had been put into effect.

For *teaching* posts there are certain exceptions to the rule that a spent offence need not be disclosed. The Rehabilitation of Offenders (Exceptions) Order 1975 designates some twenty-two categories of employment in which a rehabilitated person must disclose spent conviction when applying for appointment provided he is told at the time that he should do so.[43] Whilst he will not be liable to any penalty in law for failing to do so, there are occupations where the existence of a spent conviction is regarded as a valid reason for refusing employment, or for dismissal. It follows that, should a spent conviction come to light in these circumstances, dismissal may well follow. Teaching, whether in schools (including independent schools) or further education establishments, employment involving access to persons under the age of eighteen, the service of youth and cadet forces, appointments in social services involving access to the young or the handicapped, the National Health Service insofar as it involves access to patients, the police, and the probation service are among those listed as exceptions. In Scotland where, unlike England and Wales, there is a professional register of teachers, spent convictions may be taken into account in assessing a person's suitability for admission to the register.

Spent convictions may also be considered in dealing, among others, with applications for licences to employ persons under the age of eighteen abroad, and for the registration of homes for the elderly, disabled, handicapped and (in Scotland) children.

The Act is of great importance to teachers, partly because their profession is one in which rehabilitation does not give an unrestricted right of employment. Candidates may be asked about spent convictions; and it is important, when this is done, to remind them that .they are not protected by the Act from disclosure.

There is another aspect with which teachers, particularly heads, are concerned when they are writing references for colleagues, for pupils and for former pupils. In such circumstances it is not defamatory to make a statement that the subject of the reference has a spent conviction if, at the time of writing, it is believed to be true and is not made maliciously. This defence is destroyed under the Act if irrelevant defamatory comments of this nature are introduced gratuitously, even if they are true. Needless to say, no improper use may be made of official records for this purpose.

Spent convictions need not be mentioned in references unless the Exceptions Order applies to the occupation, appointment or licence which is being sought. It is, therefore, essential that teachers should be aware of the provisions of the Order as set out in the *Guide*.

References

1. NUT *v.* Avon County Council (1978) IRLR 55. See also Part IV Employment Protection Act 1975: Variation Order 1979, S.I. no. 958.
2. Now: Employment Protection (Consolidation) Act 1978, s. 82(6).
3. Employment Protection (Consolidation) Act 1978, ss. 81–4.
4. Employment Protection (Consolidation) Act 1978, Part IV, and the *Redundancy Payments Scheme*. (HMSO).
5. Taylor *v.* Kent County Council [1969] 2 All ER 1080; LCT 398.
6. Fishman *v.* London Borough of Redbridge (1978) IRLR 69.
7. Cole *v.* Birmingham District Council, *The Times*, 23 June 1978.
8. Lee *v.* Nottinghamshire County Council, *The Times*, 28 April 1980.

9. Taylor v. Powys County Council, *The Teacher*, 30 April 1976.
10. Employment Protection (Consolidation) Act 1978, s. 1. as amended by the Employment Act 1982.
11. Employment Protection (Consolidation) Act 1978, s. 49(1).
12. See p. 135.
13. See p. 129.
14. Employment Protection (Consolidation) Act 1978, s. 53.
15. Employment Protection (Consolidation) Act 1978, s. 3(4).
16. Teachers in schools are rarely, if ever, appointed to such contracts, but the law does not forbid it.
17. Employment Protection (Consolidation) Act 1978.
18. Ford v. Warwickshire County Council (1982) IRLR 246.
19. Rashid v. ILEA (1977) ICR 157.
20. Tayside Regional Council v. Moncrieff EAT/563/80.
21. Redundancy Payments (Local Government) (Modification) Order 1983. See also Employment Protection Act 1982.
22. Employment Protection (Consolidation) Act, 1978, s. 55(2)(c).
23. Devon County Council v. Cook (1977) IRLR 188. See also Ahmad v. ILEA, p. 127.
24. Western Excavating (EEC) Ltd v. Sharp (1978) ICR 221.
25. Roberts v. Post Office (1980) IRLR 347.
26. *Times Educational Supplement*, 19 March 1982.
27. Unless the conduct is so serious that there is no alternative to dismissal, the employee should have been informed in writing, at least once previously, that further misconduct could lead to dismissal. He should have had the opportunity to mend his ways after this warning. The incident actually leading to dismissal must be properly investigated, and the employee given an opportunity to explain his conduct. Even in cases of gross misconduct justifying instant dismissal, there should be the opportunity for explanation.
28. This was the defence advanced by the local education authority in Sandhu v. London Borough of Hillingdon, when a teacher had failed his probationary service. See p. 158.
29. In order to be valid, union membership agreements coming into operation after 14 August 1980 must be initially approved by a ballot of not less than 80 per cent of those entitled to vote. From 1 November 1984 for any union membership agreement to be relied on it must have been supported in a secret ballot by not less than 80 per cent of those entitled to vote or by 85 per cent of those actually voting. The ballot must have been

held within the five years preceding the date of a dismissal. Employment Act 1982, s. 3.

30. Employment Protection (Consolidation) Act 1978, s. 68(1).
31. Norton Tool Co. Ltd *v*. Tewson (1972) ICR 501.
32. *Daily Telegraph*, 23 March 1982.
33. These figures are reviewed annually.
34. The nationally agreed week's pay is currently £152 for this purpose.
35. Cohen *v*. London Borough of Barking (1976) IRLR 416.
36. Employment Protection (Consolidation) Act 1978, s. 61.
37. Dixon *v*. British Broadcasting Corporation (1978) ICR 387; (1979) 2 All ER 112.
38. Christopher Curson, *'Education' Guide to Industrial Relations*, Swift Publications Ltd for Councils and Education Press Ltd (1977).
39. Lake *v*. Essex County Council (1977) IRLR 24, EAT.
40. Lake *v*. Essex County Council (1979) 77 LGR 708 CA.
41. Employment Protection (Consolidation) Act 1978, s. 80.
42. These periods are halved for offenders under 17 at the date of their conviction.
43. A complete list may be found in *A Guide to the Rehabilitation of Offenders Act 1974* (HMSO, 1975).

VI
Health and Safety

1 History

At common law employment does not involve a guarantee that an employer will never expose his staff to risk, although he must take reasonable care to provide safe premises and equipment. The remedy for injuries due to negligence is by means of an action for damages. In addition, however, Parliament has, since the early years of the last century, laid an increasing burden of duty on employers to operate their workplaces safely.

The first legislation dealing with the health of people at work was the Health and Morals of Apprentices Act 1802, which required factories where pauper children were apprenticed to be properly ventilated and whitewashed annually. The Factory Act 1833 provided *inter alia* that machinery was not to be cleaned whilst in operation, and the first four inspectors were appointed to monitor the working of the Act. Early legislation, however, was principally concerned with the working hours of women and children, and it was not until the 1840s that there was a significant flow of legislation dealing with dangers to the health and safety of workers in high-risk industries. The nineteenth-century enactments were largely codified in the Factory and Workshops Act 1901, and specialist inspectors were appointed to secure the enforcement of the law in factories, mines and other places to which the Acts applied.

The Offices, Shops and Railway Premises Act 1963 was the first statute of this kind to affect schools, since its requirements extended to those parts of a school building used for administrative purposes: the school office, the head's room, and rooms set aside as offices for members of the staff. It was a moot point, never resolved, whether it applied to staff common rooms.

This Act so extended the protection of health and safety legislation that two thirds of people at work were covered by the enactments, but the law was piecemeal, being spread through some thirty statutes and almost five hundred statutory instruments. Moreover, it was only in mining that a direct criminal liability was imposed on managers as well as employers. In 1960 a committee was established under the chairmanship of Lord Robens to consider the whole question of occupational risks, including danger to the public arising from work. The committee reported in 1972, recommending that the emphasis of new legislation should be on the personal responsibility of those who created risks, and those who worked with them, rather than on external regulation. Concern for health and safety was, henceforth, to be a primary element of good management.

The report was accepted by the Government in May 1973, the Bill received the Royal Assent on 31 July 1974, and the main provisions of the Health and Safety at Work etc. Act 1974 came into force on 1 April 1975.

2   The scope of the Act

The Act is designed to secure the health, safety and welfare of all persons at work, and of all other persons, against risks arising out of the activities of people at work. This includes the control of dangerous substances and the control of noxious and offensive emissions into the atmosphere.[1] The word 'work' in the statute includes work by self-employed persons.[2]

It must be remembered that the Health and Safety at Work etc. Act is largely an enabling measure: that is to say it confers powers enabling the promulgation of regulations to secure its implementation. These regulations, if properly made, have the force of law. Thus the Act itself is concerned only with general duties in the widest terms and with the setting up of structures. The general duties do little more than reaffirm the common law. Where new regulations and codes are made in respect of forms of work already covered by the legislation listed in Schedule 1 of the Act, the previous law is repealed automatically on replacement, provided that the new requirements do not impose a lower standard. Until the new regulations are made existing law remains in force.[3]

3   The Commission, the Executive and other bodies

The Health and Safety Commission is a corporation of between six and nine persons, and is responsible to Parliament for the replacement of existing statutes and regulations by new regulations and codes, for assisting and encouraging people to fulfil the general purposes of the Act, for providing an information and advisory service, for submitting proposals for new regulations to the Government, and for investigating any accident or occurrence when it considers this to be necessary.[4]

The Health and Safety Executive (HSE) is a corporation of three persons, and is the employer of the Health and Safety inspectorate.[5] The Executive exercises any functions of the Commission which may be delegated to it, but its principal responsibility is the enforcement of the law except insofar as the Secretary of State may have delegated this duty to another authority.[6]

Local authorities exercise such enforcement roles as may be designated or transferred by regulations[7] from the Executive by the Secretary of State.

The Employment Medical Advisory Service is responsible

for advising the Government on matters of health, and for informing workers about safeguards and improvements.[8]

EDUCATION SERVICE GROUP

The Health and Safety Executive has set up an Education Service Group. The main task of that group is to co-ordinate and advise on the activities of HSE inspectors visiting educational establishments and to liaise nationally with the Education Departments and various professional bodies. This Group is at present based at the HSE's North-East London Area Office.[9] In addition to the responsibility already described, the inspectors in this Group are responsible for the health and safety inspection of educational establishments across London and also provide the secretariat for the Health and Safety Commission's Education Service Advisory Committee set up in 1982. Other authorities may, by arrangement with the Commission, be given powers to exercise functions under the Act.[10]

4   General duties (employers and self-employed persons)

Every employer must, so far as is reasonably practicable, ensure the health, safety and welfare of all his employees and, in particular, he must:

(a) provide and maintain safe plant and systems of work;
(b) provide safe arrangements for the use, storage and transport of articles and other substances;
(c) provide information, instruction, training and supervision;
(d) maintain a safe place of work, including means of access and egress that are safe and without risks;
(e) provide a safe and healthy working environment which is adequate as regards facilities and arrangements for welfare at work.[11]

In addition, every employer must prepare and, when appropriate, revise a written statement of his policy on health and safety at work, including arrangements for its implementation. He must draw the attention of his employees to this statement.[12]

Every employer, and every self-employed person, must ensure that persons other than their employees are not exposed to risks to their health or safety.[13]

An employer may not charge his employees for anything which he does or provides in discharge of his duties under the Act.[14]

5 General duties (persons in control of premises)

Duties are also imposed on those who have to any extent the control of non-domestic premises made available as a place of work or for carrying on a trade, business or other undertaking, whether for profit or not.[15] They must, so far as it is reasonably practicable, ensure that the premises under their control, including the means of access and egress and any plant or substances in the premises, are safe without risk to the health of any persons using the premises, whether employees or not. They must take such measures as are reasonable, having regard to their position, to ensure this.[16]

Under the Articles of Government, the head teacher provides the senior management of the school. However the statutory obligations imposed on the local education authority under the Act cannot be imposed on head teachers against their will and without contractual formalities. Head teachers and others do, however, have a clear obligation to assist the local education authority to carry out its obligations, and the local education authority's instructions and directions are binding on schools.

The duty of an employer to take reasonable steps to ensure the safety of the environment in which employees work formed the background to a case in the Court of Appeal. A teacher was assaulted by a violent 11-year-old pupil and in consequence was forced into early retirement. The pupil had a known record of violence. However, in order to bring an action against her employer the teacher needed access to the files on the pupil, which included the psychologists' reports. The local education authority claimed that the files were confidential and that access should be denied.

The Court of Appeal relied on section 31 of the Administration of Justice Act 1970, to the effect that '... on the application of a person who appears to the High Court to be a party to subsequent proceedings ... for personal injuries ... the High Court shall have power to order a person ... likely ... to have ... documents relevant to the issue ... to disclose whether such documents are in his possession and ... to produce those documents.' Having examined the files on the pupil, the court held that they were 'of crucial importance' in determining whether the local education authority knew, or should have known, of the pupil's violent tendencies, and whether he should have been allowed to attend the teacher's classes. The court ordered the local authority to open the files to the teacher so that she might take her action further.[17]

6 General duties (all employees)

The Act enjoins every employee, whilst he is at work, to take reasonable care for his own health and safety, as well as that of others who may be affected by his acts or omissions. He must also co-operate with his employer as regards any duty or requirement which may be imposed so far as it may be necessary for the discharge of that duty or requirement.[18]

No-one may interfere intentionally or recklessly with anything provided in the interests of health, safety or welfare in pursuance of any statutory provision.[19]

7 General duties (suppliers)

Designers, manufacturers, importers or suppliers of any article for use at work must ensure that, so far as is reasonably practicable:

(a) the article is designed and constructed so as to be safe, and without risks to health, when properly used;

(b) adequate testing and examination takes place to ensure that these requirements are achieved;

(c) adequate information is provided about its intended use, and the conditions necessary to ensure that, when used for that purpose, it will be safe and without risks to health.[20]

Installers of equipment must, so far as is reasonably practicable, ensure that it is installed so that it is safe in use.[21]

Similar requirements apply to the manufacturers, importers and suppliers of any substance used at work.[22]

8   Safety representatives

Regulations[23] have been made under the Act prescribing the circumstances in which trade unions may appoint safety representatives. The representatives are appointed on behalf of those groups of workers for whom the union has negotiating rights. By agreement between the unions concerned, a safety representative may be appointed to represent members of more than one union. They should have had at least two years' experience in similar employment. Safety representatives are expected to know the legal requirements relating to health and safety, especially insofar as they affect the colleagues whom they represent, they should be aware of the particular hazards at the place of work, and they should know their employer's health and safety policy and the arrangements made to implement it. Their duty is to co-operate between the employer and his employees, and to bring to the former's notice (usually in writing) any unsafe or unhealthy conditions or working practice, or any other unsatisfactory arrangements. No legal liability is imposed on a safety representative other than that which he has as an employee. Representatives must be allowed time off, with pay, for the performance of their duties, and for training, and they must have means of access to their employer.

Safety representatives may make inspections of a general nature, they may undertake safety sampling, or they may survey dangerous activities, processes or areas. They may make special investigations following an accident or other dangerous occurrence. Employers are required to provide them with relevant information.

9   Safety committees

If requested to do so, an employer must, in certain circumstances, establish a safety committee within three months of a request for its formation being made.[24] Such a request must come from two or more safety representatives. The committee is responsible for keeping under review the measures taken to ensure the health, safety and welfare of the employees. It is also expected to help with the development of the health and safety programme, to evaluate the effectiveness of employee training, and to liaise with the appropriate health and safety inspectorate.

Membership of the committee is settled by consultation between the management and the trade union representatives. Not more than half the committee should be drawn from the management side. They should meet as often as necessary, and copies of their minutes should be sent to each safety representative and to the most senior executive responsible for health and safety.[25]

10   Regulations and codes of practice

Regulations, such as those dealing with safety representatives and safety committees, are made by the Secretary of State for Employment in the form of statutory instruments. As such they have the force of law and it is an offence not to comply with them.

Codes of practice are issued or approved by the Health and Safety Commission. In themselves they are not legislative rules and there are no penalties for failing to observe them, except where a statute or regulation is incorporated in the code. However, a person accused of a statutory offence may find that his failure to adhere to the recommendations of the code has provided the means by which his guilt is established.

The best known code of practice is the Highway Code, and

an example from this may serve to illustrate the point. In the Code motorists are recommended not to park opposite a traffic refuge. This is not, in itself, an offence. A motorist may be charged with obstruction (which is an offence at law) and find that, because he parked opposite a refuge, his failure to observe what the Highway Code recommends as good practice is sufficient evidence of his guilt. He will, nevertheless, be convicted of obstruction, not of parking opposite a refuge.

11   First Aid regulations

The Health and Safety (First Aid) Regulations came into force on 1 July 1982, accompanied by a detailed code of practice and guidance notes.[26]

First aid must be 'adequate and appropriate', and available for employees who become ill or are injured at work. Pupils' first aid needs are not covered by these regulations. Every workplace must have 'such number of suitable persons as is adequate and appropriate in the circumstances responsible for rendering first aid', not necessarily a fully-trained first-aider, though a person is not deemed to be suitable unless he has undergone training approved by the Health and Safety Executive. Exceptionally it may be satisfactory merely to appoint a person to take charge of first aid requirements.

The appointed person must take charge in any accident or illness. The employer must provide an appointed person in all working hours and bear in mind the need to cover for the absence of appointed persons.

A duty is laid on every employer to inform every staff member of first aid arrangements. There should be at least one conspicuous notice stating first aid equipment locations and facilities with the names of people concerned. Such notices ideally should be written in all languages commonly spoken on the premises.

A useful guide to first aid is published by the British Red Cross Society, St John and St Andrew's Ambulance Association.[27]

The regulations prescribe penalties for infringement. These

depend on the court's assessment, but on conviction on indictment may extend to unlimited fine, or on summary conviction, a fine not exceeding £1,000.[28]

12   Notifiable dangerous occurrences

From 1 January 1981 every employer must give immediate notice to Factory Inspectors or other Enforcement Officers of certain notifiable dangerous occurrences.

These are mishaps which, because of their nature, have serious injurious potential or could cause serious ill health, even though they may not have caused any injury or damage to health.

Fourteen kinds of mishap are identified under Part 1 of Schedule 1 of the Notification of Accidents and Dangerous Occurrences Regulations. Clearly many of these are unlikely to occur in schools but, in principle, employers should issue guidance to schools. Such accidents would include fire or explosion involving electrical short circuit or overload; collapse or partial collapse of buildings; inhalation or ingestion or absorption of any substance − in any of which circumstances somebody could sustain serious injury.[29]

13   Protecting the public

Disasters like that at Flixborough, which occurred in June 1974 whilst the Health and Safety Bill was before Parliament, have drawn attention to the public risk attendant on large-scale industrial plants. Yet it is as great a personal tragedy for one bystander to be injured by something beyond his control which arises from the activity of a single person at work. The Act, therefore, extends its protection to 'persons other than persons at work', that is, to the public at large. Furthermore, this aspect of the statute applies as much to a one-man business as to a giant industrial concern. Needless to say, the same duty is laid on schools.

Regulations designed to protect the general public may be made under the Act, and the Health and Safety inspectorate can take this into consideration. The section covers both visitors to a workplace and persons who may be affected without coming to the premises. It is this section which protects pupils, as they are not employees.

Employers are required to take such steps as are reasonably necessary to ensure that the health, safety and welfare of persons who may be affected by their work are not injured. Those in control of premises must take similar precautions with regard to visitors, including workers and persons using equipment or substances provided on the premises for their use.[30]

14 Enforcement

THE INSPECTORATES

The supervision of the Act is entrusted to the Health and Safety inspectorate, to whom alone is given the power to prosecute for offences under the Act.[31] The initial recruitment was achieved by fusing the former specialist inspectorates who dealt with factories, mines and quarries, and so forth. In addition to the central inspectorate of the Health and Safety Executive, every enforcing authority may appoint its own inspectors to discharge the functions laid upon it by law.[32]

Inspectors have wide powers of examination and investigation. They may remove articles or substances for testing, require answers to questions which they deem necessary, and demand the production of records.[33]

IMPROVEMENT NOTICES

If an inspector forms the opinion that the Act is being, or is likely to be, contravened, he may issue an improvement notice requiring the defect to be remedied.[34] An appeal may be made to an industrial tribunal which has the power to affirm, modify or cancel the notice.[35] The notice is suspended until the appeal is determined.

PROHIBITION NOTICES

If, in the inspector's opinion, there is an imminent risk of serious personal injury, he may issue a prohibition notice.[36] The issue of a prohibition notice requires the immediate cessation of the contravention, even if this means closing down. It is possible to appeal to an industrial tribunal, but a prohibition notice is not suspended on appeal, except with the leave of the tribunal.[37]

OFFENCES

There is a long list of offences for which prosecutions may be instituted.[38] Some are triable only before a magistrates' court, and for these the maximum penalty is a fine of £1000. Others may be tried either by magistrates, or on indictment before a crown court. The maximum penalty on summary conviction is again £1000, but conviction on indictment can lead to a sentence of up to two years' imprisonment, an unlimited fine, or both. If certain offences continue after conviction, the court can order a further fine of £100 a day for each day the contravention continues.

15   Defences

The following statutory defences are provided by the Act:

(a) that the offence charged was due to the fault of another person;
(b) that the defendant had done all that was 'reasonably practicable' to avoid committing the offence;
(c) other defences which, from time to time, may be specified in regulations made under the Act.

It is not a defence to claim that the contravention was due to an act or default by someone to whom the defendant had delegated the duty. In such cases both the delegator and the delegate may be prosecuted and convicted.[39]

16   Extra-territorial offences

Her Majesty may, by Order in Council, bring acts or omissions by British subjects outside the United Kingdom within the jurisdiction of the English courts.

Should such an Order be made, it is not impossible that this could apply to overseas school journeys, including the safety of the accommodation used, the system of working, and so forth.

17   Negligence

The Act does not destroy the common law right of a citizen to claim that he is entitled to compensation for damage caused by injury arising out of another's negligence.[40] An employer or employee convicted of an offence under the Act may well find himself pursued for damages in the civil courts. The standard of proof in civil cases depends on the 'balance of probabilities' and is less strict than the requirement that criminal charges shall be proved 'beyond all reasonable doubt'. If there has already been a criminal conviction relating to a particular offence, it is most likely that a civil claim arising from the same matter would succeed. The financial risks, however, are greater for employers than employees, as in English law an employer is liable for the torts of his servants committed in the execution of their duty. Even if an employee had been convicted on a criminal count, it is most unlikely that damages would be awarded against him.

References

1. Health and Safety at Work etc. Act 1974, s. 1(1).
2. Health and Safety at Work etc. Act 1974, s. 52(1).
3. Health and Safety at Work etc. Act 1974, ss. 1(2) and 80.
4. Health and Safety at Work etc. Act 1974, ss. 10–14.
5. Local authority inspectors of offices and shops are still employed by the authorities, but they work in close liaison with the Executive.
6. Health and Safety at Work etc. Act 1974, ss. 10–11.

-7. The Health and Safety (Enforcing Authority) Regulations 1977.

8. Health and Safety at Work etc. Act 1974, ss. 55–60.

9. Maritime House, 1 Linton Road, Barking, Essex, 1G11 8HF.

10. Health and Safety at Work etc. Act 1974, s. 13(1).

11. Health and Safety at Work etc. Act 1974, s. 2(1) and (2).

12. Health and Safety at Work etc. Act 1974, s. 2(3).

13. Health and Safety at Work etc. Act 1974, s. 3.

14. Health and Safety at Work etc. Act 1974, s. 9.

15. 'Premises' are defined by s. 53 of the Act as including any place, including any vessel, vehicle or hovercraft, any installation on land or offshore, any other installation (whether floating, or resting on the seabed or its subsoil), and any tent or movable structure. For the purposes of this Act the school minibus and canoes are premises.

16. Health and Safety at Work etc. Act 1974, s. 4.

17. Campbell v. Tameside Metropolitan Borough Council (1982) 80 LGR 700; 2 All ER 791 CA.

18. Health and Safety at Work etc. Act 1974, s. 7.

19. Health and Safety at Work etc. Act 1974, s. 8.

20. Health and Safety at Work etc. Act 1974, s. 6(1)–(2) and (6)–(10).

21. Health and Safety at Work etc. Act 1974, s. 6(3) and (6)–(7).

22. Health and Safety at Work etc. Act 1974, s. 6(4)–(10).

23. Safety Representatives and Safety Committees Regulations 1977.

24. Health and Safety at Work etc. Act 1974, s. 2(7).

25. See Safety Representatives and Safety Committees (HMSO, 1977).

26. See First Aid at Work (HMSO, 1982).

27. First Aid, 1982.

28. Health and Safety at Work etc. Act 1974, s. 33.

29. See Health and Safety series booklet HS(R)5: Notification of Accidents and Dangerous Occurrences (1980) HMSO.

30. Health and Safety at Work etc. Act 1974, ss. 1(1)(b) and 3.

31. Health and Safety at Work etc. Act 1974, s. 39.

32. Health and Safety at Work etc. Act 1974, s. 19(1).

33. Health and Safety at Work etc. Act 1974, s. 19(2)–(8).

34. Health and Safety at Work etc. Act 1974, ss. 21 and 23.

35. Health and Safety at Work etc. Act 1974, s. 24.

36. Health and Safety at Work etc. Act 1974, ss. 22 and 23.

37. Health and Safety at Work etc. Act 1974, s. 24.

38. Health and Safety at Work etc. Act 1974, s. 33. The fines which

can be imposed were increased by the Criminal Law Act 1977, Schedule 6.
39. Health and Safety at Work etc. Act 1974, ss. 36 and 40.
40. See chapter XIV.

VII
Salaries and income tax

1 The salary committees

It is the duty of the Secretary of State to secure the appointment of one or more committees consisting of an independent chairman, one or more persons representing the Secretary of State, together with representatives of local education authorities and of organizations appearing to the Secretary of State to represent local education authorities, teachers, or particular descriptions of teachers. The committees must submit proposals for suitable salary scales to the Secretary of State when they think fit, or when he so requires. After the scales have received his approval, the Secretary of State makes an order binding them upon the local education authorities.[1]

The present statute, the Remuneration of Teachers Act 1965, replaced and repealed section 89 of the Education Act 1944 and an interim Act of 1963. The independent chairman is appointed by the Secretary of State, and there is provision for arbitration in default of agreement in committee. It also allows decisions to be retrospective.

When a review of salaries is projected, the Burnham Main Committee considers the salaries of teachers in primary and secondary schools. After these have been agreed, the committees dealing with other institutions meet to revise the scales for which they are responsible. These are to some extent geared to the primary and secondary scales.

After both panels of the Main Committee have agreed on a decision the scales are referred to the various bodies represented on the Committee, and are then submitted to the Secretary of State. His approval is given in a letter to the chairman of the Committee and the scales are printed for the guidance of all concerned and published by HMSO.

The constitution of the Burnham Committee was revised in 1981 and representation is currently:

Management panel		Teachers' panel	
Association of County Councils	13	National Union of Teachers	16
Association of Metropolitan Authorities	10	National Association of Teachers in Further and Higher Education	1
Welsh Joint Education Committee	2	Assistant Masters and Mistresses Association	4
DES	2	Secondary Heads Association	1
		National Association of Head Teachers	2
		National Association of Schoolmasters/Union of Women Teachers	7
		Professional Association of Teachers	1

It is something of an anomaly that the Burnham Committee can consider only the remuneration of teachers, while it is left to another body, CLEA (school teachers),[2] to advise on conditions of service. It is possible that in the foreseeable future the Act will be amended in some way to bring both sets of negotiations together, as has already been achieved in Scotland.

2   The salary structure

In 1981 the management panel of the Burnham Committee proposed radical changes in the salary structure of the teaching profession. Under these proposals, the 'points score' system would go, and promotion would be linked to teaching performance, and to clearly defined additional tasks such as supervision or co-ordination. For the first time there would be a national system of teacher assessment. At the time of writing these proposals are still 'on the table': the outline given in this section refers to the salary structure of 1983/84.

SALARY AWARDS

New salary awards normally take effect from 1 April each year. For each term's service not less than one third of the annual salary must be paid. For this purpose a term includes vacations.

INCREMENTAL DATE

The standard incremental date is 1 September each year. A teacher normally receives an increment on the standard incremental date up to the maximum of the appropriate scale. A teacher in continuous service placed on a different scale during the year, subject to the maximum of his new scale, receives a complete increment on that scale at the next standard incremental date.

PROMOTION

Promotion is defined as movement between one scale and a higher one, provided that the maximum of the new scale is at least £100 more than the maximum of the scale in the former post. A teacher who moves from one scale to another scale where the difference in the scales is £99 or less is transferred at the salary applicable to him in his former post. The following arrangements apply to teachers being promoted:

A teacher who is promoted from Scales 1, 2, 3 or 4 to another or to senior teacher scale is paid the salary applicable in the former post plus a promotion increase of 2 increments. If the promotion is to a scale higher than that next above the one previously applicable, the increase is the total of the increases which would have applied if the teacher had moved up one scale at a time, subject at each stage to the maximum of the scale.

A teacher who is promoted from Scale 2, 3 or 4 or the senior teacher scale to a head or deputy head teacher scale shall be paid the salary applicable in the former post plus an amount equivalent to 2 increments on the scale to which he is promoted.

A teacher who is promoted to a head or deputy head teacher scale from Scale 1, 2, 3 or 4 or the senior teacher scale shall be paid the salary applicable in the former post plus the promotion increase of $1\frac{1}{2}$ increments on the scale to which he is promoted.

A head or deputy head teacher who is promoted to another head or deputy head teacher scale is paid the salary applicable in the former post plus the promotion increase of $1\frac{1}{2}$ increments on the scale to which he is promoted.

INCREMENTAL CREDIT

Incremental credit is given as follows:

Qualifications

(i)   Diplomas recognized by the Burnham Committee qualify a teacher to be given one increment.

(ii) An ordinary degree or a qualification agreed by the Burnham Committee to be of ordinary degree status qualifies a teacher to be given two increments.

(iii) A good honours degree or a qualification agreed by the Burnham Committee to be of honours degree status qualifies a teacher to be given four increments.

A qualified teacher who for the first time obtains any of the above has his increments credited from the first day of service after obtaining the qualification.

Study, training and research

A teacher is given one increment for each year of study, training or research in excess of three years undertaken after the age of 18, subject to a maximum of three increments.

Experience

Teachers over 21 at the time of qualification receive one increment in respect of each period of three years in teaching, professional, clerical, social or other gainful employment. However, where a local education authority decides that such experience gained after the age of 21 is of special value to the teacher in his particular duties, the LEA may allow the teacher one increment in respect of each complete year of experience which the local education authority approves for the purpose.

Unpaid activity

Incremental credit of one increment for each completed period of three years, up to a maximum of 5 increments, is given in respect of unpaid activity after the age of 18. No allowance is given under this heading for the first three years of training after the age of 18.

SAFEGUARDING

A teacher who loses his post continues for salary purposes to hold the post he held immediately before a closure or reorganization that brought about the loss of post. The social priority allowance is not normally safeguarded unless the teacher is subsequently transferred to a similar school when he shall continue to receive the social priority allowance he was receiving. The safeguarding arrangements do not apply to a teacher who at any time unreasonably refuses to accept an alternative post in an educational establishment maintained by the same LEA.

TEMPORARY ALLOWANCES

If an assistant takes charge of a school during the absence of the head or pending a new appointment, the salary must be that which would be payable if the teacher concerned were appointed as the permanent head of the school. It is payable only during such periods as the assistant is actually in charge of the school. A local education authority may make an additional payment to a teacher in certain categories when it is considered that the salary or the scale properly payable under the Burnham Report is inadequate having regard to the special circumstances of the teacher's duties and responsibilities. A teacher whose appointment is temporary, pending the reorganization of his school, is entitled to a safeguarding of his salary from 1 July 1967.[3]

SOCIAL PRIORITY SCHOOLS

A designating committee consisting of members of the Burnham Committee decides which schools should be classed as social priority schools; a list is supplied to each LEA. An allowance is paid to teachers working in social priority schools. Following the completion of two years six months qualifying service this amount is increased.

THE GROUPING OF SCHOOLS

Schools are grouped according to size. At present there are fourteen groups. A school is placed within a particular group according to the review average which is determined at each triennial review. At the triennial review, the average of each of the three unit totals is taken. The unit total is calculated from statistics taken each January by the DES (Form 7 (schools) or Form 11 (schools)) or Welsh Office (Form Stats 1). Each

224 Teachers and the Law

Grouping of schools‡: Burnham assessment

Unit total or review average (1)	Points score range (2)	Highest scale for teachers below deputy head teacher (3)	Group of school for head and deputy head teacher purposes (4)
up to 100	0–1	2	1
101–200	0–1	2	2
201–300	0–2	2	3
301–400	2–6	2	4
401–500	2–6		
501–600	3–8	3	5
601–700	5–11		
701–800	7–13		
801–900	9–15	3	6
901–1000	10–17		
1001–1100	11–21		
1101–1200	13–23	3	7
1201–1300	14–26		
1301–1400	15–28		
1401–1600	17–33	4	8
1601–1800	21–37		
1801–2000	25–40		
2001–2200	30–44	4	9
2201–2400	35–49		
2401–2700	41–55		
2701–3000	47–60	4*	10
3001–3300	52–65		
3301–3700	57–74		
3701–4100	62–79	4*	11
4101–4600	68–83		
4601–5100	75–90		
5101–5600	81–96	4*	12
5601–6000	88–103		

6001–6100	88–103		
6101–6600	94–109	4*	13
6601–7100	101–116		
7101–7600	108–123		
Over 7600	Proportionately	4*	14

‡ Other than special schools.
* Including senior teachers.

pupil recorded on these statistical returns represents a number of units according to his age:

Each pupil under 14 years of age	2 units
aged 14 and under 15	3 units
aged 15 and under 16	4 units
aged 16 and under 17	6 units
aged 17 and over	8 units

The units are added together to form the unit total.

The chart above shows the appropriate group for each review average range. The group of the school determines the salary scale applicable to the head and deputy head teacher and the points score range appropriate to the school for the purpose of placing teachers on scales above Scale 1. The number of teachers placed on Scale 2 and above is determined by the LEA within the limits set out in the chart. Within this context, each teacher on Scale 2 counts 1 point, each teacher on Scale 3 counts 2 points, while each teacher on Scale 4 or designated as a senior teacher counts 3 points.

Special arrangements apply to schools which have been newly opened or reorganized in certain specified years.

ALLOCATION OF POSTS

The number of teachers placed on Scale 2 and above is usually determined by the local education authority within the limits of the grouping. The limits are given in the column headed 'Points score range':

each teacher on Scale 2 1 point
each teacher on Scale 3 2 points
each teacher on Scale 4 3 points
each senior teacher   3 points

The numbers of senior teacher posts that may be allocated are:

(i) up to 3 senior teachers may be appointed in a school other than a special school in Group 10
(ii) up to 4 senior teachers may be appointed in a school other than a special school in Groups 11 and 12
(iii) up to 5 senior teachers may be appointed in a school other than a special school in Groups 13 and 14

In each case the points score range must not be exceeded.

As far as deputy head teachers are concerned, a local education authority must appoint a deputy head in a school in Group 2 or higher, where the review average or unit total is 151 or more. A local education authority must also appoint a second master or second mistress in a mixed school in Group 7 or higher. The teacher appointed as second master or second mistress is treated for all purposes as if he were a deputy head and paid on the deputy head scale.

Local education authorities have some discretion as far as other deputy head appointments are concerned. They may appoint:

(i) a deputy head in a school where the review average or unit total is below 151.
(ii) a second deputy head in a school in Group 9 or higher.
(iii) a third deputy head in a school in Group 10 or 11 which was established following the closure of two or more other schools and which is situated in three or more separate locations.
(iv) a third deputy head in a school in Group 12 or higher.

EFFECTS OF REORGANIZATION ON GROUPING

For the purposes of the Burnham Report, reorganization is

defined as any action by a local education authority 'in the interests of educational organization the effect of which would be significantly to add to or to reduce the number of children who will normally be enrolled'. In a 1982 case the Court of Appeal held that a change of not less than 20 per cent in total numbers was accepted by the teaching profession generally and head teachers in particular as significant. Two head teachers, the size of whose schools had been affected by changes in their catchment areas, lost their cases for salary increases because the increase in the size of their schools did not reach 20 per cent.[4]

THE LONDON ALLOWANCES

A new scheme of allowances for teachers in and around Greater London was introduced in 1974. This provides for graduated additions to the scales to avoid the creation of a salary 'cliff' around the capital. The tiers are:

(a) The inner area. Inner London Education Authority, Barking, Brent, Ealing, Haringey, Merton and Newham.
(b) The outer area. Outer London boroughs not included above.
(c) The fringe area.
  Buckinghamshire: Beaconsfield and Chiltern
  Berkshire: Bracknell, Windsor, Slough and Maidenhead
  Essex: Basildon, Brentwood, Epping Forest, Harlow and Thurrock
  Hertfordshire: Broxbourne, Dacorum, East Herts, Hertsmere, St Albans, Three Rivers, Watford, Welwyn and Hatfield
  Kent: Dartford and Sevenoaks
  Surrey: the whole county
  West Sussex: Crawley.

Teachers serving in schools which have premises in more than one of the London areas, or partly outside the London areas, are paid on the scale appropriate to the premises in which they spend more than half their time.

  Teachers already serving in the Metropolitan Police District but outside area (a), i.e. those who received the former London allowance, are safeguarded at the highest rate.

3   Other educational establishments

Separately negotiated salary scales are published in respect of:
Universities
Technical colleges and polytechnics
Farm institutes
Colleges of education
Youth service organizers
Specialist organizers
Educational psychologists
General inspectors and advisers

4   Overpayment of salary

Overpayments of salary made as a result of a mistake of law are not recoverable from the recipient. A local authority which, for example, using the Burnham Scales wrongly assessed and overpaid a teacher's salary could not normally expect to recover the overpayment, because the Burnham Report is a statutory document.

Overpayments based on errors of fact however may be recoverable from the recipient, unless the payer has in some way led the recipient reasonably to infer that he or she is entitled to retain the moneys overpaid, as a result of which the recipient acts in some way to his or her detriment.

In the Court of Appeal in 1982 Lord Justice Eveleigh gave judgment in a case where a former teacher had been overpaid during his absence through illness: 'The plaintiffs overpaid the defendant because of a mistake ... of fact. The terms of the defendant's contract of employment and the manner in which the plaintiffs controlled the assessment of the defendant's pay show that they were under a duty to him to determine his entitlement and not to misrepresent it. They represented to him that his entitlement was those sums which they paid to him from time to time ... the plaintiffs are to be taken as having represented to the defendant that he was entitled to treat the whole of the money as his own. The defendant positively relied upon this representation.'[5]

In another case where two teachers were overpaid for periods of two and six years arising from some confusion about the Burnham Scales, it was held that the local authority had a duty of care to check salary assessments within a reasonable time after the information upon which the assessments were made became available. In both cases, in the court's view, far too long a period had elapsed. It was further held that the lapse of time in itself could be taken by the teachers as an assurance that their salaries were correct.[6]

It should be noted, however, that it is not unlawful to include in teachers' contracts a provision to the effect that salaries might be modified to recover monies paid in error, including overpayments made as a result of mistakes of law. Any clawing-back must take place during the same salary year in which the overpayment occurs.

5 Income tax

There is not space in a book of this scope to deal with the various complexities of the income tax regulations. Small handbooks which explain the current provisions are easily obtainable from any bookseller. A few common matters are dealt with below.

It should be noted that the rule which makes allowances for expenses necessarily and exclusively incurred in following one's occupation is strictly interpreted and there are few claims open to teachers under this head. *Books*, for example, are not regarded as a necessary expense since they are supplied by the local education authority. On this point, however, it seems that local tax inspectors *may* be willing to make some allowance in respect of books purchased in connection with teaching above 'O' level, if the books are needed in the classroom.

Items of equipment bought by teachers for their work in school are viewed in the same way. In a relevant case in 1983,[7] a vicar was first allowed to set against his income tax the purchase of a slide projector for use in visual sermons as being 'necessary'. When the Inland Revenue successfully appealed against the allowance, the court held that 'the commissioners had found as a fact that another vicar could have performed the religious ministry without the equipment and that this vicar would have been able to do his job without the equipment. He had purchased the equipment not in order to carry out duties which a vicar with less devotion to his work might not have thought it his duty to perform, but in order to perform his duties as vicar in what he considered to be the most effective way.' Similarly, a typewriter is likely to be regarded as neither necessarily nor exclusively obtained for the following of the profession of a teacher.

The use of *a room at home as a study* is also not allowable as a necessary expense by school teachers, although the Association of University Teachers has gained such a concession for its members. A teacher who appealed to the Tax Commissioners for an allowance in 1978 lost his case: 'It appears to us that the appellant was not obliged in performing his duties to set aside a room exclusively as a study ... section 189(1) of the Income and Corporation Taxes Act 1970 did not extend to those cases where the holder of an office incurs expenses personally and of his own volition.'[8]

With effect from the beginning of the tax year 1983–4, *examining fees from GCE and CSE Boards* are taxed at source, and expenses relating to transfer of subsistence are paid gross.

Teachers who do examination marking and who do not earn enough for tax to be paid, can apply to the Examinations Board concerned for an exemption form; the Board will then pay the fees without deduction.

If a teacher does not wish to apply directly to the Board for an exemption certificate, the P.60 substitute which will be issued by the Board at the end of the tax year to show the amount of tax deducted at source should be sent to the individual's tax office. A tax refund will then be made.

If, on the other hand, a teacher should be paying some tax above the basic rate, the local tax office will make the necessary adjustments.

Members of *professional associations and learned societies* may now claim income tax allowances against their *subscriptions*. These include not only annual fees which are payable as a statutory condition of exercising a profession, but also subscriptions to bodies which have been approved by the Commissioners of Inland Revenue. It is required that the activities of the body should be relevant to the profession concerned.

Mileage allowances at a fixed rate paid to teachers for travelling to and from unpaid, out-of-school activities on a purely voluntary basis are not taxable as 'emoluments of their employment' unless the teacher's total earnings exceed a figure currently set at £8499 per annum. A Birmingham teacher in 1981 successfully appealed to the courts against being taxed on mileage allowances paid to her for attending parents' evenings. Mr Justice Walton said:[9]

'In the present case it was clear beyond question that the teacher did not receive the allowance "for acting as an employee" for the simple — albeit surprising — reason that attendance at out-of-school activities was not something under the terms of her contract of employment she was bound to perform. It was entirely outside the duties for which she was paid as a teacher.

Still less was the allowance received "for being an employee" because in order to obtain it she had to perform duties outside her contractual duties, and if she had merely performed her contractual duties and none other she would not have received the allowance.

Those short considerations appeared to be a conclusive end to the case. However, the matter should be looked at in a slightly different way. What would have been the position if the teacher had had a contractual duty to attend out-of-school activities? In general, allowances of the nature here in question fell to be treated as additional remuneration.

But in many instances the expenditure so reimbursed might, in whole or in part, be claimed as an expenditure falling within section 189(1) of the 1970 Act.'[10]

Fringe benefits and benefits in kind are also taxable. Teachers occupying school houses owned by governors or local authorities and receiving a rent reduction in consideration of, say, living in a certain place or carrying out certain work for their employer, may find that the Inland Revenue seek to tax the value of the accommodation. However, the matter is subject to negotiations at the moment between the Inland Revenue and teachers' associations.

Teachers who must themselves provide *special clothing* for their work, such as perhaps physical education teachers, are unlikely to find a sympathetic ear at the Inland Revenue. The Court of Appeal held in 1982 that a female barrister who required traditional clothing for her court appearances could claim tax relief. The expenditure must be shown to be 'wholly and exclusively laid out or expended for the purposes of the trade, profession or vocation' of the claimant.[11] However, the barrister's claim was later rejected in the House of Lords.

References

1. Remuneration of Teachers Act 1965, ss. 1 and 2.
2. See p. 115.
3. Stott *v.* Oldham Corporation (1969) 67 LGR 520; LCT 393.
4. Vaughan and another *v.* Solihull Metropolitan Borough, *The Times*, 25 May 1982.
5. Avon County Council *v.* Howlett (1983) IRLR 171 CA.
6. Whitwell and Asquith *v.* Council of Metropolitan District of Wakefield, *Education*, 22 May 1981.
7. White (Inspector of Taxes) *v.* Higginbottom, *The Times*, 7 January 1983.
8. *Times Educational Supplement*, 22 September 1978.
9. Donnelly (Inspector of Taxes) *v.* Williamson, *The Times*, 4 November 1981. See also, on the issue of teachers' contractual obligations: Lake *v.* Essex (1979), pp. 140, 194.
10. Income and Corporation Taxes Act 1970.
11. Mallalieu *v.* Drummond, *The Times*, 15 December 1982, CA.

VIII
Leave of absence

1 Sickness

Until 1981 common law held that an employee was entitled
to his wages during temporary illness, provided that his
contract of employment was not at an end and that he was
willing, but for the illness, to return to work. However the
Employment Appeal Tribunal ruled in 1981 that payment
during sickness must be a clearly stated term in a contract and
in the absence of a clear term it would not be automatically
taken to be implied.[1]

Sickness has been defined by Mr Justice Macnaghten as 'any
morbid condition, without paying any attention to the cause'[2]
and therefore includes incapacity due to accident. It comprises
not only the illness itself but also approaching illness and the
subsequent convalescence, and was described by Mr Justice
Channell as 'not a break of contract but an act of God'.[3]

It should be noted that the contract of employment must
subsist throughout the illness. A servant who is unable to
commence fresh employment through illness is not entitled to
salary from his new employer, even though he has left the
employ of his former master.[4]

2   Sick pay regulations

Sick pay allowances are granted by local education authorities under a scheme which has been agreed between them and the teachers' professional associations. The scheme is codified in the Burgundy Book and service in one area is recognized for the calculation of benefits on transfer to another in accordance, of course, with the scheme of the new authority.

The nationally agreed minimum rates of sick pay are as follows, for the year for this purpose commencing on 1 April:

Year of Service	Working days' pay	
	Full	Half
First (after 4 months' service)	25	25
Second	50	50
Third	75	75
Fourth (and successive)	100	100

If a teacher's service begins on any date other than 1 April he is deemed, for this purpose, to have commenced duty on the previous 1 April, except that he cannot receive half pay until after four months' actual service.

A teacher who is absent on 31 March is not entitled to a fresh allowance for the new year until he has resumed duty. Sick pay already received during the year is taken into account if a teacher transfers to a new authority.

For the purpose of sick pay, two half days count as one working day.

When an illness extends over more than seven calendar days, a medical statement must be submitted to the authority. It is also necessary, in order to claim benefit, to send a 'National Health' medical certificate to the employer within seven days. If a certificate cannot be obtained within that time, the teacher should write to the Social Security office, quoting his full name, address, date of birth and National Insurance number. The letter should state that benefit is being claimed, and the medical certificate should be sent on as quickly as possible.

Some local education authorities are prepared to accept the

National Health certificate and, after recording the details, to forward it to the department. There is, however, a risk in following this procedure: if, through postal or administrative delays, the certificate is not received at the Social Security office within the prescribed time there may be a loss of benefit. Teachers may consider it worthwhile to pay for a private medical certificate for their employing authority, and to send the official certificate themselves to the Social Security office.

A teacher who is absent frequently, or for a prolonged period, may be asked to undergo a medical examination. If the teacher so wishes, his own doctor may be present during such an examination. Failure reasonably to co-operate with an employer in accepting such medical examination may form grounds for dismissal.

Teachers are strongly recommended to obtain particulars of their authority's sick pay procedure as early as possible after entering service.

3 Statutory sick pay

The Social Security and Housing Benefits Act 1982 came into force on 28 June 1982. Part 1 of the Act which set up the statutory sick pay scheme (SSP) came into force on 6 April 1983.

If an employee is absent from work because of illness or injury, he is entitled to SSP from his employer subject to a maximum of eight weeks' SSP in any tax year; and while he is entitled to SSP he is not entitled to sickness benefit from the state social security scheme. This does not apply in certain exceptional cases, notably to employees over pensionable age, and employees on short contracts.

As far as teachers are concerned, net pay remains in practice unchanged, even if they are in receipt of SSP. There may, of course, be minor income tax adjustments.

Section 1 of the Act provides that where an employee has a day of incapacity for work in relation to his contract of service with an employer, that employer is liable, if the day satisfies the qualifying conditions, to pay SSP to him for that day. Any agreement which purports to exclude the operation of the Act is void.

A day is not treated as a day of incapacity for work in relation to any contract of service unless on that day the employee is, or is deemed in accordance with regulations to be, incapable through specific disease or disablement of doing work which he can reasonably be expected to do under that contract. The regulation in question is regulation 2 of the Statutory Sick Pay (General) Regulations 1982. It provides that an employee who is not incapable of work that he can reasonably be expected to do under a particular contract of service may be deemed incapable if a registered medical practitioner states that he should abstain from work, or from work of that kind, for precautionary or convalescent reasons, or if he is excluded from work, or from work of that kind, on the certificate of a Medical Officer of Environmental Health after contact with infectious disease. It also provides that an employee is deemed incapable throughout a day if he is incapable for at least part of it, and does no work.

If a teacher is absent for four days or more a 'period of incapacity for work' is established (known as a PIW). SSP is payable once such a PIW is established, but from the fourth 'qualifying' day. A qualifying day is usually defined in the case of teachers and lecturers as a day on which the teacher would have worked but for illness. However, during periods of school closure teachers have the same qualifying days as in term time, and such illnesses must be notified in the usual way to the employer.

If a teacher falls ill, he should:

Day 1: notify the employer, *no later than the first day of illness*.
Day 4: *re*-notify the employer and submit a self-certification form.
Day 8: obtain a medical certificate for the employer.

During a longer illness medical certificates should be submitted as necessary, and always on entering and leaving hospital.

Any employee is excluded from receiving SSP if he:

(a) is over state pension age (60 for women, 65 for men);
(b) has a contract of service for three months or less, unless the contract is extended beyond three months;
(c) has done no work under the contract of service;
(d) goes sick during a trade dispute at the place of work and has no direct interest in it;
(e) falls sick during the 'disqualifying period' related to her pregnancy;
(f) has already received the maximum entitlement of SSP in the current year;
(g) is abroad outside the EEC;
(h) is in legal custody.

4 Infectious illness

All teachers who are in contact with infectious illness at home should notify the authority. As a rule they are not excluded from school except when the illness is of an exceptionally serious character, such as smallpox or poliomyelitis. If, however, they are excluded, they should forward a certificate to this effect from the Medical Officer of Health or, if this cannot be obtained quickly, from their own doctor. Full pay should be allowed, and the absence should not prejudice future entitlement to sick pay. This is reckoned as sick pay, but does not count against the teacher's entitlement.

When a teacher himself contracts an infectious illness which the authority's medical officer certifies to have been, in all probability, caught in school, full salary is allowed for the necessary absence and neither the time nor the sick pay is counted against the teacher's entitlement.

5 Accidents during teaching duty

On production of the appropriate certification, full salary is payable from the date of the accident until the date of recovery, provided this period does not extend beyond six months. The matter is then reviewed. Absence due to such accidents does not count against the sick pay entitlement.

Where an authority makes up the salary of a teacher receiving benefit as the result of an accident sustained at school, this is without prejudice to the authority's liability in the case of negligence. Any amount so paid, however, would be deducted from an award of damages, as would any sum recoverable from a negligent third party.

Accidents arising from extra-curricular or voluntary activities connected with the school should be classified under this head.

6   Accidents outside teaching duty

If a teacher's absence is due to the actionable negligence of a third party[5] he should advise the authority accordingly. The authority may advance sick pay pending the result of any action taken by a teacher to obtain compensation, but may then claim a sum to the extent of the damages recovered, not exceeding the allowances paid in respect of sick pay. If the claim be settled on a proportionate basis between the parties, the authority will determine the proportion to be refunded by the teacher.

In one case, a teacher was prevented from carrying out her duties following an accident when she was returning from her holidays. She claimed that she was entitled to her full salary for the three weeks that she was absent. The authority's case was that the sick pay regulations conferred eligibility, but not a right, to allowances as there was a clause which allowed the withholding of payments in specific cases. Judgment in the Bury County Court was given for the teacher.

7   Tuberculosis

Special arrangements are usually made for teachers who contract pulmonary tuberculosis, and those who suspect that they have developed this illness should consult the authority immediately. Full pay is normally paid for twelve months, provided the teacher undertakes an approved course of treatment. Further full or half pay may be allowed at the authority's discretion.

Circular 11/78 requires that a teacher suffering from this

illness should be suspended immediately, and not allowed to return to school until the Secretary of State is satisfied that he is fit to do so.

8 Mental illness

A teacher who has been absent for more than three months, ignoring short breaks, because of mental or nervous illness should be suspended and not be allowed to return until cleared by the Secretary of State. Before this is permitted he will be required to submit a report by a consultant psychiatrist to the DES. The consultant, who should preferably be one who knows the case, is asked to indicate whether he believes the teacher to be fully recovered, fit to teach children, and capable of being a member of a school community.

9 Epilepsy

Because of improved methods of treatment, it is not now considered necessary to suspend every epileptic. In the event of a severe seizure, or of recurrent attacks, the specialist in community medicine (child health) should be informed and his advice taken on temporary suspension pending investigation. A specialist physical education teacher found to be epileptic should be suspended. In cases where epilepsy leads to suspension, a full report must be made to the DES, including information as to whether the teacher has undertaken work involving physical risks such as physical education, home economics, woodwork or other crafts, or driving children on out-of-school activities. Before allowing a suspended epileptic to return, the Secretary of State will require to be satisfied as to the result of investigations, the prognosis, the medication required, and the treatment of the condition.

10 Maternity leave

Maternity leave is available to women with at least twelve months' continuous service immediately prior to the commencement of the maternity leave, though not necessarily with one authority. An authority can, at its discretion, apply the scheme in whole or in part to unmarried women and to adoptive parents.[6]

A woman teacher with at least two years' continuous service as a teacher, whether with one or more local education authorities, by the beginning of the eleventh week before the expected week of confinement, may remain absent for up to a period of twenty-nine weeks beginning with the week in which the date of confinement falls. The teacher must give her employer at least seven days' notice, in writing, of the date on which it is her intention to return to her job after her confinement.

The teacher may absent herself from duty not earlier than the beginning of the eleventh week before the week of expected confinement. She may continue at work, if she so wishes, until a date later than the beginning of the eleventh week before the week of expected confinement, but she may not remain at work if certified medically unfit to do so.

The teacher may remain absent for a period of eighteen weeks from the beginning of her absence for maternity, save that, in the event of a stillbirth, she may remain absent for up to six weeks after the confinement.

Salary entitlement during maternity leave is currently as follows. *The first four weeks of absence:* full pay, with deduction of flat-rate maternity allowance and, if the teacher is entitled to such additional benefits, of earnings-related supplement and/or of increased maternity allowance attributable to dependants; provided that the total weekly payment shall not be less than 9/10 of a week's salary after deduction only of flat-rate maternity allowance.

Each of the next two weeks of absence: 9/10 of a week's salary with deduction of flat-rate maternity allowance.

The remainder of the eighteen-week period of absence: half pay without deduction of maternity allowance except to the extent to which the combined pay and allowances may exceed full pay.

Any remaining period of absence up to the date of return notified by the teacher: absence without pay.

A teacher who wishes to be absent from work by reason of maternity must notify her employer, in writing, as soon as practicable and, unless she can show good cause, not less than fourteen weeks before the date of her expected confinement. The teacher must inform her employer (in writing if so requested) at least twenty-one days before her absence begins or, if that is not reasonably practicable, as soon as is reasonably practicable, of the date by which she wishes her absence to begin. Where a teacher wishes to exercise at the conclusion of her absence for maternity her right of return to work in the job in which she was employed, she shall declare that intention, in writing, *at the time of the notification of her absence.*

Subject to the provision of a medical certificate, any absence due or attributable to the pregnancy, absence due to miscarriage, and any extension of maternity leave, are treated as ordinary sick leave. If a teacher is advised by her doctor to absent herself during the early months of pregnancy because of a risk of rubella (German measles) such absence is treated as leave with full pay, unless she refuses (if asked) to serve in another school where there is no such risk.

Payment during maternity leave is normally conditional on the teacher returning to full-time (or the equivalent part-time) duty for at least thirteen weeks, which runs from the date of return, or from the date when she is certified to be fit for duty if that occurs during a holiday. The employer may, at his discretion, reduce the requirement to below thirteen weeks.

Payment of any sums due in respect of leave following the confinement, or of salary in respect of a holiday period following immediately on maternity leave, may be withheld until the teacher actually returns. If the teacher does not return, the authority may require a refund of such proportion of the payments made as it deems appropriate. This requirement may, for good cause, be varied by the authority. A woman with two years' or more continuous service as a teacher is entitled to retain the first six weeks' payment.

It is unfair dismissal to discharge an employee if the reason, or the principal reason for doing so, is related to pregnancy as distinct from incapacity.[7]

A woman can claim her employment back, on terms and conditions at least as favourable as those which applied before, up to twenty-nine weeks after the beginning of the week of her confinement or, if a doctor certifies further absence to be necessary, up to thirty-three weeks. To qualify for this provision, however, she must have two years' continuous service immediately before the commencement of the leave.

As noted, to obtain her entitlement the woman must notify her employer in writing, before leave commences, that she will be absent because of pregnancy and that she intends to return to work. The employer should inform the teacher of her rights both under the national conditions of service and under the Employment Protection (Consolidation) Act. She must give at least a week's notice of her intention to return. In 1983 the Court of Appeal held that a woman employee who gave only five days' notice of her proposal to return to work instead of the statutory seven had led her employers into thinking that they could terminate her employment because of the short notice given, and that her dismissal in the circumstances was not unfair.[8]

In general terms, the provisions of the Act always override any local conditions of service where the latter are less favourable to the employee.[9]

11 Holidays

If a teacher is on sick leave at the end of term, he continues during the holiday at the sick pay rate applicable on the last school day. The holiday period, however, does not count against his entitlement to benefit. If, during the holiday, he notifies his local authority that he is fit to return to work, he is regarded as having done so from the date of such notification, provided he is in school on the first day of term.

Similarly, a teacher who falls sick during the holidays should report the matter to the local education authority or, if in receipt of benefit rather than SSP, the DHSS. Benefits are payable and deductions are made as in term time.

12   Suspension of sick pay

Most authorities include in their schemes a provision that if sickness is due to the teacher's misconduct, failure to observe the conditions of the scheme or conduct prejudicial to recovery, benefits may be suspended. When this is done, the teacher is informed of the fact and may then make representations to the authority.

No allowance is payable in respect of injury arising from professional sport unless the authority otherwise determines.

13   Deductions from sick pay

In accordance with general practice in public employment, no teacher, during sickness, may receive from public funds an amount in excess of his full salary. When a teacher is absent on full or half pay which, together with benefits receivable from other sources, would exceed full pay, deductions are made in respect of allowances to which the teacher is eligible under the Social Security Acts.

If there is an entitlement to sick pay for the first three days of absence, a deduction is made only if that benefit is actually received.

Since 1948 teachers have been required to contribute for benefits under the Social Security Acts and it should be particularly noted that the deductions from sick pay are made by the authority if the teacher is entitled to benefit, whether he has claimed the benefit or not. It is important, therefore, that claims to full entitlement, including any benefits payable in respect of dependants, should be submitted promptly. Otherwise the teacher will suffer loss of income. As noted, short absences totalling no more than eight weeks in any year are covered by SSP and not benefit.

If a teacher, having exhausted his sick pay, is given notice of dismissal (whether on grounds of permanent incapacity or for any other reason) before returning to work, full salary with normal deductions only is payable for the period of the notice.

14   Saturdays and Sundays

Saturdays and Sundays falling within a period of sick leave do not count against the sick pay entitlement, unless they immediately precede or follow a period of leave. Exceptions may be made when a weekend comes in a period of unpaid leave of less than a week's duration.

15   Graduated contributions

When graduated contributions were introduced by the National Insurance Act 1959, teachers in general were contracted out of the scheme. They paid only the employee's share of the basic contribution to which the employer added his proportion, and bought an appropriate stamp to affix to the employee's card.

The National Insurance Act 1966 introduced a scheme of earnings-related supplements to the various benefits, financed by additional graduated contributions. These must be paid by all employees between the age of eighteen and the minimum pensionable age if their earnings exceed £9 a week. The employer collects his servants' contributions through the pay-as-you-earn tax system, adds an equal contribution of his own, and forwards it to the Collector of Inland Revenue.

Part-time and supply teachers, who do not contribute to the teachers' superannuation scheme, are liable for the full graduated contribution, not simply that part which is in respect of the earnings-related supplement.

16   Declaration as to National Insurance entitlement

All teachers are required to notify the authority of their entitlement to benefit under the Social Security Acts, and of any subsequent changes. Such entitlement is related to the number of dependants, of whom only one may be an adult.

17   Married women

The older scheme by which women could elect to be exempted from the payment of contributions other than those which they could not avoid (industrial injuries and graduated contributions above a certain weekly income) has been abolished.

A married woman who elected as above, for exemption, is not entitled on the basis of her husband's insurance to sickness benefit, unemployment benefit, maternity allowance or a full retirement pension. Nevertheless, the Teachers' Sick Pay Regulations provide that, if she is ill, the authority will deduct from her salary the full amount of the benefit to which she would have been entitled if she had paid the full contributions.

A married woman who pays contributions in full is of course entitled to full benefits. She may be entitled to claim benefits for as long as two years after exemption, in virtue of contributions previously paid or credited, and should therefore continue to submit claims until she is notified that her entitlement has expired.

18   First appointments

Teachers leaving college become entitled to sickness benefit shortly after starting work, and should claim benefit immediately if they are ill. The DHSS requires this evidence, even though benefit may not be immediately payable, in order to grant credits for contributions in respect of complete weeks of absence.

19   Leave for reasons other than personal illness

Leave of absence may sometimes be granted for reasons other than the personal illness of the teacher. Except in grave emergencies, such leave should be requested in advance through the head of the school. The question of payment of salary is at the discretion of the authority and varies widely in practice.

It has been held in the courts that a dismissal is not valid if a teacher is absent for urgent cause without the permission of the authority but with the permission of the head.[10]

Some of the grounds on which leave of absence is sometimes granted are noted below, but these must not be regarded as more than a general guide to the sort of application which may be considered by an authority. Because of the considerable differences in the practice of the local education authorities, only a general indication has been given as to whether salary is payable in any particular instance. For detailed information, the teacher must consult the rules of his own authority.

(a) *Serious illness of relative.* The usual degrees of relationship which are accepted are husband, wife, father, mother, child, brother, sister, a child of whom the teacher is guardian and, in exceptional circumstances, other persons. It is generally a condition that a doctor should certify that the illness involves serious domestic difficulties which require the teacher's presence.

(b) *Death and funeral of members of the family* in the categories listed above.

(c) *Weddings* of relatives in the same degrees.

(d) *Private or family business* – usually without pay.

(e) *Holiday with husband or wife.* This is primarily intended for cases where the teacher's spouse is serving in HM Forces or is compelled to take the main annual leave in termtime. Such leave is normally without salary.

(f) *Blood transfusions.* Teachers may be allowed to act as donors provided that they keep themselves fit for normal duties.

(g) *Conferences on purely educational matters* to which the teacher is a delegate, or of which he is a permanent official.

(h) *Courses of training approved by the authority.* Some authorities will allow leave for the final months of study for a degree.

(i) *Examinations and private study.* Most authorities pay for leave for an examination which would improve the teacher's educational qualifications, but this is not universal. Salary is not paid for private study at home without attendance at a recognized institution.

(j) *Examination duties.* Paid leave is generally allowed for absence in connection with public examination duties.

(k) *Honours, decorations and degrees.* Leave is usually granted for the ceremony of presentation to a teacher or the teacher's spouse, child or ward.

(l) *Inquests, witness and jury service.* Leave is normally with pay but any fee received should be handed to the authority which will then refund out-of-pocket expenses which are not in excess of the fee.

(m) *Days of religious obligation.* Leave is usually granted with pay on condition that the teacher may be required to make up the time in another school on a day on which his own is closed.

(n) *Interviews for appointments.* Some authorities limit the number of days' paid leave which may be granted for this purpose in a year. In some cases salary is not paid when the post sought is outside the profession.

(o) *Public duties.* Special leave may be granted for teachers who are candidates at parliamentary or local elections, or who have other public duties, including attendance at national conferences of political parties. An employer must permit an employee to have reasonable time off with pay for duties as a justice of the peace, or as a member of a local authority, a governor of a maintained educational establishment, or a water authority.[11] The statutory provisions for time off for officials of independent trade unions, and for members of appropriate trade unions, have already been noted.[12]

A teacher complained to an industrial tribunal in 1978 that his employer, Buckinghamshire County Council, had failed to give him enough time off to carry out his duties as a Justice of the Peace. The tribunal granted him a declaration under section 60 of the Employment Protection Act 1975 that he should be granted 19 days per annum off, with all days of absence over 10 unpaid. The Employment Appeal Tribunal held however that the industrial tribunal did not have jurisdiction to impose such a specific condition.[13]

In deciding what is reasonable time off in this connection, an employer may take into account all the circumstances, in particular:

(i)   how much time off is required for the performance of the duties of the office or as a member of the body in question, and how much time off is required for the performance of the particular duty;

(ii) how much time off the employee has already been permitted under this and similar releases;

(iii) the circumstances of the employer's business and the effect of the employee's absence on the running of that business.[14]

(p) *Sport and out-of-school activities.* Leave may be granted to act in a responsible capacity at sports meetings, musical festivals, etc., promoted by schools or associations of schools. Occasionally, leave may be granted to enable teachers to represent their country in international sports events or trials.

(q) *National service.* Members of the Territorial Army, the Auxiliary Air Force, the Officers' Training Corps, the Royal Naval Volunteer Reserve or the Air Training Corps may be allowed leave for annual training. Pay may be allowed for part of the absence on proof that the whole period of training has been completed.

(r) *Visits to other schools.* Leave for a limited number of days a year may be granted for purposes of observation.

(s) *Other teaching.* Teachers are increasingly involved in staffing in-service courses organized by polytechnics, universities and the DES. Some authorities expect half of any fees earned to be paid to them. The teacher, however, may be taxed on the whole fee.

20   Unauthorized leave

In 1979 a well known Welsh rugby football player and physical education teacher applied for leave of absence to play for Tredegar Rugby Football Club. The period in question started two days before his school's Whitsun holiday and ended five days after the holiday period. When subsequently the local education authority paid his salary, deductions were made in respect of the Whitsun holiday period, and the teacher appealed to the court.

The local authority argued in court that they had previously written to Mr Evans indicating that the leave of absence would be without pay, and that by going on leave Mr Evans had accepted this counter-offer, if it was one. Mr Justice Foster however did not think, in the circumstances of this case, that 'they are empowered to make any offer which is different to the application made ... to grant leave without pay for a period for which no application was made is in my judgment *ultra vires* and a nullity'.[15]

However, a teacher who effectively absents himself without leave may be liable to disciplinary procedures like any other employee, at the employer's discretion.

This case is also of considerable interest because of its possible implications for teachers' holiday entitlement.

The absence of any clear conditions of service agreement on the teacher's day, duty and holiday entitlement, together with the custom and practice that teachers might be required to undertake a reasonable amount of work out of school hours, has hitherto suggested that, in law, holidays were an act of 'grace and favour' by teachers' employers. The case of *Evans v. Gwent* appears to have destroyed this notion as far as holidays are concerned: Mr Justice Foster decided that the Gwent Education Committee, having in April 1978 fixed the terms and holidays for all Gwent schools for 1979, the holiday dates so fixed became a holiday entitlement of its teachers. This view had long been widely professed by the teachers' organizations but never before clarified in court.

The question of whether a *local education authority* may grant leave conditionally on the basis that it must also be without pay for a period for which no application has been made was not clarified in this action. The facts of the case were simply that the chairman and vice-chairman of the schools sub-committee who had dealt with Mr Evans' application had no authority delegated to them by the Gwent local education authority to attach conditions to such applications.

References

1. Mears *v*. Safecar Security Ltd (1981) IRLR 99 EAT.
2. In Maloney *v*. St Helens Industrial Co-operative Society Ltd (1932) 49 TLR 22.
3. Davies *v*. Ebbw Vale UDC (1911) 75 JP 533; LCT 75.
4. R. *v*. Wintersett (1783) Cald MC 298.
5. This might cover a whole range of accidents including, for example, being knocked down by a careless motorist, illness arising from food poisoning which can be traced to actionable negligence, etc.
6. The national scheme is contained in the Burgundy Book.
7. Employment Protection (Consolidation) Act 1978, s. 60.
8. Lavery *v*. Plessey Telecommunications Ltd, *The Times*, 25 March 1983.
9. Employment Protection (Consolidation) Act 1978, s. 118 and ILEA *v*. Nash, *The Times*, 13 November 1978, EAT.
10. Martin *v*. Eccles Corporation [1919] 1 Ch. 387.
11. Employment Protection (Consolidation) Act 1978, s. 29.
12. See p. 125.
13. Corner *v*. Buckinghamshire County Council (1978) EAT 77 LGR 269.
14. Employment Protection (Consolidation) Act 1978, s. 30.
15. Evans *v*. Gwent County Council, *Education*, 22 October 1982.

IX
Superannuation of teachers

1 Statutory provisions

The legal basis of the scheme is to be found in the Superannuation Act 1972, which applies to a wide range of persons employed in the public service.

Section 9 of the Act empowers the Secretary of State for Education and Science to make regulations dealing with teachers' pensions, allowances or gratuities, with the consent of the Minister for the Civil Service. The regulations also prescribe the conditions under which such benefits may be paid.[1]

The various matters which may be included in any regulations are specified in Schedule 3 to the Act. The Secretary of State is required, before making any regulations, to consult with the representatives of local education authorities, of teachers, and of anyone else he deems appropriate.

For the purposes of this section the word 'teachers' includes persons employed, otherwise than as teachers, in educational work which involves a substantial control or supervision of teachers and those employed in connection with the provision of education or its ancillary services.

All teachers employed in maintained schools must participate in the scheme. 'Accepted schools' are independent schools operating the scheme in the same way as grant-aided schools: full-time service in these establishments is counted as reckonable service.

Independent schools operating a modified form of the scheme are called 'admitted schools'. Service in such schools places a teacher in a position somewhat different from that in grant-aided or accepted schools, and is described in a leaflet obtainable from the DES, and known as 430 Pen.[2]

2   Contributions

Teachers in contributory service pay a contribution currently of 6 per cent of their salary during such service, and at least an equal amount is paid by the employing authority. Contributions are not funded separately but are appropriated in DES funding. An actuarial inquiry into the scheme is held every five years and, should this reveal a deficiency, supplementary contributions are payable by the employers. The contributions cover both personal and family benefits.

No contributions are payable in respect of service exceeding forty-five years' pensionable service, nor after the age of 70. Teachers are only very rarely permitted to remain in service after the age of 65.

In cases where a teacher's salary is reduced, he may opt to continue paying contributions on his previous higher rate of salary. This procedure is dealt with in section 17 of this chapter.

Contributions are deducted from salaries by the employer, who remits them to the Treasury. They are allowed as a deduction from income for tax purposes.

Deduction of correct contributions from salary is a matter between the teacher and the employer. A teacher may be asked at any time to make up under-deductions from salary. Teachers whose salary is reduced may elect to pay higher contributions to maintain retirement benefits.

3   Reckonable service

Reckonable service is, in general, all full-time service as a teacher in schools not conducted for private profit and, in certain cases, as a local authority inspector or full-time youth leader employed by a local education authority. Such service falls into four categories:

(a) *Recognized service* is full-time service as a teacher, rendered between the ages of 18 and 65.

(b) *Contributory service* (the so-called 'reckonable' service) includes full-time service, up to his 70th birthday, of a teacher in a maintained or grant-aided school, initial teacher training institution, county college, or place of further education in England and Wales. It may include periods as an inspector or adviser with responsibility for the control or supervision of teachers, or organizing or advisory work in connection with the services ancillary to education such as School Meals or Youth Service. Full-time service may include 'class supervision and subsidiary duties such as corrections, preparations, and supervision'. It may be divided between two schools under the same control or management. In general, it is held to be sufficient for the teacher to be on contract as a full-time teacher with a full-time salary.[3] Part-time service is contributory at the irrevocable option of the teacher.

(c) *Qualifying service* is employment, whether or not as a teacher, which is accepted by the Treasury for qualification for a pension. Service in independent schools which do not operate the government's superannuation scheme may be so counted, as may certain periods of service abroad. War service which does not count as recognized or contributory service is always included under this head. An application for the recognition of qualifying service should be made within three months of: (i) entry into contributory service by a person who has not previously been so employed; or (ii) entry into qualifying service from contributory service.

(d) *Approved external service* may be counted in establishing a claim to a retirement pension, but is not in itself pensionable under the teachers' superannuation scheme. It includes teaching service in Scotland and Northern Ireland, service in universities in the United Kingdom and many parts of the Commonwealth, employment in the Civil Service which is not integrated with teaching service, work as an educational officer of the British Broadcasting Corporation, employment as an educational administrator, or service recognized under the National Health Service (Superannuation) Regulations.

4   Supplementary service

Service as a supplementary teacher was not pensionable. In the case, however, of those in such employment on 1 April 1945 (or re-employed after that date) the following provisions have been made:

(a) Teachers who, within a year of being employed as supplementary teachers, were not subject to the Local Government Superannuation Act 1937, are automatically in contributory service. They may opt to count all, or part of, their previous service on payment of the appropriate contributions.

(b) Teachers who, within a year of being employed as supplementary teachers, were subject to the Local Government Superannuation Act 1937, could remain in that scheme if they chose, or withdraw their contributions, with compound interest, and join the teachers' scheme with the option to count all, or part, of their previous service on payment of the appropriate contributions.

5   Overseas service

A teacher who has been in contributory service in this country may count a period of teaching overseas as pensionable service on payment of the appropriate contributions. Such service is normally limited to six years, but the period may be extended by the Secretary of State. Teaching in schools maintained by other Commonwealth countries in Britain may be counted similarly.

To facilitate the recruitment of staff to schools overseas in which it is desirable that British teachers should be employed, a similar provision can be made, even if there is not any previous service in this country. Such service will normally be allowed for a period of up to six years, provided that the teacher enters contributory service within two years of the end of overseas service. Contributions for the period spent abroad will, in the case of teachers with no previous contributory service, be based on the salary they would probably have received under the Burnham Scale if they had been teaching in this country. The contributions payable include both the teacher's and the employer's share.

6   'Buying-in' service

Teachers who are employed in reckonable service may buy-in any years after the age of 20 and before 60 at an actuarially determined cost.[4] The limitations are:

(i)   not more than thirty years may be bought-in;
(ii) there is a special restriction on the number of years which may be bought-in by a teacher who first enters reckonable service after the age of 50;
(iii) only such service may be bought-in as will not cause the teacher's reckonable service to exceed forty years at the age of 60;
(iv) the number of years which can be bought-in, may be restricted if the teacher concerned will receive superannuation benefits from some other scheme;
(v)   the number of years which will count in the calculation of the lump sum will be restricted if the teacher's actual, reckonable service at retirement is less than twenty years;
(vi) total contributions to the superannuation scheme, including instalments paid for the purpose of buying-in added years, must not exceed 15 per cent of salary, as this is the

maximum amount which attracts income tax relief under Inland Revenue rules.

There are four methods of payment.

Method A: Payment by instalments based on a fixed percentage of salary for a whole number of years and a minimum of five years.

Method B: Payment by a lump sum based on the teacher's age and full salary at the date the Department of Education and Science receives the teacher's election to pay by this method.

Method C: Payment by fixed instalments of the lump sum determined as in Method B, plus interest over a period of five to ten years, with the payment period commencing on 1 October following the acceptance of an election.

A teacher, under age 55 on 1 October following the date on which the election is received, must complete payment by his 60th birthday and a teacher who is over 55 on 1 October must spread the payment over five years exactly.

Method D: Available only at retirement to a teacher who has made an election by Method A involving a payment period that will cease after the teacher's 69th birthday and prior to his 70th birthday.

This method has been introduced because the regulations restrict the payment period attached to a Method A election to a period which it is realistic to expect the teacher to complete, that is, before his 70th birthday, and in consequence could prevent the teacher from being able to buy-in as many past added years as he may wish. An election under this method could only be in respect of a gap in service which occurred before the Method A election had been made and provided the teacher had indicated, at the time of making the Method A election, that he may wish to consider paying for further added years by means of a deduction from his retirement lump sum.

It is possible to buy-in by a combination of methods, partly by Method A and partly by B, or partly by C and B.

A teacher who chooses Method A must declare at the time that he knows of no reason why his state of health should prevent him from completing the contract for the purchase of additional years.

If a teacher retires from teaching, changes from full-time to part-time service or leaves for any other reason (otherwise than through death or infirmity) and has not completed the payment period, he will be credited with the number of added years represented by the contributions already paid and will have the option to pay off the outstanding amount by a lump sum.

At retirement this could be effected by a deduction from the retirement lump sum.

Once made, an election to buy-in is irrevocable.

An explanatory leaflet, 374 Pen., is available from the DES (Pensions Branch).

7 War service

War service by a teacher who left contributory service for this purpose is counted as contributory service. If the authority supplemented the service pay or if the service pay was equal to, or higher than, the teacher's salary, normal contributions were paid by both teacher and employer on the full teaching salary.

If the authority did not supplement the service pay, and the latter was less than the teaching salary, no contributions are payable and the service is treated as fully contributory.

In cases where a teacher in training, or a trained teacher who had not yet entered contributory service, undertook war service, such service is treated as contributory without payment of contribution unless the service pay equalled or exceeded the amount he would have received as a teacher.

Teachers in service, or who commenced certain courses of training before specified dates in 1950, are now treated (as to one half) as being in reckonable service in respect of service in HM Forces, and certain auxiliary services, undertaken before 1 April 1949. Contributions are deducted from the lump sum.

There is no entitlement to family benefits in respect of this service. The scheme applies to existing pensioners at, but not to those who died before, 1 September 1974. It does not apply to anyone who has transferred out of the teachers' superannuation scheme.

'War service' means service in any of the naval, military or armed forces of the Crown, or any service during that period which the Education Board considered could properly be treated in the same manner as service in those forces. For the purposes of the Teachers' Superannuation (War Service) Act 1939, the war started on 1 September 1939 and ended on 31 March 1949.

NATIONAL SERVICE

The Teachers' Superannuation (National Service) Rules 1949 provide that such service will count as reckonable service only where a person was employed in reckonable teaching service immediately before undertaking national service: it must be emphasized that the teacher must actually have completed a teachers' training course and have been employed as a teacher before being called-up for national service, for this service to be counted as reckonable service.

8 Residential and other emoluments

Emoluments in kind form part of a teacher's contributory salary only if the Secretary of State is satisfied that it is impracticable or inconvenient to convert their value into cash salary. In such cases the Secretary of State must be satisfied that there is an actual legal obstacle to conversion (such as a clause in a trust regulating a school foundation which requires a teacher to occupy a rent-free house by virtue of office and not as a tenant). A contract or agreement, which may be altered or cancelled during the tenure of employment, is not usually sufficient to satisfy the Secretary of State.

Board and lodging may not normally be treated as an

emolument which may be included in a teacher's contributory salary.

Emoluments in kind which are a reward for duties beyond those of a full-time teacher (such as boarding-house supervision) are not pensionable.

9 Leave of absence

Absence on sick leave is not treated as contributory service:

(a) after continuous sick leave of more than twelve months, or eighteen months in the case of tuberculosis;
(b) after the issue of a medical certificate of permanent incapacity for further contributory service;
(c) when on less than half-pay.

Periods of leave, other than sick leave, may be treated as contributory service up to a maximum of thirty days in any financial year. If a teacher is seconded on full pay for a longer period (e.g. for further training) the time limit of thirty days does not apply.

Leave without pay, or other unpaid service, up to a maximum of one year may be counted as contributory service with the Secretary of State's permission. In this case the teacher will be required to pay both his own and the employer's share of the contributions for the period concerned, and to satisfy the Secretary of State that he intends to return to contributory service. Application for permission should be made as early as possible.

10 Re-employment after retirement

If a teacher retires, even for one day, he is entitled to claim his lump sum and to receive a pension for the period of retirement. Should he return to contributory service, or to service which would be contributory if he were under the age of 70, his pension may be suspended if his annual salary on re-employment is as great as it would have been had he remained in service. If his salary during re-employment is less, he may receive enough of his pension to make it up to the salary at the date of retirement. If he has allocated part of his pension, the salary before retirement is considered to be reduced by the amount which is equal to the allocated part of the pension.

Re-employment for a period, or periods, amounting to a full year may be taken into account for the reassessment of superannuation benefits, but the teacher's pension is not thereby reduced. Service after the age of 70 cannot be allowed for reassessment. If the service after retirement does not qualify for reassessment, the contributions are returned to the teacher.

A teacher can be re-employed on a part-time basis permanently without loss of pension, provided that his earnings plus his pension in any particular quarter do not exceed the quarterly rate of his equivalent salary on retirement.

11   Part-time teachers

Superannuation arrangements for part-time teachers do not apply to service in all educational establishments. The conditions under which such teachers may elect to have part-time service treated as pensionable are fully explained in leaflet 476 Pen., available from the DES Pensions Branch.[5]

12   Application for pension

Four months before retirement a teacher should write to the Department of Education and Science (Pensions Branch),[6] asking for the appropriate forms for application for allowances. After completion they should be sent to the employing authority who will forward the application to the DES.

The DES will not notify an assessment of the allowances before the formal date of retirement, that is, the last day on which salary is paid or, if the teacher has already retired, his 60th birthday.

13   Qualification for allowances

Retirement is optional at 60 and contributory service cannot continue beyond the age of 70. With the approval of the local education authority, however, a teacher may continue in non-contributory service beyond the latter age. Most local education authorities, under the national conditions of service, provide for automatic retirement at the end of the term in which a teacher attains the age of 65 and for extension beyond that age by mutual agreement.

In *Nothman v. London Borough of Barnet 1977*, it was held that if there is a normal retiring age for the employment group to which an employee belongs, the right to complain to an industrial tribunal of unfair dismissal applies until that age is reached. Only if there is no normal retiring age will applicants lose their right of complaint at 60 in the case of a woman and 65 in the case of a man.

The fact that an employee has reached his pensionable age (but not his normal retiring age), and can voluntarily retire, does not mean that the employer can automatically terminate his employment at that stage, unless of course a valid reason for termination exists.

Allowances are based on the number of years of pensionable service, up to a maximum of forty-five (of which only 40 may be counted before the age of 60), and on the teacher's highest salary for any successive 365 days during the last three years of service. To qualify for allowances, a teacher must have completed five years' pensionable service. They are not payable before the age of 60, except in the case of an infirmity allowance.

All service, including odd days, is taken into account in determining a teacher's entitlement to a pension.

14   The pension

The pension is a sum equal to one-eightieth of the highest salary for any successive 365 days during the last 1095 days' (three years') service, for each year of pensionable service. This is subject to a limit of forty-five years, of which not more than forty may be service before the age of 60.

Teachers who are entitled to receive a modified pension under the National Insurance scheme receive a reduced pension to which they become entitled on reaching the age of 60 in the case of women, or 65 for men. The amount of the reduction varies according to the amount of modified service, but the maximum is £67.75 a year, and this applies only where a teacher has completed forty years' modified service.[7]

The pension may be paid by draft which may be cashed at any bank, proof of life and identity being required when payment is due. Payment may, alternatively, be made by credit to the pensioner's account.

Pensions are treated as earned income for tax purposes,[8] and assessments in this connection are made by HM Inspector of Taxes, Public Departments (3), Ty Glas Road, Llanishen, Cardiff, to whom all correspondence on the subject should be addressed.

15   The lump sum

The lump sum is equal to three-eightieths of the highest salary for 365 consecutive days during the last 1095 days (three years) of service, for each year of pensionable service. This is subject to a limit of forty-five years.

In the case of teachers with pensionable service before 1 October 1956, the service before that date is calculated at the rate of one-thirtieth for each year. The limitation which applies to the pension requiring not more than forty of the qualifying years to have been completed before the age of 60 does not apply to the lump sum, but the amount attributable to service before that pensionable age must not exceed one and a half times the salary.

The lump sum is payable on application to HM Paymaster General immediately after the notification of the award.

16   Allocation of part of pension

On reaching the age of 60, or on retirement, teachers in good health who have qualified for a pension may, subject to certain conditions, surrender up to one-third of their pension for actuarially equivalent benefits payable to a wife or other dependant after their death. This may be done without interrupting service by temporary retirement, but the terms offered to 'continuing teachers' are less favourable than those for 'retiring teachers'.

A teacher may not allocate more than a third of the pension, or such an amount as would make the pension smaller than that payable to a beneficiary after their death. Neither may they allocate so small an amount that the beneficiary will receive less than a quarter of the reduced pension after their death. There are two ways of making an allocation:

Option A permanently reduces the teacher's pension by the amount of the allocation and secures a pension for the beneficiary on the teacher's death.

Option B also permanently reduces the teacher's pension, but the teacher also receives an annuity during the lifetime of the spouse. On the teacher's death the spouse receives a pension which is double the annuity.

It is equally open to a woman teacher to allocate in favour of her husband or other nominated dependant.

17   Safeguarding of amount of pension

If a teacher continues in service, but at a lower rate of salary, he may safeguard his pension at the higher rate, but only with the consent of the Secretary of State. To do so he must continue to pay contributions on the higher salary, and also pay the appropriate part of the related contribution by the authority.

18   Invalidity benefit

A teacher with a minimum of five years' pensionable service may, on the grounds of permanent incapacity, receive an invalidity benefit and lump sum. Enhancement of reckonable service for this purpose is currently as follows:

1 Actual reckonable service	2 Service counting for allowances (subject to column 3)	3 Limitation affecting column 2
5 years to 9 years 364 days	Twice the number of years of the actual reckonable service	Not exceeding the amount of service which could have been completed by 65th birthday
10 years to 13 years 122 days	20 years	ditto
More than 13 years 122 days	Either 20 years or actual reckonable service plus 6 years 243 days whichever is more favourable	ditto Not exceeding the amount of service which could have completed by 60th birthday

Lump sums paid on disablement are calculated at the rate of three-eightieths of the average salary for each year of service since 1 October 1956, and one-thirtieth for each year of contributory service before that date.

If a teacher's health breaks down before the completion of five years' service he is entitled, provided that one year has been completed, to a short service gratuity amounting to one-twelfth of his average salary for each completed year of service.

An application for a disablement allowance or short service gratuity should be made within six months of the end of a teacher's contributory sick leave. In this case, twelve months' continuous absence on not less than half pay (or as a special case, eighteen months in the case of tuberculosis) is treated as contributory sick leave. The Secretary of State has, however, the power to accept later applications.

As in the case of ordinary retirement, the salary is reckoned as the highest amount of salary received for any successive 365 days of reckonable service during the last three years (1095 days) of service. Reckonable service for invalidity benefit may be enhanced by up to six and two-thirds years of service as compensation for premature retirement, subject to a limit of what could have been completed by the age of 60, and a maximum of forty years. The Pensions (Increase) Act 1971 applies to disability benefit.

Teachers in receipt of National Insurance sickness benefit may continue to draw this after receiving invalidity benefit, but it is replaced by National Insurance invalidity benefit after 168 days. Those not receiving sickness benefit under the National Insurance scheme should register as incapable of work. Teachers signed off by their doctors whilst receiving invalidity benefit should, if they are under the age of 65, register as unemployed.

Teachers who return to contributory service after receiving a breakdown allowance will not have their pensions reduced on retirement, but the lump sum in respect of the whole period of service will be reduced by the amount already received.

It has been held that the acceptance of a short service gratuity by a teacher automatically frustrates his contract of service without the need for notice.[9]

19 Death gratuity

When a teacher dies in reckonable service, a death gratuity equivalent to the best consecutive 365 days' salary during the last three years, or the lump sum which would have been payable if the teacher had retired on an infirmity allowance at the time of his death, will be paid. This is conditional upon death taking place in contributory service or within twelve months of leaving such service, and the completion of five years' reckonable service.

There are arrangements for men who die before completing

five years' reckonable service, and for temporary payments to a male teacher's widow for a period of three months. These payments are equivalent to the teacher's qualifying salary.

20   Note on will

Every teacher should enclose with his will a note to his executors quoting his DES reference number and instructing them to write, claiming any allowances payable at his death, to the Department of Education and Science (Pensions Branch), Mowden Hall, Staindrop Road, Darlington, Co. Durham, DL3 9BG. This note should not be attached with a pin or paper clip. In one case a teacher had pinned such a note to his will, but when his executors sought to obtain probate they had to swear an affidavit to the effect that the pin-holes and the rusty mark were not caused by any attempt to tamper with the testator's wishes.

21   Widows, widowers, orphans and other dependants

The integrated scheme introduced in 1972 includes provision for dependants. If a teacher's contributions cover dependants, either because they have been paid since 1 April 1972, or because all previous service has been bought-in, the dependants' allowances are reduced proportionately. These pensions commence on the conclusion of the temporary pension referred to in section 19 above.

The pension for one dependent child is one-half of the widow's pension; if there are two or more dependent children, the pension is equal to the widow's pension.

If there are dependent children, but no widow, one child qualifies for two-thirds of the teacher's pension; if there are two or more children, the amount payable is four-thirds.

A woman teacher may nominate any financially dependent close relative (including a dependent husband) to receive these benefits.[10] An unmarried man may similarly nominate an adult dependant, but this nomination lapses on his marriage.

Within six months of marriage it is possible to purchase

previous years of reckonable service to improve widows' benefits.

22 Return of contributions

Where a teacher fails to qualify for the payment of benefits before reaching the age of 60, all contributions paid may be returned with compound interest at 3 per cent after three months[11] continuous absence from contributory service. A similar provision exists for women who marry, provided that they cease to be employed in pensionable service within one year of marriage − subject, where appropriate, to deductions in lieu of graduated contributions to the National Insurance scheme. Such payments are subject to a standard deduction of 10 per cent for income tax. The contributions of teachers who leave the profession, or who move to approved external service, are frozen until they qualify for allowances.

Contributions cannot be repaid to a teacher who:

(a) leaves reckonable service after 31 March 1977 and is qualified for pension benefits payable immediately on leaving, or at age 60; or

(b) has at any time while in reckonable service earned a salary exceeding £5000 in any year and has not been employed in reckonable service after 5 April 1980; or

(c) has the right to return to work after maternity under the Employment Protection (Consolidation) Act 1978 unless that right is not exercised; or

(d) has earned a guaranteed minimum pension which cannot be discharged by the payment of a contributions equivalent premium.

Employer's contributions cannot in any circumstances be repaid.

23 Effect of dismissal

The Secretary of State may refuse altogether, or grant at a reduced rate, any benefits when a teacher's service has ceased through grave misconduct. It would appear that in such cases the decision is at the Secretary of State's discretion and it is immaterial whether the service has been concluded by dismissal or by resignation.

24   National Insurance

Since 1948 all teachers have been required to pay National Insurance contributions. Qualification under the National Insurance Acts is additional to any benefits receivable under the Teachers (Superannuation) Acts for 'existing teachers' who opted to continue payment of the full contributions under the Teachers (Superannuation) Acts as well as those to which they are liable under the National Insurance scheme.[12]

Most teachers are contracted out of the national graduated pension scheme, but have to pay contributions at the lowest rate applicable to contracted-out employees. These contributions earn units of graduated pensions, but do not affect contributions or benefits under the teachers' superannuation scheme.

Those entering service too late to qualify for benefits under the teachers' superannuation scheme before they reach the National Insurance retirement age (60 for women and 65 for men) must pay the full graduated contributions. They pay lower contributions under the teachers' scheme, and their pensions are reduced by approximately the amount of their graduated pension.

25   Transferability

Under certain conditions it is possible to transfer pensionable service between various sectors of the public service provided there is no more than a very limited break. Unless the DES is notified within three months of any change of employment, the right to transfer may be lost.

The principal services between which transferability arrangements may, at present, be made are the teaching profession, the established Civil Service, the Post Office and pensionable employment in local government, the National Health Service and some public boards.

The Department hopes, in future, to increase these facilities, and to include moves to and from private employment.

26   Premature retirement

Regulations allow teachers who retire before the age of 60, in certain circumstances, to receive their pension on retirement. The regulations affect all teachers in the employment of local education authorities, and teachers in voluntary aided schools.

In order to qualify for premature retirement benefits a teacher must have five years' service, and his retirement must be attributable either to redundancy or to a decision that that retirement will be in the interest of the local education authority's service. Teachers under 50 years of age cannot qualify.

Such teachers are paid the benefits to which their contributions have entitled them under the superannuation provisions, and such payments are made from the Fund. Local education authorities *may*, however, augment such benefits by payment from their own funds to cover a notional addition of years of reckonable service, provided that the shortest of the following periods is not exceeded:

(a) ten years;
(b) a period equal to the total of the teacher's pensionable service;
(c) a period which would bring the teacher's pensionable service to more than forty years;
(d) a period in excess of that between the day following premature retirement and ending on the day the teacher will attain the age of 65.

There is currently no national agreement about the level of enhancement payable in individual cases and there is substantial variation between authorities. Enhancement in individual cases is negotiated between teachers and their employers. The assistance of a professional association is invaluable.

The accrued pension and enhancement are usually index-linked from the age of 55, and are paid separately – the former by the DES and the latter by the employer.

There is no automatic right to early retirement or enhancement, both of which are at the employer's discretion.

27   The Pensions (Increase) Act 1971

The purpose of this legislation is to keep pensions in the public service more or less in step with decreases in the value of money through the effect of inflation. Earlier Acts had added specific amounts or percentages to pensions commencing before particular dates, and further increases could be secured only by a further Act.

After setting out the percentages to be added to pensions beginning before 1 April 1971,[13] the 1971 Act provides that the Minister for the Civil Service shall make an annual review of official pensions against any rise in the cost of living during the review period, starting as soon as possible after 31 March 1973. If the review discloses a rise of at least 4 per cent, the Minister must make an order raising pensions beginning before the review period by the percentage disclosed. Pro-rata increases must be applied to pensions commencing after the beginning of the review period.[14]

28   Guaranteed minimum pension

The Social Security Pensions Act 1975 introduced the concept of a guaranteed minimum pension for all within the framework of the National Insurance system. Teachers have been contracted out of this scheme by the Secretary of State, and the Teachers' Superannuation Regulations have been amended to provide certain guarantees in the light of this action.

At state pensionable age, at present 65 for men and 60 for women, it is guaranteed that a teacher's pension will not be less than the guaranteed minimum pension, and that the contingent widow's pension will not be less than half her husband's guaranteed minimum pension. The pension of the widow of a teacher, when the marriage took place after retirement or withdrawal from reckonable service, is calculated at the normal rate of accrual of the husband's contracted-out service: that is, from 6 April 1978 or such later date as he may have entered such service.

At present a widow loses her pension if she remarries, or goes to live with another man. The revised regulations provide that in future the pension will merely be reduced to the rate of the guaranteed minimum pension.

Part of a pension equal to the guaranteed minimum pension can be forfeited only if the teacher or the widow, as the case may be, is convicted of treason, or one or more offences under the Official Secrets Acts 1911–39 for which there has been a sentence on the same occasion to imprisonment (whether one term or consecutive terms) amounting in total to ten years.

A pension and lump sum will be awarded to teachers who have attained the age of 60, even though they have less than five years' pensionable service.

Arrangements are also made for teachers who transfer to other schemes. If the new scheme is contracted-out, and its managers agree, a transfer value will be paid to that scheme. A transfer value will not be paid to a scheme which has not been contracted out, however, unless a teacher has insufficient service to qualify for a preserved pension. In such cases a contributions equivalent premium would have to be paid to the Department of Health and Social Security to buy the teacher back into the state scheme, and a related deduction would be made from the transfer value.

References

1. The Teachers' Superannuation Regulations 1976 (as amended).
2. All correspondence with the DES in connection with superannuation should be addressed to: The Department of Education and Science, Pensions Branch, Mowden Hall, Staindrop Road, Darlington, Co. Durham, DL3 9BG.
3. Where, with the consent of the Secretary of State, a teacher pays contributions during a break in contributory service, the

contributions are assessed on the probable salary he would have received had he remained in the same (or similar) contributory service. This does not apply to allowances which began to accrue before 10 November 1965, or to a gratuity payable before that date. If the Secretary of State's consent to payment was given before 10 November 1965, the teacher could elect to pay under the 'probable salary' clause from any date not earlier than 1 January 1962. This, however, did not apply to any period of absence falling partly or wholly before that date.

4. The Teachers' Superannuation (Amendment) (No. 2) Regulations 1982.

5. The address of the Pensions Branch is given in note 2 above.

6. See note 2 above.

7. See section 24 below.

8. Contributions made during service are exempted from tax.

9. Watts v. Monmouthshire County Council and another (1968) 66 LGR 171; LCT 77.

10. It may well ultimately be held to be discriminatory in law that a deceased male teacher's pension passes in part to his widow, but not that of a woman teacher, unless the widower is totally dependent on the wife's pension. In 1984 a seventh protocol was added to the European Convention on Human Rights guaranteeing 'Equality of rights and responsibility of spouses.'

11. This may be reduced for teachers who are emigrating.

12. 'Existing teachers' are those who on 1 July 1948:
    (a) were in reckonable service, or
    (b) had completed an approved course of training, or
    (c) had entered an approved training college, or
    (d) had been accepted for an approved course of training, or
    (e) had applied for admission to an approved course of training and, as a result of that application, later began such a course, provided that they entered contributory service within six months of completing that training.

13. Pensions (Increase) Act 1971, s. 1.

14. Pensions (Increase) Act 1971, s. 2.

PART II
TEACHERS AND
THEIR EMPLOYMENT

X
Routine Administration

1 Obligatory records

Both the Department of Education and Science and the local education authorities require certain records to be kept in schools. This chapter deals principally with those required by the DES, since the local authorities' forms differ widely. The keeping of such documents should be done with care. Some of the records, or certified extracts from them, are admissible as evidence in the courts and it is vital that they should be accurate. It is a serious reflection on a teacher when, for example, an attendance register is kept carelessly or inaccurately.

The DES requires that in every maintained and voluntary school, or every department of such a school organized under a separate head, the following records should be kept by, or under the supervision of, the head:[1]

(a) an admission register;
(b) attendance registers;
(c) the school annals (sometimes known as the log book or school record);
(d) a punishment book in which all cases of corporal punishment must be recorded.

Entries in these documents must be written in ink. They must be originals and not copies, and all alterations should be made so that both the original entry and the correction are clearly distinguishable.

Admission and attendance registers must be preserved for at least three years from the date on which they were last used. The same requirement applies to the punishment book. The school annals should be preserved at least during the life of the school.

2 Admission of pupils

The Articles of Government normally provide that the admission of pupils is under the control of the local education authority in the case of county schools and of the governors in aided and special agreement schools.[2]

A pupil may not be refused admission to, or be excluded from, a school on other than reasonable grounds. It has been held that it is not reasonable to refuse a child admission to a voluntary school merely because he does not belong to the religious persuasion providing the school. Other grounds which have been held to be unreasonable are that the child has previously been untaught, that he is shoeless and neglected, that he has been irregular in attendance or that his brothers and sisters do not attend the school.

The Race Relations Act 1976 provides that it is unlawful for anyone concerned with the provision of education to discriminate against any person by refusing or deliberately omitting to provide him with it on the grounds of colour, race, nationality (including citizenship) or ethnic or national origins. The courts have held discrimination against Sikh dress to be racial discrimination.[3] No person may on these grounds be refused access to education or treated less favourably than anyone else.[4]

Refusal to admit, or a decision to exclude, has been held to be reasonable if a child has been persistently insubordinate after suffering the usual punishments, or if there has been a refusal to submit to a medical examination in connection with the cleansing of a verminous child.[5]

A pupil may not be admitted to, or retained in, a special school unless it is suitable for him, having regard to age, sex, and his special educational needs. In cases of doubt, a pupil may be admitted for a trial period. The roll of a special school must not exceed that approved by the Secretary of State.[6]

An admission register, which may be of looseleaf or card-index form, must be kept in which the name of every pupil is entered on the day he first attends the school. The details required are:

(a) the full name of the pupil;
(b) sex;
(c) the name and address of the parent or guardian;
(d) the date of the pupil's birth, verified if necessary by reference to the birth certificate;
(e) the date of admission or re-admission;
(f) the name and address of the last school attended;
(g) in the case of schools taking boarders, a statement as to whether the pupil, if of compulsory school age, is a boarder or a day-pupil.

A child whose name is entered in the admission register becomes a registered pupil of that school,[7] and his name must be deleted only when one of the grounds noted in section 4 (p. 279) has become applicable.[8]

Children may be admitted only to schools for which they are qualified by age, ability, aptitude and any special educational needs they may have.[9] A child of primary school age may not be admitted to a secondary school.[10] The development of middle schools permitted by the Education Act 1964 has blurred the former distinction between primary and secondary schools. For administrative purposes, however, each middle school is specifically designated by the Secretary of State as either a primary, or a secondary, school.[11] Similarly, a child ascertained as having special educational needs must not be admitted to an ordinary school if the local education authority has required his admission to a special school.

Children must not be admitted to nursery schools before they attain the age of 2. In the case of nursery classes forming part of a larger school, the lower age limit is 3. They must not be retained after the end of the term in which they reach the age of 5. These limits may be varied if there are exceptional circumstances in the case of any pupil.

The Education Act 1980[12] provides that, for every maintained school, a limit shall be determined of the number of pupils to be admitted in any age group(s) in which pupils are normally admitted. This is referred to in the Act as the 'standard number'. A limit may also be set on the number of pupils to be educated in any other age group in a school. Limits in county and controlled schools are determined by the local education authority, and may not be exceeded without the authority's consent. Those for aided and special agreement schools are settled by the governing body after consultation with the authority, and may not be exceeded without further consultation. The authority decides to which age groups limits are to be applied.

If a local education authority, or the governors of a voluntary school, wish to reduce the number of pupils to be admitted to the school in any one year by 20 per cent or more of the standard number, they must go through the procedures in the 1980 Act outlined for approval of a 'significant change'.[13] These involve the formal issue of public notices and the consideration of objections.

Parents may also express a preference for admission of their child or children to a school maintained by an authority other than the one in whose area they normally reside.[14]

Since formal admission policies have generally been thought of in connection with secondary schools, it is important to note that the Act extends these provisions to all schools other than nursery and special schools.[15]

3   Admission of children from overseas[16]

Local education authorities have the same statutory duties to provide educational facilities to children from overseas as to

United Kingdom children. Similarly, as regards the education of their children, parents from overseas have the same rights and are under the same duties as United Kingdom parents. None of these rights and duties is affected in any way by the status of the children or their parents under the immigration rules. Discrimination against such children is also unlawful.[17]

Under the immigration rules a student from overseas who has gained admission to a university, polytechnic, college, independent school or any *bona fide* private educational institution may be admitted to the country on those grounds. Heads will note that maintained schools are not included in these categories of institution. It would therefore be most unwise and possibly misleading to the visitor to offer a place in a maintained school to a pupil who is not already in this country.

Visitors may remain in the United Kingdom for up to one year. Whether it is reasonable to admit children of visitors to schools for a short period is for governors and local authorities to determine in the light of each application. A visitor has the same right of appeal to the Secretary of State as a United Kingdom parent.

European Community nationals are treated as United Kingdom citizens.

4 Removal from roll

The name of a pupil must be removed from the roll of a school on any of the following grounds becoming applicable.[18] It is important that the name should not be removed until there is evidence that one of the conditions has been fulfilled. When a pupil's name has been removed, he ceases to be a registered pupil of that school and, should the parent fail to cause him to be admitted to another school, the local education authority might be considerably embarrassed in proceedings for failure to attend school.

If still of compulsory school age:

(a) if the pupil is registered at the school through the

requirements of a school attendance order, and the order is amended by the substitution of another school or revoked because arrangements have been made for the child to receive suitable education otherwise than by attendance at school;

(b) in any other case where the child has become a registered pupil of another school;

(c) in any case not falling within (a) above when the pupil has ceased to attend the school and the parent has satisfied the authority that he is receiving efficient full-time education suitable to his age, ability and aptitude otherwise than by attendance at school;

(d) when, being a day-pupil, he has removed to a place from which the school cannot be reached with reasonable facility;

(e) when the pupil is certified by the school medical officer as unlikely to be fit to attend school before becoming exempt from the obligation to do so;

(f) when the pupil has been continuously absent for at least four weeks and reasonable inquiries have failed to elicit the cause of absence;

(g) when the pupil is known to have died;

(h) in the case of a boarder, or a pupil in a school not maintained by a local education authority, when the child has ceased to be a pupil of the school;

(i) when the pupil will cease to be of compulsory school age before the next meeting of the school and it is known that he intends to leave;[19]

(j) when the pupil has been permanently excluded by the local education authority or by the governors of a maintained school.

If the Secretary of State, as the result of an appeal by the parent, determines that the child has been excluded unreasonably, the name must be restored to the roll.

If not of compulsory school age:

(a) if the pupil has ceased to attend the school or, if a boarder, he has ceased to be a pupil of the school;

(b) when the pupil has been continuously absent for at least four weeks and reasonable inquiries have failed to elicit the cause of absence;

(c) when the pupil is known to have died.

When a pupil of compulsory school age, who is not the subject of a school attendance order, has become a registered pupil at a special school under arrangements made by a local education authority, his name must not be removed from the roll of that school without the consent of the authority or, if this be refused, without a direction by the Secretary of State.

5   Suspension and expulsion of pupils

The procedure to be followed is laid down in the Articles of Government and in the regulations of the local education authority. Suspension is within the jurisdiction of the head and is usually the limit of his power, but there are some schools where the head is authorized by the Articles of Government to expel. It cannot be too strongly urged that, even where this is so, it is always wiser to choose the less final course. Suspension gives the pupil and his parent the opportunity of a constitutional inquiry, whereas there is an administrative difficulty connected with expulsion (see below) which might mean that the decision would have to be revoked, with consequent embarrassment to all concerned, except, possibly, the pupil.

Even the right of suspension should be used with the greatest discretion, and only for serious and urgent cause. When a head has decided to pursue this course he should explain carefully to the pupil that he may not attend school again until the matter has been fully considered. The suspension should be communicated at once, in writing, to the parent and to the local education authority. In the case of voluntary-aided schools the head should notify the correspondent or clerk, whose duty it then becomes to inform the authority.

The parent must be given an opportunity of attending any meeting at which the suspension is to be considered. At this meeting, unless there are cogent reasons to the contrary, it should be decided, subject to any consents which may be necessary, either to fix a date from which the suspension will be lifted on such conditions as may seem desirable, or to renew the suspension for good reason, or to expel the pupil.

It is the duty of the head to tell the parents that they have a right to appeal. In the first instance they may address their appeal to the governors and, if this proves unsuccessful, they may also state their case to the Secretary of State. If the child is expelled, they may request that he should continue as a pupil of the same school; and should the Secretary of State decide that the expulsion is unreasonable, the child must be readmitted by the school.[20] The Secretary of State might make such a decision if, for example, the parents stated that the school in question was the only voluntary school within reasonable distance to provide religious education in accordance with their own beliefs. Herein lies the danger of expulsion from an administrative point of view. If the Secretary of State's decision were to be against the governors there would be a considerable loss of face by all concerned, and the force of expulsion as an ultimate sanction would be lost.

Problems can arise when a pupil is expelled. The duty to ensure that a child receives 'efficient full-time education suitable to his age, ability and aptitude . . . , either by regular attendance at school or otherwise' resides in the parent:[21] the local education authority's responsibility is to provide a sufficient number and variety of schools for all the children it has a duty to educate, and this includes those whose presence in a particular school has become impossible. Normally, no proceedings for *non-attendance* can be taken in the courts in respect of any child who is suspended or who, being expelled, has not been admitted as a registered pupil at another school. There may be action, however, for *breach of the statutory duty to cause to be educated.*

Where, however, suspension is due to the parent's encouragement of his child's disregard of the school rules, a prosecution of the parent may be successful, as was the case in *Spiers v. Warrington Corporation* referred to elsewhere.

In view of what has been written in the last paragraph, local education authorities are naturally not over-enthusiastic about the expulsion, or even the suspension, of pupils from a maintained school, and many feel that they have a moral, if not a clear statutory duty to keep children in school.

During the past few years many authorities have established a number of special units where it is hoped that treatment can be provided for difficult children and 'school refusers' which will enable them, ultimately, to return to normal school life.

There is always the possibility that a parent may complain to the courts that the authority is failing in its own duty, and thereby preventing him from performing his under section 36. Halsbury[22] suggests that if there is an absolute refusal of admission to any school the parent may be obliged to pay for his child's education, if necessary at a private school. With the recent tendency towards the reduction or elimination of corporal punishment there has been a further tendency for suspensions to increase in numbers. Some local education authorities have shown a corresponding tendency to advise and sometimes to exert pressure on heads not to suspend pupils. During the past few years there has also been an awareness that violence, insubordination and other forms of anti-social behaviour have increased among pupils. As a result heads sometimes find themselves faced with a staff demand that a pupil should be suspended. It is also implicit in such a demand that the governors will support the head and the staff, so that expulsion will follow as a matter of course. In such a situation the head may well find himself subjected to opposing pressures from the authority and the staff.

Suspensions fall into one of two broad groups, and may arise from a specific and serious breach of school order by a pupil or, alternatively, from the cumulative effect of a long series of disruptive acts.

In law, that is according to the Articles of Government, the head's position has not changed: the decision to suspend, or not to suspend, remains his alone.

In order to avoid a large number of suspensions, it is not unknown for a local education authority to suggest that a head may consider keeping a pupil out of school for a specific period of, say, three or four days, or to surround the head's discretion with a range of the procedures described below before suspension takes place.

The Articles do not provide a head with the discretion to re-admit a pupil by ending a suspension. The first of these courses, therefore, needs· great caution and, if it is employed, great care should be taken not to refer to suspension but to exclusion. The distinction was drawn by Lord Chief Justice Goddard in *Spiers v. Warrington Corporation* in 1954. Whereas suspension is a refusal to admit to the school, exclusion, a term not known to the law in this context nor indeed used by Lord Goddard, is a willingness to admit the child at all times subject to certain conditions being met. In *Spiers v. Warrington* the condition was one which, in itself, might not nowadays find approval in the courts, namely that the girl pupil shall not wear trousers. Nevertheless, the principle of conditions, as such, remains. One condition may be, for example, that parents visit the school, perhaps, as some schools are requiring, to sign a 'good behaviour' agreement with or on behalf of their child. The pupil must be readmitted as soon as the condition is fulfilled. In view of the uncertainty as to the extent of the head's powers in this situation, exclusion should be used with the greatest of care if the head is not to be accused of unreasonably denying a pupil his rights to education. The condition must be reasonable, and must be capable of being fulfilled. It is doubtful if the passage of time *per se* is sufficient; in other words, exclusion should be designed for the benefit of the child or the school, or both, and should not be used as a disciplinary procedure equivalent to rustication in the ancient universities. It will normally be preceded by endeavours to secure parental co-operation in the issue at stake.

The 'requirement' by some local education authorities that heads should enter into a long series of procedures before suspending any pupil, including such tactics as consultation and correspondence with the parents, seeking the advice of the educational welfare service, arranging for the services of the child guidance clinic, or discussing a transfer with a colleague in a neighbouring school, is appropriate to the cumulative variety of suspension. In such a case the relationships between pupils or pupils and staff may well have broken down to such an extent that it will be in the pupil's interest, as well as that of the school, that he should move elsewhere. There are occasions when in spite of his concern for the individual pupil, his dislike for handing on his professional failures to someone else, and his care not to seem merely to cast out a difficult member of the community, a head must ask: 'Have I now reached the stage where I must place the welfare of the school as a whole, and the other pupils as individuals, above my concern for this pupil?'

It is not, however, necessarily a justifiable criticism by parents that they knew nothing of any problems at school before a suspension. Sometimes a pupil commits some offence, perhaps quite out of keeping with his character, for which there is no alternative to immediate suspension and the law will always support a head in this. Sometimes there may have been prior indications of a deterioration in behaviour which were insufficient to cause enough concern to notify the parents. If, in these circumstances and with due consideration, a head considers that suspension is the only course, he has a duty to take this step as part of his legal responsibility under the Articles of Government.

No one suggests that suspension is a procedure on which to embark lightly or prematurely. Professionally, however, delay can lead to a situation where it is difficult to distinguish one act of indiscipline from another in order to decide that suspension has become inevitable. In the end it is often staff strain which tells, and the offence which precipitates the suspension may be less serious than some of its predecessors which appear to have been condoned. It may also make justification of the suspension more difficult on the facts at law. Delay can also lead to a deterioration in the behaviour of the pupil concerned and in the good order of the school.

As was said earlier in this section, the power of suspension should be used only in the interests of the pupil concerned or those of the school as a whole, it must be firmly rooted in facts which can be established and it must be exercised strictly in accordance with the Articles of Government.

Finally, it must be remembered that in suspending a pupil a head revokes his jurisdiction to his governors who have, subject to appeal, complete discretion. If they readmit the pupil, even against his advice, he has no cause to complain nor have the other members of the staff.

6   Infectious illness

Pupils suffering from an infectious or contagious illness should be excluded from school in accordance with the regulations of the local education authority. Unless the notification comes from him, the medical officer should be informed of the illness. If a case of an unusually serious nature, such as smallpox, diphtheria, cholera, dysentery or poliomyelitis occurs amongst the pupils of a school it is advisable to telephone the medical officer and ask for special instructions.

Children in contact with infectious illnesses at home are excluded in certain cases. Contacts should be carefully watched after their return to school, in case the disease develops at this later stage.

The medical officer should be informed of verminous children in order that he may take the necessary steps for cleansing them.

The closure of schools during an epidemic is now rare. Children running about and playing together are as dangerous to each other as they are in school. Moreover, during such periods, teachers can watch for the appearance of symptoms and do much to prevent the spread of the epidemic by prompt action. Closure is a matter for the medical officer.

7   Transfer of records to other institutions

When a child ceases to attend a school and becomes a pupil at any other place of education or training, such educational information as the governing body considers reasonable shall be supplied to the new school if requested.[23]

8 Educational year and holidays

All maintained schools, including special schools, must meet, except for unavoidable cause, for not less than 400 half-day sessions in each calendar year, from which may be deducted not more than twenty for closures during term. This does not apply to nursery schools.[24]

The 1981 Regulations require that, where it is 'reasonably practical', schools should make up at alternative times any sessions unavoidably lost. This could create difficulties for schools if, as seems likely from the case of *Evans v. Gwent* discussed in chapter VIII, teachers are contractually entitled to school holidays as soon as the dates are published in advance.

Occasional closures during term, for half term or other purposes, may be granted in accordance with the Articles of Government, provided that the limits described in the first paragraph are not exceeded. It should be noted that these holidays must be taken during the course of a term, and may not be added to the main holidays.

9 School sessions

The length of an individual session is not prescribed, but on every day on which a school meets, there must be provided in a maintained school:

(a) in a nursery school or class – at least three hours of suitable activities;
(b) in a school or class mainly for pupils under 8 years of age – at least three hours of secular instruction;
(c) in a class of pupils 8 years of age and over – at least four hours of secular instruction.

This must be divided into morning and afternoon sessions unless exceptional circumstances make this undesirable. If a school meets on six days in the week, two days may consist of a single session of half the length noted above. If pupils attend a nursery school or class for half a day only, the session may be of one and a half hours' duration.

The time set aside for registration is excluded from these periods, but the necessary time for recreation, and the medical examination, inspection, and treatment of pupils (including dental treatment) may be included. In a voluntary school the time required for the inspection of religious education[25] may also be included.

Schools which seek to operate a 'continental day' (more accurately, a German day) must nonetheless keep within these regulations. There is no definition of a reasonable break at lunchtime, but it is a requirement of the Education Act 1980 that a free school meal should be available for those entitled to it at midday.[26]

10   Timetable

The long-standing regulation requiring schools to publish a timetable has been revoked.[27]

11   Size of classes

There are no regulations stipulating maximum numbers of pupils permitted on the roll of any class.

In 1980 a Nottinghamshire teacher who refused to teach a nursery class which she considered to be too large was not unfairly dismissed, decided an industrial tribunal.[28]

12   Temporary closure of schools

The HMI must be given seven clear days' notice of the closure of a school or the suspension of its ordinary work for holidays or any other cause. If, in the case of an emergency, this notice cannot be given, the closure should be notified by telegram to ARISTIDES, AUDLEY, LONDON, when the message will be transmitted to the inspector concerned. (Tel. 01–934 9260)

The purpose of this notification is twofold. It enables the DES to keep a check on the number of closures during the year, and it avoids fruitless visits by an inspector to a school which is closed.

13 School annals

This record should be kept by or under the supervision of the head, and it forms a permanent record of events connected with the history of the school. The actual form is not prescribed, but the following matters are amongst those which should be included:[29]

(a) matters of significance such as changes in the character, organization or curriculum of the school, alterations to premises, substantial changes in equipment, visits of governors, the illness or absence of members of the staff;
(b) the receipt of any report on the school sent by the DES to the authority, or to the governors, and any remarks made by the DES thereon;
(c) the receipt of any report made to the authority by the committees or officers, if so directed by the authority;
(d) the reasons for a temporary closure of the school, a substantial variation in the routine or a marked change in the average attendance.

14 Corporal punishment

All cases of corporal punishment must be entered immediately in a book which is kept for this purpose. The head is responsible for its completeness and accuracy.[30]

15 Change of pupil's name

Teachers are asked from time to time to change a child's surname in the school records. This often happens when the parents are divorced and the mother, having the custody of the child, marries or lives with another man. Care is needed in dealing with such a request.

A case came before the Chancery Division on this point in 1962.[31] The mother had changed her child's name to that of her new husband, without informing the father. When she eventually told her former husband of her action he brought a lawsuit in order to restore the child's original surname. It was held that an adult can change his name at any time, and there is no magic in a deed poll, which merely records the intention to change in a solemn form. If there is any power to change an infant's name it resides in the natural guardian, who is the father if he is still alive. An order for custody means no more than the name implies, and does not abrogate all the rights of the father. Mr Justice Buckley ordered the restoration of the father's name.

There are some indications that the law may be changing.

The mother of four children went to live with another man. After the husband set up home with a woman and the children, the mother secured custody, and arranged for them to be known by the surname of the man with whom she was living. The three eldest children settled down happily, but the youngest became disturbed and went back to his father. The mother sought to regain custody. The father appealed against her successful application.[32] Lord Justice Stamp said that the names by which children are known attract too much attention in the place where they are being brought up, and in this case it was most convenient that they should be known by the name of the head of the family. In the long term it would be important that all the children should be brought up together. Lord Justice Ormerod added that rule 92(8) of the Matrimonial Causes (Amendment) Rules 1974 was designed to prevent parents who had custody, or care or control orders, from changing names by deed poll or some other formal means; but it now troubled the school authorities and children, and a sense of proportion was necessary. Children should be protected from embarrassment by being known by a name other than the mother's, and it was to be hoped that no-one would make a point about a change of surname, and treat it as a symbol of the mother's attitude towards the children's father.

Despite this, Mr Justice Latey, in *L. v. F.* (1978)[33] declined to follow the Court of Appeal in *Rice v. Rice*, and preferred the view of Lord Justice Cairns in the Court of Appeal in 1976:[34] 'The mere fact that there has been a divorce, that the mother has remarried and has the custody of the child, is not a sufficient reason for changing that child's surname.' Mr Justice

Latey said: 'A marriage can be dissolved, but not parenthood. The parents in most cases continue to play an important role in their children's emotional lives and development .... As the years pass by the children might bitterly resent, and be disturbed by, the deprivation of their father's name at an age when they had no understanding of that decision, and no say in it. Today, divorce is commonplace. The fact that the children's surname is different from that of the mother and their half-sister would not cause embarrassment.' His Lordship ruled that the children should retain their father's name, but granted leave to appeal.

In 1980 in the Court of Appeal[35] Lord Justice Dunn took the same view. The first and paramount consideration was the children's welfare. The judge had to use his discretion to decide whether the change would be in the children's best interests, after he had heard all the evidence and had seen the witnesses, the parents, and possibly the children. Decisive importance should not be given to the wishes of young children of 10 and 12 years who would wish to avoid giving offence to their mother. The facts to be taken into account included the child's possible embarrassment at school, his link with the father, his interests on a long-term basis and the stability of the mother's marriage.

Requests to change names in records should be referred to the local education authority for advice. In any case the entry in the admission and attendance registers should be in the form, 'Smith, otherwise Jones', to enable quick cross-referencing, and to prevent, for example, the invalidation of a summons for failing to attend school.

The position is somewhat different where a child with a foreign name which is very difficult for his English classmates is known by an English name; sometimes the parents adopt an English forename without intending to make any legal or permanent change. In such cases no formality is required, but both names should appear in all registers. Entries for external examinations should always be made in the legally recognized name to facilitate the verification of qualifications against other documentation later in life.

16   Scientific dangers

Ionizing radiations. No instruction may be given in any school or further educational establishments involving:

(a) radio-active material which has an activity in excess of .002 of a microcurie per gram, or
(b) apparatus in which electrons are accelerated by a potential difference of 5 kilovolts or greater, other than apparatus used primarily for the purpose of receiving visual images by way of television, closed circuit television or the output of a computer, unless the Secretary of State has given his approval, which may be withdrawn at any time.[36]

Carcinogenic amines. Naphthylamine and other known carcinogens should not be kept in schools. The risks are greatest with beta-naphthylamine and benzidine.[37]

Lasers. Under no circumstances should laser beams be viewed directly, and their use should accord with the Ministry of Technology's Code of Practice for Laser Systems (1969).[38]

17   Bombs and explosive devices

A feature of life in recent years has been the use of explosives in civil disturbances. In the train of this development has come the practical joker who gets some satisfaction out of giving false warnings that a bomb has been placed in a particular building. Hundreds of hoaxes of this kind were perpetrated in London during the month following an explosion in the Post Office Tower.

It is now a criminal offence to communicate information, known or believed to be false by the person passing it on, which is intended to make anyone believe wrongly that a bomb (or anything else) is present in a place where it is likely to ignite or explode. It is immaterial that the hoaxer has no particular victim in mind. The penalty on summary conviction is imprisonment for a maximum of three months, a fine of up to £1000, or both; and on indictment imprisonment for a term not exceeding five years.[39] Schools have had their share of false alarms and, unfortunately, there have been sufficient explosions elsewhere to make it imperative to treat every warning as genuine until all reasonable steps have been taken to establish its true nature.

In the first place, it must be remembered that pupils are in the care of the staff *in loco parentis*, and the precautions to be taken are those which a reasonable parent would take in similar circumstances. Safety is the paramount consideration.

The school's fire drill system may be sufficient as far as the pupils are concerned, but if a spate of warnings is received it may be necessary to devise a special scheme, possibly in consultation with the police.

Immediately a warning is received the school must be cleared and all pupils escorted to the safest available place where the register should be checked to ensure that no one has been left behind. The police should be informed immediately, with as much information about the nature of the call as possible.

Unless arrangements have been agreed with the police beforehand, a search of the premises should be deferred until the police arrive. This is essential if a particular call seems particularly significant, or any suspicious object has been noticed. Assistance in searching by teaching or non-teaching staff must be a matter for individual voluntary consent, and must not be given if it has been prohibited by the local education authority. No pupils, whatever their age, should be permitted to search.

The police can rarely, if ever, say that they are completely satisfied that there is no risk in returning to the building. The head will have to take this decision, basing his judgement on the facts available to him, such as whether the call is one of a series, whether a deadline was given, the nature of the search and so forth.

No amateur attempts should be made to touch any object which arouses suspicion.

If an external examination is interrupted by an evacuation, the examining board should be asked by telephone for instructions before it is resumed. A written report should also be sent.

Sometimes a public occasion, such as a concert or prizegiving, may be scheduled to take place during a period when a school is suffering a series of hoaxes. In such cases the advice of the police should be sought as to any special precautions to be taken.

18   Age of majority

Since the age of majority was reduced from 21 to 18, secondary schools have, for the first time, numbered adults among their pupils, and this has led to a considerable degree of uncertainty about the relationship between these pupils and the school organization.

The legislation provides that a person shall reach 'full age' on attaining the age of 18,[40] and applies to all statutory provisions and rules of law unless there is a contrary definition or expression of intent. It also applies to wills and other instruments made after the Family Law Reform Act came into force on 1 January 1970. As teachers are sometimes asked by pupils about their rights in law, a summary of the principal changes is given below, and the table on pages 296–7 sets out the minimum ages for a wide variety of acts.

It is now possible at the age of 18 to marry without parental consent (section 2), to make a valid will and to benefit under intestacies occurring after 1 January 1970 (section 3). Various maintenance orders may be kept in force until attainment of the age of 21, and a son may not claim under the Inheritance (Family Provisions) Act 1938 until he reaches that age (sections 4 and 5).

Persons under the age of 18 may be described as 'minors' instead of 'infants' (section 12).

A minor, having attained the age of 16, may give consent to any surgical, medical or dental treatment which would otherwise constitute, without consent, a trespass to the person. This includes diagnostic procedures and ancillary acts including, particularly, the administration of an anaesthetic (section 8).

Schedule 2 of the Act sets out a number of miscellaneous changes effected by the Act. On attaining the age of 18 it is now possible to become a member of the committee of a trade union, a friendly society, or an industrial and provident society (membership can begin at 16) and also to vote and hold office in a building society. The powers of a guardian over the person and property of a minor[41] cease when the minor attains the age of 18. At the same age a person can apply income to maintenance and accumulate a surplus income; he may be hypnotized at a public entertainment; he may withdraw money from a trustee savings bank, and sue for wages; he may receive betting advertisements; and he may become a governor of a school.

In certain matters, however, no change was made by the Act. Under Schedule 2 it is expressly provided that the Act does not affect the Representation of the People Act 1933, so that no person under the age of 21 may be a candidate at a parliamentary election. Neither can he be a candidate in a local government election.[42] Statutory provisions relating to taxes are also unaffected by the changes in the law.

It is still an offence for consenting males to commit an act of gross indecency together, even in private, if one of them is under the age of 21.

So far as schools are concerned, the two problems which are most commonly raised are the rights and duties of the teacher *in loco parentis* towards pupils who are adults, and the power to exercise control over such pupils in cases of indiscipline.

No cases have so far come before the courts for decision on these points, and any consideration must therefore, to some extent, be a matter of conjecture. So far as the first issue is concerned, it would seem doubtful if the schoolmaster can be *in loco parentis* to an adult. Nevertheless, he owes a common law duty of care to everyone who comes to the school, as well as duties under the Occupiers Liability Act 1957 and the Health and Safety at Work etc. Act 1974. To discharge these duties he must have an adequate, fully maintained system, and in planning that system it would be prudent to remember that he has among his pupils a number of young adults and, usually, a large number of children on the premises. Any system he devises should aim to prevent injury to any person in either of those categories, and must be enforced.

Legal age limits
At the age shown in the left-hand column a person:

Minors

Children	May	Must
0	Have a bank deposit account	
6w	Be handed to prospective adoptive parents	
4½m	Be adopted	
2	Join a nursery school	
3		Be paid for on public transport
5		Begin school
10	Be charged with a crime	
12	Buy a pet	
13	Have a current bank account at the manager's discretion	

Young persons

	May	Must
14	Go into a bar with an adult	Pay full fares on public transport
	Consent to his fingerprints being taken	
	Be fined up to £200	
	Be sent to a detention centre	
	Be admitted to an 'AA' film	
	Own an air-gun	
15	Own a shot-gun	
	Join the Army, Navy, Royal Air Force or Women's Royal Army Corps with parental consent	
16	Drink cider or beer with a meal in a room with no bar	Pay National Insurance Contributions
	Leave school	Have own passport if travelling abroad (except when travelling on a collective passport)
	Buy fireworks	
	Fly a glider solo	
	Marry, with parental consent	
	Consent to medical treatment	
	Buy and smoke cigarettes and tobacco	
	Drive a moped or tractor	

16½	Receive sickness and unemployment benefit	
17	Drive a car or motorcycle Pilot a powered aircraft solo Be sentenced to imprisonment Join the Women's Royal Naval Service with parental permission	Be tried on any charge in an adult court

Adults

18	Not be adopted Buy or consume alcohol in a bar Become a blood donor Own land Be admitted to see 'X' films Enter a betting shop Marry without consent Join the Women's Royal Air Force Bring an action before the courts Give a body organ or tissue for transplant Vote in a parliamentary or local election Receive, personally, money under a will Make a will
21	Drive a lorry or bus Serve on a jury Stand for election to Parliament or a local authority

There can be little doubt that the relationship between a pupil and the school changes immediately the former attains his majority. A possible basis for discipline seems to be the acceptance by both that the pupil remains at school voluntarily, and thereby agrees to abide by the rules of the school so far as they may reasonably be applied to him. It is most doubtful whether detention or corporal punishment may be used to deal with disciplinary offences by adult pupils, in view of what has been said in the last paragraph about the position of the schoolmaster *in loco parentis* to these members of the school. If, however, their behaviour merits it, they can be suspended and, if it seems right in all the circumstances, expelled.

Various subsidiary questions are raised from time to time. If an adult pupil wishes to be withdrawn from religious education should he not make the request himself? On the face of it, this seems reasonable, but the Education Act 1944 has not been amended at this point. Parents are still expected to contribute to the maintenance of their children until they are 25 (or 21 in the case of a married daughter) if they are students, unless they have been self-supporting for three years.

To whom should a report on the work of an adult pupil be given? It is probably wiser that this should be handed to the pupil, and not sent to the parents.

In general, the rights and obligations of a parent or guardian end when the child reaches the age of majority. A parent's rights and obligations would end on the child's earlier marriage, but this would not be so in the case of a guardian whose male ward married before the age of 18.

The problems are similar to those with which universities and colleges have had to deal for a very great many years. There is no indication that the difficulties of schools have been vastly increased merely because the age of majority has been lowered. As time goes by a corpus of practice will develop. In the meantime a working relationship may be founded on the acceptance that the pupil is continuing in attendance voluntarily, and voluntary membership of any organization implies an acceptance of its rules and customs.

19   School councils

Some schools have established councils, which include members of the staff, pupils and, sometimes, non-teaching staff. Insofar as these bodies can act in a consultative capacity to achieve desirable results which cannot be attained in some less formal way there is much to commend them.

It must be pointed out however that, whatever the ideals which may lie behind the promotion of 'effective' school councils with a 'real' say in the running of a school, the law has not been changed, nor has the responsibility been shifted. A head who allows a school council to be formed cannot abdicate his legal responsibilities to it. If the council is adamant in proposing a course of action which he can reasonably foresee will lead to disaster, and disaster ensues, it will be the head and not the council who will be accountable.

20   Work experience

A pupil in his last year of compulsory schooling may be employed under regulations made by the local education authority with a view to providing work experience as a part of education. Before 1973 this was possible only for those who had reached the upper age limit of compulsory education.[43]

Pupils may not be employed under this Act in ships. Nor may they be employed contrary to any statute, by-law, regulation or other statutory provision which excludes young persons from any description of work or prescribes the conditions under which they may perform it.

21   Employment of children

Under the Employment of Children Act 1973, restrictions are placed upon the employment of children of compulsory school age with a view to safeguarding the health and wellbeing of those who have frequently proved a temptation to employers seeking cheap labour.

The Act has removed the power of local education authorities to make by-laws in respect of the employment of children, and placed the responsibility for making regulations in the hands of the Secretary of State. The supervision of the regulations remains with the local education authority.

A person who assists in a trade or occupation carried on for profit is deemed to be employed, even though he receives no reward for his labour.

Age limits. No child may be employed until he has attained the age of 13.

Time limit. On days on which he is required to attend school a child may not be employed before the end of school hours, nor for more than two hours. He may not be employed for more than two hours on a Sunday, nor before seven o'clock at night on any day. The nature of the employment must be such that he is not required to lift, carry or move anything so heavy as to be likely to cause him injury.

The Secretary of State's regulations may reduce the age limit for children employed by their parents in light agricultural or horticultural work and may permit employment for not more than one hour before the beginning of school hours. The regulations may also prohibit altogether the employment of children in certain occupations and may prescribe restrictions regarding the actual periods of employment, periods of rest and holidays. They may also prohibit employment except under and in accordance with a permit issued by the local education authority, and require employers to keep records of children so employed, and to furnish returns. Taking part in street trading is against the law for everyone under the age of 17 except that a young person with his parents may be permitted to take part by local bylaws.

It is an offence, punishable on summary conviction by fines, for any employer to fail to carry out a local education authority's lawful conditions in this matter or to fail to provide the local authority with any relevant required particulars of employment of children.

Entertainments. The regulations may not prevent a child from taking part in an entertainment under a licence granted in pursuance of the Children and Young Persons Acts, nor in a performance where, by virtue of section 37(3) of the Children and Young Persons Act 1963, no licence is required. A licence is not required if a child has not taken part in a performance of the kind mentioned in the following paragraph on more than three days in the previous six months. Neither is a licence required for a performance under arrangements made by a school, or other organization approved for this purpose by the Secretary of State, provided no payment, other than for expenses, is made to him or any other person.

In general, children are not allowed to take part in any entertainment for which a charge is made, whether for admission or not, to any member of the audience. Neither may they perform in licensed premises, or take part in a broadcast performance, or any recorded performance made for exhibition to the public by broadcast or film. A local authority may, however, grant a licence for such performances (in accordance with any conditions and restrictions which may be made by the Secretary of State for Education and Science).

Children may not be allowed time off from school for unlicensed public performances in any medium. This applies also to auditions and rehearsals. The making of recordings (except for use in a broadcast or a film intended for public exhibition) and modelling, are subject to the ordinary law regulating the employment of children, and not to the provisions dealing with entertainments.

Dangerous performances. No person under the age of 16 may take part in any performance endangering his life or limb, nor may he be trained for such performances if under the age of 12. Between the ages of 12 and 16 a licence is necessary for such training.

Performances abroad. No person under the age of 18 may be taken outside the United Kingdom and the Republic of Ireland for the purposes of singing, playing, performing or being exhibited for profit except under licence. Licences for this purpose are granted only by the Chief Magistrate at Bow Street. The prohibition does not apply to a person under the age of 18 who is not permanently resident in the United Kingdom.

Absence from school. A licence may authorize absence from school: it is for the licensing authority to determine that the holder's education will not suffer thereby.

Age limits. A child who has attained the age of 13 may be licensed for any kind of performance. A younger child may not be licensed unless:

(a) for acting the part cannot be taken except by a child of about his age;

(b) for ballet the part cannot be taken except by a child of about his age, and the programme consists entirely of ballet or opera;

(c) the performance is wholly or mainly of music, opera or ballet, and the child's part is wholly or mainly musical.[44]

Street trading by young persons below the age of 18 is controlled by regulations made by the local education authority in pursuance of the Children and Young Persons Acts as amended by the Education Acts. This includes the hawking of newspapers, matches, flowers or any other articles, singing or performing for profit, shoeblacking and other similar occupations carried on in public places.[45] Young persons below the age of 17 are prohibited altogether from street trading, unless the by-laws permit them to be employed by their parents. Children may not be so employed in any circumstances.

Enforcement of the law relating to the employment of children and young persons is the duty of the local education authority, but often the first notice which an authority has of a suspected infringement comes from a school. Teachers should therefore remember that, though they have no power to act directly in this matter, they can help by bringing apparent breaches of the law to the attention of the local education authority.

Teachers can also help in cases where children who have a licence appear to be suffering as a result of their employment. A purely factual report that a licensed child is lethargic in school will enable the authority to submit him to a further medical examination with a view to considering whether it would not be in the child's best interests to withdraw the licence, or to make it subject to certain conditions.

At any age, a child's wages are the child's property and cannot be demanded by parents as of right. However, a parent is entitled to know of the earnings since these must be declared on the parent's tax return.

22   Information for parents

The information which must be made available to parents about schools is governed by regulations made under the Education Act 1980.[46] The substance of the regulations is given in the earlier section on 'Parental choice'. The requirements are of course minima, and local authorities and schools may if they choose, go beyond these in the interests of relationships with parents and bearing in mind local conditions.

23   The school fund

The school fund contains non-official monies, that is, other than monies derived from local authority expenditure and grants, and is normally under the control of the head teacher. The local authority treasurer has authority to audit the funds, and the local education authority will have detailed regulations about the accounting procedures to be adopted.

The head teacher may be responsible to the governors for the efficient running of the school fund but neither they, nor the auditors, have statutory power to direct the purposes to which the funds are applied.

It is important to bear in mind that a school fund should be used only to provide items which are not normally provided by the local education authority, and not normally be used as a substitute for public funds. This distinction is very important, as upon it depends the willingness of local Inspectors of Taxes to regard the purpose of the fund as charitable and consequently to exempt any interest earned by the fund from income tax.

It may be possible, by arrangement with local education authorities, to register larger school funds for VAT purposes. If this is done, it might be possible to obtain VAT relief on at least part of the fund's activity.

The fund's bankers will be able to advise on the desirability of having the fund formally registered as a charity. A formally registered charity can gain the tax advantages associated with covenanted payments and is in a firmer position as regards tax on investment income. It may also accept donations from other charities and trusts.

The school fund should be insured against the usual risks. Care should also be taken to ascertain whether items purchased by the fund are covered by the local education authority's insurance policy.

References

1. Administrative Memorandum no. 531 (10 May 1956).
2. For the requirements of the Education Act 1980, see 'Parental choice' p. 21.
3. See p. 351.
4. Race Relations Act 1976. See chapter XIII.
5. Gateshead Union Guardians v. Durham County Council (1918) 1 Ch 146.
6. Education (Approval of Special Schools) Regulations 1983.
7. Education Act 1944, s. 114(1).
8. Education (Miscellaneous Provisions) Act 1948, s. 4(6).
9. Education Act 1981, s. 17 and Education Act 1944, s. 36.
10. Except in certain cases between the ages of $10\frac{1}{2}$ and 12.
11. See p. 66.
12. Education Act 1980, s. 8.
13. Education Act 1980, ss. 15 and 12.
14. Education Act 1980, s. 6(5)(a).
15. Education Act 1980, s. 9.
16. DES Circular 1/81.
17. Race Relations Act 1976, ss. 17–19.
18. Pupils' Registration Regulations 1956.
19. The names of these pupils should be removed on the last day of term: Administrative Memorandum no. 531 (10 May 1956).
20. Pupils' Registration Regulations 1956.
21. Education Act 1944, s. 36 as amended by the Education Act 1981, s. 17.
22. *Laws of England*, volume XIII.
23. Education (Schools and Further Education) Regulations 1981.

24. Education (Schools and Further Education) Regulations 1981 and DES Circular 6/83:*The Approval of Special Schools*.
25. Education Act 1944, s. 77(5).
26. Education Act 1980, s. 22(2).
27. Education (Schools and Further Education) Regulations 1981, Schedule 1.
28. See p. 149.
29. Administrative Memorandum no. 531 (10 May 1956).
30. Administrative Memorandum no. 531 (10 May 1956).
31. T. (Orse H.) (an infant) [1963] Ch. 238; LCT 133.
32. Rice *v.* Rice [1977] 1 WLR 1256.
33. *The Times*, 1 August 1978.
34. In re WG (1976) 6 Family Law 210.
35. W *v.* A (1980) LSG 24 July 1980.
36. Education (Schools and Further Education) Regulations 1981.
37. DES Circular 3/70.
38. DES Circular 7/70.
39. Criminal Law Act 1977, s. 51(2) and (3).
40. Family Law Reform Act 1969, s. 1.
41. Under the Tenures Abolition Act 1660.
42. Local Government Act 1972, s. 79.
43. Education (Work Experience) Act 1973.
44. The Children (Performances) Regulations 1968. See also The Law on Performances by Children (HMSO, 1968).
45. The term 'public place' is discussed in Chapter XVII.
46. Education (School Information) Regulations 1981.

XI
School Attendance

1 Compulsory school age

The Education Act 1944 as amended provides that a person who has attained the age of 5 years but has not attained the age of 16 is to be deemed to be of compulsory school age.[1] A pupil may not, however, necessarily leave school immediately he passes his 16th birthday, as he is not deemed for this purpose to have reached the upper age limit of compulsory education until the appropriate school leaving date.[2]

On the other hand, a child born between the Friday before the last Monday in May and the end of August may leave shortly before reaching his 16th birthday.[3]

2 Attainment of age

As the law stood until the end of 1969, a person attained a given age at the beginning of the day preceding the appropriate birthday.[4] Parliament has now acted to provide that since 1 January 1970 a particular age expressed in years is attained at the commencement of the relevant anniversary of the date of birth.[5] Schooling is compulsory from the first day of the term following the child's 5th birthday.

3 Attainment of school leaving age

For the purpose of determining whether a pupil has attained the upper limit of compulsory education Parliament has fixed two school leaving dates in the year, and a pupil may not leave until the relevant date in relation to his 16th birthday:

(a) for pupils born between 1 September and 31 January, both dates inclusive – the end of the spring term at his school;
(b) for pupils born between 1 February and 31 August, both dates inclusive – the 'May school leaving date' (the Friday before the last Monday in May) in the year in which he attains the age of 16.[6]

This law applies to all children who are registered pupils at a school at the date of their sixteenth birthday, or who have been so registered at any school within the preceding twelve months. There are certain categories of young people, however, who attain the school leaving age immediately they reach their sixteenth birthday. Those who have attended a community home during the twelve months preceding attainment of the age of 16; and those who have left schools in Scotland or Northern Ireland, or HM Forces' or other schools abroad before reaching the school leaving age under English law, are examples. The exceptions apply, of course, only to those who have at no time been registered pupils at a school in England and Wales between their 15th and 16th birthdays.

For the purposes of this section the spring term is deemed to be the last term ending before 1 May, and the summer term is the last term ending before 1 September.[7]

A child who has remained at school beyond the school leaving age may, of course, still leave at any time.

4 Presumption of age

In court proceedings for failure to attend school a child is presumed to be of compulsory school age unless the parent proves the contrary.[8]

5 Duties of parents

It is the duty of the parent[9] of every child of compulsory school age to cause him to receive efficient full-time education suitable to his age, ability and aptitude and to any special educational needs he may have, either by regular attendance at school, or otherwise.[10]

There is no obligation on a school to admit a pupil except at the beginning of term unless the child was unable to start then because he was ill, or there were circumstances beyond the parent's control, or the parent was then resident at a place from which the school could not be reached with reasonable facility. Where, under the provisions of this section of the amending Act,[11] it is not practicable for a parent to arrange for his child to become a registered pupil at a school, he is relieved of his duty under section 36 of the Principal Act until such time as he can secure admission of the child.

If a child of compulsory school age, who is a registered pupil of a school, fails to attend regularly, the parent is guilty of an offence.[12] The same section of the Act provides that the following grounds shall be a good defence in the case of day-pupils when action is taken:

(i)   that the child was absent with the leave of any person authorized by the governors or proprietor of the school.
(ii) that he was prevented from attending by sickness or other unavoidable cause. The child himself must be sick. A mother kept her daughter at home because she was herself ill. The justices acquitted her of a charge under this section. On a case being stated for appeal, the matter was remitted to the magistrates with a direction to find it proved.[13]
(iii) that the child was absent on a day exclusively set apart for religious observance by the persuasion to which the parent belongs. This matter is discussed further in the section on 'days of obligation'.
(iv) that the school is not within walking distance of the child's home and the local education authority has failed to provide arrangements for transport, for admission to a school nearer home, or for admission to a boarding school.

This defence does not hold when a child is proved to have no fixed address, unless the nature of the parent's occupation requires him to travel from place to place and the child has attended a school of which he is a registered pupil as regularly as the parent's occupation permits. In the case of a child who has attained the age of 6 this exception is no defence, unless the parent proves that the child has made 200 attendances during the twelve months prior to the commencement of proceedings. Walking distance to school is measured by the 'nearest available route.' This is two miles in the case of children under 8 and three miles in all other cases. In 1954 the Courts held that distance was the only test to be applied, but in 1984 Lord Justice Parker added to this the test of the child's safety: 'To regard Parliament as having intended that there should be regarded as an available route something, such as a public footpath, which was dangerous even for adults, and which was so dangerous for children that no responsible parent would allow a child of the relevant age to use it is, in my view, to impute to Parliament an unacceptable disregard for the safety of children.'[14]

Only the four statutory defences are acceptable. In *Jenkins* v. *Howells* referred to above the magistrates felt great sympathy with the parents, and Lord Goddard did not wonder at this: 'Parliament has not seen fit to provide that what may be called "family responsibilities" or "duties" can be relied on as an excuse for a child not attending school.... But I think "unavoidable cause" must be read in the present context as meaning something in the nature of an emergency.' In this connection the reader is referred to the section on 'Minority groups'.

FREE TRANSPORT AND ATTENDANCE

Pupils who do not live within walking distance of the nearest suitable school must be provided with free transport or payment in substitute for transport.[15] Such payment or transport should cover the whole distance from home to school, and not for part of it: from a point reasonably near the pupils' home to a point reasonably near the school.[16] Local education authorities may also allow non-qualifying pupils to occupy spare seats on a school bus provided for pupils travelling free, and may if they wish make a charge.[17]

The Education Bill 1980 contained a clause which would have allowed local education authorites to charge for transport: this was rejected, however, in the House of Lords, and did not pass into the 1980 Education Act. The major concern of the Lords was that such a change might fall disproportionately on those parents who chose denominational schools, since, on average, their children travel further to school.

A Letter of Guidance[18] issued by the DES on 15 December 1981 to local education authorities expressed the hope that local education authorities would help parents with transport costs, particularly in connection with attendance at voluntary schools, 'some of which have been associated with a local agreement or understanding about the siting of voluntary schools'.

Parents have reasons other than religious convictions for preferring a school which is not the nearest to their home, but their choice may in practice be restricted unless some assistance is given with transport. This applies especially where travelling costs to the preferred school would involve the parent in serious financial hardship. Although the local authority may feel in such cases that arrangements for free transport are not necessary, ... it may be possible to meet the need in other ways. There will also be cases where the authority would be ready to meet the cost of travel to the school nearest the pupil's home which they consider suitable for the pupil, but where the pupil chooses a more distant school. In these circumstances, but subject to what is said in the following paragraph, the Secretary of State hopes that the authority would consider meeting part of the travelling expenses to the extent, if any, that the child's attendance at the chosen school might otherwise enable the local authority to reduce its expenditure on school travel.

The Secretary of State recognizes that there will be cases in which a parent expresses a preference for a school in circumstances where the authority feel that they would not be justified in assisting with the travelling arrangements. The authority may, for example, consider that the distance or duration of travel involved may conflict with the child's ability to profit educationally from attendance at the preferred school.

The law in this respect is not entirely clear. It would seem that there is no statutory obligation on local authorities to pay for travel outside the two- or three-mile limits if a place can be made available in a closer school which is suitable in terms of age, ability, aptitude and special educational needs, where they exist. Voluntary schools are also covered by this principle. Although the issue has not yet been tested in court, it is likely that local authorities who refuse to provide free transport beyond the statutory walking distance on the grounds that there is an efficient bus service would have a good chance of winning a challenge in court.

A local authority which provides transport or payment in substitute beyond the statutory requirements may, in straitened financial circumstances, lawfully reduce its provision to the statutory minimum. Suffolk County Council previously provided free transport if children under 9 lived more than $1\frac{1}{2}$ miles from school. When this was withdrawn, a parent brought an action on the grounds that the Council had been motivated purely by the need to save money and had disregarded other considerations, notably whether free transport was 'necessary for the purpose of facilitating the attendance of pupils at school'. Mr Justice McNeil held: 'In my view it seems quite impossible to hold that the council was exercising its discretion improperly or unreasonably. It was entitled to take finance into account when making its decision and did not disregard other considerations. In no way was it unreasonable in coming to its conclusion and the decision was not unlawful.'[19]

A case heard in 1981[20] involved a parent whose daughter had been issued with a bus pass when it was thought that the school to which the daughter had been allocated was just over three miles from her home. But the facility was withdrawn when it was discovered on re-measurement that the school was in fact just less than three miles away. The parent claimed reimbursement of the fares she had paid for her daughter after the free ticket was withdrawn. The parent's medical practitioner certified that long walks, especially in the winter, would not be in the daughter's interest, but this was disputed by the county council's own doctor.

Lord Justice Lawton in the Court of Appeal said that Kent County Council had exercised its discretion under the 1944 Act[21] to grant a free season ticket to the applicant's daughter. The decision was not irrevocable: it was made under a mistake of fact, and could be reviewed. Furthermore, it was a general principle of law that the doctrine of estoppel[22] could not be used against local authorities to prevent them from using their statutory discretion.

6 Exclusion and attendance

Exclusion by the school may not necessarily be a defence. A mother persisted in sending her daughter to school wearing slacks, maintaining that the girl's health demanded this costume. The headmistress refused to admit the girl in this attire unless the mother produced a medical certificate stating that it was necessary. Although the girl had been excluded, the mother was guilty of an offence.[23]

In another case a boy ran away from school after learning that he was to be caned. His parents said they would send him back if he could be punished in some other way, but the headmaster refused. The boy was suspended and the father was convicted of failing to cause him to attend the school of which he was a registered pupil. The Queen's Bench Divisional Court upheld the conviction when the father appealed on the ground that 'leave'[24] should be construed liberally to include suspension. The greater, it was said on his behalf, included the lesser. Lord Justice Cumming-Bruce held the concept of refusing to allow a pupil to come to school is quite different from giving the pupil permission to be away. The Lord Chief Justice, Lord Widgery, said that suspension is essentially a hostile act, whereas leave is a privilege.

The father's second contention was that the parent is entitled to hold strong views which are not unreasonable. The Court held, however, as has been said above, that no defence other than those set out in section 39(2) could avail, and that on no view could the father's reason come within those bounds.[25]

At the time of writing, however, it is not clear whether this case is still a binding precedent, since the European Court of Human Rights ruled in 1980 in another case that to deny education by using the threat of corporal punishment constitutes a breach of the European Convention on Human Rights.[26]

It is held that a boarder has failed to attend school regularly if he has been absent during any part of a school term when he was not prevented from attending by reason of sickness or other unavoidable cause.

7 Education 'otherwise'

The law does not specifically require parents to send children to school. It requires them 'to cause ... to receive efficient full-time education ... either by regular attendance at school or otherwise'.[27]

A local authority is under a statutory obligation[28] to ensure that the parental duty is carried out. The authority may serve an attendance order if it appears that a child is not being efficiently educated 'otherwise', usually at home, and the efficiency of the education provided by the parents is judged in court.

It has been held that the courts may decide that a child is being efficiently educated, even if it is shown that the child may be *more* efficiently educated in some other way.[29] A parent is, of course, entitled to call evidence for the purpose of showing that he is providing efficient education for his child at home.[30]

A parent may not lawfully 'mix' the two systems; he may not choose to educate partly at school and partly 'otherwise'. If the parent chooses a school as the means of carrying out his parental duty, his child must attend 'regularly' i.e. for the full, normal school opening hours.[31]

The issue of education 'otherwise' has already been before the European Commission on Human Rights.[32] Four dyslexic children were being educated at home by their parents. The parents disliked authoritarianism in the state school system and disapproved of the use of corporal punishment.

The parents were charged and convicted of failure to comply with school attendance orders and for not having shown that the children were receiving efficient full-time education in accordance with sections 36 and 37 of the Education Act 1944. The parents appealed to the Crown Court which complimented the parents on their educational achievements for the children but found that the home education was deficient in respect of literacy and numeracy for two of the children.

The European Commission held that the European Convention on Human Rights implied a right for the state to establish compulsory schooling of a satisfactory standard whether in state schools or private tuition, and verification and enforcement of educational standards is an integral part of that right. The complaint was held to be inadmissible as it was reasonable to require the parents to co-operate with the education authority to ensure a certain level of literacy and numeracy whilst nevertheless allowing them to educate their children at home.

A self-help organization, 'Education Otherwise', which offers support, advice and information to families practising or contemplating home-based education as an alternative to schooling, has been established since 1977.[33]

8   Effect of truancy

Truancy is not a term known to English law. In common speech it is absence from school on the child's own initiative. It is the parent's duty to cause his child to receive full-time education in accordance with the requirement of section 36 of the 1944 Act and it has been held that he is guilty even if he is unaware that his child is truanting.

In 1969 the Bracknell magistrates dismissed an information against the parents of a girl who had been away from school on twenty-three half-days in two and a half months. The justices found that there was no reasonable excuse for twelve of the absences, but that the parents were not aware of them. As soon as they knew, they obtained police assistance to find their daughter and thereafter ensured her regular attendance. On appeal,[34] Lord Parker, the Lord Chief Justice, held that the bench had erred in law. The offence is absolute and 'it is unnecessary in order to create the offence to show any knowledge on the part of the parents of the child's absence or any neglect on their part to ensure that the child did regularly attend. Those are matters which, as the justices' clerk appears to have advised them, were matters wholly in mitigation and did not affect the offence at all. The real and only question here is whether the twelve occasions out of a possible 114 when this little girl was not attending school, and had no reasonable excuse for not attending, amount to a failure to attend regularly. In my judgment they do, and what is more important I read the case stated as showing that the justices were of the same conclusion.'

9 Attendance registers

The Secretary of State's requirements[35] may be summarized as follows:

(a) There must be an attendance register for each class, form or group containing the names of all pupils in that class, form or group. The register must be marked at the beginning of each morning or afternoon session at which secular instruction is given.

(b) Any pupil who is out of class for medical or dental inspection or treatment (unless he is in hospital or receiving treatment at his home) must be marked present. It is immaterial whether the treatment is arranged through the National Health Service or privately.

(c) There must be a special register for secular instruction given elsewhere than on the school premises, but this requirement does not apply to classes forming an integral part of the school, even though they are in detached buildings or another school. If such classes are under the control of the head of the school to which the pupils belong, the attendances should be marked in the ordinary class register.

Apart from these requirements, the methods of marking attendance registers is left to the discretion of the local education authority, whose regulations should be followed.

It is not necessary to record in an attendance register the presence or absence of any pupil who is a boarder in an independent school.[36]

Registers are open to inspection by HMIs, by persons authorized by the Secretary of State under section 77(2) of the 1944 Act and by authorized officers of the local education authority, all of whom may make extracts therefrom for the purposes of the Act.[37]

Moreover, attendance registers are documents from which evidence may be required in a court of law and the registers, or certified extracts from them, may be vital in a prosecution for failing to attend school regularly. Periodic returns must be made of all day-pupils who fail to attend school regularly or who have been absent continuously for two weeks unless a medical certificate has been received. This return must give the full name and address of the pupils concerned, and the cause of absence if it is known.[38]

All entries in attendance registers must be originals and in ink; any alteration should be made in such a way that both the original entry and the correction are clearly distinguishable. Attendance registers must be preserved for three years from the date on which they are last used.[39]

The duty to ensure that registers are kept as required lies with the governors or proprietor of a school. Failure on the part of any person to keep registers as required renders that person liable to a fine on conviction.[40]

10 Leave of absence

Leave of absence must not be granted to enable a child to be employed during school hours, or to take holidays during term time, subject to the exceptions noted below.[41] Employment includes assistance in any trade or occupation carried on for profit and it is immaterial whether the pupil receives any reward or not.[42]

The exceptions are: participation in work experience schemes from school approved under the Education (Work Experience) Act 1973, and employment abroad for a purpose mentioned in the Children and Young Persons Act 1933 where a licence has been granted under section 25 of that Act. The employment of children in entertainments under a licence[43] is not subject to this regulation.

At the request of the parent, a child may be granted leave for not more than two weeks in any calendar year for the purpose of accompanying the parent on his annual holiday.[44]

11 Enforcement of school attendance

Once a local education authority is satisfied that the attendance of a pupil is irregular the duty of enforcing attendance passes to the authority, which may institute proceedings against the parent. The courts may inflict a fine of £200 (or impose a month's imprisonment, or both in the case of subsequent offences).[45]

Such proceedings may be commenced only by a local education authority, which before deciding to prosecute must consider whether it is appropriate, alternatively or additionally, to bring the child before a juvenile court under section 1 of the Children and Young Persons Act 1969. If the authority merely proceeds against the parent, and there is a conviction, the court may direct the authority to bring the child before a juvenile court. If this happens, the authority must comply.

Failure to attend school is part of the care proceedings in juvenile courts. The court may make one of five orders in respect of a child if 'he is of compulsory school age within the meaning of the Education Act 1944 and is not receiving efficient full-time education suitable to his age, ability and aptitude ... and also that he is in need of care or control which he is unlikely to receive unless the Court makes an order under this section in respect of him'.

For a care order to be made, it is not necessary that a child be both not receiving education *and* in need of care or control. A father had an 'implacable objection' to comprehensive schools and refused to send his son to any of those offered by his local education authority. It was not disputed that the boy came from an excellent home. The juvenile court made a care order, with a view to ensuring the education of the boy. The parent appealed against the order, succeeded, and the local authority in turn appealed.

In the Court of Appeal Lord Denning said, 'This is a case where Duncan is not receiving sufficient full-time education. Is he in need of care and control? The Crown Court took the view that care and control ... meant ... 'physical' or 'moral' care and control, and that it did not apply to care in respect to a child's education.... I think that is far too narrow a view. ... If a child was not being sent to school or receiving a proper education then he was in need of care ... in respect of his own education. "Care" applies not only to the physical well-being of a child, but also to his proper education.' The court allowed the local authority's appeal that a care order be made.[46]

Proceedings in cases where a school attendance order is in force are discussed below.

12 School attendance orders

When a parent is apparently failing to perform his duty to ensure that his child is receiving education as required by the Act, the local education authority may require him to show that he is, in fact, fulfilling that duty. The notice served by the authority must specify the time within which the parent must reply, and this must not be less than fourteen days.[47] The notice must inform the parent which school they have in mind for the child if a school attendance order is issued. An aided or special agreement school must not be specified without the prior consent of the governors.[48]

If during the fourteen-day period the parent applies to have his child admitted to an independent school, or a school maintained by another local education authority, then, assuming that the child is admitted, that school is to be named in the school attendance order.[49] The same applies if the local education authority serving the notice offers more than one school to the parent, and the parent then applies to one of these.[50]

If, in the view of the local authority, any school named or chosen by the parent 'would prejudice the provision of efficient education or the efficient use of resources'[51] the authority can ask the Secretary of State to direct which school shall be named in the attendance order. If the school named is a maintained school, the authority and the governors must admit the pupil.[52]

Whilst the order remains in force, the parent may request the authority to substitute another school, or to revoke the order on the grounds that the child is, in fact, receiving efficient full-time education suitable to his age, ability and aptitude. This request must be complied with unless the authority is of the opinion that the change would be detrimental to the child's interests, for example where 'special educational needs' are involved.[53] In such cases an appeal lies to the Secretary of State.

Failure to comply with the requirements of a school attendance order is an offence unless the child is receiving suitable full-time education otherwise than by attendance at school.[54] A court before whom a parent appears for failing to comply with an order may revoke the order, but this does not preclude the authority from taking further action. Penalties are as for non-attendance.

School attendance orders remain in force until the child ceases to be of compulsory school age, unless revoked by the local education authority or the courts.

13   Further education

County colleges under the 1944 Act have not come into being. However, a young person who is not exempted from compulsory attendance at a county college must comply with the requirements of any college attendance notice served upon him by the local education authority.[55] In the event of failure to do so, he may be charged before the juvenile court if under 17, or before the adult court if he is older.

The Act provides that the following grounds shall provide a good defence:

(a) that he was, at the material time, exempt from compulsory attendance;
(b) that he was prevented from attending by sickness or other urgent cause;
(c) that the requirement does not comply with the provisions of the Education Acts.

The following persons are statutorily exempted from attendance for further education:

(a) those in full-time attendance at any school or educational institution other than a county college;
(b) those receiving suitable and efficient instruction, whether full-time or not, for at least 330 hours a year;
(c) those who, having been exempted under the preceding clauses, did not cease to be so exempt until they had attained the age of 17 years and 8 months;
(d) any person undergoing an approved course for the mercantile marine or the sea fishing industry or who, having completed such a course, is engaged in that industry;
(e) any person in the service of the Crown, persons of unsound mind and those detained by order of a court;
(f) any person who attained the age of 15 before 1 April 1945 and who was not, immediately before that date, required to attend a continuation school under the terms of the Education Act 1921.

14   Documents receivable in evidence

The following documents may be received in the courts and deemed to be correct in every detail without proof of the identity, signature or official capacity of the persons by whom they purport to have been signed, unless the contrary be proved:[56]

(a) those issued by a local education authority and signed by an authorized officer;
(b) extracts from the minutes of the governors of a school, signed by the chairman or clerk;
(c) certificates of attendance signed by the head of a school;
(d) certificates signed by a medical officer of a local education authority, or a medical officer whose services are made available to that authority by the Secretary of State for Social Services.

15   Lateness and full-time attendance

On 24 May 1960 the Birmingham magistrates imposed a fine in a case brought against a parent for failing to send his six-year-old son to school regularly. The father appealed to Quarter Sessions under section 39(2)(a) of the Education Act 1944, which prescribes that no proceedings may be taken if a child is absent through sickness or other unavoidable cause. The child had been present on twenty-seven out of fifty-six occasions in a period of six weeks in a school where the registers were closed at 9.45 am. In reply to the Assistant Recorder a welfare and school attendance officer said that he knew of no regulation which entitles a particular school to decide on the time for closing its register, but technically it should be closed at the time of the school assembly.

In allowing the appeal, the Assistant Recorder said, 'When this certificate says weekly attendances, it means in fact weekly attendances by 9.45 am. I don't know if there is any authority under the Act whereby a local education authority is entitled to limit weekly attendances by failure to attend by a certain time.... Unless there is any authority under the Act to limit attendance to attendances by a certain time, the first point of the case – failure to attend school – has not been established.... This certificate sets out to show a fact which I now know is not the fact at all.'

The local education authority appealed against this decision, and the case was heard in the Queen's Bench Divisional Court before the Lord Chief Justice (Lord Parker), Mr Justice Winn and Mr Justice Lawton. For the Corporation it was said that, if the Assistant Recorder's decision were allowed to stand, a boy who did not like spelling would be able to skip that lesson, but would still be entitled to have 'Present' against his name. The Lord Chief Justice said that the Assistant Recorder took the view that the headmaster's certificate was not evidence of non-attendance, although it might be evidence of unpunctuality. In the view of the Court the phrase 'full-time education' meant attendance for the period prescribed by the school authorities. The Assistant Recorder was wrong in ruling that there was no case to answer and it would be remitted.[57]

When the case came before the Court of Quarter Sessions for the second time, the father said that he now wished to appeal, not against the conviction but against the sentence. The Recorder ordered the fine to stand but, because the father said he was unemployed, ordered it to be paid at the rate of one shilling a week.

This is an important decision which defines the term 'full-time education' as meaning exactly what it says.

References

1. Education Act 1944, s. 35 and the Raising of the School Leaving Age Order 1972.
2. Education Act 1962, s. 9, as amended by the Education (School Leaving Dates) Act 1976, s. 1. See section 3 below.
3. Education (School Leaving Dates) Act 1976, s. 1.
4. See re Shurey: Savory v. Shurey [1918] 1 Ch. 263.
5. Family Law Reform Act 1969, s. 9.
6. Education (School Leaving Dates) Act 1976, s. 1.
7. Education Act 1962, s. 9. See also DES Circular 4/62.

8. Education (Miscellaneous Provisions) Act 1948, s. 9.
9. The term 'parent' includes a guardian and every person who has the actual custody of a child or young person – Education Act 1944, s. 114(1). Apparently, for this purpose, it may include the mother, even though the child is living with both parents.
10. Education Act 1944, s. 36, as amended by Education Act 1981, s. 17.
11. Education (Miscellaneous Provisions) Act 1948, s. 4(2).
12. Education Act 1944, s. 39.
13. Jenkins v. Howells [1949] 2 KB 218; LCT 168.
14. Two miles in the case of children under 8; three miles in all other cases, measured by the nearest available route – Education Act 1944, s. 39(5). In Shaxted v. Ward [1954] 1 All ER 336; LCT 193, it was held that distance and not safety is the test to be applied in defining the nearest available route. Safety was added by Rogers v. Essex County Council (1984) (unreported).
15. Education Act 1944, s. 39 and s. 55.
16. Surrey County Council v. Ministry of Education (1953) 1 All ER 705: LCT 50.
17. Public Passenger Vehicle Act 1981.
18. Not an authoritative interpretation of the law, since this is a matter for the courts.
19. Jones v. Suffolk County Council, Daily Telegraph, 12 March 1981.
20. Rootkin v. Kent County Council (1981) 80 LGR 201; All ER 227 CA.
21. Education Act 1944, s. 55(2).
22. See 'Overpayment of salary' p. 228.
23. Spiers v. Warrington Corporation [1954] 1 QB 61; LCT 165.
24. Education Act 1944, s. 39(2).
25. Happe v. Lay (1978) 76 LGR 313. This point was emphasized more recently in Jarman v. Mid-Glamorgan LEA (1984) when a parent kept a child from school to resist corporal punishment.
26. Campbell and Cosans v. UK: see pp. 313, 470.
27. Education Act 1944, s. 36 as amended.
28. Education Act 1944, s. 37.
29. Bevan v. Shears (1911) 2 KB 936.
30. R v. West Riding of Yorkshire Justices, ex parte Broadbent (1910) 2 KB 192.
31. Osborne v. Martin (1927) 91 JP 197.
32. Application 10233/83 v. United Kingdom.

33. 'EO' can be contacted at Heathermead, 25 Common Lane, Hemingford Abbots, Cambs PE18 9AN.
34. Crump *v.* Gilmore (1969) 68 LGR 56.
35. Administrative Memorandum no. 531 (10 May 1956).
36. Pupils' Registration Regulations 1956, no. 3(4).
37. Pupils' Registration Regulations 1956, nos 5 and 6.
38. Pupils' Registration Regulations 1956, no. 7.
39. Pupils' Registration Regulations 1956, nos 8 and 9.
40. Education Act 1944, s. 80.
41. Education (Schools and Further Education) Regulations 1981.
42. Employment of Children Act 1973, s. 2(6).
43. Children and Young Persons Act 1963, s. 37(3).
44. Education (Schools and Further Education) Regulations 1981.
45. Education Act 1944, s. 40(1); as amended by the Criminal Law Act 1977; s. 31 Schedule 6.
46. In re S. (a minor) (Care order – Education) (1977) 75 LGR 787 CA.
47. Education Act 1944, s. 37.
48. Education Act 1980, s. 10(1).
49. Education Act 1980, s. 10(3).
50. Education Act 1980, s. 10(2).
51. Education Act 1980, s. 10(6).
52. Education Act 1980, s. 10(7).
53. Education Act 1980, s. 10(4).
54. Apparently, however, an offence would be committed by sending the child to a school not named in the order, in spite of the fact that suitable full-time education otherwise than by regular attendance at school is a statutory defence. See p. 313, 'Education otherwise'.
55. Education Act, 1944, s. 44. This section remains on the statute book, although there is now little likelihood that any Order in Council for the establishment of county colleges will be made.
56. Education Act 1944, s. 95(2), importing into sub para (d) the amended definition in s. 114(1) of 'medical officer' required by the National Health Service Reorganization Act 1973, Schedule 4. 8.
57. Hinchley *v.* Rankin [1961] 1 All ER 692; LCT 172.

XII
Religious education

1   Freedom of conscience

In some countries, of which the United States of America is
an example, the educational system is purely secular and no
religious teaching is permitted in the state schools. This is not
so in England where the Church was a pioneer in the field of
education and religious education is an essential part of the
work of every school. In a country where there are to be found
many non-Christian religions as well as many orders within
the Christian faith, it is essential that the freedom of the
individual conscience should be strictly safeguarded on lines
such as those laid down in the 1944 Act.

The provisions of the Act are designed to protect both the
pupil and teacher. Although there must be religious education
in all schools, no child may be taught any doctrine or practice
which is repugnant to the wishes of his parent, even in a
denominational school. Parents may, if they wish, withdraw
their children wholly or partly from religious instruction.

Except in a limited number of cases,[1] a teacher's beliefs are
his own concern and he cannot be dismissed, deprived of
promotion or paid a lower salary because of his religious
opinions.[2] The conscience clauses of the act are characteristic

of the English attitude towards freedom of belief and must be strictly observed.

If the faith of a person involves limitations on food, these must be strictly observed. Indeed, the whole question of what may be called 'secondary' religious practices (practices which derive from the teaching of a particular faith) is something with which the law will have to come to grips in a society which is increasingly multicultural. Examples may be found in the Sikh's insistence on wearing a turban[3] and the Muslim refusal to send girls to a co-educational secondary school.

In this connection it is important to consider article 9 of the European Convention on Human Rights, of which Great Britain is a signatory:

(1) Everyone has the right to freedom of thought, conscience and religion; this right includes freedom to change his religion or belief, and freedom, either alone or in community with others and in public or private, to manifest his religion or belief, in worship, teaching, practice and observance.

(2) Freedom to manifest one's religion or beliefs shall be subject only to such limitations as are prescribed by law and are necessary in a democratic society in the interests of public safety, for the protection of public order, health or morals, or for the protection of the rights and freedoms of others.

The settlement in this country of large numbers of immigrants professing faiths other than Christianity has also produced a new situation, and it has been claimed that religious education should extend an equal recognition to all religions and, indeed, to ideologies such as Marxism. The Secretary of State made it plain early in 1985 that he had no intention of abolishing compulsory religious education, and that he did not envisage any other base for it than Christianity. The present legal position is unlikely to be changed: indeed it is probable that a majority of parents, even though they may not be actively involved in the life of the Church, wish their children to receive a grounding in Christian teaching. At the same time, the past three decades have witnessed an increasing tolerance of, and respect for, those whose cultures are rooted in other faiths or, indeed, in none. It seems likely that this trend will continue.

Some strict Muslims, believing that education at the secondary school stage should be in single-sex schools, hope to establish voluntary-aided schools for members of their faith, at least in areas where secondary education is entirely co-educational. It was reported in 1984 that one London council had granted planning permission for the establishment of a private Islamic school.[4]

2   The 1944 Act

The Act lays down that there must be religious education in all schools within the statutory system.[5] This and recreational and physical education are the only subjects so specified by statute. Apparently, a head could dispense with English and arithmetic in his school, so long as he could persuade HMI and the LEA that the children were receiving efficient full-time education suitable to their respective ages, abilities and aptitudes, but he may not omit religious education from the timetable.

No local education authority may issue any instruction relating to secular education to any county or voluntary school which would interfere with the provision of reasonable facilities for religious education during school hours, or with the opportunity of any pupil to receive religious education, unless an alternative time is provided.[6]

Although it is generally accepted that in framing the 1944 Act Parliament intended all pupils to receive religious education (unless their parents exercised their right of withdrawal), it may be that the Act has not been framed unambiguously. If called upon to interpret Acts of Parliament, the courts will always consider the meaning of the words, and not presume to jump to conclusions about what might or might not have been in the minds of Parliamentarians at the time.

Section 25(2) of the 1944 Act requires simply that 'religious education shall be given in every county and in every voluntary school'. Section 25(1) requires the school day to 'begin with collective worship *on the part of all pupils in attendance at the school'* (author's italics).

Although the matter has not been tested in court as such, it seems likely that a school which offered religious education perhaps only for first-year pupils, or perhaps even only as an optional subject, would not be in breach of the law. There are many precedents in law to support the view that Section 25(2), lacking as it does any reference to *all* pupils, means that a county school might not be acting unlawfully in not compelling *all* pupils to attend religious education. It cannot reasonably be argued that 'all pupils' was omitted from section 25(2) in order to allow for the right of parents to withdraw their children, since the conscience clause[7] specifically mentions withdrawal both from collective worship and religious instruction and forms a discrete sub-section in the Act.

3   The daily act of worship

The school day must begin with a collective act of worship attended by all the pupils, subject of course to withdrawal on conscientious grounds, provided that there is suitable accommodation for assembling the whole school.[8] In county schools the worship must be undenominational in character;[9] the form to be used in voluntary schools is not stipulated in the Act, but it is generally held that, like denominational instruction in such schools, it may be in accordance with the trust deed, or, where there is no such provision, in accordance with the practice in the school before it became a voluntary school.

The worship should take place on the school premises both in county and voluntary schools. The governors of an aided or special agreement school may, on a special day, make arrangements for the worship to take place elsewhere, but this must be an exception and not the rule.[10]

When it is proposed to take the school to church, due notice must be given to the parents so that they may, under the conscience clause, have an opportunity of requesting the withdrawal of their children from such worship. An announcement to the school, coupled with a written notice on the school notice board could be sufficient. It is important that this should be done, as many parents who have no objection to their children attending religious instruction in school will prefer them not to attend church.

Occasionally clergy and ministers visit a school on special occasions, e.g. for Founder's Day or for leavers' services. On such occasions a similar opportunity for withdrawal should be given.

In voluntary schools the regular daily act of worship may be led by a clergyman or minister. If this is done in controlled schools the fact should be noted in the school annals.

The Swann report on ethnic minority education, *Education for All*, recommended in 1985 that the government should review the requirement of the 1944 Act for daily collective worship.

4   The Agreed Syllabus

In county schools it has long been the law that religious education shall be 'without any catechism or formulary distinctive of any particular religious denomination'.[11] This is the famous Cowper-Temple clause named after Mr William Cowper-Temple who first introduced it as an amendment to the 1870 Act. It has been re-enacted in all succeeding legislation. The law officers of the Crown have decided that the ten commandments, the Lord's Prayer, and the Apostles' Creed are not distinctive and their use is not a violation of this clause. On the other hand, that section of the catechism known as the 'Duties' is distinctive in this sense, and may not be taught in county schools.

Soon after the first world war a number of local education authorities, of which Cambridgeshire became the best-known, produced syllabuses of religious instruction which had been agreed between representatives of the Protestant denominations as suitable for use in county schools.

Under the 1944 Act each education authority must now adopt such a Syllabus[12] in accordance with the decision of a conference representative of the religious denominations, the authority and the teachers' organizations. Such conferences were given power either to adopt a syllabus prepared by another authority, or to appoint a committee to draft a special syllabus for use in the authority's area.

Agreed Syllabuses are drawn up in general terms, and the responsibility of adapting them to the needs of a particular school is left to the staff of the school. HMIs are required to ascertain that the religious education in county schools is in accordance with the Syllabus adopted by the authority. Provision is also made for the reconsideration of the Syllabus from time to time. An authority may appoint a standing advisory council on religious education to report to the authority on matters concerning the Agreed Syllabus, to recommend books and to sponsor courses.[13]

As many parts of England contain citizens of many different faiths, Agreed Syllabuses should acknowledge this fact. The Act permits representation on to the agreed syllabus committees to be changed to reflect the new multi-faith basis of society.

5   Voluntary schools

In aided schools religious education is under the control of the governors and must be in accordance with the provisions of the trust deed or, where there is no provision of this nature in the deed, in accordance with the practice in the school before it became a voluntary school. The position in special agreement schools is precisely the same. In both kinds of school Agreed Syllabus instruction must be provided for the children whose parents request it and who cannot conveniently be educated elsewhere. If the governors fail to make such arrangements, the local education authority must do so.[14] It should be noted that the control of religious education is the responsibility of the whole governing body and not simply of the foundation governors.

In controlled schools the Agreed Syllabus must be used, but the school may, at the request of parents, give further teaching for not more than two periods a week on denominational lines. Such additional teaching may be given by clergy or ministers.[15]

In voluntary schools, regular religious instruction may be given elsewhere than on the premises. The fact must be entered on the timetable, opportunity for withdrawal given, and care exercised to see that the children return to school in time to be able to complete the minimum period of secular instruction required by the Schools Regulations. It should be particularly noted that this applies to regular instruction and not to the regular daily act of worship. The latter should normally be held on the school premises.

A proportion of the staff of controlled and special agreement schools may be appointed as reserved teachers, especially qualified for their ability to give trust-deed religious instruction.[16]

6   Inspection

HMIs and the inspectorate of a local education authority may inspect and report upon all religious instruction, whether in county or voluntary schools, where such instruction is given in accordance with an Agreed Syllabus. They may also inspect the undenominational form of worship in county schools. In aided or special agreement schools, the function of the inspector would be limited to the Agreed Syllabus instruction provided for the children whose parents requested it. Although many such schools use parts of an Agreed Syllabus for their religious instruction, such portions are really taken over and incorporated in the Syllabus approved by the governors.

In voluntary schools, denominational instruction may be inspected, on not more than two days a year, by the governors or by inspectors acting on their behalf. Fourteen days' notice of such visit must be given to the local education authority so that arrangements can be made to see that the authority's officials do not visit the school on such days. No child whose parents have withdrawn him from denominational instruction can be compelled to attend school on the day of such an inspection.

In controlled schools the Agreed Syllabus instruction would be inspected by the secular, the denominational instruction by the denominational inspector.

7 Timetable

The requirement that religious instruction should be given only at the beginning or end of the school day no longer applies, and the abolition of this rule has opened the door to specialization in religious education. If children are withdrawn, however, for denominational instruction elsewhere than on the school premises, this must be done at the beginning or end of a session.

8 Withdrawal from religious instruction

A parent may withdraw his child from any part of the religious instruction or worship of the school or from the whole of it.[17] This is the conscience clause, and once such a request has been made it must be strictly honoured unless and until it is withdrawn. It is desirable that such a request should be in writing but it is probable that an oral intimation is legally sufficient.

In 1971 the secretary of the Humanist Teachers Association complained that a boy who asked to be allowed to withdraw from religious education was first refused permission and later permitted to withdraw by sitting at the back of the room whilst taking no part in the lesson. It must be recognized that it is often difficult to make special supervision arangements for individual pupils, but it would seem that such an arrangement is contrary to the spirit, if not the letter, of the law.

A parent is not required to give a reason for requesting withdrawal and it is doubtful whether school authorities should inquire into a parent's motives. If the request is made by the child himself, however, it is probably as well to verify that it represents the parent's, and not just the child's, wish, since section 25 gives the right to the parent. This may well be challenged at some future date, since the European Convention on Human Rights to which reference was made at the beginning of this chapter grants 'everyone' (not only adults or parents) 'the right ... to manifest his religion or belief in ... practice and observance'.

When a child cannot with convenience be educated in a school providing such instruction, he may be withdrawn by the parent for religious instruction in accordance with the parent's wishes. A pupil in a county school may thus be withdrawn for denominational instruction, or a pupil in a voluntary school for instruction of a denominational kind which is not provided by that school. Adequate arrangements must be made for the withdrawal instruction, which must be given at the beginning or end of a session. It need not coincide with the provision for religious instruction in the timetable.

If a county school is so situated that arrangements cannot conveniently be made for withdrawal, the authority may provide facilities in the school for such instruction if it is satisfied that the parents desire such instruction to be given and that adequate arrangements have been made. No cost for this provision may fall on the authority.[18]

9 Days of obligation

Parents may withdraw their children from attendance at school for all or part of a day which it is the practice of their religious persuasion to set apart exclusively for religious observance,[19] e.g. Ascension Day (for Anglicans and Roman Catholics) or the Day of Atonement (for Jews). It is not certain how many such days are recognized by the Church of England; an Act of 5 and 6 Edward VI mentions seventy-nine, including Sundays, which are 'separated from profane uses'.[20]

It was decided in the 'Darfield Case'[21] that a parent has this right, even though the child does not attend any form of worship on that day. To avoid misunderstanding, it is desirable that the parent should give notice to the head and some religious bodies provide printed forms for this purpose.[22]

Teachers may also withdraw their services on such days. It is usual for leave to be granted with pay, subject to the right of the authority to use the teacher in another school on an equivalent number of days when his own is closed.

This indulgence cannot be stretched too far. Mr Iftikhar Ahmad was appointed to the service of the Inner London Education Authority as a full-time teacher, and served in a number of schools between 1968 and 1975. He did not, before making his contract with the Authority, reveal that he would, if possible, attend prayers at a mosque each Friday from one o'clock until two o'clock. The mosque was about fifteen or twenty minutes' walking distance from some of the schools in which he taught, with the result that he returned three-quarters of an hour after the session began. In January 1975 the Authority, because of his colleagues' resentment about this, offered him an appointment on a part-time basis for four-and-a-half days a week, but he refused and resigned. He then claimed that he had been exploited and humiliated by the Authority, so that his resignation amounted to constructive and unfair dismissal.[23]

Both the industrial tribunal and the Employment Appeal Tribunal found that the Authority had acted reasonably, so Mr Ahmad asked the Court of Appeal to reverse this decision. He relied on the Education Act 1944, section 30, the Authority's staff code (which allows absence on days of obligation) and article 9(1) of the European Convention for the Protection of Human Rights and Fundamental Freedoms. By a majority the Court rejected his submissions, Lord Denning, the Master of the Rolls, observing that section 30 must be read subject to the qualification 'if the school timetable so permits'. Regular absence on a working day was quite different from occasions such as Good Friday for Christians, the Day of Atonement for Jews, or Ramadan for Muslims: 'It has been so interpreted by the great majority of Muslim teachers in our schools. They do not take time off for their prayers: nor should Mr Ahmad if he wants to get his full pay for a five-day week.' Lord Justice Orr agreed, but Lord Justice Scarman dissented on the ground that section 30 must be construed broadly against the background of the Convention and the policy of modern statute law. He felt that Mr Ahmad's absence for prayers did not amount to breach of contract.[24]

Mr Ahmad's appeal to the European Commission of Human Rights was also unsuccessful. The Commission ruled that it considered he was not required by his religion to disregard contractual obligations to his employer, the ILEA.[25]

10 The Jewish Sabbath

The Jewish Sabbath begins at sunset on Friday, and Jewish children attending a school which does not cater exclusively for that faith should be allowed to leave school in time to reach home before sunset on Fridays during the winter. Some authorities issue a list of the times at which Jews may be allowed to go home on different Fridays during the shorter days.

11 Staffing

The question of reserved teachers, and the safeguarding clause dealing with the religious opinions of teachers, have already been considered in chapter IV and at the beginning of this chapter respectively.

Since 1959 it has been possible for clergy and ministers to hold any appointment on the staff of a maintained school. This does not affect the nature of religious instruction and worship in a county school. A clergyman or minister on the staff of such a school must observe the provisions of the Cowper-Temple clause, except in a voluntary-aided school or when giving denominational religious instruction in a controlled or special agreement school.

A former missionary, appointed to take charge of religious education at Rickmansworth School from September 1975, made it clear from the outset that his interpretation of the Bible was what he described as 'conservative evangelism', and that he intended to teach the book of Genesis from a literal standpoint. The Hertfordshire Agreed Syllabus laid down: 'The Genesis stories of creation, read as their writers intended them to be, and not as literalist interpreters have read them, do not conflict with evolutionary theories. They are, of course, only part of the collection of myths and legends – Hebrew religious folklore – which make up the first eleven chapters of Genesis, and they should be seen in this setting.'

The master, Mr David Watson, claimed that he was not shown the syllabus until, at the end of his first year in the school, he drew attention to the fact that he proposed to teach Genesis from a fundamentalist standpoint to the second year during the following term. He added that 'when a book like Genesis is being taught, it seems necessary to avoid unnecessary contradiction and confusion'.

The headmaster did not object to some reference to this approach, provided it was balanced by other views, but it was said that Mr Watson had already caused some 'confusion, distress and resentment among his pupils' because of his rigid views. After an interview with the head and three governors, Mr Watson refused to give a written undertaking to conform to the Agreed Syllabus and he was dismissed.

Mr Watson took his case to an industrial tribunal, claiming that he had been dismissed because of his religious beliefs and not, as the Hertfordshire Authority alleged, because he had refused a reasonable request for an assurance. The tribunal held that he was guilty of misconduct, no matter that the reason may have lain with his conscience. 'He was refusing to carry out what was a legitimate requirement of his employers, namely, to teach in accordance with the Agreed Syllabus of the county. The county council had acted reasonably in dismissing him, and he had been given ample warning both verbally and in writing. The uncompromising stand which the applicant adopted permitted of no other solution than to terminate his employment with the council, and release him to teach elsewhere in the manner and subject he preferred.'[26]

12   Visits of clergy to schools

Clergy and ministers sometimes visit schools as speakers when, for example, pupils' conferences are organized through the medium of the Christian Education Movement or similar bodies. Though these lie outside the normal religious education of the school it is as well to make the denominational allegiance of the speaker known beforehand. Attendance at such meetings must be purely voluntary, unless of course the speaker is dealing with purely secular topics.

13 Boarders

Parents of pupils who are boarders may request that their children attend worship conforming to the tenets of the religious body to which they belong.[27] Similarly they may request that their children receive denominational instruction out of school hours. Such requests must be complied with, but no expense in this connection can be met by the local education authority.

These facilities may be provided on the school premises so long as they do not entail the meeting of any expense in connection therewith from public funds.

14 Special schools

Provision must be made, so far as is possible, for every pupil to attend religious worship and receive religious instruction in accordance with the wishes of his parent. No pupil may be required to attend such worship, or receive such instruction, contrary to the wishes of his parent. These regulations apply both to boarders and day-pupils in special schools.[28]

References

1. The exceptions are the staffs of aided schools and reserved teachers in controlled and special agreement schools.
2. Education Act 1944, s. 30.
3. See p. xxxv.
4. *Education*, 15 June 1984.
5. Education Act 1944, s. 25(2).
6. Education Act 1944, s. 25(6).

7. Education Act 1944, s. 25(5).
8. Education Act 1944, s. 25(1).
9. Education Act 1944, s. 26.
10. Education Act 1946, s. 7.
11. Education Act 1944, s. 26.
12. Education Act 1944, s. 29(1) and Schedule V.
13. Education Act 1944, s. 29.
14. Education Act 1944, s. 28.
15. Education Act 1944, s. 27.
16. See p. 121.
17. Education Act 1944, s. 25(3).
18. Education Act 1944, ss. 25(5) and 26.
19. Education Act 1944, s. 39(2)(b).
20. The relevant passage in the Act is quoted in G.R. Barrell, *Legal Cases for Teachers* (Methuen, 1970), p.184.
21. Marshall *v.* Graham; Bell *v.* Graham [1907] 2 KB 112; LCT 178.
22. One such form reads as follows:

    To the Head teacher, ... School

    Dear Sir or Madam,

    I am writing to give notice that as next Thursday is Ascension Day – set apart for religious observance by the Church of England, of which I am a member – I shall not be sending my children to school on that day.

    Parent.................
    Address..........................

23. See pp. 187–9.
24. Ahmad *v.* Inner London Education Authority (1977) 75 LGR 753, p. 127.
25. *Education*, 8 May 1981.
26. Watson *v.* Hertfordshire County Council, *Education*, 16 September 1977.
27. Education Act 1944, s. 25(7).
28. Education (Approval of Special Schools) Regulations 1983.

XIII
Discrimination

1 Public policy

It is contrary to current public policy in this country that an individual should be penalized merely because of certain identifiable and more or less indelible characteristics which mark him as a member of a group against which others may be prejudiced. Such unfair treatment is, in general terms, known as discrimination.

The right not to be discriminated against is enshrined in the international conventions to which this country is a signatory. For example, the European Convention on Human Rights, article 14, provides:

> The enjoyment of the rights and freedoms set forth in this Convention shall be secured without discrimination on any ground such as sex, race, colour, language, religion, political or other opinion, national or social origin, association with a national minority, property, birth or other status.

Similarly, article 2 of the Universal Declaration of Human Rights adopted by the General Assembly of the United Nations declares:

> Everyone is entitled to all the rights and freedoms set forth

in this Declaration, without distinction of any kind, such as race, colour, sex, language, religion, political or other opinion, national or social origin, property, birth or other status.

Article 3 of the United Nations International Covenant on Civil and Political Rights goes a stage further by including a pledge given by the states who accede to it:

The States Parties to the Covenant undertake to ensure the equal right of men and women to the enjoyment of all civil and political rights set forth in the Covenant.

It is against this background that national efforts, in Britain as elsewhere, to bring law into conformity with the principles of the conventions must be viewed.

This chapter deals with two areas, race relations and sex discrimination, relatively new to statutory regulation. Because the structure of the provisions is similar, the survey is topical, differences being noted where appropriate.

2   Areas of legislation

The United Kingdom's first attempt to outlaw discrimination was made in 1965 when the first Race Relations Act reached the statute book. An amending Act was passed in 1968, and both were repealed and replaced by the Race Relations Act 1976.

The other area in which Parliament has made discrimination unlawful is sex. Because it was felt by many that unfairness on this ground was normally directed against women, the primary definition in the Sex Discrimination Act 1975 is in terms of the less favourable treatment of women.[1] The following 'mirror' section declares that *mutatis mutandis* the same provisions apply to discrimination against men.[2] The Act also incidentally deals with discrimination against married persons of either sex merely on the ground that they are married.

Two bodies have been set up at national level: the Equal Opportunities Commission and the Commission for Racial Equality. They have functions concerned with the enforcement of the law, but their primary purpose is the promotion of equal opportunity. They are required to work towards the elimination of discrimination, and to keep the legislation with which they are concerned under review. They may make proposals for amending legislation. The Commissions may conduct formal investigations and for this purpose, subject to certain conditions, they may require the production of information. They may serve non-discrimination notices, and in the case of persistent discrimination they may apply to the courts for an injunction. They have a discretion to assist an aggrieved person where his case raises a question of principle. They have a general duty to advise the Government on the working of the legislation.[3]

The functions listed above are common to both Commissions. In addition, the Equal Opportunities Commission, set up by the Sex Discrimination Act, keeps under review in consultation with the Health and Safety Commission those parts of the health and safety legislation requiring different treatment for men and women. The Commission for Racial Equality is also concerned, generally, with the promotion of good relations between people of different racial groups.

3 Discrimination

Direct discrimination occurs when someone treats a person less favourably on grounds of sex, colour, race, nationality, or ethnic or national origins, than he would treat others.[4]

Indirect discrimination is specifying a requirement which the discriminator would apply equally to all, but which is such that the proportion of those belonging to one sex or certain racial groups is considerably smaller than the proportion who do not belong to the sex or group. The requirement must be unjustifiable having regard to race or sex, and to the detriment of the victim because he, or she, cannot comply with it. Thus, the proportion of immigrant farm labourers who could produce an 'A' level pass in English is likely to be significantly smaller than the proportion of English applicants who could do so. Similarly, the proportion of women shop assistants who would be prepared to work stripped to the waist is likely to be smaller than the proportion of men willing to do so.[5]

Discrimination by victimization is less favourable treatment of a person because he, or she, has brought proceedings under the relevant Act, has given evidence in discrimination proceedings, or has alleged that anyone has committed an act which would be a contravention of the relevant Act of Parliament. The Equal Pay Act 1970 is a relevant Act for this purpose. It is not discrimination by victimization, however, to treat a person less fairly because he has maliciously made a false allegation.[6]

Discrimination against married persons is treating a person of either sex less favourably because of his, or her, marital status. Such discrimination may be direct or indirect.[7]

Fields of discrimination. The principal fields in which discrimination is illegal under both Acts are employment, education, the supply of goods, facilities and services, and treatment by the police. Special provisions in respect of certain occupations (prison officers, ministers of religion, midwives and mineworkers) are included in the Sex Discrimination Act.[8]

Part IV of both Acts deals with discriminatory practices, and advertisements, instructions or pressure to discriminate, the liability of employers and principals, and the aiding of unlawful acts.

4   Discrimination in employment

It is unlawful for an employer to discriminate on grounds either of sex or race in respect of employment in Great Britain, whether the employment be under a contract of service, apprenticeship, or a contract personally to do work.[9]

Recruitment. An employer may not make any arrangements, or give any instructions, of a discriminatory character in deciding who should be offered an appointment. If he does, a complaint may be made by any individual in a class against which the discriminatory act operates, whether or not he has actually applied for the post. The terms of any appointment offered must not be discriminatory: if, for example, they were in breach of the Equal Pay Act 1970, they would amount to sex discrimination. An employer may not refuse, or fail to consider, an application purely on grounds of sex or race. This can give rise to considerable difficulties when there is a large number of applications, all of similar merit. If, for example, there were six hundred applications from teachers leaving initial training and only one post available, it would be practically impossible to demonstrate that one who complained was not included in the short list because of sex or race. One large local education authority has advised its heads to keep a list of all applicants and the reason for interviewing, or not interviewing, each. This is a wise suggestion, for a note made at the time, when there was no cause to apprehend a specific complaint, may well provide an answer to later allegations.[10]

Great care must be exercised during the recruitment process. It may be discriminatory, for example, to insist that English language teachers must be native speakers if such a requirement could only mean that whole racial or ethnic groups were excluded. In 1979 a Miss Hafeez was awarded £200 compensation for hurt feelings on being refused an interview at an English Language school: an industrial tribunal ruled that the head had no personal prejudice, but that the school had an understandable policy of meeting the wishes of parents who did not want their children (mostly Italian) taught by other than English men and women.[11]

In *Gates v. Wirral Borough Council*[12] the Council was held to have contravened the Sex Discrimination Act 1975 because the interviewing panel's arrangements for determining who should be offered the post of head teacher discriminated against Mrs Gates on the ground of her sex. She was asked if she was separated from her husband and whether she intended to have a family in the near future. She was awarded £200 for injured feelings, since the same question was not put to the male candidates for the post.

Present employees. An employer must afford equal opportunities for promotion, transfer or training regardless of the sex or race of individual employees, and his selection procedures for these purposes must not be discriminatory. Similarly, an employer must not dismiss an employee or treat him, or her, unfavourably in any other way on account of sex or race. Discriminatory dismissal may give rise to a successful claim that the employee has been unfairly dismissed under the provisions of the Employment Protection (Consolidation) Act 1978 outlined in chapter V. Any benefits, facilities or services provided for employees must be provided for all, regardless of sex or race.

Dismissal. Dismissal proceedings are similarly covered by the Acts. Mohammed Haseen claimed racial discrimination when his extended probation was judged unsuccessful. He was dismissed from a post with Walsall Local Education Authority and the local authority recommended to the Secretary of State that he should no longer be allowed to teach. In rejecting the claim, an industrial tribunal held that the real reason for dismissal was that Mr Haseen's inadequate command of English was holding back pupils and preventing proper class control. A remark alleged to have been made by the headmaster that Mr Haseen should go home to Pakistan was held by the tribunal chairman not to be evidence of racial discrimination: it was made, if at all, in the realization that Mr Haseen's English was not improving after four years' employment as a teacher.[13]

Exceptions. Some of the general exceptions, for example employment in a private household or, in the case of sex discrimination, small firms employing not more than five persons, do not apply to educational establishments, but others are of considerable importance.

Pregnancy and childbirth. An employer may, without infringing the Sex Discrimination Act, provide special treatment for women in circumstances arising from pregnancy or childbirth, for example by allowing special leave as part of the conditions of service.[14]

Death and retirement. It is not discrimination for the employer to make different provisions for men and women in a pension scheme, or in the age at which he requires workers to retire. Since April 1978, however, the Social Security Pensions Act 1975 has required equal treatment for men and women in occupational pension schemes in relation to conditions as to age and length of service for admission to the scheme, and the voluntary or obligatory nature of the scheme.[15]

At the time of writing there is considerable concern that there is sex discrimination in the operation of the Teachers' Superannuation Regulations of 1976. A male teacher's pension is automatically transferred to his wife on his death, but a woman's partner must prove financial dependence on her before receiving the pension. It may be that this matter will have to go ultimately to the European Court.

Genuine occupational qualifications (sex). Genuine occupational qualifications, commonly known as GOQs, do not apply to discrimination against married persons or to discrimination by victimization. They are, in any case, not general exceptions, and the criteria are applied to the needs of any specific appointment. Sex is a GOQ:

(a) Where the essential nature of the work requires that it be performed by a man or a woman on physiological grounds, for example to achieve dramatic authenticity or for modelling clothes. The test is that the nature of the work would be materially different if it were carried out by someone of the other sex: a *general* difference between the sexes in stamina or physical strength is not, therefore, a GOQ.

(b) Where it is necessary to preserve decency or privacy because the work involves physical contact between the employee and persons of one sex, or the employee works in the presence of persons of one sex who are undressed or using sanitary facilities; and the persons with whom the employee works in such circumstances might reasonably object to the presence of a person of the other sex.

(c) Where the location of the work makes it impracticable for the employee to live elsewhere than on premises provided by the employer, and those premises do not have separate sleeping or sanitary provision for both men and women and the employer cannot reasonably convert the premises for use by both sexes or provide alternative accommodation for the other sex.

(d) Where the work is in a single-sex establishment (or a single-sex part of the establishment) for persons requiring special care, supervision or attention, and it is reasonable to restrict the staff to those of the same sex as those for whom the establishment is provided. The occasional admission of persons of the other sex does not, of itself, invalidate the GOQ which, however, applies to specific posts: in other words, it must be possible to prove that a particular appointment must be held by a man or a woman as may be appropriate.

In November 1984 for example the Equal Opportunities Commission lost a case against the governors of a boys' grammar school in Northern Ireland who had advertised specifically for a headmaster. The tribunal decided that because the headmaster would have to live in the school and take on some 'boarding master' responsibilities, the sex of the applicant was a GOQ.

(e) If the employee provides personal services promoting the welfare or education of individuals, and those services can more effectively be provided only by a man or a woman as the case may be.

(f) Where a particular post must be held by a man because of legal restrictions on the employment of women.

(g) Where an appointment involves work outside the United Kingdom in a country where, by law or custom, it can be done (or done effectively) only by a man or a woman as the case may be.

(h) For each of two appointments to be held by a married couple.

The GOQs apply to the whole of an appointment, notwithstanding they are strictly appropriate only to a part, unless the employer has a sufficient number of staff of the sex concerned who would be employed for the qualifying work without inconvenience.[16]

Genuine occupational qualifications (race). GOQs do not apply to discrimination by victimization, and are not general automatic exceptions. The criteria must apply to any specific appointment.

Belonging to a particular racial group is a GOQ in the following circumstances:

(a) where there is a need for authenticity in a dramatic performance, or other entertainment;
(b) where there is a need for authenticity in a model for a work of art, picture or film;
(c) where there is a need for authenticity in a place where food or drink is provided in a particular setting (the 'Chinese waiter' situation);
(d) where personal services for the welfare of a particular racial group are provided most effectively by members of the same group.

The GOQs apply to the whole of an appointment, notwithstanding they are strictly appropriate only to a part, unless the employer already has a sufficient number of staff belonging to that group who can be employed for the qualifying work without inconvenience.[17]

Discrimination by other bodies concerned with employment. It is unlawful for any of the following bodies to practise discrimination:

(a) an organization of workers[18] (one effect of this has been the mergers of teachers' associations which formerly were single-sex, such as the National Association of Schoolmasters with the Union of Women Teachers);
(b) an organization of employers;[18]
(c) an organization whose members carry on a particular profession or trade, for the purpose of which the organization exists;[18]
(d) an authority or body which confers an authorization or qualification without which a person cannot (or would find it difficult to) practise a particular profession or trade. Authorizations or qualifications, such as ordination, which are limited to one sex to comply with religious doctrine or to avoid giving offence to the religious susceptibilities of a significant number of adherents, are exempt;[19]
(e) industrial training boards;[20]

(f) the Manpower Services Commission, the Employment Services Agency and the Training Services Agency;[20]

(g) group training associations of employers;[20]

(h) any other person designed by the Secretary of State to provide facilities for training for employment;[20]

(i) employment agencies.[21]

5   Discrimination in education[22]

GENERAL SCOPE

It is illegal for the responsible body conducting a school to discriminate on grounds of race or sex. This prohibition applies to independent establishments as well as in the public sector, and to the treatment of pupils as well as staff. The Secretary of State for Education and Science has made an order designating the responsible bodies for various categories of establishments. In county schools this may be either the local education authority or the governors, depending on which has the function in question: in independent and non-maintained special schools it is the proprietor.

The position of single-sex schools is dealt with separately below.

ADMISSION OF PUPILS

It is unlawful to discriminate in terms of admission to a school or college. Different criteria for members of different racial groups, or for boys and girls, may not be used.

It should be borne in mind that indirect discrimination may occur if governors responsible for admissions give preference to the children of former pupils and the former pupils are all of one race. Similar indirect discrimination may also result, more probably in non-maintained schools, if schools select pupils for admission on personal recommendations from one ethnic group.

The reorganization of schools brought about *inter alia* by falling rolls has raised a number of issues which may ultimately come to be determined by future legislation in the field of discrimination. The transfer of an Ealing comprehensive school from the local education authority to the Church of England, for example, enabled the Diocesan Board of Education to give preference on admission to the children of Anglican parents: the effect of this would be to change sharply the hitherto multi-racial character of the school.[23] Nor is it clear at the moment how far proposals for the reorganization of schools which incidentally reduce the provision of single-sex education contravene the Sex Discrimination Act. A report commissioned by the Equal Opportunities Commission in 1980 suggested that the Secretary of State should formally enquire into the possibly discriminatory aspects of school reorganization when consultative proposals are made under the Education Act 1980.

FAILURE TO ADMIT

It is unlawful to refuse, or to omit deliberately to consider, a particular application for admission on grounds of race or sex. It is no longer possible for mixed schools to attempt to achieve what used to be called a 'balanced intake' between boys and girls. In the first place this may involve a deliberate decision to apply different criteria; secondly it is likely that such a course of action may well involve the rejection of an applicant on the ground of sex – or, possibly, in some cases, of race. This has admittedly presented some difficulties, and one local education authority has advised that it would regard an intake with a disparity greater than 6 : 4 as discrimination against the minority sex. This, however, is an administrative attempt to apply the Act in terms of practicalities, and it is by no means certain that it would be upheld in determining a complaint.

BENEFITS, FACILITIES, OR SERVICES

Having admitted a pupil or student, an education establishment must not discriminate against him, or her, because of his race or sex. This makes it unlawful to refuse to allow pupils of one racial group or sex to join a course to which others are admitted, although it is possible to refuse if the group is full, and no more pupils in any category would be admitted. Separate facilities for boys and girls are allowed, where appropriate, provided they can be regarded as equal.

This point was tested in 1979 in the Croydon County Court.[24] Pupils in a mixed 11–14 school normally progressed to one of two single-sex 14–18 schools. Home economics was taught only at the senior girls' school and craft work only at the boys', in both cases aiming at public examinations at 16 plus. It was generally agreed that the two years' study in the senior schools would not by themselves be sufficient to bring a pupil with no previous knowledge of the subject up to the necessary standard and that study of them must therefore commence in the lower school. Limitations of properly equipped classrooms and appropriate staff made it impossible to offer these subjects to more than about half the number of children in the lower school if they were to devote the necessary time to the subject. For these reasons it was the practice in the lower school to give priority to girls in admission to the home economics course and to boys for the craft work course. A girl pupil in the lower school objected to being placed in home economics instead of craft work and sued through her mother claiming discrimination on the ground of sex.

In court it was contended by an expert witness that the value of craft work was so great that to be excluded from it must constitute discrimination, even though boys were excluded from home economics. The judge rejected this on the grounds that there was an evident intrinsic value of home economics also and that it was not clear how the relative values of these very different subjects could be assessed. Moreover, it was clear that in the circumstances of this case there was an advantage to girls in that by taking the home economics in the lower school they had an opportunity to take the subject to 16 plus. If they took craft work, they had no such opportunity. The lack of choice, therefore, did not constitute discrimination against the girl.

It is important to recognize that a significant factor in this case was the relationship of the lower mixed school to the single-sex upper schools. The outcome of the case could well have been different had the dispute occurred within an 11–18 mixed school.

GROUPING OF PUPILS IN SCHOOL

Streaming, banding and setting of pupils are not in themselves unlawful, unless it can be shown that the means used to allocate pupils to groups are discriminatory. Grading or selection tests for example should not discriminate, however indirectly, on grounds of race or sex through any implicit bias.

In November 1984 in a case supported by the Equal Opportunities Commission, the London Borough of Bromley admitted unintentional discrimination in that eight girls of primary school age were 'kept down' for a year when the rest of their class was moved up. Three of the girls brought a joint action. The local education authority agreed that the girls had not been kept down for any reason connected with their aptitude, ability or individual qualities, but solely because of their sex. Each was awarded £351 as general damages, and one was further awarded the costs of the private tuition she had taken.

EXCLUSION AND OTHER UNFAIR TREATMENT

It is contrary to the Acts to exclude a pupil, or to treat him unfavourably in any other way on grounds of sex or race. Banning a Sikh pupil for wearing a turban has been held to be discriminatory.[25] Similarly the Football Association and the Nottinghamshire Football Association were held to have discriminated against a girl whose registration as a player for an under-12s football team was not accepted by them, despite her demonstrable skill and competence as a footballer.[26]

OTHER DISCRIMINATION BY LOCAL EDUCATION AUTHORITIES

Local education authorities may not discriminate in their

provision of other facilities, for example, the award of discretionary grants, the provision of social and recreational facilities, or their functions under the Employment and Training Act 1973, s. 8.[27]

GENERAL DUTY IN THE PUBLIC SECTOR

In addition to the specific duties described above, there is a general duty in the public sector to ensure that educational facilities and ancillary benefits are provided without discrimination.[28] This is enforceable by the Secretary of State for Education and Science or, in the case of Welsh schools, by the Secretary of State for Wales. An example of the responsibility in this field is the so-called sexist stereotyping of the curriculum, which is considered in 'Curricular Differences for Boys and Girls'.[29]

It may be that society can justify the striking differences that exist between the subjects studied by boys and girls in secondary schools, but it is more likely that a society that needs to develop to the full the talents and skills of all its people will find the discrepancies disturbing. Whatever differences that may continue to exist ought to be based on genuine choice.

Schools must ensure that all facilities provided by them are provided without sex discrimination. For example, timetabling and extra-curricular arrangements should be organized to ensure that this requirement is met. Single-sex classes in co-educational schools may take place provided that the facilities enjoyed by each class are equal; this means, for instance, that a co-educational establishment does not necessarily have to provide mixed classes in physical education. Schools may also make use of this provision in order to separate boys and girls for certain academic subjects, e.g. mathematics and science, where it has been demonstrated that participation and attainment are increased in single-sex groups.

Wherever, in co-educational schools, subjects are taught to pupils in single-sex groups, the educational justification for so doing should be clearly defined.

The Equal Opportunities Commission publishes useful guidelines for schools in the matter of avoiding discrimination. It also publishes an annual report, available from HMSO, which often contains valuable information about how the law on discrimination has affected schools.

WORK EXPERIENCE SCHEMES

In 1983 the Employment Appeals Tribunal found that a trainee sponsored by the Manpower Services Commission was not 'employed' by the company concerned, and, therefore, that an industrial tribunal had no jurisdiction to hear a complaint of unlawful discrimination under the Race Relations Act of 1976. The Employment Appeal Tribunal expressed the hope that the Race Relations Act would be amended to cover such situations as it was 'of utmost importance that there should be no discrimination on racial grounds against a young person engaged in a work experience scheme'.[30]

SINGLE-SEX SCHOOLS

Single-sex schools are not prohibited by the Sex Discrimination Act. A school which is basically for pupils of one sex is regarded as a single-sex establishment if the admission of pupils of the other sex is exceptional, and confined to particular courses of instruction or teaching classes. Confinement to particular classes or courses in such circumstances does not amount to discrimination. A mixed school which admits as boarders only pupils of one sex (or only comparatively small numbers of the other sex) does not contravene the Act. Similarly, protection is extended to schools which accept only limited numbers of boarders of one sex because the dormitory accommodation is restricted. Nor is it an infringement to allocate inferior dormitory accommodation to one sex, if this is necessary in the light of the exigencies of the situation.[31]

TRANSITIONAL PROVISIONS

A single-sex school which is in the process of becoming co-educational may admit pupils on a discriminatory basis during such period as may be specified in the transitional exemption order.[32]

PHYSICAL EDUCATION

It is not unlawful to practise sex discrimination in respect of courses in physical training or courses for teachers of physical training in further education.[33]

RELIGIOUS EXCEPTION

Sex discrimination is not unlawful in the provision of goods, facilities or services if it is practised in a place occupied and used for the purposes of an organized religion to the extent that it is necessary to comply with the doctrines of that religion, or to avoid offending the susceptibilities of a significant number of its adherents.[34]

EXCEPTIONS

Exception for special care, etc.

It is not illegal to practise sex discrimination in the provision of goods, facilities or services in an establishment for persons requiring special care, supervision or attention.[35]

Exception for propriety and privacy

It is not illegal to practise sex discrimination in the provision of facilities or services where it is reasonable to do so to preserve decency.[36]

Exception for non-profit making bodies

Sex discrimination in the provision of goods, facilities and services may be practised by a non-statutory, non-profit-making body, even though the membership of that body is not confined to one sex and is open to the public, or a section thereof.[37]

Exception for foreign travel

Those concerned with the organization of overseas school journeys should remember that the Acts dealing with sex and racial discrimination are generally confined to Great Britain, including its territorial waters. The Acts also apply to British registered ships, aircraft and hovercraft, unless they would conflict with the laws of another country where, or over which, the vessel might be. Arrangements for travel abroad may not be discriminatory when those arrangements are made in this country, apart from certain financial facilities including banking and insurance.[38]

Exception for charities

If a charitable instrument contains provisions for conferring benefits on members of a particular racial group defined otherwise than by reference to colour, or on persons of one sex (disregarding any exceptional or insignificant benefits for the other sex), the charity may be administered to give effect to the instrument. Since 13 June 1977, a charity provision in favour of, say, white residents of London must be operated in favour of all residents of London; and a provision in favour of coloured persons must be applied to all persons as colour is not excepted.[39]

Thus the Employment Appeal Tribunal held in 1979 that a woman was ineligible to be considered for a research fellowship at one Cambridge college because of a statute restricting such posts to men: the statute was in law 'a charitable instrument'. The college conceded that there was discrimination but denied acting unlawfully.[40]

Exception for sport

There is an exception to the provisions prohibiting sex discrimination in sports where physical strength, stamina or physique are important, so that the average woman would be at a disadvantage compared with the average man. In the field of racial discrimination, there is an exception which may be based on place of birth or length of residence when teams are selected to represent a country, place or area, or where the rules of any competition relating to eligibility would otherwise be infringed.[41]

Exception for persons not ordinarily resident in Great Britain

There is a general exception permitting racial discrimination in the case of persons not ordinarily resident in Great Britain, where it appears a person, for whose benefit education or training or ancillary benefits are being considered, does not intend to remain in Great Britain beyond the end of that period of education or training.[42]

6   Reverse discrimination

Neither Act permits discrimination in favour of one group on the ground that that group has, in the past, suffered from adverse discrimination and should be given the chance to catch up. Powers are, however, given to certain bodies to undertake certain forms of positive action. Training bodies[43] may limit access to one sex or racial group if, during the previous twelve months there were no persons, or a comparatively small proportion of persons, of that sex or race engaged in that particular form of work in Great Britain. They may also limit access in one particular area in which this condition is satisfied.[44] Similar provisions exist whereby employers may limit access to internal training, but they may not take advantage of this section to balance the sexes or races in recruitment for the particular employment concerned. The same section permits trade unions, employers' organizations and professional associations to take positive action to ensure that both sexes and all appropriate racial groups are represented at different levels; but this does not permit them to discriminate in admitting to membership or in filling particular posts.[45]

7 Other provisions

DISCRIMINATORY PRACTICES

It is unlawful to apply or to operate a practice which would call for the application of a condition or requirement which will, or is likely to, result in an act of indirect discrimination. This would include a condition which is so effective a deterrent that no person of one sex, or no person of a particular racial group could ever comply with it. In these circumstances the benefit concerned would never be refused because no-one would apply for it.[46]

In 1973 the reorganization of his school led to a headmaster being offered, and accepting, a post of general adviser for his local education authority. Under the arrangements in force for the safeguarding of salary on reorganization, it was agreed that he should remain on the Burnham Scale and on the terms of employment originally agreed as a headmaster with the authority. Other advisers for the authority were paid, as is normal, on the Soulbury Scale.

When, later, there was a substantial Soulbury award, the former headmaster found that he was earning less than two ladies employed on the Soulbury Scale for advisers. He appealed to an industrial tribunal for a declaration under the Equal Pay Act 1970.

The local education authority argued that when the former headmaster was earning more than his fellow lady advisers he had a 'vested interest' and that, in law, the ladies could not bring an action for discrimination. Their only right was to a proper pay scale for the job. The tribunal, however, held that this did not apply in reverse: 'Under the Act the applicant is entitled to like pay for like work unless he comes within one of the exceptions. Vested rights ... are only a defence to a claim for equality where it is the person with whom it is sought to compare who has the higher pay because of such rights. On the wording of the Act it cannot avail the other way round.[47]

RACIALIST ABUSE AND ENVIRONMENT

In 1983 a welfare assistant to whom a teacher referred as 'a coon' was awarded £500 for hurt feelings.[48]

In 1980 the Commission for Racial Equality supported an action against Birmingham City Council claiming that a teacher had called a boy 'Sambo' and 'nig nog'. This action failed, since the class discussion in which the words were used had been about a television programme in which they occurred.[49]

In *Chattopadhyay v. Headmaster of Holloway School and others*,[50] a well qualified and experienced history teacher failed to secure a post as head of history when the post became vacant in his school. He alleged that this was for racist reasons, drawing specific attention to the attitude of his headmaster and deputy headmaster. It was claimed that the headmaster and deputy had both indicated that Dr Chattopadhyay's promotion depended on his withdrawing complaints, that the headmaster had 'snooped' during the complainant's absence, and that the ILEA, the employer, had been sent letters suggesting that Dr Chattopadhyay should be referred to a psychiatrist.

There are three points of significance in this case. Firstly, the events described above took place *after* Dr Chattopadhyay had been interviewed and failed to gain the post for which he had applied. Nevertheless the Employment Appeal Tribunal agreed that they were relevant in determining the attitude of the head and his deputy who sat on the appointment committee and that the industrial tribunal should consider them. However, the judgment 'should not be treated as a charter for wholesale allegations of subsequent events', as Mr Justice Browne-Wilkinson advised. Secondly, it was the headmaster who was specifically named in this action and not the employer as is more usual. This seems now to be acceptable to the courts if a *prima facie* case for discriminatory behaviour is made out. Thirdly, it seems that appointments panels and report writers cannot limit their responsibility to events leading up to and including interviews themselves. Tribunals will examine behaviour very broadly.

REDUNDANCY AND REDEPLOYMENT

Both redundancy and redeployment agreements are in general subject to the law on racial and sex discrimination. It has been held, for example, in a case from outside the field of education, that a company which made redundant its part-time workforce of 60 women in accordance with a union agreement that part-time staff should be made redundant before full-time, had unlawfully discriminated.[51]

DISCRIMINATORY ADVERTISEMENTS

It is a contravention of the Acts to place or publish an advertisement which indicates an intention to discriminate, unless the relevant discrimination falls within the permitted exceptions such as a GOQ. It is open to the publisher to set up the defence that he relied on a statement by the person placing the advertisement that its terms were legitimate and that it was reasonable for him so to rely. Anyone placing an advertisement who knowingly or recklessly makes a statement to the publisher which is materially false or misleading is liable, on summary conviction, to a fine.[52]

INSTRUCTIONS, PRESSURE AND AIDING

Someone who has lawful authority over another may not instruct that person to discriminate unlawfully or procure (or attempt to procure) such an act by his subordinate.[53] Any person who induces, or attempts to induce, someone else to perform an act of illegal discrimination commits an offence, even if he does not make the suggestion directly. It is enough if it is made in such a way that the second person is likely to hear of it.[54] Any person who knowingly aids another to undertake an act of illegal discrimination[55] is guilty of the offence equally with the person who commits it. As with advertising, it is a defence to have relied on a reasonable statement by the other person that the act being aided was legitimate; and it is an offence, punishable by a fine, to attempt to secure help by a false or misleading statement.[56]

EMPLOYERS AND PRINCIPALS

A principal is liable for any illegal act of discrimination by his agent if he has given authority for it expressly or by implication, before or after the act. An employer is liable for any act of illegal discrimination by his employee in the course of employment, even if the employee acts without his knowledge or approval. In these situations the agent or employee has aided the principal or employer, and both are guilty. It is open to the employer to plead that he took reasonable steps to prevent the offence.[57]

CONTRACTS

Subject to certain exceptions, a term in a contract which contravenes the Acts, including the Equal Pay Act 1970, is void and unenforceable. If the victim of the discrimination is a party to the contract, the term is not void, but is unenforceable against him. In such circumstances a county or sheriff court may remove or modify the discriminatory term on request. No term may be enforced by a person in whose favour it would operate if it purports to exclude the Acts, including the Equal Pay Act 1970.[58]

8   Enforcement

EMPLOYMENT

Complaints to an industrial tribunal, which consists of a legally qualified chairman and two lay members, must normally be made within three months, although the tribunal may admit a complaint out of time if it appears to be just and equitable. A deliberate omission is treated as having been done at the time when the decision to make it was taken. An act extending over a period is regarded as having been done at the end of that period. An unlawful term in a contract continues throughout the duration of the contract.

The matter is then referred to a conciliation officer, who attempts to reach a friendly settlement. If this fails, the complaint is heard by the tribunal. In the event of the complaint being substantiated, the tribunal can afford certain remedies:

(a) an order declaring the rights of the parties;
(b) compensation; this is currently limited to the maximum compensatory award under the Employment Protection (Consolidation) Act 1978,[59] which is varied from time to time;
(c) recommendation of action by the respondent.

Appeals on points of law, but not of fact, are considered by the Employment Appeal Tribunal and there is the possibility of a further hearing by the Court of Appeal.

EDUCATION

The time limit for a complaint is six months, the period being calculated as for employment cases. Complaints against independent establishments follow the non-employment procedure indicated in the next paragraph, but those concerned with the public sector must first be referred to the Secretary of State for Education and Science (for England), the Secretary for Welsh Education or the Secretary of the Scottish Education Department as may be relevant. If the Secretary has not reached a conclusion within two months, the complainant may bring the issue before the courts under the non-employment procedure, even if the Secretary states that he will continue his investigation and notify his decision.

NON-EMPLOYMENT

Complaints about discrimination which are not concerned with employment, and which do not have to follow the special procedure for education in the public sector, are referred to county courts in England and Wales, or to sheriff courts in Scotland. All county courts have jurisdiction in matters of sex discrimination, but only sixteen designated courts may deal with racial issues.[60] The time limit for bringing a complaint is six months which, in the case of matters referred under the special educational procedure, runs from two months after submission to the Minister. The judge is assisted by two assessors in cases dealing with racial discrimination, and in sex discrimination cases he may appoint assessors on his own initiative or at the request of a party to the proceedings. When a case has been proved, the court may afford one of the following remedies:

(a) an order declaring the rights of the parties;
(b) an injunction, or order in Scotland;
(c) damages;
(d) removal of a discriminatory clause from a contract.

An appeal lies to the Court of Appeal in England, or the Court of Session in Scotland.

NON-DISCRIMINATION NOTICES

The Equal Opportunities Commission and the Commission for Racial Equality may undertake formal investigations on their own initiatives, and must hold them if required to do so by the Secretary of State. If, at the end of such an investigation, it appears that there has been discrimination, the Commission may issue a non-discrimination notice requiring the person to whom it is directed not to contravene specified provisions of the relevant legislation. When it is proposed to issue such a notice, the person on whom it is to be served must be given twenty-eight days' warning, and during this period he may make written or oral representations, or both. An appeal against the notice may be made to the industrial tribunal in employment matters or to the county or sheriff court in non-employment issues. If an appeal is rejected or withdrawn, or if no appeal is made within six weeks of the service of the notice, it becomes final and is effective for five years. Breach of the conditions of a notice renders the offender liable to proceedings for a court order requiring compliance.

PERSISTENT DISCRIMINATION

Persistent discrimination occurs when a non-discrimination notice has been served, or a court order made, within the previous five years and the Commission is of the opinion that it seems likely that the person on whom the notice or order was served is likely to contravene the Acts. In such cases, though this does not apply to discriminatory advertisements or pressure or instructions to discriminate, the Commission may seek an injunction from the county court or sheriff court.

DISCRIMINATORY ADVERTISEMENTS, PRESSURE AND INSTRUCTIONS

Only the Commissions may commence legal proceedings in these matters. Formal investigations, non-discrimination notices, but not the persistent discrimination procedure, are available. Legal proceedings may take the form of an application to determine whether an infringement has occurred, or a request for an order to prevent an infringement. Such applications may be made whether or not the respondent is the subject of a non-discrimination notice or the order of a court or tribunal.

9 Codes of practice

The Commission for Racial Equality, but not the Equal Opportunities Commission, may issue codes of practice. The legal force of such codes is similar to that of those issued under the Health and Safety at Work etc. Act 1974, and described in chapter VI.

10   Complaints procedure

To help an individual to decide whether to institute proceedings and to present a complaint in the most effective way a special form is available. This form may be used to question the person whose conduct is the subject of the grievance — and the questions and answers would be admissible in evidence.

A copy of the special form and advice generally on the Sex Discrimination Act 1975 and the Equal Pay Act 1970, may be obtained from:

Equal Opportunities Commission
Overseas House
Quay Street
Manchester M3 3HN

The main addresses of the Commission for Racial Equality are:

London	Elliott House 10/12 Allington Street London SW1E 5EH
Leeds	133 The Headrow Leeds LS1 5QX
Birmingham	Daimler House Fourth Floor 33 Paradise Circus Queensway Birmingham B1 2BJ
Manchester	Scottish Life House (Third Floor) Bridge Street Manchester M3 3DH

Leicester   Haymarket House
(4th Floor)
Haymarket Shopping Centre
Leicester LE1 3YG

References

1. Sex Discrimination Act 1975, s. 1.
2. Sex Discrimination Act 1975, s. 2.
3. Sex Discrimination Act 1975, ss. 53, 57, 59, 67, 71 and 75; and Race Relations Act 1976, ss. 43, 48, 50, 58, 62 and 66.
4. Sex Discrimination Act 1975, ss. 1(1)(a) and 2; and Race Relations Act 1976, s. 1(1)(a).
5. Sex Discrimination Act 1975, s. 1(1)(b) and Race Relations Act 1976, s. 1(1)(b).
6. Sex Discrimination Act 1975, s. 4; and Race Relations Act 1976, s. 2.
7. Sex Discrimination Act 1975, s. 3.
8. Sex Discrimination Act 1975, ss. 18–21.
9. Sex Discrimination Act 1975, ss. 6 and 82(1); and Race Relations Act 1976, ss. 4 and 78(1).
10. Sex Discrimination Act 1975, ss. 6(1) and 8(3) and (4); and Race Relations Act 1976, s. 4(1).
11. *Times Educational Supplement*, 3 October 1979.
12. *Times Educational Supplement*, 2 April 1982.
13. *Daily Telegraph*, 6 February 1980.
14. Sex Discrimination Act 1975, s. 2(2).
15. Sex Discrimination Act 1975, s. 6(4).
16. Sex Discrimination Act 1975, s. 7.
17. Race Relations Act 1976, s. 5.
18. Sex Discrimination Act 1975, s. 12(1); and Race Relations Act 1976, s. 11.
19. Sex Discrimination Act 1975, s. 13; and Race Relations Act 1976, s. 12.
20. Sex Discrimination Act 1975, s. 14; and Race Relations Act 1976, s. 13.
21. Sex Discrimination Act 1975, s. 15; and Race Relations Act 1976, s. 14.
22. Sex Discrimination Act 1975, s. 22; and Race Relations Act 1976, s. 4.
23. *Times Educational Supplement*, 7 December 1979.

24. Whitfield *v*. London Borough of Croydon (1979) (unreported).
25. Mandla *v*. Dowell Lee (1983) 1 All ER 1062 HL.
26. *The Times*, 2 June 1978.
27. Sex Discrimination Act 1975, ss. 23 and 15(2); and Race Relations Act 1976, ss. 18 and 14(2).
28. Sex Discrimination Act 1975, s. 25; and Race Relations Act 1976, s. 19.
29. Department of Education and Science: *Education Survey no. 21*.
30. *Education*, 25 February 1983.
31. Sex Discrimination Act 1975, ss. 26 and 46.
32. Sex Discrimination Act 1975, s. 27.
33. Sex Discrimination Act 1975, s. 28.
34. Sex Discrimination Act 1975, s. 35(1)(b).
35. Sex Discrimination Act 1975, s. 35(1)(a).
36. Sex Discrimination Act 1975, s. 35(1)(c) and (d).
37. Sex Discrimination Act 1975, s. 34.
38. Sex Discrimination Act 1975, s. 36; and Race Relations Act 1976, s. 27.
39. Sex Discrimination Act 1975, s. 43; and Race Relations Act 1976, s. 34.
40. *Guardian*, 28 July 1979.
41. Sex Discrimination Act 1975, s. 44; and Race Relations Act 1976, s. 39.
42. Race Relations Act 1976, s. 36.
43. The Manpower Service Commission, the Training Services Agency, the Employment Service Agency, and any other bodies specifically designated for this purpose by the Secretary of State.
44. Sex Discrimination Act 1975, s. 47; and Race Relations Act 1976, s. 37.
45. Sex Discrimination Act 1975, s. 48; and Race Relations Act 1976, s. 38.
46. Sex Discrimination Act 1975, s. 37; and Race Relations Act 1976, s. 28.
47. Thomas *v*. London Borough of Richmond-upon-Thames (1978), unreported.
48. *Education*, 16 September 1983.
49. *Daily Telegraph*, 4 March 1980.
50. (1981) IRLR 487 EAT.
51. Eley (IMI) Kynoch Ltd *v*. Powell, *The Times*, 28 September, 1982.
52. Sex Discrimination Act 1975, s. 38; and Race Relations Act 1976, s. 29.

53. Sex Discrimination Act 1975, s. 39; and Race Relations Act 1976, s. 30.
54. Sex Discrimination Act 1975, s. 40; and Race Relations Act 1976, s. 31.
55. This includes discriminatory practices and advertisements, and instructions and pressure to discriminate.
56. Sex Discrimination Act 1975, s. 42; and Race Relations Act 1976, s. 33.
57. Sex Discrimination Act 1975, s. 41; and Race Relations Act 1976, s. 32.
58. Sex Discrimination Act 1975, s. 77; and Race Relations Act 1976, s. 72.
59. Sex Discrimination Act 1975, s. 65(2); and Race Relations Act 1976, s. 54(2).
60. The designated courts are: Birmingham, Bristol, Cambridge, Canterbury, Cardiff, Carlisle, Exeter, Leeds, Manchester, Newcastle-upon-Tyne, Nottingham, Oxford, Plymouth, Southampton, Westminster and Wrexham.

XIV
Accidents and negligence

1 Negligence

Circumstances vary so widely that it is impossible to secure a short definition of negligence which will cover every possible situation. The court applies the law to the facts of the case so far as it has been able to ascertain them from the evidence placed before it. It must be remembered that in civil actions the decision of the court is based in the 'balance of probabilities', and not on proof 'beyond all reasonable doubt' which is required in a criminal trial. No superior knowledge or skill is required of the defendant unless he has failed in a duty of which he may be presumed to have special knowledge: thus, when an accident occurs to a child whilst he is under school discipline, the court would take into account the fact that a teacher may be presumed to have a special knowledge of children and their behaviour, and to act accordingly.

If an action for negligence is to succeed, three factors must be present. In the first place, the defendant must have owed a duty of care to the plaintiff. Secondly, he must have failed, either by what he has done or by what he has left undone, reasonably to perform that duty. Reasonably is the key term here. Finally, the plaintiff must have suffered damage through that act or omission. These tests are applied by the courts in all cases where negligence is alleged.

It follows from this that no claim for damages will succeed in respect of what is strictly an accident, i.e. an event which cannot be prevented, or which could not reasonably have been foreseen so that steps should have been taken to guard against it. In 1921 a seven-year-old blind boy was playing with other children, some of whom had full sight, in a hostel for blind children. He was injured when, without warning, another boy jumped suddenly on his back. Lord Justice-Clerk Scott Dickson said: 'What actually occurred was an unexpected, an unforeseen, and, I think, an almost unforeseeable misfortune, and even if there had been a matron or some other servant in the room where the children were playing, I do not see how that would have prevented the accident. The occurrence is described as one boy jumping unexpectedly on the back of the boy who was injured. It was the thing of a moment.... I think the case fails because the obligation which was sought to be imposed on the education authority was higher than the law imposes upon it.'[1] Although this was a Scottish case, English law is identical at this point.

Special circumstances may put a plaintiff outside the duty of a defendant's care. Such a case might occur when a pupil is compelled to play games which, because of a hidden physical defect, cause harm. If the defect were known to the teacher he would be required, of course, to exercise a sufficient degree of care to prevent injury to the pupil.

It is important that articles which might harm children, or with which they might harm each other, should not be left lying about. The case of *Williams v. Eady*[2] arose because some phosphorus was left in a conservatory. Lord Justice Kay asked, 'Was it not evidence of negligence to have left the bottle of phosphorus lying about in a place to which boys had access, knowing what boys are?'

A contractor left a mixture of sand and lime in the corner of a school playground, and a boy's eye was injured when another lad threw a lump of the mixture at him. The headmaster was found to be negligent although he had telephoned the contractor and asked him to remove the materials, and the contractor was also found to be negligent in failing to remove the 'rough stuff' within a reasonable time of the request to do so.[3]

On the other hand it was found that it was not necessary to have a protective cover, over which boys could not climb, round a heap of coke in a playground. One boy injured another by throwing a piece of coke at him. There was proper supervision. The trial judge found for the plaintiff, but his decision was reversed on appeal.[4]

Much publicity is often given to cases where there is an allegation of negligence towards children and a good deal of sympathy is aroused thereby. Mr Justice Hilbery referred to this whilst summing up in an action resulting from an accident in which a small boy lost an eye whilst a patient in a convalescent home.[5] He said, 'Our law reports show how fatally attractive children's cases have been to those who have to try them. Judges are human beings and their feelings are easily aroused in favour of the child, especially children of tender years. When they meet with an accident, any court is liable to strain the law in favour of the child, but an infant plaintiff has exactly the same burden of proving his case as any other plaintiff.'

Lord Atkin once summed up the question of negligence in words which echo the parable of the Good Samaritan.[6] He said, 'You must take reasonable care to avoid acts or omissions which you can reasonably foresee would be likely to injure your neighbour. Who then, in law, is my neighbour? The answer seems to be, persons who are so closely and directly affected by my act that I ought reasonably to have them in contemplation as being so affected when I am directing my mind to the acts or omissions which are called in question.'

2 The duty of a schoolteacher

Many school accidents occur during the course of a year and most have no repercussions, but sometimes parents consider that the school authorities have been negligent in some way and an action is brought in the courts. It is therefore vitally important that teachers should understand their responsibilities and that they should take all reasonable steps to prevent their pupils from coming to harm.

The courts have always taken a realistic view of these cases and have recognized that it is quite impossible, even if it were desirable, to watch every child during every minute of the school day. On the other hand, they expect that teachers should exercise supervision strictly enough to prevent unnecessary accidents. Mr Justice McNair, for instance, said,[7] 'A balance must be struck between the meticulous supervision of children every moment at school and the desirable object of encouraging sturdy independence as they grow up.' The danger of crushing initiative and independence in pupils was noted in another case in the judge's comment: 'It is better that a boy should break his neck than allow other people to break his spirit.'[8] These are both illustrations of what the courts have considered to be 'reasonable care.'

In one case, a child of 5 had climbed on to the glass roof of a lavatory after his class had been dismissed at four o'clock. He fell through and received injuries from which he died. The child's father maintained that an adult should have been present until the children had left the premises. The judge said, 'In the case of children under 5 attending the nursery department of this school it was thought right to have some person in actual supervision of them until they were collected by their mothers. That was not thought necessary in the case of the 5-year-olds and that was a decision taken by a responsible person. I should require strong evidence to convince me that it is wrong.' The case was dismissed.

Towards the end of the nineteenth century Mr Justice Cave defined a schoolmaster's duty in the following words:[9] 'The schoolmaster is bound to take such care of his boys as a careful father would take of his boys.' This definition was quoted by Lord Esher, then Master of the Rolls, who added that there could not be a better definition of a schoolmaster. Mr Justice Cave's statement is still the most used definition of a teacher's duty and is usually cited in cases where teachers are accused of neglect.

The doctrine of the careful parent has been followed quite literally in nearly every case since *Williams v. Eady*, but there is a general tendency in the courts to raise the standard of the duty of care, and educational cases have followed this trend. Two examples will serve to show the way in which the rising standard of care is being applied, but it must be remembered that these were settled at a lower level, and refine the rule in *Williams v. Eady* which was decided in the Court of Appeal.

In the autumn of 1962 damages were awarded against the Middlesex County Council in an action following injuries to a boy who put his hand through a pane of glass. It was held that the glass was too thin. Mr Justice Edmund Davies said, 'The test of the reasonably prudent parent must be applied not to the parent in the home, but the parent applying his mind to school life.... It may be that the consequences of the decision I have arrived at may be widespread. If this widespread nature leads to greater safety in the care of the young, then no consummation can be more devoutly desired.'[10]

In 1968 the Surrey County Council was sued for damages for negligence following injury to a boy's eye during morning break. Mr Justice Geoffrey Lane considered the duty of care *in loco parentis* in the following terms: 'The duty of a headmaster towards his pupils is said to be to take such care of them as a reasonably careful and prudent father would take of his own children. That standard is a helpful one when considering, for example, individual instructions to individual children in a school. It would be very unwise to allow a 6-year-old child to carry a kettle of boiling water – that type of instruction. But that standard when applied to an incident of horseplay in a school of nine hundred pupils is somewhat unrealistic, if not unhelpful.

'In the context of the present action it appears to me to be easier and preferable to use the ordinary language of the law of negligence. That is, it is a headmaster's duty, bearing in mind the known propensities of boys and indeed girls between the ages of 11 and 17 or 18, to take all reasonable and proper steps to prevent any of the pupils under his care from suffering injury from a combination of the two. That is a high standard.... They, the defendants, in the manner which I have described, regrettably fall short of the standards which the law demands of them.'[11]

Proceedings may be brought against the governors, against the local education authority, or against teachers acting as their servants. Only one sum, however, may be awarded in damages. Where, in an action against a teacher, the employer is made a joint defendant, the court may find against both and, under the Law Reform Act, 1935, apportion the amount of damages to be paid by each. In general, the employer would be liable for accidents arising from defective premises or equipment unless the accident is directly caused by the negligence of the servant.

It is in a teacher's own interest to report immediately any defect in buildings or equipment which may give rise to an accident and, pending action by the responsible authority, to take reasonable steps to prevent any use which might lead to a mishap. Failure to take these steps might raise the question of the teacher's negligence. The provisions of the Health and Safety at Work Act 1974 are important here also, and are outlined in chapter VI.

3 'The system'

When damages for injury arising from negligence are claimed before the courts the onus is on the plaintiff, as has already been said, to prove negligence on the defendant's part. In reaching its decision the court must judge whether the plaintiff has made out his case or whether the injuries were due to some other cause, for example an accident which could not have been prevented, or which could not reasonably have been foreseen.

In different contexts the local education authority, the governors, the head teacher and the assistant staff (including, sometimes, ancillary workers and caretakers) have a duty of care to the pupils of a school in the management of which they have a share. In the case of the teaching staff and, perhaps, to a greater or lesser extent the other groups as well, there is a common law duty of care based on the rule in *Williams v. Eady* referred to earlier in this chapter.

The matter, however, extends more widely than that. The owners of the school, be they the proprietors of an independent school, the governors of voluntary schools, or the local education authority in the case of county schools, have a duty of care for all persons on school premises whether by statute (e.g. The Occupiers Liability Act 1957), or by regulation, and some would say that it is the local education authority which stands *in loco parentis*.

Be that as it may, the Articles of Government prescribe that the head shall control 'the internal organization, management and discipline of the school'. This requirement postulates that he must create and maintain a system which, amongst other things, will be the machinery for discharging his duty of care for the safety of his pupils. It further postulates that this system will include a suitable code of rules, known to all members of the school; and, since the head cannot be everywhere at once, it follows that he has the authority to delegate parts of the supervisory system to assistant staff to carry out. This is, of course, the origin of the 'staff duty roster', known to all staffrooms. The head will himself ensure in one way or another that the system is being maintained at a fully efficient level.

This burden of responsibility is laid upon the head because he is the principal servant of his employers in the school and it is not unreasonable to assume that his professional experience is such that he is the person who will most clearly understand the special circumstances of the school. Conditions vary so widely, even between similar neighbouring establishments, that it would not be practicable to impose the same system throughout an authority's schools. In framing a scheme to meet the needs of his school a head must take into account such matters as the number and age-range of the pupils, any handicaps from which they may suffer, any special problems posed by the building, traffic and other conditions in the neighbourhood, and such other matters as may seem to him to be relevant.

One issue which must be determined as a fact by any court hearing an action for damages for negligence is whether a system existed which, so far as could reasonably be foreseen, was adequately designed to prevent such mishaps as that which gave rise to the claim. In the light of the argument which has been outlined in this section it is clear that, if such a system has not been provided, there has been negligence. The only exception would be a genuine accident which could not have been prevented if such a system had been enforced; or which was so unforeseeable that no reasonable person, having regard to all the circumstances, would have judged it necessary to guard against it.

If, however, the court is satisfied that an adequate system existed, it must then examine another matter: whether at the time of the event giving rise to the action the system was being maintained at full efficiency. If not, the court is likely to hold that there had been negligence to the extent that the system was not being observed. Three cases illustrate this point:

MARTIN v. MIDDLESBROUGH CORPORATION

An 11-year-old girl slipped on an icy playground, severing the tendons of the middle and ring fingers of her right hand and injuring the little finger on a broken piece of milk bottle lying on a drain cover. In court the headmistress gave detailed evidence of the way in which the free milk was distributed to various parts of the school, including the fact that the empty bottles were not brought downstairs until the midday break, and then under the supervision of two mistresses. The plaintiff said that they were in the playground before the end of the mid-morning break. In the Court of Appeal, Lord Justice Willmer said: 'The evidence of the headmistress (whom the judge said he found an impressive witness) was rather different from that of the plaintiff.... This conflict of evidence was never resolved by the judge. But there was evidence from the school's caretaker, which corroborated that of the plaintiff, evidence to show that quite often there were loose bottles standing on the ground alongside the crates in the playground, and this he regarded as dangerous.

'I am quite sure that the headmistress was correctly describing what was supposed to be the routine, but notwithstanding that I am left with the impression that the plaintiff probably knew more about what usually happened in practice....

'The headmistress said that when the empties were carried down by the girls and stacked outside, there were always two mistresses on duty, and they would see that the girls did it. This answer at least recognized the need for supervision if and when the bottles were brought downstairs and stacked outside. I have no doubt that there ought to be such supervision. But the evidence given by the plaintiff as to the prevailing routine for bringing the bottles down seems to show that in actual practice there was in fact no such supervision. Moreover, as I have said, the defendants did not see fit to call any mistress to prove that such supervision was in fact exercised....

'In my judgment, on the evidence, the risk of an accident such as this occurring was a reasonably foreseeable risk against which the defendants could and should have guarded by making better arrangements for the disposal of empty milk bottles. I do not think that the arrangements which they in fact made were such as would commend themselves to any reasonably prudent parent.'[12]

BEAUMONT v. SURREY COUNTY COUNCIL

At a boys' secondary school in Surrey, morning break lasted for eighteen minutes, and was supervised by two masters, four prefects, four sub-prefects and four monitors. Before going into the playground the masters were responsible for clearing the school; on the day in question this operation took some time, and break had continued for ten minutes before they reached the playground. During that time some boys had found a discarded piece of trampette elastic which they used as a catapult for the purpose of projecting their schoolmates across the loggia. The elastic either broke or flew out of the hand of one of the boys who were holding it, and one end struck another pupil in the eye, the sight of which was to all intents and purposes destroyed.

After defining the headmaster's duty of care towards his pupils in terms already quoted, Mr Justice Geoffrey Lane found that the presence of the elastic in an open wastepaper basket amounted to a failure in the standard of care required: 'It is sufficient as far as the law is concerned for the possibility to be there — for the possibility to be foreseen that some physical injury might be caused by the extension or use of, or horseplay with that piece of elastic. If such, even slight, injury is foreseeable, then the defendants must foot the bill if unforeseen and major injury occurred.'

The learned judge also found that the standard of supervision did not measure up to the high standard of care required: 'It may be that this was a particularly difficult day as Mr Clerke has indicated, it may be that the system of prefects, sub-prefects and monitors was not quite up to standard. It may be that on the one day when pupils were possibly reluctant to get out on to the playground insufficient staff were available on the loggia to supervise. Suffice it to say that had the system been working properly I have no doubt that either a prefect, sub-prefect, monitor or one of the staff would have seen or would have been summoned to see what was going on. . . .

'At all events it would have been stopped immediately, and had it been stopped immediately, or even within two or three minutes of this inception by the 11-year-olds, then this tragic matter would never have happened.'[13]

BARNES v. HAMPSHIRE COUNTY COUNCIL

At an infants' school in Hampshire, nearly 200 yards from the A30 trunk road, it was the system that those pupils who were met by their parents at half-past three were escorted to the gate by a teacher. If a parent was not there, the child concerned was instructed to return to his teacher. The children were given kerb drill, and a traffic warden was on duty on the main road.

One afternoon in 1962 a 5-year-old girl began to make her way home whilst her mother was still on her way to meet her. Attempting to cross the main road at a point 250 yards from the school gate, she was knocked down and sustained partial paralysis of the left arm and foot. A man working in his nearby garden heard the accident, walked down his drive, saw that a girl had been hurt, and ran back to his house to telephone for an ambulance. The call was recorded in the telephone exchange at 3.30 pm.

The plaintiff's claim for damages for negligence was rejected at Winchester Assizes. This judgment was affirmed by a majority of the Court of Appeal, Lord Justice Diplock observing that the school system was reasonable: 'Ordinary people in ordinary life do not carry a chronometer; and I do not think that the three to five minutes in the present case constituted a breach of duty.' The Master of the Rolls, Lord Denning, dissented. He maintained that 'The school's system depended on the parents being there to meet the children at half-past three, and the school not letting them out until that time: to let them out before the mothers were due to arrive was to release them into a situation of potential danger and, in my view, a breach of duty.'

The House of Lords reversed the decision and awarded damages amounting to £10,000. Lord Pearson said: 'I agree with the Master of the Rolls. The system proved by the evidence was as he stated it. It was the duty of the school authorities not to release the children before the closing time. Although a premature release would very seldom cause an accident, it foreseeably could, and in this case it did cause the accident to the plaintiff.'[14]

GOOD v. ILEA

A pupil of $6\frac{1}{2}$ years of age was injured in the eye in the 'junior' playground of school premises as the result of horseplay. He was struck by a sharp object obtained from a pile of sand and stone in the playground and thrown by another boy. He was blinded. School normally ended at 4 pm, most children being met at that time, but those who were not met were ushered into an adjacent play centre which opened at 4 pm. The children had been warned in assembly not to go near the sand and stones, which were to be used in the building of a swimming pool. Unfortunately, on the day in question the two boys escaped unnoticed when they were being ushered to the play centre, and the incident occurred.

The Court of Appeal held that no-one could reasonably be expected to keep an eye on the children every minute of the day. In particular there was no breach of duty by the local authority by not supervising the whole of the journey from the infants' school building to the play centre. The teachers' responsibility ended when the children left the school either to be collected by their parents or to go to the play centre.[15]

It is important to emphasize again here that the responsibility of the head teacher for the supervisory system of the school derives from the Articles of Government. Since the Articles of Government are themselves required by Act of Parliament, it follows that the head's duty is 'subsidiary legislation' and just as much the will of Parliament as the Act itself.

There is therefore a clear distinction to be drawn between the head's duty as laid down in the Articles, and teachers' conditions of service. The latter can, within the law, be freely negotiated between teachers and their employers. The head's general duty may not be, without amendment of the Articles and the orders which bring them into force.

4 Contributory negligence

At one time an action for negligence could be defeated if it were proved that the plaintiff himself contributed to the damage he sustained. In such a case the question of duty did not arise if it could be proved that the plaintiff acted without due care. The courts, however, took into account the fact that children are reckless and that it is to be expected that teachers will know this. The standard of care demanded from teachers is, however, that of the reasonably careful parent.

The law of contributory negligence was amended by the

Law Reform (Contributory Negligence) Act 1948. Under this Act, a claim in respect of damages can no longer be defeated purely because the injured person contributed to his own harm. The amount of any damages, however, must be reduced to such an extent as the court thinks just and equitable, having regard to the claimant's share of responsibility. The Act does not operate against any defence arising under a contract.

A child aged 9 was injured when he rode his bicycle into a pile of hardcore left on the road by the defendants. In an action for damages, it was held that the child, who according to the evidence was a 'good rider' of his bicycle, was guilty of 20 per cent contributory negligence. The degree to which a child could be capable of contributory negligence is a question of fact in each case.[16]

Generally speaking, however, it is difficult to establish contributory negligence on the part of a younger child.

5 Higher duty of care

A defendant who, through training or experience, may have grounds to visualize more clearly the results of his acts in a particular sphere than would be expected of the proverbial man in the street, owes what is known as a higher duty of care. Obviously a doctor would be expected to render first aid more effectively than a person who is completely untrained, and it has been noted above that teachers are expected to know more of the vagaries of children than most people do.

A case which contained this element[17] arose out of an accident which occurred when a chemistry master sent two boys across a school cloister with a bottle of sulphuric acid. Contrary to the school rules some other pupils were playing cap touch in the vicinity after the end of school. One of the players backed into the boys who were carrying the flask of vitriol with the result that it was shattered, and the plaintiff was permanently scarred. Actions were brought against the managers and the headmaster.

For the defendants it was urged that the chemistry master was competent and qualified, and that the boys carrying the jar were monitors who were well aware of the properties of sulphuric acid. The plaintiff should have left the school premises before the accident occurred. The monitors had called out in warning when they saw him running backwards towards them.

The managers were dismissed from the case, but the jury found for the plaintiff against the headmaster, who was ordered to pay damages. It was held that no steps had been taken on this occasion to ensure that boys left the premises at the end of school, and the chemistry master — with his special knowledge of the nature of the liquid — should have made sure that the cloister was clear before he sent the monitors on their errand. The school rules were sufficient, but they were not carried out. There was no contributory negligence by the plaintiff.

6 Scope of employment

An employer is liable for the acts of his servants so long as they are acting within the scope of their employment. It is difficult to say where the scope of a teacher's employment begins and ends today, for there is a multitude of out-of-school activities which would once have been considered beyond his province. It is clear that the scope of employment is not to be construed in any narrow sense. A teacher inflicting corporal punishment in defiance of the local education authority's rules would possibly be acting outside the scope of his employment and would have to take full personal responsibility for any mischance arising therefrom. The same would apply in the case of a teacher who sent a child across the road on a purely personal errand.

Some years ago, a teacher sent a 14-year-old girl to the staffroom to poke the fire and draw the damper. Whilst she was doing this her pinafore caught fire and she was burned. An action[18] was brought against both the teacher and the local education authority. The judge held that the order was given by the teacher for her personal convenience, that she was therefore acting outside the scope of her employment, and the authority had no liability in the matter. He dismissed the authority from the suit, and awarded damages against the teacher.

Two appeals followed. That by the teacher against the parent failed, but the latter appealed successfully against the dismissal of the authority from the case. Lord Justice Farwell held that the teacher was acting within the scope of her employment, and said, 'In my opinion the Education Acts are designed to provide for education in its truest and widest sense. Such education includes the inculcation of habits of order, obedience and courtesy; such habits are taught by giving orders and, if such orders are reasonable and proper under the circumstances of the case, they are within the scope of the teacher's authority even though they are not confined to bidding the child to read or write, to sit down or to stand up in school, or the like. It would be extravagant to say that a teacher has no business to ask a child to perform small acts of courtesy for herself or for others, such as to fetch her pocket handkerchief from upstairs, to open a door for a visitor, or the like.

'It is said that these are for the teacher's own benefit, but I do not agree. Not only is it good for the child to be taught to be unselfish and obliging, but the opportunity of running upstairs may often avoid punishment. The wise teacher who sees a child becoming fidgety may well make the excuse of an errand for herself an outlet for the child's exuberance of spirits very much to the benefit of the child. Teachers must use their common sense, and it would be disastrous to hold that they can do nothing but teach.'

The question of scope of employment can also affect claims for industrial injuries benefit. Some years ago a caretaker, out of sheer good will, used to play cricket with the boys and staff during the lunch break. One day he was hit on the knee by a ball bowled by a master, and claimed for industrial injuries. The answer to an official inquiry was that playing cricket was not part of his duties as a caretaker.

A favourite topic for staffroom discussions is the legality of using pupils for various duties which are for the benefit of the staff. In some schools senior pupils prepare tea for the staff at break time, and a case arising out of this practice was heard by the Court of Appeal in 1959.[19]

A 14-year-old girl was carrying a pot containing half a gallon of tea to the staffroom, and was scalded when she collided with a small boy who charged out of a room. In the county court she was awarded damages against the Corporation. For the plaintiff it was claimed that the girl was engaged in a dangerous operation, and that if the school desired free labour a greater burden of care was placed on it. She had to walk 25 yards along a narrow corridor, which gave on to a number of rooms from which anyone might properly emerge, and round three blind corners.

On appeal it was maintained that this was not a dangerous operation. The older girls had lessons in domestic science and carried out certain duties, partly in furtherance of their training and partly for the convenience of the staff. It was part of their general training for life. The girl was required to take the tea to the staffroom before the beginning of break, and was doing so on this occasion, but the county court judge had believed that children were thronging the corridors at this time. If children of 14 were to be guarded against the least physical injury, cricket would be played with soft balls, gymnastics would be abandoned, and cookery classes would cease.

In allowing the appeal, Mr Justice Hodson said that a great many domestic operations carried danger with them. There was no evidence of crowds of children thronging the corridor, and it had not been contended that it was the case. There was no reason to see that a single boy would be outside a classroom at that time. On the facts of the case there was nothing to justify a finding of negligence.

A teacher came out of her classroom and fell over a tricycle which had been left near the door by a 10-year-old boy in the course of distributing free milk. At first instance the judge found that the pupil was a servant of the local education authority whilst he was taking round milk. Holding the teacher one-fifth to blame for the mishap, he decided that the authority must bear four-fifths of the blame because of their servant's negligence. On appeal Lord Justice Orr said: 'Children should be encouraged to assume responsibilities appropriate to their age within the community of the school, just as they should be encouraged to do so within the community of their homes. The services performed by schoolchildren can take various forms. They can help serve school meals or move furniture. If an accident happened because the work being performed by a child was beyond his capacity, or was insufficiently supervised, the authority would be directly liable; but that is altogether different from vicarious liability which depends on the existence of a master and servant relationship.

'If it were right that in carrying out a task for the benefit of the community of the school a schoolboy should be considered to be a servant of the authority, it would lead to curious results. During the course of a school day a boy might be continually alternating between being a pupil of the school and a servant of the school authority. The question whether the boy was a servant of the authority falls to be decided in the context in which the service is rendered, and in that context the proper inference is that the boy was not acting as a servant.'[20]

7   Damages

The assessment of damages where a plaintiff succeeds in an action is not a matter of caprice, and potential defendants should be aware of the fact that, like everything else, they are following current inflationary trends. This must be so, for example, in considering the future loss of earnings, due to someone else's negligence, of a young person whose career had shown promise of considerable success for a further period of thirty years or more. Loss of future earnings is currently a minefield in the law.

POVEY v. RYDAL SCHOOL

In 1969 a young man confined to a wheelchair after dislocating his neck in a school gymnasium was awarded £69,998 in damages. It was said that he had been forced to give up his ambition to become a doctor, that he would never be able to stand up or walk again and that he was constantly reliant on others for all physical needs except for propelling his wheelchair. The award consisted of £14,920 for loss of earnings, £19,400 for nursing costs, £7,000 for miscellaneous costs, £25,000 for general damages, £400 for loss of expectancy of life, and £3,278 agreed special damages.[21] Special damages are disbursements actually and necessarily made before the trial including, for example, medical and nursing attention not provided by the National Health Service. They do not include the legal costs of the action, although these usually follow success. It should be noted that damages for 'loss of expectancy of life' are no longer awarded.

HAMP v. ST JOSEPH'S HOSPITAL, ALDERLEY EDGE

The damages awarded against the proprietors of a convent school were so far in excess of the insurance cover taken out by the owners that a special appeal had to be launched to save the school. The award stemmed from an incident in 1965, when an 11-year-old girl was grinding chemicals for a teacher and an explosion virtually destroyed her sight. For the next six years she underwent almost continuous medical attention, including eighteen months in a hospital in Barcelona where she had an average of an operation each month, and a corneal transplant in Houston, Texas. For long periods she had to lie in total darkness. She was awarded £76,878 in damages to include £36,000 for pain, suffering and loss of amenities, £11,000 for loss of future earnings and £5,500 for future medical expenses. Special damages were agreed at £24,378. In addition, interest of between 6 and $7\frac{1}{2}$ per cent was due on the general damages from the issue of the writ until the date of judgment nearly four years later, and at half that rate on the special damages from the date of the accident seven years previously. The father was also awarded £4,471 for his expenses in travelling with his daughter to Spain and the United States. When the costs were added the school was faced with a bill in the region of £95,000. At the time of the accident the school's insurance policy for contingencies of this kind provided cover for £25,000.

Loss of marriage prospects formed an element in the assessment of damages in this case, and when the school's appeal was heard in July 1973 it was known that she was about to marry an American electronics engineer. By this time interest had raised the damages, apart from costs, to more than £88,000, and counsel for the school submitted that the impending marriage should go to the reduction of damages. The Court of Appeal did not agree. The Master of the Rolls, Lord Denning, said that if she had children she would probably have to have paid help, and he thought 'the pecuniary loss would be more in a way when she is married than if she is unmarried'. Lord Justice Lawton thought that, if anything, the award was 'a little on the low side'.[22]

Although an employer is liable for the torts of his servants committed in the execution of his duty, there is nothing to prevent a head or assistant being joined with the employer in an action for negligence and, as has already been stated, he may be ordered to pay a proportion of the damages if there has been gross personal negligence on his part. In any case, if he is a joint defendant, he may find himself faced with costs or, at least, considerable out-of-pocket expenses when he is not condemned in damages.

If for no other reason than this, a teacher should belong to a professional association which will not only undertake his defence and pay for it, but will also insure him in respect of any damages which may be awarded against him. The only reasonable alternative is to take out an equivalent insurance policy privately, and there are underwriters prepared to do business in this field. The snag in this case is that general insurers may not have the specialized knowledge of educational law which has been built up by the professional associations.

Teachers in voluntary-aided and independent schools are not the servants of the local education authority, but of the governors or proprietor. They are in a particularly vulnerable position. Some local education authorities are unwilling to extend the same degree of protection to the staffs of voluntary-aided schools as to those in county schools; they can do nothing for teachers in independent schools. Unfortunately, these schools do not always carry sufficient cover, and it is even more essential that teachers in these establishments should take steps to protect themselves, or at least to ascertain the extent of the cover provided by their employer.

Damages awarded inevitably increase as time goes by and it is important that the financial limits of insurance cover are reviewed regularly. In June 1983, for example, an 8-year-old boy was awarded £380,000 for 'devastating' injuries received in a car crash.[23] Although not an education case, it is worth noting also that in 1982 the House of Lords held[24] that illness caused by shock to a mother who was told at home that her family had been seriously injured in a car accident two miles away, and was told that one child had been killed, was a reasonably foreseeable consequence of the admitted negligence of a driver: she was therefore entitled to damages for nervous shock.

8   General and approved practice

A common defence to an action for negligence is that the act causing harm was in accordance with general and approved practice (sometimes called 'the custom of the trade') in the circumstances. A selection of examples will show how this defence has been used in cases arising from accidents in school.

In the first,[25] some children were playing when one fell on the lance of a toy soldier with which another was amusing himself. The lance pierced the child's eye. It was held in this case that children are commonly allowed to play with these toys, and it cannot therefore be considered negligent for them to be permitted to do so in school.

In another case[26] the plaintiff was a girl of 7 who was injured in an exercise which consisted of running across the floor and jumping over an inverted wastepaper basket. The head, an assistant and a student were present. An action for damages was based on the grounds that the basket was an unsuitable obstacle, the child was not physically fitted for the exercise, no landing mat was provided and there was no stand-by. In the defence, which was based on a plea of general and approved practice, it was pointed out that the Board of Education's suggestions included running and jumping for children of this age, that the head had been at the school for two and a half years during which the exercise had been performed regularly without accident, and that there had been no accident arising from this exercise at the head's previous school. Moreover, it was contended that the rope which the plaintiff suggested as a more suitable obstacle was, in fact, more dangerous. The suit was dismissed.

During the slump in the early 1930s an unemployed youth of 17 was ordered to attend a juvenile instruction centre, as a condition of receiving unemployment benefit. Whilst engaged in physical training at the centre, he fell and injured his arm during a game of horses and riders. He sued the local education authority[27] and was awarded damages in the county court. This decision was reversed by the divisional court, whereupon Jones took the case to the Court of Appeal. Giving judgment for the Council, Lord Justice Scrutton asked whether it could be negligence to play a game which had been played for twenty years. He added that there were few physical exercises without the possibility of an accident.

9   The effect of age

It has already been mentioned that what amounts to negligence in one case may not be so in another because the age of the plaintiff must be taken into account. This may be further illustrated by a case[28] arising from an accident to a man of 19 who was using an unguarded circular saw. It was alleged that the education authority was negligent in failing to provide a guard. In an appeal from the decision of the county court, it was said that the plaintiff knew the use of the saw and voluntarily took the risk. Observing that there was no evidence of a general practice to protect saws, Mr Justice Lush added, 'If he had been a child, the case might have been different but, so far from being a child, he was a lad of 19 years of age and had been in the habit of using the saw for two years.'

The circumstances outlined in the last paragraph might amount to a breach of statutory duty if any regulations had been ignored. In *Lyes v. Middlesex County Council* already referred to, the plaintiff grounded his case both in negligence and in breach of duty.

It was held in 1968 that a college of further education is not a factory. A 16-year-old trainee printer at the Camberwell School of Arts and Crafts caught his hand in a Thomson-British auto platen machine, which he was using for the first time. Three of his fingers were broken, one being permanently shortened by a quarter of an inch.

The Court of Appeal dismissed the local education authority's appeal against the award of damages. Lord Justice Danckwerts found that the Factories Act 1961, section 14, required such machinery to be fenced, in spite of evidence that it was not usual for automatic machines to be guarded. The Act, however, did not apply in the circumstances of the case, which therefore fell to be considered in terms of common law negligence: 'It is said, of course that if no guard was provided in factories, a school of this kind could not be expected to go to the trouble, and the expense, I suppose, of obtaining a guard, which would have to be made specially for the purpose, from the manufacturers. It seems to me, however, that it is the duty of the school to provide for the safety of their pupils.'[29]

More than a century ago it was held by Lord Ellenborough that it was negligent to allow children of tender years to play with fireworks unsupervised.[30] In *Williams v. Eady*, to which reference has already been made, Mr Justice Cave said, 'To leave a knife about where a child of 4 could get at it would amount to negligence, but it would not if boys of 18 had access to it.' Charlesworth on Negligence defines this test by asking the question, 'Is the thing one of a class which children of that age are, in the ordinary course of things, not allowed without supervision?'

In July 1964 an experienced teacher was taking a class of 9- and 10-year-old girls, who were given pointed scissors to cut out illustrations during a geography lesson. Whilst the teacher was attending to one girl, another pupil waved her scissors about so that the point destroyed the sight of the plaintiff's eye. There were thirty-seven children in the class. At first instance the plaintiff was awarded damages, Mr Justice Mocatta holding that it was incumbent on the education authority to ensure that the waving about of scissors was rendered impossible by proper supervision. If personal attention was to be given to one child, it must be given either out of class, or after the class had been told to put down the scissors.

This judgment was unanimously reversed in the Court of Appeal. 'If every little child got into a difficulty', asked Lord Denning, the Master of the Rolls, 'was she to be told to come back afterwards? That did not seem practical. Nor was it practical to make sure that the rest of the class put the scissors down. Was the whole class to stop still if one little girl needed supervision? It was a large class, but that was inevitable in conditions today. The teacher conducted the class in a good and efficient way. It was a very unfortunate accident, but there was no justification for finding either the education authority or the teacher at fault. The judge had the evidence of experienced teachers that there was no fault in the system of using pointed scissors.'[31]

However, in 1983 the Court of Appeal took quite a different view in another case involving the use of scissors. A 7-year-old was allowed to choose in class between sharp and blunt-ended scissors: he chose the former and jabbed himself in the eye when his chair was jogged.

The Master of the Rolls, Sir John Donaldson, held that there was no countervailing reason why sharp-ended scissors were necessary for the pupils' task, and accepted as guidance the DES booklet *Safety at School* which said it was sensible to provide round-edged scissors for children aged up to 8 or 9. The teachers were guilty of an error of judgement and the appeal was dismissed.[32]

The question of allowing children of different ages to leave the school premises with or without an escort is dealt with in other sections of this chapter.

10 Warning of danger

A teacher who can prove that he has warned a pupil of the dangerous consequences which may follow from a particular act is in a much stronger position when sued for negligence.

FOSTER v. LONDON COUNTY COUNCIL

A teacher told an 11-year-old girl to take a pair of pincers from a drawer to remove a broken, rusty nib from a penholder. The nib broke and the child's eye was damaged by splinters. A case[33] was brought, claiming damages for personal injuries resulting from the negligence of the teacher, it being claimed that such an order should not have been given to a child. Directing the jury, Mr Justice Avory said that it was not contended that the pincers were dangerous, and the case rested on a direct order to take the pincers from the drawer in order to pull out the nib without any warning of the possible danger. Even at arm's length, the accident might have happened. The jury awarded £100 and special damages.

It will be noted that the judge stressed the fact that the girl was not warned of the danger.

CROUCH v. ESSEX COUNTY COUNCIL

The most important case on this issue was heard in 1966.[34] Four years previously a young science master had given a lesson on the reaction of the oxides of zinc, aluminium and tin to caustic soda. The first twenty or thirty minutes of the lesson were taken up with an account of the experiment, after which the pupils worked in pairs at sinks, each couple being provided with the necessary apparatus and, subject to one exception, a normal solution of caustic soda. On the master's bench was an unlabelled beaker of a much stronger solution from which a group of pupils at the back of the laboratory, who were working with the tin oxide, were required to draw a supply.

The witnesses on whom his Lordship relied principally said that Mr Ford had constantly warned his pupils of the danger of playing about with chemicals, and he certainly did so on this occasion. One quoted him: 'If you put your hand into this solution, it will turn it into a bar of soap.' It was said semi-seriously and, commented the learned judge, no doubt had a twofold purpose: partly to convey a warning, and partly to drive home the chemical lesson that the reaction between caustic soda and animal fat is the creation of soap. The witness admitted that some of the class may not have heard the warning, but she had no difficulty whatever in doing so.

The plaintiff, who was at that time aged 15, said that there was talking and squirting of water with pipettes during the lesson. He did not really know what was being taught and, soon after the practical part of the lesson started, he took some test-tubes to the front of the room to clean them and to ask as to the nature of the experiment. 'In particular, I was going to ask a couple of girls at the teacher's desk who seemed to know exactly what they were doing.' As he reached them one girl squirted a liquid into his ear; he thought it was water. Immediately afterwards the other girl squirted the concentrated caustic soda into his eyes. Through his father as next friend he claimed damages for negligence on the master's part for which, he claimed, the local education authority was vicariously liable.

The master said that he liked a free and easy atmosphere and, as far as he could, he tried not to be the strict Victorian disciplinarian. The class was a fairly well-behaved group, although there were isolated acts of horseplay, such as connecting bunsen burners to the water taps and squirting water through the burners. He often had to repeat himself because of talking. He taught that chemicals were potentially dangerous, he had warned them that alkalis are as dangerous as acids, and he remembered the reference to the bar of soap mentioned by a former pupil. He was walking about among the pupils when he heard the plaintiff scream.

Having analysed the evidence, his Lordship said: 'I accept the evidence of Mr Ford so far as the facts of the matter are concerned. I am quite satisfied that for students as advanced as these students were in March 1962, there was no danger or impropriety in allowing them to help themselves to this stronger solution of caustic soda once an adequate warning as to the nature of the solution and its properties had been given. I am quite satisfied that one cannot say, as a general rule, that 15-year-olds with this background in the study of chemistry should not be allowed to draw supplies of caustic soda of this strength without direct supervision, provided that they have had an adequate warning and are supplied with adequate materials.

'Further, I am quite satisfied that no criticism can be attached to the failure to label the beaker in the circumstances of this case because the nature of the contents had to be put over to the class by oral instruction, and, if oral instruction given by Mr Ford was inadequate for this purpose, I find it difficult to believe that a label on the beaker would have had any other effect. I am impressed by the evidence that the labelling of the beaker would primarily be a means of avoiding confusion with other liquids; and as it seems there was no other liquid available at that time, labelling seems to me to be a matter of no relevance.

'The case, therefore, really turns on whether in the circumstances of this class and these pupils it was right for Mr Ford to allow the pupils from the back bench to come up and draw this liquid in the manner which I have described. That it would have been proper for him to do so in regard to pupils generally of the status of these I have no doubt at all.

'The plaintiff's case, in brief, is that there was such lack of discipline in this class, such lack of control and such lack of responsibility, that it was a dangerous act for Mr Ford to leave the caustic soda in the position in which it was left, and to allow these irresponsible girls and boys in the back row to approach it with the tempting pipettes which they were likely to use as weapons. I have considered this aspect of the case with care overnight, and I am quite satisfied that the plaintiff's case is not made out.

'That there was some horseplay in this class I do not question. Chemistry classes seem given to that kind of activity, and possibly the teacher's position is not made easier when the class is a mixed one. I think all the witnesses who spoke in this case have been honest and have done their best, but 19-year-olds, looking back on their schooldays, will naturally remember the entertaining features rather than the dull ones, and can quite easily look back on Mr Ford's lectures after four years as an unbroken orgy of distilled water and squirting, which I am quite satisfied they were not. If that had been the kind of atmosphere which one found in this class, I have no doubt whatever that Mr Smith and Miss Veall would have disclosed it to me.

'Having listened in particular to them, I am quite satisfied that Mr Ford maintained a standard of discipline which, at any rate, was adequate from a safety point of view. It is not for me to express an opinion as to whether that type of discipline is satisfactory from an educational point of view. That is not my concern.

'Furthermore, I am satisfied that there was no particular incident on this morning which would suggest any unusual outbreak of indiscipline. Indeed, Miss Veall's account of the general hum of conversation is indicative of the fact that the class as a whole were perfectly normally well-behaved. So really, in the last analysis, one has to ask oneself whether it was reasonably foreseeable to Mr Ford, approaching his duties as being equivalent to those of a careful and prudent parent, that on this occasion not only should Miss Crispin and Miss Jackson and the plaintiff have studiously ignored everything which was said to them in the earlier part of the period, but should also have proceeded to his desk, and then proceeded to squirt a wholly unidentified liquid at the plaintiff's face.

'This conduct was a little short of lunatic, and it was utterly irresponsible, and I am quite sure on the evidence which I have heard that the general atmosphere and standard of Mr Ford's class was not such as to make that kind of conduct foreseeable. He gave an adequate warning on this occasion of the nature and properties of the caustic soda. He was not to foresee that Miss Jackson should, first of all, fail to listen; and then – which is the important point – should have proceeded to pick up this pipette and, with complete and utter irresponsibility, to have squirted it into the plaintiff's face.

'In those circumstances the allegations of negligence against Mr Ford fail; and with them, of course, any allegations against the county council as well.'

This case has been quoted in some detail not only because of its importance as an illustration of the need to give adequate warning of potential dangers, but also because it is an outstanding example of the care with which the courts examine the details of a system in applying the common sense of the common law.

NOONAN v. INNER LONDON EDUCATION AUTHORITY

In the absence of the master a boy filled a syringe with sulphuric acid from an unlabelled beaker standing on the bench, and squirted it at another boy. The victim's face was scarred permanently in several places. On behalf of the plaintiff it was alleged that the Authority was negligent in leaving unlabelled dangerous chemicals on a bench, and in leaving a class unsupervised. The master, who had emigrated to Australia before the case was heard, said in written evidence that he had warned the class not to touch anything; but this was denied by the boy who had caused the injury. Claiming that he had intended merely to play a practical joke on a friend, he said he thought the substance was water.

Awarding damages, Mr Justice Willis said: 'I am not satisfied that the class was warned not to touch anything. But, even if they had been, I think that in the case of a substance like sulphuric acid a much more graphic and specific warning than simply "Don't touch" should have been given. This was particularly the case when acids were not clearly labelled. The class had been led to expect that such substances would be clearly marked, covered, or specifically identified. The failure to give a specific warning involved a departure from the very high standards demanded.'[35]

11   Special dangers

Special dangers exist in some subjects because of the nature of the tools or materials employed. So far as the law is concerned, the tests applied by the courts are the same. The important point to watch is that all reasonable care is used by teachers in charge of such subjects.

The risk in science laboratories is highlighted in *Crouch v. Essex County Council* in the preceding section. It should be noted also that a scientist could be expected to ensure a higher standard of care in a science laboratory than would be the case if a person not highly trained in his subject were in charge. It will be remembered that this was an element in *Baxter v. Barker* in the section on 'contributory negligence'.

Other places where there is a high degree of risk include workshops where edged tools and an increasing amount of machinery are installed. A special risk is the long hair adopted by some boys, with the attendant risk that this may get caught in quickly revolving plant. Handicraft masters should take care to see that such hair is fastened back or covered adequately. Accidents of this nature not infrequently lead to the victim being scalped.

Handicraft's sister subject, housecraft, also has a comparatively high risk rate. In the leading case[36] Salford Corporation was condemned in damages arising from serious injuries to an 11-year-old girl when her apron caught fire. The particular kind of accident on that occasion is less likely to arise today, but modern equipment, such as washing machines, drying cabinets and electric food mixers, can be used in an unsafe way. Again, it is important that long hair should be kept well away from naked flames and quickly moving machinery, and that on no account should girls be allowed to wear aprons made of flammable material.

Needlework is also a subject in which injuries are relatively common. In particular danger can arise from horseplay with scissors – which, of course, are often used in other subjects as well. This question was discussed in *Butt v. Cambridgeshire and*

Isle of Ely County Council and *Black v. Kent* referred to in section 9, 'The effect of age'.

12   Safety in science laboratories

Specific legislation applies to science laboratories in school as elsewhere. Science teachers should be aware for example of the provisions of the Radio-active Substances Act 1960, and the Packaging and Labelling of Dangerous Substances Regulations 1978 as amended by the Packaging and Labelling of Dangerous Substances (Amendment) Regulations 1981. DES Regulations[37] require the Secretary of State's approval for the use in schools and colleges of:

(a) any radio-active substance which has an activity in excess of 0.002 of a microcurie per gram, or

(b) any apparatus in which electrons are accelerated by a potential difference of at least 4 kilovolts other than:

  (i) a television receiving set, or

  (ii) an apparatus designed primarily to produce visual images derived from video-recordings, closed circuit television equipment or the output of a computer. The Secretary of State may withdraw such approval at any time.

General and approved practice referred to earlier in this chapter which may provide a defence in law against an action for negligence, is usually codified into guidelines issued to heads and teachers by local education authorities or governors as employers. Such guidelines may well include reference to the series of DES booklets *Safety in Science Laboratories* or to *Safeguards in the School Laboratory* published by the Association for Science Education. The DES booklets are available free of charge, and are supplemented by regular bulletins entitled *Safety in Education*. One such bulletin in 1982 for example, drew attention to the dangers which may arise when pupils observe solar eclipses by using smoked glass, filters or dark goggles. In 1980 a pupil successfully sued a local authority for the damage suffered to his sight whilst observing an eclipse during a geography lesson.

It is very important that communication on such matters between teachers and their employers should be good: in 1977, for example, concern was expressed about the numbers of science teachers who were still unaware of a 1976 Administrative Memorandum to local authorities which suggested the immediate withdrawal of certain types of asbestos from use in school.

Generally agreed guidelines would include:

(i) Heads of science departments should ensure that science colleagues are aware of relevant safety advice;

(ii) Protective clothing and goggles should be worn by teachers, technicians and pupils at all appropriate times;

(iii) Potentially dangerous defects in equipment or premises (e.g. defective wiring) should be reported in the usual manner for the school, and a copy of the report carefully filed;

(iv) The use of science laboratories for classes taken by non-scientists should be very strictly controlled, as it is not possible to remove all potential dangers;

(v) Classes should always be supervised by a teacher in the laboratory and should not be allowed to enter a laboratory unless a teacher is present. Whether a teacher's presence in the preparation room off a laboratory amounts to adequate supervision depends entirely on the circumstances surrounding each incident.

(vi) There must be adequate lockable storage accommodation for poisonous, flammable or otherwise hazardous chemicals;[38]

(vii) Classes should be no larger than the number for which the laboratory was designed. Where reasonably practicable, teaching groups should not exceed 20. This is admittedly an ideal situation but it should be remembered that the further a school strays from it, the greater the potential liability.

The general duty to care for health and safety is imposed by the Health and Safety at Work Act 1974 and the Occupiers Liability Act 1957. If, after an injury, the plaintiff proceeds under the latter Act the teacher is not involved and the responsibility falls directly on the local education authority.

Other DES Memoranda of which all science teachers should be aware are:

3/70 *Carcinogenic Aromatic Amines in Schools and Other Educational Establishments*
7/70 *Use of Lasers in Schools and Other Educational Establishments*
2/76 *The Use of Ionising Radiations in Educational Establishments*
6/76 *The Laboratory Use of Dangerous Pathogens*

Copies of these can be obtained free of charge from the DES, Honeypot Lane, Stanmore, Middlesex, HA7 1AZ.

13   Physical education

Gymnasia and playing fields are, perhaps, the most common scenes of school accidents and there have been many cases arising from such mishaps. So far as the gymnasium is concerned, authorities are careful to prohibit the use of apparatus, as far as possible, by those who are not qualified. Disregard of such a requirement may place the teacher, and the head if he has knowledge of the infraction, outside the scope of his employment. The tests which are most likely to be applied by the courts will concern the adequacy of supervision and the following of general and approved practice. For this reason it is important in games periods that the rules of the game be adhered to strictly and dangerous play penalized.

In 1968 the DES drew attention to the danger of using apparatus giving a high rebound, especially in primary schools.[39] A more recent pamphlet by the DES[40] advises against the use of the Fosbury flop technique of high jumping, where the athlete leaps backwards over the bar and lands on his back. This can result in serious permanent injury in school sandpits, which are not designed for such a purpose. The pamphlet also questions boxing as a school activity, pointing out that the Royal College of Physicians warned in 1968 that permanent brain damage can result from the cumulative effect of injuries. To allow boys to lift weights to the limit of their capacity is another dangerous practice, which can lead to permanent injury of the spine.

There is, says the DES, no such thing as a safe firearm, and there are risks inherent in the use of large-bore starting pistols, which can be drilled to convert them into firearms (even though not actually drilled). The pamphlet advises that all starting guns should be marked with the school's name. A case[41] followed an accident when a boy fell whilst jumping from an agility stool in 1951. The boy was then aged 5 and it was claimed that he was required to jump from a stool which was almost his own height, the nearest adult being 12 to 14 feet away. For the defence it was said that there was no permanent damage to the boy's elbow, and the headmistress maintained that the whole point of the apparatus was to give the children confidence. Mr Justice Devlin said that the apparatus itself, and the way in which it was designed to be used, were safe. It was clear that the headmistress was not negligent, neither was the teacher, and he did not see what they could have done if they had seen the boy jump. There was nothing to show that it was anything but an accident.

The importance of having a 'stand-by' during vaulting cannot be too strongly emphasized. During a physical education lesson a boy fell whilst vaulting over a horse. It was held that reasonable care to prevent a fall had not been taken, and the master did not seem 'to have acted with the promptitude which the law requires'. The Court found for the plaintiff.[42] In another case there were four classes in the gymnasium when a boy fell whilst vaulting over the buck at a time when the master was dealing with another class. It was held that the supervision was in accordance with normal practice, had been safely practised for years, and that it was not negligent.[43]

Some years ago an accident in a comprehensive school pinpointed another risk arising from the diversification of activities. On that occasion some boys were practising golf strokes indoors when one pupil was killed by a blow on the head from the club being used by another boy. This emphasizes the need for care when outdoor activities are being coached in a confined space and on a hard surface.

Professional players are often used for training in the specific skills at which they are expert. It is important that they should be warned about any pupils who may indulge in dangerous behaviour; alternatively, such pupils may be removed from the group.

Bathing and boating are considered in chapter XVI.

A boy of 14 put his arm through a glass partition during a relay race at a play centre. The children had been told to touch the supervisor, and had not been told to touch the partition, as they turned at the end of the hall. There was no negligence.[44]

Allowing pupils to do gym in stockinged feet has been held to be negligent. This was held in an unreported case where a master, not having a spare pair of plimsolls of the right size, allowed a boy who had forgotten his own to wear his socks. The boy slipped and hurt himself badly. It was held that the risk of falling was greater when wearing socks than when wearing plimsolls or doing gym in bare feet.

Two clear warnings for PE teachers came from a case heard in the Court of Appeal in November 1981.[45] A girl pupil with a congenital lip defect injured her ankle attempting a handstand during a PE lesson. The mother of the pupil had made it quite clear to the school, in writing, that the girl should not on any account do any form of physical education or games. It was accepted in court as a fact that in addition to the written note to the school, a meeting had taken place between the mother and the head teacher and that at that meeting the girl's incapacity had been stressed. It was also noted in the school's records.

The difficulty arose because the girl herself was desperately keen to join in PE lessons with the class and felt left out. She on one occasion told the head of the PE department that she would soon be able to participate, and later appeared at school armed with a pair of PE shorts. She thus persuaded a teacher to let her take part in a PE lesson, and suffered injury. Her claim for damages was first rejected, but this decision was unanimously reversed by the Court of Appeal.

Lord Denning stated: 'The standard required of a teacher is reasonably high, but I am afraid this teacher did not come up to the standard required. This teacher should have decided to tell the child that it would be necessary to check with her mother before she was allowed to participate in the class and as the teacher had already had prior notice from the child the teacher should have made arrangements for the child's account to be checked with the mother before allowing her into the class.'

As to whether the teacher's supervision of the girl was adequate at the time of the incident, Lord Denning said that the girl should have been given more positive instructions because she had just joined the class, and the teacher should initially have given her closer supervision. Lord Justice Watkins, agreeing, added that the teacher had not observed the girl's movements which she had begun to make of her own volition. 'It was a case without a defence.'

Most teachers have some experience of children playing them off against parents, and for the most part nothing serious comes of it. Two points arise from this case, however. If a parent has put some proper restriction on a child on medical grounds, this must be respected until the parent lifts it; and secondly, if a child with a known or suspected disability is taking part in an unaccustomed physical activity, rigorous supervision is required.

14   Before and after school

Many teachers are concerned about their responsibility for pupils on the school premises before the beginning, and after the end, of the school day. This section does not deal with supervision during the midday break, which is dealt with below in 'Meals and midday supervision'.

BEFORE SCHOOL

Children arrive at school early for a variety of reasons; sometimes as much as an hour before the beginning of the morning session. Some are 'latch-key' children sent out by their parents when the adult members of the family leave for work;

in rural areas public transport may be infrequent, so that a child must be very early, or late; sometimes the local education authority arranges a shuttle service of privately hired coaches, the vehicles depositing their load at the school on their first journey long before opening time.

The generally accepted practice, which has no legal sanction unless it is provided for by the authority's regulations or the head's requirements as to supervision made in pursuance of his duty under the Articles of Government, is for the teaching staff to accept responsibility for pupils for up to ten minutes before morning school.

The extent of the local education authority's duty of care towards children before the beginning of school has been considered in two recent cases which are summarized later in this section. Suffice it to say that the teacher's duty is not greater than the authority's and that some of the anxiety expressed by teachers arises from moral acuity. Their employers, apparently (although not necessarily, in fact) more hardhearted, can consider only their legal liability.

One thing which a prudent head will not do is to take a unilateral decision to lock the playground or playing field gates against children. If, as a result, a child should be knocked down and injured it is doubtful if he would be held to have acted as a careful parent when he had refused the victim admission to a place of safety. It would go to mitigation if he had advised parents well in advance of his intention to do so, but every other avenue should first be explored to achieve the co-operation of the local education authority.

If a head is concerned about the safety of children who arrive early, for whatever reason, he should ask the local education authority to take appropriate action to safeguard their own position. It would also be prudent, if the cause is within the parents' control, to write to parents asking them not to send their children to school before a certain time, and pointing out the unreasonableness of expecting teaching staff to accept responsibility for an excessive period before the beginning of school.

WARD v. HERTFORDSHIRE COUNTY COUNCIL[46]

In a Hertfordshire primary school, where the playground was surrounded by an unrendered flint wall, the children were allowed into the playground from 8.15 am and played there unsupervised until they were called into school at 8.55. One day an 8-year-old boy was racing across the playground when he stumbled and crashed into the wall about five minutes before the beginning of school. A steel plate had to be inserted in his skull but, although he made a good recovery, he was not able to join in pursuits such as boxing and rugby football.

At first instance Mr Justice Hinchcliffe awarded the plaintiff £950 damages, holding that the wall was inherently dangerous and that the authority were in breach of their duty under the Occupiers Liability Act 1957 and their common law duty to take reasonable care for the safety of the children. Section 2(3) of the Act requires an occupier to be prepared for children to be less careful than adults.

On the question of supervision, the learned judge said: 'In my judgment a prudent parent of a large family would have realized that this playground, with its flint walls and sharp and jagged flints protruding was inherently dangerous. In my judgment reasonable supervision was required, not only during the working day, but also when the children were collected together in the playground before the school starts. I do not suggest that there should necessarily be a continuous supervision from 8.15 onwards, but there should have been supervision from time to time controlling any risky activity of the children having regard to the proximity of this dangerous wall: and really it is not too much to ask that there should be supervision between 8.30 or 8.45 and 8.55 when the supervision might well have been continuous.'

The Court of Appeal unanimously reversed this decision. The Master of the Rolls, Lord Denning, did not think that the wall was dangerous. A third of the village had similar walls, so had sixteen schools in the county 'and goodness knows how many in the country at large.... But this does not mean that they are dangerous. We have lived with them long enough to know.' About supervision he added: 'The headmaster said that the teachers took charge of the children from the time they were due to be in school at five minutes to nine until the time when they were let out. Before the school began, the staff were indoors preparing the day's work. They cannot be expected to be in the playgrounds too. He said that even if he had been in the playground, he would not have stopped the children playing. It often happens that children run from one side of the playground to the other. It is impossible so to supervise them that they never fall down and hurt themselves. I cannot think that this accident shows any lack of supervision by the school authorities.'

In a concurring judgment, Lord Justice Salmon said: 'The judge said that a master, if he had been present in the playground, should have prevented this racing. I am afraid I cannot agree with him. We know from the headmaster that racing between the walls had continually gone on during all the time he was there and no harm has come of it. I dare say a small boy has occasionally fallen and scraped his knees or hands or elbows on the ground, or perhaps on the wall, and hurt himself to some extent. But this is the sort of thing that happens to children in playgrounds. It would in my view be wrong to try to protect them against minor injuries of that kind by forbidding them the ordinary pleasures which school children so much enjoy. I appreciate the point that during the breaks during the day, children playing in the playground are supervised but are not supervised in the morning before 8.55. Some of the children arrive at 8.15 in the morning, and the school does not start until 8.55. For reasons which have been explained to us, there is no master in the playground before 8.55 am, although they are in school getting ready for the day's work and would hear what is going on outside. If this accident had been caused by the children fighting or indulging in some particularly dangerous game which a master should have stopped if he had been there, the fact that there was no supervision at the time might have afforded anyone who was injured in that way a good cause of action. It is not necessary to express any concluded view on that point. To my mind the fact that there was no master in the playground on this occasion is irrelevant, because even if there had been a master there I can see no reason why he should have prevented the children racing or playing as Timothy was doing at the time when he met with this most unfortunate accident.'

Although the Court of Appeal clearly thought that the trial judge had set the requirement of supervision too high, it must be observed that the court limited itself strictly to the facts of this particular case where the headmaster had said that he would not have stopped the game if he had been present. In this case, therefore, the higher court found the supervision issue irrelevant.

MAYS v. ESSEX COUNTY COUNCIL[47]

One frosty morning Royston Mays arrived at school a few minutes before nine o'clock, and joined some friends on one of a number of slides which had been made in the playground. Suddenly his feet slipped from under him and he fell, hitting his head on the asphalt. He spent the next three months in hospital, during which he had two operations to remove blood clots from the brain, and in the following year and a half he received anti-convulsant treatment and had two operations on each leg. Five years after the accident his speech was slurred, he had difficulty in walking, his right hand was stiff, clumsy and reduced in size, his chest wall was abnormal and he frequently gasped for breath. A consultant neurologist said it would be unrealistic to suppose that he would ever be more than 50 per cent physically of a normal person.

At the time of the accident the supervising teacher was in the staffroom on the other side of the school. Three weeks earlier the Essex County Council had issued a circular stating that a teacher must be on duty in the playground for fifteen minutes before morning school, and for a similar period at the end of the afternoon. This document was not distributed to schools in the Basildon area, where Royston lived, until a fortnight after his fall. The school playground was opened at eight o'clock each morning, and children were in the habit of congregating there for at least half an hour before the beginning of school, although the headmaster had written to the parents asking them not to send the youngsters too early.

The parents' claim for damages for negligence was based on allegations that the playground should have been supervised, that the supervising teacher should have stopped the sliding as a dangerous activity, and that the surface should have been treated.

The judge said that the headmaster had taken the view that the school could not, and should not, accept responsibility for the children until the time appointed for school. It was a grey area, and he felt that all concerned should do something to clarify it. 'Exact timekeeping by everybody is impossible', said the judge, 'and perhaps undesirable. Just as there would be intolerable confusion at a railway station if everyone arrived a minute before the train was due to leave, so there would be serious obstruction outside school if every parent brought his child, or children, to the gate at exactly one minute before the bell rang for lessons.'

Of the parents' claim that the sliding should have been stopped, he said: 'If I thought that any school authorities were seriously prepared to declare that sliding on ice is a dangerous game, and should be stopped, I would feel obliged to make some sort of declaration that the children of this country are free to slide on ice in a sensible and orderly manner whenever a suitable opportunity arises. They, and their elders, have been doing it for centuries, and not a single witness in this case, medical or educational, or lay, could call to mind a single instance of serious injury arising from this innocent and healthy amusement.... There is nothing with which a child cannot hurt itself. There is no game which may not develop into unruly and disorderly conduct.... Moreover, there is not a word of evidence before me to suggest that there was any disorder among the group of four or five boys of whom the plaintiff was one.... *Life is full of physical dangers which children must learn to recognize, and develop the ability to avoid. The playground is one of the places to learn.*'

The judge did not think that parents had any right to impose responsibility on teachers outside the ordinary school hours. Although many schools open their gates well before the beginning of school, is that an implied acceptance of responsibility, or an act of grace offering the comparative safety of the playground as against the hazards of the street? In this case the headmaster had not been negligent.

On the question of treating the surface of the playground, the father had alleged that, because this had been done on the day following the accident, it should have been the practice before that date. It is sometimes thought to be unwise to shut the stable door after the horse has gone in case this creates an aura of guilt. The judge did not agree: in the light of the accident it was the natural response, springing from compassion and fear at the contemplation of a recent disaster.

In this case the judge held explicitly that a local education authority is not responsible for the safety of children before the beginning of school unless it voluntarily accepts them on the premises. He reached this conclusion in the face of the fact that the gates at this particular school were open for an hour before that time. Clearly, the head's request that parents should not send their children to school unreasonably early carried considerable weight: in these circumstances the open gates were an act of grace, not an acceptance of responsibility.

Discussions about teachers' hours of duty may produce a nationally agreed statement in the future. In its absence teachers should ensure that they perform such reasonable duties of this nature, say for up to ten minutes or so, as may be required by the local education authority or their head. Nothing should be said to suggest that pupils who arrive early will be willingly accepted and safeguarded, and heads would be well advised to remind parents frequently not to send children to school unreasonably early.

AFTER SCHOOL

It is general and approved practice for the majority of pupils to be expected to leave the premises within ten minutes or so of the close of school. It is also common practice for a member of the staff to see that this is done. Failure to do so resulted in adverse judgment in *Baxter v. Barker*. With young children, who are commonly met by parents or other adults, it is necessary to have, and maintain, an adequate system, as is shown by *Barnes v. Hampshire County Council*. On the other hand, if the system breaks down because of a failure by the adult meeting the child, the school will not be held negligent if it has maintained its own part of the system efficiently: *Jeffery v. London County Council*.

If there is to be any change in the system, e.g. the time of release, whether this be permanent or temporary, it is important that parents, especially those of very young children and those who normally meet their children from school, should be given adequate warning. This does not become in any way different or less important if the change in time of release is caused by industrial action or 'withdrawal of goodwill'.

The question of supervising children crossing roads at the end of school is dealt with in the section on 'Road crossing'.

Where pupils are kept in school, whether as part of a formal or informal detention class or for any out-of-school activities, it should be the recognized practice in the school that the teacher in whose charge they are should be responsible for supervising their departure and for ensuring that they have all left the premises.

IN GENERAL

Beyond recognizing the fact that children are generally in the care of the school authorities, which for this purpose includes the staff so long as they are on the school premises, the law remains somewhat nebulous. In many ways this is unfortunate, because it is a matter which causes the gravest concern to teachers throughout the country, particularly in primary schools. What, for example, is to be done about the neglectful parent who habitually fails to collect her child, trusting that a teacher or somebody else will look after him for an indeterminate period?

The answer in such a case is that the parent, provided she

has been properly instructed, has broken the part of the system for which she is responsible, and if this can be proved there is little likelihood that the courts will find against the school, even if a very young child has been released at the proper time into a potentially dangerous situation. No caring teacher would take this risk though more from a moral and professional, rather than a legal, standpoint. Should the child be taken home? What then happens if there is no one there, or if the child has an accident whilst being escorted? Again, everything would turn on the precise facts in each case.

Some authorities have an arrangement by which the educational welfare service or the police may be telephoned and asked to deal with this situation on individual occasions. Frequently, however, there is no officer available when needed; even if there is, he may be unwilling to accept this responsibility.

The essential point is that each school must have its own system especially tailored to suit its own needs. That system must be rigorously enforced so far as the school's part is concerned, and every reasonable effort should be made to encourage the parents to shoulder their share of the responsibility.

Open-plan schools and schools standing on an open campus which may be crossed by rights of way, coupled with a less rigid control of children than was once the case, raise in teachers' minds considerable anxiety about their responsibility for the safety of a pupil who goes off the premises.

If, following an accident to a child in these circumstances, there is an action for damages for negligence, the test which will be applied will be that of the careful parent in all the circumstances. What was the system designed to prevent pupils from escaping? Was it adequate, having regard to the nature of the building, the surrounding traffic situation, and the age and propensities of the plaintiff? At the time of the escape, was it working properly? In considering what answers must be returned to questions such as these, the court will bear in mind that schools are not – indeed, should not be – designed to resemble the high-security wings of prisons, and that teachers are not expected to emulate gaolers.

Judges have constantly reiterated the principle that an important part of a child's education is to teach him to accept personal responsibility for ever-increasing areas of his life, and that this training must begin at a very early age. Every child in school, unless he suffers from some grave disability of understanding, knows perfectly well that both the school and his parents expect him to stay on the school premises for the duration of the school hours. If he leaves of his own volition, he does so in defiance of the school's requirements and his parent's wishes. This will not go to his credit as a plaintiff if the supervision has been reasonable.

Children, particularly younger ones, occasionally run home because they fear injustice or bullying. They should invariably be told, as part of the normal practice of the school, that the proper course is to seek the help of a member of the staff. Needless to say, there must be an effective system for providing sanctuary in such circumstances; though to say this does not mean that there should inevitably be a remission of punishment.

Teachers often ask if they should search for a straying child. There can be no universal answer to such a question and the teacher must make an instant professional judgement for which he is prepared to answer. Sometimes it may be right, but there are two attendant risks to be taken into account. There is always the possibility that a pupil, finding himself followed, may panic and run into traffic dangers which he would not otherwise have faced. Moreover, the situation is not precisely analogous to that of the good shepherd seeking a lost sheep. Children are less docile, and twenty-nine youngsters abandoned in a classroom, unless adequate arrangements can be made for their supervision, are more likely to create their own hazards than ninety-nine sheep left in a fold.

15 Meals and midday supervision

The positive power to require teachers to supervise school meals was removed in 1968, and Section 49 of the 1944 Act which provided that duties in connection with school meals 'shall not impose upon teachers at any school or college duties upon days on which the school or college is not open for instruction, or duties in respect of meals other than the supervision of pupils' has been repealed.[48]

All duties in connection with meals are voluntary. In 1956, a case concerned with the collection of dinner money decided the point as far as all duties *other than supervision* are concerned.

Early that year members of the National Association of Schoolmasters, after giving reasonable notice to the local education authority, had stopped collecting dinner money in Sunderland schools as a protest against the Teachers (Superannuation) Bill, then before Parliament. They were given notices of dismissal by the authority, but the notices were subsequently withdrawn, except in the case of six teachers. These teachers sought an injunction in the High Court to restrain the authority from acting on the notices on the ground that they were *ultra vires*, and a declaration that the Council was not entitled to impose on its teachers any duties in respect of meals other than the supervision of pupils.[49]

Mr Justice Barry said that he was unable to accept the authority's contention that, because the 1921 Act specifically stated that teachers need not collect dinner money and the 1944 Act had no such reference, Parliament had *intended* to change the law because teachers in many places were collecting such money. He held that the collection of dinner money was a duty in respect of meals within the meaning of section 49 of the Act, and that the service which had been given by the teachers for this purpose was voluntary service. The Council had, therefore, acted *ultra vires* in dismissing the teachers for refusing a service which the local education authority had no right to impose as a condition of appointment.

It should be noted in this case that the teachers were not opposed to the actual collection of dinner money; they had stopped doing so as a protest against something quite unconnected with school meals. Their lawsuit was based on an attempt by the local education authority to compel them, under the threat of dismissal, to perform a service which was purely voluntary and which, therefore, they could withhold at will. Such withholding, incidentally, has become a feature of teachers' industrial action (see chapter IV; 'Industrial action').

The withdrawal of the requirement to supervise school meals followed the report of a working party on school meals and midday supervision which had been established by the Secretary of State. The report recommended the abolition of the element of compulsion, suggested that free meals might be allowed in return for the performance of duties during the midday break other than meals supervision, e.g. playground supervision, coaching for games and the organization of clubs; and paved the way for an improved scale of ancillary assistance. It stated categorically that the head retained an overall responsibility for the conduct of meals as he 'does for everything else which goes on in and about his school'. This report became widely known as the '1968 School Meals Agreement' or sometimes, after its chairman, the 'Rosetti Agreement'. It can be found as an appendix in the current Burgundy Book.

Unfortunately, the result is still a considerable degree of confusion. One professional association maintained, in the meetings of the working party, that its aim was to end all compulsory duties during the midday break on the ground that a teacher is entitled to his dinner hour as much as anyone else. After the working party reported, and before any change in the regulations was made, the association advised its members that all duties during the midday break would, henceforth, be voluntary.

So far, no case has come before the court for decision precisely on this issue, and there are currently two differing views among lawyers about the matter.

One maintains that the difficulties appear to have arisen from an attempt to join together two duties which have quite distinct foundations in law. The supervision of school meals was at one time a statutory duty bound on teachers by regulations made by the Secretary of State following the provisions of section 49 of the 1944 Act which has already been quoted. As has been noted, this section of the 1944 Act was repealed by the Education Act 1980,[50] and consequently the regulations made under it no longer apply. However, at no time did this duty comprise anything more than the supervision of school meals; and it would give altogether too wide a meaning to the words 'school meals' to make them include playground supervision, chess clubs and the many other activities which go on in a school during the midday break.

Supervision of the school, the meal apart, during the period stems from a completely different root. It is the duty of the teacher, as we have seen, to take care of his pupils. It is the duty of the head to control the internal organization, management and discipline of the school. In certain circumstances, other duties arise from the Occupiers Liability Act 1957. It is necessary to have an adequate and fully maintained system to ensure that these duties are performed. Assistant staff are appointed to assist the head in discharging his legal obligations, and he can, as the law stands at present, require them reasonably to do so.

The common law duty of care is an ancient precedent, and is binding so long as there are pupils on the school premises. It may develop as a result of distinguishing cases in the courts; it can be changed only by Act of Parliament, not by statutory instrument, and not by a professional association. No steps have been taken to vary this duty by statute. Neither have the Articles of Government been varied. The duty under the Occupiers Liability Act also remains.

This seems to lead to the conclusion that the view taken by some, that the abolition of the element of compulsion in meals supervision extends to the whole of the midday break, is based on a confusion of statute and common law. The associations concerned sought to remove both compulsory meals supervision and obligatory midday supervision elsewhere in school. The first leg of this policy was achieved by regulations but that could not effect a change in the common law duty of care. The second leg remains for the associations an aim for the future.

The other view is that in common with other employees the teacher's job is defined by contract with his or her employer. The common law duty of care towards pupils applies only when the teacher is carrying out the job he is contracted to do. As noted earlier, the great uncertainty at the moment is about precisely what the job is — the Burgundy Book states that there is no agreement.

Without doubt this remains the most intractable problem concerned with teachers' conditions of service. One of the difficulties lies in the reconciliation of the law with the practicalities of the situation. It is almost twenty years since the working committee presented its report, and many of the present teaching force cannot remember the days of compulsory meals supervision. There has grown up a tradition in many schools that the whole of midday supervision is voluntary, and in these circumstances a head who tries to impose compulsory duties may find himself faced with a statement that this was not in younger teachers' contemplation when they signed their contracts. The problem bears severely on head teachers during industrial action when they themselves are not in dispute with employers.

The 1968 agreement made the assumption that teachers would *continue to volunteer* to undertake lunchtime supervision. In addition to receiving a free lunch, teachers would receive the support of paid 'ancillary helpers' on the following scale:

Infants' schools: 1 helper for every 30 children
Junior schools: 1 helper for every 75 children, but not normally exceeding 4
Secondary schools: 1 helper for every 200, not normally exceeding 5

These are, of course, recommended minima, and some local education authorities operate a more generous scale.

The use of the term 'ancillary helpers' in the 1968 agreement should be noted particularly. The agreement did not envisage that such helpers would take over full responsibility for the children at lunchtime: the analogy was more with infant helpers, or parents who came in to school in order to hear younger children read, or perhaps to help with the school play or some out-of-school activity. Where teachers do not volunteer in adequate numbers, the difficult question arises as to whether the adult personnel available constitute reasonable supervision for the numbers of children on the premises. Under the Articles of Government such a decision must lie with the head teacher, whose responsibility is for the 'internal management' of his school.

The issue came before the Birmingham Crown Court in March 1981.[51] During a wet lunchtime an 8-year-old boy was in a classroom with some thirty other pupils when he was struck in the right eye by a paper clip fired from a rubber band by another pupil. At the time of the incident one ancillary helper was supervising two adjacent classrooms, each with some thirty pupils. It was agreed that she was not present in the classroom when the clip was fired, but entered it shortly afterwards.

It was generally agreed in evidence from all the parties that the three boys who were going around firing paper clips would not have done this in the presence of a teacher or dinner lady. The head and deputy head teachers of the school gave evidence that in their view it was too much to ask of the dinner lady that she should have to supervise two classrooms with so many pupils in each and that 'the only safe system is to have one person in each class'.

Sir Basil Nield found that the authority had not discharged its duty of supervision. 'I would much regret it if Mrs Horner (the dinner lady) were to blame herself unduly for the misfortune suffered by "one of my children", to use her own warm phrase. She should have had assistance, and if there had been more supervisors the accident — and indeed the confused state of things at the two classrooms — would have been avoided.' He rejected however the second allegation made that rubber bands and clips had been left lying about in a negligent way. He was satisfied that these were normally kept in the teacher's desk. Damages totalling £6,500 plus interest and costs were awarded against the local authority.

This case emphasizes again the urgent need for a solution to the problem of lunchtime supervision. The judgment in the Blasdale case clearly indicates that the ratios of helpers to teachers recommended by the 1968 agreement are inadequate on wet lunchtimes (frequent enough in the British climate!). By implication they are also inadequate if teachers do not volunteer lunchtime help to the extent envisaged in the 1968 agreement.

With the necessary consent of governors and the local authority, some schools seek to solve the supervision difficulty at lunchtime by adopting the continental school day, and thereby shortening the break. The abolition of the duty to provide a school meal for those who want it has eased this transition. The duty to make provisions of 'milk, meals or other refreshment' ... 'in the middle of the day' for children from families 'in receipt of supplementary benefit or family income supplement' remains:[52] however 'other refreshment' is not defined in the Act and it may be that the provision of packed lunches would satisfy the law. Nor does the Act require such provision necessarily to be made on school premises. Where older pupils are concerned it might well be within the law for arrangements to be made with local eating establishments. 'Staggered' lunchbreaks seem also to be within the letter of the law. It should be noted that the regulations requiring the schoolday to have 'two sessions' do not stipulate the length of the break between them.

16 Playground duty

It is generally agreed that when a large number of children are gathered together in a playground during a break in the school session it is desirable that they should be under some form of supervision. In principle this need not be as rigid as the supervision which is exercised in the classroom. This is a matter of the internal organization and discipline of the school and, in accordance with the Articles of Government, is under the control of the head. Whilst the presence of a teacher in a playground will not prevent every accident from happening, the teacher can ensure that dangerous play is, as far as possible, avoided and he will be there to give assistance should an accident occur.

In planning supervision, including the deployment of ancillary staff, the head will have regard to the general principle that he must have an adequate system which is efficiently maintained. If there is a duty rota and a teacher has failed to perform a duty to which he has been allocated, the question of negligence might be raised in the case of an accident.

17   Road crossing

At one time it was quite usual for teachers to supervise children leaving school premises which opened onto a busy road. They have no authority over traffic, and local authorities have been given powers[53] to make arrangements for the patrolling of places where children cross roads on their way to or from school by persons other than police constables. Between eight o'clock in the morning and half-past five in the afternoon, such patrols have power to control traffic on exhibiting a sign of a size, colour and type prescribed by the Minister of Transport's regulations. Patrols must wear a uniform approved by the Secretary of State.

It is very important to note that school crossing patrols have authority *only to escort children of school age*. It would be unlawful – and conceivably dangerous – for a patrol to attempt to halt traffic to escort adults, even a mother who had taken her child to school and was returning home, across the road.

It is an offence for traffic to continue so long as the crossing patrol is properly exhibiting the sign. The Queen's Bench Divisional Court allowed an appeal by the police against the acquittal of a driver who passed behind a party of women and children who had reached the centre of the road. The magistrates had based their finding on the words 'so as not to impede their crossing'.[54] The last pedestrian had quickened his steps to avoid the car. The court held unanimously that, in the words of the Lord Chief Justice, 'if the sign was still exhibited, there was an obligation to stop which could not be released until section 25(2)(b) had been satisfied – until the sign was no longer exhibited'. The case was sent back to the justices with directions to convict.[55]

Newport (Monmouthshire) Corporation was ordered to pay very substantial agreed damages following an accident where a crossing patrol was employed to provide additional security on a zebra crossing. To ease the flow of traffic, classes were dismissed at two-minute intervals and taken to the crossing by their teachers. The driver of a furniture van saw the elderly patrol but, as he was at the roadside, he accelerated to a speed of thirty miles an hour. A 6-year-old boy 'shot out like a pea from a peashooter', and collided with the van. His claim for damages against the owners of the van was dismissed at Monmouthshire Assizes, Mr Justice Browne finding it reasonable for the driver to assume that the crossing was clear because the patrol had gone back to the pavement. An alternative claim against the Corporation was successful: the system was not as good as it should be, the teacher had not done all she should and the patrol was negligent.

Dismissing an appeal by the Corporation, the Master of the Rolls, Lord Denning, said: 'Mr Hubbard's action or inaction was decisive. Though he was well liked by the children, there was no doubt that the mothers were very nervous. The police thought that if he had really been exercising control over them and keeping them back as he should have done, it should have been possible so to handle them that there would not be the sudden dart into the road. There was ample evidence on which the judge could find Mr Hubbard negligent, and the Corporation liable for his negligence.'[56]

When children are being taken through the streets for school purposes, the teacher in charge is responsible for the safety of the pupils. It is important that any ratio of staff to pupils laid down by the local education authority is observed. If children in the party suffer from any disability, it is desirable to increase the number of accompanying teachers.

It is quite another matter for teachers to assume responsibility for seeing children across the road in the absence of a crossing patrol. A person who takes on a duty, whether obligatory, voluntary or of his own motion, is bound to discharge it as a reasonable person and to the best of his ability. As has already been said, teachers have no authority over road traffic, and in undertaking this responsibility they are accepting risks which they cannot control. At the end of the school session a teacher should confine himself, if on duty, to seeing that the children leave the premises in a reasonably orderly manner, and that they do not flood into the carriageway in a dangerous manner. The teacher is empowered to control children; but he should resist both the pressure or blandishments of others, as well as his own kindness of heart, and avoid any duty which he has no power to carry out.

18   Games

It is important that teachers supervising games should ensure that they are played in accordance with the accepted rules, and that unfair play is penalized. It is, therefore, highly desirable that staff should be acquainted with changes in the rules – and should know the difference between what is permitted, and what is sometimes seen on television! If parents assist with games on a voluntary basis, it is essential that they are made aware of the need to keep to the rules and to penalize rough play. If they are not properly briefed, the duty has not been delegated with the care which is necessary. Only if games are strictly supervised can a defence of 'general and approved practice' discussed earlier in this chapter be raised in the event of a court action following an accident.

The extent of games supervision was reviewed in a 1984 case after a boy of 15 had been injured when tackled by the teacher on the games field during instruction in rugby football. Mr Justice Hodgson said that a teacher could still take part in a game to keep the ball moving and to demonstrate the skills of the game. There was no doubt that what was perpetrated on the plaintiff ... was a high tackle which, though permitted by the rules of the game, was unlawful and dangerous. The teacher 'momentarily forgot he was playing with young schoolboys ...', 'the sort of thing which could happen to any 20-year-old who was taking part in a game with boys'. Teachers should always bear in mind the differences between themselves and pupils and not participate as in a game with adults. Accordingly the teacher, who was a wholly admirable teacher, and his employer the Inner London Education Authority were liable to the plaintiff in damages.[57]

19   Dereliction of duty

Once a teacher has undertaken a duty, whether it be obligatory or voluntary, it is incumbent upon him to perform it conscientiously. There are few heads who would burden their staffs with a multitude of unnecessary tasks, but a certain amount of supervision is necessary for the good order and discipline of a school.

The fact that duties were normally performed with care in a school influenced a judgment by Lord Justice Scrutton.[58] A boy had hit a golf ball through an open door from a playground and struck another boy in the eye, with the result that the sight of that eye was lost. The governors of the school were dismissed from the case by Mr Justice Horridge, who awarded £250 damages and £45 special costs against the headmaster.

Allowing the headmaster's appeal, Lord Justice Scrutton said that there was no evidence of lack of supervision, or that lack of supervision contributed to the accident. A golf ball is not in itself dangerous, and it was not habitual to hit them about the playground.

As was said in this case, no schoolmaster in the world can prevent a naughty boy doing naughty things on some occasions. However carefully duties are performed, it is quite impossible to ensure that accidents will not occur. Where, however, a plaintiff can show that there has been dereliction of duty on the part of a teacher, the defendant's case is seriously weakened.

By the Articles of Government, the whole internal organization, management and discipline of a school are under the control of the head. If, therefore, a teacher fails to perform a duty which the head has prescribed as necessary, he may be condemned for negligence should an accident occur.

20   The straying child

The House of Lords gave judgment, in 1955, in a case which had been before the Cardiff Assizes and the Court of Appeal.[59] In all three courts the decision was for the plaintiff who was awarded damages in respect of the death of her husband.

The accident occurred in 1951, when the plaintiff's husband was driving a lorry along a road leading past one of the Council's schools. A 4-year-old pupil ran in front of the lorry, which swerved into a telegraph pole to avoid him. The driver was killed. His widow alleged that the child would not have been in the road if the children had been properly supervised.

It was the habit of the teacher-in-charge of the school to take two nursery children for a walk and, on the day in question, she had prepared them for this. She had left them in a classroom whilst she went to the lavatory, but her absence was protracted by the fact that on the way back she met an injured child and stopped to dress his wound. In all, she was away for about ten minutes, during which time the children disappeared.

The youngsters made their way to the road, and the accident occurred when one of them tried to cross it in the path of the oncoming lorry.

In the House of Lords, Lord Chief Justice Goddard said that the question of general importance was whether the occupiers of premises adjoining the highway had a duty to prevent young children from escaping so as to endanger other persons lawfully passing upon it. By young children, he meant those whom a prudent parent would not allow to go into a street unaccompanied. He could not hold that an inference of negligence on the teacher's part should be sustained, but that did not conclude the matter. If it was possible for children at that age, when a teacher's back might be turned for a moment, to go out into a busy street, that did seem to indicate some lack of care or precautions that might reasonably be required. No satisfactory explanation had been given. The appeal was dismissed.

The interesting feature of this case is that both the Assizes and the Court of Appeal held that the teacher had been negligent. The House of Lords fixed the responsibility on the local education authority, maintaining that the gates must either have been open, or so easy to open that a child of 3 or 4 could escape.

21 Further comments on duty of supervision

It is the duty of a schoolteacher to exercise reasonable supervision over his pupils in all parts of the school premises. What is reasonable depends on the age of the children,[60] and the activity in which they are taking part.[61]

A higher degree of supervision is required during instruction than during play. A tipping lorry delivering coke to a school was standing in the playground when some pupils jumped on it and set the tipping mechanism in motion. The headmaster did not know of the lorry's arrival. It was held that there was no negligence on the part of the school, as it is not necessary to provide continuous supervision in the playground for normally healthy children of school age. The Gas Company was also exonerated as the driver could not have foreseen that the boys would jump on the lorry.[62] Similarly, when a girl of 6 was injured by a 10-year-old boy using a bow and arrow during the teacher's absence from the playground, it was held that there was no negligence in supervision.[63]

The best supervision in the world cannot prevent every possibility of accident, for a mishap may occur three feet behind the back of a teacher on duty. When a girl was about to jump from the springboard into a swimming pool, another girl who had been holding on to the board let go without warning. It was held that this was a sudden accident which could neither be foreseen nor prevented.[64] An accident which could not be prevented by supervision is not attributable to negligence, even if there has been a breach of duty, as in the case of *Gow v. Glasgow Education Authority* referred to elsewhere.

PETTICAN v. LONDON BOROUGH OF ENFIELD

At Enfield Lower Grammar School it was the practice, on wet days, for pupils who stayed for lunch to go into classrooms for the remainder of the midday break.[65] During a frolic on such an occasion a 14-year-old boy was hit in the eye by a piece of chalk, and lost the sight of that eye. In an action for damages counsel for the plaintiff complained that there was no games room, no library and no prefects; and only one master to control two hundred and forty boys. The school was negligent in not giving the boys an outlet for their high spirits, and for not providing enough supervision.

Mr Justice Kilner-Brown did not accept the evidence of the master on duty that he paid twelve visits on a patrol system during the lunch break. Neither did he accept the evidence of the boys that no master appeared at all. The boys had agreed that they might not have seen a master appear in the doorway to make a cursory glance. He held that a system of supervision was in operation on this day, and that it was being exercised: 'It has recently been said that what used to be known as the "prudent parent" test is not applicable to a large school.[66] I adopt the suggestion that the duty is to take such care as is reasonable in the circumstances of the case. It was said by the plaintiff that a reasonable system would involve a master on duty in each classroom for a period of one hour. This is not right and, even given three or four masters on duty with three or four prefects, schoolboys of 15 are perfectly able, as soon as the master's back is turned, to start fooling about. This high standard suggested by the plaintiff puts an intolerable burden on schoolmasters. They are not policemen or security guards or prison officers. The case of *Beaumont v. Surrey County Council* discussed earlier is not analogous: that case involved injury to an eye by a piece of elastic which had been carelessly discarded. The risk of injury in those circumstances was foreseeable. It was argued by the plaintiff that the risk of injury from the blackboard and chalk was just as likely a foreseeable consequence arising from a frolic. In my view, this sort of suggestion was getting very near to placing on a local authority an absolute liability.

'The phrase used by one of the schoolboys who gave evidence, "I knew that there was authority about", summed up the position exactly. The boys knew perfectly well that there was a master about, and that is what supervision is all about. I have looked at the case broadly, and common sense says that supervision is the implanting of the feeling that there is authority about, that is, that there is some control and sanction.'

Apart from the definition of supervision at the end, this judgment is interesting in that it shows the way in which the courts distinguish one case from another, the distinction turning on the precise facts. In *Beaumont v. Surrey County Council* there was a much more comprehensive system of supervision, as a system, but it was not fully enforced, and the fact that the trampette elastic had been discarded in a place to which pupils had access, created a foreseeable risk. In *Pettican v. Enfield* the system itself was less rigid, but was held to be adequate to protect against foreseeable risks in all the circumstances of the case.

It should be noted that the events which gave rise to this action took place before the implementation of the 1968 school meals agreement described earlier in this chapter under 'Meals and midday supervision'.

22   Criminal negligence

The cases which have been considered are civil matters where an action has been brought by a person who has suffered damage and seeks redress for himself. These are cases of the kind most likely to affect teachers. If, however, it is maintained that conduct has been so reckless as to amount to a crime, the action would be brought before the criminal courts. It is necessary to prove a much greater degree of negligence to establish criminal liability. More commonly, a fatality brings about a criminal charge of manslaughter.

Few teachers are likely to act so recklessly, but it is possible to imagine a hypothetical case which might be held to constitute a crime. A teacher brings a party of junior children to London for the day from the heart of the country. On arrival, he tells them to amuse themselves until six o'clock, and goes off alone to watch a test match. During the afternoon one of his pupils is knocked down and killed. It is probable that in such circumstances — admittedly so extreme and unknown that it is difficult to imagine any teacher being so rash — a criminal charge might be brought.

Failure to observe the law relating to the risk of burning may well result in a criminal action. The section is worth quoting in full:[67]

> If any person who has attained the age of sixteen years, having the custody, charge or care of any child under the age of twelve years, allows the child to be in any room containing an open fire grate or any heating appliance liable to cause injury to a person by contact therewith, not sufficiently protected to guard against the risk of his being burnt or scalded without taking reasonable precautions against that risk, and by reason thereof the child is killed or suffers serious injury, he shall on summary conviction be liable to a fine....
>
> Provided that neither this section, nor any proceedings taken thereunder, shall affect any liability of any such person to be proceeded against by indictment for any indictable offence.

The warning of the last paragraph is perfectly plain: if a child is killed in this way, the law may hold the negligence to be gross enough to sustain a charge of manslaughter.

A child or young person who is a member of a household in which this offence has been committed may be brought before a juvenile court as being in need of care or control.

23   Accidents away from school

BETWEEN SCHOOL AND HOME

When a pupil meets with an accident on his way to or from school there is no liability on the part either of the teacher or of the authority. It would be quite impossible to care for each child's safety from the time he shuts his front door behind him in the morning until he arrives back in the afternoon, so far as the journey is concerned. This does not mean that the school is unable to deal with indiscipline on the way to or from the school.[68] The supervision of pupils on public transport is the concern of the transport authority. If the local education authority hires coaches for this purpose under contract, responsibility is a matter for negotiation between the authority and the operator. In one case a boy was injured by a pellet on a bus hired in this way. The local education authority provided an adult supervisor on buses for very young children and on those used by sub-normal children. In this particular case supervision was in the hands of prefects. Finding that the behaviour was not 'abnormally boisterous or undisciplined', Mr Justice Waller applied the test laid down in *Lyes v. Middlesex County Council* referred to earlier of the careful parent of a large family applying his mind to school life where there is a greater risk of skylarking. He found the system adequate, and dismissed a claim for damages.[69] In another case, a woman supervisor on a school bus deposited an 8-year-old deaf and dumb pupil on the pavement. In crossing the road the pupil was struck by a van. Although the driver of the van was held 80 per cent to blame for the injury, the woman supervisor was held partly responsible in that she had been at the other end of the bus when the pupil had alighted, and had not taken any steps to see that the road was clear for the pupil to cross.[70]

In 1980 the Court of Appeal ruled that in hiring an independent contractor to transport children to school, a local education authority did not make itself liable for any negligence by that contractor.[71] A taxi firm had a contract with Essex County Council to transport two boys regularly from their home to a special school at Brentwood four miles away. On one occasion the taxi driver did not obey instructions. He dropped the boys in a lay-by on the opposite side of a busy main road to where their home lay. The judge said that it was 'quite outrageous', to leave the boys there. One boy was injured in crossing the road.

Lord Denning held that the local education authority had fulfilled its duty under statute and common law when the contract was made with the taxi firm. The authority had behaved as a reasonably careful father would, since it was reasonably common for parents to get together to get a taxi to take their children to school. The local education authority was not liable, but the finding in negligence against the driver of the van which struck the boy was good.

Occasionally a local education authority allows teachers, as a matter of convenience, to travel free on contract coaches, expecting, in return, some supervision on the journey. A teacher considering such an offer should obtain its precise terms in writing from the local education authority and, if it seems desirable, consult his professional association before accepting.

VISITS TO CLINICS, ETC.

If a child visits a clinic on his way to or from school at either end of a session there is no liability on the school authorities. If a child is sent from school during the course of a session, the teacher should make arrangements for an escort if he considers it necessary, having regard to the age of the pupil and the nature of the route. In any case no child under the age of 8 should be allowed to undertake such a journey on his own. Even in secondary schools it may be desirable to provide an escort (who may be a prefect) in suitable cases, when, say, a first-year child is leaving the school officially. The position is similar with regard to practical subjects centres, swimming baths and the like.

ERRANDS

Children should not be sent away from the school premises on personal errands for teachers. A teacher who takes this responsibility is acting outside the scope of his employment and would probably be liable personally in the event of an accident.

GAMES AND EDUCATIONAL VISITS

The teacher in charge is *in loco parentis* and this responsibility continues even though the normal school time has ended. Sometimes teachers who take children on visits which extend beyond the normal school hours dismiss the pupils from the place visited. Probably this would not render the teacher liable for negligence in the case of older pupils who might reasonably be expected to reach home safely, but much depends on the facts of the case. If, for example, it is proposed to dismiss a party from a railway station, the parents should be asked to agree to this in advance. If any parent objects, that parent's child must be brought back to the school, or some agreed nearby point.[72]

SCHOOL JOURNEYS

Teachers in charge are *in loco parentis* twenty-four hours a day and seven days a week. It should be remembered, that once a person undertakes a voluntary duty he accepts a legal obligation to carry it out to the best of his ability for as long as he has undertaken to perform it. The standard of care which is exacted by the court in these circumstances is that which would be applied by a reasonable and prudent man in the conduct of his own affairs.

WORK EXPERIENCE

Pupils in their last year of compulsory schooling can take part in work experience schemes under the Education (Work Experience) Act 1973. It is very important that any local authority guidelines are closely followed. The authority will confirm the arrangements and indemnify the employers against negligence by pupils. Where teachers accompany pupils the question of legal responsibility where injuries occur depends as usual on the facts of the incident. It may be the teacher and the local authority, or the employer under the Health and Safety at Work etc. Act 1974. DES Administrative Memorandum 22/67 sets out the position as regards liability.

24   Commencement of proceedings

Actions for damages for negligence, nuisance or breach of duty, which include a claim for damages in respect of personal injuries, must be commenced within a period of three years. It is immaterial whether the duty is contractual or statutory.[73]

The period of three years runs either from the date on which the cause of action accrues, or from a date on which the plaintiff first learned:

(a) that the injury in question was significant, that is serious enough for him to commence an action against a plaintiff who did not dispute liability and was able to satisfy a judgment, and

(b) that the injury was wholly or partly attributable to the act or omission which is alleged to constitute negligence, nuisance or breach of duty, and

(c) the defendant's identity, and

(d) if it is alleged that the act or omission was that of a person other than the defendant: the identity of that person, and the additional facts supporting a claim against the defendant.

Knowledge that any acts or omissions did, or did not, in law involve negligence or breach of duty is irrelevant. If an injured person dies before the expiry of the period, time runs (if a cause of action survives him) from the date of his death or from the date when his personal representative first learns the facts set out above.

Knowledge includes facts which the plaintiff can himself observe, or ascertain with such medical or appropriate expert advice as it is reasonable for him to seek. A person is not fixed with knowledge of a fact ascertainable only through expert advice if he has taken all reasonable steps to obtain that advice and, if appropriate, to act on it.

The court may override the limits if it appears equitable, having regard to the extent to which the provisions would prejudice the plaintiff, and a decision to override would prejudice the defendants or their representatives. In considering applications the court must look at the length of, and reasons for, the plaintiff's delay, the effect of the delay on the possible cogency of evidence, the conduct of the defendant, the duration of any disability of the plaintiff, the promptitude with which the plaintiff acted after learning that he might have a cause of action, and the steps taken by the plaintiff to secure expert advice together with the nature of the advice received.

BRIDEN v. ASHBY

The Court of Appeal held in December 1973 that there had been inexcusable delay on the part of a plaintiff's solicitors after a Registrar had dismissed an action for want of prosecution in the previous March. The plaintiff alleged negligence by the local education authority in appointing as a prefect a boy known to be of a bullying disposition. He alleged that in June 1965 the prefect treated him in such a way that he was concussed, and had to have stitches in his head. The plaintiff's father had admitted that his son had been cheeky to the prefect when requested to leave a room. The Master of the Rolls, Lord Denning, said it was a most serious delay: 'Memories grow dimmer all the time, especially when the witnesses were small boys. One witness is in Canada. There must be a risk that a fair trial is no longer possible. The last year's delay was inexcusable: it was far more than marginally prejudicial to everyone.'[74]

With certain exceptions, a person suffering from a disability which prevents him from pursuing an action at the time a cause of action accrues may commence an action at any time up to three years after the end of that disability.[75]

25 Delegation of duty

It is sometimes necessary for a person on whom a duty is laid to delegate all or part of that duty to someone else. Indeed, it is the function of the assistant staff of a school to accept reasonable delegation of responsibility from the head: as the Articles of Government are structured at present, he is responsible for the entire internal organization, management and discipline of the school. Manifestly, he cannot personally undertake all these duties in detail, but it is through him the staff receive their authority.

The question then arises as to how far, having delegated duties to the teaching staff or to ancillary workers, he is liable if a person to whom a duty has been delegated fails to perform it properly.

Again, much must depend on the facts in each case, but it is possible to lay down certain guidelines to be taken into consideration at the moment of delegation.

In the first place he must be satisfied that the person to whom the responsibility is being given is capable of discharging it. Secondly, he must ensure that that person understands fully what is required of him. Thirdly he must be reasonably certain that the person is not only able to carry out the delegated duty, but also that he can do so for the period required. Finally he should, by one means or another, satisfy himself from time to time that the duty is actually being undertaken efficiently.

Similar considerations apply in delegating responsibilities to prefects, their ages and dispositions being matters to take into account. Assistant teachers will also do well to give some thought to these matters when delegating responsibility to junior colleagues, ancillary helpers and pupils.

WRIGHT v. CHESHIRE COUNTY COUNCIL

If all these things are taken into account in choosing the duties to be delegated to another there is little to fear although, once again, everything will depend on the precise facts. During group activities in a gymnasium, one exercise consisted of vaulting over a buck. As the master moved round from group to group, and the pupils were trained and experienced, he delegated his duty to see that boys made a safe landing after the vault to the pupils in the group itself. Whilst the master was at the other end of the gymnasium, the bell went for the end of the lesson and the 'stand-by' ran off to the changing room. A boy in mid-vault landed badly and sustained serious injuries. The defendants pleaded general and approved practice.

The Court of Appeal rejected the plaintiff's claim. Lord Justice Singleton said: 'The bell was an indication of a break for playtime. In the ordinary course the boys, on the sound of the bell, would receive an order to go to the corner at which their squad paraded before being dismissed. Why should the defendants apprehend that on this or any other occasion the boy would run away when the plaintiff was in the act of vaulting? So far as we know, that sort of thing had never happened before. The boys all had experience, seven months, in this school, and the plaintiff (and no doubt the other boys) had been in a junior school before and had taken part in physical exercise and drill.' Earlier in his judgment, he had pointed out: 'There may well be some risk in everything one does or in every step one takes, but in ordinary everyday affairs the test of what is reasonable care may well be answered by experience from which arises over the years a practice adopted generally, and followed successfully over the years so far as the evidence in this case goes.'

Lord Justice Birkett added: 'For my own part, if I were asked what a reasonable and prudent man would do, I think, first of all, he would have regard to the nature of the exercise; and the nature of the exercise, as I see it, requires care, but it is not in itself a dangerous operation, and I think further that, if there had been a system in vogue, as there was here, whereby a boy waited to support the boy vaulting, a reasonable and prudent man would say: "If the boy has been made proficient by his training, there is no negligence in not having an adult there." It is, I think, impossible to avoid the conclusion that it was a most unfortunate, unforeseeable, and quite unpredictable thing which occasioned the accident on this day.... It appears that this was the first time such a thing had happened. In those circumstances I find it is impossible to say on the facts that any negligence was shown on the part of the defendant.'

26   When an accident occurs

Circumstances vary greatly and it is impossible to give advice except in very general terms, but it is as well to remember that not only may emergencies be caused through negligence, but also that it is possible to be negligent in the treatment of such situations.

The teacher's first duty is to the children in his charge. If there is still danger to pupils who are uninjured, as when dangerous gas is escaping in a laboratory, they must be removed from the possibility of harm at once.

Suitable action must be taken in the case of children who are hurt. First aid should be rendered, remembering that it is first aid and that detailed treatment in a serious case is a matter for the doctor. Whenever it appears prudent to do so, a doctor must be called and, if necessary, an ambulance summoned. If the child's own doctor attends, the local education authority will not pay a fee in respect of the visit; in any case, the teacher calling the doctor should state that he is acting as the agent of the child's parents and that he is not personally responsible for the payment of fees.

A teacher should use his own judgement as to the need for summoning further assistance. If possible, another teacher should be asked to look after the children who are not hurt, and the head should be notified at once.

Unless the incident is manifestly trivial – and a teacher should err on the side of caution – the first opportunity should be taken of notifying the child's parents. If the child is removed to hospital, or has to be taken home or to a doctor, he should be accompanied by a teacher, or other responsible person, who will remain until a parent arrives or the doctor says that the child may go home. This may sound overmeticulous but, should there be a charge of negligence later, evidence of attention to detail of this kind would greatly strengthen the teacher's case. Even more important, in a borderline case where a parent is perhaps likely to sue, a teacher is more likely to gain his goodwill and so, possibly, avoid action altogether if the parent is assured that everything possible is being done for his child.

The local education authority will require a report on the accident which will be passed to their solicitor so that he is ready should action be contemplated at a later date. The head should also be fully acquainted with the facts and a note made of any details for future reference. Memories are often short.

In the event of a serious accident, or one which, though trifling, looks as though it may lead to legal difficulties, a teacher should consult his professional association before forwarding any report, even to his local education authority. If the police are called in, he may also deem it wise to consult his association before making any statement. In speaking to the professional association's legal advisers, the teacher must give a full and frank account of the facts so far as they are within his knowledge. A similar precaution should be taken if the local education authority appears to be making any moves towards disciplinary action against the teacher.

In the event of a complaint by a parent about an accident, the teacher should take care not to admit liability in any way. The safest course is to express regret, and to say that the accident occurred whilst the teacher was acting in accordance with general and approved practice.

27 Religious convictions and medical treatment

From time to time a teacher is faced with the problem where, in his opinion, skilled medical treatment is essential, but where it is known that the child belongs to a religious body to which such treatment is repugnant. Normally, of course, it is possible to get in touch with the parent who will take appropriate action in accordance with his conscience and, where possible, this should be done. Sometimes, however, the matter may appear extremely urgent and the parent is not available. This applies *a fortiori* to school journeys abroad.

How is the teacher to deal with this *in loco parentis*? It is not generally permissible to probe into a family's religious beliefs, but in such cases they are usually known. If a child is being taken on a school journey, and it is reasonable to apprehend that medical treatment may — under normal circumstances — become necessary, it is as well to discuss the matter quite frankly with the parents, and to point out that apparent medical neglect might well cast a reflection on the teacher's care for the child as a careful parent. Unless the parent is prepared to give written instructions, and an indemnity, the teacher might well consider whether the child should be taken away.

Nevertheless, such drastic action would be repugnant to most teachers, and certainly gives an aura of religious prejudice. The position with regard to Christian Scientists and Jehovah's Witnesses is not nearly as difficult as popular misunderstanding suggests. For this reason it is dealt with fully in chapter XVI.

As the United Kingdom becomes increasingly multicultural, teachers will have to deal with a wider variety of practices rooted in religious belief. It must be admitted that this is a thorny problem, and the best advice which can be given is that the teacher should use his judgement to find a solution which will, as far as possible, avoid violence to another's conscience without a breach of his duty to act as a prudent parent or, at the same time, causing disadvantage to a pupil. In the final analysis the interest of the child to whom the teacher owes a duty of care is paramount.

28   Accidents to visitors

Until 1958 the duty of care owed to a visitor depended upon the relationship between a guest and the occupier of the property, a distinction being drawn between invitees (who visited the occupier in pursuance of some common material interest) and licensees (who were permitted to visit the premises, but were not there for material interest). It has been held that pupils at a school are invitees,[76] as are parents who visit the school for an exhibition of pupils' work.[77] The ruling relating to parents was given in a case which arose out of an exhibition of work during which the floor collapsed. On the other hand a guest who is invited to a private house is a licensee.

Whilst these distinctions remain for certain purposes, an Act has substituted a 'common duty of care' which an occupier owes to all visitors other than trespassers, unless he has extended, modified, or excluded it in any case, whether by agreement or otherwise.[78] This duty requires him to see that his visitors will be reasonably safe in using the premises for the purpose for which they are invited, or permitted, to be there.

The Act provides that an occupier must be prepared for children to be less careful than adults, and also that a visitor in the exercise of his calling will appreciate and guard against any special risks incidental to that occupation. Thus, an electrician would be expected to take necessary precautions in dealing with defective wiring.

In deciding whether an occupier has discharged his duty, all the circumstances must be considered. A warning of danger, by itself, may not be sufficient unless, in all the circumstances, it is enough to enable the visitor to be reasonably safe. In the case of accidents due to faulty construction the extent of the occupier's liability is fixed by his good faith in assuring himself that the contractor was competent, and the work properly done.

An occupier is not liable in respect of risks willingly accepted by a visitor.

Trespassers are those who enter the property of another with no legal right or justification. They have no redress for any damage they may suffer from the defective state of the premises, but the occupier must not create a new danger whilst they are there, neither may he deliberately harm them: there is a general duty of common humanity. Unauthorized persons who have no business on the premises, licensees whose leave to remain has been withdrawn, and children who have broken bounds by going to a forbidden part of the premises, are trespassers.

A person entering premises under a statutory right is regarded as having the occupier's permission whether, in fact, he has received it or not.

In the event of a visitor suffering damage through the

defective state of a school or its equivalent, the local education authority may be responsible or, in certain cases, the governors of a voluntary school. The owner who is also an employer will be liable for damage arising through the negligence of his servants in the course of their employment. Where danger is known to exist, liability may to some extent be avoided by suitable warning notices and guards.

29   *In loco parentis*

This chapter must end where it began by reminding the reader that he is *in loco parentis* to the children in his charge, and that the law asks merely that he should act reasonably in this capacity. Provided that his actions are in accordance with general and approved educational practice, and provided that he takes such care of his children as a careful father would take, he has little to fear from the mischances of school life.

A year or two before the war, some grammar school pupils were playing, contrary to the school rules, with a cricket-pitch roller which ran over one of them. The parents sued the governors and the master in charge, claiming damages for negligence.[79] Mr Justice Hilbery carefully defined the role of the careful and prudent father: 'It was not suggested for the plaintiff that anybody could reasonably say that a master must watch boys, not merely in classes, but throughout every moment of their school lives.

'What has a reasonably careful parent to do? Supposing a boy of yours has some other little boys, who are friends of his, coming to tea on a Saturday afternoon and you see them all playing in the garden. Suppose your garden roller happened to be there. Would you consider you had been neglectful of your duty to the parents of those other boys because, for five minutes, you had gone into the house and two of them had managed to pull the roller over the third?

'Would you think that, in those circumstances you had failed to exercise reasonable supervision as a parent? These things have got to be treated as matters of common sense, not to put on Mr Johnson any higher standard of care than that of a reasonably careful parent.

'If the boys were kept in cottonwool, some of them would choke themselves with it. They would manage to have accidents: we always did, members of the jury — we did not always have actions at law afterwards.

'You have to consider whether or not you would expect a headmaster to exercise such a degree of care that boys could never get into mischief. Has any reasonable parent yet succeeded in exercising such care as to prevent a boy getting into mischief and — if he did — what sort of boys should we produce?'

Finally, in 1983 the Court of Appeal heard a case with implications for teachers, although not directly involving a member of the profession. A girl of 7 was playing with a friend on a bluff on a mountainside which sloped steeply down to a main road. On the other side of the road were blocks of flats. The girl launched herself on a blanket to slide down the slope and fell 30 or 40 feet, sustaining severe personal injuries. The bluff was unfenced. The trial judge had held that the area constituted a danger to children and should have been fenced.

Lord Justice Dunn said that it was quite clear that the girl's father did not think that the bluff was dangerous: 'It never entered his head that his little girl would try to slide down that slope on a blanket, and the slope was dangerous only if somebody tried to do that.'

There was no reason why the council should be required to apply a higher standard of care than a reasonably prudent parent. If the council were required to fence off that ground, it would be required to fence every bluff which was near a housing estate.

It would be reasonable for such occupiers to assume that the parents would warn their children and would not allow them to play there unless the children had appreciated the danger.

The trial judge had given insufficient weight to the ability of children to look after themselves. A prudent parent would warn his children of natural hazards.

It seems therefore, subject to what is described in section 5 on the 'higher duty of care', that the duty of a council to take reasonable care is no higher than that of a parent. Although the case was brought under the Occupier's Liability Act 1957 and not directly on the ground of *'in loco parentis'*, the general principle applied would no doubt be applied also in actions for professional negligence.[80]

30   *In loco parentis* in the future

Although for the foreseeable future the courts will continue to react to actions for professional negligence using the criteria discussed in this chapter, it is likely that in the longer term a different basis in law for teachers' responsibility may have to be sought. The *loco parentis* doctrine is rooted in a different social climate from that of the later twentieth century: a hundred years ago and longer it made sense to think of the private tutor being selected and hired by parents to carry out their wishes in the education of their children, and being intentionally endowed with quasi-parental status, duties and rights. This seems increasingly inappropriate in the era of mass compulsory education and an increasingly unionized and regulated teaching profession. The idea that teachers, like parents, have no job description but always act in the best interests of their children and do what has to be done as it arises, is starkly at odds with current pressures for definitions of contractual and non-contractual duties and more precise regulation of hours. Also, in the context of corporal punishment the European Court seems to be asserting that teachers do not have the right to chastise by analogy with a child's natural parents. For a further discussion of this aspect the reader is referred to chapter XV.

References

1. Gow *v*. Glasgow Education Authority [1922] SC 260, LCT 295.
2. Williams *v*. Eady (1893) 10 TLR 41 CA; LCT 240.

3. Jackson *v.* London County Council and Chappell (1912) 28 TLR 359; LCT 293.
4. Rich and another *v.* London County Council [1953] 2 All ER 376; LCT 308.
5. Marston *v.* St George's Hospital, Hyde Park Corner, *Daily Mail*, 1 May 1956.
6. In Donoghue *v.* Stevenson [1932] AC 562.
7. Jeffery *v.* London County Council (1954) 119 JP 43; LCT 242.
8. Suckling *v.* Essex County Council, *The Times*, 27 January 1955, LCT 245.
9. In Williams *v.* Eady (1893) 9 TLR 637; 10 TLR 41 CA; LCT 240.
10. Lyes *v.* Middlesex County Council (1963) 61 LGR 443; LCT 198.
11. Beaumont *v.* Surrey County Council (1968) 66 LGR 580; LCT 246.
12. Martin *v.* Middlesbrough Corporation (1965) 63 LGR 385; LCT 316.
13. Beaumont *v.* Surrey County Council (1968) 66 LGR 580; LCT 246.
14. Barnes *v.* Hampshire County Council (1969) 67 LGR 605; LCT 403.
15. Good *v.* ILEA (1980) 10 Family Law 213.
16. Minter *v.* D & H Contractors (Cambridge) Ltd, *The Times*, 30 June 1983.
17. Baxter *v.* Barker and others, *The Times*, 24 April 1903.
18. Smith *v.* Martin and Kingston-upon-Hull Corporation (1911) 2 KB 775.
19. Cooper *v.* Manchester Corporation, *The Times*, 13 February 1959.
20. Watkins *v.* Birmingham City Council, *The Times*, 1 August 1975.
21. Povey *v.* Governors of Rydal School, Colwyn Bay, *The Times*, 13 March 1969.
22. Hamp *v.* Saint Joseph's Hospital, Alderley Edge (1972) *Daily Telegraph*, 19, 23 and 24 October 1972; *Daily Telegraph*, 26 and 27 July 1973.
23. *Guardian*, 29 June 1983.
24. McLoughlin *v.* O'Brien and others, *The Times*, 7 May 1982, HL.
25. Chilvers *v.* London County Council (1916) 80 JP 246; LCT 259.
26. Reported in the *School Government Chronicle*, 19 February 1925.

27. Jones and another *v.* London County Council (1932) 30 LGR 455; LCT 277.
28. Smerkinich *v.* Newport Corporation (1912) 76 JP 454; LCT 265.
29. Butt *v.* Inner London Education Authority (1968) 66 LGR 379; LCT 268.
30. King *v.* Ford (1816) 1 Stark NP 421; LCT 256.
31. Butt *v.* Cambridgeshire and Isle of Ely County Council (1970) 68 LGR 81.
32. Black *v.* Kent County Council, *The Times*, 23 May 1983.
33. Foster *v.* London County Council, *The Times*, 2 March 1928, LCT 255.
34. Crouch and another *v.* Essex County Council and another (1966) 64 LGR 240.
35. Noonan *v.* Inner London Education Authority, *The Times*, 14 December 1974.
36. Fryer *v.* Salford Corporation [1937] 1 All ER 617; LCT 271.
37. Education (Schools and Further Education) Regulations 1981.
38. This is a requirement of the Health and Safety at Work Act 1974, s. 2(2).
39. Administrative Memorandum no. 2/68: *Physical Education Apparatus in Schools and Colleges.*
40. *Safety in Physical Education* (HMSO, 1973).
41. Webb *v.* Essex County Council, *Times Educational Supplement*, 12 November 1954, LCT 290.
42. Gibbs *v.* Barking Corporation [1936] 1 All ER 115; LCT 279.
43. Wright *v.* Cheshire County Council [1952] 2 All ER 789; LCT 284.
44. Cahill *v.* West Ham Corporation (1937) 81 SJ 630; LCT 280.
45. Moore *v.* Hampshire County Council (1982) 80 LGR 481.
46. Ward *v.* Hertfordshire County Council (1969) 67 LGR 418; (1970) 68 LGR 151.
47. Mays *v.* Essex County Council, *The Times*, 11 October 1975.
48. Education Act 1980, Schedule 7, and Education Act 1944 s. 49.
49. Price and others *v.* Sunderland County Borough Council [1956] 1 WLR 1253, 3 All ER 153; LCT 377.
50. Education Act 1980, s. 38(6) and Schedule 7.
51. Blasdale *v.* Coventry District Council (1981) (unreported).
52. Education Act 1980, s. 22.
53. Road Traffic Regulation Act 1967, s. 25, which incorporates the general provisions of the School Crossing Patrols Act 1953.
54. Road Traffic Regulation Act 1967, s. 25(2)(a).

55. Franklin v. Langdown, *The Times*, 27 July 1971.
56. Toole (an infant) v. Sherbourne Pouffes Ltd and another, *The Times*, 29 July 1971.
57. Affutu-Nartoy v. Clarke and another, *The Times*, 9 February 1984.
58. Langham v. Wellingborough School Governors and Fryer (1932) 147 LT 91; LCT 297.
59. Lewis v. Carmarthenshire County Council [1955] 2 All ER 1403; LCT (as Carmarthenshire County Council v. Lewis) 326.
60. See Jeffery v. London County Council, p. 371.
61. Camkin v. Bishop [1941] 2 All ER 713; LCT 334.
62. Rawsthorne v. Ottley [1937] 3 All ER 902; LCT 300.
63. Ricketts v. Erith Borough Council [1943] 2 All ER 629; LCT 304.
64. Clarke v. Bethnal Green Borough Council (1939) 55 TLR 519; LCT 281.
65. Pettican v. London Borough of Enfield, *The Times* 22 October 1970.
66. See Lyes v. Middlesex County Council.
67. Children and Young Persons Act 1933, s. 11, as amended by the Children and Young Persons (Amendment) Act 1952, s. 8.
68. Cleary v. Booth, pp. 427, 451; and R. v. Newport (Salop) Justices *ex parte* Wright, pp. xxxii, 452.
69. Jacques v. Oxfordshire County Council and another (1968) 66 LGR 440; LCT 330.
70. Ellis v. Sayers Confectioners and others (1963), 61 LGR 299 CA.
71. Myton v. Wood and others, *The Times*, 11 July 1980, CA.
72. See chapter XVI.
73. Limitation Act 1939, s. 2A, as inserted by the Limitation Act 1975, s. 1.
74. Briden v. Ashby and West Sussex County Council, *The Times*, 6 December 1973.
75. Limitation Act 1939, s. 22, as amended by the Limitation Act 1975, s. 2.
76. Woodward v. Hastings Corporation (1944) 2 All ER 565; [1945] KB 174; LCT 65.
77. Griffiths v. Smith [1941] AC 170 HL; LCT 63.
78. Occupiers Liability Act 1957, s. 2.
79. Hudson v. Governors of Rotherham Grammar School and Selby Johnson, *Yorkshire Post*, 24 and 25 March 1938; LCT 303.
80. Simkiss v. Rhondda Borough Council, *The Times*, 28 February 1983.

XV
Punishment

1 General

Since the 1970s substantial queries have been raised about the basis in law of traditional sanctions in United Kingdom schools. Increasingly sanctions against pupils are being seen as a general human rights issue, and the European Court of Human Rights has been involved on several occasions. Although the focal point of the disputes has so far been almost entirely corporal punishment, there is no reason to suppose that, gradually, other forms of sanction will not fall to be considered.

At the time of writing there is still some uncertainty as to how the law on punishments is evolving. The first part of this chapter therefore is devoted to the traditional position of the teacher in law: a later section deals with possible future developments.

2 The teacher's traditional authority

The law has always recognized the right of the teacher to inflict reasonable punishment on his pupils. In a leading case, Mr Justice Phillimore laid down the principles by which the law judges a teacher's punishment in these words: 'My brother,

Mr Justice Walton, and I have considered the matter carefully and I will read a sentence which he has been good enough to compose: "The ordinary authority extends not to the head teacher only but to the responsible teachers who have charge of classes." In other words, if I may add anything to what he has written, a teacher of a class has the ordinary means of preserving discipline and, as between the parent of the child and the teacher, it is enough for the teacher to be able to say, "The punishment which I administered was moderate, it was not dictated by any bad motives, it was such as is usual in the school and such as the parent of the child might expect that it would receive if it did wrong".'[1]

The teacher's powers in this matter stem from the fact that he is considered to be *in loco parentis* to the children in his charge and thereby assumes some of the rights — and duties — of the natural parent. The latter's duty in this matter was defined by Mr Justice Field, who said, 'It is his duty, if the child will not do what he advises it to do, to take whatever steps he considers necessary for its correction. But he must act honestly in this course; there must be a cause which a reasonable father believes justifies punishment.'[2]

Parliament endorsed the views of the judges in this matter by a clause in the Prevention of Cruelty to Children Act 1904, which was re-enacted in a later statute.[3] 'Nothing in this section shall be construed as affecting the right of any parent, teacher or other person having the lawful charge of a child or young person to administer punishment to him.'

3 The canons of punishment

There are three standards by which punishment, generally, must be judged. In the first place it is retributive — an expression of the displeasure of society at the offence for which a person is punished. Secondly it is deterrent — an example to prevent others from committing the offence for which punishment is meted out. Finally, it should be reformative — an attempt to turn the offender into an acceptable member of the community.

Modern practice has tended to place the greatest emphasis on the last of these principles.

The exact forms of punishment to be used in schools are not laid down by Parliament. Teachers are left largely to their own discretion and they would do well to bear a double criterion in mind. Not only should their punishment come within the scope both of Mr Justice Phillimore's summing up in *Mansell v. Griffin* quoted above and local education authority regulations, but they should also apply the test of the canons cited in the last paragraph in order to assure themselves that their motives are right.

4 Local education authority regulations

All local education authorities have some regulations dealing with punishment. These are usually concerned chiefly with the more severe forms such as corporal punishment, suspension and expulsion. Minor punishment, as a rule, is left largely to the discretion of the teacher, although some guidance may be given on certain points such as the length of time for which it is reasonable to detain a child. Teachers must know the rules of their own authority and be careful to observe them. A further consideration must be that teachers will abide by the limits of the disciplinary policy for the school, which must be included in the 'Information for Parents' required by regulation.[4]

Two forms of action against the teacher may follow the use of punishment and, as they are quite independent, a particular case may lead to either or both. A case may be brought in the courts, either as a civil action claiming damages, or as a criminal charge of assault. The second course is for the local education authority to take disciplinary measures against the teacher for breach of its regulations.

In the latter case, the authority is concerned merely with the fact that its rules have been broken and the teacher's contract, which includes a requirement that he shall serve in accordance with the rules of the local education authority from time to time in force, thereby breached. This may be so, even where there has been no offence of which the courts can take cognizance; indeed, legal action against the teacher may have failed. This was so in *Gill v. Leyton Corporation* referred to in chapter IV on 'Dismissal'. In accepting appointment the teacher has undertaken to obey the authority's code and, if he fails to do so, he has broken the terms of his agreement. It is for this reason that a newly appointed teacher cannot be urged too strongly to acquaint himself with his authority's rules.

The fact that a teacher has broken the authority's regulations does not, however, necessarily deprive him of a defence in the courts, though it may weaken his case. In *Mansell v. Griffin*, Mr Justice Phillimore said, 'It did not, in our view, necessarily follow because, as a matter of internal government, the teacher was prohibited from administering corporal punishment herself that she was necessarily without defence when it came to a question of an action brought by the pupil against her for trespass to the person or of an indictment for assault. It seems to us that the question must be deeper and must rest on more general considerations. It was admitted that the question depended on the delegation of parental authority to administer moderate corporal punishment to a child, but it was contended for the plaintiff that a parent could only be considered as delegating his or her authority to a headmaster or headmistress.... The fact that the teacher herself did not know of the restrictive regulation is probably immaterial, although it does have a bearing on the teacher's good faith.'

It is very possible that, before long, a test case will come before the courts in the area of an authority which has prohibited the use of corporal punishment. Parents sometimes authorize a teacher to use corporal punishment when his authority has forbidden him to do so. It will be interesting to see how the courts react in such circumstances when, in all other respects, the punishment in question was reasonable. It is not impossible that the courts might hold that such a teacher was acting outside the scope of his employment[5] as a teacher, and therefore not covered by the traditional immunities.

In another case a teacher used an unorthodox instrument — a blackboard pointer — to cane all but one of her class of thirty-eight children. Eight parents took out summonses against the teacher, of which seven were adjourned when the teacher decided to appeal against a fine on the first case. Allowing the appeal, the Recorder said, 'I think it was most regrettable that this prosecution was launched.... The only point I was concerned with has not given any difficulty. I have concluded that what she did to the child did not amount to excessive punishment.'[6]

Nevertheless, the use of an unorthodox or forbidden method of punishment is bound to imperil the teacher's position, and it can afford no defence against disciplinary action by the local education authority. In 1979 it was reported that the headmistress of a primary school had been suspended, *inter alia*, for making two mischievous 6-year-old boys dress as girls: despite other forms of dissuasion the boys had persisted in visiting the girls' toilets.[7]

In December 1971 a young probationary teacher, said to be 'of above average ability', was fined by the West Ham magistrates for gagging and binding an 11-year-old boy with adhesive tape. The boy was said to be a disruptive influence about whom parents, as well as other teachers, had complained. The teacher pleaded guilty, although prosecuting counsel said: 'I am not suggesting that the Sellotape hurt him. After speaking to the boy twice about his behaviour, with no success, the teacher stuck some tape across his mouth and stood him in a corner. When he fidgeted with the tape she fastened his hands to his sides, later slapping him and sending him home. She had previously tried to control the boy by giving him lines and detention.'[8]

The power of a local authority to regulate the use of corporal punishment in its schools was the subject of legal action in October 1982.[9] Manchester local education authority passed a resolution in April 1982 to ban corporal punishment in all its schools and was challenged as to the legality of that resolution.

Under the Articles of Government of Manchester schools at that time, matters affecting 'the general education system' were for the local authority to decide, while matters affecting 'the general direction of the conduct of the school' fell to the governors. Under which of these headings did a ban on corporal punishment come?

Lord Justice Griffiths '... had no doubt that it fell into the latter rather than the former phrase. It was not easy to give a comprehensive definition of that which was comprised in the former phrase but it would clearly include such matters as the sex and age range of the pupils to be taught and principles of selection. Read in their context, those words, wide as they were, did not include a decision as to whether or not a particular form of punishment was to be used in a school. That decision fell naturally within the words "general direction of the conduct of the school".' That being so, the judge held that the decision should have been taken by the governors, in consultation with the teaching staffs as required by the Articles.

It seems from this judgment that, subject to whatever appears in individual Articles of Government, the courts see corporal punishment as a matter of school administration and not of education in the wider sense. Presumably, by analogy, the same would apply in instances where local education authorities seek to ban the wearing of school uniform. It could however be that at some future date the courts might hold that corporal punishment is an integral part of the process whereby a school seeks to achieve the object for which it was established – the moulding of the character and mental power of its pupils. If so it would come under the 'general educational character' of a school, and as such fall to be determined by the local education authority. Such a development could have far-reaching consequences for the status and autonomy of schools and teachers.

5 Unreasonable punishment

It has already been mentioned that any punishment inflicted in school must be reasonable. If it is so, a teacher is not liable for accidental injury to a pupil.[10] The consequences of a mischance during excessive or illegal punishment were clearly pointed out by Lord Chief Justice Cockburn in a case concerning a boy who died after being beaten by a schoolmaster with a thick stick and a skipping rope, 'secretly in the night' for two and a half hours. The Lord Chief Justice said, 'If it [corporal punishment] be administered for the gratification of passion or rage, or if it be immoderate or excessive in its nature or degree, or if it be protracted beyond the child's power of endurance, or with an instrument unsuited to the purpose and calculated to produce danger to life or limb: in all such cases, and if evil consequences ensue, the person inflicting it is answerable to the law and – if death ensue – it will be manslaughter.' In this case the jury did convict of manslaughter. The fact that the father had authorized punishment was irrelevant as he did not, and no one can, authorize excessive punishment.[11]

Happily, cases of excessive punishment are now rare. In 1964 the headmaster of a grammar school and the senior mistress pleaded guilty to assaulting two girl pupils aged 17 and 18, and were fined. The punishments were administered after the girls had been caught kissing and cuddling a sixth form boy and another youth in the school's green room. The two members of the staff spanked the girls on their bare buttocks with a hairbrush. Two days later one girl had 72, the other 33 square inches of bruising. In her defence the senior mistress pleaded that she had to take orders from the headmaster, otherwise she would undermine his authority.[12] In 1979 a schoolmaster pleaded guilty to two charges of assault: one was on a 15-year-old boy, a difficult pupil, on whose back thirteen long weal marks inflicted by a bamboo cane were found. The teacher was fined for punishment 'far in excess of reasonable chastisement'.[13] In 1981 a London teacher was fined for hitting a 13-year-old boy with a tennis racquet,[14] and in 1983 the Court of Appeal upheld the conviction of a teacher who threw an exercise book at a 12-year-old boy 'occasioning actual bodily harm'. Mr Justice Nolan stated: 'Reasonable chastisement involved a controlled, if not an entirely cool, response, and the throwing of an exercise book could not come within that category.'[15]

6 Authority out of school

Some cases concerning punishment are brought by parents who maintain that the schoolmaster's writ does not run beyond the school's walls. The courts have laid it down clearly that the authority is not so limited, but the precise bounds of that power have never been defined. In general it may be said that the teacher may exercise such control over the pupil as is necessary to maintain the implied contract between parent and teacher. If this is so, the teacher's jurisdiction extends to all matters which may affect the welfare of the school.

It is important to distinguish between matters where the child is the offender and those where the parent has exercised control over the child to prevent him from acting in accordance with the school rules. In cases falling in the latter category the child must not be punished, although it is possible to consider suspending him with a view to expulsion if it appears that the parent's action is so subversive of school discipline as to break the contract to educate. This is possible because the law presumes that a parent, in sending his child to school, has *chosen* that school and accepts the rules of the school.[16]

A boy threw some putty at a fellow-pupil on the way to school. The latter complained to the headmaster who caned the assailant. The justices convicted the headmaster of assault, but the Divisional Court quashed the verdict.[17] Mr Justice Collins said, 'It is clear that a father has the right to inflict reasonable personal punishment on his son. It is equally the law, and is in accordance with very ancient practice, that he may delegate this right to the schoolmaster. Such a right has always commended itself to the common sense of mankind. It is clear that the relation of master and pupil carries with it the right of reasonable corporal punishment. As a matter of common sense, how far is this power delegated to the schoolmaster? Is it limited to the time during which the boy is within the four walls of the school, or does it extend beyond that limit?

'In my opinion, the purpose with which the parental authority is delegated to the schoolmaster, who is entrusted with the bringing-up and discipline of the child must, to some extent, include an authority over the child while he is without the four walls.

'It may be a matter of fact in each case whether the conduct of the master in inflicting corporal punishment is right. Very grave consequences would result if it were held that a parent's authority was exclusive right up to the door of the school and then, and then only, the master's authority commenced. It would be a most anomalous result to hold that, in such a case as the present, the boy who had been assaulted had no remedy by complaint to his master who could punish the assailant by thrashing.... It is obvious that the desired impression is best brought home by a summary and immediate punishment.... In my opinion, parents do contemplate such an exercise of authority by the schoolmaster. I should feel very sorry if I felt myself driven to come to the opposite conclusion, and am glad to say that the principle shows that the authority delegated to the schoolmaster is not limited to the four walls of the school.'

In another case[18] a headmaster caned a boy for smoking in the street and the father brought an action on the grounds that the boy had parental permission to smoke. The case was dismissed by the magistrates and the father was ordered to pay costs. He asked for a case to be stated, but the magistrates certified the application as frivolous. A rule nisi was then obtained to allow a hearing in the High Court on the grounds that the magistrates were wrong in allowing that the defendant had authority to inflict corporal punishment on the boy, that the boy was at the material time under the authority of his father and that, since the father had given the boy permission to smoke, the headmaster had no power to inflict punishment on him for so doing.

Lord Hewart held that the rule forbidding pupils to smoke during term time, whether within the school precincts or elsewhere in public, was a reasonable rule. The boy knew of the rule and deliberately broke it; the punishment administered was a reasonable and proper punishment for the breach of the rule.

In one case a boy ran across the road on the way to school, just in front of a teacher's car. The headmaster, who had frequently spoken to the children about road safety, caned the boy and the parents brought a case against him for assault. The magistrates dismissed the case and ordered the plaintiff to pay costs.[19]

As Mr Justice Collins said in *Cleary v. Booth*, it is a matter of fact in each case as to whether the schoolmaster's authority extends far enough to justify his interference. It is probable that it would be held not only that it was within his power but that it was his duty to deal, for example, with any of his scholars engaged in street feuds with pupils from a neighbouring school. It is most unlikely, of course, that he would be thought to be controlling the internal organization, management and discipline of his school if, seeing one of his pupils not wearing the school uniform on a private holiday in Ibiza, he waited until the beginning of term and then punished the boy for that breach of the school rules!

7 Trespass against the person

The two forms of punishment which give rise to the greatest number of legal problems are detentions and corporal punishment. Both of them lie within that field of the law in which they would, were it not for the special status of the teacher, constitute trespasses against the person. Either may, in general, be punished as a crime or be the root of a civil action as a tort.

In common speech the word 'trespass' is usually employed today to refer to trespass to land, and it is often forgotten that there may also be trespass to goods and trespass against the person. Trespass is an ancient legal concept to describe a 'direct and forcible' entry or injury, and, so far as trespass against the person is concerned, includes assault, battery and false imprisonment.

The criminal aspect of these matters was largely, though not entirely, removed from the realm of common law to that of statute by the Offences against the Person Act 1861. Civil law retains the element that a plaintiff in an action for trespass does not have to prove that he has suffered damage: he can recover compensation, often purely nominal, merely by proving the act of trespass.

The total restraint of another person's liberty, whether by force or show of authority, is false imprisonment. This act usually involves assault and battery in addition, but this is not true in all cases: if a person walks willingly into a room, and is then forced to remain there because the door is locked behind him, that would be false imprisonment. In an Australian case it was held to be false imprisonment to detain a passenger against his will in a car by driving too fast for him to be able to alight.

The essential element in false imprisonment is that the restraint must be entire. No degree of permanence is involved and complete temporary restraint, even for a few moments, is false imprisonment. The restraint need not be the personal act of the defendant, nor need he personally know of it at the time. Once the restraint has been proved, the onus is on the defendant to show that it was lawful, e.g. that he had a reasonable and honest belief that the detention was justified. Such a defence may be grounded in the duty of every citizen to arrest a person provoking a breach of the peace, about to commit a crime, reasonably suspected of committing a crime or escaping from legal authority. In all such cases the person detained must be taken to a magistrate or the police with all reasonable despatch.

An assault is an unlawful attempt, offer or threat to do violence to another in such a manner as to cause him reasonably to believe himself to be in immediate danger. Thus to wave a cudgel threateningly at someone whilst within arm's length is an assault; it would not be so if the parties were a hundred yards apart. It is an assault to threaten another by pointing an unloaded gun at him unless at the time the complainant knew that it was unloaded.

Immediately a threat is translated into action, battery is added to assault. The least touch is sufficient.

There are several general defences. One is *volenti non fit injuria* (no one suffers injury from that to which he has consented): thus, a person using a public highway is presumed to have consented to people brushing past him. One may also take reasonable ,steps to defend oneself, one's family, one's property and possibly anyone else. What is reasonable is a question of fact in each case, having regard to the gravity of the circumstances. Similarly a citizen may use such force as is reasonably necessary in all the circumstances in exercising his duty of arrest. Alternatively it is possible to plead that a battery was an 'inevitable accident'.

A civil action for assault or battery cannot be brought against a person who has been summarily convicted of that particular commission of either act.

A defence to false imprisonment or assault and battery may be set up on the ground of lawful parental discipline. The success of the defence will depend on the facts of the case; what, for example, is reasonable in the case of a 7-year-old child might be held to be unreasonable when he is ten years older. Nevertheless, a parent has a legal duty to exercise proper custody and control over his children, and he will be supported by the courts if he reasonably forces them to remain under his roof or uses corporal punishment.

By analogy these powers are transferred to the schoolmaster *in loco parentis*. 'This power is not limited to corporal punishment, but extends to detention and restraint.'[20] The power may, on occasion, include trespass to goods as, for example, when a master took away a boy's notebook containing the names of the ringleaders in a plot to disturb order.[21] It used to be held that the schoolmaster's powers were derived from the parent by delegation, but it is doubtful in these days, when a parent is by law required to provide efficient full-time education for his children of statutory school age, whether this is the soundest basis, in spite of the precedents. The difficulty in relying on the principle of delegation is that delegation is usually a voluntary act: a power which is delegated can presumably be taken back by the delegator. There is currently some doubt as to whether for example it is lawful to administer corporal punishment to a pupil whose parents have specifically informed the school that the authority to punish is not delegated. The matter is considered further in the section 'The disciplinary future': in the meantime it is sufficient to note that the courts have so far accepted reasonable punishment by a teacher *in loco parentis* as a defence both in cases of detention and of corporal punishment.

8   Detention

As has been said above, the total restraint of another's liberty by force or show of authority is false imprisonment and actionable before the courts. Of this, Mr Justice Phillimore said, in *Mansell v. Griffin*, 'It is, I suppose, false imprisonment to keep a child locked up in a classroom, or even to order it to stop under penalties in a room for a longer period than the ordinary school time without lawful authority. Could it be said that a teacher who kept a child back during play hours to learn over and say a lesson, or who put upon him a dunce's cap – could it be said that such a person would be liable in an action for trespass to the person? The cases I have instanced are not cases of the infliction of blows, but they are cases of interference with the liberty of the subject and it seems to me that the principle must be the same for all these cases.'

The right of a teacher to detain a child was also referred to by Mr Justice Field,[22] when he said, 'The law, therefore, does justify a parent in a case where he honestly considers correction necessary, in administering blows in a reasonable and proper manner. This power is not limited to corporal punishment but extends to detention and restraint.' A teacher has the power by analogy.

Teachers should be aware of any regulations of their employing authority which may limit the period for which a child may be detained, and should ensure that they comply with them. In any case the tests applied in *Mansell v. Griffin* referred to at the beginning of this chapter, are equally appropriate in dealing with all punishments. The variable criterion is that the punishment should be moderate and reasonable: this is a matter of fact in each case, and includes such factors as the offence which is being punished, the age of the child, the distance and quality of the travel facilities between the school and the home, traffic and other dangers, and the child's ability to cope with the journey in question alone and at an unusual hour.

The use of detention in a school should be included in the school rules and brochures and made known to parents when their children are admitted. In areas where there is particular danger much parental worry can be avoided, and parental support may often be secured, if the performance of a detention is not required on the day it is awarded. A note of advice that a child will be late on the following day, incorporating a space for the parent to sign, may be helpful. It must be stressed, however, that such a note does not seek the parent's consent to the detention. This is not required since the teacher's legal right to detain his pupils does not arise from parental delegation, and parents should be clearly aware of this fact.

A parent who wilfully refuses to co-operate in this way may be breaking the contract to educate.

9 Corporal punishment

By far the greatest number of cases concerning discipline arise from the use of corporal punishment. The courts have consistently upheld the teacher's right to administer reasonable physical chastisement, but perhaps the best summary is to be found in the words of Lord Chief Justice Cockburn. 'By the law of England, a parent or schoolmaster (who for this purpose represents the parent) may, for the purpose of correcting what is evil in the child, inflict moderate and reasonable corporal punishment – always, however, with this condition: that it is moderate and reasonable.'[23]

Mass corporal punishment is to be deprecated, albeit on professional rather than legal grounds. In the case of *Hazell v. Jeffs*, already quoted, the punishment of a large number of children was involved and, in a similar case, where a master had caned a whole class four times because particular offenders failed to own up, the magistrates dismissed the case, commenting that the teacher had acted reasonably in the interests of discipline.[24] It is doubtful whether magistrates would take the same view in the 1980s.

Opinions vary widely on the question of the most suitable part of the body for the infliction of corporal punishment, and teachers with authority to use the cane should make certain of any directions by their local education authority. Some years ago, a bench convicted a schoolmaster who had caned a pupil on the hands, because the justices felt that the risk of injury was grave, even though none had resulted in that particular instance. Quashing the conviction, Mr Justice Charles said, 'When Parliament lays down a chart showing the particular region of the body to which corporal punishment in schools shall be confined, the court will take care that those limits are not overstepped. At present there is no such chart.'[25]

In the former Approved Schools the Home Office laid down strict regulations regarding corporal punishment and, although these have never bound other schools, they are of interest as the only statement ever published showing *to some extent* what may be officially regarded as reasonable. The following is a summary:[26]

BOYS

(a) Only a cane or tawse of an approved pattern may be used.
(b) Only a cane may be used on the hands, and the number of strokes must not exceed three on each hand. No boy over 15 may be caned on the hands.
(c) When applied on the posterior, either a cane or a tawse may be used over the boy's ordinary cloth trousers, and the number of strokes must not exceed six for boys under 15 or eight for boys of 15 and over, with the proviso that the managers may authorize up to twelve strokes for a boy in the higher age-group.
(d) In the case of boys with any physical or mental disability the prior approval of the medical officer must be obtained.
(e) It must not be inflicted in the presence of other boys.

GIRLS

(a) Only a cane of an approved pattern may be used.
(b) Only girls under 15 may be caned, and the number of strokes may not exceed three on each hand.
(c) In the case of girls with any physical or mental disability the prior approval of the medical officer must be obtained.
(d) It must not be inflicted in the presence of other girls.

Legally there is no discrimination between boys and girls in this matter, so far as ordinary schools are concerned. Most authorities have their own rules which normally lay down that it may be inflicted on girls only by a woman. In general, it is confined to the hands.

Local authority regulations normally forbid the use of corporal punishment by probationary, supply or temporary teachers, and some require several years' experience before they will authorize a teacher to use the cane. All irregular forms of punishment, such as boxing the ears and shaking, are strictly forbidden. Some authorities forbid the caning of children under 8.

The Articles of Government of voluntary-aided schools do not, in general, require the school to be conducted in accordance with the regulations of the local education authority, except insofar as there may be special requirements dealing with finance and other matters. In such cases a head would be wise, in his own interests, to ask his governors to adopt and make known a policy on corporal punishment in the usual way.

10 Punishment by prefects

The use of prefects is nowadays less common than it was. However the law regards prefects as part of the disciplinary system of a school. Punishment which is otherwise legal does not become unlawful merely because it has been administered by a duly authorized prefect. There is, however, a duty to ensure that the penalties enforced by prefects are reasonable and moderate.

11   Suspension and expulsion

The technical procedure for dealing with cases where suspension or expulsion has become necessary is contained in the Articles of Government for each school, and has already been noticed. Since these penalties are the ultimate sanctions which can be employed by a school, it is important that they should not be used lightly or unadvisedly. Even if the Articles of Government give the head the power to expel, it is most desirable that he should suspend in the first instance in order to give the pupil and his parents the opportunity of a constitutional hearing.

On this subject, Lord Chief Justice Cockburn said, 'It is incidental to the authority of a headmaster to expel from the school over which he presides any scholar or student whose conduct is such that he could not any longer be permitted to remain without damage to the school. This is, however, not to be exercised arbitrarily. It may be questioned and, although no doubt a large discretion must be allowed, it must not be exercised wantonly or capriciously.'[27]

The judge's latter point cannot be stressed too strongly. The discretion to ban children from school is couched in much broader terms than the very specific grounds permitting parents to keep their children from school and referred to in chapter XI. Unhappiness at school, for example, is something very real to many children, yet not admissible as a ground for non-attendance. From the school's point of view these cases do not involve them being 'in the dock', for the legal issue is seen simply as whether or not the parent has complied with a statutory duty. The court will not debate the unhappiness as such. Moreover, if the unhappiness leads to the pupil becoming disruptive, the pupil may be banned from school: the disciplinary proceedings involving the governors are again much more likely to revolve around the nature of the offences against school discipline and the effect on other pupils than around why the child was unhappy at school.

A difficulty arises in connection with the future education of pupils who are expelled. Many local education authorities regard themselves as under a duty to find another school place for expelled pupils: some, suspecting that this might be difficult, advise governors and head teachers not to expel for that reason, and a few have been known to make expulsion conditional on the expelling school finding a place elsewhere.

Local education authorities have a *moral* obligation to see to the education of all children in their area, and a general duty under the Act[28] to promote education. As far as education provided in schools is concerned, the Act requires local education authorities to provide schools 'sufficient in number, character and equipment' for the 'different ages, abilities and aptitudes' of pupils.[29] The Education Act 1981 added the requirement that local education authorities secure provision for children with 'special educational needs'.[30] Disruptiveness on its own, however, is not a 'special educational need'.

If, therefore, a local educational authority has provided a school place for a pupil, it has satisfied the law. If a pupil is then expelled lawfully from that place, no duty to find a place reverts to the local education authority. In law, the duty to educate falls back on the parent at that stage, and, if the duty is not carried out, care proceedings are a possibility. The reader is referred to chapter XI, 'Attendance'.

The options open to local education authorities in caring for expelled pupils include, of course, special units for difficult pupils, home tuition and specialized boarding schools.

12 Exclusion

A head teacher's right reasonably to exclude is not restricted to cases where pupils have contagious diseases. In *Spiers v. Warrington* Lord Chief Justice Goddard drew a distinction between suspension and exclusion: a pupil may be excluded for failure to fulfil a reasonable and lawful condition, but the head teacher must at all times be willing to receive the pupil back when that condition is fulfilled. In the case in question, the condition was that the pupil be appropriately dressed.

In practice some confusion has arisen over the distinction between exclusion and suspension, and it remains unclear. Lord Chief Justice Goddard implied in *Spiers v. Warrington* that an exclusion need not, unlike a suspension, be reported to the chairman of governors. Thus there is no right of appeal to the governors by the parents as is granted in the Articles of Government in cases of suspension. It would be unwise of a head teacher to use exclusion rather than suspension solely to avoid a hearing for the parents, however.

Exclusion probably differs from suspension in the nature and degree of offence to which it is applied. A pupil arriving at school wearing extreme 'punk' or, perhaps, neo-fascist regalia, or a girl pupil wearing a provocative see-through blouse are probably best dealt with by exclusion, since the pupils and their parents can probably put matters right very quickly. There is no element of punishment intended here.

Suspension is really time for reflection by the school authorities. The pupil's offence must be sufficiently serious to merit immediate removal from the school premises, while those in authority decide what further steps to take. A decision should be reached as soon as reasonable and practicable and communicated to all concerned. Indefinite suspension is probably unlawful: some local education authorities wisely limit suspension to a fixed number of days. This is not intended in any way to inhibit head teachers and governors, but rather to ensure that regular meetings take place of the interested parties to discuss the case. Re-suspension is a possible outcome of such a meeting, if circumstances justify it.

Exclusion is perhaps most frequently thought of as only partial. A pupil may be excluded temporarily from a class for misbehaviour or, on safety grounds, from a laboratory or workshop if long hair is worn unsatisfactorily. Repeated exclusions may of course provide grounds for suspension and more serious action.

Concern has been expressed as to whether the head teacher's power to exclude extends also to children whose behaviour during school meals at lunchtime is unacceptable. This issue has perhaps become more pointed since the passing of the 1980 Act which put children from poorer families into a special category as regards the provision of food and drink. The Child

Poverty Action group has expressed concern about this aspect of heads' authority.[31]

The position in law may be summarized as follows. The regulations governing the provision of milk and meals in schools[32] ceased to apply after the power of the Secretary of State to make such regulations was partly revoked by the Education Act 1980. Those regulations stipulated that they were '... without prejudice to the exercise by the head teacher of a school, under the Articles of Government ... of any function relating to the internal discipline of the school.'[33] For this purpose no distinction was made in the regulations between those pupils receiving free school meals and others.

In the vacuum left by the withdrawal of these regulations, the authority of the head teacher must again derive directly from the Articles of Government. Here again, no distinction is made between children from poor homes and any others. However, it must be noted that the length and reasonableness of an exclusion, and whether it was temporary or not, would, if challenged, be a matter for the courts to decide.

In May 1985 a Government White Paper on the government of schools[34] proposed limiting heads' power to debar pupils from schools to a maximum of three days in any term, before which the local education authority and governors would have to be informed. Either of these bodies could instruct a head to readmit a debarred pupil. If a pupil were debarred from a public examination, the local authority and governors must be informed immediately. The White Paper proposed also that heads should have to 'have regard to guidance' from governing bodies in securing acceptable standards of behaviour from pupils.

At the time of writing, this document is still under discussion.

13   Confiscation

It is an offence 'dishonestly to appropriate property belonging to another with the intention of permanently depriving the other of it'.[35] Teachers' general powers of discipline can afford them a defence against actions for theft,[36] provided that confiscated property is returned as soon as the reason for the confiscation is past. If the confiscation lasts unreasonably long, even inadvertently, the wish to deprive the owner of it permanently in the wording of the Act may, depending on the circumstances, be inferred.

Confiscated property must be looked after as a teacher would look after his own property. If such property is negligently lost, compensation may be payable.

Dangerous items such as drugs and knives should not be returned after confiscation, but the parents or the police, or both, contacted. A flick knife has been held to be an offensive weapon for the purpose of the Prevention of Crime Act 1953.[37] In effect this means that, in criminal proceedings for possession of an offensive weapon, the burden is on the defendant to show that he had a lawful excuse to carry it. If it were not offensive by definition, the burden would be on the prosecution to show that the defendant had an offensive purpose in mind.

The kirpan is a ceremonial dagger which is sometimes carried by pupils of the Sikh religion. It is a religious symbol and not an offensive weapon. Nevertheless the law gives it no special position with regard to teachers' discretion and the safe conduct of schools.

14   Civil actions concerning punishment

It is, of course, open to a plaintiff to bring a civil action for damages arising out of punishment. In 1965 Judge Duveen held at Slough County Court that a parent's claim must be rejected. The father had said that the corporal punishment administered to his son was excessive and sadistic, and the mother gave evidence that her son suffered from nightmares and bedwetting afterwards. The judge said, 'There is no doubt in my mind that the punishment was made to fit the crime.'[38]

15   Violent pupils

Before proceeding to a discussion in the next section on the effect of some current thinking on the practice and development of deterrents in schools, an account of several cases will indicate the general approach when the problem of violence reaches proportions which remove it from the school's disciplinary procedures to the Queen's courts.

In December 1971 a 15-year-old pupil smoked during morning break, made rude gestures at the head of the physical education department, swore at him, kicked him in the stomach, and then ran away. The master gave him a light blow, which broke his jaw. The boy was later found to have taken half a tablet of the drug LSD before morning school. The master was charged with assault and causing grievous bodily harm, the more serious charge being dropped during the trial at Birmingham Crown Court. He was also suspended from duty. Summing up to the jury, Mr Justice Ackner said: 'Have we really reached the stage in this country when an insolent and bolshie pupil has to be treated with all the courtesies of visiting royalty? You may think we live in strange times. Whatever may be the view of our most advanced, way-out theoreticians, the law does not require a teacher to have the patience of a saint. You may think that is a good thing, too. You may think that a superabundance of tolerance fails to produce a proper degree of self-discipline in any pupil.

'Nothing has happened to the boy concerned, although he could be brought before a juvenile court and receive a wide range of penalties. Yet a schoolmaster, "a man of exemplary character and an able, efficient and conscientious teacher" has been brought before the court. That is why I say we live in very strange times. The issue before you is not whether we suffer nowadays from an excess of sentimentality or sloppy thinking with regard to the criminal responsibility of the young. It is whether the prosecution has proved the master guilty.'

The master was acquitted.[39]

During the same week a master in the south of England was cleared of assault by a bench of magistrates. The court was told that the class had been in an uncontrollable uproar for thirty-five minutes. 'It was like trying to stop a riot,' said the master. He added that when he told a boy to stop fighting, the complainant made a very provocative remark which was the last straw. 'I meant to cuff him,' he said, 'but not with the board rubber.' He was sorry that he had cut the boy's forehead, but thought that his actions were justified in the circumstances.[40]

Five months later the Bristol Juvenile Court heard the story of two 16-year-old boys who admitted causing grievous bodily harm to a master in a comprehensive school by punching his head. They also spat on him, emptied the contents of a wastepaper basket over him and wrecked science apparatus. The master's skull was fractured, and he would have died if surgery to remove a clot near the brain had not been performed immediately. Because he was a Quaker the master did not retaliate. At the time of the trial his speech was still impaired, and it was not certain whether there was brain damage which would render him permanently unfit to teach. The boys said they believed the master had prevented them from being entered for their Advanced Level examinations.

The chairman said: 'In this court we believe that mercy is part of justice. We have to consider the possibility of you being taken away from society and the community for a considerable time. Maybe we are wrong in deciding otherwise. Your behaviour has been offensive and arrogant; the school had done everything possible for you, and no one had tried to stop you taking your A levels.'

The boys were sent to a detention centre for three months, followed by a year's after-care order.[41]

In December 1973 a boy was acquitted at the Old Bailey both of the murder and manslaughter of an older and much larger boy in a classroom. The boy who died was said to be 'hot-tempered, quick to take offence, and a bit of a bully'. He often kicked the defendant unnecessarily during football matches, and referred to him as a 'yellow bastard' and a 'mongol'. On the day following a serious scuffle on the football field, the younger boy, who had come to this country from Hong Kong some three years previously, took a knife to school to frighten his tormentor. The older boy picked a quarrel and raised a chair above his head as though to throw it at the immigrant boy. However, he flung the chair to the floor and lunged forward on to the knife which was being held towards him. The defendant tried to pull the knife back but, before he could do so, it penetrated his assailant's heart.[42]

The cases cited above may be isolated incidents, but three salient points emerge. It is certain that a new form of aggravated violence, reckless of life or limb is, at least occasionally, manifesting itself in the schools of this country, and that the ordinary means of controlling discipline are inadequate to prevent this on some occasions. It is also clear that the courts are prepared to take a strong line with the perpetrators of this violence when they appear before them. Finally there must be considerable concern among head teachers, charged with a legal duty to control the internal discipline of their schools and a common law duty *in loco parentis* to take all reasonable steps to prevent any of their pupils from suffering unavoidable harm, that it is becoming increasingly difficult to discharge their responsibilities at a time when their authority to do so is subject to constant challenge.

An action will not normally lie against the parent of a pupil who has injured a teacher or damaged his property. For such a case to succeed it would be necessary to prove that the parent ordered or approved the action in question, or that it would not have taken place except for the parent's negligence. This matter is discussed further in chapter XX.

16 The disciplinary future

The post-war years have witnessed a shift of emphasis in dealing with recalcitrant children from punishment to treatment, a movement which has gained considerable impetus since 1967. In society at large the age of criminal responsibility was raised from 8 to 10, and there are some who think that 12, or even 14, would be more appropriate. The Children and Young Persons Act 1969 made it very difficult to bring a child before the courts charged with an offence other than homicide, unless it was also possible to allege that he was also in need of care or control.

In the schools the battle has been waged largely over the issue of corporal punishment. In 1967 the Plowden report on primary education recommended that the then Schools Regulations be amended 'to provide that the infliction of physical pain as a method of punishment should not be allowed'. The committee also suggested that legislation should deny registration to any independent school in which 'the infliction of physical pain is a recognized form of punishment'. Although the committee's terms of reference restricted its deliberations to the primary sector of education, these recommendations gave the appearance of being applicable to the secondary schools as well.

The Secretary of State at that time, Mr Patrick Gordon Walker, expressed similar views, and in the following year the Cardiff education authority decided to ban corporal punishment in its schools for an experimental period of twelve months. Opposition from the teaching profession, notably the National Union of Teachers and the National Association of Head Teachers, led to the lifting of the prohibition after two months. A survey revealed that only four out of sixty-four primary schools were in favour of abolition in the conditions prevailing at that time, although forty-four were in favour of phasing out.

The year 1968 also saw the formation of the Society of Teachers Opposed to Physical Punishment. The Society is dedicated to the abolition of corporal punishment, pointing out that of the European countries only the United Kingdom, the Republic of Ireland and parts of Switzerland have retained its use. Within the Commonwealth it is still employed in Canada, Australia and New Zealand. It is also used in the Union of South Africa and parts of the United States of America.

The argument for abolition is based on a number of grounds. It is said to be degrading both for the teacher and pupil. It is psychologically dangerous, and leads to disturbance later in life. The frequency with which some names appear in the punishment book is proof that it is ineffective. It produces school phobia. It is used too frequently on the recidivist (on whom it has no effect) and the maladjusted (who should never be caned). It gives an opportunity to a sadistic teacher to gratify his perversion. Above all, violence begets violence and destroys the possibility of a satisfactory relationship between teacher and taught.

The first effective step towards abolition was taken by the ILEA which announced in 1971 that it proposed to ban the use of all corporal punishment in its primary schools from the beginning of 1973. Since they are not subject to the Authority's regulations, the prohibition does not apply to voluntary-aided schools in which the position varies considerably. In 1972 the Shropshire Authority forbade the use of the cane in infants' schools, but did not go so far as the ILEA in that it decided to allow slapping to continue in certain restricted circumstances.

In 1973 Baroness Wootton of Abinger introduced the Protection of Minors Bill 1973 in the House of Lords. The bill sought to end corporal punishment by all persons having the custody, care or control of a child, including all teachers, through the creation of a statutory offence to be known as wilful assault on a minor; that is, any person under the age of 18. The bill proposed to exempt natural, adoptive and foster parents and legal guardians and their spouses in each case, but not the employees of a local authority in charge of a child committed to the care of that authority. The bill proposed the abolition of the defence of reasonable corporal punishment. The proposed penalties were a fine or four months' imprisonment, or both, on summary conviction; or on indictment a larger fine or one year's imprisonment, or both. The motion for the second reading was rejected by sixty-seven votes to fifty-one.

Early in 1976 a further attempt was made to ban corporal punishment when leave was sought under the ten minute rule to introduce the Education (Abolition of Corporal Punishment) Bill. Alternative forms of punishment, including Saturday morning detention and community service, were proposed. Leave was refused.

On all sides it is being said that discipline in schools is more difficult than ever before, and problems which were once peculiar to secondary schools are now increasingly appearing in the primary sector. Some would retain, even increase, the sanctions already available; others wish to see them diminished and replaced by suitable treatment. The supportive social services are labouring under increasingly heavy case loads, and are not yet adequately staffed with experienced workers to take over the treatment of all pupils who have become problems in school. Indeed, in spite of promises, the problems appear to be increasing in number and severity faster than the services created to deal with them.

Since the late 1970s the trend towards abolition has gathered momentum and it is likely that in the foreseeable future a majority of local education authorities will have abolished the practice. Abolition has not always been greeted with instant enthusiasm by local teachers' associations,[43] particularly where teachers have feared that inadequate supportive services, or reductions in staffing levels resulting from financial cutbacks would leave them very exposed.

The scene of the legal debate has shifted now emphatically away from the United Kingdom to the European Court of Human Rights in Strasbourg. In March 1983 the United Kingdom Government was ordered by the Court to pay almost £13,000 in compensation and legal costs to two Scottish families who brought joint actions concerning corporal punishment in Scottish schools.[44]

The background to the first case was that a mother could not obtain from the Strathclyde Regional Council a promise that her son at primary school would not in any circumstances receive corporal punishment. The boy was, in fact, never punished at any time during his stay at the school and there was no indication that he was personally threatened with it.

The second family, Cosans, had a 15-year-old boy who was caught trying to take a short cut home along a prohibited route through a cemetery. On his father's instructions he refused to accept corporal punishment and was suspended. After some three months the local education authority felt that the long absence from school was in itself sufficient punishment, and offered to readmit the boy subject to an undertaking that he would in future accept school discipline. As with the Campbell family, the local authority would not give an assurance that the boy would never be tawsed: consequently the boy remained out of school until he reached school-leaving age four months later.

Supported by the Scottish Council for Civil Liberties, the parents filed a complaint with the European Commission of Human Rights. The submissions were made under articles of the European Convention of Human Rights which prohibit inhuman or degrading treatment (Article 3), and respect the right of parents to ensure that education is in conformity with their own religious and philosophical convictions (Article 2 of Protocol No. 1).

The Commission decided that there had been a failure to respect the parents' convictions, that there had been no violation of Article 3, and that it was unnecessary to consider whether Jeffrey Cosans had been unlawfully denied his right to education under the Convention. At this stage the usual procedure is to invite the parties to achieve a 'friendly settlement'. This reconciliation turned out to be impossible and the matter was then referred to the European Court of Human Rights.

The Court held that the mere threat of punishment may breach the Convention, provided it is real and immediate. However, Jeffrey Cosans' feelings of apprehension about the tawse were not in themselves sufficiently strong to violate the Convention: the Court confirmed that there had been no breach of Article 3.

Corporal punishment was held to be a matter of 'philosophical conviction'. 'Convictions' must attain a certain level of 'cogency, seriousness, cohesion and importance'. They must, according to the Court, be worthy of respect in a democratic society, and not incompatible with human dignity: they must not conflict with the fundamental right of the child to education.

The applicants' views relate to a weighty and substantial aspect of human life and behaviour, namely the integrity of the person, the propriety or otherwise of the infliction of corporal punishment and the exclusion of the distress which the risk of such punishment entails. They are views which satisfy each of the criteria listed above: it is this which distinguishes them from opinions that might be held on other methods of discipline or on discipline in general.

The Court held that there had been a failure to respect the parents' philosophical convictions. Moreover, the Court, unlike the Commission, did hold in the case of Jeffrey Cosans that the right to education had been infringed. He could have returned to school, argued the Court, only if his parents had acted against personal convictions which the United Kingdom Government had a duty to protect. He was awarded £3,000 for lost schooling.

It is important to emphasize that in this case the argument was not about the actual use of corporal punishment, but about the threat of its use, and that the United Kingdom Government did not provide sufficient schools without corporal punishment. However the DES in 1982 saw fit to warn local education authorities that the *use* of corporal punishment may amount to inhuman or degrading treatment *in certain circumstances*.[45] This followed the conclusion of a 'friendly settlement' (as attempted in *Campbell and Cosans*) between the United Kingdom Government and the mother of a schoolgirl who was severely caned by her headmistress. The mother was paid £2,200 in compensation and legal costs.[46] However it seems that in this case the degree of the punishment was an important factor.

A consultative document issued by the DES in 1983 stated that the 'Government is obliged by the (European) Court's judgment to change the law in England and Wales as it relates to corporal punishment in schools.'

The proposal in the document is to 'oblige a maintained school to enable a parent to exempt a child from corporal punishment', which includes 'slaps and similar physical chastisement, whether formally or informally administered'. The stated intention is formally to recognize parents' 'philosophical convictions'.[47] However, the proposed legislation may well be overtaken by events. In March 1984 the European Commission on Human Rights ruled as admissible a complaint from an English mother about the punishment of her daughter who was caned on the hand causing blood vessels to be broken and two blood blisters.

The girl brought a civil action for damages for assault in 1981, which a county court dismissed, holding that the corporal punishment complained of was not 'improper, inappropriate or disproportionate'. The European Commission however held the complaint admissible on three grounds: the philosophical objections of the parents, the claim that corporal punishment is inhuman and degrading, and the fact that there was no effective way in which the applicants could remedy their claim in Britain.[48]

This case could well herald a total ban on the use of corporal punishment in schools: the Government's proposed opting-out scheme would in all probability be unlawful.

Space does not permit a detailed analysis of the likely impact of such judgments on the law as it affects the education system of England and Wales and the teachers who work in it. Briefly the problematical areas are:

APPLICABILITY

In its consultative document the DES states: 'The Court's judgment is binding on the United Kingdom.' This may not, however, be the end of the matter. Campbell and Cosans was concerned with children in the Scottish education system, and there are significant differences in the law of Scotland. There the English common law principle that the teacher is in loco parentis does not operate to the same extent: Scottish law derives from the old Roman law from which, significantly, the Continental system also comes. Arguments about the in loco parentis principle were not presented to the European Court although the court did uphold the independent right of the teacher to impose discipline. A further consideration is that under the law a parent is deemed to have chosen the school which his child attends: that being so, the parent does not have the power to place terms or conditions on the child's attendance.

It should be noted that at the time of signing the Convention the United Kingdom made a formal reservation to Article 2. In effect, the principle of Article 2 is affirmed 'only so far as it is compatible with the provision of efficient instruction and training, and the avoidance of unreasonable public expenditure'. The Court, however, held that it did not believe that to exempt certain pupils from corporal punishment would either interfere with efficient instruction and training, or cause unreasonable expenditure.

A major issue also, but beyond the scope of this book, is whether the British Government should accept the European Convention in its entirety, which might mean amending many hundreds of statutes and regulations, or merely have regard to it in matters of interpretation. To do this would, of course, call into question the sovereignty of Parliament, a major constitutional and political issue. However, member states under the Convention do have a 'margin of appreciation'. In another case[49] the Court emphasized: 'The main purpose of the Convention is to lay down certain international standards to be observed by the Contracting States in their relations with persons under their jurisdiction. This does not mean that absolute uniformity is required.'

IN LOCO PARENTIS

As noted elsewhere in this chapter, the teacher is endowed at common law with such of the natural parent's duties and powers as are necessary for him to do his job. By contrast, the teacher under the civil law of Continental Europe is a public official charged only with such duties and rights as are given by his masters. He is employed to teach, but sometimes, for example in parts of France, not even to maintain order in his own classroom.

In *Campbell and Cosans* therefore, by taking the continental view of the teacher's status, the Court has struck at the professional stature of British teachers. In the present authors' view this should lead, with some haste, to the establishment of a General Teaching Council, a compulsory register and a code of conduct as a means of safeguarding teachers' professionalism and standing.

The European Court of Human Rights sat in January 1978 to consider the Commission's report on an application under Article 3 by Mr Anthony Tyrer. Six years previously, when he was 15, the applicant received three strokes of the birch following conviction of assault causing bodily harm.

In Tyrer's case the Commission refused the applicant's leave to withdraw the issue, as it believed general questions were raised which required further examination. The government of the United Kingdom was in a difficult position, as the Isle of Man (where punishment took place) is the only part of the Kingdom where judicial birching continues. There was a strong feeling against abolition among the people of Man, but the Commission did not feel able to find any significant social or cultural differences which were relevant to Article 3. By fourteen votes to one the Commission found birching degrading and, as a friendly settlement could not be reached, the matter was referred to the European Court.

The Court, which consisted of seven judges, announced its findings in April 1978. It was held that the pain inflicted was not sufficient to support a decision that the punishment was inhuman; but, the British judge alone dissenting, the Court found that the punishment was degrading. In the Court's view the humiliation or debasement was greater than what is usual, indeed almost inevitable, in all judicial punishments. Judicial corporal punishment, however, involves the institutionalized infliction of physical violence by one human being on another, and in this case amounted to an assault on his dignity and physical integrity in addition to the mental anguish of anticipating that violence. The administration of the birch to the bare posterior aggravated the degradation, but was not the only, or the determining factor. The matter was made worse by the fact that those carrying out the sentence were total strangers to the complainant.

The Court rejected, unanimously, the submission that local public opinion was sufficient to establish that corporal punishment was necessary to maintain law and order in the

Isle of Man, and the present practice of the great majority of member states of the Council of Europe cast doubt on this need. Even if it were necessary, no member state could employ a punishment contrary to Article 3.

The attitude of the European Court to corporal punishment has therefore remained consistent from *Tyrer* to *Campbell and Cosans*. However, there is considerable difference between judicial corporal punishment and that used in schools in Britain, since they have different bases in law. Nevertheless both cases are bound to lend a good deal of moral force to the anti-corporal punishment lobby, even in advance of the cases currently waiting for judgment at Strasbourg.

PHILOSOPHICAL CONVICTIONS

Much here depends on how elastic the Court's definition of a 'philosophical conviction' is found to be as time goes by and more cases are heard. The judgment may have opened up the way for other parents to take their views to Strasbourg. Distinct possibilities are anti-sex-educationalists, opponents of single-sex or co-education, even of comprehensive schools. The matter of compulsory sex education in Denmark has already been before the Court in 1976, but failed, *inter alia*, because the Danish system of education left open an escape route for parents who objected to compulsory sex education, namely the possibility of sending their children to private schools where there is no similar compulsion and which are heavily subsidized by the State.[50] If a number of these issues do in time achieve the official status of 'philosophical convictions', local education authorities will face insuperable difficulties in making the required provision of schools and head teachers no less in running them.

Finally, the European Court of Human Rights may well have brought about the beginnings of a shift from collective to individual decision-making in education – a trend also noticeable in the sections of the Education Act 1980 relating to parental choice and discussed in chapter I. In both *Tyrer* and *Campbell and Cosans* it was held that it was immaterial whether or not a majority, even a large majority, of the population, approved of the practice in question. This contrasts with the 1967 judgment that comprehensive education (and by implication other large matters of principle) were for the ballot box and not for individual insistence.[51] This seems not to have been seriously taken into account by the present government. The Education (Corporal Punishment) Bill was introduced into Parliament in late 1984 which would allow parents to opt out of corporal punishment on behalf of their children. The Secretary of State, Sir Keith Joseph, told the House that the Government was not proceeding with total abolition of corporal punishment because more teachers and parents supported it than opposed it.

Under the Bill, which it is proposed to bring into force in September 1986, schools would be required to ask parents individually whether they wished to opt out. Those who did not reply would be deemed not to have opted out. A slap would be included in the definition of corporal punishment. The Bill would not apply to public schools, except in the case of pupils on music or ballet or assisted places schemes, i.e. assisted from public funds.

Perhaps even before this Bill becomes law the European Court will rule under Article 3 (see p. 471) that the practice is totally illegal.

References

1. Mansell *v.* Griffin [1908] 1 KB 947; LCT 216.
2. In Hutt *v.* Governors of Haileybury College (1888) 4 TLR 623; LCT 226.
3. Children and Young Persons Act 1933, s. 1(7).
4. Education (School Information) Regulations 1981.
5. See p. 381.
6. Hazell *v.* Jeffs, *The Times*, 11 January 1955.
7. *Daily Telegraph*, 14 July 1979.
8. *Times Educational Supplement*, 24 December 1971.
9. R. *v.* Manchester City Council *ex parte* Fulford, *The Times*, 26 October 1982.
10. Scorgie *v.* Lawrie (1883) 10 R Ct of Sess 610.

11. R. *v.* Hopley (1860) 2 F and F 202; LCT 220.
12. *Daily Telegraph*, 3 July 1964.
13. *Daily Telegraph*, 26 April 1979.
14. *Times Education Supplement*, 6 February 1981.
15. R. *v.* Taylor, *The Times*, 28 December 1983.
16. See p. 21.
17. Cleary *v.* Booth [1893] 1 QB 465; LCT 235.
18. R. *v.* Newport (Salop) Justices *ex parte* Wright [1929] 2 KB 416; LCT 237.
19. Cook *v.* Attock, *Evening Standard*, 13 January 1955.
20. Hutt *v.* Governors of Haileybury College (1888) 4 TLR 623; LCT 226.
21. Fitzgerald *v.* Northcote (1865) 4 F and F 656; LCT 148.
22. Hutt *v.* Governors of Haileybury College (1888) 4 TLR 623; LCT 226.
23. In R. *v.* Hopley (1860) 2 F and F 202; LCT 220.
24. R. *v.* Dennis, *The Times*, 19 November 1954.
25. Gardner *v.* Bygrave (1889) 53 JP 743; LCT 224.
26. The Approved School Rules 1933, nos 35 and 36.
27. In Fitzgerald *v.* Northcote (1865) 4 F & F 656; LCT 148.
28. Education Act 1944, s. 1.
29. Education Act 1944, s. 8.
30. Education Act 1981, s. 2.
31. *Times Educational Supplement*, 13 March 1981.
32. Provision of Milk and Meals Regulations 1969 (as amended).
33. Provision of Milk and Meals Regulations 1969. Reg. 6(2).
34. 'Better Schools' Cmnd 9469 HMSO, 1985.
35. Theft Act 1968, s. 1.
36. See Fitzgerald *v.* Northcote. p. 463.
37. Gibson *v.* Wales, *The Times*, 2 November 1982.
38. Daly *v.* Buckinghamshire County Council, Marchant and Buckland, *Daily Telegraph*, 22 December 1964, and *Evening News*, 5 January 1965.
39. R. *v.* Higgitt, *The Times*, 17 March 1972.
40. *Daily Mail*, 16 March 1972.
41. *Daily Telegraph*, 8 and 22 August 1972.
42. *Education*, 14 December 1973.
43. See, for example, R. *v.* Manchester City Council *ex parte* Fulford, p. 470.
44. Campbell and Cosans *v.* UK (1976). Applications nos 7511/76 and 7743/76.

45. *The Times*, 6 March 1982.
46. Mrs X *v*. United Kingdom (1982). Application no. 7907/77.
47. DES, *Corporal Punishment in Schools: A Consultative Document*, 28 July 1983.
48. Mrs X and Ms X *v*. UK (1981). Application no. 9471/81.
49. *Sunday Times v*. UK Series A, no. 30, European Court of Human Rights.
50. Kjeldsen, Busk Madsen and Pedersen *v*. Kingdom of Denmark (1976).
51. Wood and others *v*. Ealing London Borough Council (1967) 65 LGR 282; 3 All ER 514; LCT 143, 358.

XVI
School journeys and educational visits

1 General

Schools planning journeys have three basic methods of organization available to them. One is to make use of one of the commercial travel agents who specialize in school journey work. Many of these undertake the full responsibility of organizing travel, hotels, visits, and other necessary details. If a school intends to plan a journey in this way it must, of course, accept the necessity of verifying the experience and quality of the organizers in this field. Those who are members of the Association of British Travel Agents are governed by that Association's code of conduct.

The second possibility is to use the services of one of the reputable voluntary bodies established for the promotion of school journeys. The School Journey Association of London was one of the earliest, and organizes a large number of visits to centres at home and overseas. Some may find the international services of the Youth Hostels Association more appropriate to their needs; and there are specialist organizations dealing with working holidays abroad, vacation study, cultural holidays and other activities.

Thirdly, a school may decide to 'go it alone', a course not

recommended unless the party leader is experienced in school journey organization, with particular reference to the kind of visit planned. Schools who decide to follow this practice may still obtain advice from the School Journey Association of London, if they are in membership, and this country has the only national organization in the world established to foster overseas journeys: the Central Bureau for Educational Visits and Exchanges, which was set up by HM Government in 1948 and is financed entirely from public funds. The Bureau has linked more than 2,500 schools in this country with counterparts in Europe, and works with more than ninety countries throughout the world. The Bureau publishes a comprehensive list of reputable agencies working in the school travel field.

Teachers undertaking responsibility for educational visits and school journeys are responsible for the pupils in their care throughout the whole period; in the case of a journey for twenty-four hours a day and seven days a week. It is therefore essential to have an adequate staff competent to deal with any emergencies which may arise. If there are both boys and girls in the party, the staff should also be mixed. To attempt a visit or journey with insufficient teachers is the most ardent way to court disaster.

2 Educational visits

All local education authorities have regulations dealing with educational visits, and these should be thoroughly understood and observed by any teacher undertaking such a visit. It is particularly important to observe any requirements as to the pupil–teacher ratio. Some years ago a headmistress organized a visit which took place during the spring half-term holiday. Not wishing to spoil the holiday of any of her colleagues, she took the twenty-one pupils herself; the authority's regulations permitted a maximum of twenty pupils to one teacher. On the way a boy was knocked down by a car which failed to stop at a zebra crossing. Fortunately the lad was not seriously hurt; but the headmistress, in the kindness of her heart, had laid herself open to discipline by her authority. Had the accident been more serious, she could have been in grave difficulties.

The responsibility of a teacher for the welfare of his pupils is not lessened by the fact that he has undertaken the duty voluntarily whether he is on, or away from, the school precincts. Neither is such liability affected by the end of the normal school hours. In all cases where he has accepted the care of children, he must take reasonable precautions for their safety.

The East Ham Corporation was sued in 1926 following an incident at the British Empire Exhibition at Wembley. During the dinner-hour, the master in charge of a school party gave the boys permission to amuse themselves for a while. One boy caught his foot between the platform and the train on the Never-Stop Railway, and was so badly injured that he spent nineteen weeks in hospital. Despite a contention that a reasonable father would have allowed a 14-year-old boy to go on the railway, the jury found that negligence had been proved and awarded damages against the Corporation.

In cases where a teacher voluntarily takes charge of children out of school hours in an *unofficial* capacity, i.e. an activity which is not organized by the school, it should be made clear by the head to the parents in advance that such an arrangement is purely between themselves and the teacher as an individual. In such cases the school authorities can accept no responsibility. Despite the good intentions which lie behind such unofficial activities, they are probably best avoided altogether. In any case, many such unofficial activities can with a little thought be made official and the activity given the full backing of the local education authority.

Teachers taking parties of children to concerts, sports meetings and similar events where there are large gatherings of children from many schools should be especially watchful of their charges. On such occasions there is normally a corps of experienced stewards who are concerned with the general oversight and marshalling of parties, but the discipline of each group remains the responsibility of the teachers escorting it. Quite apart from the fact that it creates a thoroughly bad impression if teachers settle down to enjoy themselves and allow their pupils to do as they please, it should be remembered that with large crowds there is always the risk that small children may be lost and, furthermore, in the event of a mischance, panic spreads rapidly. Rigid supervision is especially necessary on staircases.

General guidance on educational visits has been given by the DES in a booklet, *Safety in Outdoor Pursuits*. The booklet is divided into sections dealing with safety on land, afloat and in the air. It also contains general guidance on arranging large school trips. A section on 'Safety at school: general advice', deals with travel abroad. The booklet says that children should be warned about the dangers of rabies, which can result from bites or the saliva of dogs and cats, and also of the possibility of prosecution if animals are brought into this country without authority. Children should also be warned against bringing fireworks home from abroad as these often do not satisfy United Kingdom requirements and can be dangerous.

An Administrative Memorandum, *Liability for Pupils and Students Visiting Industry*,[1] deals with liability arising from accidents or damage to property taking place during visits to industrial firms. Local education authorities are advised to take out appropriate insurance to cover this kind of risk. It is also recommended that parental consent should be obtained in the case of minors, though this might not be necessary on every occasion unless special risks are involved. If a firm asks for indemnity against accidents or damage caused by visitors not in their employment, this may be given provided it does not relieve the firm of liability arising from its own negligence or that of its employees. Section 4 of the Health and Safety at Work etc. Act 1974 also imposes a duty on those in charge of industrial premises to look to the safety not only of employees but also of others on the premises.

Visits falling within the scope of the Education (Work Experience) Act 1973 have been dealt with in chapter X.

Schools, particularly those in the south-east of England, sometimes arrange day visits to the accessible parts of the Continent, usually Calais or Boulogne. The general provisions relating to school journeys must be observed, as must the appropriate parts of the requirements relating to overseas school journeys. Customs concessions are now available even for travellers who have been out of the country for less than twenty-four hours. It is also important to ensure rigid compliance with the conditions set out in the travel documents. On one occasion a school visited Calais on a day excursion which allowed three and a half hours between the time of landing and the time of return sailing: the ticket specified that passengers should be at the quay an hour before sailing time. Feeling that the time ashore was somewhat inadequate, the party arrived on the quay a quarter of an hour before the ship was due to leave, only to find that it had already sailed. In order to get the party home at a reasonable time the staff had to book a crossing with another line but, as the conditions had been broken, British Rail refused a refund on the unused return tickets.

3 Standard of care

On both educational visits and school journeys, the ordinary standard of care *in loco parentis* applies. Teachers may, however, be concerned about accidents arising as a result of defective premises or equipment which are outside their control. In 1961 a pupil at an approved school took part in a confidence course established by the Outward Bound organization at Reigate. Whilst using an aerial ropeway, the wire cable snapped, and he fell to the ground. He was disabled until his death (which was not connected with the accident) five years later. The cable was found to be rusted internally, but the defect could not have been discovered without dismantling. The warden who, without the knowledge of the owner of the site or the school, was no longer employed by the Croydon Outward Bound Group, was ordered to pay damages for failure in his duty under the Occupiers Liability Act 1957 and at common law. The owner and the school were dismissed from the suit.

Mr Justice Nield said: 'Where a school must take their pupils to other premises, they discharge their duty of care if they know the premises and if the premises are apparently safe, and if they know that the premises are staffed by competent and careful persons. They further discharge their duty if they permit their pupils there to use equipment which is apparently safe, and is under the control of competent and careful persons who supervise the use of such equipment. They do not in such circumstances have an obligation themselves to make an inspection.'[2]

4 Parental permission

Although, as has already been said, it is not essential to have parental permission for every short educational visit not involving special risk, many teachers feel it advisable. If, on a perfectly legitimate educational visit, an accident happens to a child whose parent believed him to be safely on the school premises the situation can, to say the least, be embarrassing. If children are undertaking a series of visits in connection with a particular course, a general permission given at the beginning would be sufficient. Everything depends on the nature of the visit, and the age and capability of the pupils.

It is essential, and many authorities have a regulation to this effect, to obtain permission in writing before taking children on a school journey. In the case of overseas school journeys the Passport Office may require to see the written parental permissions.

When taking children abroad it is desirable, also, to obtain the parent's consent to any necessary medical treatment. The special circumstances which arise in the case of Christian Scientists and Jehovah's Witnesses are dealt with later in this chapter. Consent is essential in the case of a pupil known, for example, to have a grumbling appendix. The party leader should compile a list of emergency contact addresses, with telephone numbers if possible. It is sometimes practicable to make arrangements with the school caretaker to pass on urgent messages, and the police are always willing to assist in such circumstances. As a matter of good personal relationships it should be explained to the parent that the teacher is *in loco parentis* and must be free in a pupil's interest to take such decisions as a prudent parent would take in connection with his own child. It is also wise to say that the natural parent's consent will be obtained if possible, but that, in a sudden emergency there may be insufficient time to do so. A suitable form of words to be added to the parental consent would be:

> I authorize the leader of the party, or any other member of the school staff who may be present, to consent to such medical treatment (including inoculations, blood transfusion or surgery) which in the opinion of a qualified medical practitioner may be necessary during the course of the journey.

A pupil who has attained the age of 16 may himself give consent to medical treatment (see 'Age of majority').

A child who is the subject of a court order may not be taken out of the country without permission of the court. This applies to school journeys, and if it is proposed to include any such pupil in a party, it is necessary to make an application to the court in good time.

5   Discipline on school visits

As has already been noted, teachers in charge of school parties are *in loco parentis* and therefore have the usual delegated authority over their charges.

On overseas visits it is always well to explain to parents in advance what the policy will be on potentially contentious issues such as smoking, consumption of alcohol and times of going to bed. Although the alcohol, drugs and smoking laws may be different in many countries to be visited, the authority of the teacher in charge remains. Although teachers will not wish to spoil an enjoyable trip by over-rigorous disciplinary procedures, the fact that a trip to, say, Austria is seen essentially by all as a holiday rather than an exclusively educational visit does not require those in charge to permit standards of behaviour which would not be tolerated in the United Kingdom.

In 1983 the Ombudsman dealt with a complaint from the

parents of three boys who were sent home after repeated misbehaviour during a school trip to Belgium. They had been generally beyond control, smoking, drinking and abusive. Despite reprimands from the staff, they had so abused the hotel manager and his reasonable requests that the manager would not permit them to remain. The boys were put in the charge of a purser on the cross-channel ferry: in Dover the harbour police escorted them ashore.

While not condoning their sons' behaviour, the parents raised questions about the staff—student ratio on the visit. They wanted to know why the teacher in charge had sent one boy home when it was known that his parents were on holiday, and argued that contact should have been made with all parents before the boys were despatched. The headmaster of the school spent 'many hours' explaining matters to the parents: they remained dissatisfied however and complained to the Ombuds-man.

The Ombudsman found it 'regrettable' that the parents were somewhat hostile towards the headmaster who had shown a proper concern: 'I am satisfied that he treated the parents' concern seriously.' The Ombudsman felt that it would have been better if Avon Council had provided full written answers to the parents' questions, but the Council's failure to do so did not amount to maladministration.[3]

6   Letters of indemnity

For many years it has been the common practice of schools taking children away to ask their parents to sign a form indemnifying those concerned with the organization of the journey against all claims arising through accident, illness or any other cause. As was said in earlier editions of this book, such letters could not prevent a parent from issuing a writ if he believed that there had been negligence.

It seems certain that such indemnities are void by virtue of the provisions of the Unfair Contract Terms Act 1977. The Act specifically states that 'a person cannot by reference to any contract term or to a notice given to persons generally or to particular persons exclude or restrict his liability for negligence except insofar as the term or notice satisfies the requirement of reasonableness. Where a contract term or notice purports to exclude or restrict liability for negligence a person's agreement to, or awareness of, it is not of itself to be taken as indicating his voluntary acceptance of any risk.'[4] Liability for negligence causing personal injury is wholly unavoidable.

The real protection is insurance, and no teacher should consider taking a school journey party away without adequate third party cover. Some insurance companies specialize in this particular cover, and can give sound advice on the subject. It is not so essential to arrange for personal accident insurance for the children. If this is not to be covered, it is worthwhile mentioning this to the parents, and offering to put them in touch with the company which is insuring the journey.

7   School journeys

Whatever form school journeys take, whether they be field study weeks, travel experience, archaeological expeditions, or simply holidays, there are certain basic principles which apply to them all.

The duty of care *in loco parentis* has already been mentioned, and the regulations of the local education authority on staffing, as on all other matters, must be rigidly followed. In order that a due succession of qualified leaders may be retained in a school, it is valuable practice to give subordinate leadership experience to a number of younger members of the staff. The leader, however, must have some experience, and it is important to remember that the standard of care imposed is that of a reasonably careful parent. The standard of conduct which should be exacted is similar and, although these standards may be modified over the years, it must be remembered that the great majority of parents do not expect their children to be encouraged to develop behaviour patterns which are lower than those of their homes merely because they appeal to a teacher who may not be much older than the pupils, and who has no personal experience of bringing up children in a family.

Relationships between pupils and staff are usually more relaxed than they are in school, and it is good that they should be so, but the journey location is essentially an extra-mural extension of the school, and the rules of the school may still be applied. Of course, in any country, aliens are subject to the domestic law of their hosts.

The numerical adequacy of the school journey staff is also important. The benefit and enjoyment of the journey may well be lost if the programme has to be seriously reduced because staff sickness has reduced the ratio below the permitted limit for any particular activity. It is always useful to have a reserve member of the staff standing by, willing to travel at short notice in the event of serious illness which reduces the school journey staff to a level which would vitiate the success of the journey.

Most countries now have a national tourist office in London, and the staffs of these bureaux are always willing to give considerable help in the planning of overseas visits. Further assistance can be obtained by joining one of the cultural exchange organizations which exist, such as the Anglo-Austrian Society.[5]

In planning overseas journeys it is essential to take the length and means of travel into account in relation to the age of the children and the facilities available on the way. During the past decade large numbers of primary schools have extended their activities to the Continent. Setting on one side the problem that, if their experience is widened too rapidly, these children may, when they reach their secondary schools, sit down like Alexander and weep because there are no more worlds to conquer, there is a problem of stress. As improved means of transport have made the Continent more accessible, it would be churlish to suggest that primary schools should not undertake overseas travel. It would seem wiser, however, to restrict their activities to those parts of Europe nearest to the British Isles, so that the overland journey following the crossing is reasonably short. The author remembers seeing an exhausted party of 9-year-olds from Scotland sleeping on the platform at Basel. They were on their way to Rome, no couchettes had been arranged, their only food consisted of the sandwiches they had brought with them, they still had some hundreds of miles to go and, as they waited for their connecting train, they were utterly exhausted. This hardly seems the standard of care of a prudent parent, and the first two days after arriving at their destination must have been wasted whilst they recovered from travel fatigue.

Couchettes are well worth the extra cost for any journey involving all-night train travel on the Continent, and arrangements for adequate meals should be made in advance.

It is not good practice for staff to carry travel-sickness pills for indiscriminate distribution, as some children suffer from side-effects as a result of taking such drugs. At least one authority forbids teaching staff to dispense these unless they have been obtained by a parent on the advice of the family doctor. In making arrangements with parents, it is wise to ask whether there are any medical points which should be watched so far as individual children are concerned. Parents should be encouraged to hand over any drugs, together with the appropriate instructions, to the party leader to ensure that they are taken at the correct intervals without risk either of under- or over-dosage.

If an all-night train journey is involved, it is essential to know if there are any sleep-walkers in the party, otherwise there is a risk of such a pupil walking on to the track instead of finding the toilet door. In any case the staff should arrange for a supervision rota by which a sufficient number of teachers is on duty at all times during the night to deal with any emergency.

8   Booking conditions

Schools who book holidays through travel agents should first make themselves aware of the agent's booking conditions, and ensure that parents are notified of any important conditions. In particular, if a travel agent makes it a condition that deposits are not returnable in the event of cancellation and a school does not make this clear to parents before the deposit is paid, there is the strong possibility that a parent might be able to reclaim the deposit from the school if he has to cancel.

9   ABTA Code of Conduct

The Association of British Travel Agents[6] together with its specialist sub-group the School and Group Travel Association (SAGTA) provides substantial protection for customers against the effects of the financial collapse of any member agent. This protection does however not extend to holidays taken wholly within the United Kingdom.

The SAGTA Code of Conduct is available free of charge. The major obligations it imposes on member travel agents are:

Alterations to booked journeys: schools must be informed immediately and an offer made to refund money paid promptly.
Surcharges: schools must be given information about the sort of surcharges which might be made. Surcharges may be imposed only for reasons beyond the agent's control.
Cancellation: the conditions affecting cancellation should be made clear at the time of booking. When the balance of the cost of the trip has been paid, the agent may cancel only for reasons beyond his control. If no agreement about a substitute trip can be reached, there must be a speedy refund of money paid. In such a case the agent may deduct reasonable costs already incurred.

10   Complaints about holidays

ABTA provides a free conciliation service where schools complain about its members. SAGTA will also convene a special panel to investigate disputes. Another possibility is to use the independent arbitration scheme for the travel industry.

A third possibility is to take action through the courts of law. An interesting development here in recent years has been the willingness of the courts to award compensation for disappointment and trauma suffered as the result of a bad holiday. In a 1983 case,[7] a school had booked and paid for a seven-day, two-centre holiday for a school party comprising 43 pupils and five teachers. Each pupil paid £98. In Paris the food provided was uninteresting and insufficient in quantity. The coach which was to be available for evening use was not available one evening and could only be used for a short time on the other. At the second centre the party could not stay at the hotel which they had booked. The substitute was very cold, dirty and had inadequate heating. The showers and toilets were so dirty that the female teachers had to clean and disinfect them before they could be used. The bedrooms were damp and musty with peeling paper and mould on the walls. The beds and bedding were so damp that the party slept, fully clothed, on the beds, not in them. The food was served almost cold, was insufficient to satisfy the appetites of teenage children and was of poor quality. The pupils therefore bought food elsewhere. The party leader spent much time phoning the tour company's representatives and complaining to the hotel proprietor, who told them they should leave if they did not like it.

The judge at Neath and Port Talbot County Court awarded damages to the children 'for diminution in value and loss of enjoyment', to the teachers for 'extra worry and responsibility', and to the party leader for 'extra worry, responsibility, work and unpleasantness in dealing with complaints'.

Schools may not go both to arbitration and the courts. Professional associations are usually willing to advise on the better course to take in each case.

11   VAT on official school visits

The application of Value Added Tax to school journeys is a complex matter, largely because the term 'educational' is in a very real sense infinitely elastic in meaning. Local education authorities have a wide and flexible discretion in their work: HM Customs and Excise on the other hand must, under the Finance Act 1972, produce clear, workaday definitions. Local VAT offices are usually very willing to give helpful advice to schools.

The current general position is that school visits are not liable to VAT if:

(i) they are provided without charge to the pupils, or where the cost is subsidized by the local education authority from public funds. It is important that the subsidy comes from the local authority: other sources (for example the school fund or a grant from a PTA) do not carry the same exemption.

(ii) despite the fact that the pupils pay the full cost, the following conditions are satisfied:

    (a) the visit must be part of the school's general educational curriculum. If sporting or recreational activities are involved, the Customs and Excise Department may seek evidence that the visit is in fact part of the general educational curriculum.

    (b) the visit should involve preparatory work in school time and follow-up work similarly.

    (c) the pupils taking part in the visit must be supervised by suitably qualified persons.

Difficulties sometimes arise in connection with visits to commercially run holiday camps. HM Customs and Excise must be satisfied that *most* of the activities during the stay satisfy the conditions outlined above. It is not sufficient merely to rely on the description 'educational week' or something similar.

12   Mountaineering

In 1971–2 three fatal accidents overtook school parties, one in the Cairngorms, one in Snowdonia and one in the Lake District. After the Cairngorms incident, in which five children died, the inquest returned a verdict that the children died of cold and exposure, but ascribed no blame. The jury made, however, a number of recommendations:

(a) more care should be exercised in fitness and training;

(b) parents should be more fully informed about, and asked to acknowledge, such activities;

(c) qualified teachers should accompany the parties and the actual expeditions should be led by qualified and long-experienced instructors;

(d) certain areas should be designated as suitable for summer or winter expeditions by children;

(e) the removal, or otherwise, of high-level bothies should be left to experts;

(f) mountain rescue work should be furthered, financially and otherwise;

(g) the education authority should maintain closer liaison with parents in the event of disaster.

Following these tragedies, local education authorities reviewed their regulations, and teachers who are considering such activities should observe the requirements of their own authority.

A summary of the regulations of the ILEA for hill walking and mountaineering provides a general guide. By reason of altitude, terrain, remoteness and climate, the Authority has defined the following areas as subject to these rules:

Dartmoor	Peak District
Exmoor	Pennines
Bodmin Moor	North Yorkshire Moors
Black Mountains	Lake District
Brecon Beacons	Cheviots
Central Welsh Mountains	Southern Uplands
Snowdonia	Highlands and Islands

In these areas any departure from metalled roads is defined as hill walking, and only instructors holding the Mountain Leadership Certificate and approved by the ILEA may lead expeditions involving these activities. Leaders who have passed the introductory course may act under the general supervision of a MLC leader. Parties using centres run by the Field Studies Council are exempt if the Warden is satisfied that the programme conforms to his safety precautions. The same conditions apply to areas of similar potential hazard outside the United Kingdom.

There must be at least one teacher for every eight pupils; and at least two teachers (normally one at the front and one at the rear) must accompany all expeditions into high or remote areas.

Equipment must be of the kind approved by the Authority. All parties walking or camping in mountains must take 120 feet of no. 13 rope with them, and all pupils must wear suitably soled boots and suitable protective clothing which must be examined by a teacher before setting out. All pupils must carry a whistle, spare clothing, food for an emergency and a polythene bag measuring 8 by 4 feet. At least two members of the party must each carry a torch, map, compass, first-aid kit, knife and watch.

All pupils must be instructed in basic emergency procedures and signals. A reliable local weather forecast should be obtained before setting out on any expedition.

13   Minibuses

Many schools now have their own minibuses or coaches. It is obviously important that such vehicles are kept in a serviceable condition and comply with all the regulations, whether those of HM Government or the local education authority. Local education authorities will designate a responsible individual in each school with a minibus, and it is vital that that individual is aware of the full extent of his responsibilities, particularly where routine checks before journeys are concerned.

Adequate comprehensive insurance must be arranged, including injury or damage to other road users and their vehicles as a result of the actions of passengers.

If fares are charged, and the vehicle is constructed or adapted to carry more than sixteen persons in addition to the driver, it becomes a public service vehicle. This means that it must comply with the more stringent requirements relating to such vehicles, and the driver must have a public service vehicle licence. These requirements apply whether the passengers are charged directly or indirectly for their travel. Local education authorities have drawn up rules or memoranda of guidance for schools which have their own vehicles, and any school planning to purchase one should study these carefully. There are many snags, some of which do not appear until misfortune strikes unless one has taken the trouble to be forewarned.

The Minibus Act 1977, subject to certain conditions, exempts vehicles seating from eight to sixteen passengers, exclusive of the driver, from the requirements relating to public service vehicles, if such vehicles belong to an educational, religious, or social welfare organization, or to some other body providing activities for the good of the community. To qualify for a permit under the Act, an organization must be non-profit making, although a permitted vehicle may be used in the course of fund-raising.

The Act enables the Secretary of State for Transport to make regulations authorizing the issue of permits by designated bodies to defined organizations, or to individuals representing those organizations. Local authorities are designated for this purpose, and will control the permits issued to schools: the other designated bodies are all national organizations of one kind or another. A permit specifies the body or individual to whom it is granted, identifies the vehicle in question, and sets out the conditions under which it may be used. A disc, supplied with the permit, must be displayed on the vehicle. There is a fee, to which the designated body may add a further charge for administration.

The effect of the permit is that the minibus may be used without a public service vehicle licence, and driven by a person who does not hold a PSV licence, even though passengers are being charged directly or indirectly for riding in it. The vehicle may not be used for the carriage of the public at large, and the classes of passengers who may be carried are set out in the permit. For schools and colleges these will normally be pupils or students, staff attendants and members of parent–teacher associations. A separate permit must be obtained for each vehicle, and in cases where more than one eligible body uses the minibus a separate permit must be valid for each body. A permit is not transferable, even to a temporary replacement vehicle. In the case of schools the permit is normally granted to the head teacher. There is no specified period of validity.

Vehicles must not be used under permit for the transport of pupils between the school and their homes without the permission of the local education authority and the traffic commissioners.

An applicant for a permit must undertake to maintain the vehicle in a fit and serviceable condition at all times, to arrange regular preventive maintenance inspections, to make arrangements for drivers to report any defects of which they are aware, to remedy any defect promptly, to insure the vehicle for the purposes for which it is to be used, and to ensure that all drivers are experienced, hold a full licence and are over 21. The requirement as to the qualifications of the driver applies whether or not passengers are being carried. Needless to say, a current MOT test certificate must be held in respect of vehicles more than three years old.

Conditions of fitness regulations incorporate the safety requirements relating to public service vehicles. Regulations in force are concerned with the marking, position and operation of emergency exits, signs showing the maximum number of passengers which may be carried, and the provision of fire extinguishers and first aid equipment.

In addition to the usual documents, every permitted vehicle must carry:

(a) a driver's notice specifying the conditions under which the permit is valid, fixed inside the vehicle where the driver can read it;

(b) the disc which must be fixed inside the vehicle in such a position that it can be read from the outside.

The positioning of these documents must not, of course, interfere with the driver's control of the vehicle.

Any breach of the conditions causes the permit to be entirely ineffective. It may also lead to prosecution under the Road Traffic Act 1960 for causing or permitting the vehicle to be used without a PSV licence; the driver may also be prosecuted for not holding a PSV licence. Presumably, although the regulations do not mention it, the permit may be revoked under section 2(3) of the Act.

There is no change in the law relating to vehicles for fewer than eight passengers (to which PSV requirements have never applied) or those constructed or adapted to carry more than sixteen (which still require PSV licences if passengers are carried and make a contribution towards the cost of the journey).

Bearing in mind the occasionally boisterous behaviour of children in groups, it is a wise precaution to fit safety belts to all seats in minibuses.

14   EEC regulations

One of the advantages of joining the EEC is that the insurance 'green card' is no longer necessary for travel within the Common Market by cars registered in a member state. Without a 'green card', however, only the minimum insurance cover required by the law of the countries visited is provided and there may be difficulties over what is called 'non-insured loss'. One of the authors was involved in an incident in Germany where the British driver was at fault, and had no 'green card'. The German driver, whose car was under repair for several weeks, claimed the cost of a hire car for that period. He was entitled to this under his German policy. The British insurance company, however, claimed that this was more than was implied by 'minimum cover' and passed the bill directly to be paid by the British driver. The motoring associations will give advice on this matter: it seems, however, a wise precaution to take a 'green card'.

If a vehicle is equipped to carry ten or more persons, including the driver, special requirements apply. This is so also for journeys to Eire.

Under EEC Regulation No. 117/66, school journeys taken in a minibus or coach owned by the school would normally be classified as 'occasional closed door tours', i.e. services where the vehicle makes a round trip back to its starting point, carrying the same group of passengers throughout. The destination of such a tour is regarded as the member state where the point of departure lies: for a school journey, the destination will be the school!

The control document for these journeys is a book of fifty waybills in duplicate, valid for five years in respect of any vehicle operated by the person to whom the book is issued. A duplicate waybill must be completed by the person responsible for the tour before its commencement, and the top copy must be carried on the vehicle throughout the journey. This exempts the vehicle from domestic licensing in member states, and must be produced on demand. The duplicate remains in the book. The penalty for non-compliance is, in this country, a fine.

Provided the vehicle is registered in a member state, and its destination is a state within the Common Market, the waybill is valid for crossing Austria, Norway, Portugal, Spain, Sweden, Switzerland, Turkey and Yugoslavia. It should be observed, however, that if the vehicle takes a party to a country outside the EEC and returns empty, the destination is not held to be within the Common Market and advice should be sought from the school's Traffic Area Office. Books of waybills can be obtained free of charge from the Traffic Area Office or, in Northern Ireland, from the Ministry of Development.

On completion of the journey the top copy of the waybill must be sent to the Department of the Environment or, in Northern Ireland, to the Ministry of Development. Failure to do so can entail a fine. The duplicate waybills must be retained in the book throughout the period of its validity.

EEC Regulation No. 543/69 deals with the drivers of vehicles equipped to carry ten or more persons, including the driver. It applies to international journeys within the EEC, including those to Eire and within the United Kingdom. On such a journey the driver must be at least 21 years of age, hold a valid British driving licence, and have had at least one year's driving experience. Before setting out the driver must send the appropriate form and his driving licence to a Traffic Area Office to obtain a certificate of age and experience. This is not needed by holders of a public service vehicle or heavy goods vehicle driver's licence. The requirements apply to that part of an international journey which lies within the country of origin, and contravention will lead to prosecution. For offences within the United Kingdom the maximum fine is £75 together with endorsement and possible disqualification.

The driver must carry an individual control book in which to enter his driving record during the journey. Except in cases of emergency, provided that road safety is not endangered and to the extent which it is necessary to reach a suitable stopping place at the end of the journey and ensure the safety of the passengers or vehicle, driving hours are rigidly controlled. A driver must not drive for more than eight hours a day (without an extension of one hour twice in any period of seven consecutive days), nor for more than forty-eight hours in any consecutive period of seven days, subject to a maximum of ninety-two hours in a fortnight. He may not drive for more than four hours without a break of at least half an hour (or two breaks of twenty minutes, or three breaks of fifteen minutes). At any moment he must have had a break of at least ten consecutive hours during the preceding twenty-four hours. Alternatively he may take eleven hours, reducible twice a week to nine under certain conditions. The daily rest period must normally be taken outside the vehicle unless there is a bunk and the vehicle is stationary. He must have a period of twenty-nine consecutive hours' rest during each period of seven days and this must be immediately preceded or followed by a daily rest period.

Between 1 April and 30 September the weekly rest period may be replaced by one of at least sixty consecutive hours in any consecutive fourteen days. This must be immediately preceded or followed by a daily rest period. The rest period of twenty-nine hours may be reduced to twenty-four, provided the loss is made up during the same week.

If there are two drivers there must have been for each a break of ten consecutive hours during the preceding twenty-seven if there is no bunk, or eight hours during the preceding thirty if there is a bunk.

15   Tachographs

In all EEC countries and Austria, Czechoslovakia, German Democratic Republic, Norway, Soviet Union, Sweden and Yugoslavia, a tachograph must be fitted to minibuses with 10 or more seats. In Great Britain one must be fitted to minibuses with 16 or more seats.

It is important to remember that drivers' hours are calculated from the start of the journey i.e. the home town or school, and not merely from the point of arrival in mainland Europe.[8]

A valid United Kingdom driving licence is sufficient for most countries in western Europe. Teachers planning journeys which involve driving in more exotic countries should ascertain whether an international driving permit is required. The permit costs £1, and is valid for a year in every country except that in which it is issued. International driving permits may be obtained from the Automobile Association.[9] A passport-type photograph must be enclosed with the application.

16   Lorries

To save expense, school parties are sometimes transported by lorries. No charge may be made by the owner of the lorry for this service but he may, if his vehicle is properly licensed and insured, charge for the carriage of luggage and equipment. The lorry must be correctly insured for the purpose for which it is used, and the tax paid must be adequate for the conveyance of the children. *The owner is not, however, obliged to insure against accidents to passengers travelling free of charge* and, if he does not have adequate cover, teachers are strongly advised to take out a policy in respect of such risks.

17   Bathing and boating

When bathing or boating form part of the activities of a school excursion, it is desirable to seek — and follow — local advice regarding currents, tides and general safety. In bathing it is a good rule to have two strong swimmers as pickets. The pickets should be changed and ready for any emergency, but they should not enter the water, unless an emergency arises, until all the other bathers have left. This is the rule of the Scout movement and is based on long experience. In the case of school Scout camps it must be observed.

It is also useful to obtain specific permission for swimming from parents of each child. Those with any defect which may be aggravated by bathing should in no circumstances be allowed to enter the water.

In a recent tragic accident, two children during a properly organized swimming class collided head-on in the water. One was stunned and sank to the bottom, unnoticed until it was too late. The teachers were in the water with the pupils giving assistance when the accident happened. The swimming rules of the local education authority now require there to be at all times an adult observer, either a colleague or a teacher, in a position to be able to survey the whole pool.

18   The law of waterways

Canoeing and boating are becoming increasingly popular with school parties, and it is necessary, if trespass is to be avoided, to know something of the law of waterways.

Tidal waters are public highways and their ownership is vested in the Crown. They may be used freely by anyone who does not interfere with the similar rights of others.

Non-tidal waters are vested in the owners of the adjacent land and there is no right of passage across them unless, in specific cases, it has been granted by Act of Parliament or has become customary through immemorial use. Such a right is similar to the usage of a public footpath across a field and is primarily for passage from one place to another; it confers no right to recreation, to fishing or to landing on the banks. Where no right of way exists, entry to non-tidal waters is trespass.

Canals are the property of the authority to which they belong, and passage along them may be granted on payment of the appropriate dues, subject to observance of the regulations.

19   Treasure trove

The development of field studies, sometimes with active participation in archaeological excavation, makes it possible that from time to time school parties may discover hoards of valuable items. In general, gold or silver, whether in plate, coin or bullion, which has been hidden in the ground or a building, and of which the owner cannot reasonably be traced, is regarded as treasure trove and is the property of the Crown.

It is important, therefore, that any such finds should be reported to the police, as HM Coroner has a duty to hold an inquest to determine whether the find is treasure trove. He may find that the goods have been abandoned by their owner, in which case they belong to anyone who cares to claim them; they may have been lost, in which case it would be theft not to return them to their rightful owner. Treasure openly buried, like the Sutton Hoo burial hoard, belongs to the owner of the ground.

The test applied by the coroner is whether, so far as can be discovered, the treasure was hidden by its owner with the intention of recovering it at some future time. It is this category which is treasure trove and, if its find is reported immediately to the police, the finder is allowed its full market value. Concealment is an offence. In Scotland all finds are treasure trove, and the intention of the owner to recover his property does not have to be proved.

Only gold and silver are treasure trove.[10] An urn full of third-century Roman coins discovered in Lincolnshire in 1975 was held to contain insufficient silver to be regarded as treasure trove. The coins were obviously intended at the time of minting to look like silver and indeed contained some silver mixed with an alloy. Without laying down a precise figure the court held that the coins did not contain sufficient silver to justify the claim of treasure trove.

20   Ancient monuments

Schools taking part in field studies or archaeological excavations should be aware that the Ancient Monuments and Archaeological Areas Act 1979 reaffirms from earlier legislation the authority of the Department of the Environment to 'schedule', and thereby to protect, any monument which, in the view of the Secretary of State is of public interest for historical, archaeological or other reasons. The Secretary of State may also under the Act designate 'areas of archaeological importance'. There are penalties for damaging or destroying any protected monument.[11]

It should be noted that the use of a metal detector on the site of a scheduled monument requires written permission in advance from the Department of the Environment.

The schedule includes not only a large variety of buildings and structures, but also barrows, forts, earthworks and other remains from ancient times. No scheduled monument may be destroyed, altered, or added to without the Department's consent. Unauthorized excavation is also forbidden. To deface an ancient monument renders the offender liable to a fine or imprisonment, together with compensation for the damage.

Schools undertaking work in this field should enlist the help of the local archaeological society who will always support serious research. Advice can also be obtained from the Chief Inspector of Ancient Monuments at the Department of the Environment.

21   Medical requirements

Many local education authorities require that all pupils should undergo a medical examination by a medical officer whose services are made available to the authority by the Secretary of State for Health and Social Services. Alternatively, they may produce a medical certificate of fitness for the journey from their own doctor.

The Department of Health and Social Services recommends everyone travelling abroad to be vaccinated against smallpox, and to have other inoculations appropriate to the countries being visited. From time to time countries enforce protection against certain diseases if there has been an epidemic in their own country, or in any place where an immigrant has recently lived or visited. At the time of vaccination against smallpox it is possible to obtain an International Vaccination Certificate from the doctor, whose signature must be verified by the local health authority's official stamp. The certificates are normally valid for three years.

It is not considered good medical practice, except as an emergency, to give a smallpox vaccination to anyone suffering from eczema, or who is being treated with steroids, or to a pregnant woman. In such cases the doctor will provide a certificate stating the reason for the traveller's failure to be vaccinated.

22   Insurance

When taking children away for educational visits, school journeys or camps, inquiry must be made to ascertain whether the local education authority or the organization sponsoring the visit has an *adequate* policy to cover possible claims. If not, a special policy should be arranged with an insurance company, the premiums being chargeable to the cost of the journey.

Some authorities which do not carry bulk insurance for such activities require evidence that the organizers of the journey have taken out adequate cover. Where the authority does provide its own insurance, teachers should ensure that their own interests are covered as well as those of the authority and the pupils and if in doubt they should consult their professional association.

For some educational visits and school journeys, where special risks are involved, e.g. canoeing or mountaineering, an additional premium may be payable, and such proposed activities should be disclosed when effecting the insurance.

If a journey is arranged through a commercial travel agent or a school journey organization, the promotion booklet may refer to the fact that 'full insurance' is included in the cost of the tour. This is not good enough: the organizer should require the agent to disclose the full terms of the policy to see whether it complies with the local education authority's minimum requirements, or whether it will need to be supplemented by additional insurance arranged by the school. The minimum cover required is set out in the following list which represents the standard terms of insurers experienced in the school journey field, although some, obviously, apply only to overseas journeys:

(a) the death or disablement by accident of any member of the party;

(b) loss of or damage to personal luggage and loss of money;

(c) expenses incurred due to the unforeseen extension of the visit or to any forced change in the planned route of the journey;

(d) additional expenses incurred in connection with the return home of any person in the party due to the death, serious injury or illness of a member of the family;

(e) medical, surgical, nursing and other similar expenses which might have to be met;

(f) expenses incurred as a direct result of remaining with a sick or injured person;

(g) additional expenses incurred in transporting home on medical advice any sick or injured person or, in the event of death, the body or ashes of the deceased;

(h) expenses necessarily incurred by the parent or guardian of any sick or injured person travelling on medical advice to visit such person.

It will be noted that personal accident insurance of the kind which provides, for example, £5,000 in the case of death, £1,000 for the loss of one limb, and so forth, is not included in the suggestions listed above. There is no reason why a school should not take out a personal accident policy and add the premium to the cost of the journey. Many schools, however, prefer to advise parents that insurance of this nature is their responsibility and that, if they wish for this cover, they should make arrangements privately.

23   Passports

All persons taking part in visits to countries outside the United Kingdom of Great Britain and Northern Ireland must be protected by valid passport documentation without which both admission to a country overseas will be refused, and re-admission to the United Kingdom will be difficult.

DAY VISITS

For France, post offices issue an excursion document for visits not exceeding 60 hours. It costs £2, lasts for one month and a verified photograph is needed. For Belgium and Holland, simple identity cards from the Passport Office are sufficient.

PARTY LEADER

If a collective passport is used, the party leader must be the holder of a valid full British passport. (A British Visitor's passport is not sufficient.) These are issued to British subjects who are also citizens of the United Kingdom and Colonies, British subjects without citizenship and British protected persons. They are valid for ten years, and cost currently £15. Regular travellers to countries requiring a visa may now obtain a 'jumbo-passport' containing ninety-four pages instead of the usual thirty. These cost £30 and are heavy and bulky. A wife or husband may be included in the spouse's passport. If the marriage took place after 1 January 1949, a wife may be included only if she was a British subject at the time of the marriage, or has become a British subject by registration. A wife who is a citizen of another Commonwealth country cannot be included unless she is also a citizen of the United Kingdom and Colonies. Children under the age of 16 may also be included on a parent's passport; an individual passport is issued to a child under 5 only in exceptional circumstances. Children under 16 cannot travel without the person to whom the passport has been issued.

Although it is more economical for a husband and wife to

have a family passport, a problem can arise in the case of illness as, although the person to whom it has been issued can travel alone on such a document, the spouse cannot; and should they have to travel separately in such circumstances, special arrangements will have to be made through the nearest British consulate. The deputy leader of a party must also hold a full passport.

Foreign-born spouses of British subjects, who have retained the nationality of their birth, should take careful steps to verify their position before applying to be included in a British passport. Not all countries have accepted the concept of dual nationality; and a citizen of the Netherlands, for example, would lose Dutch nationality merely by applying alone or jointly for such a document.

OTHER ADULTS

Other adults travelling in the party may hold a full British passport as described above; alternatively, they may travel on a British Visitor's passport which is valid for one year. British Visitor's passports are valid for visits of up to three months to the following countries, but may not be used for taking up employment or for gainful activity:

Andorra	Italy (i)
Austria	Liechtenstein
Belgium	Luxembourg
Bermuda (j)	Malta
Canada (a)	Monaco
Denmark (b) (c)	Netherlands
Federal Republic of Germany (d)	Norway (c)
Finland (c)	Portugal (e)
France (f)	San Marino
Gibraltar	Spain (g)
Greece (h)	Sweden (c)
Iceland (c)	Switzerland
	Turkey (h)

Notes

(a) A British Visitor's passport must be valid for three months beyond the last day the visitor is in Canada, and is not valid for travel to the United States of America.

(b) Including the Faroe Islands and Greenland.

(c) Visits to this group of countries as a whole must not exceed three months in any period of nine months.

(d) And, for travellers by air only, the western sector of Berlin.

(e) Including Madeira and the Azores.

(f) Including Corsica.

(g) Including the Balearic and Canary Islands.

(h) Visitors travelling overland to Greece and Turkey through bordering countries require a full British passport.

(i) Including Sicily, Sardinia and Elba.

(j) Not valid for the United States of America.

COLLECTIVE PASSPORTS

Collective passports are issued for approved parties of students, and members of the Scout and Guide movements. Not less than five, nor more than fifty, persons may be included in a collective passport, which is not acceptable in some countries where the members of the party are staying in separate households (see section on 'Visas etc.'). The leader and deputy leader must be at least 21 years of age, and must hold valid full British passports.

Only the following may be included in a collective passport:

British Citizens. It is important to note in this connection that a child *may* not be a British Citizen *even if born in the United Kingdom*. If it is known that the parents or responsible parent have come from overseas, the party organizer should contact the local Passport Office. Possession of a British birth certificate is not on its own sufficient proof.

British Dependent Territories Citizens.

British Overseas Citizens.

British Protected Persons.

Foreign, Commonwealth and Irish Citizens should obtain passports from their own authorities. It is very important for party organizers to check whether such passport holders, although travelling with a British party, nevertheless still need a personal visa in order to enter the countries to be visited.

Every person included in a collective passport who will be 16 years of age on the date of re-entry must carry a personal identity card bearing his photograph. These cards, signed by the head teacher, must be submitted, with the photograph attached, for authorization with the application for the collective passport.

The application must be accompanied by a supporting letter from the governors or the head of the school. Maintained schools should obtain the support of their local education authority, independent schools must state that they are registered, provisionally registered or deemed to be registered by the Registrar of Independent Schools at the DES. The Passport Office may also require written evidence of the consent of the pupils' parents or legal guardians, which must in any case be obtained.

The fee for a collective passport is currently £30; there is no charge for the supporting identity cards.

Whilst it is a general rule that no person may hold, or be included in, more than one United Kingdom passport, there is no objection to the inclusion of an individual passport holder on a collective passport. Individual passports can cause delay at frontier controls, and there is always a risk that they may be lost. Each has to be collected in advance of the journey for currency control entries to be made. In general it is preferable to include all eligible pupils on the collective passport, and to persuade them to leave their individual documents at home.

All persons named in a collective passport must travel and remain together. If a member of the party becomes separated, or is unable to return with the party, the leader must inform the local authorities, and must report the fact to frontier passport controls. The nearest British consul must also be informed so that he can make arrangements for the issue of individual travel documents.

The application for the collective passport must name all countries to be visited, even if only for a day excursion. It is also a useful practice to include countries through which a diversion may be necessary. If, for example, a journey to Italy is planned by rail through France and Switzerland, and is disrupted at the last moment by, say, a railway strike in France, it might be possible to re-route the party through Belgium, Holland, West Germany and Austria if these countries are named in the collective passport.

For some countries visas or more than one copy of the collective passport may be required. In some countries every pupil must carry an identity card. The current details are set out in the next section.

Teachers from independent countries of the Commonwealth, or who are citizens of Eire or foreign nationals, should ensure that their papers are in order to permit re-entry before leaving the country with a school journey party. They can receive advice on the appropriate action to be taken from their High Commission, Embassy or Consulate.

ISSUE OF PASSPORTS

The Passport Offices are:

London: Clive House, 70 Petty France, London SW1H 9HD.
    Tel. 01–213–5041/7075.
Liverpool: 5th Floor, India Buildings, Water Street, Liverpool L2 0QZ.
    Tel. 051–237–3010.
Newport: Olympia House, Upper Dock Street, Newport (Gwent) NPT 1XA.
    Tel. 0633–56292.
Peterborough: 55 Westfield Road, Peterborough PE3 6TG.
    Tel. 0733–895555.
Glasgow: 1st Floor, Empire House, 131 West Nile Street, Glasgow G1 2RY.
    Tel. 041–332–0271.

Applications should be forwarded at least four weeks before

the passport is required. A duty officer is available for very limited periods on Saturdays to deal with passports required for an emergency such as death or serious illness. The applicant must produce documentary proof of the emergency.

24   Visas, etc.

No visas or additional copies of the collective passport are required in the following countries:

Austria (a)	Liechtenstein
Belgium (b)	Luxembourg
Bulgaria (a)	Malta
Canada	Monaco
Federal Republic of Germany (d)	Netherlands (b)
France (e)	Portugal
Greece	Spain
Iceland	Switzerland (c)
	Tunisia

Notes

(a) Each child, including those under 16, must carry an identity card with a photograph.
(b) If the children are staying in individual households, each child, including those under 16, must carry an identity card with a photograph.
(c) If the children are staying in individual households, a collective passport is not acceptable.
(d) These arrangements also apply to parties travelling by air to the western sector of Berlin.
(e) If children are staying with individual families, they must be within the limits of the same city and each child must have a copy of the collective passport. Paris is taken to include Hauts-de-Seine, Seine-St. Denis and Val-de-Marne.

Copies of the collective passport must be produced at the

points of entry and departure in the following countries, but no visa is required:

Denmark (a)	Italy (c)
Finland (a) (b)	Norway (a)
	Romania (d)

Visas are required by the following countries:

Czechoslovakia (a) (e)   Yugoslavia (a) (f)

An endorsement is required if Sweden (a)(b) is the first Nordic country to be visited. The Nordic countries are Sweden, Norway, Denmark and Finland. The application for endorsement, enclosing the collective passport and one copy for each point of entry and departure, should be sent to the Swedish Consulate-General, 23 North Row, London W1.

Notes

(a) Each child, including those under 16, must carry an identity card with a photograph.
(b) The minimum number of persons to be included in a collective passport is ten.
(c) A copy of the collective passport is required at the point of entry only.
(d) Two copies of the collective passport are required at the points of entry and departure.
(e) A visa to cover the collective passport must be endorsed on the leader's passport.
(f) Enquiries should be made of the Yugoslav Consulate, 19 Upper Phillimore Gardens, London W8.

Schools taking part in cruises should consult the shipping company responsible for the organization.

In the case of visits planned to countries other than those listed above, schools should ask the Consulates concerned whether collective passports are accepted, and what requirements must be met concerning visas.

25 HM Customs

Smuggling is a crime, and the penalties are heavy. Teachers travelling with school journey parties should make it a point of honour to observe the Customs regulations, and to ensure that the pupils follow their example.

Before the journey begins, teachers should advise children not to bring home with them large quantities of goods which attract customs duty or value added tax. The pupils should be instructed to make a complete list of all items which they have obtained abroad, with their approximate value, so that this can be handed to the customs officer should the traveller be stopped. Receipts or guarantees should be carried if valuable items such as foreign cameras and watches are being taken abroad, to establish proof either that they were purchased in this country, or that duty had been paid on them previously.

Counterfeit coins, dangerous drugs, firearms and ammunition, flick-knives, plants and bulbs, radio transmitters (including walkie-talkies), meat and poultry not fully cooked, and live animals are prohibited or restricted.

Travellers from a country in membership of the EEC, but not the Channel Islands, may bring the following items into the United Kingdom without paying duty:

(a) 300 cigarettes, or 150 cigarillos, or 75 cigars, or 400 grammes of tobacco. This does not apply to persons under 17.

(b) 4 litres of still table wine and $1\frac{1}{2}$ litres of alcoholic drink over 22 per cent vol or 3 litres of alcoholic drink not over 22 per cent vol, or fortified or sparkling wine. This does not apply to persons under 17.

(c) 75 grammes (3 fluid ounces) of perfume;

(d) 3/8 litre of toilet water; and

(e) other goods not exceeding £163 in value.

Travellers from a country outside the European Economic Community may bring the following items into the United Kingdom free of duty:

(a) 200 cigarettes, or 100 cigarillos, or 50 cigars, or 250 grammes of tobacco;
(b) 2 litres of still table wine and 1 litre of alcoholic drink over 22 per cent vol, or 2 litres not over 22 per cent vol or fortified or sparkling wine;
(c) 50 grammes (2 fluid ounces) of perfume;
(d) 1/4 litre of toilet water; and
(e) other goods not exceeding £28 in value.
Similar restrictions on persons under 17 also apply.

Goods bought in a duty- and tax-free shop in the Common Market, or under similar conditions of sale on a ship or aircraft, are treated as though they were purchased outside the EEC, and the lower level of allowances applies.

Any traveller entering Britain with goods acquired abroad (whether by purchase or gift) in excess of the allowances quoted above must pass through the red channel at the Customs control in order to declare the excess. Those bringing back items entirely within the duty-free allowances may go through the green channel, but they may be stopped by a Customs officer in the course of a spot check.

The allowances are only for travellers' *own* purchases. On no account should teachers in charge of school parties bring through customs cigarettes or alcohol which pupils have bought, perhaps as presents for their parents.

26 Exchange visits

Schools often arrange exchanges by which a pupil from overseas spends some time staying with an English family in this country in return for a visit on a reciprocal basis. Every endeavour should be made to ensure that the exchange is well matched, and that the British home has the facilities necessary for a successful visit to this country. It is also wise to make some inquiries about the visitor from overseas.

It should be pointed out to the parents that such arrangements, by their very nature, are of the order of 'blind dates', and the school can accept no responsibility for any mischances which may arise.

27   Finance

SCHOOL JOURNEY ACCOUNTS

All money received must be paid promptly into a separate bank account, and a careful record must be made. Most local education authorities include school journey accounts in their routine audits. If this is not done, it is desirable that the accounts should be audited by at least two persons not connected with the organization of the journey. Under no circumstances should such funds be placed, even temporarily, in a private account.

Some local education authorities lay down very tight guidelines for the book-keeping procedures connected with school trips. It is essential that all concerned adhere very closely to these.

POCKET MONEY

In the case of foreign journeys it is sometimes possible to get a better rate of exchange by collecting pocket money with the school journey subscriptions, and changing in bulk. It is useful to have a regular time each day for the issue of pocket money, and to warn pupils who appear to be overspending early in the journey so that they are not out of funds before the visit ends.

CURRENCY CONTROLS

The law relating to exchange control and, of course, the exchange rate, vary from time to time in accordance with the economic climate. Those responsible for the organization of school journeys abroad should consult their bankers at an early date so that arrangements for the transfer of currency can be made in good time. Penalties for breaking the law in this respect are heavy.

EMERGENCY FLOAT

The organizer of a school journey abroad must have sufficient funds available to meet any emergency which might reasonably be expected to arise. Although the United Kingdom now has reciprocal agreements in the social security field with a large number of countries (outlined in chapter IV), these arereciprocal agreements in the social security field with a large number of countries (outlined in chapter IV), these are intended to apply to British nationals living in those states and, in any case, they do not cover such matters as medical attention or hospital fees. It is by no means unusual for these fees to be demanded in advance in continental countries. It is no good assuring the medical authorities that the members of the party are adequately insured: payment has to be made on the spot, and the insurance issue settled later. A teacher, one of whose pupils has acute appendicitis which needs immediate surgery, is in an impossible position if he cannot find perhaps £500 or more to get the boy admitted to hospital. Other unforeseen snags have been expensive bail bonds. Drivers of minibuses should be aware that the infringement of minor motoring regulations can attract on-the-spot fines. These are intended to be punitive and can be extremely high, especially in France. For example, there may be fines for crossing a white line, ignoring traffic lights, failing to observe speed limits or overloading vehicles beyond the manufacturer's standards. Long-distance emergency phone calls are expensive, and may not be recoverable from insurance.

Occasionally the British consulate may be able to help, but the diplomatic service, as many stranded Britons have found, is not in business as a moneylender. People travelling abroad are expected to exercise reasonable prudence in planning for all contingencies.

EUROCHEQUES

Holders of British Eurocheque cards can cash cheques at banks in Europe which display the Eurocheque symbol. Cheques are drawn in sterling to a maximum of £50, payment being made in any currency desired and available, subject to the bank's deduction of commission. One large British bank operates the full Continental European Eurocheque scheme, whereby cheques may be drawn in the currency of the country visited and are then converted to sterling by the UK bank and debited to the sterling account. Although bank charges for this type of account may be slightly higher, there are advantages over the more common British Eurocheque scheme in that hotel bills and the like can usually be settled abroad by cheque rather than by large sums of cash. This could be particularly valuable out of banking hours abroad, or in villages with, perhaps, no easy access to a bank.

28 The law abroad

Many teachers with long experience of taking school parties abroad have also had some experience of dealing with the forces of law and order at sometime or another.

Pupils must be reminded that so long as they are guests in another country they are amenable to its law, without being released entirely from their obligations under the law of their homeland.

Not only do continental legal systems differ widely from our own; police methods are also different, and the language barrier may make problems seem even more intractable.

In the event of serious difficulty a teacher should get in touch with the nearest British consulate. This is especially important if an arrest is threatened.

In some countries, particularly those with totalitarian governments, arrest and imprisonment before trial is more common than in the United Kingdom. Party organizers should take this into account in their planning, since it could involve additional expenditure and possibly affect the supervision of the party.

29 Christian Scientists

Teachers are sometimes concerned about the legal risks involved when pupils who are Christian Scientists are included in the party. Party leaders feel that, should such a pupil need medical attention of a kind which they would provide for their own children, they are fettered in their discretion to act *in loco parentis* by the conscientious rejection of usual medical treatment. If they call in a doctor they have offended the religious conviction of the pupil and his parent; if they fail to do so, and the child dies, will they be held legally responsible?

These fears are completely groundless. Christian Scientists rely on the practice of their religion for healing because they find it efficacious; they do not neglect conditions which others would treat medically and, since most European countries have a number of Christian Science practitioners, parents would expect teachers in charge of school journey parties to seek the assistance of such a practitioner with the same urgency with which they would consult a doctor in the case of a pupil who is not a Christian Scientist.

The Christian Science Committee on Publication for Great Britain and Ireland have produced a form of request for exemption from medical treatment which indemnifies both the teaching staff and the local education authority. The form gives the name and address of the nearest Christian Science practitioner to the school journey base, and is so clearly worded that it is worth reproducing in full:

> I wish my son/daughter ...., on religious grounds, to be exempted from emergency operations, from all medical treatment, vaccination and/or immunization (except where legally required for entry into a foreign country) in connection with the proposed school journey to .... To the best of my knowledge and belief he/she is and has been in normal good health and is free from all communicable diseases.
>
> In consideration of these exemptions, it is understood that I accept complete responsibility for the health of this minor, and I hereby release the local education committee

and those in charge of the school journey from any liability for unforeseen circumstances which might arise during the approved journey, by virtue of these exemptions. I request that, should an emergency arise, the person in charge of the school party shall first try to contact me by telephone or the Christian Science practitioner named below. In the event that neither the undersigned nor the practitioner can be immediately located, the school authorities may take such measures as on medical advice appear to them to be absolutely necessary for the protection of life, having regard to my wishes as expressed above.

This form should remove any qualms. In the first place the party leader is asked to act strictly in accordance with the dictates of the parent's conscience, a procedure which is strictly in accordance with the spirit of the 1944 Act. Secondly, both he and the local authority are indemnified for so doing. This is different from any kind of indemnity issued by the school for the parent to sign, because in this case the indemnity is offered by the parent, and not requested by the school. Thirdly, if the channels of healing desired by the parent are not available, it is recognized that the teacher must make a responsible and conscientious decision *in loco parentis* which may involve recourse to ordinary medical treatment. If there is any difficulty in obtaining the indemnity form locally when it is known that a Christian Science pupil is taking part in a school journey, a copy can be supplied from the office of the Christian Science Committee on Publication, Ingersoll House, 9 Kingsway, London WC2B 6XF.

So far as immunization is concerned, Article 83 of the International Health Regulations enables those with conscientious objections to claim exemption, even in unusual circumstances.

Nor need a head, or the parents of children who are not Christian Scientists, have any fears about allowing a teacher who is a Christian Scientist to take charge of a school journey party. If a member of the party were taken ill such a teacher would not allow his religious convictions to intrude and he would arrange for medical treatment such as the child's natural parent would wish.

30   Jehovah's Witnesses

Some teachers are also concerned about including Jehovah's Witnesses in a school journey party because of a fear of complications should a child need medical treatment.

Jehovah's Witnesses have no code of rules, each individual being guided by his own understanding and application of Biblical principles. They accept any form of treatment which does not involve the introduction of blood or blood fractions into the body. Jehovah's Witnesses freely accept blood substitutes. All forms of immunization are acceptable.

It is for parents who are Jehovah's Witnesses to make their wishes clear to leaders of school journey parties in advance. No such parent would authorize a teacher to override his religious convictions, and it would be most unwise for a party leader *in loco parentis* to do so. Since the only problem is one of blood transfusion, and there are now several substitutes which are acceptable both to the medical profession and to Jehovah's Witnesses, the problem should not arise in any reasonably foreseeable circumstances.

Jehovah's Witnesses do not eat food which has not been bled, such as some poultry, or which is partly made of blood, such as black pudding. A Jehovah's Witness who is in doubt about food which is set before him will merely leave it.

In general, a teacher who is a Jehovah's Witness in charge of a school journey party will follow the wishes of a pupil's parent with regard to medical treatment. It is possible, however, that he might not feel able to authorize treatment which he believes to be contrary to the law of God. Again, since this is confined to one area where medically acceptable substitutes are available, this should cause no worries.

References

1. Administrative Memorandum no. 22/67. Also 12/69.
2. Brown *v.* Nelson and others (1971) 69 LGR 20.
3. *Education*, 25 February 1983.
4. Unfair Contract Terms Act 1977, s. 2.
5. 46 Queen Anne's Gate, London SW1H 9AU.
6. 55 Newman Street, London W1P 4AH.
7. Hunt *v.* Hourmont: *Current Law*, April 1983.
8. Fuller details may be found in leaflets issued by the Department of the Environment, 2 Marsham Street, London SW1 3EB.
9. Fanum House, 7 High Street, Teddington, Middlesex TW11 8EQ.
10. Attorney General of the Duchy of Lancaster *v.* G. E. Overton (Farms) Ltd, *The Times*, 19 November 1981, CA.
11. Ancient Monuments etc. Act 1979, s. 28.

XVII
Concerts, fetes and plays

1   Licensing of hall

STAGE PLAYS

Before a hall is used for the public presentation of stage plays,
a licence must be granted by the licensing authority[1] to the
owner or licensee of the premises. It should be noted that the
admission of parents (with or without payment) is sufficient to
constitute a public performance. In the case of a school, the
licence is normally taken out by the head. The procedure for
dealing with applications for licences varies somewhat from
county to county, and some authorities grant only an occasional
licence for halls which are used by amateurs. In such cases a
fresh application must be made for every production. Others
also grant what is called a restricted licence which authorizes
the use of the hall for dramatic presentations on not more than
a specified number of nights during its currency, normally a
year. In some cases an authority issues the licences through
its administrative machinery; others require an application to
be made through a magistrates' court.

In Greater London the Greater London Council is the
licensing authority; elsewhere in England and Wales the district

council has been given the responsibility of issuing such licences.[2] Applications for licences should be made to the chief executive officer of the appropriate council.

An applicant for the grant or transfer of a licence must give at least twenty-one days' notice to the licensing authority and to the chief officer of police of his intention to apply, and must provide such particulars as are required. In the case of an application for renewal not less than twenty-eight days' notice of the intention to apply must be given.

If the application is for one or more specified occasions only, the period required for notice of intention to apply (whether an original application, or one for transfer or renewal) is reduced to fourteen days, and the chief officer of police need not be informed.[3]

The Secretary of State (in this case, the Home Secretary) prescribes the scale of fees to be charged for licences; except that no fee is payable if the licensing authority are satisfied that the play or plays to be performed will be of an educational or other like purpose.[4]

Before a licence is granted, the hall is inspected to ensure that the safety of the public is adequately secure by the provision of sufficient exits, gangways, fire extinguishers and emergency lighting. The licence is granted subject to such conditions as may be endorsed upon it, and these must be rigidly observed. The police, the fire, and the licensing authorities may enter the hall at any time during a performance to satisfy themselves that the conditions are being observed.

Such an inspection may be very thorough. One fire officer refused to accept an assurance that the scenery had been fireproofed in accordance with the regulations and tried the effect of his cigarette lighter on some flimsy and combustible-looking flies. They stood up to the test but, with only forty minutes to go before the curtain rang up on the first performance, it is not difficult to imagine what the effect would have been if they had not been treated.

On the death of the licensee the licence continues in the name of his personal representatives for three months unless it is transferred, cancelled or revoked in the meantime. It then expires, unless the licensing authority is satisfied that an extension is necessary for winding up the deceased's estate. This last contingency might conceivably occur in an independent school: in a maintained school steps should be taken to transfer the licence within the period.[5]

The licence may be cancelled on the holder's application. In the case of premises which are being constructed, extended or altered, the licensing authority may grant a provisional licence. This does not become effective until it has been confirmed on completion of the building operations.[6] The licensing authority may impose any restrictions they consider necessary in the interests of physical safety or health, or in connection with an exhibition, demonstration or performance of hypnotism within the meaning of the Hypnotism Act 1952.[7] On the licensee's application the authority may vary the terms of the licence, subject to any conditions or restrictions within the terms of the Act, as they see fit to impose.[8]

> Any person concerned in the organization or management of a public performance of a play, or any other person knowing or having reasonable cause to suspect that such a performance will be given who allows, lets or otherwise makes available unlicensed premises for that purpose is guilty of an offence.

So is the holder of a licence or any person who knowingly allows any of the terms of the licence to be broken. The licensee is not guilty if he can prove that the breach took place without his consent or connivance, and that he used all due diligence to avoid it. The penalty on summary conviction of these offences is a fine of up to £200, or a maximum of three months' imprisonment, or both. If the licensee is convicted, the licensing authority may revoke the licence.[9]

If an offence is committed by a body corporate and is proved to have been committed with the consent or connivance, or is attributable to the neglect, of any director, manager, secretary or similar officer, or any person purporting to act in such a capacity, that individual is guilty, as well as the body corporate, and he may be prosecuted and punished accordingly.[10]

MUSIC, DANCING AND OTHER PUBLIC PERFORMANCES

The stage play licence does not cover the use of the building. For public dancing, music, contests, exhibitions or display of boxing, wrestling, judo, karate or similar sport a separate licence is needed.[11] Such licences are also issued by the appropriate district council.

Where annual licences are obtained for these purposes, it is advisable to apply for them as a matter of routine at the same time each year. This avoids the possibility of the application being overlooked immediately before a performance.

It is an offence not to have the appropriate licence or licences. Any person concerned in the management or organization of a performance or entertainment must check this carefully. A head teacher who allows the premises to be used in such a way either knowing or having reasonable cause to suspect that a licence is not in force is guilty of an offence.

2   Public performance of plays and their direction

A play is (a) any dramatic piece, whether involving improvisation or not, which is given wholly or in part by one or more persons actually present and performing; and in which the whole, or major proportion of what is done by the person or persons performing, whether by way of speech, singing or action, involves the playing of a role; and (b) any ballet given wholly or in part by one or more persons actually present and performing whether or not it falls within paragraph (a) of this definition.[12]

'A *public performance* includes any performance in a public place within the meaning of the Public Order Act 1936 and any performance which the public or any section thereof are permitted to attend, whether on payment or otherwise.'[13]

A *public place* is defined as 'any highway, public park or garden, any sea beach, and any public bridge, road, lane, footway, square, court, alley or passage, whether a thoroughfare or not; and includes any open space to which, for the time being, the public have, or are permitted to have, access, whether on payment or otherwise'.

For the purposes of the Act the word *premises* includes any place,[14] and it is explicitly stated that no other licence is necessary for any premises merely because plays are presented there. In this context any occasional music played at a performance of a play is treated as part of that performance provided the time taken by the music on any day is less than one quarter of the time taken by the performances on that day.[15] This of course applies to incidental music, and not to music which forms an integral part of a performance such as the accompaniment to a ballet. Provided that the incidental music is confined within the specified limits, a music and dancing licence is not required for the performance of a stage play.

A person is not treated as presenting a play merely because he takes part as a performer; but if, as a performer in a play directed by someone else, he performs without excuse otherwise than in accordance with that person's direction, he will be treated as a person directing the performance. The director of a play shall be held to have directed a performance notwithstanding the fact that he was absent from that particular performance. This definition is necessary for precision in connection with sections 2 (obscene performances), 5 (incitement to racial hatred) and 6 (provocation of a breach of the peace). A person who is merely a performer shall not be held to have aided or abetted an offence under one of these sections merely by reason of being a performer.[16]

A performance or entertainment is not public in the eyes of the law if steps are taken not to admit the public freely. Adequate precautions for schools are probably to arrange for admission to be by personal invitation to parents and friends only. It should not be possible for members of the public to obtain tickets by payment or otherwise as a result of advertising.

3 Bars at school functions

Provided that the local education authority or the governors of voluntary-aided schools have given general or specific permission, the most common practice is to make arrangements with a local publican to run a bar on the school premises. In such cases the publican is responsible for obtaining the necessary permission.

A further possibility was opened up by the Licensing (Occasional Permissions) Act 1983. An 'officer of an eligible organization', the latter being defined as an organization not conducted for private gain, can apply for an occasional licence to sell liquor. Only four such applications can be made in one year, and on each occasion the period for which the licence is granted must not exceed 24 hours. Schools may make use of this legislation for parent-teacher meetings and social functions, summer fetes, fund-raising activities and the like.

The Clerk to the Licensing Justices in each area will supply the necessary details. It is necessary to satisfy the Justices in several ways about the manner in which the bar will be conducted, and that the person applying is a fit and proper person to sell intoxicating liquor. There is nothing to prevent local residents, who feel that they may be adversely affected in some way by the function, from lodging formal objections which will be taken into account by the Justices. It is always courteous of schools to consult such neighbours beforehand.

4 Intoxicating liquor as prizes

Schools sometimes run raffles, tombola and other fund-raising activities, perhaps organized by parent-teacher associations, where wines and spirits are included among the prizes.

It may be an offence to do this without a licence. Section 160 of the Licensing Act makes it an offence if any person not holding a justices licence 'sells or exposes for sale by retail any intoxicating liquor' or does it other than 'at the place for which that licence authorizes him'.

Schools contemplating such activities should take the

precautionary measure of checking this with the local police or licensing authority. The Act stipulates penalties on conviction of a maximum of six months' imprisonment or a £200 fine or both.

5 Censorship of plays

Prior to the operation of the Theatres Act 1968 no stage play could be produced publicly until it had been licensed by the Lord Chamberlain, in accordance with the Theatres Act 1843, which was completely repealed by the new statute. In granting a licence, a licensing authority may not impose any term, condition or restrictions as to the nature of the plays to be presented or as to the manner of their performance. This prohibition is subject to the proviso already mentioned dealing with physical health, safety and hypnotism.[17]

Nevertheless, certain restrictions remain. Within one month of the first performance of a play based on a script, a free copy of the script must be delivered to the British Museum, in default of which the person presenting the performance may be fined a sum of up to £5. This requirement applies only to plays which have not been publicly performed.[18]

The removal of the Lord Chamberlain's powers of censorship has not produced a state of affairs which allows complete licence to those who present plays, The 1968 Act has substituted a number of statutory offences in a number of fields:

OBSCENE PERFORMANCES

A performance is obscene if, taken as a whole, its effect would be such as to tend to deprave and corrupt persons likely to attend. So far as teachers are concerned, an important circumstance which the courts would consider would, of course, be the age of members of the audience. Under this section no person may be prosecuted for a common law offence alleging that the performance was obscene, indecent, offensive or injurious to morality; nor for the common law offence of conspiring to corrupt public morals. A person cannot be convicted under this head if it is proved that the performance was justified as being for the public good in the interests of drama, opera, ballet or any other art, or of literature or learning. Expert evidence as to the artistic, literary or other merits of the production may be called by the prosecution and defence.

DEFAMATION

Defamatory words spoken during the performance of a play, although impermanent in form, are now statutory libel both for civil and criminal purposes. So, in similar circumstances, are pictures, visual images, gestures and other methods of signifying meaning.[19] The crime remains a common law offence. The law of defamation is dealt with in chapter XX.

INCITEMENT TO RACIAL HATRED

It is an offence if a play performed in public involves threatening, abusive or insulting words intended to stir up hatred against any section of the public in Great Britain distinguished by colour, race, ethnic or national origins. It is also an offence if the tendency of the performance as a whole is likely to stir up hatred against such groups. It should be noted that for the first of these offences it is necessary to prove intention, whereas for the second the mere likelihood of fomenting racial hatred is sufficient. In either case the person responsible is the person who presents or directs the play, whether for gain or not. The amateur producer is as vulnerable as the professional. The penalty on summary conviction is a fine or imprisonment, or both; on indictment a fine of up to £1,000, a maximum of two years' imprisonment, or both.[20]

PROVOCATION OF BREACH OF PEACE

It is an offence if a play produced in public involves threatening, abusive or insulting words or behaviour and either the person (whether for gain or not) who presented or directed the performance intended to provoke a breach of the peace; or the performance, taken as a whole, was likely to occasion a breach of the peace. The person presenting or directing the performance is liable in either case. On summary conviction he can be fined or imprisoned for a maximum of three months, or both. On indictment the maxima rise to £500 or twelve months' imprisonment, or both.[21]

INSTITUTION OF PROCEEDINGS

Prosecutions for the statutory offences set out in the Act or for the common law offence of libel in the course of the performance of a play may be commenced only by, or with the consent of, the Attorney-General.[22] This does not, of course, affect the right of anyone believing himself to have been libelled to commence a civil action. In the case of a play based on a written script, which for this purpose includes the music and stage or other directions, that script is admissible in evidence and the performance is held to have been in accordance with it unless the contrary be proved. If a police officer of above the rank of superintendent believes that one of the statutory offences has been, or is likely to be, committed he may make an order requiring the script to be produced and the opportunity to make a copy. A copy so made will be accepted by the court as the script on which the performance was based. Failure, without reasonable excuse, to comply with such a requirement can lead to a fine on summary conviction.[23]

6 Infringement of copyright

The law of copyright is dealt with generally in chapter XVIII. In connection with plays and concerts it should be noted that whilst it is not an infringement to write a short extract on the blackboard, or an overhead projector transparency, for teaching purposes, it is illegal to duplicate copyright material or reproduce substantial portions, e.g. parts of plays, so that the purchase of copies becomes unnecessary.

7   Royalties on stage plays

It is a condition of the performance of most stage plays in which copyright still subsists, that a fee known as a royalty should be paid to the author. This is usually done through his agents.

Royalties must be paid in advance, and a licence is then issued for the performance. Authors are sometimes asked to waive the fees due to them for the production of their plays, particularly when they are being presented on behalf of charity. Unless there is a note in the printed copies to the effect that the playwright is prepared to do this in particular circumstances, such requests are grossly unfair. No author wishes to appear ungenerous, but royalties are the due reward which a writer receives for his work, and at least he should be allowed to choose for himself the charities to which he wishes to subscribe.

In some cases, even when royalties are paid, it may be a condition that an announcement appears in all printed matter stating that the play is produced by arrangement with a particular agent. Failure to observe the conditions of presentation may result in action being taken against the school.

Some copyright plays carry a statement that they may be freely produced by amateurs provided that the ownership of the copyright is acknowledged. This may be taken as a general licence, subject to any conditions stated.

8   The Performing Right Society

Under the Copyright Acts, the performance of copyright musical matter is subject to a fee similar in nature to the stage play royalty. Most composers and music publishers belong to the Performing Right Society which acts as their agent to collect and distribute their fees. Through its links with similar organizations in more than thirty countries, for which it is the agent in Great Britain, it is able to license performance of the works of nearly 200,000 composers, authors and music publishers of many nationalities.

Schools affiliated to the Music Masters' Association of the

Incorporated Society of Musicians may take out an annual licence covering all performances for a very low fee. In other cases the form should be obtained from the Society, and when this has been completed the performer will be notified of the fee to be paid. Failure to ensure that these formalities have been completed, at least a week before the performance, will result in action by the Society.

Individual application is not necessary if the proprietor of the hall has an annual licence, or the local education authority has a similar arrangement. In such cases, a return should be made on the appropriate form to the licensee, who will forward it to the Society which then makes arrangements for the composer and publisher to receive their fees.

The Performing Right Society does not make a charge for performances in churches during religious worship, or at competitive musical festivals. Fees are, however, payable in respect of winners' or other concerts at the end of such festivals.

The address is: Phonographic Performance Ltd, 62 Oxford Street, London W1N 0AN.

9   Broadcast music

It is an offence under the Copyright Act 1956 and the Performers' Protection Acts 1958 and 1963 to make records of broadcasts, or videotapes or records of telecasts, other than for private purposes, without the prior approval of the broadcasting authority. Neither may a telecast be shown in public to a paying audience. If, for some particular reason, it is wished to do this, it is essential to obtain permission in advance from the broadcasting authority, the owners of any copyright material and the performers taking part. Both the British Broadcasting Corporation and the Independent Television Authority are protected by the Acts.

10   Private performances

The private performance of a copyright play by a school company to an audience composed entirely of members of the school is not an infringement of copyright. The admission of one member of the public however (and for this purpose parents, unless they are directly connected with the school organization, are treated as members of the public) would render the school liable in damages. The point at issue is that the author's rights might be injured if such a person, because he had seen the play at the school, failed to go to a performance at a theatre where royalties are paid.

In all cases of doubt about the nature of a private performance, it is advisable to consult the author or his agents in advance.

11   Use of schools by outside bodies

Under the Local Government (Miscellaneous Provisions) Act 1982, any person concerned in the organization or management of a function *who allows the premises to be used* without the appropriate licence or licences or in contravention of any conditions laid down in the licences is guilty of an offence.

Head teachers should therefore clarify with their local education authority, or governors in the case of aided schools, who is responsible for ensuring that outside individuals and bodies using the school have complied with the law. Many such functions have only very little, if any, connection with the life of the school and heads are strongly advised, when approached for the use of a school for entertainments by outside bodies, to pass such requests to the local education authority or governors as may be appropriate, and to do nothing which might be construed as suggesting that they had taken part in the organization of the entertainment, or that they had purported to act on behalf of the owners of the school.

It is for the authority or governors to require the hirer to provide such assurances, indemnities and evidence of adequate insurance as may seem necessary.

12 Performances by children

The law relating to professional public performances by children has already been dealt with in connection with the employment of children and young persons in chapter X. These restrictions do not, of course, apply to children taking part as amateurs in school productions.

References

1. Theatres Act 1968, s. 12(1).
2. Theatres Act 1968, s. 18(1)(a); and (b) as amended by the Local Government Act 1972, s. 204(6).
3. Theatres Act 1968, Schedule 1. 2.
4. Theatres Act 1968, Schedule 1. 3(1)
5. Theatres Act 1968, Schedule 1. 4.
6. Theatres Act 1968, Schedule 1. 5 and 6.
7. Theatres Act 1968, proviso to s. 1(2).
8. Theatres Act 1968, Schedule 1. 7.
9. Theatres Act 1968, s. 13.
10. Theatres Act 1968, s. 16.
11. Local Government (Miscellaneous Provisions) Act 1982.
12. Theatres Act 1968, s. 18(1).
13. Theatres Act 1968, s. 18(1).
14. Theatres Act 1968, s. 18(1).
15. Theatres Act 1968, s. 12(2) and (3).
16. Theatres Act 1968, s. 18(2).
17. Theatres Act 1968, s. 1.
18. Theatres Act 1968, s. 11; see also s. 7(2)(a) and (b).
19. Theatres Act 1968, s. 4.
20. Theatres Act 1968, s. 5.
21. Theatres Act 1968, s. 6.
22. Theatres Act 1968, s. 8.
23. Theatres Act 1968, ss. 9 and 10.

XVIII
Copyright

1 Copyright and schools

In 1970 the secretary of the Publishers' Association complained that many educational establishments were unintentionally breaking copyright law by the use they were making of photocopying apparatus: 'If the practice is allowed to an unlimited degree', he said prophetically, 'the time will quickly come when no one can afford to publish anything.' In his book,[1] he added: 'The fact that it is cheaper to steal someone else's property rather than buy it does not make it right to steal.'

In earlier editions of the present book the law of copyright was dealt with in less than two pages. Almost three decades, however, have witnessed a remarkable escalation in the amount of copying undertaken in schools, much of it undoubtedly illegal. Teachers may claim that they are acting only in the interests of their children, but this defence availed little to a father who pleaded in the nineteenth century that he had stolen bread for his starving offspring. In the light of recent developments and the current discussions designed to control and regularize modern practice, it is now necessary to devote a whole chapter to this subject.

The intensification of dishonest copying practices in educational institutions in recent years is due to a number of factors. Inflation has had a marked effect on the price of books and other copyright learning materials. Capitation allowances have not kept pace with rising costs and increased amounts spent by schools represent actually a cutting back in the number of copies bought. A second factor is the development of teaching techniques which postulate greatly increased flexibility, and the use of a vast amount of instant topical source material obtained much more quickly by copying than by waiting for the supplies department to deal with a requisition. Thirdly, there has become available a large range of relatively cheap and versatile reproductive hardware such as photocopiers, video and tape recorders. Finally, the growth of teachers' centres, often equipped and staffed to prepare material of this kind, and the appointment of media resource officers in many schools and colleges, have increased the facility with which material may be reproduced.

2   History of copyright

The concept of copyright dates back to the invention of printing, when it first became possible, on a large scale, to make multiple copies of the actual form in which an author had put his thoughts on paper. From time to time the common law right was reinforced by statute, and extended to include engravings (1734), sculpture (1814), performing rights in plays (1833), similar rights in musical works (1842), paintings, drawings and photographs (1862) and gramophone records (1911).

The need for the reciprocal international recognition of copyright holders' rights led to the Berne Convention of 1885, effect being given to its decisions in English law by the International Copyright Act 1886. A further convention was held in Berlin in 1905, after which the Copyright Act 1911 consolidated the law and expressly put an end to common law copyright. The Berne Convention was revised in Rome in 1928 and in Brussels in 1948, the latter meeting paving the way for the present statute, the Copyright Act 1956, which repealed the whole of the 1911 Act with the exception of three sections, one of which is that dealing with the delivery of copies of works to the British Museum.

The United Kingdom is also a signatory of the 1952 Geneva (Universal) Copyright Convention, commonly called the UCC.

The rights of performers are protected by the Dramatic and Musical Performers' Protection Act 1958 and the Performers' Protection Act 1963. The latter Act gives effect in the United Kingdom to the International Convention for the Protection of Performers, Producers of Phonograms and Broadcasting Organizations agreed in Rome in 1961.

3 The nature of copyright

The law of copyright is based on the assumption that the creator of intellectual material is entitled, just as much as any other craftsman, to control the use of what he has produced and to benefit from its use by others. Copyright is therefore a valuable property and the law gives its owner an exclusive power to do, or to authorize others to do, certain acts in respect of the protected material.

If there were no law of copyright, publishing, in all its forms, would quickly come to an end; for, as soon as a particular and valuable piece of work came into existence, anyone would be free to reproduce it without let or hindrance. The author or originator would not receive the due reward accruing from such acts of piracy; neither would publishers be prepared to undertake the financial risks inherent in their work if the author could not assign to them a right sufficiently wide to protect their interests.

As has been said above, copyright may be owned not only by writers, but also by painters, artists, sculptors and composers. For the sake of brevity the word 'author' when used in this chapter without qualification may be taken to include all originators of material in which copyright subsists.

Also protected by the Copyright Act 1956 are the makers of sound recordings, films and videotapes to safeguard their rights in these forms. Videotapes are not specifically mentioned in the Act because the process had not been developed at the time the legislation was passed: presumably, however, there is an analogy between them and films. As has already been mentioned, performers are protected by the Dramatic and Musical Performers' Protection Act 1958 and the Performers' Protection Act 1963.

There is no copyright in ideas; but immediately an author commits his ideas to some material form, that expression of his ideas becomes copyright without further formality. Publication is not necessary, indeed it has been held that an author dictating work to his secretary who takes it down in shorthand has already established his copyright. The essential element is that the ideas must be established in a material form.

There is no copyright in titles, although a title must not be taken with the purpose of passing a work off as the original.

By United Kingdom law, copyright may be acquired only by 'qualified persons'. A qualified person is an individual who is of British nationality, or who is domiciled or resident in the United Kingdom or in any country to which the Berne and Universal Copyright Conventions extend. Similar rights extend to corporate bodies in these countries and the domestic law of these states gives similar protection to the owners of copyright in all the subscribing states.

Generally speaking, the original copyright is the property of the author who has the exclusive power to deal in and assign any of the rights given to him by law. If, however, the original work is produced in the course of the author's employment, the copyright, subject to any specific terms in the contract of employment, is vested in the employer. This proviso is clearly of some importance to teachers and is dealt with in a later section, 'In the course of employment'.

The rights reserved to the author of a literary, dramatic or musical work are:

(a) reproduction in any material form;
(b) publication;
(c) performance in public;

(d) broadcasting;
(e) transmission through a diffusion service;
(f) adaptation;
(g) any act in relation to adaptation falling within any of the categories (a) to (e).[2]

Adaptation includes any conversion of a non-dramatic into a dramatic work (or vice versa), whether in the original language or another; translation; or a version wholly or mainly in pictures suitable for publication in a book, newspaper, magazine or similar periodical. In the case of musical works it includes an arrangement or transcription.[3]

For copyright purposes an artistic work is (irrespective of artistic merit) a painting, sculpture, drawing, engraving, photograph, work of architecture (whether a building or a model for a building) or any other work of artistic craftsmanship not included in these categories.[4]

The rights reserved to the copyright owner are:

(a) reproduction in any material form;
(b) publication;
(c) inclusion in a television broadcast;
(d) transmission of a television broadcast including the work through a diffusion service.[5]

The maker of a sound recording, film or videotape owns a separate copyright in the recording itself which is additional to the rights of the author. Videotape recording is an invention since the passage of the 1956 Act but 'the majority opinion is that a videotape recording must be treated legally as though it were a film'.[6]

For copyright to subsist, the maker must be a qualified person at the time the recording or film is made. In the case of a sound recording it is the person who owns the recording at the time of making, in the case of films and videotapes the person or corporate body arranging for it to be made.[7]

In the case of sound recordings the rights reserved are:

(a) making a record embodying the recording;
(b) performing the recording in public;

(c) broadcasting the recording.[8]

The restricted acts in the case of films (and, by analogy, videotapes) are:

(a) making a copy;
(b) causing it to be seen or heard in public;
(c) broadcasting;
(d) transmission through a diffusion service.[9]

Similarly, an additional copyright subsists in every published edition of a work where the publisher is a qualified person. It is a breach of copyright to make 'by any photographic or similar process ... a reproduction of the typographical arrangement of the edition'. This applies only to editions published since 1 June 1957, and is the domestic law in the United Kingdom and Australia; it does not form part of the Berne or Universal Copyright Conventions.[10] Thus, to photocopy an edition of *David Copperfield* would not infringe Charles Dickens's 'copyright' in the work, since this has expired. (See section 7, 'Duration of copyright'.) If the edition were published after 1 June 1957, however, the publisher's permission would be needed to avoid an infringement of his right in the edition.

4   Transfer of copyright

Any person in whom copyright is vested may sell, give away, or otherwise dispose of his rights, e.g. by will. In the case of intestacy copyright forms part of the estate and is dealt with according to the law in such cases.

There have been many cases where authors in urgent need of ready cash have parted with their property in this way, and the publisher has made profits vastly exceeding the amount he has paid for the rights. Once he has sold the copyright, however, the author has no further financial interest in his work. Regrettably, in the past, some publishers put pressure on authors to part with their rights in work which was obviously going to be a moneyspinner; but this has never been the practice of reputable houses, and has become much more rare as a result of the vigilance of the Society of Authors. The address of the Society is 84 Drayton Gardens, London SW10 9SD.

The more usual practice is for the copyright owner to issue a licence granting those rights which he wishes to transfer. The licensee is then responsible for acting strictly within the terms of the licence.

Authors need to exercise particular care in submitting articles to journals. If they make it clear that they are offering only 'first serial rights', the journal concerned may publish the article, but the copyright remains with the writer, and he may have it republished elsewhere in any form. There are journals, however, including some of high repute, who take the copyright of all freelance material submitted. The contributor may know nothing of this until his cheque arrives with a form of receipt on the back assigning the copyright to the publishers. If he has specified that he is offering only 'first serial rights', he should refuse to sign this; the periodical should not have proceeded to publication on a basis not offered by the author. This matter is dealt with further in the section on school magazines.[11]

Artists taking part in a recorded, filmed or videotaped performance are protected by the rights granted to them under the Performers' Protection Acts 1958 and 1963.

Lectures, addresses, speeches and sermons are defined as 'performances',[12] but copyright in these can subsist only if expressed in literary form, i.e. in print or writing,[13] and there is no copyright in an extempore speech. If the speech is made from notes, publication of the speech might infringe the copyright of the notes. The delivery of a lecture does not amount to publication, and a lecturer would probably be held to have licensed publication if he delivered a lecture knowing that reporters were present.

A letter is an original literary work. No matter how poor its literary quality, it is protected by copyright.[14] The writer of a letter can restrain publication unless the circumstances imply a licence to publish. Unless specific limitations are imposed the receiver of a letter has an unqualified title to the physical document, which he may keep, destroy or sell for wastepaper or the value of the signature. Whilst the signature is not a literary work, its reproduction might in some cases be protected as an artistic work. A long series of precedents going back for more than two hundred years[15] has settled the law that the one thing the receiver cannot do is to publish the ideas in their particular verbal expressions.

5 'In the course of employment'

Where a literary, dramatic or artistic work is made by the author in the course of his employment by the proprietor of a newspaper, magazine or similar periodical under a contract of service or apprenticeship, and is made for the purpose of publication in a newspaper, magazine or similar periodical, the said proprietor shall be entitled to the copyright in the work insofar as the copyright relates to publication of the work in any newspaper, magazine or similar periodical, or to reproduction of the work for the purpose of its being so published; but in all other respects the author shall be entitled to any copyright subsisting in the work by virtue of this Part of this Act.[16]

Subject to the last preceding subsection, where a person commissions the taking of a photograph, or the painting or drawing of a portrait, or the making of an engraving, and pays or agrees to pay for it in money or money's worth, and the work is made in pursuance of that commission, the person who so commissioned the work shall be entitled to any copyright therein.[17]

Where in a case not falling within either of the last two preceding subsections, a work is made in the course of the author's employment by another person under a contract of service or apprenticeship, that other person shall be entitled to any copyright subsisting in the work by virtue of this part of this Act.[18]

Each of the three last preceding subsections shall have effect subject, in any particular case, to any agreement excluding the operation thereof in that case.[19]

The four subsections of the Copyright Act 1956 quoted above are clearly of great importance to teachers, not only in schools but also in universities where research and its publication form an integral part of the work of the academic staff. Subsection (5) clearly permits the exclusion of the employer's right to copyright whether by operation of the general terms of the contract of service or by a special agreement referring to a specific piece of work.

It is an essential feature of a contract of service that the master has a right 'in some reasonable sense to control the method of doing the work'.[20] If a man employs another, and leaves it to the servant to decide how the work should be done, the contract is not one of service, but for services: 'In each case the question to be asked is, what was the man employed to do? Was he employed upon the terms that he should, within the scope of his employment, obey his master's orders, or was he employed to exercise his skill and achieve an indicated result in such manner as, in his judgement, was most likely to ensure success?'[21] As far as is known, the courts have not been called upon to consider whether a teacher's contract is a contract of service or for services. Generally, most people would probably regard it as the former because the requirement to comply with the reasonable instructions of the head suggests a measure of control. In very recent years, however, some teachers have claimed that neither the governors nor the head have any right to interfere with the way in which they carry out their professional duties. This may one day be a matter for the courts to decide; it is certainly not, in the present climate, a matter on which the authors of this book or individual teachers can pronounce authoritatively.

The work must be made in the course of the employment under a contract of service. A translation by a member of a newspaper staff[22] or lectures prepared by an accountant employed under a contract of service,[23] in each case in their spare time, were held not to have been carried out in the course of their employment.

The problem has shown up in its most acute form in educational circles in the preparation of material for closed circuit television programmes produced by local education authorities. In at least one case the authority has seconded members of its teaching staff to work as members of production teams. It is clearly envisaged that work produced during such periods of secondment should fall within the scope of the teacher's employment, but members of the teams have complained that much of their work, particularly the writing of scripts, has to be done outside normal working hours.

The authority claims that it is impossible to distinguish between the contributions of different members of a team and that, in the course of preparation, original scripts are so altered by the co-operative thinking of the team that the original is no more than an idea in which, of course, there is no copyright. Following this line of argument, it seems that the copyright of the material is vested in the employing authority.

There is, certainly, one important issue which, at the least, should be the subject of a special exclusion agreement under section 4(5) quoted above. It may be that a teacher is preparing, in his own time, a book or teaching pack including diagrams or other material suitable for inclusion in a programme, and allows the local education authority to make use of them. It would be obnoxious if he were, by such an act of grace, to lose control of the copyright. If material of this kind taken from a work already published is to be included, the teacher's contract with his publishers will probably have given them a sufficiently exclusive licence to control this use. The authority will then have to negotiate with the author's publishers who will watch his interests as well as their own.

6   Micro-computer programs

The increased use of micro-computers in schools in recent years has inevitably brought with it a greater interest among teachers in writing programs for use in school. Some of these programs undoubtedly have considerable value if sold to publishers of educational materials.

If a teacher, during the day at school, writes a program on a machine belonging to his employer and, moreover, stores it on a disk or tape belonging to his employer, then the employer has a major interest in the copyright, and the teacher, if he wishes to market the program, should consult his employer first. The same would be true if the teacher, with permission, borrowed a micro-computer from school and created a program at home. It is most unlikely that an employer would regard this activity in the same light as writing a school textbook.

If programs are written by a teacher employed in a local authority or school resources centre, or perhaps in a post such as head of computer studies, then it is most likely that writing programs is an integral part of the work he is contracted to do: in this case the copyright belongs to the employer.

7 Duration of copyright

LITERARY, DRAMATIC, MUSICAL AND ARTISTIC WORKS

Fifty years from the end of the calendar year in which the author dies in the case of works published during his lifetime; in the case of posthumously published works, fifty years from the end of the calendar year it was first published, performed in public or offered for sale as a recording.[24]

PHOTOGRAPHS

Fifty years from the end of the calendar year of first publication:[25] copyright is therefore perpetual until publication, which consists of the issue of reproductions to the public (not necessarily for value) but does not include the exhibition of an artistic work.[26]

SOUND RECORDINGS

Fifty years from the end of the calendar year of first publication.[27]

CINEMATOGRAPH FILMS

Fifty years from the end of the calendar year of registration in the case of films registrable under Part II of the Films Act 1960; in other cases for fifty years from the end of the calendar year of its first publication. In the case of newsreels copyright is not infringed by performance after fifty years from the end of the calendar year in which the principal events depicted occurred, though it might still be an infringement to reproduce them.[28] Films made before the 1956 Act came into force are protected as dramatic works (if fiction) or photographs (if non-fiction).

PUBLISHED EDITIONS

Twenty-five years from the end of the calendar year of the first publication of the edition.[29]

TELEVISION AND SOUND BROADCASTS

Fifty years from the end of the year in which any broadcast is made by the British Broadcasting Corporation or the Independent Television Authority, and in any country to which section 14 of the 1956 Act has been extended by the European Agreement on the Protection of Television Broadcasts 1964 (France, Sweden and Denmark), and by Orders in Council made in 1961 and 1964.[30] The term of copyright is not extended by the repetition of a broadcast, although any new material included would presumably acquire its own copyright. As broadcasts made before 1 June 1957 are specifically excluded, the first repeat after that date of a broadcast originally made before the commencement of the Act would count as a new broadcast, and copyright would run from the date of that repetition.[31]

CROWN COPYRIGHT

Perpetual until publication and then for fifty years from the end of the calendar year of first publication in the case of literary, dramatic or musical works, engravings or photographs made by or under the direction of the Crown or a government department. Fifty years from the making of other artistic works, or photographs taken before 1 June 1956. Crown copyright in sound recordings and cinematograph films is the same as for other holders of these rights.[32]

PERPETUAL COPYRIGHT

By the Copyright Act 1775 the Universities of Oxford and Cambridge, the four universities in Scotland, and the colleges of Eton and Westminster (to which, by a later Act, Trinity College, Dublin, was added) were given perpetual copyright in books given or bequeathed to them for the advancement of useful learning and other purposes of education. Such books had to be printed by the universities and colleges on their own presses and for their own benefit. Perpetual copyrights still in existence at the commencement of the 1956 Act continue, but all proceedings in respect of them must be in accordance with the terms of the 1956 Act. No new perpetual copyrights may be acquired.[33]

JOINT WORKS

Fifty years from the end of the calendar year in which the last surviving author dies; except in the case of any literary, dramatic and musical work or engraving which has not been published, performed in public, offered for sale as records or broadcast during the lifetime of the last surviving author: in such cases copyright continues for fifty years from the end of the calendar year in which one of these acts is first done.[34]

Joint authorship involves a collaboration in which the work of each author is not separate from that of the other author or authors.[35]

ANONYMOUS AND PSEUDONYMOUS WORKS

Fifty years from the end of the calendar year of first publication (except in the case of a photograph). If before the expiry of this period it is possible for a person without previous knowledge of the facts to ascertain the identity of the author by reasonable inquiry, copyright will run in the usual way from the date of the author's death. A work published under two or more names is not pseudonymous unless all those names are pseudonyms.[36]

8 Minors

Minors, that is persons under the age of 18, are not specifically mentioned in the Copyright Act 1956. Nevertheless, since copyright is a valuable property, they must be able to own this right, though they may not sell, deal in, or otherwise dispose of it except through their parent or legal guardian.

In default of any decided cases it must be assumed that the copyright of any original work produced by pupils in the course of instruction is vested in the author. A child is not employed by a school under a contract of service, and the school authorities can hardly be regarded as the child's employer. Neither do they, in the ordinary course of school work, commission work for money or money's worth. It seems most unlikely that the school authorities can lay any claim to copyright in such material: it is quite certain that no such right can pass to any individual teacher. These aspects of the law are particularly worth noting in connection with the growth of micro-computer games. There is currently quite a substantial trade in such games, often written by youngsters using programming skills acquired at school, and sometimes even using school equipment. Commercial firms are willing to pay quite large sums for suitable programs.

It is the 'custom of the trade' for schools to solicit and accept original work for publication in school magazines. No payment is usually, if ever, made for such publication. The practice is so long-established that it is doubtful if it would be considered a breach of copyright, and it could, in any case, be regularized by a simple form of consent signed by the parent or guardian. Whether or not this is done, the acceptance by the school should not be regarded as more than acquiring 'first serial rights', and the copyright must remain with the pupil. The reader is referred in this context to chapter XXI, 'The school magazine'.

9   General exceptions

The 1956 Act provides a number of exceptions to the general prohibition of infringement of copyright. Those which are purely concerned with educational use are dealt with in later sections. The principal reliefs from infringement in the ordinary affairs of life are considered here.

FAIR DEALING

'No fair dealing with a literary, dramatic or musical work for purposes of research or private study shall constitute an infringement.'[37] A further section extends this to artistic works.[38] 'No fair dealing with a literary, dramatic or musical work shall constitute an infringement of the copyright in the work if it is for purposes of criticism or review, whether of that work or of another work, and is accompanied by a sufficient acknowledgement.'[39] Similar provisions extend to artistic works.[40] For literary and dramatic works, 400-word quotations are acceptable to the law.

'Sufficient acknowledgement' is 'an acknowledgement identifying the work in question by its title or other description and, unless the work is anonymous or the author has previously agreed or required that no acknowledgement of his name should be made, also identifying the author'.[41]

The Act, however, is silent on the meaning of fair dealing

since this is a matter of fact for the courts to determine in each case, and depends on a number of elements. In 1983 the Council for Educational Technology stated:[42] 'Anyone may, for their private study, make or have made copies of all or part of a work, provided the number of copies made, the proportion taken and the circumstances are "fair" to the copyright owner.... Reference to the special educational provisions (of the Act) suggests that teachers may not make copies for distribution to their pupils although each pupil may make or have made a copy for personal use. There is no restriction on the method used, so photocopying is permitted. No guidance is given in the Act on what factors should be considered when deciding if a certain act of copying is "fair" but apart from the volume of copying a court would probably wish to know if the material was readily available for purchase and to what extent the copying was detrimental to the copyright owner's interests. The fair dealing provisions also apply where material is copied for research, whether private or not, but since the word is fairly elastic a court would probably interpret it narrowly and be hard to convince that a school did in fact engage in "research".'

The Society of Authors and the Publishers Association in 1958 stated that objection could not normally be taken to a quotation in a book, criticism or review of a single extract up to 400 words, or a series of extracts (none of which exceeds 300 words) totalling up to 800 words. In the case of poetry, an extract or extracts up to 40 lines would be acceptable, but in no case exceeding one quarter of any poem.

SUBSTANTIALITY

'Any reference in this Act to the doing of an act in relation to a work or other subject matter shall be taken to include a reference to the doing of that act in relation to a substantial part thereof....'[43] The Act does not define the term 'substantial part' which is, again, a matter of fact in each case. Much will depend upon whether an alleged infringement would compete with the original, or make the purchase of copies of it unnecessary. The test is: 'Is the act one which will damage the copyright owner?' The reproduction *in toto* of a diagram summarizing the argument of a book will almost certainly do so. The Council for Educational Technology puts the point succinctly: 'Courts tend to interpret "substantial part" rather carefully, taking the view that if it's worth copying, it's worth protecting.'

LIBRARIES

In 1957 the Board of Trade issued the Copyright (Libraries) Regulations[44] empowering the library of any school, university, college or other establishment of further education, any public library, any parliamentary library or that of any department of government, or any library conducted for ... facilitating or encouraging the study of religion, philosophy, science (including any natural or social science), technology, medicine, history, literature, languages, education, bibliography, fine arts, music or law to make for their readers a copy of a single article from any one periodical or a 'reasonable proportion' of any other copyright work. Before this is supplied the applicant must personally sign the following declaration:

> I, ... of .... hereby request you to make and supply to me a copy of ....
> which I require for the purposes of research or private study.
>
> I have not previously been supplied with a copy of the said article/the said part of the said work by any librarian.
>
> I undertake that if a copy is supplied to me in compliance with the request made above, I will not use it except for the purposes of research or private study.

If a librarian (including a school librarian) is asked for multiple copies of copyright work, he must, by law, seek the approval of the owner of the copyright. The exception provided by the regulations does not extend to libraries conducted for profit.[45] The library must make a charge for this service and, even for a single copy, the owner of the copyright must be approached if his whereabouts can be reasonably ascertained.

COLLECTIONS FOR SCHOOLS

It is not an infringement of copyright to include a 'short passage' of a copyright work in a collection intended for school use. The collection must be described as intended for this purpose, but the extract must not itself have been published for this purpose. 'Sufficient acknowledgement'[46] must be made, and the bulk of the collection must consist of material which is out of copyright. Not more than two extracts may be included from one author's copyright works.[47]

The Act does not define the meaning of 'short extract' but the Society of Authors and the Publishers Association stated in 1958 that they would regard this as not more than 750 words from a prose work or 75 lines from a poem, provided that the extract did not exceed one-third of the whole poem, essay, story or other literary or dramatic work.

10 Educational exceptions

It is not an infringement to reproduce a copyright literary, artistic, dramatic or musical work in the course of instruction so long as this is not done by a duplicating process. Apparently a teacher may write copyright material on a blackboard, and his pupils may copy it individually, but he may not hand out multi-copies prepared in an unauthorized manner. Neither is it an infringement of copyright to include, and reproduce in multiple form, such material in an examination question or answer. It would be a breach of copyright, say, to copy out the parts of a copyright play so as to deprive the copyright owner of his livelihood by making it unnecessary to purchase or hire copies.

It is not an infringement to perform a copyright literary, dramatic or musical work in class or otherwise in the course of the activities of a school, provided that both performers and audience are members of the school. Any other members of the audience must be directly connected with the activities of the school, and a person is not held to be so merely because he is the parent or guardian of a pupil.[48] The same exemption extends to sound recordings, cinematograph films and television broadcasts.[49]

It is, however, an infringement to make a copy of a film, or to exhibit it publicly, without the appropriate consent. Such actions violate the conditions under which the distributors make their products available to schools, film societies and other institutions.

Public performances of copyright literary, dramatic and musical works, including the use of recorded material, are dealt with in chapter XVII.

It must be emphasized that the 'educational exceptions' are very limited in scope, and all concerned should exercise great caution. It is not a defence in law that illicit photocopying in schools is done with pupils' best interests at heart and with no intention of profiteering by anyone. This defence failed in 1981 when the Music Publishers Association successfully sued Oakham School for infringement of music copyright. The school had produced its own book of carols, putting works together from various sources without the permission of the copyright holders. The school was ordered to give a perpetual undertaking not to infringe the copyrights of any member of the Music Publishers Association, to deliver up all the offending materials and to pay £4,250, including exemplary damages, under the Copyright Act 1956. In 1980 Wolverhampton Local Education Authority was obliged to pay £1,300 damages together with very substantial legal costs in a similar action. There have also been reports of actions against other local education authorities. Teachers who are not fully aware of the limitations of copyright where music is concerned should consult the 'Code of Fair Practice' available from the Music Publishers Association, 73/75 Mortimer Street, London W1N 7TB.

Teachers' associations and the Educational Publishers Council have been exploring the possibility of some sort of licensing system to which reference is made later in this chapter. In the meantime, the associations representing owners of copyrights show every sign of pursuing their rights under the law more aggressively than in the past. In a 1982 leaflet, *Copying and*

Copyright (from the Publishers Association, 19 Bedford Square, London WC1), the Education Publishers Council makes its attitude clear: 'Exactly the same financial pressures which teachers experience through cuts and restrictions in capitation are felt by the writers and publishers of the material in its original form. If teachers and other educationalists switch from book-buying to photocopying, it could soon become uneconomic for books to be written at all, or published.'

The costs of copying are often hidden, but in real terms compare unfavourably with the price of books. The photocopying, collating and binding of ten copies of a 16-page workbook costs at present (1982) between £4 and £5 when the same workbook would cost under £3. In addition to this, if illegal copying is challenged in a court of law, the cost of defending would be likely to prove embarrassingly high, whatever damages were awarded if the claim succeeded. In a recent case (1980) a local authority was required to pay £10,000 including costs − 70p per page illegally copied!

11   Broadcasting and television

Reference has already been made to the duration of copyright in broadcasts and telecasts by the British Broadcasting Corporation, the Independent Television Authority and in countries to which section 14 of the 1956 Act has been extended, but it has been felt wiser to leave a review of the nature of this particular form of copyright to a separate section in which it is possible also to discuss its effect on educational use. It must be remembered that this right is independent of, and additional to, any other rights vested in authors, makers of recordings and performers.

It is a breach of copyright to make a cinematograph film (or a copy of such a film) of a telecast insofar as it consists of visual images or, in the case either of a sound or television broadcast insofar as it consists of sound, to make a sound recording or a record including such a recording. It is not a breach of copyright to do any of these acts for private purposes. It is also a breach of copyright to cause a telecast to be seen or heard in public by a paying audience; or to rebroadcast it on a sound broadcast.[50]

The restrictions apply to breaches by the reception of the broadcast or telecast itself, or the use of any record, print, negative or tape on which the broadcast or telecast has been recorded.[51] In the case of telecasts any sequence of images sufficient to be seen as a moving picture is sufficient to breach copyright.[52]

A recording is not made for private purposes if it is made for the sale or hire of any copy of the film or record embodying the recording; broadcasting the film; broadcasting the film or recording; or causing the film or recording to be seen in public.[53]

A television broadcast has been heard or seen by a 'paying public' if they have been admitted for payment to the place where it is to be seen or heard, or to a place of which that auditorium forms a part; or who have been admitted to a place in circumstances where goods or services are supplied at a higher price than is usual there, such enhancement being attributable to the facilities for hearing or seeing the broadcast or telecast. The first part of this definition does not apply to residents or inmates of the place in question, or if persons are admitted as members of a club or society where the only payment they make is the membership subscription, and the broadcasting and telecasting facilities are only incidental to the main purposes of the club or society.[54]

In order to facilitate the use of broadcasts and telecasts transmitted for educational purposes, the British Broadcasting Corporation and the Independent Television Authority have made arrangements with the British Record Producers Association and with certain performers' unions to enable these programmes to be recorded off the air. In the case of schools, recordings may be used only on the same premises, not themselves copied again, and destroyed within three years. Since 1975 this facility has been extended to local education authority resource centres which are designated by an authority for this purpose. A licence must be obtained by the authority for this purpose from the Mechanical Copyrights Protection

Society Ltd, and a record kept of all material copied. In the case of a resource centre, circulation of recorded material to schools and colleges must also be recorded. Material on loan must be returned within four weeks. The recordings must be erased within three years of being made or, in the case of BBC radio vision programmes, by the end of the third school year.

The British Broadcasting Corporation requires no formalities in connection with this facility, but the Independent Television Authority issues an annual licence to local education authorities and other appropriate bodies, such as universities, for a fee of £5. The local education authority may determine which schools within its area may make use of the facilities afforded by the licence, and this may include independent schools within its boundaries.

It must be clearly understood that this facility applies only to educational programmes advertised as such, and confers no right to record any other material put out by the broadcasting authorities. Open University broadcasts are not regarded as educational programmes for this purpose; and the consent of the University, as owner of the copyright, must be obtained before a re-recording is made.

Not all local education authorities have taken out Independent Television Authority licences, and schools should ensure that they do not record programmes put out under the aegis of that body unless the licence has been obtained.

In recent years the practice has grown in many schools of providing children with 'end of term treats' in the form of showing video cassettes, sometimes hired from High Street dealers, sometimes even naïvely borrowed from friends or colleagues. There is of course the technical problem of whether video tape is covered at all by the 1956 Copyright Act since magnetic imprints are not 'visual images'. However, on the assumption that copyright does subsist – and most people think that it does – the practice of showing such cassettes or tapes clearly involves a breach, as the label on most commercial video cassettes clearly points out.

The Copyright Act is part of the civil law: a violation of the Performers' Protection Acts is a criminal offence. To make an 'off-air' recording without the appropriate permissions might then offend against both Acts.

The Council for Educational Technology believes that it would not be a *major* infringement of the Copyright Act if a recording were to be made specifically for a single teaching purpose, was not made for open access but used within the institution and destroyed immediately after use.

It should be stressed, however, that this procedure would not prevent action under the Performers' Protection Acts 1958 and 1963.

12   Records and pre-recorded tapes

With the limited exception of recorded material included in broadcasts and telecasts referred to in the last section, it is an offence to re-record, without licence, any record or pre-recorded tape for public, educational or private use.

The leading recording companies have formed a company, Phonographic Performance Ltd, to control the use of their recordings by the issue of licences and to distribute the fees received from public performances among the various owners of the rights. The use of recordings at public performances given by schools has been discussed in chapter XVII, and this section is concerned with the use of recordings and with re-recording in schools.

Phonographic Performance Ltd is concerned only with the rights of recording companies. Those of composers, authors and publishers are the concern of the Performing Right Society which licenses the public performance, broadcasting and diffusion of copyright music, and collects and distributes royalties on behalf of its members. The Society is not concerned with non-musical plays or sketches, ballets, operas, musical plays or other dramatico-musical works performed in full by living persons on the stage. Again, the function of the Society in connection with public performances by schools is dealt with in chapter XVII.

Neither Phonographic Performance Ltd nor the Performing Right Society make any charge in respect of the use in accordance with the educational exemptions granted under section 41 of the Copyright Act 1956.

In this country the necessary negotiations for permission to re-record (as distinct from playing the actual record by arrangement with Phonographic Performance Ltd) are conducted on behalf of copyright holders by the Mechanical Rights Society Ltd. The collection and distribution of the fees arising from negotiated licences is undertaken by an associated company, the Mechanical Copyrights Protection Society Ltd whose address is 41 Streatham High Road, London SW16. Teachers who wish to make recordings for use in their own homes, in amateur tape recording clubs or for amateur recording competitions may not be aware that the MCPS will issue to anyone an amateur recording licence. The licence authorizes recording of musical works owned by members of the Society which have previously been released on gramophone records. Since 1974 it has covered re-recording on sound tape, from records issued under labels and/or trademarks owned or controlled by members of the British Phonographic Industries Copyright Association.

In August 1973 the Council for Educational Technology announced a proposed form of licensing for re-recording records and pre-recorded tapes for curricular purposes. These licences are issued by the Mechanical Copyright Protection Society on behalf of the British Phonographic Industries Copyright Association and the British Copyright Council. The licences permit the use of re-recorded material in an establishment used for the curricular purposes of the institution where it is made, e.g. during teaching practice in schools.

The licences are of two kinds. The first kind are available to local education authorities to enable re-recordings to be made in their maintained institutions for use in the institution in which the recording is made. The licence waives the restriction that the re-recording shall be made in the course of instruction as required by section 41 of the 1956 Act. Since many secondary schools and further education establishments have their own media resource officers, the new licence enables re-recordings to be made for curricular purposes in the institution's resource centre – a course of action not previously possible as this could hardly be considered as falling within the restriction. Local education authorities pay a fee which consists of a basic sum together with an addition for every fifty institutions to be covered. No addition is charged for institutions in excess of one thousand. The licence also permits the recording of the live performance of copyright music, provided that the consent of the performers had been obtained in writing.

The same form of licence may be obtained by independent schools and universities.

The second kind of licence is designed to waive the restriction that re-recordings must be used only by the copying institution. It provides that teachers' centres and resource centres, maintained by the licensee to augment the resources and facilities of a group of educational institutions, may copy recordings as parts of a composite sound programme of short extracts from commercially published records and pre-recorded tapes. A single extract must not exceed four minutes in duration, and the licence does not cover re-recording on the sound track of a cine film or videotape, for which special arrangements must be negotiated with the owners of the copyright. Any visual images included in the programme must be stills, and physically separate from the re-recording, e.g. a sound tape accompanied by slides or film strips. The original may not be copied on the sound track of a film or videotape. The original record or tape from which the copy is made must be the property of the licensee at the time of copying.

Copies may be made and used only on the licensee's premises, or on premises used for the licensee's curricular purposes. The recording remains the property of the institution where it is made. The label must show the distinguishing label mark, number and title of the original, and must state that copyright is reserved. The label must also state that the recording is produced only for the curricular purposes of the institution. The copy may not be used for extra-curricular purposes or for students' recreational activities.

VAT is payable on the licences. The Mechanical Copyright

Protection Society Ltd (41 Streatham High Road, London SW16 769–4400) (1985 Directory) and the British Copyright Council (29 Berners Street, London W1 580–5544) (1984 Directory) grant the necessary rights on behalf of the copyright holders of the recorded works, and the Phonographic Industry Copyright Association (33 Thurloe Place, London SW7) are the representatives for the copyright owners of the originals. The Society is endeavouring to negotiate terms for the extension of similar facilities to individual domestic licensees.

13 Photocopying

The accessibility and convenience of photocopying and other facilities for making multiple copies of printed material has undoubtedly led to a great deal of illegal copying of books, magazines, music and diagrams for which the permission of the copyright owner should have been sought.

In 1965 the Society of Authors and the Publishers Association issued a joint statement setting out what they considered as 'fair dealing' in the case of single copies made for research or private study. Under the terms of this statement it is not unfair to make a single photocopy from a copyright work of a single extract not exceeding 4,000 words, or a series of extracts (none of which exceeds 3,000 words) to a total of not more than 8,000 words. In neither case may the total exceed 10 per cent of the whole work. Poems, essays and other short literary works are whole works in themselves and not 'parts' of the volumes in which they appear. An unlimited number of copies may be made by hand.

It is probable that the making of a single photocopy of a diagram for use in transparency form on an overhead projector is an extension of the former practice of projecting such diagrams by means of an episcope. The episcope did not involve any physical reproduction, and therefore could not infringe copyright. The Society of Authors and the Publishers Association have indicated that they would not regard the making of single copies for projection transparencies within the terms of section 41 of the 1956 Act (solely for instruction

in a school or other educational establishment) as an infringement of copyright.

The making of multiple copies is an infringement unless the
permission of the owner of the copyright has been obtained.
It is clearly difficult, however, to avoid constant breaches of
copyright of this kind, and in the autumn of 1973 the Council
for Educational Technology and the Publishers Association
conducted an experiment to discover whether a licensing
scheme might be necessary or desirable to legalize the practices
which had developed.

Those responsible for the experiment recognized that there
was no reliable assessment of the extent of multiple copying
in breach of copyright. Obtaining consent in each case is a
cumbersome procedure, and the terms on which permission is
granted by different copyright owners are by no means
identical. Some, for example, may give permission freely, others
may charge a fee. Information was required about the extent
to which multiple copying would be used if the copyright
owners granted bulk licences to local education authorities
enabling all their schools to reproduce material on specific
terms and conditions, without the need to seek individual
permission on each occasion.

For the purpose of the experiment the Publishers Association
gave the Council for Educational Technology permission to
select a number of schools which, for a limited period, were
'licensed' to copy for curricular purposes all the published
printed material which they needed, British or foreign,
textbooks, work cards, examination papers, sheet music,
newspapers and periodicals. The schools were asked to complete
a simple return giving details of the title and form of the work
copied, the proportion of the work used, the number of copies
made and the method used. The results showed that an average
of 25 copies per primary school child and 35 per secondary
school child were taken.

14   The experimental licensing scheme 1984-5

Following on advice given in a Government Green Paper of 1981, the Copyright Licensing Agency Ltd concluded an agreement in 1984 with the Associations representing local authorities in England, Scotland and Wales — the Association of County Councils, the Association of Metropolitan Authorities and the Convention of Scottish Local Authorities — to operate an *experimental* licensing scheme for a twelve-month period to assess the amount and type of copying of copyright material. Payment during the twelve months is a notional sum paid by each LEA which bears no relation to the actual amount of copying estimated to take place. In total the sum for the year 1984-5 is £350,000. At the time of writing, the London Borough of Bromley, the County of Avon and Derbyshire are not members of AMA or ACC: the scheme, therefore, is subject to separate negotiations in those areas.

Educational institutions fully controlled by the authorities within the associations, are covered by the licence during the experimental year, provided that they copy only within the terms of the licence. Polytechnics, however, because of the differences in their copying practices, will be treated separately.

Records will be required to be kept by a representative sample of institutions of all copies made from copyright material. The records will be returned to CLA at regular intervals to form the basis upon which CLA and the Associations will negotiate a licensing scheme for the future.

The experimental licence stipulates that:

(a) The proportion of the work which can be copied will be limited to 5 per cent of a book or to one article from a periodical at any one time.

(b) The number of copies that can be made will be limited to 30, or to the number required for a class of students and their instructor. Copying for stocking purposes will not be permitted.

(c) The works covered by the licence include all books, periodicals and journals with UK imprints, with the exception of:

Printed music

Maps, charts and books of tables

Tests and examination papers whether published individually or in collections

Work cards and assignment sheets

Workbooks

Privately owned documents issued for tuition purposes and limited to clientele who pay fees

Newspapers

House journals and other free publications for employees of commercial businesses, industrial undertakings or public services

Any work on which the copyright owner has expressly stipulated that it may not be copied under this licence

Any work produced by any copyright owner listed as not participating in this licensing scheme

Permission to make copies of works or numbers of copies outside the terms of this licence must be requested in writing from the respective copyright owners.

All institutions, whether in the sample or not, receive notices of conditions of the licence to attach to copying or duplicating machines and notice boards.

It must be stressed that, at the time of writing, this scheme is experimental for one year, 1984–5 and implies no permanent change in the law.

15   Language laboratories

It is the essential nature of work in a language laboratory that a master tape is repeatedly copied on the students' tapes. In order to safeguard the copyright in such tapes the publishers charge a higher price for the master tapes than would normally be applicable to a similar commercial tape. This 'levy' is distributed among the owners of the various rights, and in consideration of this the purchaser is licensed to make copies in such numbers, and as frequently as may be necessary, within the laboratory.

16 Closed circuit television

Some local education authorities and many educational establishments now have closed circuit television systems. The exposure of work by a television camera does not amount to reproduction, and does not infringe copyright. If, however, the work is reproduced in material form the consent of the owner of the copyright must be obtained. Few closed circuit television programmes are 'live', the majority being transmitted on videotape, and in all such cases consent must be obtained.

17 Juke boxes

Juke boxes installed for entertainment are not exempt.

18 The future of copyright

The law of copyright is complex, and is not made simpler by the necessary international conventions to protect rights not only in the country of origin, but also throughout as wide a part of the earth's surface as possible. It is also constantly changing. During the 1960s problems arose in the developing countries because of their need for ready access to educational material. The Paris Revisions of 1971, which are in the process of ratification, provide that such countries will be able to apply compulsory licensing for educational use after specified periods which vary between one and five years. Royalties must be paid on such licences.

In this country, and particularly within our educational system, the biggest problems posed at present are those arising from the sudden development of facilities for copying print, sound and vision. In its pamphlet *Copyright and Education* the National Council for Educational Technology (now the Council for Educational Technology for the United Kingdom) examined several possible changes.

One was a proposal that the exemptions granted to schools by the 1956 Act should be extended to other educational institutions. The difficulty about this solution is that it would conflict with the international conventions to which the United Kingdom is a party. Another idea was the imposition of a levy on copying hardware (photocopiers, tape recorders, etc.), or on software (such as copying paper or tapes), the purchaser being authorized by payment of the levy to copy copyright works, and the levy being distributed among copyright owners. In Western Germany a levy of 5 per cent has been placed on tape recorders for domestic purposes and, as has been said earlier, this is already the practice in this country in the case of language laboratory tapes. The Council's objection to this scheme is that it would bear hardly on the many purchasers of tape recorders and blank tapes who have no intention of using them for recording copyright material.

Possibly the most acceptable solution is the further development of 'blanket' agreements within the framework of the 1956 Act, such as those concluded in 1973 and outlined earlier for re-recording in educational establishments and centres, and also those which it is hoped may grow from the multiple copying experiment in 1984–5.

A committee under the chairmanship of Mr Justice Whitford spent almost four years unravelling the complexities of the law of copyright, and considering what changes may be desirable. The report, one of the best-written and most readable documents of this character, made sweeping proposals for revision, including streamlining of the provisions for the duration of various forms of copyright, adoption of the German system of levy licensing, and an extension of blanket licensing.[55]

19 *Caveat praeceptor*

In the meantime let the teacher beware. If he wishes to reproduce material which he may have reasonable grounds to believe to be subject to copyright, he should make careful inquiries before doing so. Ignorance is no excuse for breaking the law and, in the case of published material, an inquiry to the publishers is the best way of discovering whether the work concerned is still protected and, if so, the name of the owner of the copyright from whom it will be possible to secure details

Before you copy: questions to ask and answer

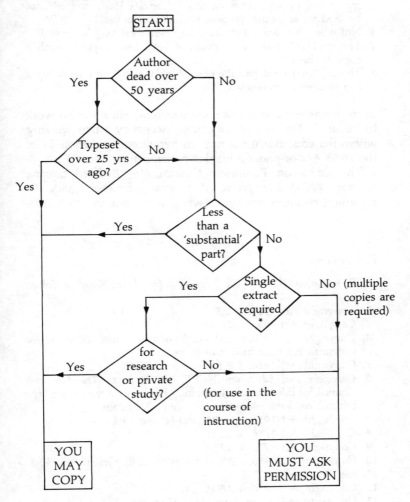

* At this stage, copies may be obtained from libraries, subject to these provisions:

1. One copy of an article from a periodical may be taken.

2. The applicant must provide a signed statement that the copy is for his/her own personal research or private study and will not be used for any other purpose (e.g. classroom use).
3. Not more than one article from any periodical may be copied.
4. The applicant must not previously have been supplied with a copy of the article.
5. The applicant must pay the cost of making the copy including a contribution to overheads.

of the terms and conditions upon which he will allow his work to be used. This is not, of course, necessary when working within the educational exemptions permitted by section 41 of the 1956 Act or under a blanket agreement.

The Education Publishers Council (19, Bedford Square, London WC1) has produced a straightforward guide to copyright clearance procedure which is reproduced on p. 567.

References

1. R. E. Barker, *Photocopying Practices in the United Kingdom* (Faber, 1970).
2. Copyright Act 1956, s. 2(5).
3. Copyright Act 1956, s. 2(6).
4. Copyright Act 1956, s. 3(1). Works of architecture and of artistic craftsmanship must have artistic merit.
5. Copyright Act 1956, s. 3(5).
6. *Copyright and Education* (NCET, 1972), p. 6. The National Council for Educational Technology has become the Council for Educational Technology for the United Kingdom.
7. Copyright Act 1956, ss. 12(1) and (4) and 13(1).
8. Copyright Act 1956, s. 12(5).
9. Copyright Act 1956, s. 13(5).
10. Copyright Act 1956, s. 15; and Australian Copyright Act 1968.
11. See pp. 639–40.
12. Copyright Act 1956, s. 48(1).
13. University of London Press Ltd *v.* University Tutorial Press Ltd [1916] 2 Ch 601.
14. Walter *v.* Lane [1900] AC 539; British Oxygen Co. Ltd *v.* Liquid Air Ltd [1925] Ch 383.

15. Pope *v.* Curl (1741) 2 Ark. 341 to Philip *v.* Pennell [1970] 2 Ch. 577.
16. Copyright Act 1956, s. 4(2).
17. Copyright Act 1956, s. 4(3).
18. Copyright Act 1956, s. 4(4).
19. Copyright Act 1956, s. 4(5).
20. Per Lord Thankerton in Short *v.* J. and W. Henderson Ltd (1946) 39 BWCC 62.
21. Per Buckley, LJ, in Simmons *v.* Heath Laundry Co [1910] 1 KB 543.
22. Byrne *v.* Statist Co [1914] 1 KB 622.
23. Stevenson, Jordan & Harrison Ltd *v.* Macdonald & Evans (1952) 1 TLR 101.
24. Copyright Act 1956, ss. 2(3) and 3(4).
25. Copyright Act 1956, s. 3(4)(b).
26. Copyright Act 1956, s. 49(2)(a). Photographs taken before the 1956 Act came into force are protected for fifty years from the date they were taken.
27. Copyright Act 1956, s. 12(3). Sound recordings made before the 1956 Act came into force are protected for fifty years from the date they were taken.
28. Copyright Act 1956, s. 13(3) and (8).
29. Copyright Act 1956, s. 15(2).
30. 1961, no. 2460 and 1964, no. 690.
31. Copyright Act 1956, s. 14(2) and (3).
32. Copyright Act 1956, s. 39(1), (2) and (3).
33. Copyright Act 1956, s. 46(1).
34. Copyright Act 1956, Schedule II, 1, 2 and 3; Schedule III, 31.
35. Copyright Act 1956, s. 11(3).
36. Copyright Act 1956, Schedule II.
37. Copyright Act 1956, s. 6(1).
38. Copyright Act 1956, s. 9(1).
39. Copyright Act 1956, s. 6(2).
40. Copyright Act 1956, s. 9(2).
41. Copyright Act 1956, s. 6(10).
42. CET Information Sheet No. 6, Sept. 1983: *Copyright*. Available from 3 Devonshire Street, London W1N 2BA.
43. Copyright Act 1956, s. 49(1).
44. Under the Copyright Act 1956, ss. 7(1), (3) and (7); 15(4) from which they derive their statutory force.
45. This subject is dealt with fully in R. E. Barker, *Photocopying*

Practices in the United Kingdom (Faber, 1970), pp. 23–7; and *Copyright and Education* (NCET, 1972), pp. 42–9, which reproduces the relevant section of the British Copyright Council's statement *Photocopying and the Law* (1970).

46. See p. 550.
47. Copyright Act 1956, s. 6(6).
48. Copyright Act 1956, s. 41(3) and (4).
49. Copyright Act 1956, s. 41(5).
50. Copyright Act 1956, s. 14(4).
51. Copyright Act 1956, s. 14(5).
52. Copyright Act 1956, s. 14(6).
53. Copyright Act 1956, s. 14(7).
54. Copyright Act 1956, s. 14(8).
55. *Copyright and Designs Law* (HMSO, 1977). Readers who are interested in the educational proposals of the report are referred to G. R. Barrell 'Photocopying – a new look' (*Education Today*, College of Preceptors, Autumn 1977).

XIX
Children in trouble

1 The juvenile courts

Since 1909 a special system of juvenile courts has existed to
deal with children (under the age of 14) and with young
persons (14 and under 17). Originally conducted in much the
same way as adult petty sessions, the juvenile courts have in
the course of time become much more concerned with reform
and rehabilitation than with punishment, in pursuance of the
statutory duty laid on them in the following terms: 'Every
court in dealing with a child or young person who is brought
before it, either as an offender or otherwise, shall have regard
to the welfare of the child or young person.'[1] In this chapter
the word 'juvenile' is used to describe features of the system
common both to children and to young persons as defined in
this paragraph.

Juvenile courts are less formal than their adult counterparts.
If a juvenile court uses the same room as any other court, its
sittings must be separated from those of the other by an
interval of at least an hour.[2] Only members and officers of the
court, and parties to the case being heard, with their advocates
and witnesses, bona fide reporters and other persons specially
authorized by the court may be present. Press reports are

restricted and nothing may be printed which might lead to the identification of the juvenile or of his school, except by direction of the Secretary of State or of the court in cases where it appears to be in the interests of justice to dispense with secrecy.[3]

Outside the metropolitan area the court consists of two or three justices selected from a panel of juvenile court magistrates, specially chosen for their suitability to sit in juvenile courts. Any stipendiary magistrate with jurisdiction in the area is ex-officio a member of the panel and may, in special circumstances, sit alone. Unless there is a specific direction by the Lord Chancellor, lay justices must retire from the panel on reaching the age of 65. At any hearing the bench should include both a man and a woman unless this is impossible because of unforeseen circumstances.

The chairman of the panel, nominated by the Lord Chancellor, may be either a metropolitan stipendiary magistrate or a lay justice. The chair is taken by the chairman or deputy chairman unless unforeseen circumstances make it impossible.[4]

In the Inner London area, including the City of London, the court consists of three justices selected from a panel of juvenile court magistrates nominated by the Lord Chancellor. There must be a man and a woman on the bench at each sitting. If, however, on any occasion the bench is not fully constituted, the chairman may sit with one magistrate, of the same sex if this is necessary, to prevent an adjournment. A metropolitan stipendiary magistrate may sit alone.[5]

2   Definitions

Different Acts of Parliament, and even different sections of the same Act may assign different definitions to particular words. This is particularly confusing in the various meanings given to the terms 'child' and 'young person'. Some definitions essential to an understanding of the law relating to children and young persons are given below.

Child:
(a) a person under the age of 14: Children and Young Persons Acts 1933 to 1969 (generally) except as below;
(b) a person under the age of 10: Children and Young Persons Act 1969, ss. 5(8) (notification of offences to the local authority), 7(7) (orders of the court on a finding of guilt), 7(8) (remission to the juvenile court of young persons found guilty of an offence by an adult court), 9(1) (investigations by local authorities), 23(1) (remand of juveniles convicted of homicide), 28(4) and (5) (special arrangements for detention and release of children arrested), and 29(1) (further detention or release of juveniles);
(c) a person under the age of 12: Children and Young Persons Act 1969, s. 13(2) (designation of a child's probation officer by the court only if the local authority so requests, and a probation officer is, or has been, in touch with the family), s. 34(2) and (3) (passage of responsibility to make pre-hearing inquiries from local authority to probation officer);
(d) a person under the age of 16: Education Act 1944 (a person who is not over compulsory school age);
(e) a person under the age of 18, or who has attained that age and is the subject of a care order: Children Act 1948 (orphans, lost or abandoned children, children living away from their parents, children with parents unfit or unable to take care of them), Children and Young Persons Act 1969, ss. 27 (children in care), 63 (functions of children's committees), 64 (financial liability for Secretary of State's expenses in providing homes with special facilities), and 65 (grants to voluntary bodies);
(f) a person under the age of 18: Children and Young Persons Act 1963, s. 1, Children Act 1975.

Young person:
(a) a person who has attained the age of 14 and is under 17: Children and Young Persons Acts 1933 to 1969 (generally) except as below;
(b) a person who has attained the age of 10 and is under 17: Children and Young Persons Act 1969, ss. 5(8) (notification

of offences to the local authority), s. 7(7) (orders of the court on a finding of guilt), 7(8) (remission to the juvenile court of young persons found guilty of an offence by an adult court), 9(1) (investigations by local authorities), 23(1) (remand of juveniles convicted of homicide), 28(4) and (5) (special arrangements for detention and release of children arrested), and 29(1) (further detention or release of juveniles);

(c) a person who has attained the age of 12 and is under 17: Children and Young Persons Act 1969, s. 13(2) (designation of a child's probation officer by the court only if the local authority so requests, and a probation officer is, or has been, in touch with the family), s. 34(2) and (3) (passage of responsibility to make pre-hearing inquiries from local authority to probation officer);

(d) a person who has attained the age of 16 and is under 18: Education Act 1944, s. 114, with reference to the upper limit of compulsory education;

(e) a person who attains the age of 17 whilst court proceedings are pending or taking place (in such cases the juvenile court retains its jurisdiction until the end of the proceedings): Children and Young Persons Acts 1963, s. 29; and 1969, ss. 7(8) and 16(11).

Protected child: A protected child is one below the upper age limit of compulsory education who is in the care and possession of a person (other than his parent, guardian or other relative) who proposes to adopt him, and someone else (not being his parent or guardian) takes part in the adoption arrangements; or alternatively in the care and possession of a person who has given notice of intention to apply for an adoption order under the Adoption Act 1958, s. 3(2) and s. 37.

Guardian: Any person who has, for the time being, the actual charge of, or control over, a juvenile.

Legal guardian: A person appointed to be a juvenile's guardian by deed or will, or by an order of the court. A local authority may exercise legal guardianship.

Local authorities:

(a) Employment of juveniles: local education authorities;

(b) Local authorities' functions and powers under the Adoption Act 1958, Parts II and IV are exercised by a Social Services Committee.[6] The authorities for this purpose are the Common Council of the City of London, the London boroughs, the non-metropolitan counties and the metropolitan districts.

Place of safety: A place of safety includes a community home provided or controlled by a local authority, a police station, a hospital or surgery, or any other suitable place whose occupier is willing to receive a juvenile temporarily.

3 Offences by juveniles

The Children and Young Persons Act 1933 provided: 'It shall be conclusively presumed that no child under the age of 8 can be guilty of an offence.'[7]

Thirty years later Parliament substituted 10 as the age below which criminal proceeding could not be brought.[8] Considerable pressure was then brought to raise the age to 14, 16 or even 18, and the current Act states: 'A person shall not be charged with an offence, except homicide, by reason of anything done or omitted while he was a child.'[9] This section, however, has not been brought into force, and children can still be prosecuted from the age of 10. The common law doctrine *doli incapax* presumes that a child under 14 has not reached years of discretion, and is therefore incapable of forming a guilty intention. In the face of strong evidence, however, the common law doctrine does not necessarily avail a defence. In 1971 a 12-year-old boy was said to have plotted the murder of a Southwark octogenarian, and to have goaded his mother's lover into committing the crime whilst he watched. The man was sentenced to life imprisonment for murder; the boy was acquitted of homicide but found guilty of conspiracy. Sentencing him to six years' detention, Mr Justice Ackner commented: 'What the law says is that there is a presumption that between the ages of 10 and 14 the child is incapable of criminal intention. It is a presumption that weakens as the child moves up in years towards 14. It is a presumption that can be rebutted – eliminated.'[10]

In 1983 on a charge of criminal damage, it was held that a 14-year-old girl who set fire to a shed by pouring white spirit onto the shed floor and throwing a lighted match onto the spirit was guilty of an offence under section 1(1) Criminal Damage Act 1971 notwithstanding that, because of her age and lack of experience in dealing with inflammable liquid, she would not have appreciated the risk if she had given thought to the matter.[11]

On being arrested, a juvenile must be bailed unless he is brought immediately before the court. He can be detained however if he is charged with homicide or some other grave crime, or if it is in his own interest to remain in custody, or if his release would defeat the ends of justice or if, having been arrested without a warrant, he is unlikely to surrender to his bail.[12]

The court may require the juvenile's parent to attend and must do so if it thinks it desirable. The father may be compelled to attend as well as the mother and at least one person who may be needed in court should be informed immediately a juvenile is arrested. The parent's attendance may be ordered by summons or warrant, or he may be included in the juvenile's summons.[13]

A juvenile charged with homicide must be remanded for trial to the Crown Court; he may be sent for trial on other charges if he is charged jointly with a non-juvenile and the court believes it necessary to commit them both in the interests of justice. A young person (but not a child) may be committed for trial if charged with an offence for which an adult could be imprisoned for fourteen years or more and the court considers that (if found guilty) it should be possible for him to be detained for a period up to the maximum sentence available for an adult.

The procedure of the court is kept as simple as possible; the nature of the charge must be explained in simple terms, the parent or guardian, or some other relative or adult, must be allowed to represent the juvenile, and the court must do everything in its power to assist any unrepresented juvenile. If it appears to the court, when dealing with care and related proceedings, that there is a conflict of interest between the parent and the child, the court may order that the parent shall not represent, or otherwise act for, the child. The court may then consider whether it is appropriate to appoint a guardian *ad litem* for this purpose. *Ad litem* means 'for the suit', and the responsibility of a person so appointed ends with the case. When parents make an unopposed application for the discharge of a care or supervision order, the court must appoint a guardian *ad litem* unless satisfied that it is not necessary to do so to protect the child's interests.[14] Reports are received on the juvenile's conduct, home, school work and so forth, and the court must tell the child or parent of any relevant matter contained in these reports which would help in avoiding further trouble.

The terms 'conviction' and 'sentence' are not used, being replaced by 'finding of guilt' and 'order made upon a finding of guilt'.[15]

It is the duty of the court to have regard to the welfare of the juvenile brought before it.[16]

It should be noted that the courts will be reluctant to hear a civil action against a young offender who has already been dealt with by the juvenile courts. In 1982 a plaintiff brought civil proceedings for mental anguish against two juveniles who had broken into his house and caused damage worth £1,000 after they had been sentenced to three months' detention.

He was awarded £500 damages: the juveniles appealed.

Lord Justice O'Connor allowed the appeal on the ground that the judge had erred in his interpretation of section 38 of the Powers of Criminal Courts Act 1973 with regard to his award of £500 damages.

His Lordship could well understand the plaintiff's fury at the way the defendants had behaved. But they had been punished, given custodial sentences, and their parents had paid the maximum compensation orders that could be awarded. He should have been content.[17]

4   Orders of the court (offences)

The Criminal Justice Act 1982 prohibits the imposition of custodial sentences for young offenders, unless the court be satisfied that there is no other way of dealing with them.[18] The court must be satisfied in such cases that a non-custodial penalty would be ineffective, or that the public would be at risk or that the offence was so serious that only a custodial sentence would be appropriate.[19]

On a finding of guilt the court may make one of the following orders.

DETENTION CENTRES

A young male of between 14 and 21 years of age found guilty of an offence which, if he were an adult, might involve imprisonment, may be sent to a detention centre for a period of not more than four months and not less than three weeks.[20] Detention centres are establishments where the inmates are subjected to extremely rigid discipline. The number of such centres is very restricted. A juvenile who has been to borstal may be sent to a detention centre only in special circumstances.

YOUTH CUSTODY SENTENCE[21]

The offender must be not less than 15 but under 21 years of age for a male: females must be at least 17. The offence must be one for which imprisonment would be appropriate if the offender had been over 21. The minimum term is four months, and the maximum the same as the maximum term of imprisonment that the court could impose for that offence. If an offender is under 17 the term of youth custody may not exceed twelve months. There is a provision for a young offender convicted of murder (or any other offence for which the sentence is fixed by law) to be sentenced to custody for life.[22]

Before a court can impose a custodial sentence on a young offender, it must consider that it is the 'only appropriate method of dealing with him'.[23] All relevant information as to his circumstances, character, physical and mental condition must be taken into account.

ATTENDANCE CENTRES

A juvenile found guilty of an offence punishable for an adult with imprisonment may be sent to an attendance centre for a number of periods of up to three hours on each occasion, totalling not less than twelve hours (unless he is under fourteen), nor more than twenty-four hours. The centre provides suitable employment or instruction. In the case of failure to attend, or a serious breach of the rules, the juvenile may be brought back to court and dealt with as though the attendance centre order had not been made. Those who have previously been to prison, borstal, a detention centre or an approved school cannot be sent to an attendance centre. The centre must be reasonably accessible.[24]

SUPERVISION ORDER

An offender may be placed under the supervision of a local authority or, if he has attained the age of 13, of a supervisor, not necessarily a probation officer, whose function it is to 'advise, assist and befriend'.

The court may include requirements in supervision orders.[25] The offender may be required to live at a particular place, to report regularly to someone or to participate in certain activities. The maximum period during which such detailed requirements may operate is ninety days. There is the possibility also of a 'night restriction order', by which offenders under 17 must stay at home during specified hours unless accompanied by a parent or other suitable person. He may also be prohibited from certain activities at certain times, for example, football matches.[26]

The Act contains a requirement that the parent or guardian of the offender should consent to the order and give full co-operation.

CARE ORDER

A care order commits the juvenile to the care of the local authority, which then assumes the powers of the parent or guardian.[27] Subject to certain conditions a local authority may, by resolution, transfer the parental rights and duties to a voluntary organization which has the actual care of a child. This transfer may be similarly withdrawn.

The powers of guardianship transferred to a local authority by a care order do not permit the authority to bring up a child in any religion other than that in which he would have been brought up if the order had not been made.

A juvenile who is the subject of a care order may be placed in a community home, boarded out or, in some cases, allowed to remain at home. If a further serious offence is committed while the offender is being permitted to live at home, the court may restrict the power of the local authority to give permission to live at home.[28]

In criminal proceedings the court may make a residential care order only subject to certain conditions. First, the juvenile must have been found guilty of an imprisonable offence; secondly, the offence must be serious and, thirdly, the juvenile must be in need of care and control.[29]

A care order lasts until the juvenile reaches the age of 18 if the order is made before he is 16, otherwise it continues until he is 19. It can, however, be varied or rescinded.

Provisions exist for dealing with those who fail to comply with the requirements of a supervision order.

COMMUNITY SERVICE

An offender may be required to carry out unpaid 'community work' to a maximum of one hundred and twenty hours within one year. Offenders must be over 16 years of age and are usually supervised by the probation service. If the order is breached, the offender may be fined up to £200.

HOSPITAL OR GUARDIANSHIP ORDERS

Where a juvenile is convicted of an offence for which an adult could be imprisoned on summary conviction, and two doctors certify that he is suffering from a mental illness, psychopathic disorder, subnormality or severe subnormality, the court may make an order for detention in hospital if the offender can be admitted within twenty-eight days. Mental disorder in this sense is defined by the Mental Health Act 1959, section 4.

Alternatively, the court can commit such a person to the guardianship of the local authority, or any person willing to receive him.

If the court, in the interests of the public, deems that a hospital order should restrict the offender's discharge, he must be committed to the Crown Court which may then make a hospital order with or without restriction.

ABSOLUTE DISCHARGE

After a finding of guilt the court may order the offender to be discharged absolutely. No further action may then be taken in respect of this offence, but it should be noted that an absolute discharge is to be distinguished from a discharge after acquittal. The court may order an absolute discharge if it feels that it is not desirable to inflict punishment and that a probation order is not appropriate. It may also be a mild rebuke to the prosecution.

CONDITIONAL DISCHARGE

The court may order the offender to be discharged on condition that he commits no further offence during such period as it may order which does not exceed three years. The offender must be told that, should he commit another offence during that period, he will be liable to punishment both for that and for the offence in respect of which he is discharged. The court may allow a consenting person to enter into a security for the child's good behaviour during the period of the discharge. The court may combine the discharge with orders for costs or compensation.

FINE

If an indictable offence is tried summarily, the court may impose a fine, as it may for an offence for which an adult could be fined. Since May 1984 a 10- to 13-year-old may not be fined more than £100, a 14- to 16-year-old no more than £400 — but neither can be more than an adult would pay for the same offence.[30]

The parent or guardian may be ordered to pay the fine, and this must be done in the case of a child unless the court is satisfied that the parent has not neglected to exercise reasonable care and control.[31] Parents have a right of appeal in this case.[32] Changes in the value of money have made it necessary to revise fines upwards. Under the Criminal Law Act 1977, section 61, and the Criminal Justice Act 1982 this is now brought about by delegated legislation rather than by changing the principal Act in Parliament. In May 1984 the Home Secretary told the House of Commons that after the passing of the Criminal Justice Act 1982 the number of fines paid by parents rose from 700 in 1982 to 4,000 in 1983.

It was held until 1982 that if a child is the subject of a care order, the local authority, acting *in loco parentis*, might be ordered to pay the fine. In July 1971 a 13-year-old boy was placed under a supervision order, and ten months later was committed to the care of the Croydon local authority. In September 1972 he was again before the court charged with six motoring offences, burglary and wilful damage to a telephone box. The justices ordered the local authority to pay the fines, and this was upheld in the Queen's Bench Divisional Court.[33]

This decision, however, was overruled by the House of Lords in 1982. A boy of twelve in the care of Leeds City Council was allowed to stay with his parents for a weekend, during which he attacked and robbed an old woman. The juvenile court ordered the local authority to pay the compensation awarded to the old woman.

In the House of Lords, Lord Scarman agreed that if the local authority was in charge and control of the child, then the authority would indeed have to pay the compensation. However 'the reason for reaching the contrary conclusion was that, on a fair reading of the legislation, and the legislative history, that could not have been the intention of Parliament when section 55 (of the Children and Young Persons Act 1933) was enacted. Nor was there any public policy which required, in order to make the statutory system of child care effectual, that the courts should take the contrary view, namely, that when Parliament introduced the system of child care it intended to subject those public authorities on whom it laid the duty to the penalties and liabilities imposed in an earlier era on parents and *de facto* guardians whose neglect or offence had brought the child to the notice of the criminal courts.' Leeds City Council was therefore not liable to pay. The victim's remedy was instead an application for compensation to the Criminal Injuries Compensation Board.[34]

In the two cases outlined above the offenders were already subject to care orders. A case heard in 1979 involved a 12-year-old boy who was on remand before sentence for trespass in a local school. Evidence in court that the boy had a history of fire-raising activities was given by the police. However, the social worker concerned with the case, who was present in court, failed to pass the information on to the community home: the boy later escaped from the home and set fire to a church.

The court held that the county council was in effect *in loco parentis*. Its duty of care extended to the consideration of the consequences of failure to exercise proper control. It had not exercised this properly, since the important information about fire-raising had not been passed on. The church authorities were awarded damages totalling £77,000.[35]

COMPENSATION

An aggrieved person may ask for compensation for personal injury, loss or damage arising from an offence. This is limited to £1,000 for each offence, and the order is suspended until the time limit for an appeal has expired. A compensation order may be made either in its own right, or as an adjunct to another order.

Where such an order is made, the interests of the victim prevail over the interests of the Crown. Priority is given to the payments of compensation rather than to the payment of a fine where an offender cannot afford to pay both.[36]

Theoretically there is no limitation to the prosecution costs which may be awarded against an offender, except in the magistrates' court, where if a fine is to be paid by the juvenile himself, costs may not exceed the amount of the fine.[37]

If young people default in payment, they can be sent to attendance centre, or the court can, if it is reasonable, order parents to pay — or alternatively if the parents consent they can enter into a recognizance to ensure payment. The court may order fines to be paid in instalments, which may be varied at a later date.

BINDING-OVER

The court may require the parent or guardian to enter into a recognizance to take proper care and exercise proper control in a sum not exceeding £1,000.[38] Binding-over may last for up to three years, or until the offender reaches the age of 18. The parents' consent is needed. Young offenders can also be bound over for up to one year to keep the peace in the sum of £50.[39]

Young people under 17 cannot be forced to be bound over. In 1980 Bristol police preferred complaints against six defendants all aged 14 and 15, alleging a likely breach of the peace. All six refused to be bound over to keep the peace, in the sum of £100 each. The justices felt that they had no sanction to secure compliance with their order, and that they had no alternative but to let the defendants go.

Dismissing an appeal by the prosecutor, Lord Chief Justice Lane said: 'To suggest that such an order required consent before it was effective was almost a contradiction in terms.

Moreover, a consent which could be compelled, in the case of a person over seventeen, by the threat of imprisonment was hardly the sort of consent which, in other circumstances, the court would look upon with favour.... There was nothing in the books which suggested that justices had any power to impose an obligation to be bound, except, indirectly, by threatening imprisonment. If they had such a power, it was strange that the much more drastic sanction of imprisonment should have become so firmly rooted in the law at such an early stage. The form of recognizance into which a person was required to enter had remained in substantially the same language for centuries. By that language the person acknowledged that he was indebted to the Queen in the sum fixed. It was now far too late to argue that the acknowledgement was a mere formality which could be dispensed with when occasion demanded. Acknowledgement of the indebtedness was an essential ingredient in the binding-over process.'[40]

DEFERRED SENTENCE

With the offender's consent, the court may defer sentence after a finding of guilt for not more than six months. This will give the court an opportunity to test the offender's conduct (including the making of reparation where appropriate). The hearing may, of course, be brought forward if the juvenile's conduct during the deferment is unsatisfactory. Magistrates can now commit offenders to the Crown Court for sentence at the end of the period. The Crown Court may defer again, if it so wishes.[41]

5 Remission to the juvenile court

If found guilty of an offence by another court, a juvenile may be committed to the juvenile court. This must occur if the court which has tried the case is a magistrates' court other than a juvenile court unless the adult court has discharged him absolutely or made one of a number of specified orders. There is no right of appeal against remission, but the juvenile may, after the decision of the juvenile court, appeal to the Crown Court which may vary or rescind the order, or direct that the case be heard by different justices.

6   Appeals

A juvenile may appeal to the Crown Court against a finding of guilt, or against an order, or both. If he pleaded guilty he may appeal only against sentence, but even then he may not do so if the order was a conditional discharge. A parent or guardian may also appeal to the Crown Court against a fine or other order for payment.

7   Care proceedings

A local authority, a constable, or other authorized person (such as an officer of the NSPCC) may bring a juvenile before the court if he is reasonably satisfied that the juvenile is in need of care (including protection and guidance) or control (including discipline). The court may make one of the orders listed in section 4 of this chapter if it considers that the juvenile will not otherwise receive care or control, and one of the following conditions applies:[42]

(a) his proper development is being avoidably prevented or neglected, or his health is being avoidably impaired or neglected, or he is being ill-treated;

(b) it is probable that he will so suffer because a person convicted of an offence mentioned in Schedule I of the Children and Young Persons Act 1933 is, or may become, a member of the same household;

(c) he is a member of the same household as a person found by the juvenile court to be suffering as in (a), and, having regard to this, he is likely to suffer similarly;

(d) he is exposed to moral danger;

(e) he is beyond the control of his parent or guardian;

(f) he is of compulsory school age, and is not receiving efficient full-time education;

(g) he is guilty of an offence other than homicide.

A summons or warrant may be issued, but if an arrested juvenile cannot be brought to court immediately he may be detained in a 'place of safety' for not more than seventy-two hours, during which period he must be brought before a justice who may make an interim order. If a constable believes that one of the first four conditions outlined above is applicable, the juvenile may be held in a place of safety for up to eight days, subject to a right by him or his parent or guardian to apply for release.

A justice may order detention in a place of safety for up to twenty-eight days if he is satisfied that one of the first five conditions mentioned above is fulfilled.

Proceedings for failure to receive full-time efficient and suitable education may be brought only by the local education authority.

A parent may not bring a juvenile before a court as being beyond control, but he may request the local authority to do so. If the authority does not act within twenty-eight days the parent may ask the court to direct them to do so.

If reasonable, the parent or guardian's attendance may be required and enforced. The juvenile must be told the purpose of the hearing, but he may be excluded from the court whilst certain evidence is given, other than that relating to character or conduct. The parent or guardian, however, has a right to remain, but may in certain circumstances be excluded whilst the juvenile is giving evidence. Reports are received, as in the case of juveniles alleged to have committed an offence.

In attendance cases the head's certificate is admissible evidence.[43] When a parent appears before an adult court charged with failure to cause his child to receive efficient full-time education, the child or young person may be remitted to the juvenile court even though the parent is acquitted. Truancy *per se* without the need for care or control is no longer sufficient for prosecution of a juvenile. A child may be brought to court under the care procedure in such cases, provided he has reached the age of criminal responsibility, and even though he is old enough to be prosecuted. The standard of proof and the rules of evidence are the same as in a criminal case. If the offence be proved, the need for care or control must then be established on the basis of the civil burden of proof. In a criminal trial the case must be proved beyond all reasonable doubt; in a civil action the court will proceed on the balance of probabilities.

In general, any juvenile court may hear care proceedings but, unless the case is dismissed, the juvenile must be sent to the court in whose area he lives for an order to be made.

8   Orders of the court (care or control)

The orders which can be made in care proceedings are similar to those in the case of offences outlined above, and the details in such kinds of orders are not repeated here.

CARE ORDER

SUPERVISION ORDER   see section 4

HOSPITAL OR GUARDIANSHIP ORDER

BINDING-OVER

Parents may be bound, provided they consent, to enter into a recognizance to exercise proper care and control. Where a young person is found guilty of an offence he may agree to be bound over to keep the peace and to be of good behaviour for one year in a sum of up to £200. There is no appeal against this order.

COMPENSATION

Compensation of up to £1,000 may be ordered if there is a finding of guilt arising from an indictable offence. This may be in addition to a care, supervision, hospital or guardianship order. The parent of a young person may be ordered to pay the compensation, and the parent or guardian of a child must be so ordered unless he has not conduced to the offence by neglect to exercise proper care or control.

INTERIM ORDER

A court may commit a juvenile in care proceedings to the care of the local authority for not more than twenty-eight days if it has not decided how to deal with the case. Further interim orders may be made, and an unruly young person may be sent to a remand centre if one is available. The High Court may discharge an interim order and there is a right of appeal against it to the Crown Court.

9 Reporting restrictions

Juveniles involved in court proceedings may not be identified in the press. Name, address, school or any other fact which may lead to identification must remain confidential to the court.[44] Confidentiality remains whether the juvenile is defendant or witness. The magistrates or the Home Secretary may lift reporting restrictions, but only in the interests of the juvenile concerned: the power is rarely used.

10 Juveniles and jury trial

Under the Magistrates' Courts Act 1980 a defendant who has attained the age of 17 may elect for trial by jury.

In the case of a juvenile who reaches the age of 17 while legal proceedings are being taken against him, the point at which the decision about jury trial is taken is not the occasion of the first court appearance, but the occasion when the court makes a specific decision about the matter.[45]

11 Educational reports

Heads may be asked to provide a local authority with information to assist in making a decision whether to bring a child before the court. Any written report for this purpose should be clearly marked as not intended for use as a report for the court. When there has been a finding of guilt, or the justices have found proved a case in which there is an offence by the juvenile, the court is provided with reports on the child's general conduct and home surroundings, his school record and his medical history. The provision of the school report is the duty of the local authority but it is prepared, in the first instance, in the child's school. If the report is not immediately available, the court may remand the juvenile, either in custody or on bail, until it is received.

The purpose of these reports is to put the court in possession of the child's whole background so that it may deal effectively with the case and have regard to its duty to consider the welfare of the youngster before it. It is therefore important that the reports should be both factual and full. They are marked 'Confidential' but the parent has a right to be told the substance of any part which reflects upon the home surroundings, and the child must be told of anything which deals with his conduct. This is not a breach of confidence: neither the parent nor the child can be expected to correct things which are wrong unless they are told what those things are.

In some cases a juvenile is remanded in custody for a special report which can be made only whilst he is under the supervision of a remand home for some time.

It cannot be too strongly emphasized that reports emanating from the school should be strictly factual, confined to the juvenile's school career and to matters which have a direct bearing on school life upon which the teacher is qualified to comment. Heads may be required to justify their statements in court and should avoid subjective opinions. A working party of the National Association for the Care and Resettlement of Offenders recently reported on the significance of school reports in sentencing in juvenile courts. The report deplored unsubstantiated allegations of criminal behaviour made in many reports: 'pejorative and unsubstantiated remarks would not be permissible in an adult court'. The report stressed that teachers should not 'yield to the understandable temptation to use the report as a forum for the expression of frustration about, or even anger towards, a child who is a nuisance at school'.[46] A teacher who submits a written report to the courts may be required to attend the court.[47]

12 Parental rights and duties, and custody

The concepts referred to here were defined in the Children Act 1975 and, except as regards actual custody, will apply to all subsequent legislation unless the context otherwise requires.

PARENTAL RIGHTS AND DUTIES.

This term includes all the rights and duties which, by law, the father and mother have with regard to a legitimate child and his property, including a right of access and any other element included in a right or duty. In the absence of a court order depriving either or both of custody, the parents of a legitimate child do not hold the rights and duties jointly: they each, under the Guardianship Act 1973, have the same rights and authority in relation to their child and those rights and authority are exercisable separately. Where two or more persons have a parental right or duty jointly, either may exercise or perform it without the other if disapproval has not been expressed by the other (or others). The rights and duties in respect of an illegitimate child reside exclusively in the mother, and the putative father has neither rights nor duties unless he has custody and access by virtue of a court order. A person with a parental right or duty cannot divest himself of it, either by surrender or transfer, except under a separation order. In the event of death the rights and duties pass to the survivor exclusively, or to the survivors jointly. If there is no survivor, the duties lapse but may be acquired by someone else under other legislation. If the rights and duties are vested in a body corporate, the dissolution of that body has the same effect as the death of a person.

LEGAL CUSTODY

Legal custody includes those rights and duties which relate to the person (but not the property) of a child, including the place and manner in which his time is spent. The custodian's duties, not defined in the Act, include the duties to feed, clothe and shelter the child and to protect him from harm. A legal custodian, however, cannot effect or arrange a child's emigration, unless he is the parent or guardian.

ACTUAL CUSTODY

Actual custody means possession of the child's person. Such possession may be enjoyed by one person, or shared. An actual custodian has the same duties as a legal custodian, even though he may not possess that status. In the Act 'the person with whom a child has his home' is the actual custodian, disregarding temporary absences including time spent in a hospital or boarding school.

IN THE CARE OF A VOLUNTARY ORGANIZATION[48]

A child is in the care of a voluntary organization, not being a public or local authority or an organization conducted for profit, if that organization has actual custody or, having had actual custody, has transferred it to a person who is not a legal custodian in respect of that child.

RIGHTS OF PARENTS AFTER DIVORCE

Both parents after a divorce continue to have equal access to information about their child or children, regardless of which parent has custody. Schools should make information such as school reports available on an equal footing.

References

1. Children and Young Persons Act 1933, s. 44(1), as amended by the Children and Young Persons Act 1969, Schedule 6.
2. Children and Young Persons Act 1933, s. 47(2) as amended by the Children and Young Persons Act 1963, s. 17(2).
3. Children and Young Persons Act 1933, s. 49.
4. Children and Young Persons Act 1963, Schedule 2, Part I.
5. Children and Young Persons Act 1963, Schedule 3, Part II. The

City of London is included in this area by the Justices of the Peace Act 1949, s. 11(5).

6. Local Authority (Social Services) Act 1970, s. 2(a).
7. Children and Young Persons Act 1933, s. 50.
8. Children and Young Persons Act 1963, s. 16(1).
9. Children and Young Persons Act 1969, s. 4.
10. *The Times*, 30 October 1971.
11. Elliott *v.* C (a minor) (1983) 2 All ER 1005.
12. Children and Young Persons Act 1969, s. 29.
13. Children and Young Persons Act 1969, s. 34.
14. Children and Young Persons Act 1969, ss. 32A and 32B, as inserted by the Children Act 1975, 3. 64.
15. Children and Young Persons Act 1933, s. 59.
16. Children and Young Persons Act 1933, s. 44(1).
17. Berry *v.* Cooper, *The Times*, 30 March 1983.
18. Criminal Justice Act 1982, s. 1(1) and (3).
19. Criminal Justice Act 1982, s. 1(4).
20. Criminal Justice Act 1982, s. 4.
21. Criminal Justice Act 1982, s. 6.
22. Criminal Justice Act 1982, s. 8(1).
23. Criminal Justice Act 1982, s. 6(1).
24. Criminal Justice Act 1982, ss. 19 and 17.
25. Children and Young Persons Act 1969, s. 12.
26. Criminal Justice Act 1982, s. 20.
27. Children and Young Persons Act 1969, s. 7(7).
28. Criminal Justice Act 1982, s. 22.
29. Criminal Justice Act 1982, s. 23.
30. Magistrates' Courts Act 1980, s. 36.
31. Criminal Justice Act 1982, s. 26.
32. Criminal Justice Act 1982, s. 55.
33. R. *v.* Croydon Juvenile Court Justices (1973) 1 QB 426.
34. In re Leeds City Council, *The Times*, 22 January 1982, HL.
35. Vicar of Writtle and others *v.* Essex County Council (1979) 77 LGR 656.
36. Criminal Justice Act 1982, s. 67.
37. Costs in Criminal Cases Act 1973, s. 2.
38. Criminal Justice Act 1982, s. 28 and Criminal Penalties (Increase) Order 1984.
39. Children and Young Persons Act 1969, ss. 1 and 3.
40. Veator *v.* Glennon (1981) 2 All ER 304.
41. Criminal Justice Act 1982, s. 63.

42. Children and Young Persons Act 1969, s. 1.
43. Education Act 1944, s. 95(2)(c).
44. Children and Young Persons Act 1933, s. 49.
45. R. *v.* Islington North Juvenile Court *ex parte* Daley, *The Times*, 26 July 1982, HL.
46. *School Reports in Juvenile Courts*, NACRO, 169 Clapham Road, London SW9.
47. Summary Jurisdiction (Children and Young Persons) Rules 1933: Rule 22.
48. Children Act 1975, s. 88.

XX
In Confidence

1 General

In the course of their duties, teachers collect a mass of confidential information of a widely varied character. On professional as well as on legal grounds it is vital that they should not abuse the confidence thus reposed in them.

Some of these items concern the work of their employers, as it is often necessary for a local education authority to take the advice of the schools, and particularly of the heads. Not infrequently this consultation is for the benefit of the profession and the inevitable result of a breach of confidence would be a tendency to withdraw similar confidences in the future.

Most confidential information, however, relates to pupils, and through it teachers learn a great deal about the history, character and homes of the children. It is grossly unfair to the children that such knowledge should be revealed, except where there is a duty laid upon the teacher to do so. There may also be occasions when information concerning colleagues should not be given, except under necessity of duty. The law relating to defamation of character is involved and it is desirable that teachers should know something of this subject.

2   Libel and slander

Defamation of character is the publication of matter which may bring a person into the hatred, contempt or ridicule of other reasonable individuals, or which may cause him to be shunned by such people. It may take two forms, according to the permanence of its nature, spoken defamation being generally known as slander, whilst the more permanent forms, as for example, written words, are known as libel. Defamation by broadcasting, although the words are spoken, is statutorily libel,[1] as are words spoken, pictures, visual images, gestures and other methods of conveying meaning during the performance of a play.[2]

Where the defamation is transient in nature, as in spoken words or by gesture, it is slanderous and is always a civil, as distinct from a criminal matter. To bring a successful action, the person defamed must prove 'special damages', that is, some actual pecuniary loss which is capable of valuation. It is not sufficient for the plaintiff to establish a risk of loss, or loss of a kind which cannot be valued, such as the loss of friends or health. There are, however, four classes of slander which are exceptions to this general rule, and which are actionable without proof of special damages:

(a)   an implication that a woman is unchaste;
(b)   an assertion that a person has committed a crime for which he could be imprisoned;
(c)   a statement that a person is suffering from an infectious or contagious disease which would make him unfit for decent society;
(d)   words which would disparage a person in his trade, business, profession or calling, even though the words do not refer directly to his conduct in that capacity.

Defamation of a more permanent character, as in writing, picture, effigy, cinematograph film or gramophone record, is known as libel and may be either a civil or, in certain circumstances, a criminal matter. The offender may be sued for damages by the person affronted, prosecuted by the Crown, or both. Libel becomes criminal if it is gross, often repeated, or likely to lead to a breach of the peace.

It is not a sufficient defence to maintain that there was no intention to defame, or even that the defendant had no knowledge of the plaintiff's existence. If the words might be considered by reasonable persons to refer to the plaintiff, they may be held by the courts to be defamatory. Some relief is given to a defendant who has defamed someone innocently, and it is possible to make an offer of amends. This may include an apology and, perhaps, a notification of the falsity of the statement to anyone to whom it has been made. Even if such an offer is not accepted, it will stand a defendant in good stead provided that he makes it as promptly as possible. This course is only open in the case of innocent, as distinct from careless, defamation.

Some years ago, a newspaper published a fanciful article about a motor rally at Dieppe, in which were described the amorous continental adventures of an imaginary Peckham churchwarden named Artemus Jones, 'the life and soul of the party that haunts the casino and turns night into day'. The writer probably thought that he had chosen a sufficiently unusual combination of names to avoid any real person but, unfortunately for him and the publishers, the article came to the attention of a barrister of the same name, who sued for libel. Both the jury and the House of Lords[3] found for the plaintiff. Under the Defamation Act 1952, it is probable that this would now be a set of circumstances in which an offer of amends would be accepted.

In May 1970 an anti-authoritarian publication called *Schoolkids' Oz* appeared. It included a letter, signed by a pupil at Owen's School, Islington, in which it was claimed that one of the masters of the school liked caning people, and that the writer had been caned by him. The letter was headed 'School Atrocities', and a large picture beside it contained unpleasant insinuations. The master issued a writ for damages for libel against the publishers, editor, distributors and eight other persons concerned with the publication. After the defendants had withdrawn any imputations, apologized for the embarrassment and humiliation caused, and agreed to pay substantial damages, the court gave leave for the record to be withdrawn.[4]

Defamation becomes actionable immediately the offending matter has been published, that is, the words spoken or the document shown to some person other than the complainant, or the spouse of the defamer, but not before. The posting of a libellous postcard is actionable because, even though it is addressed to the person defamed, it may be read by someone else in the course of the post. Several years ago, a schoolmaster took a boy into his private room and spoke to him about his character. The boy told his father, who threatened to sue for slander. Such an action could not succeed, because the words complained of were not overheard by a third party.

No action for defamation can lie when the subject of the matter complained of has consented to its publication.

In libel and slander actions, the judge rules that the words spoken or written are capable of being defamatory, while the jury decides whether they were so.

In 1979 the Queen's Bench Divisional Court ruled that a trade union could not bring an action in its own name for damages for defamation of its reputation, nor could it maintain an action for damages on behalf of each and every one of its members in the name of the union without identifying any particular member or members.[5] Although this case involved a manual trade union, there is no reason to suppose that this does not apply to teachers' associations equally.

The truth of the matter complained of is a complete answer to an action for defamation, provided that the truth is complete and an answer to the whole defamation. A further defence is that the matter complained of is fair comment on a matter of public interest. A third line of defence is privilege and, since this might well be a teacher's answer should he be sued for defamation, the question must be considered in some detail.

3   Privilege

The law recognizes that, on certain occasions, it is so necessary to be able to speak or write freely, that statements made in these circumstances are privileged and not actionable for defamation.

Privilege is of two kinds, absolute and qualified. Absolute privilege is restricted to a limited class of speeches and documents and, within that class, the speaker or writer is protected even if the statements were made maliciously. It applies only to speeches in Parliament, reports published by order of either House, statements made during proceedings in courts and other tribunals recognized by law (whether by judges, parties, witnesses, counsel, solicitors and jurors), fair and accurate contemporaneous newspaper accounts of court proceedings (certain details of matrimonial cases and indecent matters arising in court proceedings are not privileged[6]) and communications between officers of state in the course of their duty.

Qualified privilege covers reports made, whether written or spoken, in the execution of a public or private duty, provided that they are made without malice, that is, absence of right motive. This defence may be used, therefore, in the case of testimonials and references, reports on children to parents, reports made by teachers to the courts or to youth employment officers, and in other circumstances where there is a duty to pass on information received. In the example quoted above, where a schoolmaster rebuked a boy, he might have reported his conversation with the boy to the headmaster. Had the boy's father then taken action on the ground of publication, the defence could have maintained that it is a schoolmaster's duty to acquaint his head with certain facts about the boys in his care; and that the occasion was privileged, since the schoolmaster had the boy's welfare at heart and the report could not therefore be construed as malicious.

BRYANSTON FINANCE v. DE VRIES

In a majority decision the Court of Appeal held that the dictation of a letter by an employer to his secretary is privileged. Lord Denning, the Master of the Rolls, said: 'The correct principle is that when a letter is dictated as being the accepted mode of writing it, the dictation is a privileged occasion which is not to be defeated except on proof of express malice, and is not otherwise actionable.'[7]

In order to claim privilege, it is necessary for the person making the statement to believe, at the time he makes it, that the substance of what he says is true. To make a defamatory statement knowing it to be false, is patently malicious and unworthy of the protection of such a defence.

HUME v. MARSHALL

This is illustrated by a nineteenth century case in which the second master of a school reported a colleague's drunkenness to the headmaster. Lord Chief Justice Cockburn held that the occasion was privileged but, since the report was exaggerated, he remitted the case to the jury for consideration of damages. The plaintiff was awarded forty shillings.[8]

M'CAROGHER v. FRANKS

In another case it was held that there may be circumstances in which the secretary of an Old Boys Association has a duty to speak to pupils of the school about a member of the teaching staff, in which case malice must be proved if an action for defamation is to succeed. It was alleged that the defendant, a magistrate, churchwarden, former city councillor and founder of the association had said of a member of the staff to six 13-year-old pupils: 'She is abnormal. She has been like that for three years. Women of that age are often like that. She is a rotten teacher.' Mr Justice Paull instructed the jury: 'There are occasions when a person ought to speak out about what he really thinks, and I have held that this is a proper case for Mr Franks to say what he really believed, provided that what he said was reasonable. If you find that Miss M'Carogher has not proved that Mr Franks acted maliciously ... unless you think that Mr Franks was speaking because, for some reason, he had a down on her, he is entitled to the verdict.' The jury found for the defendant.[9]

BLACKSHAW v. LORD AND ANOTHER

In the Court of Appeal in 1983 Lord Justice Dunn said that there was no defence of 'fair information on a matter of public interest' in defamation proceedings. His colleague Lord Justice Stephenson added that there must be 'a duty to publish it'. 'Public interest and public benefit were necessary but not enough without more. There had to be a duty to publish to the public at large and an interest in the public at large to receive the publication; and a section of the public was not enough.

'The subject matter had to be of public interest and its publication had to be in the public interest. The nature of the matter published and its source and the position or status of the publisher distributing the information had to be such as to create a duty to publish the information to the intended recipients.

'Where damaging facts had been ascertained to be true, or been made the subject of a report, there might be a duty to report them provided the public interest was wide enough. But where damaging allegations or charges had been made and were still under investigation or had been authoritatively refuted there could be no duty to report them to the public.'[10]

Although this case involved a senior civil servant and a national newspaper, it clearly has implications for the growing practice of 'leaking' to the press reports on schools by local authority inspectorates, as well as for reports published officially by the DES of HMI inspections of schools.

TRAPP v. MACKIE

The headmaster of a school in Scotland was dismissed by his local education committee.[11] A local inquiry into the matter, properly constituted by the Secretary of State, heard evidence from the chairman of the education committee. The headmaster, believing that the evidence given by the chairman was defamatory, brought an action against the chairman. The Court of Session held that the action must fail because the evidence was protected by absolute privilege. The headmaster appealed to the House of Lords.

The basis of the appeal was that the protection of privilege extended only to courts of law and not to tribunals such as the one in question. Lord Diplock ruled, however, that absolute privilege extended to evidence before tribunals which, though not courts of justice, acted in a manner similar to them. Lord Fraser agreed: the factors which determined that the tribunal had acted like a court of justice were (1) that it was set up under a statutory authority (in this case, the Education (Scotland) Act 1946); (2) it was set up to decide a specific issue and nothing else; (3) the chairman was a Queen's Counsel, sitting in public, with the power to compel witnesses to attend and to administer an oath; (4) there was the normal legal practice of examination, cross-examination and re-examination of witnesses. Lord Diplock did, however, add that he was 'far from suggesting' that the presence of only one of these characteristics would be sufficient to attract the protection of privilege, or that the absence of only one would rule out a claim. The headmaster lost his appeal.

4   Teachers and defamation

The law of defamation may affect teachers in two ways. From time to time, slanderous statements are made about teachers; most of these issue from parents in the heat of anger but, where professional damage could follow, a teacher may consider taking action in the courts. He cannot be too strongly urged to consult his professional association before doing so and to abide by its advice. An ill-considered and hasty legal action may well do him more harm in the long run, professionally as well as financially, than he would suffer if he swallowed his pride and left the matter alone. If the circumstances warrant it, the association's solicitor will send a warning letter or, in some cases, the local education authority may be prepared to do this.

BARRACLOUGH v. BELLAMY

Letters about teachers written by parents to the local education authority are probably privileged, unless malice is proved. A successful action was brought by the headmaster and headmistress of a school, following a 'round robin' sent to the authority by a number of people, some of them neither ratepayers nor parents of pupils in the school. The letter complained of the school's treatment of Empire Day, and the fact that the children had not saluted the flag on that occasion. The petition, described by Mr Justice Swift as 'a highly dangerous, cruel document, highly defamatory of the headmaster and headmistress', was held to be malicious, and damages were awarded.[12]

RIPPER v. RATE

In another case,[13] a subscriber to a school complained to the local education authority that the headmaster's corporal punishment was excessive and amounted to cruelty. The court held that the occasion was privileged and that the letter was actuated not by malice but by a sincere desire to help towards the truth. The question of whether there had, or had not, been excessive corporal punishment was immaterial.

HARDWICK v. DAILY EXPRESS

The courts are frequently very ready to uphold a professional reputation which has been maligned, but if the harm is not serious the damages awarded may seem a small return for the strain and time accompanying a High Court action. In December 1970 the *Daily Express* published the story of a small girl who was sent home to change when she appeared in a trouser suit at the infants' Christmas party at a Lincolnshire primary school. When she did not return, the headmaster suggested that she should come to the juniors' party on the following day, an invitation which was taken up.

The girl's mother complained to the press, and an article was published under the headline: NO TROUSERS – THE

HEAD BANS JULIE, 6, FROM SCHOOL CHRISTMAS PARTY
An apology was refused on the ground that the story
represented the truth. The story was repeated in a feature
article a month later and the headmaster had to have his
telephone disconnected because of the abusive calls he received.

In court it was said that the articles painted the headmaster
as 'an unreasonable and unfeeling man which was a complete
antithesis of the truth'. He tried to maintain a happy atmosphere,
encouraging conventional dress without requiring school
uniform, and he did not like children to feel deprived when
others wore 'way-out fashionable gear'. The pupils had been
warned beforehand that trouser suits would not be allowed.
Awarding damages of £1,000, Mr Justice Bean said: 'It was a
trivial, unimportant, insignificant incident, capable of so many
quiet solutions; but it was blown up by the national press into
a *cause célèbre* with specially posed photographs of the girl.'
There had, however, been no serious aggravation of libel.[14]

BATES v. DAILY EXPRESS

A number of newspapers published statements that the
headmistress of a Church of England primary school bullied
and frightened her pupils to such an extent that one girl would
only attend school with her mother. It was alleged that, despite
a petition by the parents of some twenty children, she forced
children to eat up their dinners. The managers and the local
education authority conducted an investigation, and were
satisfied both that there had never been a rule that children
must eat everything on their plates, and that there was no
evidence that a child had become psychologically ill as the
result of such a rule. In addition to the reports, one paper
carried a cartoon of a child crossing out the words 'Dining
Room' and substituting 'Torture Chamber'. The High Court
was told that all four newspapers accepted that the allegations
had been wrong and apologized to Miss Bates for the
embarrassment caused to her. Undisclosed damages were
agreed.[15]

WALDRON v. ARCHER

The warning at the beginning of this section not to rush headlong into a libel action is illustrated by a case in which the teacher plaintiff was successful. Nine parents wrote to the local education committee complaining that a teacher in a Kidderminster school had slapped her pupils, poked them with pencils, called them liars, and had sworn at them. The teacher had been forced to resign her appointment following a disciplinary inquiry based on the complaint. Mr Commissioner Gibbens found that there had been intense antagonism between the plaintiff and her headmaster who had told the education authority of complaints about her nagging and bullying. She was 'more of a strict disciplinarian than usual', but the parents complained that she ruled by 'sheer terrorism'. They had based their allegations on complaints by their children, but a child of 7 or 8 is an unreliable informant. 'With every day memory fades and imagination grows. The parents dredged every recess of memory and imagination for every pebble they could sling at the plaintiff. She was sometimes moody and sharp, but was popular.'

As has been said above, letters written about teachers by parents to their local education authority are privileged: but, as in this case, the defence of privilege is destroyed by malice on the part of the writer. The Commissioner found that the parents had acted recklessly out of 'anger, prejudice and ill-will', and the teacher was awarded £500 in damages with costs estimated at £5,000 to £10,000.

The sequel, however, was less happy for the teacher. Her new post was eighteen miles away from her home, involving her with extra expenditure of £20 a month in fares and £10 for a dogsitter. Five months after the hearing the damages had been paid into court, but some of the mothers were saying they could not afford their share of the costs; and that their husbands, who were not signatories to the libellous petition, were not liable. In the meantime the successful plaintiff had found it necessary to borrow money to meet her additional expenses.[16]

Slander and libel on schools and staffs is still unfortunately far from uncommon in the local and national media. In 1981 a newspaper conducted an interview with the National Front which claimed that a named teacher was a Marxist and that he abused his position to indoctrinate his pupils. Another newspaper claimed that a head teacher taught her pupils black magic. A women's magazine described three schools as 'rough, violent and disorganized, with low educational standards, inadequate discipline, indifferent and unhappy children'. In all these cases, damages and legal costs were awarded against publishers.

5   Reports by teachers

At times teachers may have, in the course of their duties, to make comments on the work or character of other persons. When, in the nature of things, such reports must be adverse, it is possible that the issue of defamation may arise in some degree. If the reports are made in the execution of a duty, whether it be public, private, legal or moral, they are protected by qualified privilege, provided that they are not actuated by malice. In such cases, no action can succeed against the teacher. More than a century ago, Mr Justice Wightman, speaking of the importance of letters of character, said, 'It is of importance to the public that characters should be readily given. The servant who applies for the character and the person who is to take him are equally benefited. Indeed, there is no class to whom it is of so much importance that characters should be freely given as honest servants. It is for that reason that the communications are protected.'[17]

So far as teachers are concerned, such reports fall into five main categories: testimonials, references, school reports, reports on teachers, and reports to the juvenile courts. The last group has already been considered in chapter XIX; the others must be treated in some detail here.

6 Testimonials

A testimonial is an open letter of recommendation which becomes the property of the person to whom it refers immediately it is given to him. There is no obligation on a teacher to give a testimonial to a pupil, nor on a head to write one for an assistant. If he does so, however, it must be a fair report. There is no need to assign any reason for refusal and, indeed, it is unwise to do so, but it is advisable to point out that this does not necessarily mean that the testimonial, if given, would therefore be adverse. When a testimonial is refused, it is reasonable to give a certificate of service which states the period and capacity in which the writer has known the applicant.

It should be remembered that actions arising from testimonials may be initiated from either of two directions. The recipient may claim that the document is malicious and sue for libel. If, on the other hand, it is over-generous and the new employer suffers thereby, he may bring an action for damages.

Testimonials may be withdrawn if, at any time subsequent to their issue, the writer learns of any fact which would materially affect his opinion. This course should be taken only in extreme cases and after the writer has consulted his professional association, since withdrawal may lead to the threat of an action for defamation.

The practice of giving testimonials to pupils by assistant teachers varies from school to school. In some, the head prefers that the official testimonial, over his signature, should stand alone because of the embarrassment which may arise when there are marked differences between the head's and an assistant's opinion of a pupil. In such cases it would be unprofessional for an assistant to act contrary to the head's wishes.

Testimonials for pupils are less common than was once the case, having been replaced to a large extent by the pro forma required by the careers service. Nevertheless, it is still not uncommon for a school-leaver to ask for an open testimonial. More often such a request comes from a former pupil who may have left a decade or more earlier, so that few of the staff can remember his achievements clearly if, indeed, they ever knew him. It is therefore important in secondary schools to retain indefinitely an adequate record about every pupil who has passed through the school in order that verification can be provided at any time.

When civil servants and others employed in work involving national security are being screened intensively, it is by no means unusual for the authorities to investigate their school lives, even when they have reached the middle of their careers. On such occasions it is greatly to the benefit, not only of the nation but also of the ex-pupil, to be able to retrieve the necessary information.

An open testimonial for a pupil or former pupil should include the following points:

(a) clear evidence to identify the subject (e.g. if there has been a change of name by marriage or otherwise), including date of birth and the dates of admission to, and leaving, the school;

(b) an outline account of the pupil's record, with an indication as to whether he stayed beyond the age of compulsory education; application to and quality of work; external examination results if applicable;

(c) a note on the pupil's general development throughout his school career, including any factors beyond the pupil's control which may have accounted for erratic progress, e.g. a protracted period of ill-health;

(d) a summary of the pupil's contribution to the school in out-of-school activities, on the sports field, or in special responsibilities undertaken or offices held;

(e) a positive comment on character and conduct: this is especially important in the case of pupils who have struggled to achieve even moderate results against over-whelming odds.

In large secondary schools it is now usual for the official school testimonials to be written (and even signed) by the house or pastoral staff. There is no reason why pupils should not be asked to provide a list of any achievements which they wish to have included. When there is doubt as to whether a particular point should be included it is wise for the writer to consult as many appropriate staff as possible, especially if there is a risk that the resulting comment might be held to be derogatory.

In selecting those who will be asked to write testimonials for them, teachers should remember that appointing bodies expect to see an up-to-date recommendation from the head under whom they are serving at the time of the application. Local education authorities will often write for a confidential statement if there is no testimonial, even though the head may not be named among the referees. Those who feel diffident about their head's reaction to a request for a testimonial should remember that it may be less favourable if the first news he has that one of his staff is on the wing comes through an inquiry from another school.

It is always useful to include testimonials from people whose names or positions carry weight, if the candidate is really well known to them, but a sound testimonial from someone relatively unknown will do the candidate far more good than a vague statement by some eminent individual who has manifestly met the applicant casually and infrequently.

It is an increasingly common practice, especially in large secondary schools, for heads to ask teachers for a note of any points which they may wish to have included and, particularly, for a list of their special contributions to the life and work of the school beyond the ordinary calls of duty. It is also now not unusual for a head to show a draft to the teacher concerned or, at least, to give him a specific opportunity to discuss it if he feels there might be any relevant omissions. This does not mean that teachers are asked to write their own testimonials. It is very easy, particularly when a teacher has served in a school for a number of years, to forget at the moment of writing some signal contribution which the teacher feels with every justification to merit inclusion. It is often those who have rendered most meritorious service in this way who would be most diffident about appearing to criticize an appraisal of their work. Yet they are bound to feel hurt that something which they believe to have been worthwhile has been overlooked.

A testimonial given to a serving teacher should contain some reference to such of the following points as are applicable:

(a) the professional relationship between the writer and the subject and the period for which they have been known to each other;

(b) the work done by the teacher in the school including the subjects and the age-range of the pupils taught, details of external examination work, the posts of responsibility held (including, with dates, any internal promotions);

(c) courses attended, additional qualifications gained during service in the school, and a note of additional relevant experience, e.g. evening work in education;

(d) an assessment of the quality of this work, of the teacher's relationships with children, colleagues and parents, including a reference to the teacher's classroom management skills;

(e) a note on any out-of-school activities connected with the school and, if of some importance, in the neighbourhood generally;

(f) an assessment of the teacher's character and general suitability for the profession;

(g) an expression of regret (if this is so!) that the teacher is seeking another appointment, and an offer to answer any specific questions.

It is sometimes thought that this final offer is designed by an unscrupulous head to give him an opportunity of 'playing down' what is written in the testimonial, but this is not so and, indeed, the reverse is often the case. It should be remembered that a testimonial may be used for a considerable number of applications; further inquiries may enable the head to make a particularly strong recommendation in view of the specific requirements of a particular appointment.

A testimonial often speaks most clearly through what is omitted, rather than through what is actually written. For this reason it is important to ensure that no material details are missed. The absence of a reference to discipline in a teacher's testimonial is a case in point and may – though by no means necessarily – mean that the holder is a poor disciplinarian. Since testimonials are open documents, they tend to refer to the strengths of those on whose behalf they are written, and to make no mention of weaknesses. It is open to a teacher who has received a testimonial which does not cover such a detail to ask for its inclusion, but he can hardly then complain if the reference is uncomplimentary provided, of course, that it is not malicious.

Testimonials, whether for staff or pupils, should be as factual as possible. Anything which might be regarded as a slur should be omitted. It is wiser to refuse a testimonial if, when honestly given, it is likely to be more of a hindrance than a help to the subject. In short, an open testimonial should 'accentuate the positive'.

The owner should not part with the original of a testimonial, as some authorities do not return documents enclosed with applications; in any case there is always a risk of loss in the post. A typed, duplicated or photocopied copy should be forwarded, and this must be an exact copy, without addition or omission. The original should be taken to any interview in order that it may be compared with the copy if the appointing body wishes to do so.

7 References and reports on teachers

Whereas testimonials are general appraisals of an individual either in a professional or personal capacity, references are confidential letters of recommendation. They constitute an attempt, within the honest judgement of the writer, to assess the suitability of the subject for a particular appointment for which he has applied. They remain the property of the person to whom they are addressed. In the nature of things they may be much more frank and detailed than testimonials, but they also must be fair and without malice. When the writer of a testimonial is also asked for a reference, he should take care that the two are not inconsistent; a brilliant testimonial followed by a mediocre reference reflects more clearly on the character of the writer and his inability to judge that of others, than on the capabilities of the person about whom he is writing.

On the other hand the writer of a reference should not feel completely inhibited by this warning. Situations arise where someone who is, in general terms, a most acceptable person, uses a testimonial to apply for a post for which he is not a suitable candidate or for which he is not yet, perhaps, sufficiently experienced. In such cases the referee must be utterly frank, whatever his general approval of the candidate's qualities which he has praised sincerely in an open testimonial.

In recent years there has been a growth of opinion that a teacher is entitled to see everything which is written about him. It is argued that this course would avoid the malicious reference, or one by which a head seeks to retain a valuable member of his staff by preventing his success in applications elsewhere. It is argued also that, if what is written in the reference is true, no one will be harmed by disclosure.

There are several objections to this practice. Human nature being what it is, there is always a risk that a referee may be malicious or prejudiced, but such cases are extremely rare. The generality of the statement is an unjustified slur on the great majority of educational referees, most of whom go to a great deal of trouble to write honest reports in the belief that their confidence will be respected. If a referee believes that a candidate has overreached himself in an application he must remember that he has a duty not only to the applicant, but also to the prospective employer. If, however, the contents of a reference given in such circumstances are revealed to the teacher who is the subject they may, quite unnecessarily, destroy his self-confidence, inhibit his professional development, damage his relationship with the referee, lead to unjustified accusations of bias and make continuation in his existing post difficult, if not impossible. The NUT in its Code of Professional Conduct recognizes this need for confidentiality and exempts such documents from its general rule that it is unprofessional for one teacher to make a report upon another without at the time acquainting him with its nature. No teacher is obliged to show a reference he has written.

All parties to the reference, the author, the subject and the recipient, should be in agreement beforehand as to whether or not it is to be, and to remain, permanently confidential. In asking a referee for his support, a teacher should make it clear whether or not he would like to see his reference. Similarly, if a local authority has a policy under which teachers may see their personal files at County Hall, this should be made clear by the authority when references on applicants are taken up. If a referee writes 'confidential' on a report, it should be at all times accepted by the recipient that it is offered in good faith on that basis. If a local authority has an 'open file' policy, or a governing body wishes to discuss references with candidates on interview, and yet a 'confidential' reference is received, the correct procedure is first to attempt to clear the publication of the contents with the author. Teachers who find this being abused should take the matter up with their professional association.

8   Student teachers

A particular difficulty may arise in connection with reports on the work of students in school during initial teacher-training courses. Some head teachers, anxious to be consistent with their general policy of showing references and reports to the subjects of them, may show reports to students. Other heads, of course, may reasonably take the opposite view. Where this happens there can be friction within the training institution, since some students will have seen their reports, others not; the training institution cannot equalize matters, since many heads will have written in good faith 'in confidence'. It is important therefore for heads and training institutions to agree on a common policy. In this connection it should be noted that universities in particular tend strongly to regard such reports, like all other assessment procedures inside the university, as confidential. A further consideration is that a student teacher may well during his course have worked in two or even three different schools, and received perhaps two very mediocre reports and one slightly better. If he has been shown only the better report and the judgement of the examiners is that he should fail overall, the training institution cannot reasonably explain the failure to the student without breaching the confidence in which the two mediocre reports were written.

The question of showing reports on probationer teachers is now the subject of DES guidelines and is dealt with in chapter III.

Some employers ask for a reference after they have made an offer of employment to a candidate. If the referee knows this to be so, he should send a courteous note explaining that it is not his practice to give references in such circumstances, since an adverse report might lead to a withdrawal of the offer (or to dismissal, if the employee has started work) and a consequent action for defamation of character. He may add a certificate of attendance (in the case of pupils) or of service (in the case of staff) and, if able to do so, a statement that the candidate's conduct was satisfactory. He should express no view as to the suitability of the candidate for the post which has been offered. Employers who follow this practice have been roundly condemned by the teachers' associations, but in spite of this there are still some who continue to make such inquiries.

When a head is called upon to reply to categorical questions about a pupil and the answer must be adverse, it is often worthwhile to see the child's parent before doing so in order to explain the circumstances. Presumably, now that the age of majority has been lowered, it would be more correct to hold this discussion with the pupil himself if he has reached the age of 18.

References should be addressed personally to the inquirer, and the envelope should be marked 'Private and Confidential'.

As a general rule, references should follow the broad lines of a testimonial, but, as has been indicated above, they are structured to show to the best advantage the candidate's suitability for the post in question. Unlike testimonials, it is practically impossible to withdraw them for, whereas a testimonial may be used for successive applications over a period of some years, a reference is usually acted upon finally within a matter of weeks, or even days, from the time of writing.

Inquiries are sometimes made by telephone. Exceptional care should be taken in answering questions in this way, particularly if there is a chance that the call may be intercepted. Adverse answers should not be given over the telephone, the inquirer being advised that a reply will be sent in writing.

When it is the practice to return copy testimonials to unsuccessful candidates, care should be taken to see that references are not inadvertently enclosed. The author once received a request from a candidate for the return of references on the ground that she did not wish to trouble her referees again. To have returned the documents under such circumstances would have been a breach of confidence.

Teachers proposing to use a person's name for reference purposes should remember that it is discourteous to do so without previous inquiry as to the willingness of that person so to act.

Requests (from employers) for references will often refer the referee to the provisions of the Rehabilitation of Offenders Act 1974 and specifically to the 1975 Exceptions Order, viz.

'In order to protect the public, the post for which application is being made is exempt from section 4(2) of the Rehabilitation of Offenders Act 1974 (Exceptions) Order 1975. It is not therefore in any way contrary to the Act to reveal any information you may have concerning convictions which would otherwise be considered as "spent" in relation to this application and which you consider relevant to the candidate's suitability for employment. Any such information will be kept in strict confidence, and used only in consideration of the suitability of this applicant for a position where such an exemption is appropriate.' It should be noted that the gratuitous introduction of unnecessary and irrelevant information about convictions could be libellous, even though factually accurate.

Finally, a reference written in connection with a particular application to a particular school should not be used for any other purpose without the prior consent of both the referee and the teacher concerned. There is a growing practice, particularly where it is known that a teacher or probationer wishes to gain a post in one particular area, of passing applications and references from school to school directly. This is often totally unhelpful to the applicant and the interviewing school, since the referee might well have written a different report, perhaps even more supportive, had he known the exact nature of the post in question at the time of writing. There is of course nothing to prevent a local authority specifically from seeking a general report on a teacher or probationer: the referee then accepts that the local authority will use its discretion in using that report.

9   School terminal reports

Some firms make a practice of writing to schools to ask for copies of the recent terminal or earlier reports on a pupil who has applied to them for a post, or asking a candidate to take them to the interview.

Such reports are confidential as between the head of the school and the parent of the pupil. The nature of the comments and the standards employed are usually such that they are not readily comparable between schools, or even between different classes in the same school. They are thus likely to present a misleading picture to an employer who does not really understand their true purpose. A note explaining this will sometimes be sufficient, but if the firm is pressing the head should consult his professional association.

It has to be remembered that terminal reports are written in bulk at times of the year when teachers are subject to great pressure. Their function is to keep open a formal channel of communication between the school and the parent for the benefit of a particular pupil. As a rule every teacher who has a hand in a child's education at any given time will have his other hand in the preparation of the report. To some extent, therefore, these documents consist of a number of subjective statements which the form-master, pastoral head or head tries to draw into a coherent whole in a short comment at the end.

Sometimes an able pupil, who is going through a period when he is not giving of his best, may have a poor report which is intended as a spur to greater effort. If, as a result, he reforms and thereafter produces work of a standard commensurate with his ability, it is both unfair and embarrassing that his lapse in, say, the third form should be subjected to the scrutiny of a prospective employer several years later. *Per contra* a pupil of limited ability may receive a glowing report for a massive effort which has taken him near the top of a remedial form. It is rare, moreover, for terminal reports to reveal some underlying causes of bad patches in a pupil's career such as personal illness, the death of a parent or, perhaps, staffing difficulties in school.

On one occasion a head received a visit from the father of a pupil who had just left school. On the following Monday she was due to start work as a junior clerk in one of the best known corporations in the country, and had been asked to take her school reports, not to the interview, but on her first day of employment! The school report card was issued annually and in this particular case there were two poor reports: one, unhappily, for her last year at school. The purpose of the father's visit was to put a request for a modified and more satisfactory replacement. 'Let's face it,' he said, 'would you employ anyone with a report like that?' He clearly foresaw his daughter's first post lasting one day. Even had it been possible to comply with his wish (some of the staff who had signed the card were scattered to the four corners of the earth), it would have been thoroughly dishonest to do so. A telephone call to the staff controller of the organization safeguarded that particular girl's career and, after a lengthy correspondence, the corporation agreed to drop the practice.

Enough has been said to indicate that terminal (or yearly, or half-yearly) reports are inadequate and unreliable predictions of a pupil's likelihood of success or failure in any given career. It is the cumulative school profile, reference or careers service report which is designed, and most likely, to provide a balanced assessment of the pupil in his future working life.

If, in the end, the only chance of a successful candidature is the production of the report, this is the responsibility of the parent. Under no circumstances should the head forward the document, and he should advise any parent who proposes to do so of its limited purpose.

10   Addresses of staff, pupils and governors

The addresses and telephone numbers of staff and pupils should not be divulged to any outside person by a teacher. If asked by a police officer, in the course of his duty, for the address of a child, the head should consult his local education authority before giving it. If the officer objects, he should give the information, note the objection in the school annals, and inform the authority.

When persons unconnected with the school organization request the addresses of members or former members of the staff, they should be instructed to write to the teacher at the school so that the letter may be forwarded.

The names of the head teacher and chairman of governors must be easily available to parents.[18] It is good practice to display the names prominently where they can be seen by visitors to the school. Many schools, by agreement with governors, also display the names of the current parent governors, and some indication of how they or the chairman may be contacted.

11   Press, radio and television: employers' confidence

Some local education authorities have a clause in their staff code which restricts the activity of their employees in making public statements on any work which is the concern of the authority. When such a clause exists it is implied in the teacher's agreement. This does not apply to the staffs of voluntary-aided schools unless the code is part of their agreements.

Quite apart from this rule, it is inadvisable for teachers to

give to the press any information which they may have
acquired through their employment whenever such information
may cause embarrassment or distress to anyone whether
employer, pupil, parent or colleague. Most authorities allow
certain noncontroversial news items to be disseminated by the
schools. It is, for example, usually permitted to release the
news that some distinguished figure has visited the school, but
extremely risky to admit to the press, even when the editorial
staff already have wind of the fact, that a 13-year-old girl is
pregnant or that there was a riot in the dining hall at lunchtime.
In 1981 a Liverpool teacher had disciplinary action taken
against him for copying pages from the school's punishment
book in order to reveal to an outside organization the extent
of corporal punishment in his school.[19]

In the contract of employment of those employed in
education there is an implied term that the employee shall
render 'faithful and honest service'. This clearly covers theft of
school property, using the school to run a private business and
so on, but it also covers not divulging confidential information.

'Confidential' implies privacy and the limitation of circulating
confidential information solely to those with an established
right to know. Those breaching the employer's confidence
sometimes attempt to defend their actions on the grounds that
disclosure is in the 'public interest'. This is a difficult and
unclear area of the law, but it must be recognized that the
courts do not in general like the 'public interest' defence. They
will usually investigate very closely the motives behind the
disclosure. Self-seeking publicity or selling a story to the media
would almost certainly cast grave doubt on the defence.

A thin line exists between the right to free speech and an
employee's duty not to injure the employer's reputation. To
describe one's chief education officer as a 'raving loony' or a
report by the local education authority as a 'distortion of the
truth' could be defamatory unless basically accurate, or it could
be shown that this was fair comment on a public issue. If the
head of a grammar school, for example, were to launch a public
attack on his employer's policy of selective education the

employer could legitimately doubt whether the head was holding the most suitable post for his views.

If an authority requires its staff to dissociate their books or articles from the views of the authority and to make it clear that the work is purely individual, care should be taken to see that this is done.

This is an area where practice has tended to leave precept far behind. For many years teachers complained that the mass media took no interest in what went on in schools; today the complaint is more often heard that education has become too much a subject of discussion of the wrong kind. Those authorities which restrict public pronouncements by their teachers do not always enforce their regulations, even when statements are damaging to the authority, its schools, its teachers and the children whose education is in their care.

Unfortunately bad news is often more acceptable than good news; and there is a tendency to emphasize what is wrong and to ignore what is right in the public services. The mass media also give considerable opportunity to those who seek to promote themselves by denigrating others. Furthermore, as everyone who has made statements knows only too well, the most carefully considered comment can be transformed to suit editorial policy by blue pencil or scissors.

Strictly speaking, teachers are bound by any regulations which apply to them. If, because regulations do not exist (or are not applied), they find themselves free to express their views and to reveal information acquired in the course of their duties, it is to be hoped that they will use their discretion to avoid damaging others with whom they are professionally concerned.

12   Access to pupils' records

The practice is growing of permitting parents to see school records on their children, and of permitting pupils of over 18 to see their own files. At the moment there is no statutory right of access although a handful of local education authorities, in consultation with their head teachers, have 'open file' policies for their area.

It is likely that schools may increasingly use micro-computers for storing data on present and former pupils. The Data Protection Act currently passing into law will affect this practice. The reader is referred to Chapter XXI.

References

1. Defamation Act 1952, s. 1.
2. Theatres Act 1968, s. 4.
3. E. Hulton & Co. *v.* Jones [1910] AC 20.
4. Butler *v.* Oz Publications (UK) Ltd and others, *The Times*, 30 June 1972.
5. Electrical, Electronic, Telecommunication and Plumbing Union *v.* Times Newspapers and others, *The Times*, 14 December 1979.
6. The Judicial Proceedings (Regulation of Reports) Act 1926.
7. Bryanston Finance Co. Ltd and others *v.* de Vries and another, *The Times*, 19 February 1975.
8. Hume *v.* Marshall (1877) 42 JP 136; LCT 338.
9. M'Carogher *v.* Franks, *The Times*, 25 November 1964; LCT 349.
10. Blackshaw *v.* Lord and another, *The Times*, 21 February 1983, CA.
11. Trapp *v.* Mackie (1978) 1 WLR 377.
12. Barraclough *v.* Bellamy and others, *The Times*, 18 July 1928; LCT 350.
13. Ripper *v.* Rate, *The Times*, 17 January 1919; LCT 342.
14. Hardwick *v. Daily Express, Daily Telegraph*, 19 and 21 December 1972.
15. Bates *v. Daily Express* and others, *Daily Express*, 1 August 1975.
16. Waldron *v.* Archer and others, *Guardian*, 16 February 1971; *Education*, 26 February and 16 July 1971.
17. In Gardener *v.* Slade [1849] 13 QB 796.
18. Education (School Information) Regulations 1981.
19. *Education*, 30 January 1981.

XXI
Miscellaneous

1 Official visitors

All schools today receive a large number of official visitors. Many of them are concerned only with the head; others will also wish to meet the assistant staff.

Governors may visit the school from time to time in order to see for themselves what is happening in the establishments for which they are responsible. The visits of HMIs (and the penalties for obstructing them) have already been noted. There are also callers who are concerned with such matters as audit, buildings and equipment, and local education authority advisers or inspectors.

From time to time, specially invited guests may come to a school as the principal speaker at a prizegiving or on other similar occasions.

In most cases there is no doubt about the identity of the visitor, but it is not unknown for unauthorized persons to attempt to gain access to schools by pretending to have official business there. There is no discourtesy in asking an unknown person to produce evidence of his authority in case of doubt. This is particularly important if the visitor seeks any contact with the pupils.

It is a good practice to keep a visitors' book to be signed as deemed appropriate.

The increase in the number of ancillary services has produced a corresponding rise in the number of people who call at the schools from time to time. The medical staff, meals staff, youth organizer, welfare officer and careers officer all pay more or less frequent visits. If children are subject to court orders, it is not uncommon for the supervising officers to look in from time to time for an up-to-date progress report on the children in whom they are interested.

2 Publishers' representatives and others

Some heads and, to a lesser extent, some assistants are concerned about their position in dealing with representatives who visit schools to promote, or sell, the products of a commercial undertaking. Their fear may be based on an unfortunate personal experience or on reports which they have heard of colleagues who have suffered at the hands of unscrupulous salesmen.

Local education authorities vary in their attitude to representatives' visits to schools and heads should be aware of the rules and practice of their own authority.

There are, however, certain general guidelines, and in discussing this subject it is convenient to distinguish between those who operate on a freelance basis and the accredited representatives of the principal educational publishing houses.

There are various practices which are dubious from an ethical point of view. A very small number of photographers give schools a good deal of trouble, either by failing to produce promised discounts for the school fund, or by insisting that the school pay for any copies not returned or paid for by pupils. Vigilance on the part of the professional associations seems to be solving this problem and, in recent years, schools have suffered more from the purveyors of plastic labelling tape or some other consumable.

In this trade a representative may visit the school or, and this is more usual, a telephone call may be made offering a free embossing machine or some additional piece of equipment which is attractive to a school struggling to cope on a limited capitation budget. Some time after the order is delivered another telephone call advises the head that 'the next part of your order is now ready for delivery' and, if he protests, he is told that he has ordered a considerable quantity, sometimes running into some hundreds of pounds in value. In a large school the head should verify at this point that no other authorized person has placed the order.

Occasionally, if the protests continue, the head is told that unless he accepts the order the local education authority will be informed. It is most unlikely that this would be done and the person who should do so (the head concerned) often refrains through fear of appearing incompetent, naïve or downright foolish. Unless he does advise either the authority or his professional association, the next consignment will undoubtedly arrive, and the next....

Sometimes, in reply to an inquiry about goods which are attractive to a particular school, a firm will send additional products which have not been ordered. In one case the head's protest brought a photocopy of the order form she had sent. The tick inserted by the description of the unwanted item was, even on a photostat, plainly made by another hand with another pen.

A person who receives unsolicited goods may, after six months, treat them as an unconditional gift. This is contingent on the proviso that he has not agreed to acquire or return them, that the sender did not take possession within that period, and that the recipient did not refuse the sender reasonable permission to take his goods back. Furthermore the recipient must, at least thirty days before the end of the six months, advise the sender of his name and address, the address from which the goods may be collected, and that the goods were unsolicited. The notice may be sent by post. It is an offence to demand payment or to threaten (or take steps towards) any process to recover the value of unsolicited goods. Unsolicited goods are defined as goods received by a person who has not requested them, or on whose behalf no request has been made.[1]

Without implying that all of the others are rogues (indeed, most are honest and helpful) there is one body of representatives about whom schools need have no qualms. The representatives of the leading educational publishers may belong to their own professional body, the Association of Publishers' Educational Representatives. Most of them do belong, and are bound by the strict code of conduct laid down by an organization which is jealous of the reputation of its members, their profession and their employers. The code is as follows:

(a) An educational representative is one authorized by his firm to visit schools, colleges and any other educational institutions to display therein the books and/or materials produced by his firm for use in schools, and to assist the staff in evaluating their suitability.

(b) He enters any school, college or other educational institution under the authorization of the director of education and/or at the invitation of the principal, either or both of which may be withheld at any time. In certain areas the authorization of the director to the representative to visit schools controlled by the authority takes tangible form, i.e. a printed permit which is issued to the firm and which expires annually. The director is fully at liberty to refuse to issue or renew such permits and is not obliged to give his reasons for so doing. A representative may not visit any school controlled by such an authority without having in his possession a valid permit.

(c) It is accepted practice that the representative shall not interview subordinate members of the staff without the approval of the principal, nor interview any pupil or student.

(d) The representative shall at no time attempt to canvass for orders or to take orders, or attempt to make a direct sale of any book or item of material either on or off the premises of any school, college or educational institution, except in so far as he has been instructed by his firm to visit authorized wholesalers or retailers for that purpose.

(e) It is accepted practice that the representative shall not normally make more than one visit in any one academic year to any school, college or educational institution.

(f) The representative shall at all times use his best endeavours to promote the sale of the books and/or materials published or manufactured by his firm, but none the less he shall answer to the best of his ability any questions relating to the books and materials, published or manufactured by a firm other than his own, put to him by members of the teaching profession.

(g) The representative shall not in the course of business call upon any member of the teaching profession at his private address unless expressly requested so to do by the teacher concerned.

The code was drawn up jointly by the Association and the Educational Publishers Council. The latter body is closely associated with the Publishers Association and, as all the principal educational publishers are in membership, it therefore has the approval of the representatives' employers.

The Association will investigate any complaint that one of its members has broken the code, whether made by a teacher individually, or through his local education authority or professional association. The address of the Honorary Secretary is at present: Sergeant's Yard, Horningsea, Cambridge.

The educational publishers' representative does not visit a school to sell books; indeed, the code prohibits him from direct selling. His primary function is to provide a service which enables teachers to discuss books and materials from different publishing houses in their own schools. This is of great advantage to the staff of a school: the representative can give them his full attention without distraction from other customers and the whole staff of a department can make a leisurely appraisal together as to the best possible use of the limited resources at their disposal.

Teachers often complain that they cannot find the right

books or materials. The representative is the publisher's ear to the ground, in the unique position of being able to feed back to his house the changing needs of teachers as he is confronted with them in discussion. He can prevent publishers and teachers from working in isolation and so enable the production of material of the kind and quality required in schools.

Teachers must, of course, observe any rules applicable to them and they should not admit persons wishing to sell articles to pupils, that is, to use the school as a market, unless it is definitely known that the authority has given permission in a particular instance. At least one authority is prepared to license icecream vendors to sell their wares in playgrounds.

To summarize, teachers should seek advice from the local education authority or their professional association before entering into any contract. If they feel at any stage in the course of business that they are not being dealt with honestly, they should seek similar advice immediately. On the other hand, with the exception of schools to which the ILEA regulation applies, they need not be concerned about the admission of accredited publishers' representatives. In the very rare event of such a representative being in breach of his code, retribution will be both rapid and effective.

3   Unwelcome visitors

Many education authorities have by-laws concerning nuisances and intruders on educational premises. Recent legislation specifically concerned with educational premises however takes the matter further.[2] It creates a new offence, punishable at the moment by a fine of up to £50, for creating a nuisance or disturbance on educational premises. A police constable or a person authorized by the local education authority may remove such a person from the premises. This power also extends to the removal of such persons from further education establishments. In the case of voluntary schools, the consent of the governors is necessary for the authorization of a person to exercise the power of removal. The consent of the governors is needed also before any proceedings can be brought concerning offences on the premises of voluntary schools.

4   Parents in school

Parents are by far the most frequent visitors to a school and they come for a wide variety of reasons. Generally speaking, this is to be welcomed, for it tends to produce a friendly atmosphere between staff and parents. It must, however, be borne in mind that parents have no right of entry to a school and that their presence is entirely at the discretion of the head. A parent, just as much as any other visitor, becomes a trespasser immediately that leave is withdrawn.

Under no circumstances should any parent be allowed to abuse a member of staff; such conduct should be reported at once to the local education authority. If an assault is threatened, the teacher may also wish to consult his professional association.

Difficulties sometimes arise when attempts are made to remove the child of a broken marriage by the parent who has not been granted custody. Great tact is needed in dealing with a situation which can rapidly turn to the child's detriment. It is always wise to inform the authority so that, if the parent's conduct becomes persistent, arrangements can be made to restrain him or her.

It should go without saying that a pupil must never be released into the custody of a stranger.

5   Complaints by neighbours

Much of what has already been said about other visitors applies to visits by persons who come to a school to make complaints about pupils. Such complaints should be received courteously, with a promise that they will be investigated. The names and addresses of pupils should not be given to the complainant as, in a case of mistaken identity, there may be serious results from such action. Under no circumstances should the visitor be allowed to hold an identification parade unless the local education authority has given permission for this to be done because of the gravity of the complaint in a particular case.

Complaints by neighbours that their property has been damaged by pupils should be referred to the authority's legal department. Care should be taken not to say anything which could be construed as an admission of liability in dealing with a complaint of this nature.

Where property has been damaged, the owner may seek first and foremost compensation. Schools have no authority to compel pupils to pay compensation and it is a very risky practice indeed to threaten pupils or parents with police action unless they pay up. Furthermore, if the school exercises its right to take disciplinary action against such pupils, this fact may well be taken into consideration by the police in determining whether or not charges should be brought before the magistrates to seek a compensation order.

6 Lettings

A local education authority, as the owner of school premises, may lay down the terms, conditions and cost of letting rooms for use by outside groups. The governors of aided schools, unless they otherwise agree, have similar powers.

It is usual to seek the consent of the head teacher for outside lettings, since these may in several ways impinge on the normal running of the school. Such consent may however not be withheld unreasonably.

USE OF SCHOOLS FOR ELECTION MEETINGS AND ELECTIONS

A candidate in a parliamentary election has a statutory right to hold a public meeting in furtherance of his cause in a suitable room in the premises of any school, the expense of maintaining of which is payable wholly or mainly out of public funds, i.e. county and voluntary schools. Those hiring the room may be required to pay no more than the actual costs of preparing, warming, lighting and clearing the room and restoring the room to its usual condition after the meeting. They must also defray the cost of any damage done to the room, the premises or the furniture.[3] A returning officer during an election may make use of a room under similar conditions.[4]

There is no statutory provision that a school may be closed while in use as outlined above. The local education authority in charge of the letting may so arrange matters that there is no interference with the normal running of the school.

Head teachers often have misgivings about lettings to undesirable or extremist groups. The right to hold such a meeting is not absolute: premises may be refused if there is some prior booking, some school activity or evening class activity would be disrupted or the room is occupied for maintenance purposes, e.g. decorating or floor re-polishing.[5] The use must also be confined to a suitable room.[6] Those refused a letting have a right of appeal to the Secretary of State for Education and Science.[7] A local authority or the governors of an aided school are entitled to ask for a surety or deposit against the possibility of damage.

7   Police investigations

From time to time, police officers visit schools in connection with investigations which they are conducting into alleged offences. It is an offence to obstruct a police officer in the course of his duty, but the head of a school also has a duty to his pupils and their parents.

Interrogations carried out by the police should be in accordance with the principles laid down by Her Majesty's judges in the 'judges' rules' which also deal with giving cautions and taking statements.

The present rules were adopted in 1964 by a meeting of all the judges of the Queen's Bench. They are designed to prevent investigations from taking a form which would render the resulting evidence inadmissible. They do not affect (a) the duty of every citizen to assist in the discovery and apprehension of offenders, (b) the fact that the police (except on arrest) cannot compel anyone to come to (or remain in) a police station, (c) the right to consult a solicitor privately at every stage, (d) the need to charge without undue delay, or (e) the essential need for all statements to be voluntary.

The administrative directions which accompany the rules include the following statement:

> As far as possible children (whether suspected of crime or not) should only be interviewed in the presence of a parent or guardian, or, in their absence, some person who is not a police officer and is of the same sex as the child. A child or young person should not be arrested, nor even interviewed, at school if such action can possibly be avoided. Where it is found essential to conduct the interview at school, this should be done only with the consent, and in the presence, of the head teacher, or his nominee.

In 1977 a juvenile accused of two burglaries was interviewed by the police with a social worker standing in for the parent. The social worker told the boy: 'Do not admit something you have not done. But it is always the best policy to be honest. If you were at the house, tell the officers about it.... If you were concerned tell him about it and get the matter cleared up for your own sake.' The judge ruled that these comments amounted to enticement to confess, and should have been refuted immediately by the police officer. Since they were not, the boy's evidence was ruled inadmissible and verdicts of not guilty to both charges were entered on the judge's direction.[8]

As a rule the principle laid down above is followed today in all investigations as it is realized that a visit by the police to a witness at his place of work may cause embarrassment or injury to his reputation.[9] Police visiting a school in the course of an investigation usually arrive in plain clothes.

Whilst a minor is in school the senior member of the staff present is *in loco parentis* to him and, except in certain circumstances, can refuse to produce the pupil for interrogation or to allow him to be removed to a police station. In cases where the police wish to interview a particular child, the pupil may be asked whether he has any objection to being questioned in the absence of his parents. If so, the police should be asked to defer the examination until they have an opportunity of conducting it in the parents' presence. If they refuse to wait, the head should be present *in loco parentis* through the interview. The matter should be recorded in the school annals, and the local education authority informed. If the head is a man, and a girl is being interrogated, a mistress should also be present. The head should not allow a pupil to be searched, except in the presence of the parent, unless the circumstances are such that it would be unreasonable to object.

If, on arrival, the police are armed with a warrant for search or arrest, the head must allow it to be executed; to resist would be obstruction. It is also not possible to refuse to co-operate if the police are acting under statutory powers which authorize them to bring a child in need of care or control before a juvenile court.

A head should insist on obtaining the instructions of his local education authority before allowing the removal of a child from the school or the holding of an identity parade on the premises. He should insist that written statements should be taken only at a police station with the consent of the parents.

The police may be informed of pupils' addresses.

8 Police and Criminal Evidence Act 1984

The parts of the Act which relate most directly to children and young people do not come into force until January 1986. Confidential records on pupils kept by schools will come within a 'category of excluded material' and will thereby be exempt from compulsory disclosure during searches for evidence.

Policy with regard to interviewing or arresting pupils at schools, which is contained at present in the 'judges' rules',[10] will, under section 66 of the Act, be contained in Codes of Practice.

9   Data Protection Act 1984

The purpose is to protect individuals whose personal data is stored on computers.

There will be a Data Registrar who will keep a register of computer bureaux and personal data users and who will have powers to regulate the use of personal data. There will also be a right of access by the individuals concerned to their private data. The use of computers for storing school records of pupils is still in its infancy but it seems likely that it will increase in time, and is subject to the provisions of the Act.

The Act contains exemptions covering information about health, and data gathered in connection with social work. Schools with computer records on pupils must register with the Registrar, stating the precise purposes for which the record is being held. It must also be made clear who the data users are to be, where the information is to be obtained, who will have access to the data and how the subject of the data may have access to it. Once this information has been registered, it is an offence to deviate from it in any way without prior application to the Registrar.

The data held on computer must be adequate, relevant and not excessive, bearing in mind its purpose. It must be kept up to date and be accurate, and destroyed when its purpose has been served. The user is responsible for the general security of the data bank.

At the time of writing, the Act is not fully in force. When it is, however, data subjects will be entitled to know by computer printout what information about them is held. A fee for access may be charged and access must be granted within forty days. If the subject of the data has any complaints which cannot be met by the data user, he or she may refer them to the Registrar. Should inaccurate or misleading data be found to have damaged or distressed the data subject in some way, compensation may be payable. The Registrar also has power to order access to data where he believes permission to have been wrongly withheld.

Public examining boards are covered by the Act only to the

extent that they cannot be compelled to release data to applicants until after the publication of results: at that point the forty day provision applies.

The Act does not require the records of any organization to be held totally on computer and schools are thus free to hold only part of pupils' records in that way if they so choose. Data stored manually is not open to inspection.

Care should be taken by schools using computer records that the data to which a subject has access under the Act does not, however inadvertently, contain information about another data subject, say another pupil in the same school. This could be 'unauthorized disclosure' under the Act.

10   School rules

In cases where negligence is imputed against the school, the defence is materially assisted if it can be proved that a school rule existed forbidding the conduct by which the plaintiff contributed to his accident or loss.

There is no need for the school rules to be codified or circulated to parents, although both these courses may be deemed desirable, especially when rules are of an unusual character. It is generally assumed that parents, in sending their children to a particular school, have implicitly accepted its rules, even though they have not seen them.

The question of school uniform has been dealt with earlier. A local education authority may require its schools not to insist on school uniform, but such a ban cannot be imposed if it is contrary to the provisions of the Articles of Government.

In cases where local education authorities have decided not to support the wearing of school uniform, or to inform parents of their right to free choice, schools may reasonably use the schools' esprit de corps as a form of gentle pressure. However sanctions may not be applied for non-compliance.

Long hair uncovered, or soft-topped shoes which offer no protection against heavy objects accidentally dropped, may reasonably be banned from workshops. This is done on safety grounds, not uniform. Similarly, provocative clothing occasionally worn by girls is a matter of internal school discipline, not of school uniform.

Despite decreasing enthusiasm for school uniform or in some cases even for school dress, it is not the case that teachers *in loco parentis* have lost all authority to try to influence pupils' appearance. Tidiness, cleanliness and appropriate dress are still teachers' concern: just as a parent would advise his son not to attend for a job interview with bright green hair, so might also a teacher.

The proposition that the school rules constitute part of the law of the land for the pupils of that school has been discussed in the introductory chapter.

11 Homework

In sending children to school, parents hand over a portion of their authority to the schoolteacher, and are assumed to assent to all reasonable school rules. It is probable that the courts would decide, at least in the case of pupils of secondary school age, that a requirement that a child should do a moderate amount of homework is a reasonable requirement and that, where such a rule exists, a parent may not order his child to break it. A head proposing to introduce homework in a school where it has not been the practice to require it would be well advised to seek the support of the governors (in the case of an aided secondary school) or the local education authority (in all other maintained schools), as the body responsible for the secular instruction.

One well known writer states that 'detention after school hours for not doing home lessons is not permitted, at least if the school is administered by a local authority under the Education Act 1944, since that Act does not authorize the setting of home lessons'.[11] This view is based on a case decided in 1884[12] where it was held that the Elementary Education Acts 1870 and 1876 did not authorize the setting of lessons to be prepared at home by children attending a board school, and the detention of a child for not doing home lessons therefore rendered the master who detained the child liable to be convicted for an assault.

It must be remembered that this case was heard in the early years of compulsory education, when strenuous attempts were made to confine the elementary education given by the board schools within narrow limits. In the Cockerton judgment, some years later, it was held to be outside the legal powers of a school board to provide science and art schools, or classes in day schools, at the expense of the ratepayers.[13] The Cockerton judgment galvanized Parliament into legislative activity on behalf of education at a speed which has never been equalled before or since. The result was the Education Act 1902 which abolished the school boards and set up local education authorities which, if they were the councils of counties or county boroughs, were empowered to establish secondary schools.

From their beginnings the new secondary schools introduced homework, following the practice of the ancient grammar schools, and punished their pupils for failure to perform the tasks set. The powers given to local education authorities by the 1944 Act are wide, homework was a well-established practice in 1944 and, if Parliament had wished to proscribe it or to make it unenforceable as a matter of discipline, it would surely have done so in precise terms.

It is interesting to note that current regulations require that a school's arrangements for homework should be included in the information given to parents, a statement which, at the least, suggests that homework is not a concept which is condemned by the DES.[14]

12   Modern disciplinary problems

VIOLENCE. It is frequently said, probably with some degree of truth, that violent behaviour in schools is increasing. A clause in the rules forbidding the possession of dangerous weapons and substances by pupils on the school premises might reduce the risk of serious incidents.

PREGNANCY

Happily, the pregnant pupil is a comparatively rare phenom-enon, and the solutions to individual problems lie within the home and the supportive welfare services. It is certainly not for the school to cast blame. Nevertheless, it is generally undesirable for a girl to return to her former school, if another is reasonably available; and this is an even stronger consideration if she should decide to bring up the child.

DRUGS

The mere possession of 'controlled' drugs, which include amphetamines, cannabis, heroin, LSD, methadone, morphine, opium and pethidine, is an absolute offence unless the person in whose possession they are found is lawfully authorized. It is also an offence to produce a controlled drug, to supply (or offer to supply) such a drug to another person, or to allow premises to be used for producing or supplying such a drug.

The available defences to charges on drug offences are very restricted. They include prescription by a doctor, a licence to manufacture, or the removal of a drug to prevent the commission of an offence by someone else provided it was then destroyed or handed to a responsible authority.

Setting on one side the professional care of a teacher for the pupils in his charge, and having regard to the disastrous effects of the misuse of drugs, it is clear that a schoolteacher (and this applies with particular force to the head) runs considerable risks if he believes that drugs are being brought into the school, but does nothing about it.

Clearly, the parents of any pupil concerned should be brought in as quickly as possible. Any drugs found in school should be impounded immediately and, if controlled, handed to the police. No schoolteacher likes 'shopping' children in his care, but the arrival of controlled drugs in the school leaves him with no alternative, especially if he has reason to suspect that a 'pusher' is operating in or near the school. His first concern must be to protect all his pupils, and particularly to prevent any who are not involved from being drawn into the net of addiction.

GLUE-SNIFFING

This is not in itself a criminal offence although, if severe enough, it might be a major factor in taking the young person into care. Nor is it an offence to sell solvents or polythene bags, although where these are sold openly as glue-sniffing kits the police may be willing to consider an action for conduct likely to lead to a breach of the peace.

It is likely that legislation to deal with the problem of glue-sniffing will be introduced shortly. An excellent handbook, *Solvent Abuse: A Guide for the Professional* is available from Brighton Health Education Unit, Royal York Buildings, Old Steine, Brighton, East Sussex BN1 1NP. The Intoxicating Substances (Supply) Bill, introduced in late 1984, provides for imprisonment of up to six months and/or a fine of up to £2,000 for aiding and abetting glue-sniffing. In Scotland the Solvent Abuse Act (Scotland) 1983 came into force during that year.

The sale of scented erasers has been banned by order until January 1985. There is every likelihood that the ban will continue after that date.

13   School badges

Most schools have adopted an emblematic device for use on pupils' uniforms, and for display in other appropriate ways. These are usually known as school badges, although they do not conform to the strict definition of a badge according to the rules of heraldry.

In heraldry, badges are simpler and more primitive than arms and crests; they are not mounted on a shield as are arms, neither do they issue from a wreath as do most crests.

The right to bear armorial ensigns is authorized by letters patent which are issued by the Kings of Arms after obtaining a warrant from the Earl Marshal in respect of each grant.

A fee of £840 is payable for a grant of arms and crest for private persons, or £6,000 for corporate bodies and, at the discretion of the Kings of Arms, for certain non-corporate associations of suitable standing. Since 1 January 1978 registered charitable bodies, a term which includes many educational bodies, pay a concessionary fee of £1,500 instead of the usual £2,000.

Colleges, schools, and other scholastic bodies may now apply for the grant of a badge in addition to their arms, or to their arms and crest. If a badge is assigned in the same letters patent there is an additional fee of £350, but the fee for the grant of a badge in a separate patent is £550.

It should be borne in mind that many of the devices in use by schools would not be accepted for registration from an heraldic point of view, and the Kings of Arms would not be prepared to make a grant in respect of them until such designs were revised to conform to heraldic law.

In general, arms can be granted only to corporate bodies with perpetual succession, but schools are an exception to this rule and a grant may be made to the owners or trustees for the use of the school.

Schools wishing to consider making an application for a grant should write to the College of Arms, Queen Victoria Street, London EC4V 4BT.

14   School magazines

Cases arise occasionally where a pupil submits previously published work as an original contribution to a school magazine. The editor should take every possible care to ensure that plagiarism of this kind does not slip past him. Under the Copyright Acts, the British Museum is entitled to be supplied with a copy of every book published in this country, and it has been held that this right includes school magazines. Such a copy must be delivered within one month of publication.[15]

Editors of school magazines are advised to read the chapter on copyright, particularly the section dealing with copyright vested in minors. It would seem to be the custom of the trade that material handed in by contributors is, by the act of delivery, licensed by the owner of the copyright for publication in one issue of the magazine. It is also accepted that no payment is made for such publication. This has the effect of transferring, free of charge, first serial rights to the school. The school can undertake no further publication of the work without permission from the owner of the copyright and in terms agreed with him. In the case of a minor such terms must be negotiated with the parent or guardian.

Editors must remember that it is an offence to stir up hatred against any section of the public in Great Britain distinguished by colour, race, or national or ethnic origins by publishing or distributing written matter (including any writing, sign or visible representation) which is threatening, abusive or insulting, and likely in all the circumstances to stir up hatred against any racial group. The maximum penalty on summary conviction is six months' imprisonment, or a fine not exceeding £1,000 or both; on indictment up to two years' imprisonment may be imposed or an unlimited fine or both.[16]

15   Care of property

A local education authority will not accept liability for the loss of personal property in a school, whether by pupils or staff. It is desirable to display notices to this effect at suitable points. Teachers who have personal items of value in school are advised to insure themselves against possible loss.

If a teacher takes charge of property on behalf of a pupil, he may be liable in damages if he fails to exercise reasonable care in its custody. In such cases, reasonable care would amount to the degree of care which a prudent person would exercise with regard to his own property.

Occasionally a local education authority will make an ex gratia payment in respect of property lost through no fault of the owner. Professional associations carry insurance on behalf of their members, but claims are examined carefully and often rejected if the owner has been careless, e.g. by leaving a handbag in an unlocked drawer in an unlocked room.

Householders' comprehensive policies may be so arranged that a stated percentage of the amount insured is covered whilst temporarily removed from the policyholder's house. A teacher who loses money in school, therefore, may be able to claim against his own policy, though as a rule this extension applies only to goods and does not include money.

Care should be taken to ensure that items purchased for the school by individual parents or perhaps the parent-teacher association are covered by the local education authority's insurance policy. If not, separate cover should be arranged, possibly through the National Confederation of Parent Teacher Associations at 43 Stonebridge Road, Northfleet, Gravesend, Kent, DA11 9DS.

16 Lotteries and money-raising activities

Consideration of this matter falls into two distinct parts. School voluntary funds are raised in a number of ways. Some schools have used raffles as such a means. It is for a school to decide whether such a method is consistent with the principles which should be inculcated in the young.

If it is felt that such means are permissible morally, care must be taken to ensure that the method employed is permissible legally.[17] Raffles must be purely incidental to some other entertainment and the whole of the proceeds, after deducting expenses and a sum not exceeding ten pounds for prizes, must be given to a purpose other than private profit. Money prizes are forbidden. All the tickets must be sold, and the result declared, at the entertainment to which the raffle is incidental.

The suggestion has been made recently that to offer wines and spirits as prizes in a raffle without the appropriate licence may be unlawful. If in doubt, schools should check this with the local licensing authority.

The law relating to street collections, which includes door-to-door collections, requires that permission must be obtained from the police before such a collection is made. All collectors must carry an authority signed by a responsible person and no person under the age of 16 may act as a collector.

In all money-raising activities, care must be taken to see that the law relating to the employment of children is not broken. The reader is referred to chapter X. The legality of charging fees is dealt with in chapter I.

17   Television licences

One licence taken out by the school covers the use of any number of sets in the same block of buildings, provided they are installed for the use of the licensee or the general use of the pupils. It does not cover private sets owned and used by employees.

18   Tuck shops

A tuck shop is not taxable on its profits so long as it complies with the conditions of mutual trading, but it may be assessed in respect of investment income. If the investment belongs to the school and the profit is used only for the benefit of the school, tax will possibly be avoided and it is therefore desirable to create some form of trust by which the investments are automatically handed over to the school.

Most tuck shops are relatively small concerns, but the position with regard to VAT should be verified if the turnover of the school's commercial enterprises shows signs of approaching £10,000 a year.

It is also important to ensure that the items offered for sale in the tuck shop are fit for human consumption. In 1971 a pupil took home some crisps he had bought during break at his infants' school. They were covered in green mould and his parents reported the matter to the health inspector, who telephoned the headmistress to tell her she had committed an offence under the Food and Drugs Act 1955. No prosecution followed in this case but, as responsibility for the quality of food offered for sale rests with the retailer, the headmistress could have found herself in an embarrassing difficulty.

19   Vending machines

Problems sometimes arise over vending machines leased to schools on contracts without a termination clause. Some local education authorities have rules about the installation of electrical equipment without the clearance of its engineers: in such cases the authority must be informed before any contract is signed. The contract should also be examined by the authority or the head's professional association before signature. Such contracts frequently include an absolute liability to pay the rental for a fixed period. The risk here lies in economic inflation. The head is usually advised by the supplier on the price to be charged for various drinks, and the machine is adjusted accordingly. When the cost of new supplies to the school rises, the operation may become uneconomic unless the machine is readjusted to charge more.

In one case the fixed charge brought in only a minimal profit at the time of installation; when it became uneconomic the headmistress took the machine out of use, but the supplier failed to alter the charging mechanism in spite of repeated requests. When the head who had signed the contract retired, her successor was told by the supplier that she was bound by its terms, and faced with an account for more than £600 arrears of rental.

Properly costed, however, vending machines can be a blessing but great care should be taken with accounting procedures. Subject to the considerations outlined above, there is no reason why arrangements should not be made to include the provision of staff refreshments and cigarettes. Schools have for many years installed machines to sell sanitary towels. The advantage of the machine is the time saved in setting up shop by people who are already busy.

20   Confiscation of property

Confiscation of pupils' property is a long-established practice in schools. Sometimes a teacher is exasperated because a pupil is misusing his personal property, or articles of high value are removed because of the risk of loss. Sometimes pupils bring things to school which are forbidden by the school rules; and, occasionally, pupils are found in possession of items which a prudent parent would consider they should not have, or which are plainly illegal. The last-named categories might include for example the possession of cigarettes by a pupil under 16, contraceptives, flick-knives and drugs.

Teachers should remember that anyone who 'dishonestly appropriates property belonging to another with the intention of permanently depriving the other of it' is guilty of theft.[18] The law makes no exception in the case of confiscation by teachers, and schools should therefore design a suitable code of practice for dealing with such items.

ARTICLES OF VALUE

There is a tendency for pupils to bring valuable property to school, including 'bleeping' watches, jewellery, expensive pens, personal stereos and portable radios. Long-playing records and tapes may also fall within this category. It is most unwise to keep these beyond the end of the school day on which they are confiscated. The question of care of other people's property is considered earlier in this chapter and this applies to confiscated items. A teacher must take all reasonable care of pupils' property whilst it is in his possession and the longer he retains it, the greater the risk of loss. If such articles are kept in school overnight there is always the risk that they may disappear during a burglary. The teacher may then be personally liable.

ARTICLES WHICH PUPILS SHOULD NOT HAVE

These should be returned to the pupils' parents.

ILLEGAL ARTICLES

In certain circumstances it may be necessary to call in the police; in others the articles can be destroyed after explaining to the pupil why this is being done. Responsibility for dealing with property falling within this class should be exercised personally by the head, and the parents should always be informed.

21 Children's nightdresses

Regulations were made under the Consumer Protection Act 1961 and are primarily concerned with nightdresses offered for sale. Needlecraft departments would do well to impress the restrictions on the pupils' minds and to ensure any garments made in the department conform to the standards laid down. This is, of course, essential if it is likely that any of the garments might be offered for sale in any way.[19]

22 Use of private cars

From time to time teachers are faced with the problem of getting a sick child to a doctor or hospital in circumstances where an ambulance or other official conveyance is not easily available. This raises an important point in connection with insurance, since teachers' cars are normally covered only for private use, that is, for social, domestic and pleasure purposes.

Most insurance companies and underwriters have inserted a clause which extends the definition of private use to 'official use by the policy holder in person'. This would appear to give some cover to a teacher using his car in such circumstances, but it must be remembered that an insurance policy is a contract which must be construed as a whole, having regard to all the facts in a particular case. A policy arranged through a scheme agreed between an insurer and a professional association would normally cover use by the policy holder in connection with his duties as a teacher, but not for any other business use. 'Official use by the policy holder in person' may be regarded as requiring the presence of the policy holder, but he need not necessarily be driving.

The underwriters of one of the teachers' policies have agreed that the policy is effective, even though the policy holder has lent the car to a colleague for use in connection with a school accident or emergency. The underwriters have not stated whether use in such circumstances is official or unofficial: but they would not regard the official use clause as having been breached.

Some education authorities have advised teachers against using their own cars in such emergencies, others have forbidden them to do so. At least one, however, has specifically stated that a sick child may be taken to a doctor or hospital in a teacher's own car, whether the teacher is authorized to use the car on the authority's official business, or not. The same authority has laid down that this procedure may be followed when a doctor has advised that a child should be taken home, and that the teacher may claim reimbursement on the basis of the appropriate mileage allowance.

Even though a local education authority may have advised teachers not to use their cars in this way, or even prohibited such use, a teacher is still covered for the use, in a private capacity, of a car which he has insured, provided that he accepts no fee or reward other than an official allowance.

If the authority has specifically stated that the practice is approved, the teacher is clearly acting within his official capacity and any action arising out of an accident might lie against him and the authority as joint tortfeasors. Teachers frequently carry children in connection with educational activities which may or may not be 'official' in the sense that a teacher is 'required' to do so by his employer. A policy holder may not lend his car to a colleague to take children on school activities without specific arrangement with his insurers. This use is distinct from use in an emergency referred to above.

If a private motorist accepts any fee or reward for the conveyance of a passenger he violates the terms of a private car policy, but the policies issued under arrangements concluded between insurers and professional associations permit the receipt of an allowance for official use from the teacher's employers. An allowance of this kind does not establish 'hiring'. Payments may be accepted for car-sharing, when giving lifts to friends or colleagues. A profit must not be made.

It is by no means unknown for teachers to give children

lifts to a games field, or to pick them up from a bus stop on the way to or from school. In such cases, especially since they often occur out of school hours, it is probable that such courtesies would come within the scope of private use and the policy would provide adequate indemnity.

A policy holder whose car is insured under arrangements made between an insurer and a professional association is covered, no matter in what kind of school he is serving. The advantageous terms of his policy arise from his professional status as a teacher.

In general, car insurance policies do not distinguish between liability to passengers and liability to other third parties. The policy therefore covers claims made by a passenger and claims arising from the negligence of a passenger.

Every teacher would be well advised to make a careful study of the terms of his policy in this connection, and to remember that in the last resort the application of these conditions to a particular situation can be determined only by a court of law on evidence of the facts.

The matter of travelling expenses is dealt with in chapter IV.

23 Minority groups

The law, as a matter of public policy, seeks to protect the rights of members of minority groups in this country. The operation of the conscience clause in religious matters, as well as the provisions of the Race Relations Acts, have been noticed elsewhere. Schools must observe the letter of the law in matters of this nature and it is to be hoped that they will also promote the spirit which lies behind it. The promotion of harmony may well begin in primary schools with the unspoken acceptance of integration, for young children are less inclined than adults to accentuate differences. In secondary schools any teaching should be directed towards recognition of common humanity and an understanding and tolerance of differences.

The classroom is not the place for the promotion of a teacher's personal views; it is not a policy-making chamber, but a place where individuals work and play together. All pupils, whatever their origins, have an equal claim on the teacher's care and professional skills.

The situation has changed considerably since the passage of the 1944 Act, largely because of the considerable number of people from overseas who have made their home in these islands. The integration of people from other countries is no new experience in the United Kingdom, but the two new factors are the arrival of many people whose skins are darker than those of the people who have been settled in this country in the past and the fact that many of these new citizens come from a non-Christian heritage. With the exception of the Jewish people, this second element has previously affected only very limited areas of the country.

Two groups are selected here for consideration. The first has been represented in Britain for many years, but its cultural background and way of life have prevented it from seeking complete integration into the life of the people. The second, not previously living here on a large scale, is distinguished by differences both in skin colour and religion from the majority of United Kingdom citizens, and there are signs that it wishes to preserve its own identity and ethos.

GYPSIES

Attempts to educate gypsy children go back almost two centuries. The difficulty has stemmed not merely from the wandering nature of the lives of the travellers, as they prefer to call themselves, but also from their desire to preserve their own culture. Travellers are well aware of the need for literacy in modern life, but they believe that the state system of education should be sufficiently flexible to allow their children to reap its benefits without destroying their way of life.

The National Gypsy Education Council was formed in 1969. It includes both gypsies and non-gypsies in its membership and has Lady Plowden as chairman. The purpose of the Council is to concentrate on the advancement of education for gypsy children and adults and to collect and disseminate information.

The children of travellers are subject to the law relating to school attendance in the same way as all children. It is said, however, that educational welfare officers do little to persuade travellers who do not live on caravan sites to send their children to school and that heads have sometimes refused to have them. Children may of course be absent from school for not more than two weeks in a year to accompany their parents on their annual holiday and there are special provisions for children whose parents' work requires them to travel (see chapter XI 'Attendance'). There is no equivalent in England and Wales to the Scottish law which sets out a minimum number of days in which the children of 'tinkers' are required to attend.

The travellers' way of life is based on the family and the extended family. Their children tend to view the strange life inside a building with mistrust born of their experience of free life out-of-doors, where there is little restriction on movement. Before all else, they need to become confident in a new environment. The National Gypsy Education Council at 61 Blenheim Crescent, London W11 2EG, will be pleased to give advice to teachers.

MUSLIMS

In the past Muslims have appeared to settle into the western way of life and into school with comparative ease. In 1972 a father was fined for not causing his daughter to receive full-time efficient and suitable education, because he had refused to allow her to attend a co-educational school.

Towards the end of 1980 publicity was given to the story that a Muslim parent had sent his family back to Pakistan rather than allow his daughter to go to a mixed school. In the following January the Muslim Parents Association was formed in Bradford, where one in ten pupils belonged, at that time, to that faith. Bradford had been phasing out single-sex schools for some time and officers of the local education authority said they had made concessions in dress and meals.

From puberty, Muslim girls are not allowed to mix with

males who are not close relatives and the stricter families from Kashmir regard the 'uncivilized exposure of the body', and acts 'encouraging demoralization' of Muslim children as unacceptable. An official of the Muslim Education Trust has said, 'The morals of society in Britain are not acceptable to us; we are planning our own school because we believe prevention is better than cure. Education authorities only think about education. We are thinking of the moral and religious health of future generations.'[20]

It was said that the Trust was hoping to establish its own secondary schools on a voluntary-aided basis.

24   Parent-teacher associations

Many schools have parent-teacher associations and, properly organized, they can do much to promote a good relationship between the groups they represent. Many such associations have been of tremendous benefit to the schools to which they are attached and have often raised funds for equipment and journeys which would not otherwise have been possible.

It should, however, be clearly understood that, in a maintained school, such a body has no executive power. Under no circumstances can it usurp the functions of the governors and the head as laid down in the Articles of Government.

Parent-teacher associations have grown both in number and strength in recent years, and their activities are by no means confined to money-raising. Discussions with the school staff and listening to visiting lecturers form part of the staple diet of many such bodies. In some cases they add weight to the views of the staff in negotiations with the local education authority and help in fostering public interest in and developing public opinion on educational matters in their locality.

Many parent-teacher associations belong to the National Confederation of Parent-Teacher Associations which encourages the development of associations and local federations. The Confederation was one of the founding bodies of the Home and School Council and is represented on a number of national bodies concerned with education. It works closely with the teachers' professional associations.

The National Confederation is in membership of the Confederation Internationale des Parents on which most European countries are represented, as well as Canada, Venezuela, the Ivory Coast and Senegal.

If difficulties arise from the operation of parent-teacher associations, it is not unusual to find their origin in inadequate planning in the early stages. Many of these snags could be avoided by the adoption of a constitution which defines the associations' terms of reference clearly. Teachers and others concerned with the formation of an association would do well to consider using the draft constitution issued by the National Confederation, which is reproduced below with permission. Modifications may be made to suit local conditions, provided that the clauses which establish the charitable nature of the association (nos. 2, 18 and 21) are included without alteration.

1. The name of the Association shall be....................
   ....

2. The objects of the Association are to advance the education of the pupils of the school by providing and assisting in the provision of facilities for education at the school (not normally provided by the local education authority) and as an ancillary thereto and in furtherance of this object the Association may:
   (a) foster more extended relationships between the staff, parents and others associated with the school; and
   (b) engage in activities which support the school and advance the education of the pupils attending it.[21]

3. The Association shall be non-political.

4. The president of the Association shall be the head teacher.[22]

5. The names of the vice-presidents shall be submitted at the annual general meeting.[23]

6. The annual subscription shall be (.....) per household, becoming due at the annual general meeting.[24]

7. The management and control of the Association shall be

vested in a committee which shall consist of the following:

The head of the school and the following officers, who shall be elected annually at the AGM:

1. Chairman
2. Treasurer (parent)
3. Secretary

Other members from the following sources: parents representing the first and subsequent years, members of the staff of the school, members from friends of the school.[25]

8. (......) members of the said committee shall constitute a quorum for the committee.
9. Committee meetings shall be held at least once each term at such times and places as the committee shall direct.[26]
10. The annual general meeting of the Association shall be held on (......) of each year. At the annual general meeting the chair shall be taken by the Chairman, or in his/her absence by the vice-chairman of the committee. Additional meetings shall be held of the sub-sections of the Association, and these may be in addition to those called by the convenor from time to time.
11. (......) members shall constitute a quorum at the annual general meeting.
12. The committee shall have the power to co-opt up to (......) members, and to appoint any sub-committee, and shall prescribe the function of any such sub-committee.
13. A special general meeting shall be convened at the request in writing, to the secretary, of ten members of the Association. Such a meeting shall be held within thirty days of the request. Agenda and motions submitted shall be circulated to all members.
14. Casual vacancies on the committee may be filled by the committee by co-option. Any person so co-opted shall serve only while the person in whose place he/she is co-opted would have served.
15. At the first committee meeting after the annual general meeting the committee shall elect a vice-chairman from among its members.

16. Where a child leaves school during the year then the parent, being a fully paid member of the Association, shall be deemed to continue as such until the next AGM.

17. Where parents no longer have children at the school, but wish to continue their interest in the school through the Association, such parents may be accepted as Friends of the School, on payment of the annual subscription, and shall be entitled to full membership with the exception that they may not hold office as chairman, secretary or treasurer, or serve on the committee.

18. No alteration of the rules may be made except at the annual general meeting or at a special meeting called for this purpose. No alteration or amendment shall be made to the objects clause or dissolution clause which would cause the Association to cease to be a charity at law.[27]

19. The honorary treasurer shall keep an account of all income and expenditure and shall submit accounts, duly audited, at the AGM. The banking account shall be in the name of the Association on the signature of any two of the following:
    (a) Chairman
    (b) Treasurer
    (c) Secretary

20. Two auditors, not being members of the committee, shall be appointed annually at the annual general meeting to audit the accounts and books of the Association.

21. Any assets remaining on dissolution of the Association after satisfying any outstanding debts and liabilities shall not be distributed amongst the members of the Association but will be given to the school for the benefit of the children of the school in any manner which is exclusively charitable at law.[28]

22. The Association shall take out public liability insurance to cover all its meetings and activities.[29]

23. That any matter not provided for in the constitution shall be dealt with by the committee, whose decision shall be deemed final.

It must be realized that on all educational matters the head teacher has the ultimate responsibility. Should an association wish to mention this in its constitution, an additional clause could be inserted, e.g. 'The head teacher shall have the ultimate decision on all educational matters.'

25   Politics and law

As was stated in the preface, the main purpose of this book is to provide the practising teacher with an outline of the ever-widening implications of the law for his profession. To a large extent, therefore, it is descriptive of the way in which education is brought within the sovereignty of the Rule of Law. Law is concerned with rights, but every right has a correlative duty: to avoid one's duty is frequently to deny someone else his rights.

Midway through the second half of the twentieth century, it is clear that principles and concepts once sacrosanct are being assailed. Moreover, the structure of society is changing more rapidly than at any time in history. It is inevitable that, in these circumstances, the law is being moulded to take account of developments of thought and structure.

At one time it was firmly held that a teacher should keep his political views to himself within the context of his professional activity: this has been challenged. It was once considered beneath the dignity of a learned profession to indulge in strikes and other industrial action: this has been challenged. The whole relationship between the schoolteacher and his charges has been based on the concept that one is *in loco parentis* and the others *in statu pupillari*: this also has been challenged.

The segregation of powers is historically fundamental to English law. It is for the executive to implement the law, for the judiciary to enforce it, but the power to make it is reserved to Parliament. Only by delegation from the legislature may any other body or individual presume to create law. The essence of the wisdom of Parliament, enshrined in law, is distilled from public policy; and public policy is forged on the anvil of politics.

Since the first edition of this book was published, some hundreds of thousands of young people have been enfranchised by the lowering of the age of majority. The television cameras have brought the living, walking, talking images of policy makers into most homes and schools. In the industrial field the Rule of Law has been openly defied. In schools there has been a demand for consultation and participation by teachers, parents and pupils. Truancy, an offence at law, is publicly condoned and blamed on the schools. Teachers may be found who will approve, if not encourage, pupil demonstrations.

These circumstances have imposed a testing time on educational institutions; and political activity, once confined to colleges and universities, has moved into the schools. Those charged with their direction find themselves caught between the lower millstone of demands for greater freedom and wider rights, and the upper stone of the law as it exists. Ever seeking to promote the claims of those who feel themselves underprivileged, the mass media have accorded much publicity to those who see the schools as an arena in which new liberties can be won. On the other hand, it is by no means certain that the great majority of the public would agree with some of the views so insistently expressed.

For the teacher, the dilemma lies in the uncertainty of the future. There is no indication, at present, of any change in public policy so settled that it is likely to issue in radical legislative action. Until it does, a teacher is well advised to work strictly within the framework of the law as it stands, and not as he thinks it ought to stand.

26 Complaints about broadcasts

Incorrect or misleading radio or television reports about schools or individuals may be defamatory and can be dealt with as such.

Under the Broadcasting Act 1980 there has now been set up a Broadcasting Complaints Commission at 20 Albert Embankment, London SE1 7TL, to deal with complaints, very much in the same way as the better known Press Council deals with the press.

It is not possible to take action *both* through civil action in the courts and through the Commission. Professional associations will advise in each case which is more likely to succeed.

27 Public Lending Right

Under the Public Lending Right Act 1979 payment is made to authors (writers and illustrators) whose books are lent out from public libraries. The amount each author receives is proportionate to the number of times (established from a sample) that his books were lent out in the previous year. The money is paid from a fund set up by Parliament: at present £2 million annually is allocated to the fund. The system is administered in such a way as to prevent an excessively high proportion of the money from going to relatively few widely read authors.

Books should be registered on the appropriate form available from the Registrar at the Public Lending Right Office, Bayheath House, Prince Regent Street, Stockton-on-Tees, Cleveland TS18 1DF.

References

1. Unsolicited Goods Act 1971.
2. Local Government (Miscellaneous Provisions) Act 1982, s. 40.
3. Representation of the People Act 1949, s. 82.
4. Representation of the People Act 1949, Schedule 2.
5. Representation of the People Act 1949, s. 5.
6. Representation of the People Act 1949, s. 82(1)a.
7. Representation of the People Act 1949, Schedule 7.
8. *The Times*, 18 January 1978.
9. Report of the Royal Commission on Police Powers and Procedure, 1929.
10. Judges' Rules: Home Office Circular 89/1978.
11. H. K. Bevan, *The Law Relating to Children* (Butterworth, 1973).
12. Hunter *v.* Johnson (1884) 13 QBD 225.
13. R. *v.* Cockerton, *ex parte* Hamilton [1901] 1 KB 726; LCT 30.

14. Education (School Information) Regulations 1981.
15. Copyright Act 1911, s. 15.
16. Public Order Act 1936, s. 5A; as inserted by the Race Relations Act 1976, s. 70, amended by the Criminal Law Act 1977, Schedule 6.
17. Betting, Gaming and Lotteries Acts 1963 to 1971.
18. Theft Act 1968, s. 1.
19. Children's Nightdresses Regulations 1964; see also British Standards Specification, BS 3121, 1959.
20. *Times Educational Supplement*, 11 January 1974.
21. It is essential that this clause be adopted without alteration. This wording has been agreed between the Chief Inspector of Taxes, the Charity Commissioners and the Department of Education and Science as being acceptable for use by parent-teacher associations. Any variation could render an Association liable to income tax on their investment income.
22. This clause is not essential. For example, some head teachers are chairmen of their associations.
23. These are usually people the Association wishes to honour.
24. A growing number of PTAs no longer have subscriptions, thinking they are restrictive and difficult to collect and administer. Where subscriptions are levied, the amount is usually 25p per family.
25. This is a possible arrangement, and can be varied in many ways. For example, in some schools the secretary is a member of the staff, appointed and paid for that duty. Again, while some schools have committee members representing year groups, others have class representation, or, more usually, election of those parents generally considered suitable.
26. It may also be thought desirable to specify the frequency of ordinary meetings.
27. This is another essential clause that must not be varied.
28. This is another essential clause that must not be varied.
29. Membership of the National Confederation of PTAs automatically provides this.

APPENDIX I
Table of statutes

References are to page numbers in the present book.

APPENDIX II
Table of cases

References are to page numbers in the present book.

(LCT denotes that the case is reported in G. R. Barrell *Legal Cases for Teachers*, Methuen, 1970)

APPENDIX III
Addresses of professional associations

The national associations whose names are included in this list are concerned with the professional status of their members. Those which are purely academic in character have not been noted.

Assistant Masters and Mistresses Association (1978)
29 Gordon Square, London WC1H 0PX.
A professional association and recognized independent trade union, AMMA has 90,000 members mainly in secondary schools but with a growing further education and primary school membership.

Association of Agricultural Education Staffs
Cumbria College of Agriculture and Forestry, Newton Rigg, Penrith, Cumbria, CA11 0AH.

Association of Career Teachers (1974)
Hillsboro, Castledine Street, Loughborough, Leicestershire.
The Association was formed to encourage high professional and educational standards among teachers of moderate views, and to campaign for a career-based structure of salaries.

Association of Principals of Colleges
East Herts. College, Turnford, Broxbourne, Herts.

This Association was formerly known as the Association of Principals of Technical Institutions.

Association of Principals of Sixth Form Colleges (1979)
Brockenhurst College, Brockenhurst, Hants.

Association of Polytechnic Teachers
Throgmorton House, 27 Elphinstone Road, Southsea PO5 3HP.

Association of Teachers of Domestic Science (1896)
Hamilton House, Mabledon Place, London WC1H 9BB.

British Association of Organizers and Lecturers in Physical Education
23 Quadring Road, Donington, Lincolnshire, PE11 4TD.

British Association of Teachers of the Deaf
The Rycroft Centre, Royal Schools for the Deaf, Stanley Road, Cheadle Hulme, Cheshire SK8 6RF.

College of Preceptors
Bloomsbury House, 130 High Holborn, London WC1V 6PS.
The College is the oldest society of teachers in England, and has always been noted for its pioneer work in many aspects of education. It received its Royal Charter in 1849 and, throughout its history, it has shown a high regard for the status of teachers.

The College is actively engaged in the field of higher professional education for serving teachers through courses and examinations. Qualifications awarded on the authority of the Royal Charter are Associate (ACP), Licentiate (LP) and Fellow (FCP). The LCP is recognized for salary purposes as the equivalent of a university first degree by the Burnham Main Committee (Primary and Secondary). The College has provided a series of graduate level diplomas, notably the Diploma in School Management Studies, and courses are being provided for these by an increasing number of institutions of further and higher education.

The title of Fellow is also conferred annually in March in a Charter list on a small number of persons eminent in education at home and overseas.

The College's Regional Executives arrange a programme of short courses and seminars on various aspects of the teacher's work and, in particular, on school management studies.

The annual Joseph Payne and Sir Philip Magnus lectures are sponsored by the College.

Its publications include a termly digest of current educational literature, *Education Today*.

Any teacher holding one of the College diplomas may become a subscribing member, and receive a copy of all College publications.

The Headmasters' Conference (1869)
29 Gordon Square, London WC1H 0PS.
Membership of this body is limited to headmasters of schools which fulfil certain conditions. Generally speaking, the schools whose headmasters are in membership must be independent though there is provision for the election of a limited number of headmasters of other types of school when it is thought that their personal contribution to the thought and affairs of the Headmasters' Conference would be useful. In considering applications for membership the Committee will have regard to the degree of professional and administrative independence enjoyed by the headmaster, and the academic standards obtaining in the school as indicated by the size of the sixth form in relation to the total number of pupils achieving a defined standard of success at GCE 'A' level. Although there is no official definition of the term, it is commonly held that schools whose headmasters are within the membership of the Headmasters' Conference are to be recognized as public schools.

Incorporated Association of Preparatory Schools
138 Kensington Church Street, London W8 4BN.

Independent Schools Association Incorporated
1 Chynington Lane, Seaford, Sussex.

National Association of Head Teachers (1897)
Holly House, 6 Paddockhall Road, Haywards Heath, West Sussex RH16 1RG.

This is an association of heads of all kinds of schools which are recognized as efficient by the Department of Education and Science.

National Association of Schoolmasters and Union of Women Teachers (1976)
Hillscourt Education Centre, Rosehill, Rednal, Birmingham B45 8RS.
The Association was formed by a merger of the National Association of Schoolmasters (1919) and the Union of Women Teachers (1965). It exists to safeguard and promote the interests of career teachers in all types of schools and colleges, and to protect and promote the interests of education generally.

National Association of Teachers in Further and Higher Education (1976)
Hamilton House, Mabledon Place, London WC1H 9BB.
Formed by the amalgamation of the Association of Teachers in Colleges and Departments of Education (1943) with the Association of Teachers in Technical Institutions (1904), this Association caters for teachers in all institutions of further and higher education.

National Association of Teachers in Wales (Undeb Cenedlaethol Athrawon Cymru) (1940)
Prif Swyddfa U.C.A.C., Pen Roc, Rhodfa'r Mor, Aberystwyth, Dyfed.

National Federation of Continuative Teachers' Associations
5 Naseby Close, Fairfax Road, London NW6.
The Association exists to promote the development of adult and non-vocational education, and to protect the professional interests and status of part-time teachers in this field.
National Society for Art Education (1973)
Champness Hall, Drake Street, Rochdale, Lancashire OL16 1PB.

National Union of Teachers (1870)
Hamilton House, Mabledon Place, London WC1H 9BB.
This is the largest of the associations, and comprises in its membership teachers in every kind of school and college and

also in education administration. The interests of the various groups are safeguarded by the formation of sections and advisory committees within the Union.

Physical Education Association of Great Britain and Northern Ireland (1899)
Ling House, 162 King's Cross Road, London WC1X 9DH.

Professional Association of Teachers
99 Friar Gate, Derby DE1 1EZ.
The Association seeks to maintain high professional standards among teachers, and eschews all forms of industrial action which would have an adverse effect on the children in their care.

Secondary Heads Association (1978)
29 Gordon Square, London WC1H 0PS.
The Association was formed by the merger of the Incorporated Association of Head Masters and the Association of Head Mistresses Incorporated. It is concerned with the professional status of the heads of secondary schools and with the maintenance of high educational standards in these establishments.

Society of Assistants Teaching in Preparatory Schools
The Old Malthouse, Langton Matravers, Dorset.

Standing Conference of Principals and Directors of Colleges and Institutes of Higher Education
Worcester College of Higher Education, Worcester WR2 6AJ.
The Conference is committed to the maintenance of their share of public sector higher education by the non-polytechnic institutions.

APPENDIX IV
Voluntary educational bodies

Baptist Union of Great Britain and Ireland: Department of Mission
Baptist Church House, 4 Southampton Row, London WC1B 4AB.

British Council of Churches Education Consultation
2 Eaton Gate, London SW1W 9BL.

Catholic Education Council
41 Cromwell Road, London SW7 2DJ.

Central Joint Education Policy Committee (Anglican, Roman Catholic and Free Church)
Church House, Dean's Yard, London SW1P 3NZ.
41 Cromwell Road, London SW7 2DJ.
27 Tavistock Square, London WC1H 9HG.

Church of England General Synod Board of Education
Church House, Dean's Yard, London SW1P 3NZ.

Faculty for the Training of Teachers (Jewish)
2 Egerton Gardens, London NW4.

Free Church Federal Council Education Committee
27 Tavistock Square, London WC1H 9HG.

Methodist Division of Education and Youth
2 Chester House, Pages Lane, London N10 1PR.

Moravian Provincial Board
Moravian Church House, 5 Muswell Hill, London N10 3TJ.

Muslim Educational Trust
130 Stroud Green Road, London N4 3RZ.

Quaker Social Responsibility and Education Department
Friends' House, Euston Road, London NW1 2BJ.

United Reformed Church (Congregational and Presbyterian)
86 Tavistock Place, London WC1H 9RT.

APPENDIX V
Select bibliography

1 Government publications

A complete and up-to-date list of Government publications on education will be found in Government Publications (Sectional List): Department of Education and Science. Another useful guide is the annual *Index to Department of Education and Science Circulars and Administrative Memoranda*, which lists all current publications under these heads. All publications of this nature are obtainable from any bookseller or from the Government Bookshop, Holborn, London WC1V 6HB.

2 Other publications

EDUCATIONAL LAW

Neil Adams, *Law and Teachers Today* (Hutchinson, 1983)
  A well-written and informative hardback by an experienced head teacher, with a particular eye to those issues which cause teachers some concern virtually every day. The style is non-technical and the content up-to-date.
Herb T. Appenzeller, *From the Gym to the Jury* (Michie, Charlottesville, Va., 1970)

A fascinating introduction to the legal problems of Physical Education by the Athletic Director of Guildford College, Greensboro, North Carolina. It must be remembered that, though American common law is derived from its English counterpart, and though judgments from the English courts are quoted with approval in the United States, statutory modifications have led to some changes. Nevertheless, the family likeness is recognizable in this book and *mutatis mutandis* it contains much wise advice.

G. R. Barrell, *Legal Cases for Teachers* (Methuen, 1970, out of print)

A collection of nearly 150 cases dealing with educational matters. Many of the cases touched on in this book are dealt with in more detail in Barrell's. Every effort has been made to present the cases in an interesting and relevant manner, without sacrificing legal accuracy.

G. R. Barrell, 'Teachers and the European Law' (College of Preceptors: *Education Today*, Summer 1976)

A survey of the effect of the structures of the Council of Europe on educational law, including a summary of relevant cases.

Kenneth Brooksbank (ed.), *Educational Administration* (Councils and Education Press, 1980)

Written by members of the Society of Education Officers, this book gives clear and accurate information on committee structures, the legal and financial constraints under which local authorities work, and relations with central government.

Kenneth Brooksbank and James Revell, *School Governors* (Councils and Education Press, 1981)

Two former Chief Education Officers give clear and accurate information on the powers, rights and responsibilities of school governors in the light of the Education Act 1980 and the aftermath of the Taylor report on school government.

Brooksbank, Revell, Ackstine and Bailey on behalf of the Society of Education Officers, *County and Voluntary Schools* (Councils and Education Press, 6th edition, 1982)

An analysis of sections of the Education Acts as they affect the administration of different kinds of schools.

Barbara Bullivant, *School Governor's Guide* (Home and School Council, 1981)

This 29-page booklet details the requirements of the 1980 Education Act and gives advice to governors, and especially those representing parents, in carrying out their duties. It includes a glossary of educational terms.

Charlesworth on Negligence (Sweet and Maxwell, 7th edition by R. A. Percy, 1983)

The standard work on this subject. The current edition devotes part of a chapter to negligence in schools.

Geoffrey Harrison and Duncan Bloy, *Essential Law for Teachers* (Oyez Publishing Ltd, 1980)

A relatively inexpensive paperback by two practising law lecturers with an obvious interest in schools and teachers. Particularly good on teachers' conditions of service and relationships with employers.

D. M. Hart (ed.), *The Head's Legal Guide* (Croner Publications, 1984)

A comprehensive compendium, invaluable to head teachers.

Kenneth Ireland, *Illness and Injury at School,* (Schoolmaster Publishing Co., Kettering, 1977)

Kenneth Ireland, *Teachers' Guide to the Health and Safety Act* (Schoolmaster Publishing Co., Kettering, 1979)

Kenneth Ireland, *Teachers' Rights and Duties* (Macmillan Education, 1984)

Easy-to-read brief guides to complex subjects.

Janner's Compendium of Health and Safety Law, Greville Janner QC MP (*alias* Ewan Mitchell)

This is the third edition of this standard work formerly known under the title of *The Employer's Guide to the Law on Health, Safety and Welfare at Work* and brings together the entire area of law and practice in this crucial industrial and commercial field. It contains new chapters and sections on the latest law on health and safety at work.

P. Liell and J. B. Saunders (eds.), *The Law of Education* (Butterworth, 9th edition, 1984)

The standard work on the Education Acts 1944 to 1984 with other relevant statutes and the instruments and circulars.

John Partington, *Law and the New Teacher* (Holt-Saunders, 1984)
    Intended for student teachers, probationers and those in
    their early professional life. Attempts an easy-to-read style
    and makes extensive use of case studies.

L. B. Tirrell, *The Aided Schools Handbook* (National Society and
    SPCK, 2nd edition, 1969, revised 1974)
    A useful commentary on the law relating to, and the work
    of, these schools by a former Director of Religious Education
    for the Dioceses of London and Southwark. Though primarily
    intended for governors, teachers interested in aided schools
    will find much useful matter here.

E. C. Wragg and J. A. Partington, *A Handbook for School
    Governors* (Methuen, 1980)
    Described by a reviewer as 'witty and wise', this book is
    intended for all school governors. It deals with matters of
    general school and curriculum concern to governors and
    contains a section on tricky legal problems which can arise.

CHILDREN AND THE LAW

P. Austin, *Notes on Juvenile Court Law* (Barry Rose Publishers,
    10th edition, 1978)
    The most concise, yet authoritative, guide. This is an
    invaluable booklet for teachers whose pastoral responsibilities
    bring them into contact with the juvenile courts.

H. K. Bevan, *The Law Relating to Children* (Butterworth, 1973)
    A conveniently arranged work, which is of particular value
    to teachers concerned with pastoral care.

Winifred E. Cavenagh, *Guide to Procedure in the Juvenile Court*
    (Barry Rose Publishers, 1982)
    A concise account of the work of the juvenile courts. This
    is, perhaps, the best written introduction to the subject, and
    will be invaluable for teachers who have to deal with the
    courts in the course of their work.

Children and Young Persons in Custody (Barry Rose Publishers,
    1977)
    The report of a working party of the National Association

for the Care and Resettlement of Offenders under the chairmanship of Peter Jay.

Children at Risk in School (Barry Rose Publishers, 1975)
A report of the proceedings of a one-day conference of NACRO.

B. Cox, *The Law of Special Educational Needs* (Croom Helm, 1985)
A detailed guide by a practising barrister.

M. D. A. Freeman, *The Rights and Wrongs of Children* (Frances Pinter, 1983)

Clarke Hall and Morrison, *The Law Relating to Children and Young Persons* (Butterworth, 9th edition, 1977)
The standard work on all aspects of this subject, monumental in its conception and meticulous in its presentation.

Brenda M. Hoggett, *Parents and Children* (Sweet and Maxwell, 2nd edition, 1981)
A concise guide to those areas of family law particularly concerned with children, including the legal relationship between parents and their children, substitute care, delinquency, child abuse, step-parents, and adoption.

G. H. F. Mumford, *A Guide to Juvenile Court Law* (Shaw, 8th edition, 1974)
An exceedingly valuable reference book which covers all aspects of the subject and is invaluable when heads have pupils who are in trouble with the courts. The book now includes a separate treatment table in respect of juvenile court procedure, incorporating an age table. This has been revised, and can be obtained separately.

G. H. F. Mumford and T. J. Selwood, *A Guide to the Children Act 1975* (Shaw, 1975)
A brief, fairly formal outline of the provisions of the Act.

Roger Smith, *Children and the Courts* (Sweet and Maxwell, 1979)
Good on court procedure, legal aid, evidence, care orders and sanctions in general.

Jennifer Terry, *A Guide to the Children Act 1975 as amended* (Sweet and Maxwell, 2nd edition, 1979)
An outline of the effects of an important statute which deals

with children in the care of local authorities, adoption, and the new status of custodianship.

Michael Zander, *Social Workers, their Clients and the Law* (Sweet and Maxwell, 3rd edition, 1981)

Teachers share many clients with social workers, and this book will help them to understand the legal framework within which the functions of the departments of social services are set.

EMPLOYMENT AND CONDITIONS OF SERVICE

Christopher Curson, *'Education' Guide to Industrial Relations* (Swift Publications Ltd for Councils and Education Press Ltd, 1977)

The author was formerly a member of the staff of the Local Authority Conditions of Service Advisory Board and of the Burnham secretariat. The book is slanted towards employment in education.

Christopher Waud, *Guide to Employment Law* (Daily Mail Publications, 1985)

A quick-reference, easy-to-read guide by a chairman of industrial tribunals.

COPYRIGHT

G. R. Barrell, 'Copyright – A New Look' (College of Preceptors: *Education Today*, Autumn 1977)

A commentary on the Whitford proposals with particular reference to their effects on educational practice.

Geoffrey Crabb, *Copyright Clearance – A Practical Guide* (Council for Educational Technology, 2nd edition, 1981)

An algorithmic route through the minefields of current legislation.

Michael Flint, *A User's Guide to Copyright* (Butterworth, 2nd edition, 1985)

Particularly practical and useful for those working in schools and colleges.

Index